WILLIAM OCKHAM
I

PUBLICATIONS IN MEDIEVAL STUDIES
THE MEDIEVAL INSTITUTE
UNIVERSITY OF NOTRE DAME
EDITED BY
RALPH McINERNY

*A Series Founded by Philip S. Moore, C.S.C. †, Joseph N. Garvin, C.S.C. †,
and A. L. Gabriel*

XXVI/I

MARILYN McCORD ADAMS

WILLIAM OCKHAM

VOLUME I

UNIVERSITY OF NOTRE DAME PRESS
NOTRE DAME, INDIANA 1987

Library of Congress Cataloging-in-Publication Data

Adams, Marilyn McCord.
    William Ockham.

    (Publications in medieval studies ; 26)
    Bibliography: p.
    Includes index.
    1. William, of Ockham, ca. 1285–ca. 1349.
I. Title. II. Series.
B765.O34A62   1987   189'.4   86-40337
ISBN 0-268-01940-1 (set)

Manufactured in the United States of America

For Bob

Contents

Preface   ix
Acknowledgements   xi
A Note on Ockham's Life and Works   xv
Abbreviations   xix

Part One: Ontology

Chapter   1:   The Problem of Universals   3
Chapter   2:   Universals Are Not Things Other Than
               Names   13
Chapter   3:   Names and Concepts   71
Chapter   4:   Universals, Conventionalism, and Similarity   109
Chapter   5:   Ockham's Ontological Program   143
Chapter   6:   Quantity   169
Chapter   7:   Relations   215
Chapter   8:   Quality   277
Chapter   9:   Evaluation of Ockham's Ontological
               Program   287

Part Two: Logic

Chapter 10:   The Properties of Terms   317
Chapter 11:   The Logic of Propositions   383
Chapter 12:   Arguments   437

Part Three: Theory of Knowledge

Chapter 13:   Conceptual Empiricism and Direct Realism   495
Chapter 14:   Certainty and Scepticism in Ockham's
               Epistemology   551

Preface

In the publication of a book of this size, miracles have been multiplied, but not without necessity: the first miracle was the writing; the second, finding a publisher willing and able to finance it; the third, preparing the bulky piece for printing; the fourth, the actual production! Since I finished the book in 1983, various other secondary causes have made substantial contributions to this project. I am grateful to my friend (and favorite Thomist), Ralph McInerny, former director of the Medieval Institute, at University of Notre Dame, for working out arrangements for co-publication with Notre Dame University Press. Robert Anderson spent countless hours combing the manuscript with remarkable care and patience, to free the text and the references from many errors and inconsistencies. And Kim Waterman diverted herself from the pleasures of summer to check entries in the bibliography. I am happy to thank them both.

Marilyn McCord Adams
February 27, 1987

Acknowledgements

One of the rewards of writing a book is the opportunity to acknowledge many professional debts. I now claim that prerogative.

"A student is not above his teacher...it is enough if he is like his teacher." When I took Max Fisch's Greek philosophy course twenty years ago, I learned that philosophy, like religion, begins in wonder and ends in awe. He also taught me that a historian of philosophy must never depend exclusively on secondary literature but must begin and end by listening to the primary sources. His integrity, thoroughness, and openness to new interpretations are a model and an inspiration. Norman Kretzmann introduced me to medieval philosophy and to William Ockham in 1963. I cut my teeth as a medievalist working with him on *Ockham's Predestination, God's Foreknowledge, and Future Contingents*, and learned far more than I noticed at the time or could account for now. He has put many other opportunities for professional development in my path, and I want to thank him for his continuous support and encouragement. Nelson Pike showed me the importance of the medieval tradition for theology and philosophy of religion. He also taught me most of what I know about philosophical writing, and this book owes whatever clarity and organization it has to him. My greatest philosophical debt, is, of course, to Ockham himself. When I meet him in the next life, I shall have to thank him for many lessons in metaphysics, epistemology, and theology, and for a decade of entertainment!

An historian of philosophy cannot work without texts. In this regard, all Ockham scholars have been blessed with the work of the Franciscan Institute at St. Bonaventure, New York. Following on the pioneering work of Philotheus Boehner, Fr. Gedeon Gál, OFM, has directed a team of editors in preparing critical editions of Ockham's non-political (philosophical and theological) works. The first volume was published in 1967, and by the time this book appears all volumes should be printed or in press. We can expect the dissemination of these accurate texts, and the translations they spawn, to produce an explosion in Ockham studies at all levels. The Institute's hospitality to me over the last dozen years has been a paradigm of Franciscan generosity. Much of my work antedated or was concurrent with their preparation of the critical editions. During my frequent visits (since 1971), the editors cheerfully made their resources available to me—transcriptions of manuscripts, advance type-scripts of the critical edition, new discoveries about Ockham's sources and opponents, etc. Their assistance has improved the present book in countless ways. The readiness—especially of Fr. Gedeon Gál, OFM, general editor; editors Girard Etzkorn and Rega Wood; and the Institute's director, Fr. Conrad Harkins, OFM—to share their work, their knowledge, their homes and dining rooms, and their friendship is all too rare in the academic world and best repaid by following their ex-amples.

Over the last ten years, my colleagues and students at UCLA have patiently endured someone struggling with a big manuscript. I am grateful to my colleague Tyler Burge for reading some chapters and setting me straight on a number of issues related to the philosophy of language. Montgomery Furth, through his writings and discussion, taught me a lot about Aristotelian hylomorphism. Donald Kalish, who loves logic, has patiently reviewed with me many and varied points. Jim Read wrote a fine paper on Scotus's theory of causality, from which I learned a lot. During his visits to UCLA over the last several years, Fr. Allan Wolter, OFM, has tried to teach me about Duns Scotus, whom Ockham regarded as his most distinguished opponent. No doubt, I could have learned more, had I not stubbornly clung to my own interpretations! My hus-band and colleague, Robert Adams, now knows more about Ockham than he ever dreamed he would: his comments, philosophical and editorial, have been invaluable; his toleration for and encouragement of this project, *sine quibus non*.

During my sabbatical at Princeton in 1979–1980, I enjoyed

the chance to participate in an Ockham-reading group, organized by Calvin Normore and including Michael Frede, Paul Streveler, (sometimes) John Boler, Peter King, and Chris Martin. Our detailed philosophical discussions of these texts and Ockham's positions were a rare treat, which has shaped my views of Ockham's metaphysics, logic, and epistemology in many and subtle ways. I cannot thank them enough for the experience.

Materially, this book has been heavily subsidized by UCLA in the form of salary, numerous travel grants, a research assistant and a sabbatical year in 1979–1980. At the end, our chairman David Kaplan moved administrative mountains to get the manuscript typed; Diane Wells, Brooks Vedder, and others at Central Word Processing spent hours at their keyboards; and my research assistant Steven Livesay patiently endured the task of changing hundreds of references from the incunabula editions to the new critical editions. I am grateful to all of them for their support and help.

All good things come from God. Last and most of all, I am happy to thank Him for allowing me to work on this project and for anything that is of value in it. The remaining mistakes are my own responsibility.

Marilyn McCord Adams
May 9, 1982

A Note on Ockham's Life and Works

William Ockham was born before 1290 (c.1285), probably in the village of Ockham near London, and entered the Franciscan order at an early age. The first certain date in his life is February 26, 1306, when he was ordained subdeacon of Southwark, in the Diocese of Winchester. He was licensed to hear confessions on June 19, 1318. If he followed the normal course, Ockham began his theological studies at Oxford in 1309. After five years of work, he would have given cursory lectures on the Bible for two years. Between 1317–1319 he commented on Peter Lombard's *Sentences*, thereby arriving at the rank of formed bachelor (*baccalarius formatus*), and in the following two years he completed the requirements for the degree of master of theology. Ockham never became a regent master (*magister actu regens*), occupying the Franciscan chair at Oxford, partly because there were many in line ahead of him and partly because of the opposition of the chancellor of the university, John Lutterell. Following his studies, Ockham probably went to the *studium generale* of the London Custody, where he taught and wrote philosophy until 1324, finishing all of his non-political works. It is likely that he lived in the same house as Walter Chatton, and the running debate between them is reflected in the writings of both philosophers. In 1323 Lutterell went to the pope in Avignon with a list of 56 allegedly heretical theses extracted from Ockham's writings. Ockham was summoned to Avignon to answer these charges in 1324. Two years later a papal commission declared 51 propositions open to censure, although none of them were formally condemned by the pope. During his stay in Avignon, Ockham got involved in the controversy between the pope and the Franciscan order regarding Franciscan poverty. The minister general of the order, Michael of Cesena, assigned Ockham to research the issue. Ockham concluded that John XXII was contradicting the Gospels and earlier papal pronouncements and therefore was no true pope. After committing these accusations to writing, they left Avignon with the seal of the Franciscan order and were subsequently excommunicated. In Pisa they accepted the protection of Louis of Bavaria, whose election as Holy Roman Emperor the pope did not recognize. Ockham settled with Louis at Munich and there composed numerous political treatises against John XXII and his successors. According to his epitaph, Ockham died at Munich on April 10, 1347, perhaps of the Black Death.

Works. After the ground-breaking efforts of Fr. Philotheus Boehner, OFM, the first critical edition of Ockham's philosophical and theological works is now nearing completion under the direction of Fr. Gedeon Gál, OFM, at the Franciscan Institute, St. Bonaventure, New York. Opera Theologica I–IV contains the *Ordinatio* (the prologue and Book I of Ockham's commentary on Peter Lombard's *Sentences*); Opera Theologica V–VIII, the *Reportatio* (Books II–IV of the *Sentence*-commentary) and miscellaneous questions; Opera Theologica IX, *Quodlibeta septem*; Opera Theologica X, *De corpore Christi* (the treatises on quantity); Opera Philosophica I, the *Summa logicae*; Opera Philosophica II, the *Expositio aurea* (*Expositionis in libros artis logicae prooemium* and *Expositio in librum Porphyrii de praedicabilibus*, *Expositio in librum Praedicamentorum Aristotelis*, and *Expositio in librum Perihermenias Aristotelis*) and *Tractatus de praedestinatione et de praescientia Dei respectu futuris contingentibus*; Opera Philosophica III, *Expositio super libros Elenchorum*; Opera Philosophica IV–V, *Expositio in libros Physicorum*; Opera Philosophica VI, the *Summulae in libros Physicorum* and the *Quaestiones in libros Physicorum*; and Opera Philosophica VII, dubious and spurious works.

While the exact chronological order of Ockham's works is not known, partly because many of them were composed during the same short period, the following groupings are clear. (1) *1317–1319*: The earliest of Ockham's writings is the *Reportatio* (Books II–IV of his *Sentence*-commentary), which survives in two incunabula editions—Strasbourg 1483 and Lyons 1495—as well as in the new critical edition. (2) *1321–1323*: The *Expositio aurea* was composed during this time and printed by Marcus de Benevento, Bologna 1496. The *Expositio super libros Elenchorum* was written during the same year as the *Perihermenias*-commentary; so were Books I–IV of the *Expositio in libros Physicorum*. At some point during this period, Ockham revised the first book of his *Sentence*-commentary, the so-called *Ordinatio*, which was printed in the Strasbourg 1483 and the Lyons 1495 editions. (3) *Before 1324:* Ockham composed the *Summa logicae,* his principal work on logic: the *Tractatus de praedestinatione et de praescientia Dei respectu futuris contingentibus*; the two treatises on quantity; the rest of the *Expositio in libros Physicorum* (Books V–VII); and the *Quodlibeta*, which were printed in Paris 1487–1488 and Strasbourg 1491. The authenticity of two shorter works once attributed to Ockham—viz., the *Tractatus logicae minor* and the *Elementarium*—has now been dismissed, and the *Tractatus de successivis* is an abridgement by another hand of parts of Ockham's *Expositio in libros Physicorum*. (4) *After 1324*: The political writings of Ockham constitute a separate corpus and are being edited by the Manchester University press under the title *Guillelmi de Ockham, Opera Politica*; so far, three volumes have been published.

Where possible, I have given page references to the new critical edition: to Opera Theologica I–IX, as well as to Opera Philosophica I–III. A few references to the *Reportatio* are to the Lyons 1495 edition, and question numbers follow the Lyons ordering. The new critical edition will often have a different numbering, but will provide a chart of correspondences. Where Ockham's *Physics*-commentaries are concerned, I have used the Bologna 1494 edition of the *Summulae Physicorum*; the Firenze Naz. Conv. Supp. B.5.726 manuscript of the *Expositio*; and the forthcoming critical text of the *Quaestiones*. Since the pagination of the critical texts is as yet unavailable, I have indicated the forthcoming volume numbers for each, so that readers can locate the relevant critical texts in the future. I have referred to T. B. Birch's edition (Burlington, Iowa, 1930) of the two treatises on quantity.

Abbreviations

The following list consists of titles of works by Ockham, Scotus, and Aquinas which, on account of their length and frequent citation, have usually been abbreviated in this book. Complete references for these works are included in the bibliography.

Ockham:

De praedest.:	*Tractatus de praedestinatione et de praescientia Dei respectu futuris contingentibus*, (OPh II).
De successivis:	*Tractatus de successivis*, (Boehner ed., 1944).
Expos. Elench.:	*Expositio super libros Elenchorum Aristotelis*, (OPh III).
Expos. Periherm.:	*Expositio in librum Perihermenias Aristotelis*, (OPh II).
Expos. Physicorum:	*Expositio in libros Physicorum*, (OPh IV–V).
Expos. Porphyr.:	*Expositionis in libros artis logicae prooemium et Expositio in librum Porphyrii de praedicabilibus*, (OPh II).
Expos. Praedicam.:	*Expositio in librum Praedicamentorum Aristotelis*, (OPh II).
Ord.:	*Ordinatio*, (OTh I–IV).
Quaest. Physicorum:	*Quaestiones in libros Physicorum*, (OPh VI).
Quaest. variae:	*Quaestiones variae in libros Sententiarum*, (OTh VIII).
Quodl.:	*Quodlibeta septem*, (OTh IX).
Rep. II–IV:	*Reportatio*, (OTh V–VII).
Summulae Physicorum:	*Summulae in libros Physicorum*, (OPh VI).

Scotus:

Opus oxon.:   *Opus oxoniense*, (Wadding V–X).
Ord.:   *Ordinatio*, (Vaticana I–VII) and
                                 Lectura in librum primum Sen-
                                 tentiarum, (Vaticana XVI–XVII).
Quaest. miscellaneae: *Quaestiones miscellaneae de for-*
                                 malitatibus, (Wadding III).
Quaest. subtil. Meta-
physicorum: *Quaestiones subtilissimae super*
                                 libros Metaphysicorum, (Wad-
                                 ding IV).
Quodl.:   *Quodlibeta*, (Wadding XII).

Aquinas:

In Boethii de trin.:   *Expositio super librum Boethii*
                                 De trinitate, (Decker ed., 1955).
In I–III de anima: *In Aristotelis librum De Anima*
                                 commentarium, (Marietti, 1959).
In I–XII Metaphys.:   *In duodecim libros Metaphy-*
                                 sicorum Aristotelis expositio,
                                 (Marietti, 1950).
In I–VIII Physic.:   *In octo libros Physicorum Aris-*
                                 totelis expositio, (Marietti, 1954).
In I–IV Sent.:   *Commentum in quattuor libros*
                                 Sententiarum, (Parma VI–VII) or
                                 Scriptum super libros Senten-
                                 tiarum Magistri Petri Lombardi,
                                 (Mandonnet and Moos ed., (1929).

Part One

Òntology

1

The Problem of Universals

Ockham's philosophical focus, whether he is doing logic, natural science, or theology, is on the branch of metaphysics commonly called "ontology." His insights and arguments are perennially controversial, although his syllabus was set by medieval reactions to Aristotle: the framework of the ten categories occasioned their discussion not only of the problem of universals (or the ontological status of properties) but also that of quantities, relations, etc.; and the hylomorphism of the *Physics* and *Metaphysics* was further elaborated in debates about the metaphysical structure of material things, the nature of qualitative change, and the ontological status of motion and time. Reserving the latter topics for Part Four below, I shall devote Part One to Ockham's views regarding the first two. In the present chapter, I shall briefly set out the medieval formulation of the problem of universals and sketch "Platonist" (so-called "extreme realist") and "Aristotelian" ("moderate realist") solutions to it. In chapter 2, I turn to Ockham's extensive critique of moderate realism, and in chapters 3 and 4 to his own "nominalist"/"conceptualist" solution, for which he is so notorious.

1. THE PROBLEM OF UNIVERSALS

The *locus classicus* for medieval discussions of the problem of universals is Boethius's commentary on Porphyry's *Isagoge*, or introduction to Aristotle's *Categories*. Once in that work (4, 1b25ff), Aristotle distinguishes ten categories: substance, quantity, quality, relation, place, time, being-in-a-position, condition, action, and passion. Porphyry understands these to be highest genera under which a hierarchy of species are distinguished by means of differentia. And he traces the famous Porphyrian tree under the category of substance, which divides into the species corporeal and incorporeal substance; corporeal substance (or body) into animate and inanimate; animate into plants and animals; animals into rational and irrational; and rational animals into mortal (or man) and immortal.

Aristotle's own remarks suggest at least two ways of arriving at this list. The first is to isolate a set of basic questions that collect distinct and non-overlapping ranges of answers. The suggestion is, for example, that answers appropriate to the question "Where?" are never suitable for the question "When?" and vice versa. A second approach is to examine the various kinds of answers one gets when the question "What is it?" is pressed. For example, if I ask what Socrates is, the first answer may be "a man." If I inquire further what a man is, and so on, the answers will be "a rational animal" and so on until one gets to the last answer, "a substance." Again, if I ask what chartreuse is, the answer may be first "a shade of green," then "a color," but ultimately "a quality."[1] It is at least arguable that Aristotle did not have much invested in this precise list or its length; at any rate, he never defends it or the above mentioned strategies for developing it. And medievals, too, came to challenge some of the later entries.

Given some such distinction among categories, however, the question naturally arises, "categories of what?" Both Porphyry and Boethius take it for granted that Aristotle meant to distinguish categories of *things*.[2] Further, Porphyry understands them to be categories of *predicables* and regarded genera, species, differentia, propria, and accidents as five kinds of predicable things. But Aristotle says that particular individuals are neither in nor said of a subject. Porphyry concludes that particulars are not among the things categorized and

1. See notes to chap. 4. 78–80 in *Aristotle's 'Categories' and 'De Interpretatione'*, (Oxford, 1963), translated with notes and glossary by J. L. Ackrill. Ockham notes this first approach in *Summa logicae* I, c.41, (OPh I, 107).

2. Ackrill joins this interpretation (*op. cit.*, 71–73 and 75–76).

identifies man, not Socrates, as the least species.[3] If so, Porphyry admits it is a puzzle what genera, species etc.—as non-particular predicable things—could be, although not one he is willing to pursue in an elementary textbook. Commenting on Porphyry, Boethius paraphrases,

> ...At present, he says, I shall refuse to say concerning genera and species whether they subsist or whether they are placed in the naked understanding alone; or whether subsisting they are corporeal or incorporeal; and whether they are separated from sensibles or placed in sensibles and in accord with them. Questions of this sort are a most exalted business and require very great diligency of inquiry.[4]

Taking up this challenge, Boethius notes that Porphyry has suggested four different answers to his original question: (i) *Genera, species, etc. are placed in the understanding alone.* Both Porphyry and Boethius take it for granted that we have genus-concepts (e.g., the concept 'animal'), species-concepts (e.g., the concept 'man'), etc. The question is, what extramental things correspond to such concepts? One answer would be that none do. (ii) *They subsist and are corporeal.* Unpopular in the middle ages, this option was taken up by Abelard's teacher Roscelin, whose doctrine that a universal is only a spoken sound (*flatus vocis*) was ridiculed by Anselm and Abelard alike. (iii) *They subsist and are incorporeal and separated from sensibles.* This was held by Plato, for whom the Forms or Ideas subsist independently not only of sensible particulars but also of any and every mind.[5] (iv) *They subsist and are incorporeal and placed in sensibles and in accord with them*, which Boethius considered to be the Aristotelian option.

3. Ackrill thinks Aristotle's first approach does exclude individuals from the things classified, but that the second does not (*ibid.*, 80). Moody notes that Porphyry departs from Aristotle's doctrine in the *Topics*, when he regards species as one of the predicables (*The Logic of William Ockham*, (London, 1935), chap.3, 66–73).

4. *The Second Edition of the Commentaries on the Isagoge of Porphyry*, in vol.1 of *Selections from Medieval Philosophers*, ed. and trans. Richard McKeon, (New York, 1929), sec.10, 91.

5. *Ibid.*, sec.11, 98.

Boethius observes that the distinguishing feature of genera, species, etc. is that they are or can be common to numerically many particulars. But there are several ways in which something can be had in common. (a) We have the room in common in the sense that many particulars may each occupy part of the room at one and the same time. Again (b) there is the case in which "a single thing passes at different times into the use of those having it, so that it is common as a servant or a horse is";[6] (c) "or else it is common to all at one and the same time, not however that it constitutes the substance of those to which it is common, but like some theatre or spectacle, which is common to all who look on."[7] A genus or species is not common in any of these ways, since each can be possessed wholly and completely by numerically many particulars simultaneously in such a way as to constitute the essence of each.[8]

Boethius then presents three aporetic arguments from the fact that genera, species, etc. are common and that none of (i)–(iv) can be accepted in answer to Porphyry's question. (1.1) First, he argues that none can be numerically one. For what is common can exist wholly and completely in numerically many simultaneously, and nothing that can exist wholly and completely in numerically many simultaneously is numerically one itself. Behind the latter premiss lies the assumption

(T1) If A is wholly in x at t_1, and B is wholly in y at t_1, and x is wholly outside y, then A is wholly outside and numerically distinct from B.

Where 'in' and 'outside' are understood in senses analogous to their spatial senses (T1) is highly plausible, although not—as we shall see—uncontroverted. (1.2) If a genus or species is not numerically one, existing as it can in numerically many particulars simultaneously, could it not be real by virtue of being numerically many? Boethius thinks this assumption would re-

6. *Ibid.*, sec.10, 94.
7. *Ibid.*
8. *Ibid.*

quire us to assume infinitely many genera where we thought there was only one. For suppose the genus animal is numerically n animals. Still, Boethius insists, we shall have to concede that the n animals have something in common. But what can this mean? By argument (1.1), not that numerically one animality exists in numerically n animals. Rather, Boethius says, that "they have something similar, yet not the same."[9] Yet, it seems that

(T2) if x is similar to y, there must be something z (where z is not identical to x or to y) with respect to which x and y are similar to each other.

So if animal$_m$ is similar to animal$_n$, there is something—animality—with respect to which they are similar. Yet the latter claim is ambiguous between 'The animality of animal$_m$ is numerically the same as the animality of animal$_n$', which is excluded by (1.1), and 'The animality of animal$_m$ is similar to the animality of animal$_n$'. By (T2), however, if the latter is true, there must be something—call it animality'—with respect to which the animality of animal$_m$ resembles the animality of animal$_n$. By argument (1.1), the animality' of the animality of animal$_m$ cannot be numerically the same as the animality' of the animality of animal$_n$. But if they are merely similar, we shall have to posit another animality" in respect of which they are similar, and so on to infinity. Since a genus or species was supposed to be one over many particulars, Boethius evidently finds absurd the notion that infinitely many genus-things should correspond to each higher branch of Porphyry's tree. The combined result of (1.1) and (1.2) is that, since every extramental thing is either numerically one or numerically many, genus or species is not an extramental thing, and answers (ii)–(iv) to Porphyry's original question are mistaken.

(1.3) Boethius then turns to argue that the first answer (i) is unacceptable as well. For every idea or concept is, necessarily, an idea or concept *of* something; and every idea or concept

9. *Ibid.*, sec.10, 93.

represents its object either exactly as it is in reality or not exactly. Not the first by (1.1) and (1.2). Boethius maintains, however,
that

    (T3) if an idea or concept fails to represent its object exactly
           as it is in reality, it is vain and false,

apparently in the sense that nothing falls under or satisfies that
concept. If there are no extramental genus-things or spe-
cies-things, our genus-concepts and species-concepts will not
represent extramental things exactly as they are and will thus
be "vain and false." This consequence seems the more preni-
cious when viewed against the common assumption of Plato
and Aristotle that having such genus- and species-concepts is
our means of having knowledge properly speaking. For they
hold that knowledge properly speaking and definition are of
what is universal and real; if nothing real is universal, scepticism
is the result.

2.   AN "ARISTOTELIAN" SOLUTION

   Since Boethius is dealing with a commentary on Aristotle's
Categories, he finds it appropriate to follow "out the opinion of
Aristotle very diligently" by showing how an Aristotelian, Alexander of Aphrodisias would solve the problem of universals formulated in arguments (1.1)–(1.3). (His is only one
"Aristotelian" answer; we shall examine others in detail in
chapter 2 below.) Boethius thinks that Alexander would object
to all three arguments. Most obviously defective is (1.3), resting
as it does on the simple-minded principle of representation in
(T3). Alexander distinguishes two ways in which an idea or concept can fail to represent things exactly as they are. One is by
composition—i.e., by conceiving together properties that do
not exist together in reality, as in our idea of a golden mountain
or a round square. Another is by division or abstraction—i.e., by
conceiving separately or in isolation properties that could not
exist separately in reality. Ideas or concepts of the first sort are

vain and false, in that nothing real falls under them, but abstract ideas or concepts need not be empty. And Alexander explains that our genus-concepts and species-concepts are formed by abstraction and division. Thus, Boethius reports his view that

> ...Since genera and species are thought, therefore their likeness is gathered from the individuals in which they are, as the likeness of humanity is gathered from individual men unlike each other, which likeness conceived by the mind and perceived truly is made the species; again when the likeness of these diverse species is considered, which cannot be except in the species themselves or in the individuals of the species, it forms the genus...[10]

By division and abstraction, the mind singles out those features which provide the basis for the similarity between Socrates and Plato. And even though these features cannot, on the Aristotelian view, exist all by themselves in reality but only in conjunction with others, this abstract likeness is enough for Socrates and Plato to fall under the concept.

Alexander's alternative to (T3) is further clarified by his replies to (1.1) and (1.2). The latter arguments combine the thesis (T2) that resemblance must be grounded in identity with the assumption that the same thing cannot be both numerically one and numerically many. But this overlooks the fact that something may have a double mode of existence, in the intellect as an object of thought and in reality in particulars. According to Boethius, Alexander holds that

> genera and species *are in individuals*, but they are *thought universals*; and species must be considered to be nothing other than the thought collected from the substantial likeness of individuals unlike in number, and genus the thought collected from the likeness of species. But this likeness when it is in individual things is made sensible, when it is in universals it is made intelligible; but in the same way when it is sensible it remains in individuals, when it is understood, it is made universal. Therefore, they subsist in sensibles, but they are understood without bodies...[11]

Just as the same line can be both concave and convex, so the

10. *Ibid.*, sec.11, 97.   11. *Ibid.*, (italics mine).

same subject—the genus or species—can be both particular and numerically multiplied and universal.

> ...So too for genera and species, that is, for singularity and universality, there is only one subject, but it is universal in one manner when it is thought, and singular in another when it is perceived in those things in which it has its being.[12]

Alexander would thus replace (T3) with

> (T4) the genus or species existing in thought represents all those particulars in which it really exists.

(T1) is acceptable, and it can be admitted that genus or species is not numerically one but numerically many insofar as it exists in reality in numerically many particulars. But (T2) can also be granted, because the respect in which Socrates and Plato or Socrates and Brownie the donkey resemble each other—i.e., the species man or the genus animal—is one and universal when it is thought, and the pernicious run to infinity is therewith halted.

3.   A "PLATONIST" SOLUTION

Although Boethius thinks that Alexander's approach would resolve the difficulty well enough for an Aristotelian (a conclusion with which Ockham will disagree; see chapter 2 below), he does not himself accept this solution because he is a Neoplatonist. He thought that for Plato a genus or species is something incorporeal that exists independently of human minds and of sensible particulars. It is universal, not particular in reality; nevertheless, it is individual and numerically one in reality as well. In defense of his position, a Platonist would first attack the argument in (1.1), which assumes that a genus or species is in its particulars in a way analogous to the spatial 'in', by (T1). A Platonist will refuse to think of humanity existing in Socrates on the model of a peanut existing in a jar and will say

---

12. *Ibid.*, 98.

instead that Socrates and Plato are both men because they both participate in the Form Man. And while the notion of participation is notoriously obscure, it was at least partially cashed by Plato and his successors in terms of an imperfect resemblance between the spatio-particulars and the Form. The contention is that there is no more problem in numerically many particulars imperfectly resembling one and the same really existing Form than in numerically many people watching one and the same spectacle in a theater. To the extent that a Platonist analyses participation in terms of resemblance, however, he will avoid positing an infinite progression of genera and species only if he also rejects (T2), the assumption undergirding (1.2). For according to the Self-Predication assumption, the Form of F is F. Thus, if Socrates resembles the Form Man, by (T2), they resemble each other in something, viz., man. But, by (T2), not the man that is Socrates or the man that is the Form Man. Therefore, with respect to some third man, and so on to infinity. Conceding some intuitive appeal to (T2), a Platonist might plausibly replace it with

   (T5)   where x and y are spatiotemporal particulars, if x is
          similar to y, there must be some property F-ness or
          Form of F in which x and y both participate,

but insist that the Form Man resembles Socrates through itself.

4.   NOMINALIST/CONCEPTUALIST SOLUTIONS

Besides Roscelin, Abelard and Ockham defended the first answer to Porphyry's question—viz., (i) that genera and species exist in the understanding alone and cannot be found in or identified with any extramental things other than conventional names. Abelard says that the universal man is the spoken word 'man' taken together with its signification, the concept 'man', whereas Ockham maintains that the species man is primarily to be identified with the concept 'man' itself and secondarily with the spoken or written word (see chapter 3 below). These

nominalist/conceptualists joined moderate realists in rejecting
(T3) and analysing the representation of abstract ideas or concepts in terms of similarity. Nevertheless, Abelard and Ockham
part company with moderate realists who try to sustain (T2)
with the thesis that genera and species exist not only in thought
as universal but also as numerically multiplied in extramental particulars. Rather Abelard and Ockham outdistance the
Platonists in rejecting both (T2) and (T5) and insisting that
similarity is a primitive, two term relation that is not to be further analysed in terms of identity (see chapter 4 below).

The heart of the medieval problem of universals is thus found
in the twin issues of whether similarity must be grounded in
identity as in (T2) or (T5), and whether universal concepts supply us with any knowledge of reality. Now that we have pre-
viewed the principal solutions, we are ready for a detailed look
at Ockham's defense of the nominalist/conceptualist answer.

2

Universals Are Not Things
Other Than Names

Ockham regarded the view that universals are real things
other than names as "the worst error of philosophy,"[1] not
primarily on grounds of ontological parsimony, but because he
found it contradictory. Aristotle had convinced most thirteenth
and fourteenth century philosophers that Platonism was un-
reasonable, because "no one in his right mind" would hold
that the natures of particulars exist in separation from them the
way Platonic ideas do.[2] Ockham therefore concentrates his fire
on moderate realism, the virtually unanimous opinion of his
contemporaries:

> ...everyone I know of agrees in maintaining that the nature, which is
> somehow universal—at least potentially and incompletely—really ex-
> ists in the individual...[3]

Ockham examines no fewer than six versions of it, including
those of his most eminent predecessors, Thomas Aquinas and
Duns Scotus.

1.   MODERATE REALISM AND INDIVIDUATION

In maintaining that genera and species really existed in particulars, moderate realists were affirming that genera or species
are metaphysical constituents of particulars. Since they also in-

---

1. *Expos. Periherm.* I, Prooemium, (OPh II, 363).
2. *Ord.* I, d.2, q.4, (OTh II, 117).
3. *Ibid.*, q.7, (OTh II, 226).

sisted that genera and species were common to numerically distinct particulars, they could not say that genera or species were the only metaphysical constituents of particulars. For if human nature were the only metaphysical constitutent of any particular man, it would seem that there could not be more than one man. And if human nature is a constituent in each of Socrates and Plato, so that they have a constituent in common, then, since they are numerically distinct men, they each must have a constituent that is not common to the other and that makes them distinct from each other. Most moderate realists[4] thus concluded that particulars were composites of a nature that is somehow common to numerically distinct particulars and individuating principles that were distinct in numerically distinct particulars.

Just what the individuating principles were, was a matter of considerable dispute. Abelard's teacher, William of Champeaux, seems to have held for a time that what individuates particulars of the same species from one another is that they have different accidents.[5] What makes Socrates different from Plato is in part that one has a different height, weight, hair color, and shape of nose from the other. Abelard released a battery of five arguments against this opinion, one of which was based on Aristotle's dictum that accidents cannot be naturally prior to substance. Generally speaking, if x is naturally prior to y, then y depends on x for its existence and not vice versa. Aristotle wanted to say that accidents depend for their existence on the existence of substance and not vice versa. But if accidents were what made Socrates a numerically distinct particular from Plato, then Socrates would depend on these accidents to be Socrates and hence would depend on them for *his* existence. Thus, if the individuating principles were accidents, accidents would be naturally prior to substance—which is the opposite of what

<hr>

4. It is not so clear, as we shall see, that the last view examined below—that of Henry of Harclay—fits this pattern. But it is also not obvious that he belongs with the moderate realists any more than Ockham does.

5. See selections from *The Glosses of Peter Abailard on Porphyry*, in vol.1 of *Selections from Medieval Philosophers*, ed. and trans. Richard McKeon, (New York, 1929), 222–24.

Aristotle claimed. This argument enjoyed a widespread acceptance in the thirteenth and fourteenth centuries as a refutation of the view that the individuating principles are accidents.

As we shall see in more detail later (see Part Four, chapter 16 below), Aquinas thinks that matter is what individuates. Not prime matter, however. According to Aquinas, prime matter is neither a substantial nor an accidental property but is pure potentiality that has no actuality of its own. As such, he reasons, it is just as indeterminate and determinable as the nature is and so could not serve by itself to individuate the species. Quantity, as an accidental property, could not serve by itself either, for the reason just given in the preceding paragraph.[6] Aquinas concludes that the individuating principles are matter signed by quantity—i.e., matter taken together with quantitative dimensions.[7]

Scotus rejects Aquinas's position on the ground that it is tantamont to saying that accidents individuate.[8] Further, Scotus held that only what is distinct and determinate in and of itself can individuate, insisting that

> ...no matter what common things are simultaneously conjoined, it is never contrary to the whole aggregate of itself that it should exist in something other than that in which it exists...[9]

And he concludes that neither matter by itself, existence, or any combination of accidents can individuate.[10] On the other hand, Scotus argues that the individuating priniciples must be something positive. For a particular has a more perfect unity (numerical unity) than a nature has (specific unity). Hence, what gives it that unity must have an actuality of its own. Scotus concludes that what individuates or "thisness" (*haecceitas*) is some positive principle that has an actuality of its own and that

---

6. *Summa theologiae* I, q.76, a.6, ad 2.
7. *Ibid.*, q.75, a.4 and 7; *De ente et essentia*, c.2.
8. *Ord.* II, d.3, q.4, n.111, (Vaticana VII, 446).
9. *Quaest. subtil. Metaphysicorum* VII, q.13, (Wadding IV, 417–18).
10. *Ord.* II, d.3, q.5, 3, and 4, respectively.

does not fall—except by reduction—under any of the ten
categories.[11]

What is important for present purposes, however, is that
moderate realists conceive of particulars as having at least two
metaphysical constituents: a common species or nature and individuating principles.

2. REAL DISTINCTION, DISTINCTION OF
REASON, AND FORMAL DISTINCTION

Whether or not it is possible for natures that are in any way
universal to exist in particulars, however, depends entirely on
how the connection between them and the individuating principles is explained. Of the versions of moderate realism examined by Ockham, the first two say that the nature and individuating principles are really distinct; the third, that of Duns
Scotus, that they are formally distinct; and the last three, that
there is a distinction of reason between them, although they are
really the same. Thus, before proceeding any further, it is
necessary to see how these different types of distinction were
understood.

(2.1) *Real Distinction*. Most straightforward among them is
real distinction, which, properly speaking, is a distinction
among real things (*res*).[12] Ockham, in effect, takes the Indiscernibility of Identicals—i.e., the principle that for every individual x and y and every property F, if x is identical with y,
then x is F if and only if y is F—to be a necessary truth about and
our primary criterion of distinction for real things. Thus, he says
that contradiction is "the most powerful way" of proving a
distinction among real things,[13] and insists that if we allow one

11. *Ibid.*, q.6, n.169–170, (Vaticana VII, 474–75).
12. Ockham twice recognizes a loose sense of 'really distinct' according
to which those that are formally distinct are said to be really distinct, because
they are distinct prior to any activity of the intellect (*Ord.* I, d.2, q.11, (OTh
II, 370); *Quodl.* I, q.2, (OTh IX, 12)). For Ockham's understanding of 'formally distinct', see Part Five, chapter 22 below.
13. *Ord.* I, d.2, q.11, (OTh II, 374).

and the same real thing to have contradictory properties simultaneously, "every method of proving distinction or nonidentity between any entity whatever would perish."[14] Further, Ockham seems to assume that nothing is contingently really the same as or contingently really distinct from a given real thing. Rather if x is really the same as y, x is necessarily identical with y; and if really distinct, necessarily really distinct (where proper names, demonstratives, or rigid designators are substituted for 'x' and 'y'). Thus, Ockham implies that if x and y are really the same, it is not logically possible that x should exist without y or vice versa, even by divine power.[15]

Paradigm cases of really distinct things are distinct substances such as Socrates and Plato. But Scotus and Ockham will maintain that Socrates' matter is really distinct from Socrates' form, and Ockham will argue that Socrates' sensory soul is really distinct from his intellectual soul (see Part Four, chapter 15 below). And most of their contemporaries would contend that his qualitites are really distinct from his substance (see Part One, chapter 8 below). It is widely assumed that real distinction went together with separability or the logical possibility that at least one of the pair of really distinct things should exist without the other. Ockham often makes use of the principle that

(A) ...Every real thing (*res*) that is prior to another real thing really distinct from it can exist without it...[16]

It follows from (A), together with the Aristotelian claim that substance is naturally prior to accidents, that a substance can exist without any accident that is really distinct from it. Ockham's contemporaries generally believed that Aristotle would not have granted the converse—that a particular accident can exist without the substance in which it inheres. But the doctrine of transubstantiation seemed to require that particular accidents

14. *Ibid.*, q.1, (OTh II, 16).
15. *Ibid.*, q.6, (OTh II, 193).
16. *Ibid.*, q.4, (OTh II, 115); cf. q.6, (OTh II, 193) and *Treatise on Quantity* I, q.3, (Birch ed., 96–98).

can exist without inhering in any substance at all and do so miraculously in the sacrament of Holy Communion or the Eucharist (see Part One, chapter 6 below). Thus, in at least some cases, the naturally posterior of really distinct things can exist without the naturally prior.

There is reason to think that Ockham would not endorse the following general principle, however:

> (B) If x and y are really distinct and neither is a part of the other, it is logically possible that x should exist without y and logically possible that y should exist without x.

For he explicitly asserts in *Reportatio* IV, q.14, (OTh VII, 324), that God is really distinct from a created real thing. Yet, he adheres to dogma in affirming that "a creature cannot exist when God does not exist"[17] and that "it is a contradiction for a man to exist and not God."[18] Indeed, Ockham thinks that God exists necessarily and so could not fail to exist, whether anything else exists or not.[19] Remarks throughout his works would, however, suggest his assent to an analogous general principle restricted to creatures:

> (C) If x and y are really distinct created real things, neither of which is part of the other, then it is logically possible that x should exist without y and logically possible that y should exist without x.

The above mentioned assertion—viz., that for each accident really distinct from substance, it is logically possible that the substance should exist without the accident—does not seem to entail that a substance can exist without having any accidents at all. Yet, Ockham does maintain that

> (D) When a real thing (*res*) is really distinct from other real things and can exist without each of them taken one by

17. *Ord.* I, d.27, q.3, (OTh IV, 242).
18. *Ibid.*, d.30, q.1, (OTh IV, 307).
19. *Ibid.*, d.8, q.7, (OTh III, 259–260).

one, it can exist without any and all of them taken
together,[20]

in attacking the view that universals are real, and (D) is used by
Walter Chatton as a weapon against Ockham's own position
(see Part One, chapter 3 below). And Ockham does explicitly
use (D) to argue that "substance can exist without any quantity."[21]

(2.2) *Distinction of Reason*. Whereas a real distinction between things involves the logical possibility of separate existence in reality, a distinction of reason between beings involves mere separability by a thinking mind. Thus, it was held
that there is a distinction of reason between x and y, if and only
if x and y are thought of by means of distinct concepts.

A number of Ockham's predecessors found this distinction
especially fruitful for solving philosophical and theological
problems. For often there is a strong motive for asserting that x
and y are not really distinct but are the same real thing (*res*) and
at the same time for saying that x and y are somehow distinct.
For example, the doctrine of divine simplicity forbids the claim
that divine wisdom and divine goodness, or the divine essence
and the divine persons are distinct real things. Nevertheless, the
former have different definitions and the latter have contradictory properties (e.g., the Son is begotten, but neither the divine
essence nor the Father is begotten). Thus, Aquinas says in each
case that they are really the same, but there is a distinction of
reason between them (see Part Five, chapter 21 below). Similarly, adherents of the last three versions of moderate realism find
reason to say that the nature and individuating principles in a
particular thing are really the same, but there is a distinction of
reason between them.

Ockham recognizes that there are distinctions of reason as
well as real distinctions among beings. But he thinks that, literally construed, claims of the form 'x is really the same as y, but
there is a distinction of reason between x and y' are fundamen-

20. *Ibid.*, d.2, q.4, (OTh II, 15).
21. *Rep.* IV, q.9, (OTh VII, 159).

tally confused, because they violate what Ockham regards as a fundamental principle about identity and distinction:

> (E) ...being the same or distinct are properties (*passiones*) that immediately pertain to that to which they pertain. Consequently, they pertain to it, everything else left aside.[22]

Ockham acknowledges that there are many features a thing may have through the agency of something extrinsic to it, and some (e.g., the property of being understood or thought of) that it can have through the activity of the intellect. But identity and distinction are not among such features.[23] Thus, he charges, it is absurd to suppose that Socrates is made really the same as Socrates and really distinct from Brownie through Plato.[24] A fortiori, Socrates is not made the same as or distinct from anything else by an activity of the intellect.[25] Likewise, divine goodness and divine wisdom are not changed in any way by virtue of being understood. If they were in no way distinct prior to the activity of the intellect, they were in no way distinct after it either.[26]

Again, philosophers who make such claims start with an ontology that includes only real things (*res*), which exist, or at least can exist, in reality, and conceived objects or concepts, which have a non-real mode of existence as objects of thought. In more Aristotelian terminology, "the first division of being is into real beings and beings of reason," just as the first division of substance is into corporeal and incorporeal.[27] Thus, "a real being and a being of reason are more distinct than two real beings..."[28] Thus, if, strictly speaking, identity and distinction of reason apply to beings of reason only, and real identity and

---

22. *Ord.* I, d.2, q.7, (OTh II, 229).
23. *Ibid.*, q.2, (OTh II, 63–64).
24. *Ibid.*, q.6, (OTh II, 184).
25. *Ibid.*, q.2, (OTh II, 63).
26. *Ibid.*, (OTh II, 56).
27. *Ibid.*, (OTh II, 54).
28. *Ibid.*, (OTh II, 75).

distinction to real things (*res*) only, then "no being of reason is really the same as or distinct from any being of reason" and "nothing real is the same as or distinct in reason from anything real..."[29] It is, in effect, a category mistake to say that divine wisdom and divine goodness are really the same, but there is a distinction of reason between them. For if divine wisdom and divine goodness are really the same, then they are a real thing and so not the kind of being that can be the same as or distinct in reason from another. But if there is a distinction of reason between divine wisdom and divine goodness, then they are beings of reason and so not the kind of beings that can be really the same. Similarly, for other statements of this form.

As we shall see in the next chapter, Ockham was initially inclined to accept an ontology that includes only real things (*res*) and beings of reason. And leaving aside until later (see Part Five, chapter 22 below) the relation of the divine persons to the divine essence, Ockham thinks that there are only four ways in which one being can be distinct from another:[30] (i) as one real being from another, in which case there is a real distinction; (ii) as one being of reason from another, in which case there is a distinction of reason; (iii) as a real being from a being of reason, in which case the distinction is strictly neither a distinction of reason nor a real distinction, but an intermediate distinction,[31] although in a broad sense it may be called a distinction of reason;[32] or (iv) as an aggregate of a real thing and a being of reason from a real thing or from a being of reason or from another aggregate, in which case there is neither a distinction of reason nor a real distinction.

When Ockham gave up the notion that some beings have a non-real mode of existence, he came to hold that "to be distinct in reason is only to have different descriptions,"[33] and therefore that a distinction of reason obtains "only between

29. *Ibid.*, (OTh II, 65).
30. *Ibid.*, q.3, (OTh II, 78).
31. Cf. *ibid.*, q.11, (OTh II, 370).
32. *Ibid.*, q.2, (OTh II, 65).
33. *Quodl.* III, q.2, (OTh IX, 209); cf. *Summa logicae* III–4, c.7, (OPh I, 784).

names, since definitions are only of names."[34] And, since all beings are really existent in Ockham's later theory (see Part One,
chapter 3 below), all names are real beings and there can be a
distinction of reason between names that are really distinct.[35]
He does not say whether an ambiguous name such as 'bank' is
really the same but distinct in reason from itself by virtue of its
different definitions.

Thus, Ockham suggests that when the authorities contain
statements of the form 'x and y are really the same, but there is a
distinction of reason between x and y', what they really mean to
assert is that one and the same real thing is genuinely signified
by or falls under both.

(2.3) *Formal Distinction*. Scotus found it impossible to deal
with philosophical and theological problems without resorting
to formal nonidentity or distinction, as contrasted with the real
distinction that obtains between real things (*res*) and the distinction of reason that depends on the intellect's activity of conceiving. Scotus's works contain at least two importantly different accounts of this alternative sort of nonidentity or distinction, however.[36]

(2.3.1) According to the first and earlier version, there often
is, within what is really one and the same thing (*res*), a plurality
of entities or property-bearers whose nonidentity or distinction
in no way depends upon the activity of any intellect, created or
divine. Scotus found a double motive for adopting this supposition. (a) The first is epistemological. Like Ockham, Scotus
thought that if in reality, prior to every act of the intellect, x and
y are in every way the same, the intellect could not make x
and y in any way distinct. But contrary to Ockham's whole

34. *Quodl.* I, q.3, (OTh IX, 20).
35. *Ibid.*, III, q.2, (OTh IX, 209–210).
36. Some order has been introduced into a confusing textual picture by
Hester Goodenough Gelber, in her excellent discussion *Logic and the Trinity: A Clash of Values in Scholastic Thought, 1300–1335*, (Ph.D. dissertation,
University of Wisconsin, 1974). For some reactions to her interpretation,
and to that of D. P. Henry in "Ockham and the Formal Distinction," *Franciscan Studies* N.S. XXV (1965): 285–292, see my article "Ockham on Identity
and Distinction," *Franciscan Studies* N.S. XXXVI (1976): 5–74.

philosophy, Scotus insists that distinctions in conceived objects must be mirrored by distinctions within real things, if the real things are to fall under distinct concepts simultaneously. Take the claim that whereas the genus and differntia of a given species are in no way distinct in reality, they are correctly conceived of by distinct concepts. Scotus reasons that when the intellect conceives of genus and differentia, respectively, either it has something of the thing (*res*) that is the species as its object or not. If the latter, then it seems that the concepts of genus and differentia are not of anything real and so are entirely fictitious. On the other hand, if in conceiving of genus and differentia, the intellect does have something of the thing (*res*) that is the species as its object, then, since there are no distinctions at all in that thing (*res*), these concepts must have altogether the same content—in which case they will not be distinct concepts after all. Nor will it do any good to say—as Henry of Ghent does[37]—that the conceived objects can be distinct, even though prior to every act of intellect there is no actual distinction between them in reality, because that thing is apt to cause distinct concepts in the intellect. For it is one thing to be the cause of these conceptions and another to be the object of the intellect when it conceives them.[38] Thus, Scotus does not see how those distinct concepts can genuinely signify the real thing (*res*) unless there is some nonidentity or distinction in the thing (*res*) corresponding to the distinction in conceived objects. Since there are cases in which prior to every act of intellect, what is really one and the same thing (*res*) is apt to fall under or be genuinely signified by distinct concepts, Scotus concludes that prior to every act of intellect, there must be some sort of nonidentity or distinction among entities within the real thing.

(b) Scotus's other motive is logical or metaphysical. He, too, was sensitive to the fact that often in philosophy or theology there is reason to deny that x and y are really distinct things (*res*) and yet apparent cause to affirm that x is F and y is not F. But

37. *Summae quaestionum ordinariarum*, A.27, q.1, (Paris, 1520, T.1, fol.162r O).

38. *Quaest. subtil. Metaphysicorum* VII, q.19, n.5 (Wadding IV, 727).

the Indiscernibility of Identicals, which unquestionably applies to everything that exists in reality, implies that nothing real that is in every way the same can be both *F* and not *F*. If it were possible to distinguish within what is really one and the same thing (*res*) nonidentical or distinct property-bearers, the way might seem open for a solution to such problems.

Scotus variously labels the nonidentical entities within what is really one and the same thing (*res*) "realities" (*realitates*), "formalities" (*formalitates*), "aspects" (*rationes*), "formal aspects" (*rationes formales*), "intensions" (*intentiones*) or "real aspects" (*rationes reales*). Similarly, because he says that such entities are formally distinct, different, diverse, or not the same, the relation between such entities is best known as formal nonidentity or distinction.

How can we tell when there is such a plurality of entities within the same thing (*res*)? Scotus's criterion of formal nonidentity or distinction is best inferred from what he says about formal identity. First, for Scotus, "formal unity follows real unity"[39] and so restricts the relations of formal identity and distinction to entities that are or are in what is really one and the same thing (*res*). Further, he explains that "those are formally the same which are so related that one falls under the definition of the other" or would so fall if they were definable in the strict Aristotelian sense in terms of genus and differentia.[40] Since man, by definition, is rational animal, it follows that rational animal is formally the same as man. Sometimes, he allows that rational is also formally the same as man, but other times he prefers to speak of rational's being formally included in man.[41] Given this understanding of what it is for *x* and *y* to be formally the same, we can infer a corresponding criterion of formal nonidentity or distinction:

   (F) *x* and *y* are formally nonidentical or distinct, if and only if
       (a) *x* and *y* are or are in what is really one thing (*res*); and

---

39. *Lectura* I, d.2, p.2, q.1–4, n.275, (Vaticana XVI, 216).
40. *Ibid.*; *Ord.* I, d.2, p.2, q.1–4, n.403, (Vaticana II, 356–57).
41. *Ibid.*, d.8, p.1, q.4, n.193, (Vaticana IV, 261—62).

(b) if *x* and *y* are capable of definition, the definition of *x* does not include *y* and the definition of *y* does not include *x*; and (c) if *x* and *y* are not capable of definition, then if they were capable of definition, the definition of *x* would not include *y* and the definition of *y* would not include *x*.

Does the existence of a plurality of formalities within what is really one and the same thing (*res*) render that thing composite? Not necessarily, according to Scotus. For he maintains that a thing is composite in the strict sense, only if it contains two things (*res*), one of which is in potentiality with respect to the other. For example, Socrates is a composite substance in the strict sense, because he is made up of more than one thing—matter and a plurality of substantial forms; body and soul—the former of which is in each case in potentiality with respect to the latter.[42] Alternatively, Scotus recognizes that a thing (*res*) might be seen to be composite in a less proper sense if it contains realities or formalities one of which is in potentiality with respect to the other. For example, he maintains that "the reality from which the specific difference is taken is in potentiality with respect to the reality from which the individual difference is taken..." And where genus and differentia are formally but not really distinct, the reality from which the genus is taken is nevertheless in potentiality with respect to the reality from which the specific difference is taken.[43] In these cases, the formally distinct entities are not the same "by identity" but are only "the same thing,"[44] analogous to the way distinct parts are not the same as one another but only the same whole. On the other hand, Scotus maintains that an infinite entity is (i) the same as any entity that is compossible with it and (ii) in poten-

---

42. *Ibid*. II, d.3, p.1, q.5–6, n.189–190, (Vaticana VII, 484–85); *Lectura* I, d.8, p.1, q.3, n.102–103, (Vaticana XVII, 34–35).

43. *Ibid*., (Vaticana XVII, 34–35); n.118, (Vaticana XVII, 41); q.4, n.189, (Vaticana XVII, 68–69); cf. *Ord*. I, d.8, p.1, q.3, n.106–107, (Vaticana IV, 201–202).

44. *Lectura* I, d.8, p.1, q.3, n.103, (Vaticana XVII, 35); q.4, n.189, (Vaticana XVII, 68–69).

tiality with respect to none. He concludes that where one or more formally distinct entities is infinite, they do not form a composite of any sort. Thus, while infinite goodness and infinite wisdom are not formally the same in God,[45] their existence in the divine essence does not make for any composition there, because each perfection is infinite.[46] And speaking of simple things that contain a plurality of formalities, he says that the latter are the same "by identity" or "really the same" or "the same thing,"[47] and not merely that they are *in* what is really one and the same thing (*res*).[48]

(2.3.2) Despite such reassurances from Scotus, his opponents at Paris apparently remained unconvinced that assuming a plurality of formalities or property-bearers in God was compatible with divine simplicity. Perhaps this is why Scotus adopted a different stance in the *Reportata Parisiensia* IA, d.33, q.2–3 and d.34, q.1, and in his *Logica*.[49] In these works, he continues to insist on the recognition of some distinction in reality (*ex natura rei*) and prior to every act of any intellect, but alternative to the real distinction between one thing (*res*) and another. Yet, he now denies that this involves distinguishing a plurality of entities or property-bearers within what is really one and the same thing (*res*).

Scotus elaborates this idea by contrasting absolute distinction (*distinctio simpliciter*) with distinction *secundum quid*. According to him,

> (G) *x* is absolutely distinct from *y*, if and only if (a) each of *x* and *y* is fully actual rather than having some sort of

45. *Ibid.*, q.4, n.175, (Vaticana XVII, 63); cf. *Ord.* I, d.8, p.1, q.4, n.193, (Vaticana IV, 261–62).

46. *Lectura* I, d.8, p.1, q.4, n.186, (Vaticana XVII, 69); cf. *Ord.* I, d.8, p.1, q.4, n.213, (Vaticana IV, 271); n.215, (Vaticana IV, 272–73); n.220, (Vaticana IV, 275); and II, d.3, p.1, q.5–6, n.190, (Vaticana VII, 484–85).

47. *Lectura* I, d.8, p.1, q.3, n.189, (Vaticana XVII, 69); d.33–34, q.u, n.4, (Vaticana XVII, 443); d.2, p.2, q.1–4, n.274–75, (Vaticana XVI, 216–17); *Ord.* I, d.8, p.1, q.4, n.217, (Vaticana IV, 274); *Lectura* I, d.2, p.2, q.1–4, n.272, (Vaticana XVI, 215).

48. *Ord.* I, d.2, p.2, q.1–4, n.406, (Vaticana II, 357).

49. Cf. Gelber, *op. cit.*, 80ff.

diminished being; (b) each of x and y has formal as opposed to merely virtual existence; (c) each of x and y has its own distinct existence and not confused or mixed existence; and (d) x is absolutely nonidentical with y.[50]

(a)–(c) of (G) concern the ontological status of the relata; (d), the relation of nonidentity between them. Really distinct things (*res*) satisfy all four conditions.[51] Thus, there is an absolute distinction between Socrates and Brownie the donkey, among Socrates' matter and his substantial forms, etc. On the other hand, a distinction between x and y may fail to be absolute on one of two counts: the ontological status of a relatum or the relata may fall short of that prescribed in (a)–(c) of (G); or the relation of nonidentity between the relata may be diminished in some way.[52] Thus, unproduced effects that exist only virtually in their causes cannot be absolutely distinct (by condition (b)); neither can the elements—earth, air, fire, and water—in "chemical" compounds of the same (by condition (c)). Likewise, forms that exist only potentially in matter and beings of reason that have only the diminished mode of existence in the intellect cannot be absolutely distinct from anything (by condition (a)).

Scotus makes clear that really distinct things (*res*) and distinct beings of reason alike satisfy condition (d) of (G). Thus, what makes real distinction an absolute distinction and distinction of reason not, is entirely a difference in the ontological status of their respective relata. Like Ockham, Scotus affirms that the relation of nonidentity is the same in the two cases.[53] Whereas Scotus's first account of formal distinction suggested that the same relation of absolute nonidentity is found between a third sort of entities, viz., formalities, his second account rejects such analogies and proposes instead that x and y are relatively

---

50. *Reportata Parisiensia* IA, d.33, q.2, n.9, (MS. Vat. Borg. 325, fol.83ra). This manuscript is described in Scotus, *Opera Omnia*, (Vaticana I, 145*).

51. *Quaest. miscellaneae*, q.1, n.12, (Wadding III, 444).

52. *Reportata Parisiensia* IA, d.33, q.2, fol.82vb–83ra.

53. *Quaest. miscellaneae*, q.1, n.12, (Wadding III, 444).

distinct when each satisfies conditions (a)–(c) of (G), but jointly
fail to satisfy condition (d) of (G). Thus, if *x* and *y* are distinct
secundum quid, it is not their being, but their mode of nonidentity that is diminished or reduced.[54]

Scotus informs us that nonidentity *secundum quid* is
twofold: (i) lack of formal identity, and (ii) lack of adequate
identity. (F) remains his criterion of formal nonidentity.[55] But
whereas on his first account, (F) seemed to serve as a criterion
for when to admit a plurality of property-bearers within a single
thing (*res*), the second account explicitly rejects such implications. In his *Logica*, Scotus maintains that '*A* is not formally *B* '
or '*A* is not formally the same as *B* ' no more entails '*A* is not *B* '
than 'An Ethiopian is not a white man' entails 'An Ethiopian is
not a man'. The reason is that both 'formally' and 'identity' fall
within the scope of the negation, so that it is only a certain
mode of identity, not absolute identity, that is denied. Further,
'*A* is not formally *B* ' or '*A* is not formally the same as *B* ' entails
'*A* is formally distinct from *B* ' only where the negation implicit
in 'distinct' is understood as negating 'formally' and not 'identity' alone. Finally, 'Formality *A* is distinct from formality *B* ' or
'Formality *A* and formality *B* are two distinct formalities' follow
from the above mentioned propositions, only if they are taken
in such a way that the mode of distinction is diminished or the
mode implicit in 'formality' is denied by the negation implicit in
'distinct'; but not where they are taken to imply that two formalities are absolutely distinct.[56]

Scotus says that *x* is not adequately identical with *y* when one
of them exceeds the other and vice versa, either according to
predication or according to perfection. Thus, animal is not adequately identical with man, because the former is predicated of
more things than the latter is, while the latter is more perfect
than the former is (presumably because the genus is in potentiality with respect to the specific difference, but species is not;
and actuality is more perfect than potentiality).[57]

54. *Reportata Parisiensia* IA, d.33, q.2, fol.83ra.
55. *Ibid*.
56. *Quaest. miscellaneae*, q.1, n.1–11, (Wadding III, 441–44).
57. *Reportata Parisiensia* IA, d.33, q.2, fol.83ra.

Scotus concludes that the Indiscernibility of Identicals does not necessarily hold where x and y are really the same but lacking in formal identity, and that the Transitivity and Symmetry of Identity do not necessarily apply where x and y are really, but not adequately the same.[58]

With these preliminaries in mind, let us turn to Ockham's critique of moderate realism. Ockham obviously views Scotus as his principal adversary: for he takes the trouble to argue against two misinterpretations of Scotus, before trying to refute Scotus's own position. His consideration of theories according to which there is a distinction of reason between the universal and particulars is much more abbreviated. We shall consider each in turn.

3. THE FIRST VERSION OF MODERATE REALISM

The most promising version of moderate realism considered by Ockham was in fact championed by his contemporary and arch-rival Walter Burleigh.[59] Ockham never quotes the *Doctor Clarus et Perspicuus*, however, but probably draws the following summary from a question disputed by Henry of Harclay:[60]

...One opinion is that any univocal universal whatever is a certain thing (*res*) that really exists outside the mind in any particular whatever, and is really distinct from any particular whatever, and from any other universal whatever. Thus, the universal man is one thing (*res*) that really exists outside of the mind in any man whatever and is really distinct from any man whatever and from the universal animal and the univer-

---

58. *Ibid.*, fol.83rb.

59. *Super artem veterem Porphyrii et Aristotelis*, (Venice, 1507, fol.5va–6ra).

60. See Gedeon Gál, "Henricus de Harclay: Quaestio de significato conceptus universalis," *Franciscan Studies* N.S. XXXI (1971): 178–234. Scotus himself considers a similar view and rejects it on the ground that "it seems impossible that any really existing thing should be numerically the same intelligible thing and thus attributed to different things" (*Quaest. stubtil. Metaphysicorum* VII, q.18, n.4, (Wadding IV, 722)).

sal substance, and so on with respect to all genera and species, whether they are subalternates or not...and all of these things, in themselves in no way multiplied, however much the particulars are multiplied, are in any individual whatever of the same species.[61]

This view contains three principal theses:

(T1) The universal is a thing (*res*) that exists in reality as a metaphysical constituent of particulars;

(T2) The universal exists (or can exist) in reality in numerically distinct particulars simultaneously without being numerically multiplied itself;

and

(T3) The universal is really distinct from particulars and other universals; genus is really distinct from species and from other genera; species from genera and other species; and both genera and species from particulars.

According to this theory, Socrates is a compound or aggregate of many, really distinct universal things—presumably the genus-thing substance, together with several differentia-things that combine with it to make the aggregate species-thing man—along with something else that is the individuating principle. The latter does not individuate the genus or species, so that animal or man in Socrates is numerically distinct from animal or man in Plato. Rather, the universals remain numerically unmultiplied, no matter how many particular men, animals, or substances they exist in. And they combine with one individuating principle to make Socrates and with another to make Plato.

Ockham's confident reaction to this opinion is that it is "absolutely false and absurd";[62] indeed, he contends, "that no universal is a substance existing outside the mind, admits of evi-

---

61. *Ord.* I, d.2, q.4, (OTh II, 100–101).
62. *Ibid.*, (OTh II, 108).

dent proof."[63] (3.1) To begin with, Ockham attacks (T1) on the ground that it makes universals parts of a particular, in which case

> ...Socrates would be no more a particular real thing (res) than a universal thing (res), since the whole is no more denominated from one of its essential parts than from another; just as a composite is no more said to be form than matter, or vice versa, even though form is the more principal part.[64]

This argument does not so much derive a contradiction from the view that Ockham opposes, as it represents a confrontation between two fundamentally different conceptions of the metaphysical structure of a particular. Advocates of this first opinion conceive of particulars as aggregates of really distinct properties at least some of which are universal. Abelard had already queried William of Champeaux's suggestion that a cluster consisting entirely of universals—some from the category of substance and others from accidental categories—could ever constitute a particular. If one aggregate of universals could, why not any and every such?[65] If, on the other hand, the aggregate includes some universals such as animal and rational, and some that are particular in and of themselves, Ockham does not see why the whole cluster should not have just as much title to the predicate "universal" as to the predicate "particular". Aggregate-theorists might have responded that there is a reason for identifying particulars with some property-aggregates and not others—viz., that particulars are fully determinate, while not every property-aggregate is complete enough to be so identified. For example, the one that includes only the genus substance and the differentiae animate and mobile is not, because every particular animal is determinate, not only with respect to being mobile, animate

63. *Summa logicae* I, c.15, (OPh I, 50).
64. *Ord.* I, d.2, q.4, (OTh II, 118); cf. *Expos. Praedicam.*, c.8, (OPh II, 165).
65. *The Glosses of Peter Abailard on Porphyry* in vol.1 of *Selections from Medieval Philosophers*, ed. and trans. Richard McKeon, 222–27.

substance, but also with respect to being rational or non-rational, mammal or reptile, two-legged or four-legged, etc. Adhering for a time to some nontrivial version of the Identity of Indiscernibles, William of Champeaux in effect held that a maximal aggregate could be obtained by adding more and more universals, while Burleigh appears to believe that a maximal aggregate is reached only when some non-sharable property is added to the full complement of universals. His answer to Ockham's challenge is that one unsharable property is enough to make the cluster as a whole unsharable, but one sharable or universal property does not make the whole universal.

(3.2) Focussing on (T3), the claim that universals and the particular or its individuating component are really distinct from one another, Ockham argues that in that case each will be able to exist without the other. (3.2.1) First, that the universal thing will be able to exist without the particular thing or individuating principles:

> ...(i) Every real thing (*res*) prior to another real thing (*res*) really distinct from it can exist without it. But according to you, (ii) this real thing is prior and is really distinct. Therefore, (iii) it can exist without that particular thing.[66]

Behind premiss (i) lies the Aristotelian definition of natural priority, according to which x is naturally prior to y if and only if y depends on x for its existence but not vice versa. (ii) refers to the fact that, according to this theory, a particular man such as Socrates depends for his existence on the existence of universal human nature, which is part of his essence; but universal human nature does not depend for its existence on the existence of Socrates. Without further argument, however, we might question why the conclusion in (iii) should seem so outrageous. After all, it seems perfectly reasonable, for an adherent of this position to say that universal human nature could exist without Socrates or his individuating principles, since it might continue to exist in Plato after Socrates' demise, in Aristotle after Plato's demise, etc. Ockham thinks, however, that if we apply another

---

66. *Ord.* I, d.2, q.4, (OTh II, 115).

acceptable principle to this conclusion, more objectionable consequences ensue.

> ...(iv) When some real thing (*res*) really distinct from other things can exist without each of them taken dividedly, and it can so exist by its nature, and it does not essentially depend on any of them, it can exist without each of them taken in conjunction—and this by divine power. But according to them, (v) the universal real thing that is signified by 'man' can really exist without each particular man. Therefore, (vi) by divine power, that universal real thing (*res*) could exist without any particular real thing (*res*)...[67]

(iv) is taken for granted by Scotus and Ockham and would perhaps have been accepted by an adherent of the position under attack. It is not obviously true, however: for it does not follow from the fact that this air can exist without occupying four cubic feet, and this air can exist without occupying five cubic feet, and so on for each volume, that this air can exist without occupying any volume at all. Why should such an inference hold where the independent existence of various things is concerned? Ockham further assumes that the conclusion in (vi) will come too close to Platonism for the comfort of a moderate realist. But (vi) does not contradict any of the theses contained in Ockham's summary of the opinion under discussion. (T1) says only that universals *do* exist in particulars—something which Plato would have regarded as impossible—not that they cannot exist without being part of any particular. An adherent of this opinion might simply reply that while universals never do exist in the natural course of things except as parts of particulars, Ockham is right in drawing the consequence of (T3) that it is logically possible for them to do so.

(3.2.2) Conversely, Ockham observes that "...according to them, the individual adds something to the nature, and this something combines with the universal thing (*res*) to make what is one *per se*," and he concludes that "therefore, it does not seem contradictory that what is added should be conserved by God without the approach of any universal nature—which

67. *Ibid.*

seems absurd.''[68] But what Ockham finds absurd, adherents of this position might regard as merely unusual. They could say that while individuating principles never do exist without being combined with some universal, it is indeed logically possible that they should do so and that this is no stranger than the logical possibility of the universal human nature existing in separation from any and every particular.

(3.3) Ockham argues that (T2) is impossible on two grounds, the first of which is theological. He reasons that "creation is absolutely out of nothing in such a way that nothing essential and intrinsic to the thing absolutely precedes it in real existence."[69] And "when something is annihilated, nothing intrinsic to the real thing (*res*) will remain in real existence—either in it or in anything else."[70] Consequently, if any such universal thing pertained to the essence of numerically distinct particulars of a given species, no individual of that species could be created at a time when some individual of that species already existed. Similarly, if some individual of that species were annihilated, every member of that species would be destroyed. But it is logically possible that some individual of a given species should be created at a time when some member of that species already exists; and logically possible that some individual should be annihilated without all members of its species being destroyed.[71] Adherents of this position could reply that

> ...something is created or annihilated. Nevertheless, it is not necessary that the nature that is common to it and others should be created or annihilated then.[72]

This time, however, Ockham's definitions are the ones that accord with traditional intentions. And insisting on this, Ockham maintains that

> ...The universal real thing (*res*) is just as essential to the individual as any particular real thing (*res*) is. For according to them, it is just as

68. *Ibid.*
69. *Ibid.*
70. *Ibid.*, (OTh II, 116).

71. *Ibid.*, (OTh II, 115–116).
72. *Ibid.*, (OTh II, 116).

essential to Socrates that he is a man as that he has this matter and this form. Therefore, just as Socrates cannot be annihilated or created unless both this matter and this form were created or annihilated, so Socrates cannot be created or annihilated unless this thing that is essential to them is nothing beforehand and absolutely nothing afterwards.[73]

Alternatively, this position might deny the assumption that it is logically possible that one individual of a given species should be created when some member of that species already exists or annihilated when some member of that species remains. Clearly, the latter is not an assumption that could be established by empirical evidence. For no matter how often we experience that, for example, a man comes into existence at a time when other men already exist or goes out of existence while other men remain in existence, this will give us no reason to believe that creation and annihilation are possible in such circumstances. For experience gives us no reason to believe that these are not merely cases of generation and corruption rather than creation or annihilation. Ockham's commitment to this premiss may in the end rest on a conception of the particulars of a given species as logically independent of one another. But adherents of the view under discussion conceive of them differently, as all sharing a single real thing that pertains to the essence of each, and so would not be compelled by Ockham's picture to accept the assumption or, for that matter, the conclusion of the argument based on it.

(3.4) Finally, Ockham thinks that (T2) will lead to contradiction when it comes to accounting for the relation between substances and accidents. According to Aristotle, substances are susceptible of contraries. And it is implicit in Ockham's original statement of the opinion under discussion that

(T4) A particular substance exists only if the real things (*res*) that are its genera and species in the category of substance really exist in that particular.

Further, in arguing for (T2), adherents of this position have im-

73. *Ibid.*, (OTh II, 116–117).

plied that the property (*passio*) risibility inheres in Socrates, only by virtue of the universal property (*passio*) risibility existing and inhering in the universal substance man.[74] Ockham suggests that in the same way they will maintain that

(T5) Particular contraries do not really exist unless the common universal contrary real things (*res*) exist,

and

(T6) A particular accidental property inheres in a particular substance only by virtue of the universal accident's inhering in the universal substance.

But Ockham thinks that it is easy to reduce the conjunction of (T2), (T4), (T5), and (T6) to an absurdity. For it often happens that one of a pair of contraries inheres in one member of a given species and the other in another member of that species at one and the same time. For example, Socrates may be white all over and an Ethiopian black all over at one and the same time. But in that case, it follows, by (T2), (T4), (T5), and (T6), that the universal blackness and the universal whiteness simultaneously inhere in the universal man at one and the same time. And in general it follows that contraries can simultaneously inhere in what is really one and the same thing (*res*)—which is a contradiction. Likewise, it follows that the universal man is susceptible of change. For just as the accidental properties that inhere in particular men vary from time to time, so the universal accidents that inhere in the universal man will vary from time to time.[75]

Further, the conjunction of (T2), (T4), (T5), and (T6) entails certain absurdities in theology. For according to Christian doctrine, human nature is united to the Divine Word in Christ to form one person. But it follows from the above mentioned theses that numerically the same universal man pertains to the essence of Christ and to the essence of Judas and others who are damned and miserable. Thus, it follows from these theses that

74. *Ibid.*, arg.6, (OTh II, 105).
75. *Ibid.*, (OTh II, 120).

> ...something intrinsic and essential to Christ would be damned and miserable both with the misery of guilt and the misery of punishment. For the nature common to Christ and to other men is informed both by happiness in general and by misery in general—both the misery of guilt and the misery of punishment...[76]

Yet,

> ...nothing united to the Divine Word is damned or miserable. Therefore, no such universal nature that can receive contraries—say of happiness and misery—is in Christ.[77]

Again, if something that pertains to the essence of Christ is equally informed by happiness in general and by misery in general, it seems that there is no more reason to say that Christ is happy than that He is miserable.[78] Ockham's conclusion is that there cannot be any such universal substance things (*res*) that inhere in such universal substances.

I think that adherents of this position would have accepted Ockham's development of their theory through theses (T4), (T5), and (T6), and would have granted the conclusion that the universal blackness and the universal whiteness, the universal happiness and the universal misery can simultaneously inhere in the numerically unmultiplied universal man. But they should have denied that this consequence is contradictory or in violation of the Indiscernibility of Identicals. Everyone agrees, they might point out, that contrary accidents can inhere in the same real substance successively. And no one denies that at a given time a single particular may have contraries inhering in different parts of it—e.g., a table may have a white top and black legs. This is because the predication of the contrary accidents is relativized to times and to spatial parts, respectively. In the same way, they will insist, general ascriptions of accidents to universal substances must be understood as relativized to the particulars at which it has them. Thus, just as 'white *simpliciter*' and 'black *simpliciter*' are incompatible properties, but 'white

76. *Ibid.*, (OTh II, 121).
77. *Ibid.*
78. *Ibid.*

all over at t_1' and 'black all over at t_2' or 'white on top' and 'black on the bottom' are not; so 'white all over at Socrates' and 'black all over at Plato' are not incompatible properties when asserted of universal substances.

Indeed, it is somewhat surprising that Ockham overlooked this line of escape from contradiction, since he avails himself of it in another context. As we shall see (in chapter 6 below), most of Ockham's predecessors and contemporaries thought that it was logically impossible for a single physical object to exist wholly and completely in discontinuous places simultaneously. In defense of this conclusion, they argued that if a physical object could so exist, it would be logically possible that it have some accident at one of the places that it lacked at the other. For example, it might be heated at one place by a fire that is near to the one place but too far away from the other place to affect it there; or something might cause it to be white at the one place, but be too far away to affect its color at the other place. Ockham replies that if a physical object did exist wholly and completely in two discontinuous places simultaneously, then it could have an accident at one of the places that it lacked at the other place. Yet, he denies that this is a contradiction, because we have to understand the predications of such accidents as relativized to place: 'white *simpliciter*' and 'black *simpliciter*' are incompatible predicates, but 'white all over at p_1' and 'not white all over at p_2' are not incompatible.[79] If Ockham makes this move himself, he must—barring further argumentation—allow the analogous step to his opponents. And when de does, this attempt to reduce the conjunction of (T2), (T4), (T5), and (T6) to contradiction will fail.

4.   THE SECOND VERSION OF MODERATE REALISM

The second view discussed by Ockham resembles one mistakenly attributed to Duns Scotus by William of Alnwick

---

79. *Rep.* IV, q.6, (OTh VII, 98–99); q.7, (OTh VII, 131–32); cf. *Quaest. Physicorum,* q.32, (OPh VI).

(d.1332), a Franciscan and independent-minded member of the Scotist school.[80] Like the first, it maintains that

(T7) The nature is somehow common to many in reality.

And true to the spirit of moderate realism, it holds that

(T8) The nature can exist in reality *only* as part of a particular.

Since in the strict sense of 'part', distinct parts of a whole must be really distinct from each other, it follows the first position in asserting that

(T9) The universal is a real extramental thing that is really distinct from the contracting difference

or individuating principle.[81] But it concedes Ockham's principal contention against the first view—viz., that numerically the same nature cannot simultaneously pertain to the essence of numerically distinct particulars—and so endorses the opposite of (T2):

(T10) The nature is numerically multiplied by the contracting differences in distinct particulars.

Thus, according to this position, there will be numerically as many humanities as there are numerically distinct particular human beings.

Ockham, of course, agrees with the consequence that there are numerically as many humanities as there are numerically distinct particular human beings, but contends that the quadruple of assertions in (T7)–(T10) is contradictory.

(4.1) First Ockham reasserts his contention that particulars must be homogeneously particular and therefore charges that (T7) is incompatible with (T8):

...There is always a proportion between the whole and a part, in such a

80. *Ord.* I, d.2, q.5, (OTh II, 154, note 1).
81. *Ibid.*, (OTh II, 154).

way that if the whole is particular and not common, any of its parts is, in the same way, proportionately particular. For one part can be no more particular than another. Therefore, no part of the individual is particular or every part is. But it is not the case that no part is particular. Therefore, every part is particular.[82]

Unlike the first position, however, the view under consideration does not assert that particulars have any parts that are not particular. For although (T7) says that the nature is common, (T10) says that it is individuated and made particular by the contracting difference. A combination of these is what Ockham assails in (4.3) below.

(4.2) Again, Ockham maintains that (T9) entails the denial of (T8). For

> ...if there were two such really distinct things in an individual, it seems there would be no contradiction in one being able to exist without the other. And in that case, the individual degree could exist without the contracted nature, or vice versa—each of which is absurd.[83]

What follows from (T9), however, is merely that human nature can exist without Socrates' contracting difference if it continues to exist together with Plato's or someone else's; or that Socrates' contracting difference can exist without human nature as when it continues to exist together with the corporeal nature of Socrates' corpse. It does not follow that either human nature or any contracting difference could exist without being part of any particular whatever, and it is only the latter that (T8) denies. To derive a denial of (T8), Ockham would have to appeal to the further premiss

(H) When some real thing (*res*) really distinct from other things can exist without each of them taken dividedly, and it can so exist by its nature, and does not essentially depend on any of them, it can exist without each of them taken in conjunction,

82. *Ibid.*, (OTh II, 158–59).
83. *Ibid.*, (OTh II, 159).

which seems at best dubious, as noted above.

(4.3) In another objection, Ockham argues that the conjunction of (T8) and (T10) entails the denial of (T7). He asks what the term 'man' stands for in the proposition 'Man is a species'. Either for some particular humanity, such as the humanity of Socrates or the humanity of Plato; or for some humanity distinct from these. If the first, then it will stand no more for one particular humanity than for another and so will stand for all of them, in which case there will necessarily be numerically as many species as there are particulars—which is absurd. If the second, it has to be asked whether this distinct humanity is something real or only something in the mind. But to say that it is something real, distinct from particulars, and existing separately from them contradicts (T8). And to say that it is something real that is numerically unmultiplied in numerically distinct particulars contradicts (T10). Yet, if it is not something real, distinct from, and existing separately from particulars, or something real, distinct from, and existing in particulars and numerically multiplied as the particulars are multiplied, or something real, distinct from, and existing in particulars and not numerically multiplied as the particulars are multiplied, it seems it cannot be anything real at all. But that is to say that it is only something in the mind is contrary to (T7).[84]

(4.4) The most important of Ockham's attacks on this position is his argument that (T9) entails the denial of (T10). Ockham makes it a fundamental axiom of identity that

(J) Nothing is individuated through anything extrinsic to it; rather being identical with itself and being distinct from everything else are properties that a thing has in and of itself.

But what is really distinct from a thing is extrinsic to it. Consequently, by (J), the alleged contracting difference cannot individuate a nature that is really distinct from it.[85]

84. *Ibid.*, (OTh II, 156–57).
85. *Ibid.*, (OTh II, 154).

It might be objected that Ockham's appeal to (J) begs the question. For it merely asserts his rejection of the idea that particulars are metaphysical composites of a nature and a contracting difference. No adherent of the view under attack would grant (J) as a premiss.

Whatever may be true about (J), only a more limited instance of it is needed to sustain Ockham's argument:

> (K) Nothing individuates or is individuated by what is *really distinct* from it.

And (K) has considerable intuitive plausibility, which Ockham tries to reinforce by means of the following argument:

> ...according to you, the humanity of Socrates is really distinct from the difference that contracts that humanity. Therefore, either it is really distinct of itself or through that contracting difference. Not through the contracting difference, since nothing is made distinct from *a* through *a* but rather is made the same as *a* through *a*. Therefore, this humanity is distinct from the contracting difference of itself. Therefore, these two are really distinct of themselves. But this is possible only if each is numerically one. Therefore, the humanity that is really distinct from the contracting difference is numerically one and numerically distinct of itself...[86]

If there is any initial plausibility in saying that the combination of common human nature with distinct contracting differences makes Socrates' humanity really and numerically distinct from Plato's humanity, there is no plausibility in saying that it is the combination of humanity with a contracting difference that makes the humanity really distinct from that contracting difference itself. And the theory under discussion assumes no further entities by means of which the nature is made really distinct from the contracting difference and vice versa. Thus, according to this theory, they must be really distinct from one another of themselves. And if they are two really distinct things of themselves, then, Ockham reasons, each must be numerically one of itself, so that humanity is not made numerically one by

86. *Ibid.*, (OTh II, 155).

combining with a contracting difference after all. Further, if Socrates' humanity is really and numerically distinct from Plato's humanity, then—since each is numerically one of itself and not through a really distinct contracting difference—they are numerically distinct from each other of themselves as well.

5.   THE OPINION OF DUNS SCOTUS

The third opinion considered by Ockham is that of Duns Scotus, "the Subtle Doctor, who excels others in subtlety of judgment." Ockham, because of his high regard for Scotus, and because he thought that the latter's position had often been misrepresented, gives this view a detailed and accurate statement, "without changing the words that he uses in various places."[87]

Like the second opinion, Scotus bases his theory on the conviction that the nature must somehow be common in reality, even though it cannot exist apart from any and every particular. For instance, he believes that "the unity that is required in the foundation of a relation of similarity is real. And it is not numerical, since nothing one and the same is similar or equal to itself."[88] Conversely, real opposition between numerically distinct things requires real extremes of the opposition.[89] Again, if Socrates is to be more similar to Plato than to a donkey, it must be that some real thing is common to the former two that is not common to Socrates and the donkey.[90] Similarly, "if nothing existed in the intellect, fire would produce fire and destroy water. And there would be some real unity of form between the producer and the product, because of which unity the production would be univocal..."[91]

If the nature is essentially something real that exists in and is

---

87. *Ibid.*, q.6, (OTh II, 161).
88. *Ibid.*, (OTh II, 170).
89. *Ibid.*, (OTh II, 171).
90. *Ibid.*, (OTh II, 170).
91. *Ibid.*, (OTh II, 173).

common to numerically distinct real things, Scotus argues that the nature cannot be numerically one of itself. Thus, he writes that

> If one of a pair of opposites pertains to something of itself, the other of the pair of opposites is incompatible with that thing of itself. Therefore, if the nature of man were of itself this, the nature of man would be this man in whatever it is in.[92]

Or again,

> If one of a pair of opposites pertains to something of itself, the other of the pair of opposites is incompatible with that thing of itself. Therefore, if the nature of itself is numerically one, numerical multiplicity is incompatible with the nature of itself.[93]

But, like the second opinion discussed above, Scotus thinks that human nature is numerically one in Socrates and really varied and multiplied in numerically distinct particulars. He concludes, therefore, that there must be something that individuates it, and argues further that it must be something positive that is distinct and determinate of itself.[94] And these individuating principles or thisnesses, which are numerically one and particular of themselves, contract the nature, which is common of itself, so that it, too, is made numerically one and particular. But since the nature is numerically one only through the individual difference, it is said to be one denominatively the way Socrates is said to be white denominatively by virtue of the inherence of whiteness. Unlike adherents of the first two positions, however, Scotus does not think of the nature and the contracting difference as really distinct in such a way that it is logically possible for one of them to exist without the other. Rather a particular real thing such as Socrates can be distinguished "into many formally distinct realities of which this formally is not that, and this formally is the entity of the particular and that formally is

---

92. *Ord.* II, d.3, p.1, q.1, n.4, (Vaticana VII, 393), quoted by Ockham in *Ord.* I, d.2, q.6, (OTh II, 167).

93. *Ibid.*

94. *Ord.* II, d.3, p.1, q.2–6, (Vaticana VII, 410–494).

the entity of the common nature...''[95]

Just as the nature is not numerically one and particular of itself, so Scotus maintains that "nature of itself is not completely universal."[96] Indeed, if it were, it would be impossible for the nature to be numerically one and particular in reality. Further, the nature is not completely universal insofar as it exists in a real thing. For nothing real is such that it can be truly predicated of each and every particular simultaneously in propositions of the form 'This is that'.

> ...For although it is not incompatible with any nature of itself which exists in a real thing to exist in a different particularity from the one in which it exists, nevertheless, it cannot be truly asserted of any inferior whatever that any whatever is it...[97]

Only the nature insofar as it exists in the intellect as an actual object of thought is thus apt to be predicated of each and every particular that has that nature. Thus, nature is "completely universal insofar as it exists in the intellect."[98]

Scotus's theory of universals could thus be summarized in the following five theses:

(T11) The nature of itself is common and is also common in reality;

(T12) The individuating principles or contracting difference is numerically one and particular of itself and cannot be common to numerically distinct particulars;

(T13) Neither the nature nor the contracting difference can exist in reality except as a constituent of a particular;

(T14) The nature and the contracting difference are not really distinct, but formally distinct;

95. *Ibid.*, q.5–6, n.188, (Vaticana VII, 483–84), quoted by Ockham in *Ord.* I, d.2, q.6, (OTh II, 162).
96. *Ibid.*, (OTh II, 165).
97. *Ibid.*
98. *Ibid.*

and

> (T15) As a result of its combination with a contracting
> difference, the nature is numerically one and is nu-
> merically multiplied as the particulars are multiplied.

Having laid out Scotus's opinion and his arguments for it at
some length, Ockham remarks that "there are two possible
ways of arguing against this opinion."[99] The first is to reject the
formal distinction that Scotus employs to explain the relation
between the nature and the contracting difference in a real
thing. The second is to show how the position is contradictory,
even if the formal distinction is granted. Ockham follows each
in turn.

6.   OCKHAM'S CRITIQUE OF THE
FORMAL DISTINCTION

Scotus maintains that in reality, prior to every act of intellect,
x and y may be formally nonidentical or distinct even though x
and y are really the same or at least in what is really the same
thing (*res*). Ockham argues, on the contrary, that it is impossible
for any creatures to be formally distinct without being really
distinct.

> ...I argue this way: (i) Wherever there is any distinction or nonidentity
> [between beings], there some contradictories can be truly asserted of
> those beings. (ii) But it is impossible that contradictories should be truly
> asserted of any things, or of those for which they supposit, unless they
> are (a) distinct real things (*res*) or (b) distinct concepts (*rationes*) or be-
> ings of reason (*entia rationis*) or (c) a thing (*res*) and a concept (*ratio*).
> But if (iii) they all exist in reality, (iv) they are not distinct concepts. (v)
> Nor are they a thing and a concept. Therefore, (vi) they will be distinct
> things (*res*).[100]

  99. *Ibid.*, (OTh II, 173).
100. *Ibid.*, q.1, (OTh II, 14); cf. q.6, (OTh II, 173).

As Ockham himself points out, premiss (i) is trivially true:

> ...For if *a* and *b* are not in every way the same, then both of the propositions '*a* is in every way the same as *a*' and '*b* is not in every way the same as *a*' are true...[101]

Premiss (iii) is part of Scotus's view. The crucial premiss (ii) rests on two assumptions. Of these, the uncontroversial one is the Indiscernibility of Identicals, which stipulates that it cannot be simultaneously true that x is F and y is not F, unless x and y are somehow nonidentical or distinct. The other is that (a), (b), and (c) is an exhaustive list of the alternatives under which such nonidentity or distinction might obtain. If it were complete, Ockham's desired conclusion—that no creatures can be formally distinct without being really distinct—would be assured, since (iv), (v), and (vi) would follow, given the conjunction of (i), (ii), and (iii). The principal thrust of Scotus's position, however, was to insist on a fourth and/or fifth alternative: (d) x is not formally the same as or is formally distinct from y; or (e) x and y are relatively distinct. Ockham must justify his exclusion of these alternatives, if he is to avoid begging the question. Let us consider his reaction to each of (d) and (e) in turn.

(6.1) The list of (a), (b), and (c) is based directly on Ockham's ontology, according to which real things (*res*) and beings of reason or concepts are the only beings there are. In particular, his ontology does not include any real beings that are not real things (*res*). Scotus's first account of formal distinction presupposes an ontology in which the category of real beings is not exhausted by real things (*res*). Rather it begins with formalities or realities that can have a double mode of existence: they can exist in reality as constituents of real things (*res*) or they can have a non-real mode of existence in the intellect as objects of thought or concepts. Some properties are true of the formalities of themselves—viz., their essential properties; other are predicated of the formalities only insofar as they exist in one mode of existence or the other. For example, Scotus says that

---

101. *Ibid.*, q.1, (OTh II, 14).

the nature man is, of itself, rational, mortal, and animal. Further, man is universal insofar as it exists in the intellect and is apt to be predicated of many, but particular insofar as it exists in reality. On the other hand, man of itself is neither universal nor particular, but indifferent to each.

With such a wider ontology, Scotus could identify mind-independent property-bearers of which propositions of the form '*x* is *F*' and '*y* is not *F*' are true with nonidentical or distinct formalities. And he could insist that there is no more problem about their existing in what is really one and the same thing (*res*) than there is about a table's having a completely white top and a completely black bottom.

In at least one place, Ockham seems to acknowledge that Scotus could have had such a contrasting ontology in mind. For criticizing Scotus's assertion, following Avicenna, of the proposition 'Equinity of itself is indifferent with respect to being universal and indifferent with respect to being particular', Ockham asks what 'equinity' stands for in that proposition. If it stands for the concept 'equinity', the proposition will be false, because the concept 'equinity' is not indifferent with respect to being particular, but can in no way be particular. On the other hand, if 'equinity' stands for particular horses, the proposition is still false, since particular horses are not indifferent with respect to being particular either. Thus, if 'equinity' can stand only for a concept or being of reason, on the one hand, or for particulars on the other, the proposition 'Equinity of itself is indifferent with respect to being universal and indifferent with respect to being particular' will be false. Ockham concludes his statement of this reasoning with

> ...Therefore, it seems that besides the supposition for the concept and for the particular thing, it would be necessary to assume a third in which the term supposits for the quiddity that is absolutely indifferent to each...[102]

But, unlike some of his predecessors, Ockham admits no such

102. *Ibid.*, q.6, (OTh II, 219).

supposition, since his ontology admits no such entities.[103]

Apparently, Ockham's principal objection to such an ontology is that it leaves us with no resources for proving a real distinction among really existent beings. He reasons that all contradictories are equally contradictory. Thus, if some propositions of the form 'x is F' and 'y is not F' can be true about really existent property-bearers that are only formally distinct, it would seem that any pair of contradictories can. "...And so every way of proving real distinction or nonidentity among any beings whatever would perish..." For example, if 'Divine wisdom is formally divine wisdom and divine goodness is not formally divine wisdom' entails only 'Divine wisdom and divine goodness are formally distinct', then what reason is there to suppose that 'A man is rational and a donkey is not rational' entails 'A man and a donkey are really distinct' and not merely 'A man and a donkey are formally distinct'? And in general, what would bar the conclusion that everything is really one thing (*res*) within which many formalities can be distinguished?

Ockham realizes what Scotus's reply would be: viz., "that real nonidentity can be proved through primary contradictories, but this cannot be done through other contradictories."[104] Propositions that are implicitly or explicitly of the form 'x is formally F' and 'y is not formally F' are not primary contradictories,"[105] however, because the 'formally' diminishes the supposition from the thing (*res*) of which x and y are alike constituents, to the constituent formality x and y, respectively. Ockham's recurrent answer, that "all contradictories are equally incompatible"[106] and that 'formally' and 'really' cannot function to distract or diminish the supposition, represents a persistent begging of the question against Scotus's ontology.

---

103. For a fuller account of Ockham's doctrine of supposition, see Part Two, chapter 10 below.

104. *Ord.* I, d.2, q.6, (OTh II, 174).

105. *Ibid.*   106. *Ibid.*

(6.2) If the *Lectura-Ordinatio* account removes the contradiction by finding distinct subjects for the contradictory predicates to be asserted about, the *Reportata*-position, which abolishes the notion of a plurality of entities or formalities within what is really one and the same thing, will have to provide an alternative solution. Recall that for Scotus, *x* and *y* are distinct *secundum quid*, if *x* and *y* are really the same but lack formal or adequate identity. Following (F), *x* and *y* lack formal identity if and only if they are really the same and, where they are definable, neither falls under the definition of the other or, where they are not definable, neither would fall under the definition of the other if they were. Focussing on Scotus's claim that infinite divine wisdom and infinite divine goodness are not formally the same by this criterion, Ockham writes,

> ...When it is said that if infinite wisdom were definable, and likewise infinite goodness, their definitions would be distinct, I reply that this is absolutely false...[107]

To be sure, he allows, the concepts of infinite wisdom and infinite goodness, which are formed by adding the concept of infinity to the concepts of wisdom in general and goodness in general, respectively, have distinct nominal definitions. Abandoning the, to Ockham's mind, incorrect view that infinite wisdom and infinite goodness are distinct realities or formalities within the divine essence, we will have to conclude that divine wisdom and divine goodness are in every way the same in reality. And while Ockham grants, contrary to the premiss of Scotus's epistemological argument, that what is in every way the same real thing can genuinely fall under the distinct concepts of infinite wisdom and infinite goodness, still there would be only one real definition (*quid rei*) there, because there would be only one reality there to be defined. And in general, no *x* and *y* that were in every way the same in reality would receive distinct real definitions, if they were definable.

Again, for *x* and *y* to lack adequate identity is for *x* and *y* to be

---

107. *Ibid.*, q.1, (OTh II, 30–31).

really the same and yet for one to exceed the other in predication or perfection. For example, human nature and the contracting difference Socrateity would lack adequate identity; for
while they are really the same, man is predicable of more than
Socrateity is. This is tantamount, however, to saying that x and
y lack adequate identity where x and y are really the same, but
for some F, x is F and y is not F. Where x and y are thought of as
distinct entities within the same real thing (*res*), there is at least
the appearance that the incompatible properties were being
asserted about distinct property-bearers. But once that ontology
is abandoned, Scotus is left asserting contradictories about what
is in reality one and the same thing (*res*). And Ockham will again
object that this is to abandon the Indiscernibility of Identicals as
a criterion of real distinction and thus to lose every way of proving distinction among real things.

Scotus could reply that even on his second account, he is not
left asserting contradictories about what is *in every way* the
same in reality. Rather he allows that contradictories may be
true about x and y, where x and y are really the same, only if x
and y lack formal or adequate identity.

This defense seems circular. For according to the *Reportata*,
the lack of formal or adequate identity itself partially consists in
the assertion of contradictories about really the same thing; the
lack of formal or adequate identity cannot, therefore, be
invoked to explain how those very predications are possible.
Perhaps the thrust of Scotus's *Reportata*-position is to convert
the formality-names of the *Lectura-Ordinatio* into adverbial
modifiers. Thus, whereas the *Lectura-Ordinatio* would find
'Divine wisdom is really the same as divine goodness, but divine
wisdom would be definable by D_1 and not D_2, whereas divine
goodness would be definable by D_2 and not D_1' consistent
because divine wisdom and divine goodness are distinct formalities within the same divine essence, the *Reportata* would
expound the claim by saying that one and the same divine
essence is wisdom-wise definable by D_1 and not D_2, but
goodness-wise definable by D_2 and not D_1, where 'wisdom-wise
definable by D_1' and 'not goodness-wise definable by D_1' are
no more contradictory than Ockham would say 'color-wise

similar' and 'not shape-wise similar' are. Once again, I do not
see how Ockham could be fair in disallowing this move to
Scotus.

7. SCOTUS'S THESES ARE MUTUALLY INCONSISTENT

Granting the formal distinction for the sake of argument,
Ockham tries with mixed success to argue that Scotus's theory
of universals is internally inconsistent. (7.1) First, Ockham
maintains that (T13) is inconsistent with (T11) on the now
familiar ground that particulars must be homogeneously particular in the sense of having no constituents that are not particular. Unlike the first view but like the second view examined
above, Scotus would reply that he does not claim that particulars have any parts that are not particular. By (T12),
Socrateity is numerically one and particular of itself; and by
(T15), human nature in Socrates is numerically one and particular denominatively. It is just that he adds that human nature
of itself is common and that it is common in reality—in (T11).

(7.2) To this last, Ockham objects that the conjunction of
(T11) with (T15) has the absurd consequence "that there are as
many species as there are individuals." For according to Scotus,
this commonness or unity less than numerical unity pertains to
the nature *per se* in the second way and so will accompany it
wherever it exists. Thus,

> ...just as there are really two natures in Socrates and Plato, so there will
> really be two lesser unities. But this lesser unity is either commonness
> or inseparable from commonness, and consequently inseparable from
> being common. Therefore, there are two common entities in Socrates
> and Plato, and consequently two species. Consequently, Socrates
> would be under one common and Plato under another, and so there
> would be as many common [entities]—even of the most generic en-
> tities—as there are individuals, which seems absurd.[108]

This argument seems to misrepresent Scotus's position, how-

---

108. *Ibid.*, q.6, (OTh II, 182–83).

ever. For the latter does not identify species with the common nature existing in reality, but with the nature insofar as it exists in the intellect as an abstract general concept. The nature insofar as it exists in reality in particulars is only incompletely universal. Hence, Scotus is not committed to the view that as many are completely universal as are particular.

(7.3) Again, Ockham contends that Scotus's theory of universals, like the second position examined above, contradicts Ockham's own fundamental axiom of identity

(J) Nothing is individuated through anything extrinsic to it; rather being identical with itself and being distinct from everything else are properties that a thing has in and of itself.

But the conjunction of (T14) and (T15) imply that the common nature is individuated by what is formally distinct from it. To say that one thing is formally distinct from another is to imply that neither falls under the definition of the other and so that neither is an essential constituent of the other. Hence, it seems that (T14) and (T15) are incompatible with (J).

Ockham's contention that a thing is not made the same as itself and distinct from others by virtue of something *really* distinct from it and from each of its essential parts seems highly plausible and would have been granted by Scotus. But the latter would have rejected (J) as false where the putative individuator is only formally distinct from but really the same as what it individuates. And nothing in Ockham's present argument would compel him to abandon his own intuitions about identity and distinction in favor of Ockham's.

(7.4) If the above three arguments are indecisive, I believe that Ockham's fourth attack is fatal to Scotus's theory. Ockham maintains that (T11)—the claim that the nature of itself is common and is also common in reality—is inconsistent with the conjunction of (T13)—the claim that neither the nature nor the contracting difference can exist in reality except as a constituent of a particular—and (T15)—the claim that as a result of its combination with a contracting difference, the nature is numerically

one and is numerically multiplied as the particulars are multiplied. His objective is to convict Scotus's notion that the
nature is incompletely universal in reality, which was invoked
in reply to (7.2) above, of unintelligibility.

Scotus, in his effort to show that the nature is not *this* of
itself, has endorsed the principle that

> (L) If one of a pair of opposites pertains to something of
> itself, the other of the pair of opposites is incompatible
> with that thing of itself...[109]

Thus, by (L), if the nature were *this* of itself, being *that* would be
incompatible with it of itself and so it would not be common of
itself. For the nature would be common only if existence in
another were compatible with it. Again, if the nature were
numerically one and particular of itself, numerical multiplicity
would be incompatible with it of itself, and so it would not of
itself be common or one by a unity less than numerical unity.
Ockham contends that Scotus ought, in like manner to grant the
following:

> (M) ...Whenever one of a pair of opposites really pertains to
> something in such a way that that thing is truly and really
> denominated from it, whether they pertain to it of itself
> or through something else—this fact remaining un-
> changed—the other of the opposites does not really per-
> tain to it, but will be absolutely denied of it...[110]

But by (T13), the nature does not exist otherwise than together
with some contracting difference or other; and by (T15), the
nature is numerically one and particular, as a result of its combination with a contracting difference. Thus, by (M), no nature
can simultaneously be common the way (T11) asserts it to be.

Ockham considers the objection that "the two unities are not
really opposed."[111] But this seems contrary to Scotus's own

---

109. *Ord.* II, d.3, p.1, q.1, n.4, (Vaticana VII, 393).
110. *Ord.* I, d.2, q.6, (OTh II, 177).
111. *Ibid.*

claims. For the latter says that "Multiplicity that cannot stand together with the greater unity because it is opposed to it, can without contradiction stand together with the lesser unity."[112] And he has used this fact to justify substituting 'commonness' and 'numerical unity' or 'particularity' in (L) to derive the result that if the nature is common of itself, it cannot also be numerically one and particular of itself. Thus, Ockham reasserts the analogous argument based on (M):

> Further, whenever the consequents are incompatible, the antecedents will be incompatible. But the inferences 'a is common or one by the lesser unity; therefore a stands together with the multiplicity that is opposed to the greater unity—viz., numerical multiplicity' and 'a is one by the greater unity; therefore the opposed multiplicity—viz., numerical multiplicity—does not stand together with a' both hold. But 'Numerical multiplicity stands together with a' and 'Numerical multiplicity does not stand together with a' are incompatible. Therefore, 'a is one by the lesser unity' is false, taking 'a' for the nature which you say is always one by the lesser unity...[113]

A defender of Scotus might reply, alternatively, that while (L) holds good, viz., that if x is F of itself, not-F is incompatible with x of itself, it is not the case that if x is F—no matter whether of itself, *per se*, or denominatively—not-F is incompatible with x. For a man is white denominatively, and a white is white *per se*. But "...blackness stands together with a man and does not stand together with a white. Nevertheless, a man is white, and a is a man and white."[114] In the same way, being *that* may be compatible with the nature, even though being *that* is not compatible with being *this*—e.g., being Socrates' humanity is compatible with human nature even though it is not compatible with being Plato's. And numerical multiplicity may be compatible with the nature of itself, even though numerical multiplicity is incompatible with a particular.

   Ockham thinks that this is likewise mistaken:

---

112. Quoted by Ockham in *ibid*.
113. *Ibid*., (OTh II, 178).
114. *Ibid*.

...For taking 'to stand' in the same way [in each premiss], one of them is false. Taking 'to stand' actually, then it is false that blackness stands together with Socrates, if Socrates is white. But taking it potentially, then it is false that blackness does not stand together with a white, since blackness can stand together with a white inasmuch as a white can be black or have blackness. Thus, even though blackness is incompatible with whiteness, nevertheless it is compatible with that which is white. Consequently, it is compatible with a white, since the two terms 'white' and 'that which is white' convert.[115]

If Socrates is white, blackness is not actually compatible with Socrates, because it is a contradiction to say that Socrates is white and Socrates is black. But blackness is potentially compatible with Socrates, because even if Socrates is in fact white, it is logically possible that whiteness not inhere in Socrates and blackness inhere in him instead. Similarly, if humanity in Socrates is *this* humanity denominatively, it is not actually, but at most potentially compatible with Plato's contracting difference. And if humanity in Socrates is numerically one and particular, it is not actually, but at most potentially compatible with numerical multiplicity.

Scotus might reply, however, that this is all that he intended to claim: viz., that just as Socrates is not black while he is white, so humanity is not *that* while it is *this*, or numerically many while it is numerically one. Nevertheless, just as it is possible that Socrates should exist without whiteness inhering in him and have blackness inhering in him instead, so it is possible that the humanity in Socrates should not be combined with Socrates' contracting difference, that it should be combined with Plato's contracting difference instead, and that humanity should not be numerically one but should be numerically many instead. And it is the fact that any humanity in reality is only potentially compatible with each of a plurality of thisnesses and only potentially compatible with numerical multiplicity, but not actually compatible with them, that makes Scotus say that the nature in reality is only common and incompletely universal, not completely universal.

115. *Ibid*., (OTh II, 179).

Ockham thinks that Scotus's position, so interpreted, is still unsatisfactory, given his assertion of (T14). For if humanity in Socrates is formally but not really distinct from Socrateity, it follows that it is not logically possible for the former to exist in a thing (*res*) without the latter existing in the same thing, the way it *is* logically possible for Socrates to exist without whiteness inhering in him and to have blackness inhering in him instead. Consequently, it is not even logically possible for humanity in Socrates to exist without being determinately Socrates' and so not even logically possible that it should be determinately Plato's instead. Again, it is not even logically possible that it should actually exist in numerically many at once. Thus, Ockham writes,

> ...his claim that a multiplicity opposed to the greater unity can, without contradiction, stand together with the lesser unity seems incompatible with his other claim that the nature and the individual difference do not really differ. For when any two are really the same, whatever can, by divine power, really be one of them can be the other. But this individual difference cannot be numerically many really distinct things. Therefore, neither can the nature, which is really the same as the contracting difference, be many really distinct things. Nor, consequently, can it be any thing (*res*) other than the contracting difference. Thus, the nature is not without contradiction compared to numerical multiplicity.[116]

Since the individual difference cannot exist in many things (*res*) and the nature is really the same as Socrates' individual difference and cannot exist in anything without that individual difference, it follows that the nature cannot exist in many things (*res*) either. Hence, neither existence in another nor existence in many is even potentially compatible with any nature in reality and none is common in reality, where for the nature to be common is for existence in another to be compatible with it or for numerical multiplicity to be compatible with it. And (T11) is inconsistent with the conjunction of (T12), (T13), (T14), and (T15).

116. *Ibid.*

It might seem that Scotus could circumvent this complaint of Ockham's by simply retracting the contention (T15) that as a result of its combination with a contracting difference the nature is numerically one and really varied and multiplied by distinct contracting differences. Given the first version of the formal distinction, his theory would then distinguish within what is really one and the same thing, two formalities or realities, one of which is proper of itself and the other of which is common. No contradiction would arise, because the contradictory properties would be born by distinct property-bearers. Further, the nature, as unvaried and unmultiplied in many, would be completely, as opposed to incompletely, universal; and so genus and species could be identified with something real.

Initially attractive as this proposal might seem, it will not fare any better in the end given Scotus's assertion of (T14), that while the nature and individual differences are formally distinct, they are, or are constituents of really the same thing, in such a way that it is logically impossible that either should exist without the other. Thus, it would be logically impossible for humanity in Socrates to exist without Socrateity, and logically impossible for humanity in Plato to exist without Plato's individual difference. But if by hypothesis human nature is not really varied and multiplied by the individual differences, then it will follow that it is the same humanity that is in both Socrates and Plato and hence that it is logically impossible for Socrates to exist without Plato existing and vice versa. Indeed, given a commitment to possible particular men, it will be impossible for any possible man to exist without each and every other man existing—which is absurd. It seems, then, that Scotus could not, without difficulty, retain (T14), while maintaining that humanity is not really varied and multiplied in Socrates and Plato.

He could in addition give up (T14) and replace (T13) with (T1), in which case his position would collapse into the one Ockham first examines in *Ordinatio* I, d.2, q.4. This would not make Scotus's theory of universals any more palatable to Ockham. But, as I have argued in section 3 above, Ockham's efforts to reduce the first version of moderate realism to a contradiction are unsuccessful. His arguments serve more to articulate the contrasting conceptions of the metaphysical structure of particulars than to refute his opponents.

Alternatively, Scotus could avoid both of Ockham's complaints by giving up (T11), the notion that the nature is common either of itself or in reality. But of all his contentions, that is the one that Scotus was most eager to preserve.

8. UNIVERSAL AND PARTICULAR ARE REALLY THE SAME BUT DISTINCT ACCORDING TO REASON

Some moderate realists believed that every really existent thing is particular and recognized that the universal and particular cannot be in every way the same. Accordingly, they concluded that "the universal and particular are really the same thing and that there is only a distinction of reason between them."[117] Ockham examines three versions of this view. (8.1) The first is similar to one stated by Thomas Aquinas and his Dominican follower Hervaeus Natalis (d.1323).[118] It asserts, among other things, that

> ...specific form of itself is one simple thing, and as such is universal. But the form as signed in this suppositum is particular...[119]

(8.2) The second assumes

> ...that a real thing (res) according to its actual existence is particular. And the same real thing (res) according to its existence in the intellect is universal. Thus, the same real thing (res) according to one existence or consideration is universal and according to another existence or consideration is particular.[120]

117. *Ibid.*, q.7, (OTh II, 229).
118. Thomas Aquinas, *Opuscula* XXVII, tractatus I, *De universalibus*, and Hervaeus Natalis, *Commentaria in quattuor libros Sententiarum* II, d.3, q.3, (Paris, 1647, 111). See *Ord.* I, d.2, q.7, (OTh II, 226, note 1).
119. *Ord.* I, d.2, q.7, (OTh II, 227).
120. *Ibid.*

(8.3) The third was held by Henry of Harclay, who supposed that "the same real thing (*res*) is universal under one concept and particular under another concept."[121] The suggestion is that a particular such as Socrates can cause a variety of different concepts in the intellect. Socrates can cause a distinct concept of himself in particular. But he can also cause a confused concept by means of which the intellect cannot distinguish Socrates from Plato. Harclay wants to say that Socrates distinctly conceived is particular; but Socrates confusedly conceived is universal.[122]

The general difficulty that Ockham finds with all three of these positions is that each of them tries to devise a way of predicating the contradictory properties of being particular and being universal of what is really one and the same thing. But Ockham argues that since the latter are contradictory properties, they must, by the Indiscernibility of Identicals, be born by distinct property-bearers. And these philosophers do not recognize the formal distinction, but rather believe that real things (*res*) are the only really distinct property-bearers there are. Hence, they cannot consistently say that contradictories are born by what is really one and the same thing (*res*).[123]

Adherents of (8.1) and (8.2) will reply that while being particular is a property that things have insofar as they exist in reality, being universal is a property that they have only in relation to their being understood. Ockham counters that the activity of understanding is extrinsic to any real thing. And there are only certain properties that a thing can have by virtue of something extrinsic to it. A man, for instance, can be white by virtue of the inherence of something extrinsic to him—viz., whiteness. Again, a man can be tall in relation to other men who are extrinsic to him. But according to unaided natural reason, neither the inherence of nor the relation to anything extrinsic could make it true that a man is a donkey or a cow, or in general that a man has any property incompatible with any of his essential proper-

121. *Ibid.*
122. *Ibid.*, (OTh II, 228); cf. (OTh II, 227–28, note 1).
123. Ockham's 2nd general counter-argument, *ibid.*, (OTh II, 236).

ties. And Ockham insists that it is essential to every real thing to be particular, so that being universal is just as contrary to the essence of any real thing, as being a donkey or a cow is to the essential properties of being a man. Thus, Ockham reasons,

> ...When something is incompatible with another by the nature of the thing, it cannot pertain to that thing through anything extrinsic. But being common to another thing (*res*) is incompatible with each thing (*res*) of itself. Therefore, commonness cannot pertain to anything (*res*) through anything extrinsic...[124]

And although there are certain properties that can be truly asserted of a thing by virtue of its relation to the intellect—that of being thought of, being conceived of, etc.—nevertheless, "whether or not the thing that is particular is understood, it will not be able to be common or universal according to any existence."[125]

Again, each of the three versions of the opinion stated by Ockham tries to remove the contradiction by inserting adverbial modifiers into the predication statements, so that we have not '*x* is *F*' and '*x* is not *F*', but '*x* of itself is *F*' and '*x* signed by suppositum is not *F*'; or '*x* according to one existence is *F*' and '*x* according to another existence is not *F*'; or '*x* confusedly conceived is *F*' and '*x* distinctly conceived is not *F*'. But Ockham insists that this will not work either. For on his view, adverbial modifiers could remove the contradiction only if they served to alter the supposition of the subject term, so that it stood for different things in the different propositions and the resultant statements asserted the contradictory properties about different property-bearers. But this will happen only if the supposition of the term is diminished or distracted from its usual supposition to something else. And Ockham thinks that this can happen only in a certain narrow range of cases. Thus,

> ...a determination diminishes [the supposition] when some part of the whole is expressed and denominated by that determination, as is clear

---

124. Ockham's reply to (8.2), *ibid.*, (OTh II, 241).
125. *Ibid.*; cf. Ockham's reply to (8.3), *ibid.*, (OTh II, 243, 249).

> when one says that an Ethiopian is white with respect to his teeth. For
> there the denominated part is expressed. For if the denomination of
> such a part is not sufficient to determine the whole, then the deter-
> mination diminishes the supposition...[126]

Thus, 'An Ethiopian is white with respect to his teeth' does not
entail 'An Ethiopian is white', but only 'An Ethiopian has white
teeth'. But the above mentioned adverbial modifiers do not
mention a part of the subject and so do not diminish the supposition of the subject term, so that it stands for a part instead of
the whole. Again, Ockham maintains that

> ...these determinations do not distract [the supposition], since the
> determination that distracts [the supposition] is sometimes absolutely
> incompatible with the thing (*res*) or at least with the existence of that to
> which it is added. But it denominates it, because it properly and truly
> denominates something that was its part. This is clear, for example, of
> 'dead', when something is called a dead man. For it is impossible that a
> man exists and nevertheless that he is dead. But it is said, according to
> ordinary usage, that a man is dead because the body that was part of
> him was truly dead. It is clear that this is not the way it is in the case at
> hand, however. Therefore, these determinations do not distract the
> supposition.[127]

In Ockham's view, being universal is absolutely incompatible
with any really existent thing. But unlike the first and second
versions of moderate realism, the views under discussion now
do not admit that the universal is part of a particular; rather they
say that it is really the same as a particular. Thus, the adverbial
modifiers cannot be seen to distract the supposition in the
above described way. Ockham's conclusion is that

> ...there is always a formal inference from a determinable taken together
> with a determination that neither distracts nor diminishes the supposi-
> tion to that determinable taken absolutely. Thus, 'A thing under such a
> concept is universal; therefore, a thing is universal' is a formal in-
> ference...[128]

---

126. Ockham's reply to (8.3), *ibid.*, (OTh II, 244).
127. *Ibid.*, (OTh II, 245).
128. *Ibid.*, (OTh II, 244).

Or again, that

> ...it is not good to make such claims as the following: that the same thing under one intention is particular and under another is universal; or that according to such and such existence is a man and according to another existence is not a man but something else; and many other similar claims—say that if a thing (*res*) is considered one way, then it is this, but considered in a different way, it is another. For such propositions, which include such determinations, imply propositions that absolutely lack such determinations. For if this were not so, I could say equally well that man according to one existence or consideration or intention is a donkey, and under another is a cow and under another is a lion—which is absurd. Therefore, such claims represent an altogether improper way of speaking and a departure from all scientific modes of expression.[129]

On the other hand, Ockham argues that this position cannot admit that the universal and particular are somehow distinct without conceding that the universal is a being of reason and not a real being after all.

> ...(i) opposites necessarily pertain primarily to distinct things. But (ii) universality and particularity are opposites of this kind, according to all of them. Therefore, (iii) distinct things are primarily and immediately denominated by them. Therefore, (iv) either (a) they are formally distinct—which was disproved earlier [in *Ordinatio* I, d.2, q.6]; or (b) they are distinct things (*res*)—and hence we return to the first or second opinion disproved in the first questions [i.e., in *Ordinatio* I, d.2, q.4–5]; or (c) they are distinct beings of reason; or (d) distinct as a real being and a being of reason. (v) Certainly what is primarily and immediately particular is not a being of reason. Therefore, (vi) what is primarily and immediately denominated universal is merely a being in the mind. Consequently, (vii) it is not a thing.[130]

Ockham hopes by such an argument to reduce the "common opinion" to his own.

The allegedly exhaustive disjunction in (iv) reflects Ockham's ontology according to which real things (*res*), which can exist in

---

129. *Ibid.*, (OTh II, 248).
130. Ockham's 1st general counter-argument, *ibid.*, (OTh II, 235–36); Ockham's reply to the 1st version, (OTh II, 240).

reality, and beings of reason which have a non-real mode of existence as objects of thought, are the only beings there are. And (iv) presupposes another assumption, made more explicit in Ockham's critique of the first version of this opinion, that

   (iv) There can be a distinction of reason between x and y only if at least one of x and y is a being of reason,

which in turn rest on Ockham's contention that, strictly speaking, real sameness and distinction are relations that obtain only between real things (*res*), while sameness and distinction of reason are relations that obtain only between beings of reason. Strictly, there is an intermediate distinction between a real thing and a being of reason, but in a broad sense there can be said to be a distinction of reason between them (see section 2 above). Thus, from Ockham's point of view, it is absurd to say that the universal and particular are really the same but there is a distinction of reason between them. For if they are both really the same, then they must both be real things and therefore not the kind of thing that can be either the same or distinct according to reason. But if there is a distinction of reason between them, then at least one of them is a being of reason and so not the kind of thing that can be really the same as or really distinct from anything else.

   Ockham's double-pronged attack is not clearly successful against any of the three versions he discusses, however. (R8.1) For one thing, it is not clear from Ockham's statement of the first version, that it starts with an ontology exhausted by real things and beings of reason rather than with an ontology of properties like Scotus's. According to the latter, natures are included in the ontology, whether or not they exist at all, and those features of a nature that are essential to it can be truly predicated of that nature without presupposing it to exist. Nevertheless, each nature can have a double mode of existence—in reality or in the intellect as an object of thought—and other predicates truly apply to it insofar as it exists in these modes. If the first version of this position did presuppose such an ontology, the criticisms Ockham actually gives would be ineffective against it. But he could still reject it for one of the same reasons he rejects Scotus's position: viz., that the essential properties of a nature accompany it in all of the modes of its existence. Therefore, just as man is animal both of itself and insofar as it exists in reality, so it would be universal both of itself and insofar as it exists in reality. Hence it would be both universal and particular in reality — which Ockham claims is contradictory.

(R8.2) From Ockham's account of it, the second version, too, may have presupposed an ontology like Scotus's rather than Ockham's. Further, it does not create trouble for itself by asserting that a species is universal of itself, but maintains only that it is universal according to its existence in the intellect and particular according to its existence in reality. Ockham replies that this position is contradictory because 'Man according to its existence in the intellect is universal' entails 'Man is universal', and 'Man according to its existence in reality is particular' entails 'Man is particular'. The latter contention rests on Ockham's assumption that the only way the adverbial phrases 'according to its existence in the intellect' and 'according to its existence in reality' could function to remove the contradiction is by serving to change the supposition of the subject term, so that it stands for different things in different propositions. And adherents of this position would agree with Ockham that the latter phrases do not so function. Nevertheless, they might maintain that there is more than one way of showing that apparently contradictory statements are not really contradictory: one can argue that although predicates are genuinely contradictory, they are not really predicated of the same thing; or one can maintain that although the predications are made about the very same thing, they are only apparently contradictory. Ockham leaves the second of these alternatives completely out of account here, the way he did in dealing with the first version of moderate realism (see section 3 above). But adherents of this position might contend that the above mentioned adverbial phrases function, not to alter the supposition, but to condition the predications in such a way that they are not genuine contradictories. One could think of these adverbial phrases as acting to condition the predication the way that modal operators are supposed to do. Thus, just as 'Possibly x is F' and 'Possibly x is not F' are not contradictory, although 'x is F' and 'x is not F' are; so 'In the intellect, x is universal' and 'In reality, x is particular' would not be contradictory, although 'In reality, x is universal' and 'In reality, x is particular' would be. Alternatively, one could develop the position by saying that while the predicates 'universal' and 'particular' appear to be one-place predicates, they are really two-place predicates—one place of which is satisfied by the thing in question and the other by a mode of existence. Thus, symbolizing 'x according to its existence in the intellect is universal' by 'Universal (x, existence in the intellect)' and 'x according to its existence in reality is particular' by 'Particular (x, existence in reality)', it could be pointed out that 'Universal (x, existence in the intellect)' and 'Particular (x, existence in reality)' are no more contradictory than 'Taller (x, y)' and 'Shorter (x, z)' (where y ≠ z). The latter approach has a disadvantage by comparison with the former in that it quantifies over modes of existence, and some explanation would have to be given of what they are. But either approach would circumvent the criticisms Ockham offers.

(R8.3) Henry of Harclay, by contrast, seems to accept Ockham's ontology of real things and concepts and to abandon the notion that the same thing might exist in and have contradictory properties in different modes of existence. Rather he suggests that the same thing can have those apparently contradictory properties even insofar as it exists in reality, because even insofar as it exists in reality, *in* can be conceived of under different concepts. And it is open to Henry to reject Ockham's charge that 'Socrates confusedly conceived is particular' entails 'Socrates is particular', by insisting that the predicates 'universal' and 'particular' are not one-place predicates, but two-place predicates, the first place of which is satisfied by a real thing such as Socrates and the other of which is satisfied by a concept caused to exist in the mind by Socrates. Thus, 'Universal (Socrates, confused concept caused by Socrates)' and 'Particular (Socrates, distinct concept caused by Socrates)' would be no more contradictory than 'Taller (Plato, Aristotle)' and 'Shorter

(Plato, Socrates)' are. Further, if 'universal' and 'particular' are so construed, a good sense can be given to the claim that "the universal and particular are really the same thing (*res*) and differ only according to reason":[131] viz., that 'Universal (..., α, where α is a concept caused by...)' and 'Particular (..., β, where β is a concept caused by...)' can be true of one and the same thing, provided that appropriately different concepts caused by that thing are substituted in the second argument place of each predicate. No doubt, Ockham would regard this move to transform 'universal' and 'particular' into two-place predicates as perverse. He would think it better to admit that one and the same real thing, viz., Socrates, genuinely satisfies a confused concept and a distinct concept caused by him, and to make 'universal' a one-place predicate satisfied by the confused concept, and 'particular' a one-place predicate satisfied by the real thing. But to reject Henry's way of talking as misleading, is not to convict him of a mistaken ontology. And it is clear that he and Ockham are in complete agreement about what things there are.

9.   SUMMARY

Ockham's discussion of moderate realism thus turns out to be a battle of conflicting intuitions about identity and distinction in which the opposing sides are forced to expose their war machinery and there are a few casualties but no clear winners. Ockham's arsenal is stocked with three main weapons. First, there is the notion, which he mobilizes against the first view, that the existence of any particular of a given species is logically independent of the existence of any other particular of that species. And accessory to it is the insistence that no particular has anything common or universal as one of its constituents. This picture has considerable appeal, but it has to face the opposition picture of all the particulars of a given species as bound together by a common component or some sort of real unity of

---

131. *Ibid.*, (OTh II, 229).

nature. Second, there is Ockham's fundamental conviction that nothing can individuate or be individuated by anything extrinsic to itself. Ockham wields this principle against the contentions of Scotus and adherents of the second opinion that the nature is individuated and numerically multiplied by contracting differences that are formally or really distinct from it; and in general against claims that there is a distinction of reason between the nature and individual differences, even though the latter are really the same thing. This claim seems effective against the second opinion, but by itself has no more fire power than Scotus's contrasting intuitions about individuation. And in the end it does not really seem relevant to Henry of Harclay's position. Finally, Ockham thinks his really invincible weapon is the principle that it is impossible for contradictories to be simultaneously true about one and the same being—that, in effect, the Indiscernibility of Identicals is the criterion of distinction for real beings. He contends that all of the views he discusses run counter to this principle in one way or another. Surprisingly, he is most successful in making this charge stick against one of his most distinguished opponents, viz., Scotus. Most of the others are more imaginative than Ockham fully appreciates in circumventing violations of this principle. For when contradictories seem to be asserted about one and the same real being, there are two ways to show that this is not the case. One is to argue that while the properties are genuinely contradictory, they are not predicated about one and the same real being. Scotus makes this move with his first version of the formal distinction, which Ockham shows to be unacceptable. Alternatively, one can maintain that while the predications are made about one and the same real being, they are not genuinely contradictory. This can be done by inserting adverbial phrases into the predication statements which function either analogously to modal operators or serve to relativize the predications. This strategy is implicitly in the first opinion and is explicitly employed by the last two views discussed by Ockham; it would also be required for a full development of Scotus's view. As Ockham sees it, the first approach fails because it requires more troops than a correct ontology will make available. And his failure to envision the second in this context partially explains his eventual abandonment of his own stance, that in addition to real beings, there are beings that have a non-real mode of existence as objects of thought. It is this topic that we must consider in detail in the next two chapters.

3

Names and Concepts

Ockham identifies universals with universal names and denies that there are any universal things other than universal names. In this chapter, I shall try to arrive at a more precise understanding of Ockham's nominalism by asking what sorts of names he thinks there are and what sorts of things names are.

1. THREE KINDS OF NAMES

Ockham adopts the traditional distinction, stated in Boethius but inspired by Aristotle's remarks in *On Interpretation*, chapter 1, 16a1–8, among three kinds of names: spoken, written, and mental.[1] Spoken and written signs are conventional signs; but mental signs, which belong neither to Greek nor to Latin nor to any other conventional language,[2] are natural signs. According to Ockham, conventional signs neither signify, nor signify precisely what they signify, of themselves, but rather "by voluntary imposition." And their signification could change, or they could cease to be significant "at the pleasure of the language users."[3] Natural signification, by contrast, does not depend upon voluntary institution, nor does it change at the pleasure of anyone.[4]

Ockham's doctrine of natural signification is interesting and complex and will be the center of attention in the next chapter. The issue of what it is to signify by convention, a subject of lively contemporary debate, is not one on which Ockham dwells at

1. *Summa logicae* I, c.1, (OPh I, 7); *Ord.* I, d.2, q.4, (OTh II, 134–36).
2. *Summa logicae* I, c.1, (OPh I, 7); *Quodl.* I, q.6, (OTh IX, 37).
3. *Summa logicae* I, c.1, (OPh I, 8).
4. *Ibid.*

any length. No doubt when he says that spoken and written signs have their signification "by voluntary imposition" or "at the pleasure of" the language users, he wants to emphasize first that there is or need be no logically or causally necessary connection between a given set of sounds or inscriptions that serve as linguistic signs and the things they signify, and second that it is the habits of the linguistic community that establish the conventional connection between sound-types and inscription-types and the thing signified. The former is attested to by the existence of different conventional languages that use different sound-types and inscription-types to signify the same things; the latter by the fact that such sound-types and inscription-types sometimes change their significance or lose it altogether as the habits of the linguistic community change or the linguistic community dies out.

What is the nature of the convention by virtue of which spoken and written signs signify anything? According to Ockham, a conventional relation is first established between spoken sounds and concepts—which he alternatively refers to as "intentions" or "affections" (*passiones*) of the mind—and then between written inscriptions and spoken sounds. Like most of his predecessors since Boethius, Ockham quotes with approval the Aristotelian formula that spoken sounds are "notes" of concepts and written marks are "notes" of spoken sounds.[5] But where Boethius and Aquinas had understood this to mean that words such as 'man' signify concepts primarily and things only secondarily, Ockham follows the construal of Duns Scotus and Walter Burleigh: that words signify things directly.[6]

> ...Spoken sounds and written marks are ordered signs and signify all of their significata immediately. But they are ordered in such a way that a written sign signifies whatever a spoken sound signifies; and if the spoken sound were to change its significatum, the written sign will also

5. *Ibid.*, (OPh I, 7–8); cf. *Expos. Periherm.* I, Prooemium, (OPh II, 347).

6. See Armand Maurer, "William of Ockham on Language and Reality," read at the sixth international congress of the Société Internationale pour L'Étude de la Philosophie Médiévale, September 2, 1977.

change, and not vice versa. And a spoken sound signifies whatever a concept signifies, and if the concept were to change its significatum, the spoken sound would change its significatum, but not vice versa. For a concept naturally signifies the things of which it is predicated, but spoken sound and written signs signify conventionally.[7]

Just as the concept 'man' signifies things, so the spoken and written signs also signify things. Nevertheless, since what spoken and written signs signify is defined in terms of what concepts signify, concepts are said to be terms or words primarily and conventional signs secondarily.[8] Similarly, since propositions are complexes of terms, mental propositions are the primary propositions; spoken and written propositions the secondary ones. And in general, it is the naturally significant mental language, not conventional spoken and written language, that is the primary language.

2. THE ONTOLOGICAL STATUS OF CONCEPTS

Since Ockham identifies universals primarily with naturally significant names or concepts, it is perhaps less misleading to say that he was a conceptualist rather than a nominalist about universals. And to understand fully what ontological status he assigns to universals, it is necessary to investigate what he thinks concepts are.

So far as we can tell from his writings,[9] Ockham changed his

7. *Rep.* III, q.10, (OTh VI, 346); cf. *Ord.* I, d.2, q.4, (OTh II, 140) and *Summa logicae* I, c.1, (OPh I, 8).

8. *Ibid.*, c.12, (OPh I, 41); *Expos. Periherm.* I, Prooemium, (OPh II, 347).

9. It has been pointed out to me by Fr. Gedeon Gál that the latest works in which Ockham discusses this issue—the *Quodlibeta* and the *Quaestiones in libros Physicorum*—are records of actual debates. And it is conceivable that in the course of such exercises, Ockham should have defended an opinion or made use of an argument to which he would not have given his wholehearted endorsement. Thus, Ockham's attacks on the objective-existence theory and defense of the mental-act theory in these works do not provide conclusive evidence that Ockham ever gave the mental-act theory his full support. On the other side, it should be noted that in these questions

mind about the ontological status of concepts.[10] He began by holding that concepts have a non-real mode of existence as objects of thought. (I shall label this the "objective-existence theory," because Ockham usually dubs the non-real mode of ex-

as we have them, Ockham consistently adopts a favorable attitude towards the mental-act theory and a negative to derogatory attitude towards the objective-existence theory.

10. Ockham's progressive changes of mind have been traced by Boehner, who found them an important tool for dating Ockham's works (see "The Relative Date of Ockham's Commentary on the Sentences," *Collected Articles on Ockham*, #9, 96–110, and "The Realistic Conceptualism of William Ockham," *Collected Articles on Ockham*, #13, 168–174), and by Gál (see "Gualteri de Chatton et Guillelmi de Ockham Controversia de Natura Conceptus Universalis," *Franciscan Studies* N.S. XXVII (1967): 191–212, especially 192–99). Some corrections in Boehner's chronology have been suggested by Gordon Leff in his book *William of Ockham: The Metamorphosis of Scholastic Discourse*, (Manchester, 1975), chap.2, 78–94. Briefly, their conclusions are as follows: When Ockham first commented on the *Sentences*, he held the objective-existence theory to the exclusion of any others. The text of Books II–IV (the *Reportatio*), which Ockham never revised for publication, dates from this period. When he made his first revision of Book I, d.2, q.8, (OTh II, 266–289), he acknowledged the mental-act theory as not utterly improbable, but still preferred the objective-existence theory. In his *Expositio in librum Perihermenias Aristotelis*, Ockham allows the objective-existence theory and the theory that concepts are real mental qualities as alike defensible (I, Prooemium, (OPh II, 363–64) and (OPh II, 371)), and in an added section declares the mental-act theory to be the most probable of the mental-quality theories and shows at length how it could deal with objections raised against it (OPh II, 363–69). At some point after this but probably before he made his final revision of Book I, d.2, q.8, Ockham inserted at Book I, d.27, q.3, a lengthy critique of a similar theory held by Peter Aureol (see sections 5 and 6 below). Ockham's final changes in the first book of his *Commentary on the Sentences* (the *Ordinatio*) regard the objective-existence theory and the mental-quality theory as equally defensible. In the *Summa logicae* I, c.12, Ockham notes that the principle of parsimony favors the mental-act theory over the view that mental signs are ficta or mental qualities distinct from acts of understanding (OPh I, 42–43). And where relevant he mentions what a mental-quality or mental-act theorist would say, omitting the objective-existence theory from further consideration, (c.14, (OPh I, 48); c.15, (OPh I, 53); c.40, (OPh I, 113)). Finally, in the *Quodlibeta* and the *Quaestiones in libros Physicorum*, he explicitly attacks the objective-existence theory as mistaken, thereby sustaining his endorsement of the mental-act theory in these works.

istence "objective existence.") Early on, he came to believe it equally probable that concepts were some kind of really existent mental qualities. Partly because of his own contemporary and fellow Franciscan Walter Chatton, Ockham eventually abandoned the objective-existence theory in favor of the view that concepts are really existent acts of intellect (*intellectiones*) (hence labelled the "mental-act theory"). Since these theories involve rather different ontologies, Ockham's change of mind may be viewed as a reasoned ontological conversion.

In what follows, I shall begin by considering Ockham's arguments in favor of the objective-existence theory. His reasons for changing his mind—of which we shall examine four—represent a surprising mixture of insight and confusion. By the end of chapter 4, I think it will appear that Ockham weighed the disadvantages of the objective-existence theory more carefully than the consequences of the mental-act theory and in fact had better reason to abandon the former than to adopt the latter.

3. THE DISTINCTION BETWEEN OBJECTIVE AND REAL EXISTENCE

Ockham's first view is that concepts have, not real existence, but have a non-real mode of existence as objects of thought. His arguments for distinguishing a kind of existence distinct from real existence rest on the observation that we are able to think of three kinds of things that do not and/or cannot really exist. (i) First, we think of things as having contradictory properties. Ockham's examples are chimeras and goat stags,[11] but the round square might strike the modern reader as a better case. (ii) Other things, not thought of as having contradictory properties, nevertheless are not the kind of thing that can really exist. For Ockham, these include the objects of logic: propositions and

11. *Ord.* I, d.2, q.8, (OTh II, 273); *Expos. Periherm.* I, Prooemium, (OPh II, 364).

syllogisms,[12] relations of reason—such as that of being the subject or the predicate of a proposition—which are produced by
some mental act of comparison,[13] and universals.[14] (iii) Finally,
there are things that can exist but in fact do not. Ockham mentions creatures thought of by God prior to their creation and
merely possible creatures that God eternally thinks of but never
makes.[15]

Ockham assumes that whatever is thought of must have some
sort of ontological status. When we think of something that
really exists, its ontological status is straightforward. What
about things we think of that do not and/or cannot really exist?
Ockham insists that even these must be something that is not
nothing. Otherwise, we would be thinking of nothing.[16]
Ockham says that such unreal objects of thought have "objective,"[17] "intensional," or "cognized" existence,[18] as opposed
to "subjective" or real existence.

Ockham's reasoning could thus be formulated as follows.

1. We think of objects of sorts (i)–(iii).

2. If we think of something, it has some sort of existence

---

12. *Ord.* I, d.2, q.8, (OTh II, 273); *Expos. Periherm.* I, Prooemium, (OPh
II, 369).
13. *Ord.* I, d.2, q.8, (OTh II, 274).
14. *Expos. Periherm.* I, Prooemium, (OPh II, 369).
15. *Ord.* I, d.2, q.8, (OTh II, 274, 283); d.35, q.5, (OTh IV, 491–92);
d.38, q.1, (OTh IV, 585, 587); *De praedest.* q.2, a.4, (OPh II, 529–530).
16. Thus, in *Expositio in librum Perihermenias Aristotelis* I, Prooemium, (OPh II, 352–53), Ockham begins an argument against the mental-
act theory in favor of the objective-existence theory as follows: "First, take
the common or confused intention that corresponds to the token sound
'man' or 'animal'. I ask whether something is understood by that cognition or
nothing? It cannot be said that nothing is. For just as it is impossible that there
be an act of seeing and nothing seen or that there be a desire and nothing
desired, so also it is impossible that there should be a cognition and nothing
be cognized by that cognition..." Cf. *Ord.* I, d.2, q.8, (OTh II, 268, lines
7–13).
17. *Ord.* I, d.2, q.8, (OTh II, 271–74).
18. *Expos. Periherm.* I, Prooemium, (OPh II, 370).

—viz., either objective existence or real existence.

3. Objects of sorts (i)–(iii) do not and/or cannot really exist.

4. Therefore, objects of sorts (i)–(iii) have objective existence.

5. Mental acts, mental qualities, and the mind itself really exist.

6. Therefore, objects of sorts (i)–(iii) are distinct from mental acts, mental qualitites, and the mind itself.

2 is presumably regarded as a necessary truth. And the conclusion in 6 indicates an analysis of what goes on when we think of something unreal into two components: the really existent mental act and the objectively existent object.

Once one has arrived at such an analysis, it is natural to extend it to thoughts about real things, so that really existent things also have objective existence when they are thought of. And while Ockham does not explicitly do so in passages where he is arguing for the distinction between objective and subjective existence, there is some textual evidence that he took such an extension for granted when he first commented on the *Sentences*. (a) The clearest indication comes in his remarks about God's awareness of creatures, where he implies that creatures have objective existence in God's mind even when they are real. For he says that the "ideas" of all creatures are "eternally and immutably understood by God."[19] And he has previously identified divine ideas with the creatures themselves *insofar as they have objective existence in the divine mind*.[20] It seems to follow that all creatures have objective existence in the divine mind eternally and immutably, even though some of them are real at times. And since there is no theoretical reason

19. *Ord.* I, d.35, q.5, (OTh IV, 497–98); cf. Part Five, chapter 24 below.
20. *Ibid.*, (OTh IV, 493).

why God's awareness should differ from creatures' in this respect, this is some reason to think that Ockham's objective-existence theory applied to all thoughts. (b) Further evidence comes in Ockham's reference to an intuitive cognition of a particular as an awareness of *a term* in a contingent proposition about that particular. Ockham never thought that particulars—other than conventional signs (and on the mental-act theory) mental qualities—could, insofar as they existed in reality, be a term in a proposition. If, when he held the objective-existence theory, he thought that particulars such as Socrates, this whiteness, or this body, could be the terms of propositions, it must have been because he supposed them to have objective existence. And since intuitive cognitions cannot be produced naturally unless the object really exists, he must have thought that the objects of such cognitions have objective existence even when they really exist (see Part Three, chapter 13 below).

Contemporary philosophers may be struck by the similarity between Ockham's view and those generally ascribed to Alexius Meinong. They would be even more similar if Ockham had said that what has objective existence has it independently of whether it is ever thought of. In fact, he says the opposite. He claims that things that have "only objective existence" are such that "their to be is to be known or cognized."[21] Thus 'x has objective existence' entails 'Someone is thinking of x' or 'An act of thinking of x really exists'. This does not necessarily mean that the objective existence of things is interrupted, however. For Ockham seems to imply that everything—actual, possible, or impossible—has objective existence eternally and immutably in the mind of God.[22]

Conclusions 4 and 6 distinguish two elements involved in our thought of nonexistents: really existent mental acts or qualities of mind, and objects that have objective existence (in Meinong's terminology, subsist or have *Aussersein*). Presumably, there is

21. *Ibid.*, d.2, q.8, (OTh II, 273); *Expos. Periherm.* I, Prooemium, (OPh II, 359).

22. *Ord.* I, d.38, q.1, (OTh IV, 587); cf. d.35, q.5, (OTh IV, 479).

also a relation between them, which Ockham (see Part One, chapter 7 below) and Meinong agree is not any real thing.[23] Is anything else involved? Meinong thinks that there must be, even though most of the time we are not aware of anything else in our experience.[24] Otherwise there would be nothing in what really exists to account for the fact that acts of thought are directed towards one object rather than another. It would be purely contingent that such relations held at all and held between a given object and a particular mental act. Unwilling to accept this consequence, Meinong supposes that there is some real feature of an act of thought that necessarily directs it to its object. He calls such features "contents."

Does Ockham posit anything analogous to Meinong's contents? His older contemporary Peter Aureol does in defending a theory similar to Ockham's. Ockham quotes him as offering the following argument:

> ...An act of intellect is very similar to the thing it is about. Therefore, through this likeness either the thing seizes some existence, or it is merely denominated. But it cannot be said that it is merely denominated, so that the existence in the intellect is a certain denomination, just as Caesar depicted is denominated by a picture; for through this denomination Caesar is not present to the picture, nor is he an object for it, nor does he appear to it. Therefore, it is necessary to say that the thing seizes a certain existence through the act of understanding insofar as [that act] is very similar to the thing, so that understood existence is not a mere denomination, but a certain diminished intensional or apparent existence...[25]

Aureol's idea is that the act of intellect is a likeness of the thing and this similarity of the act to the thing "produces" the thing in intensional existence and presumably directs the act towards the object thus produced. Ockham does not like to speak of a

---

23. Findlay, *Meinong's Theory of Objects and Values*, (London, 1963), chap.1, 35.

24. "Über Gegenstande höhere Ordnung und ihr Verhältnis zur Innern Wahrnehmung," quoted in J. N. Findlay, *op. cit.*, chap. 1, 22; cf. 22–32.

25. *Ord.* I, d.27, q.3, (OTh IV, 235).

thing's being *produced* in objective existence (see Part Five, chapter 24 below). But there is some hint that when Ockham first held the objective-existence theory, he agreed with Aureol that the similarity of an act towards a thing is in part what directs the act towards its object and towards one object rather than the other. In *Reportatio* II, q.12–13, Ockham considers an objection based on the postulate of Greek epistemology that ''all knowledge is by assimilation.''[26] It is observed that every mental act or cognition is equally similar to numerically distinct particulars. And the conclusion is drawn that we never have a cognition that is proper to one particular alone. Ockham replies that the similarity of the act to the thing will not suffice by itself, but one must add in the fact that the act is caused or apt to be caused to exist by one of the particulars and not the others. In taking the objection to be relevant and replying as he does, Ockham implies that a mental act's similarity to and actual or possible causal connection with a thing is what directs it towards one objectively existent object rather than another. For the objective-existence theory, a cognition will be proper to one particular alone provided it is directed towards that particular in objective existence and that particular alone. Any observation about how similar the mental act is or is not to the particular would seem to be irrelevant, unless the similarity of the act to the thing is thought to play a role in directing the act towards one objective existent rather than another. Hence, he seems to allow these features on an act to fill the role of Meinongian contents.[27]

Ockham clearly takes the objective-existence theory to have an ''ontological commitment'' to unreal entities. Perhaps the notion of an ontological commitment calls for some explanation. For Quine, a theory has an ontological commitment to the entities that must be taken to be the values of the individual variables if the theory is to be true. And a philosopher

---

26. (OTh V, 287).

27. For a fuller discussion of what makes an act of thought to be a cognition of one particular rather than another, see Part One, chapter 4 below.

NAMES AND CONCEPTS   81

has an ontological commitment to those entities, if he accepts the theory. An analogous account is available within Ockham's logic: for Ockham, we may say, a theory has an ontological commitment to entities of a certain sort if, in order for the theory to be true, a term must be taken to supposit or stand for such entities in a proposition included in the theory.[28] Thus, the objective-existence theory has an ontological commitment to really existent particular men and animals because the terms 'man' and 'animal' stand for such things in the proposition 'A man is an animal'. Likewise, it has an ontological commitment to objectively existent entities. For according to it, the proposition 'Man is a species' cannot be true unless both the term 'man' and the term 'species' supposit or stand for the objectively existent universal man.

Nevertheless, a philosopher might make use of a theory that had an ontological commitment to entities in the sense just explained, while holding the metaphysical belief that they are reducible to something else. For instance, a phenomenalist might make use of a system in which terms are allowed to stand in a proposition for physical objects, even though he holds the metaphysical belief that physical objects are ultimately reducible to perceptions or sense data. And he might or might not hold that it is in principle possible to formulate a language whose terms can stand in a proposition only for sense data. Did Ockham, while he held the objective-existence theory, believe that objective existents are somehow reducible to real existents?

Although he does not explicitly address himself to this issue, I think it is pretty clear that he did not. I think the only reduction it is plausible to see him envisioning would be one that identifies the objective existence of a thing with the real existence of a mental act with a certain content. After all, he does appear to think that a statement of the form 'x has objective existence' entails and is entailed by the statement that a mental act with a certain content really exists. Since objectively existent entities are

28. For a detailed discussion of Ockham's supposition theory, see Part Two, chapters 10–11.

the immediate objects of thought, according to the objective-existence theory, this would be tantamount to identifying the immediate object of thought with an act of intellect with a certain content. That Ockham would not accept such a reduction, is implied by an argument he offers against the mental-act theory. He argues that every act of understanding must have an object, even when it is a thought of a universal that cannot really exist, since otherwise our thought would be a thought of nothing. But he says that the object of thought cannot be identified with the act of intellect, because then the act of intellect would be an act of understanding itself—which he finds absurd.[29] If he had envisioned any other sort of reduction of objectively existent entities to acts of intellect, fairness to the mental-act theory would have required him to bring it up here.

Further evidence that he does not want to reduce objective existents to the real existence of certain mental acts—or, for that matter, of anything else—comes in an argument he raises against the objective-existence theory itself in *Quodlibeta* IV, q.35. Because God is necessarily conceptually omniscient, endorsing the objective-existence theory would require us to conclude that "from eternity there was a coordinate" of as many objectively existent entities "as there can be of different intelligibles, which were so necessarily existent that God could not destroy them."[30] This consequence was theologically objectionable, because medieval theologians hesitated to say that anything other than God was coeternal with God. (See Part Five, chapter 24 below.) If the objective existence of creatures from eternity were reducible to the real existence of the divine act of cognition from eternity, that would not involve positing anything other than and coeternal with God. That Ockham raised this objection is evidence that he did not envisage such a reduction of the coordinate of objectively existent entities to the real existence of mental acts.

In sum, then, Ockham's objective-existence theory analyses acts of thought into a really existent mental act and an objective-

---

29. *Expos. Periherm.* I, Prooemium, (OPh II, 353).
30. (OTh IX, 473).

ly existent object. The mental act is thought of as directed towards an objectively existent entity by similarity and/or actual or possible causal relations to the object. And the objective existence of something is not thought of as reducible to the real existence of something else.

4.   OBJECTIONS TO THE OBJECTIVE-
    EXISTENCE THEORY

In arguing for the distinction between objective and real existence, Ockham concentrates on our thoughts of things that cannot really exist—whether because they are abstract or because they have contradictory properties. But since premiss 2 is perfectly general, there seems to be no reason why the objective-existence theory should not apply to our thoughts of particulars as well. And we have seen evidence that Ockham does extend the theory in that direction. Nor was he the first philosopher to claim that particulars have a non-real mode of existence as objects of thought. Henry of Harclay (d.1317) suggests such a view in an early question on divine ideas,[31] and Ockham was considerably influenced by this discussion in formulating his own position. By his own account,[32] Ockham was less familiar with the views of another older contemporary, Peter Aureol, who had argued that the objects of sensation—both veridical and illusory—as well as objects of thought have a non-real mode of existence. Apparently, it was partly as a result of examining Aureol's opinion that Ockham became convinced that the objective-existence theory was false as applied to thoughts of particulars. His arguments are set out in a lengthy critique of Aureol which he inserted into the *Ordinatio* at d.27, q.3, probably even before he made the final additions at d.2, q.8,[33] which acknowledged the mental-act theory as equally

31. Edited by Armand Maurer, in "Henry of Harclay's Questions on the Divine Ideas," *Medieval Studies* XXIII (1961): 163–193, at 166–172.

32. *Ord.* I, d.27, q.3, (OTh IV, 238).

33. (OTh II, 289–292).

defensible where thoughts of universals are concerned.[34] And in d.27, q.3 itself, he expresses neutrality between the two theories as applied to thoughts of universals.[35] It was under the influence of criticisms from his contemporary and fellow Franciscan, Walter Chatton, that Ockham eventually abandoned the objective-existence theory altogether in favor of an alternative analysis of what it is to think of something.[36]

In what follows I shall consider four different objections to the objective-existence theory, three of which are actually raised by Ockham and his contemporaries. The first, urged by Ockham against Aureol and by Chatton against them both, together with the second reveal the asymmetry Ockham saw between thoughts of particulars and thoughts of things that cannot really exist. The third set of difficulties takes off from Quine's worries that there would be no criteria of identity and distinction for unreal entities of the sort assumed by the objective-existence theory. The fourth contends that such unreal entities are theoretically superfluous. I shall postpone consideration of a theological objection to Part Five, chapter 24 below.

5. THE OBJECTIVE-EXISTENCE THEORY AND DIRECT REALISM IN EPISTEMOLOGY

Ockham was a staunch defender of direct realism in epistemology. In fact, he insists that our mental life *begins* with an immediate awareness of mind-independent particular physical objects (see Part Three, chapter 13 below). If the objective-existence theory conflicted with this, he would have a powerful reason for rejecting it. Yet, Walter Chatton charged that the similar theories of their older contemporaries Henry of

---

34. Gedeon Gál, *op. cit.*, 196, note 14.

35. (OTh IV, 243).

36. Gedeon Gál demonstrates this influence in his article "Gualteri de Chatton et Guillelmi de Ockham Controversia de Natura Conceptus Universalis." Chatton's arguments are spelled out in his *Reportatio* I, d.3, q.2 and more fully in his *Lectura* I, d.3, q.2. In his article, Gál edits the former with supplementary quotations from the latter.

Harclay and Peter Aureol threatened direct realism in epistemology. Chatton insisted against them "that besides the
act of intellect and the mind-independent thing cognized by the
intellect, there is no fictional being (*ens fictum*) that is mean and
is the immediate term of the act instead of the mind-independent thing..."[37] And in *Quodlibeta* IV, q.35, Ockham turns this
criticism against his own earlier view:

> Further, such a *fictum* hinders the cognition of a thing. Therefore,
> *ficta* should not be assumed to explain cognition. Proof of the premiss:
> The *fictum* is neither the cognition nor the whiteness beyond the thing
> cognized nor both together, but some third thing that is a mean be-
> tween the cognition and the thing. Therefore, if the *fictum* is under-
> stood, the mind-independent thing is not understood...[38]

The argument here is puzzling, however. The following two of
its premises are implicit:

1.   *Ficta* are always the immediate objects of thought and
     awareness.

2.   If x and y are distinct, then an immediate awareness of x
     is not an immediate awareness of y, and vice versa.

But the third,

3.   *Ficta* are not the same either as the act of intellect or the
     mind-independent thing,

is stated. And from 1–3, we can infer that

4.   Mind-independent things are never the immediate ob-
     jects of our awareness,

which is clearly a denial of direct realism in epistemology. I
shall return to 2 later. The appropriate response to 1 and 3

37. *Ibid.*, 203, note 26; cf. 201–203.
38. (OTh IX, 473).

depends upon how the word '*fictum*' is understood. If it is being used here the way it was used by Ockham when he first formulated the objective-existence theory, then it stands only for
those objectively existent entities that cannot exist in reality.
On this interpretation, 3 is clearly true, but 1 is false on the objective-existence theory. For as long as he was an adherent of
the objective-existence theory, Ockham would have held that
ficta are the immediate objects of thought and awareness in
some cases only: viz., when we think (a) of things having incompatible properties, or (b) of abstract objects such as universals,
but not when we think (c) of things that can really exist but in
fact do not. He explicitly notes that where our thoughts of
universals are concerned, these *ficta* do come between us and
really existent particulars naturally signified by them. But, as he
recognized, this fact presents no challenge to his version of
direct realism in epistemology. For the latter theory claims only
that we are sometimes—viz., in intuitive cognition and the
abstractive cognition that immediately follows it—immediately
aware of particulars, not that we *always* are. And according to
the objective-existence theory, no *fictum* is the immediate object of thought in intuitive cognition. Rather the objectively existent particular itself, which is identical with the really existent
particular, is.[39]

On the other hand, if '*fictum*' is used for any putative entities
in a non-real mode of existence, Ockham's objective-existence
theory is committed to 1, but not to 3. For the objectively existent entities that are the immediate objects of our awareness in

---

39. Even in *Ordinatio* I, d.27, q.3, where Ockham has been attacking
Aureol's similar theory about our awareness of particulars, principally on the
ground that it compromises direct realism, Ockham continued to allow as
defensible the opinion that when I conceive of man in general 'only a certain
fictum common to all particulars' and not any particular is the immediate object of my thought (OTh IV, 242). As we shall see, Ockham ultimately
eliminates the *fictum* in these cases too, but on grounds of superfluity. For he
comes to see how a mental-act theorist might maintain that conceiving of
man in general is not a matter of his having a universal rather than a particular
man as the immediate object of thought, but rather a matter of conceiving of
particular men in a different way—viz., confusedly rather than distinctly (*Expos. Periherm.* I, Prooemium, (OPh II, 354–55)).

intuitive cognitions, are the particulars themselves. Either way, Ockham's objective-existence theory does not maintain both 1 and 3, and the objection seems to fail because of a false premiss.

Ockham's general arguments against Aureol's similar theory include a different version of this reasoning. Focussing on a veridical visual awareness of whiteness, Ockham argues first that the whiteness and its apparent existence (Aureol's analogue of objective existence) are not really the same.

> ...I ask about the apparent existence in which the whiteness is constituted when the whiteness appears. Either it is really the same as the whiteness, or it is not really the same. If it is said that it is really the same, on the contrary, when some things are really the same, they are simultaneously generated and corrupted, according to the Philosopher in *Metaphysics*, Book IV. Consequently, whenever it should happen that the existence appear, the same whiteness will come into existence. Similarly, whenever some things are really the same, it is impossible that one should exist while the other does not. But this (where the whiteness is indicated) cannot be that (where that apparent existence, which does not exist, is indicated). Otherwise, that apparent existence would exist apart from a vision.[40]

He then assumes, parallel to 2, that

> 2'. If whiteness and its apparent existence are not really the same, then an immediate awareness of one is not an immediate awareness of the other,

and parallel to 1, that

> 1'. Apparent existence is always the immediate object of our awareness.

It follows that in the visual awareness in question, we are not immediately aware of the mind-independent particular whiteness, and that its apparent existence would always be a mean between the whiteness and the visual act.

This version of the argument seems even stranger than the first, however. To begin with, it seems inappropriate to ask

40. *Ord.* I, d.27, q.3, (OTh IV, 239).

whether the apparent or objective existence of something is *really* the same as the mind-independent whiteness. For most frequently Ockham uses the terms 'really the same' and 'really distinct' in such a way that it makes sense to say only of real things (*res*). For the whole point of such a theory is to distinguish a non-real from a real mode of existence in such a way that the former is not reducible to the latter. Thus, the existence of a thing in a non-real mode would not be something that occurs in the real mode, but rather in the non-real mode of existence.

In this argument, Ockham seems to depart from his normal usage and, in effect, to allow that the apparent or objective existence of the whiteness really exists if and only if it is true that the whiteness has apparent existence. On this understanding, he correctly reasons that since it is logically possible that the whiteness should really exist when there is no visual awareness of it and hence when its apparent existence does not really exist and vice versa, the whiteness is not really the same as its apparent existence.

The difficulty is that this conclusion is doubly irrelevant to the issue at hand. For the theory under attack will be seen to compromise direct realism in epistemology only if it further endorses 1'—which neither Ockham's nor Aureol's theory explicitly does. Secondly, where 1' is incorporated into the theory, the question about direct realism will be whether I can be immediately aware of the whiteness, not whether the whiteness can exist in reality without having apparent existence and vice versa. Direct realism will be threatened, only if the answer to the first question is negative. For it seems impossible that I should have the apparent existence of this whiteness—as opposed to the apparent existence in general—as an immediate object of my thought without simultaneously having this whiteness as an immediate object of my thought. If so, 1' and the supposed real distinction of whiteness and its apparent existence are compatible with direct realism and Ockham's argument fails. Nevertheless, this does not settle the question of whether the objective-existence theory and direct realism are compatible. For we shall see that one way in which the objective-existence theory might be altered to meet the next objection involves giving up direct realism in epistemology.

6.   THE OBJECTIVE-EXISTENCE THEORY AND ONTOLOGICAL PARADOX

Not only did Ockham come to see Aureol's theory, as well as his own objective-existence theory, as leading to an incorrect epistemology, he also thought that the general principles used to infer the existence of something in a non-real mode from the fact that someone thinks of or is aware of it, had paradoxical consequences of the sort raised for Anselm's and Descartes's ontological arguments by Gaunilo's perfect-island argument and Caterus's existent-lion objection. Ockham's argument occurs in his critique of Aureol's theory, and to appreciate the objection, it is necessary to have a brief look at what Aureol has to say.

Unlike Ockham, Aureol defends his theory in the first instance by an argument from sensory illusion.[41] He begins with the premiss, familiar from more recent philosophy, that what appears must be *something*, even in sensory illusion. But while some philosophers have since identified what appears with a sense datum and others with a false proposition that appears true, Aureol insists that it is the thing and its properties that appear. And if either or both do not really exist but are merely apparent, then they will have to have a non-real mode of existence. He elaborates this reasoning in connection with eight examples of sensory illusion; but for present purposes it will be enough to consider two. (a) Someone is being carried along the water on a boat. The trees on the shore seem to that person to move. Nevertheless, Aureol supposes, contrary to modern physics, the trees do not really move. Evidently assuming (although not explicitly stating) a principle of the form

(G) If something x seems (some things x, y etc. seem) to be F,

41. *Scriptum super primum Sententiarum*, (Buytaert ed.); cf. I, d.3, a.1, sec.14, (Buytaert ed., vol.2, 696–98).

G, etc., then that instance (those instances) of *F*-ness,
G-ness, etc. must be (in some sense),

where 'in motion' is substituted for '*F* ' and 'motion' for
'*F*-ness' and 'the trees' for '*x*', '*y*', etc., he concludes that since
the observed motion does not really exist in the air or in the act
of vision, the motion must have some non-real mode of existence, which he variously labels "intensional," "seen," or
"adjudged" existence.[42]

  (b) A stick is swung rapidly around in the air; a circle appears.
Nevertheless, the circle will not be anything real in the stick,
because the stick is straight. Nor is it anything real in the air. Nor
can it be in the act of vision or in the eye, since the circle appears to be in the air, while the act of vision and the eye are not
located there. Tacitly assuming a priniciple of the form

  (H) If something *x* appears (some things *x*, *y*, etc. appear) to
       be *F, G,* etc., then that thing *x* (those things *x, y,* etc.),
       having some sort of existence, is (are) *F, G,* etc.,

where 'the circle' is substituted for '*x*' and 'in the air' for '*F* ', he
concludes that the circle "that has intensional existence or that
is in apparent, adjudged, or seen existence, is in the air."[43] Having argued that non-veridical acts of sense perception always
posit something in a non-real mode of existence, Aureol extends
this conclusion to veridical sensations, acts of imagination, and
acts of intellect.[44]

  Aureol's arguments from sensory illusion parallel Ockham's
about our thoughts of universals and chimeras quite closely.
Both argue that unreal objects of cognition must have some
mode of existence. And Aureol's principles (G) and (H) seem
analogous to Ockham's premiss 2 above. Thus, in raising difficulties with Aureol's principles, Ockham is posing problems
for his own theory as well.

  Ockham focuses on the first example and challenges Aureol's

  42. *Ibid.*, 696, quoted by Ockham in *Ord.* I, d.27, q.3, (OTh IV, 231).
  43. *Ibid.*, 696–97.
  44. *Ibid.*, 698.

tacitly assumed principles of inference:

> ...'The trees appear to move; therefore some motion appears or has objective existence' no more follows than 'The trees appear to move in reality; therefore, a real motion appears or has objective existence' follows. For the mode of arguing is analogous. But everyone agrees that the second inference does not hold good. Therefore, neither does the first...[45]

Consider the principle instantiated by the first inference:

(J) If something x appears (some things x, y, etc. appear) to be F, G, etc., then an instance (those instances) of F-ness, G-ness, etc. has (have) objective existence.

Ockham says that (J) is equivalent to that employed in the second inference and replaces (G) once Aureol's theory is extended to cover veridical as well as illusory sensations. Ockham's point is that if (J) held good for all substitutions for 'F', 'G', 'F-ness', and 'G-ness', then—substituting 'really ϕ' for 'F' and 'real ϕ-ness' for 'F-ness'—we could infer 'Real ϕ-ness has objective existence' and hence 'Some ϕ-ness is real' from 'Something seems to be really ϕ' and thus produce ϕ-nesses in real existence simply by imagining something as or by having something appear to be really ϕ—which is absurd.

I think we can get clearer about the structure of Ockham's objection if we apply his reasoning to (H) and its extension

(K) If something x appears (some things x, y, etc. appear) to be F, G, etc., then that thing x (those things x, y, etc.), having objective existence, is (are) F, G, etc.

Aureol seems to reason that since the circle appears in the air, it has the property of being in the air and is not to be identified with anything, real or unreal, that lacks this property. In contemporary terms, it is as if Aureol were operating with a system whose universe of discourse is neutral between existence in

_____

45. *Ord.* I, d.27, q.3, (OTh IV, 244–45).

reality and existence in a non-real mode and so includes everything that really exists in either or both modes. Within this system, statements of the form 'x is F' do not, in general, entail statements of the form 'x exists in reality', nor do they, in general, entail statements of the form 'x has objective existence' but only statements of the form 'Either x exists in reality or x has objective existence'. Given such a system, which allows items in the universe of discourse to exists in two modes, the way is open to relativize the predications to one mode of existence or the other. As indicated in our discussion of moderate realism (see Part One, chapter 2 above), this might be done by regarding such phrases as 'in reality' and 'in objective existence' as analogous to modal operators in having a single argument place satisfied by a proposition. Alternatively, one could construe 'is in motion' and 'is in the air', which appear to be one place predicates, as two place predicates, one of whose places is satisfied by a mode of existence. But it is clear from Aureol's reasoning that he is not exercising either of these options. In Aureol's system, the predications are not relativized to one mode of existence rather than the other, but attach absolutely. Thus, Aureol says that the circle is in the air; he does not say that it is in the air in the mode of objective existence or that it is in the air in the mode of real existence. Aureol's conclusion might be formalized in such a system as follows:

(Ex) (x is a circle & x is in the air & x has objective or apparent existence).

'Is a circle' and 'is in the air' and 'has objective existence' all attach to 'x' absolutely, not relative to a mode of existence. While statements of the form 'x is F' do not in general entail statements of the form 'x exists in reality' or 'x has objective existence', such entailments will hold for some substitutions for 'F'. For instance, suppose that 'really existent' or 'objectively existent' or 'really existent ϕ' or 'objectively existent ϕ' is substituted for 'F'. Then we will get entailments of real or objective existence, respectively. What Ockham has done, in effect, in dealing with (J) is to understand 'Real motion has objec-

tive existence' to be a statement formalizable in the above
described system as

(Ex) (x is motion & x is real & x has objective existence)

—which does, of course, entail that motion really exists. This
result is absurd enough, but matters become even worse when
we substitute 'really existent chimera' or 'really existent round
square' instead. Further, it is easy to see how a similar difficulty
would follow from substituting 'really nonexistent ϕ' for 'F' in
(H) and (K). And if in their analogue for intellectual acts of
awareness—

(L) If something x is (some things x, y, etc. are) thought of as
     F, G, etc., then that thing x (those things x, y, etc.) having
     objective existence is (are) F, G, etc.

—we substitute 'lacking in objective existence' for 'F', it
follows that if something is thought of as lacking in objective existence, as it might be by someone actively rejecting the objective-existence theory, that thing both has and lacks objective existence—which is a contradiction.

The latter paradoxical consequences might seem easily
averted by simply disallowing 'really existent', 'really existent
ϕ', 'really nonexistent', 'really nonexistent ϕ', lacking in objective existence' and 'ϕ lacking in objective existence' etc. as
legitimate substitutions for 'F'. However this move might
otherwise fare, it would do nothing to obviate a more general
difficulty which arises especially in connection with cases of
sensory illusion or intellectual misapprehension in which a really existent particular is perceived or mistakenly thought to have
properties that it does not really have. Reconsider the trees that
appear to move but do not. From the latter clause, we can infer
'These trees are not in motion'. But (H) entitles us to infer
'These trees are in motion' from the fact that they appear to be
in motion. Within the system Aureol seems to be presupposing,
both predications are made absolutely and not merely in relation to one or another mode of existence. Thus, (H) together

with the assumption that something appears to have a property that it does not really have, entails a contradiction. Similarly, for (K) and (L).

Although it is perhaps less obvious, the same general difficulty arises for (G) and (J). Substituting 'white dog' for '*F*' and 'white caninity' for '*F*-ness' in (J), we derive 'If something appears to be a white dog, then that particular white caninity has objective existence'. Suppose that what appears to be a white dog is really a brown dog, so that the particular caninity that appears white is brown. Then, given that (J) requires that the same caninity has objective existence and is white as has real existence and is brown, if the predicates are not relativized to modes of existence, we shall have to conclude that the same particular caninity is both white and brown.

The trouble with these principles is that they all specify that the same particulars that appear to have certain properties are the ones that actually have those properties. If this stipulation is combined with the assumption that the predicates attach to their subjects absolutely and not merely in relation to a mode of existence, then sensory illusion and intellectual misapprehension become impossible, since they would involve the same particular in both having and lacking the same properties. And this difficulty will arise no matter what is substituted for '*F*', '*G*', etc., and hence cannot be removed by restricting permissible substitutions.

Short of completely abandoning the theory that the particulars we are aware of or think of have a non-real mode of existence, Aureol could modify his theory in one of two obvious ways. (i) First, he could retain the assumption that predication is not relativized to a mode of existence, but drop the specific requirement in (G)–(L) that the same particulars that exist in reality and have certain properties, have objective or apparent existence and have other, incompatible properties. For example, one could say that when the trees appear to move but do not, the trees that have objective existence and move are not the same particular trees as those that really exist and do not move. If Aureol modified his theory in this way, however, it would fall prey to Ockham's earlier charge that it compromises a direct realist position in theory of knowledge. If the objectively existent moving trees are not the same particular trees that really exist, then in such cases of sensory illusion and intellectual misapprehension, we are not immediately aware of the real trees.

(ii) Alternatively, Aureol might retain the requirement that the same particulars that really exist and have certain properties, objectively exist and have certain other properties, while providing for predications to be relativized to modes of existence. This approach would involve replacing the above principles with

(M) If something x appears (some things x, y, etc. appear) to be F, G, etc., then in some mode of existence, x is (x, y, etc. are) F, G, etc.

and its analogue

(N) If something x appears (some things x, y, etc. appear) to be F, G, etc., then in the mode of objective existence, that thing x is (x, y, etc. are) F, G, etc.

Here 'in the mode of objective existence' functions as a sort of operator on the whole proposition and qualifies the predication by indicating that the predicate attaches to the subject in the mode of objective existence; similarly for 'in reality'. On this scheme, one can say without contradiction of the same particular trees that in reality the trees exist and are not moving, while in the mode of objective existence they exist and are moving. And one can thus account for sensory illusion and intellectual misapprehension without in any way compromising direct realism. Similarly, the substitution of 'really existent' and 'really nonexistent' for 'F' in these principles can be construed in a non-problematic way. For just as some things are real and others are only imaginary or thought of, so some things are thought of as real and others are thought of as only imaginary. Thus, 'In the mode of objective existence, x does not really exist' might be construed as logically equivalent to 'In reality, someone thinks of x as really existent' and 'In the mode of objective existence, x does not really exist' to 'In reality, someone thinks of x as really nonexistent'. But the former does not entail 'In reality, x exists' any more than the latter entails 'In reality, x does not exist'. Finally, 'In the mode of objective existence, x is lacking in objective existence' will be construed as logically equivalent to the noncontradictory proposition 'In the mode of objective existence, no one is thinking of x'.

It would not be necessary to stipulate that all predications within this system must be relativized. In fact, one would wish to allow for some non-relativized predications so that one might assert relations between things that exist in different modes. For the claim that objectively existent things are somehow similar to mind-independent particulars is crucial to a theory of natural signification (see Part One, chapter 4 below).

If Aureol's theory could be rescued in either of these ways, the application of Ockham's objective-existence theory to our awareness of thoughts of particulars could be saved as well. But it is clear that Ockham would reject the first way. And it is equally clear from our discussion in the previous chapter (see Part One, chapter 2, sections (3.2) and 8 above) that he completely overlooks the second way of removing apparent contradictions. In so doing, he passes over the most promising way of developing the objective-existence theory. It is not surprising, therefore, that Ockham finds this objection, together with the others he brings against Aureol, decisive for showing that the objective-existence theory is incorrect as applied to our intuitive and abstractive cognitions of particulars. But since in his view universals cannot exist in reality as well as objectively, neither of the above two objections refutes the objective-existence theory as applied to thoughts of universals.

7.   A LATTER-DAY OBJECTION

Even if Ockham had replaced (G) and (H) with (M), he would not thereby have guaranteed the objective-existence theory against paradox. For, as he himself contends in criticizing Scotus's formal distinction, an ontology will be seriously defective if it fails to provide criteria of identity and distinction for real things. In the same way, a theory that posits unreal entities must assure us that such criteria are available for them. In recent times, this challenge has been thrust upon lovers of rich ontologies by W. V. O. Quine in his essay "On What There Is." Quine expresses general suspicion of and scorn for the doctrine that whatever is thought of has some sort of being—if not real, then unreal.

> This is the old Platonic riddle of non-being. Non-being must in some sense be, otherwise what is it that there is not? This tangled doctrine might be nicknamed *Plato's beard*: historically it has proved tough, frequently dulling the edge of Occam's razor.
>
> It is some such line of thought that leads philosophers like McX to impute being where they might otherwise be content to recognize that there is nothing.[46]

Speaking of the subclass of unactualized possibles, Quine charges that the

> ...slum of possibles is a breeding ground for disorderly elements. Take, for instance, the possible fat man in the doorway; and again, the possible bald man in that doorway. Are they the same possible man, or two possible men? How do we decide? How many possible men are there in that doorway? Are there more thin ones than fat ones? How many of them are alike? Or would their being alike make them one? Are no two possible things alike? Is this the same as saying that it is impossible for two things to be alike? Or finally, is the concept of identity inapplicable to unactualized possibles? But what sense can be found in talking of entities which cannot meaningfully be said to be identical with themselves and distinct from one another. These elements are incorrigible. By a Fregean therapy of individual concepts, some effort might be made at rehabilitation; but I feel we'd do better simply to clear Whyman's slum and be done with it.[47]

So far as I know, Ockham does not explicitly consider such an objection against the objective-existence theory. But he would have felt its force, and—so far from being intimidated by Quine's string of rhetorical questions—would have set about

46. *From a Logical Point of View*, (Cambridge, MA, 1953), 1–2.
47. *Ibid.*, 4.

trying to answer them. In fact, in a number of places, Ockham implies that the Indiscernibility of Identicals is a criterion of distinction for beings of reason, just as much as it is for real beings. For he reasons that if a is F and b is not F, there are only three alternatives: a and b are distinct real things; or a and b are distinct beings of reason; or a and b are distinct as a real thing and a being of reason. By excluding the possibility that a and b are the same being of reason, he suggests that it is impossible for one and the same being of reason to have contradictory properties simultaneously, just as for the same real thing to do so. (See Part One, chapter 2 above.)

Now when Quine asks about the bald man and the fat man, it is quite clear that he has partially indeterminate objects in mind. And where indeterminate objects are concerned, Ockham can simply say that indeterminate object a is identical with indeterminate object b, if and only if a is determinate with respect to all and only the same properties as b is vice versa. By this criterion, when we think of a man, leaving all of his characteristics other than rational mortal animality indeterminate and determinable, the object we have before our minds is distinct from the one we have before it when we think of a man as bald, or think of a man as fat, leaving all of his other characteristics indeterminate and determinable. Similarly, the indeterminate object bald man will be a distinct object from the indeterminate object fat man, because the former is determinate with respect to being bald and indeterminate and determinable with respect to being fat, while the latter is determinate with respect to being fat but indeterminate and determinable with respect to being bald.

Where unactualized possible particulars are concerned, Ockham could say that the criteria of identity and distinction for them are the same as those for real particulars. Just as where a and b are distinct really existent particulars, a is distinct from b in and of itself and vice versa, so where a and b are distinct unactualized possible particulars, a will be distinct from b in and of itself and vice versa. And if the criterion of distinction in the case of real particulars is the Indiscernibility of Identicals, so he could say that the criterion of distinction for unactualized possible particulars is the Indiscernibility of Identicals.

Turning to Quine's question, "How many *possible* men *are* there in that doorway?" Ockham might reply by distinguishing two interpretations of the question. If he is asking how many men are actually standing in that doorway, then we have our answer simply by counting the number of actual men in that doorway. If, on the other hand, the question asks how many unactualized possible men can stand in that doorway, the answer is surely "each of the unactualized possible men—infinitely many of them." For each possible man is such that it is logically possible that he should be standing in that doorway. Further, each possible man is such that it is logically possible that he should be both fat and standing in that doorway, and logically possible that he should be thin and standing in that doorway. Hence there are not more fat ones than thin ones, but infinitely many of each. Again, when Quine wonders whether two possible men are alike, the reply will depend on what he means by 'alike'. If he means 'alike with respect to all properties, including those of identity and distinction', then Ockham would say with everyone else that no two are alike. For the Identity of Indiscernibles—the principle that for all x, y, and F, if x is F if and only if y is F, then x is identical with y—is trivially true, if all properties including identity and distinction enter into the comparison. But I know of no evidence that Ockham subscribed to any nontrivial version of the Identity of Indiscernibles. So if Quine means 'alike with respect to all properties that are taken into consideration in a nontrivial formulation of the Identity of Indiscernibles', Ockham would reply that numerically distinct possibles are alike and their being alike does not make them one. Although he does not address himself to the issue of how many possible men would be thus alike, it is difficult to see what reason he would have to specify one finite number rather than another. Perhaps it best accords with this theory to say that infinitely many are.

Nevertheless, Quine's worries cannot be laid to rest quite so easily. For if both indeterminate objects such as man and unactualized possible particulars can be thought of, so indeterminate objects such as round square, chimera, and goat stag can be thought of. Similarly, particulars such as Socrates can be thought of as having incompatible properties simultaneously. And according to the objective-existence theory, if such things are thought of as having such properties, then in the mode of objective existence they exist and have such properties. Hence, it is incumbent on the objective-existence theory to supply us with criteria of identity and distinction not only for nonexistent possibles, but for beings with incompatible properties as well. And if some beings of reason thus have incompatible properties, it will not be legitimate for Ockham to appeal, as he apparently did, to the Indiscernibility of Identicals as a criterion of distinction between them.

Perhaps Ockham could claim that indeterminate objects involving incompatible properties are individuated in the same way as those that do not. For instance, the indeterminate object round square is a distinct object from the indeterminate object round, because the former is determinate with respect to being square, while the latter is not. Similarly, the indeterminate object round triangle, because the former is determinate with respect to being square and not with respect to being triangular, while the latter is determinate with respect to being triangular but not with respect to being square.

But how will objectively existent particulars be individuated, when some of them have incompatible properties? Perhaps it will be said that if this particular table is distinct from that one, it will be so in and of itself. And this fact is unchanged by the former table's being simultaneously round and square. So the fact that some objectively existent particulars have incompatible properties will pose no further problem for the individuation of such particulars.

Ockham could not have been satisfied with this reply. And in any case it is inadequate. For while 'In objective existence, x is a round square' is not itself contradictory any more than 'It is impossible that something is a round square' is, nevertheless, the statement that falls within the scope of the operator is contradictory. Thus we shall be able to infer that everything obtains within the mode of objective existence: that the moon both is and is not made of green cheese, that Socrates is not identical with himself, etc.

A different approach would be to reexamine the assumption that 'x is a round square' is or entails a contradiction. First, consider an affirmative categorical proposition such as 'x is round' and distinguish its external negation, which is obtained by negating the entire statement—i.e., 'It is not the case that x is round'—from its internal negation, which is obtained by negating its predicate—i.e., 'x is non-round' or 'x is not-round'. The usual way of showing that 'x is a round square' entails a contradiction begins with the observation that it entails each of 'x is round' and 'x is square'. But 'x is square' entails 'x is non-round', which in turn entails 'It is not the case that x is round'. Thus, 'x is a round square' entails 'x is round and it is not the case that x is round'—which is a contradiction. This argument supposes that the internal negation 'x is non-round' entails the external negation 'It is not the case that x is round'. But it may be claimed that this is not necessarily so. For while it is true that what is non-round in reality cannot simultaneously be round in reality, what is non-round in the mode of objective existence may be round as well. Thus, 'In reality, x is non-round' entails 'In reality, it is not the case that x is round', but 'In objective existence, x is non-round' does not entail 'In objective existence, it is not the case that x is round'. Consequently, 'In objective existence, x is a round square' will not entail the contradictory statement 'In objective existence, x is round and it is not the case that x is round'. And if not, no violations of the Indiscernibility of Identicals will follow from the objective existence of a round square; nor will we be able to infer that everything is true in the mode of objective existence.

Whatever else may be said about this solution, it will be inadequate by itself because it fails to deal with all of the problematic cases. For just as someone might think of the same object as being simultaneously both round and square, so someone might think of the same object as having the schema '...is round' and 'It is not the case that...is round' simultaneously true of it. No appeals to a distinction between internal and external negation will remove this contradiction. And when we add that God eternally and immutably thinks of everything, such problematic examples multiply to infinity.

If Ockham had been firmly committed to the objective-existence theory, he might simply have retracted his claim that the Indiscernibility of Identicals applies to beings of reason as well as to real beings. And he could have denied that any of the above mentioned consequences of the objective-existence theory is genuinely problematic. After all, he could remind us that the mode of objective existence was invented to house the impossibles that are thought of but cannot exist in reality. If we allow the objective existence of one impossibility, why should we worry further if there are infinitely many of them? And why should we be surprised if everything is true about the mode of objective existence? Nevertheless, I think it is extremely unlikely that Ockham would, if confronted with such apparent difficulties, have had the courage of the objective-existence theorist's convictions. For, so far as we can tell from his writings, Ockham gave up the objective-existence theory in the face of a much weaker objection raised by Walter Chatton.

8.   THE OBJECTIVE-EXISTENCE THEORY
AND OCKHAM'S RAZOR

Ultimately, Ockham gave up the objective-existence theory—both where thoughts of particulars and thoughts of universals are concerned—because Walter Chatton convinced him that the objective-existence theory violated the principal of parsimony better known now as Ockham's Razor.[48]

Ockham's early expositions of the objective-existence theory make it clear that only what is thought of by someone can have objective existence. But these discussions do not seem to rule out the possibility that two people might have the same objectively existent entity before their minds. That is, nothing Ockham says earlier suggests that the objectively existent entity before my mind is numerically distinct from the one before

48. See Gedeon Gál, *op. cit.*, 191–212.

yours, just because the one is before *my* mind and the other is before *yours*. Instead, when someone objects that if Ockham's theory were true, "then there would be as many universals as intellects," he brushes the issue aside, replying "I do not care for the present whether or not a figment (*figmentum*) or concept is varied as the intellects are varied," so long as my concept and yours are "one through equivalence," i.e., equivalent in signifying.[49] Chatton argues, however, that the theory must make this assumption. For he maintains that if the objective existence of a thing does not logically presuppose the real existence of any act of this kind in particular, then it cannot presuppose the real existence of some act or other of this kind.[50] Chatton's inference is of the form 'This *A* does not logically presuppose this *B*, and so on for each *B*; therefore, this *A* does not logically presuppose the existence of some *B* or other'—which is not in general valid. Nevertheless, Ockham agrees with Chatton and offers the latter's argument as his own in *Quodlibeta* IV, q.35.[51] If objectively existent entity *a* logically presupposes the real existence of my act of intellect and objectively existent *b* logically presupposes the real existence of your act of intellect, then since my mental act can continue to exist when yours ceases and vice versa, it follows that *a* can continue to exist when *b* does not exist and vice versa. The conclusion is that there are two objectively existent entities, just as there are two acts of intellect.

It will be a violation of Ockham's Razor to posit such a coordinate realm of objectively existent entities in addition to really existent acts of intellect, however, only if the former serve no necessary theoretical function. So long as Ockham retains the premiss,

> 2. If we think of something, then it has some sort of existence—viz., either real existence or objective existence,

49. *Ord.* I, d.2, q.8, (OTh II, 284–85).
50. Gedeon Gál, *op. cit.*, 202, lines 2–12.
51. (OTh IX, 472–73).

objectively existent entities are needed, because we sometimes think of things as having properties that no real things can and/or do have. Further, once the theory is extended to cover thoughts of things that do exist, it is claimed that it is the fact that an act of intellect is directed to an objectively existent entity and to this one rather than that one, which accounts for the fact that it is a thought of something and of this rather than that.

Chatton argues that objectively existent entities are superfluous because they cannot possibly fill the latter theoretical role, while the real things posited by the theory can do so, unassisted by such objectively existent entities. To begin with, he contends that "there is no apparent contradiction in an act of intellect's remaining in existence without any such fictum."[52] Chatton presents the latter, not so much as a consequence of Ockham's theory but as something everyone would agree to. He reasons that if the real existence of an act of intellect is logically independent of every other really existent thing, then a fortiori it must be logically independent of the objective existence of anything. His second premiss is that "it is a contradiction to suppose that there is an act of intellect unless something—namely, its term—is understood."[53] Necessarily, every act of thought has an object. If it is not necessary that an act of thought is directed towards some objectively existent entity (as it cannot be if it is not necessary that some entity have objective existence whenever an act of thought exists), then that the thought is directed towards the objectively existent entity and towards one rather than another, cannot be what accounts for its being a thought of something and of this rather than that. Some alternative explanation must be found.

A devotee of the objective-existence theory would no doubt accept Chatton's second premiss and use the objective-existence theory's analysis of thought to argue that his first premiss is false. By the time Ockham wrote the *Quodlibeta*, however, he had come to endorse Chatton's argument as his own.

52. Gedeon Gál, *op. cit.*, 202, lines 21–22.
53. *Ibid.*, lines 22–24.

Chatton thinks that an adequate analysis of what happens when we think of something can be given in terms of the really existent things admitted by the theory. If we think of a round square or a chimera, it is not necessary that there be (in some sense) anything that is a round square or a chimera. It is enough if a really existing thing has a different property—viz., the property of being of-a-round-square or the property of being of-a-chimera. Thus, Chatton writes,

> ...The mind can imagine (*fingere*) many things, such as a golden mountain, a chimera, etc. But this is nothing other than for it to have an act of understanding by virtue of which I could judge that its nature would be of this sort if it existed, as was said above.[54]

Such properties are no doubt to be identified with those real features of mental acts that Meinong labelled "contents" and that Ockham acknowledges even on the objective-existence theory. And Chatton wants to say that it is just such features that make thoughts to be one thing rather than another. Ockham accepts Chatton's conclusion and—abandoning the distinction between objective and real existence—identifies concepts with really existent acts of intellect.

9. SUPERFICIAL OBJECTIONS TO THE MENTAL-ACT THEORY

We will be in a better position to assess the adequacy of the mental-act theory as compared with the objective-existence theory—and hence to say whether the latter really does with more what the former does as well with fewer—after we have examined their respective accounts of natural signification in the next chapter. For now, let us simply note how Ockham explains away some of the more obvious odd consequences of the mental-act theory.

On his new theory, Ockham will be identifying each universal with a really existent mental act. But in creatures at least, a

---

54. *Ibid.*, 207, lines 25–29.

mental act is a quality and hence an accident inhering in a mental substance.[55] Further, Ockham has insisted that only particulars really exist. Hence, each mental act is particular. It follows that all universals—genera, species, differentia, propria, and accidents—are particular qualities, and therefore that the most generic genus of substance is a particular quality and hence an accident and that the most generic genus quantity is a particular quality, etc. Similarly, being in general will be a particular quality.[56]

These conclusions would seem absurd to philosophers who thought that universals were things other than names. For on their view, genera and species would be universal and be sorted into one of Aristotle's ten categories rather than the other, on the basis of what sort of things they are. If all genera and species are particular qualities, it would seem that they are not universal after all, but particular, and that they are all sorted into the same category—the category of quality.

Ockham, by contrast, is insisting that universals are nothing other than names. And if we identify the primary names (concepts), as well as conventional names, with real things, it will turn out that all universals are particulars. Further, they will all be qualities. But Ockham finds nothing absurd in this, because he thinks that what makes names universal and what sorts them into one category rather than another is not what they *are*, but what and how they *signify*.[57] Thus, 'man' is universal, not because it is not a particular thing, but because it signifies numerically distinct particulars equally in such a way that it signifies one no more than another. And what makes it fall into the category of substance is not that it is itself a substance, but that it signifies only substances. Similarly, the most generic genus substance is, like the most generic genus quality, a particular quality. Nevertheless, the concept

55. *Summa logicae* I, c.17, (OPh I, 58, 60); *Quodl.* V, q.13, (OTh IX, 521).

56. Such objections are raised against all theories that say that the universal is something real in *Ordinatio* I, d.2, q.8, (OTh II, 266).

57. *Ibid.*, (OTh II, 290–91); *Quodl.* V, q.13, (OTh IX, 532–34); *Summa logicae* I, c.13, (OPh I, 45–46).

'substance', with which the genus substance is identified, does not fall into the category of quality, because it does not signify qualities but signifies only substances. As we shall see in succeeding chapters, this shift of attention from what universals are to what and how they signify, is of crucial importance in Ockham's attempts to show that all that really exists are particular substances and particular qualities.

4

Universals, Conventionalism, and Similarity

Whenever the nominalist-conceptualist thesis—that only names or concepts are universal, while every mind-independent thing is particular—is advanced, some see in it the seeds of metaphysical disaster. Boethius had charged that if it were true, our ideas of genera and species would be "vain and false." His argument had rested on the assumption that an idea stands for something only if the latter is exactly as the former represents it to be, from which it follows that ideas of genera and species can signify only universals. If there were no universal things, as Ockham claims, then such ideas and the corresponding conventional names would be empty—which they plainly are not. Nominalists-conceptualists easily disposed of Boethius's objection, however, charging that it rested on an overly narrow conception of representation, rejected by many realists as well.

More subtle is the contention that if there are no universal things corresponding to general terms, then which concepts count as genus- and species-concepts, and which particulars count as co-generic and co-specific will be arbitrary and subjective. The argument runs as follows:

1. No distinct universal things correspond to abstract general concepts C_i-C_n.

2. Therefore, which concepts count as generic and specific depends in part on human convention. (1)

3. Convention or use depends on contingent human free choices.

109

4.   What depends on contingent human free choices is ar-
     bitrary and subjective.

5.   Therefore, which concepts count as generic and specific
     is arbitrary and subjective. (2, 3, and 4)

6.   Therefore, the fact that certain particulars are co-
     generic and co-specific is arbitrary and subjective. (5)

Ockham rejects each of the conclusions in 2, 5, and 6. Citing the
possible position that

> nothing is universal of its very nature, because nothing of its very
> nature supposits for or is truly predicated of another thing—e.g., a
> spoken word is not—but only by voluntary conventions...[1]

his review is cryptic and negative. He says that if it were true,
"then nothing would be a species or genus of its very nature"[2]
—a conclusion that Ockham is unable to swallow.

Ockham's view is that neither the extension of general concepts such as 'animal' or 'man' nor the co-specificity of particulars is arbitrary and subjective, because both can be accounted for in terms of similarity. Opponents who regard the
above argument as decisive beg the question against the
nominalist-conceptualist by denying him access to widely
agreed upon theorems about similarity. In what follows, I shall
look briefly at what Ockham has to say about similarity and use
it to explain his account of co-specificity. Then I shall examine
his doctrine of the natural signification of such concepts both
from the viewpoint of the objective-existence and that of the
mental-act theory. My provisional conclusion will be that
Ockham's theory is inadequate, but for reasons that tell as much
against his moderate realist opponents as against him. His success in rejecting step 2 of their objection ultimately depends on
whether or not he can consistently maintain that similarity relations are not arbitrary and subjective. In my opinion and

---

1. *Ord.* I, d.2, q.8, (OTh II, 271).
2. *Ibid.*

Ockham's his views about universals by themselves pose no insurmountable obstacles. But a final verdict on this issue will
have to wait until chapter 9 below.

1.   OCKHAM ON THE NATURE OF SIMILARITY

Ockham insists that to deny that universals or common
natures are anything other than names or concepts is not to be
saddled with the conclusion that similarity relations are arbitrary and subjective. (1.1) *Similarity and Common Nature.*
Moderate realists and nominalists-conceptualists divide over
Boethius's assumption that similarity is always founded on
some kind of unity. The former hold with Boethius that the
similarity of x and y is to be metaphysically analysed in terms of
their having a metaphysical constituent in common. Ockham
accuses Burleigh's version of implying that Socrates and Plato
are similar in being human because numerically the same human
nature exists in both, while Scotus says that human nature existing in Socrates and Plato has a real unity less than numerical
unity (see chapter 2 above). Having argued that moderate
realism inevitably leads to contradiction and other absurdities,
Ockham, like any nominalist-conceptualist, is compelled to reject this analysis. Replying to Scotus's argument that since
Socrates and Plato really agree more than Socrates and a donkey
do, "Socrates and Plato agree in something real in which
Socrates and a donkey do not really agree," Ockham replies that
they do not literally speaking agree *in* any thing or things but
rather agree in and of themselves (*seipsis*).[3] Thus, similarity is a
two term relation between two things and not a three term relation between two things and a common nature. Of course,
Ockham would be willing to accomodate ordinary-language as
well as some philosophical tendencies to speak of similarity as
similarity *in* something. For example, we may say that a blue
square patch resembles a blue circular patch in color but not in
shape, or that Socrates and Brownie the donkey resemble each

---

3. *Ibid.*, q.6, (OTh II, 211–12).

other in being animals but not in being rational, while Socrates and Plato resemble each other in being man. But, like all nominalists-conceptualists, Ockham would understand the phrase 'in shape' or 'in being animals' to be referentially opaque, adverbial modifiers of 'resemble' or 'similar'. Just as 'shape' is a genus term relative to 'square' and 'circular', so 'similar' is to 'shape-wise similar' and 'animal-wise similar'. So construed, these statements involve no reference to a metaphysical constituent common to the relata.

Nevertheless, Ockham does not see how it is supposed to follow from the mere fact that a relation is primitive and two termed that it is arbitrary and subjective. (1.2) *Not Arbitrary*. According to Ockham, similarity is what Duns Scotus labelled an "intrinsic relation": i.e., one such that the existence of its relata is logically sufficient for the relation to obtain. Thus, Ockham writes, "God cannot produce two white things without producing two similar things, because the similarity is the two white things themselves."[4] Since God is omnipotent, He could make two white things without their being similar if this were logically possible. Identity and distinction are likewise relations of this type.[5] For anything x is identical with itself, and it is logically impossible for x to exist and not be identical with itself. Again, if x and y are numerically distinct, it is logically impossible that x and y should exist and not be numerically distinct (where substitutions for 'x' and 'y' are proper names or rigid designators). Thus, given the relata, such intrinsic relations obtain, not only independently of the human will, but of the divine will as well; they are thus not arbitrary in any straightforward way.

(1.3) *Not Subjective*. Ockham insists that similarity is a real relation. According to him (see chapter 7 below), to say that a relation R is a real relation is not to imply that R-ness is a thing (*res*) really distinct from and inhering in its relata. Rather he maintains that

---

4. *Rep.* II, q.1, (OTh V, 9); cf. q.2, (OTh V, 35).
5. *Ibid.*, (OTh V, 39).

(T1) *R* is a real relation if and only if given the existence of *x* and *y*, *x* and *y* can be *R*-wise related apart from any activity of the intellect comparing and contrasting them,[6]

and thus regards such intellectual activity as neither necessary nor sufficient for a real relation to hold between two things. By contrast, Ockham will say that

(T2) *R* is a relation of reason if and only if given the existence of *x* and *y*, *x* and *y* are *R*-wise related if and only if some activity of the intellect thus relates them[7]

so that such intellectual activity is both necessary and sufficient for a relation of reason to obtain.

Ockham finds the notion that similarity is a relation of reason absurd. He writes,

> ...Similarity is called a real relation because of the fact that one white thing, *by the nature of the thing*, is similar to another white thing, and the intellect no more brings this about than it brings it about that Socrates is white and Plato is white.[8]

On the other hand, if the intellect's activity of comparing them and finding them similar were sufficient for a relation of similarity to hold, then the intellect could never be mistaken about the similarity of things—which is absurd.[9]

Nor does Ockham take back this claim when from time to time he allows that Socrates and Plato agree in the concept 'man'. For he does not intend thereby to replace the moderate realists' *analysis* of '*x* is similar to *y*' by '*x* and *y* have the same metaphysical constituent in common' with '*x* and *y* are apt to be signified by some common concept *C*'. Given his account of natural signification in terms of similarity (see section 3 below),

---

6. *Ord.* I, d.30, q.5, (OTh IV, 385).
7. *Ibid.*
8. *Ibid.*
9. This sort of argument is offered for the claim that creation is not a relation of reason in *ibid.*, (OTh IV, 382–84).

an analysis of similarity in terms of natural signification would be circular. Ockham would deny that the similarity of Socrates to Plato any more *consists in* their similarity to a concept than the similarity of Socrates to the common concept 'man' is shorthand for 'man' is a certain common [concept] that can be predicated of Socrates and Plato."[10] That is, if x and y are similar, x and y can be signified by a common concept C, should C exist. And where concepts such as 'man' are concerned, the fact that Socrates and Plato can be signified by it depends on features they have quite apart from any activity of the intellect. Thus, so far as the logic of 'similarity' is concerned, Ockham adheres to his contention that similarity is a two term real relation and hence not subjective in a straightforward sense.

(1.4) *Similarity Comes in Degrees.* It might be objected that similarity cannot explain the extension of genus- or species-concepts or be what makes certain particulars co-generic or co-specific, because everything is trivially similar to everything else. Take any two things x and y. Suppose x has the property F and y has the property G. Then even if y is not F and x is not G, x and y will have some property in common—viz., the disjunctive property of being either-F-or-G. Since x and y are any individuals you like, and F and G any properties you like, it follows that everything is somehow similar to everything else. Yet, it is not the case that everything is co-generic or co-specific with everything else, nor do genus- and species-concepts signify anything and everything.

So far as I know, Ockham never explicitly considers the above argument that everything is trivially similar to everything else. But it is clear that when he and his contemporaries spoke of genus- and species-concepts signifying by resemblance and co-specific and co-generic particulars resembling one another, they did not have in mind similarity with respect to such disjunctive properties alone. And since the negative property of not-being-both-not-F-and-not-G is equivalent to the disjunctive property of being-either-F-or-G, they must not have been thinking of mere similarity with respect to such negative prop-

10. *Ibid.*, d.2, q.6, (OTh II, 212); cf. d.30, q.1, (OTh IV, 314).

erties either.

Ockham's view is that similarity comes in degrees ranging from trivial to maximal and including species-wise and genus-wise similarity. His hope is to account for the extension of genus- and species-concepts and for the fact that certain particulars are co-generic or co-specific in terms of nontrivial similarity relations.

2. SIMILARITY AND CO-GENERIC AND CO-SPECIFIC PARTICULARS

Drawing on the above theses about the nature of similarity, Ockham can reason as follows:

7.   Similarity is a real relation that, given the existence of the relata, holds independently of any will—human or divine—and hence of any conventions.

8.   Similarity comes in degrees ranging from trivial to maximal and including generic and specific similarity.

9.   What makes it the case that certain particulars are co-generic or co-specific is that they are similar genus-wise or species-wise.

10.   Therefore, that certain particulars are co-generic or co-specific is independent both of any intellectual activity comparing them and of any will—human or divine—and hence of any conventions. (7, 8, and 9)

11.   Therefore, that certain particulars are co-generic or co-specific is neither arbitrary nor subjective. (10)

11 is a denial of step 6 of the above objection.

Moderate realists would not quarrel with Ockham's premisses, although they defend them differently. 7 is true, they say, because, given the existence of the relata x and y, x and y are similar by virtue of having a common metaphysical constituent that exists in them in reality, prior to and independently of the intellect's comparing them as well as any human conventions. Again, they would grant 9, while pointing to the metaphysically more fundamental fact that particulars are similar species-wise because the same specific nature exists in them as a metaphysical constituent of both. As for 8, Scotus himself says that Socrates is more similar to Plato than he is to Brownie the donkey, thereby implying that he is in some degree similar to Brownie the donkey. It is in denying him premisses 7 and 8 that Ockham would say the moderate realists have begged the question against him, and he has insisted that these premisses stand apart from the moderate realists' explanations of them.

Nevertheless, Ockham's opponents might charge that his interpretation of the premisses will not yield the conclusion. For 7–9 imply that similarity relations among particulars are not arbitrary and subjective: e.g., the fact that the blue square patch is similar to the blue circular patch color-wise but not shape-wise, or that Socrates resembles Brownie animal-wise but not rational-wise. But if according to 8 similarity comes in degrees, and there are no common specific natures in things to pick out one degree as species-wise similarity as opposed to others, it will be arbitrary and subjective which degree of similarity counts as species-wise similarity.

To this Ockham would have a twofold response: (a) First, it tells as much against his opponents as against him. For if moderate realists accept 8 and hold that any and every degree of similarity is founded on common metaphysical constituents, they will face the analogous difficulty of saying which common constituent or combination thereof is the specific and which the generic nature. Only those moderate realists[11] who declare species to be the only common metaphysical constituents are able to solve this problem more easily than Ockham, and they have already joined him in rejecting Boethius's intuitions about

11. Those mentioned by Ockham in *ibid.*, d.2, q.7, (OTh II, 226); cf. footnote 9 above.

similarity.

(b) Second, he would identify species-wise similarity with the same degree of sort of similarity as his moderate realist opponents do: viz., perfect similarity without any dissimilarity with respect to all essentials.[12] Thus,

(T3) x and y are similar species-wise, if and only if x and y are similar, and not dissimilar, with respect to all essentials.

To identify species-wise similarity with any other degree would not be arbitrary and subjective but mistaken, while grouping Socrates and Plato in the same species because Socrates' human nature is altogether similar to Plato's is the obvious and reasonable move to make.

Ockham intends this sorting proposal to apply both to substance-things and accident-things (see chapter 5 below), but recognizes complication where accidents that come in degrees are concerned. For he maintains (see Part Four, chapter 17 below) that qualities such as heat and whiteness come in different intensities, and yet the more and less intense degrees of heat or whiteness are members of the same most specific species. Yet, is there not a sense in which whiteness in the fourth degree is more similar to other whitenesses of the fourth degree than to whitenesses of the third degree? And in that case, fourth degree whiteness is not maximally similar to third degree whiteness.

Ockham observes that "if fourth degree whiteness and third degree whiteness were not altogether similar, nevertheless, nothing is to be found in one whiteness that is dissimilar to anything in another whiteness."[13] On Ockham's theory, a quality is made more intense by adding on more parts of it to those that were already there. Thus, he imagines that fourth degree whiteness might be divided into essential parts—say whiteness in the third degree and whiteness in the first degree—none of which would be in any way dissimilar to whiteness in the third

12. *Rep.* III, q.10, (OTh VI, 335–36).
13. *Ibid*, (OTh VI, 336).

degree or to some essential part thereof, just as each essential part of Socrates is altogether similar to some essential part of Plato. By contrast, Socrates does have an essential part, viz., his intellectual soul, to which no essential part of Brownie the donkey is altogether similar.

What about generic similarity? Remarking on the similarity of animals of different species, Ockham says vaguely that "they are neither altogether similar nor altogether dissimilar" and observes that "although their specific forms are not of the same kind, their matter is of the same kind, so that they agree in some essential part and differ in another."[14] This suggests

(T4) x and y are co-generic if and only if some essential part of x is maximally similar to some essential part of y and some essential part of x is somehow dissimilar to some essential part of y.

But (T4) covers composites only and does not apply to the sorting of angels that are not maximally similar to each other into the genus of spiritual substance or of men and angels into the genus substance. Nor will it do any good to replace (T4) with

(T5) x and y are co-generic if and only if (i) if one of x and y is composite, then some essential part of x is altogether similar to y, and some essential part of x is not altogether similar to y or some essential part of y; or (ii) if x and y are both simple, x and y are similar but not maximally similar

for two reasons: (i) will not sort men and angels into a common genus because the intellectual soul of man is not maximally similar to any angel; whereas (ii) will sort God into a genus with any simple creature and God is not supposed to fall under any genus. The latter difficulty plagues the following proposal

14. *Ibid.*

(T6) x and y are co-generic if and only if x and y are similar
but not altogether similar

as well.

Although Ockham goes along with the theological consensus that God is not in any genus, (T6) really expresses the spirit of Ockham's view. Putting God in a genus causes trouble, only when combined with the moderate realist assumption that co-generic things have a common metaphysical constituent (see Part Five, chapter 21 below). When (T6) is combined with the recognition 8 that similarity comes in degrees, it seems to allow for many—even infinitely many—genera between the traditional most specific species man and donkey and their traditional proximate genus animal. Once again, this consequence need not disturb Ockham unduly for two reasons: (c) First, his theory shares his difficulty with the moderate realists'. Those who think there is a common metaphysical constituent grounding every degree of similarity, will have to hold that there are as many common constituents as there are degrees of similarity, and will have to say whether all or only some of them are genera. Those who hold that only the most specific species is a common constituent will have to admit varying degrees of similarity among things of different species nonetheless, and will still face the task of saying whether some or all of them represent genera.

(d) Second, Ockham might well find nothing sacred in Aristotle's identification of animal as the proximate genus of man and donkey. If there are infinitely many degrees of similarity, there may be no such thing as proximate genus. If each degree of similarity less than perfect similarity counts as generic similarity, then the fact that things are generically similar is still neither arbitrary nor subjective.

Why, then, did Aristotle identify animal as the proximate genus of man and donkey? Even granting that there are infinitely many genera, and the fact that particulars fall under them is neither arbitrary or subjective, the fact that we focus on some genera rather than others may well be dictated by pragmatic considerations. Ockham seems to hold (see Parts Two and

Three below) that our minds, by their very natures, can form some concepts and not others. For example, he thinks we can form simple concepts of man and animal but only composite concepts of caucasian man and negroid man; perhaps he also believes we can form only composite concepts of mammal and reptile as well. This psychological fact could well be part of the reason we and Aristotle focus on the genus animal rather than that of mammal. By themselves, these psychological considerations are not arbitrary, because, according to Ockham, which concepts we form depends on the natures of the particulars and the nature of the human mind and not on any contingent free choice—created or divine. And it would be misleading to say they are subjective, since such limitations on concept formation are common to all members of the species. Nevertheless, Ockham would doubtless allow that our interests, which may be arbitrary and subjective, are among the other factors that influence our choices.

Whatever may be said in favor of (T6) from Ockham's viewpoint, *Reportatio* III, q.9 finds him making a different suggestion. Instead of appealing to his belief that simple things may be somehow similar and somehow different, he suggests that things might be sorted into the same genus, not because of any maximal similarity among their intrinsic essential parts, but because of similarity with respect to something extrinsic. Thus, he suggests that men and angels belong to the common genus substance, not because "they agree in anything intrinsic," "but because they agree in something extrinsic, since they have accidents of the same kind—e.g., acts of understanding and will."[15] Similarly, whiteness, and blackness fall under the genus color, not because they agree in anything intrinsic, but because any subject that can have the one inhering in it can have the other inhering in it.[16] Thus, he seems to be proposing

(T7) x and y are co-generic if either (i) x is (can be) the subject of the same sort of accidents as y is (can be), or (ii) x

15. *Ibid.*, q.10, (OTh, VI, 336–37).
16. *Ibid.*, (OTh VI, 337).

does (can) inhere in something of the same sort as y does (can).

(T7) is extremely broad, sorting not only whiteness and blackness but heat and whiteness into a common genus. This will not trouble Ockham, who insists that all really inherent accidents fall under the common genus quality and all subjects of inherence under the common genus substance (see chapters 5–8 below). But his opponents who maintain that there is a distinct kind of thing for each of the nine categories of accident would have to reject (T7). For (T7ii) would make all accidental forms co-generic, but things in different categories cannot fall under a common genus, because the categories are the highest genera.

3.   OCKHAM'S DOCTRINE OF NATURAL SIGNIFICATION

Whereas the objector in steps 1–6 used

2.   Which concepts count as generic and which specific depends in part on human convention

to establish

6.   The fact that certain particulars are co-generic or co-specific is arbitrary and subjective,

Ockham can use his denial of 6 to arrive at the negation of 2 as follows:

11.   That certain particulars are co-generic or co-specific is neither arbitrary nor subjective (i.e., not 6).

12.   A concept is a genus-concept or a species-concept if and only if each member of its extension is co-generic or co-specific with each other member of its extension.

13.   Concepts are natural signs that signify by virtue of real relations that obtain or not independently of any

will—human or divine.

14.   Therefore, which concepts count as generic or specific is neither arbitrary nor subjective. (11, 12, and 13)

Step 2 is consistent with 11; for if concepts got their extension in part by convention, then, given 12, whether or not a concept was a genus- or species-concept would depend in part on convention. But Ockham joins the virtual consensus among medieval philosophers in maintaining 13, that concepts are natural signs. The success of his rebuttal of 2 thus depends upon whether Ockham is any the less entitled to this assumption than his opponents are. To answer this question, it is necessary to examine Ockham's doctrine of natural signification.

(3.1) *Signs and Natural Relations.* One thing is the sign of another if there is a relation between them that renders the first apt to make the second known. If the relation is a natural relation, the sign is a natural sign.

What sort of relation counts as a natural relation? The most obvious example is causality. Ockham thinks that one kind of natural sign is a sign in the sense of being something

...the apprehension of which causes something else to be cognized, although it does not cause the mind's first cognition of it, but causes an actual cognition in the mind after a habitual cognition...[17]

A is a natural sign of some other thing *B* in this sense if (i) the apprehension of *A* causes the apprehension of *B* and (ii) this causal relation is based on habitual association. The mind may make this habitual association because it becomes aware of a causal relation between *A*'s and *B*'s themselves (as it does in the case of smoke and fire), or because it has mastered a convention (as in the case of written and spoken words and what they signify). Thus, Ockham remarks that in this sense of 'sign'

...a spoken sound signifies naturally, just as any effect signifies at least its own cause, and just as a circle signifies wine in the tavern...[18]

17. *Summa logicae* I, c.1, (OPh I, 8–9).
18. *Ibid.*, (OPh I, 9).

Because this causal relation between the apprehension of this sort of sign (A) and the apprehension of what it signifies (B) is necessarily based on habitual association, it is obvious that the apprehension of an A cannot cause one to apprehend B for the first time. For example, one could not acquire a concept of man for the first time simply by hearing a token of the noise pattern 'man'. Rather, one conventionally associates the noise pattern 'man' with the concept 'man', so that when someone who has made this association hears the noise, the concept comes to mind.

According to Ockham, concepts are not natural signs in this first sense. For example, a concept of Socrates does not bring Socrates into cognition, because the thinker habitually associates the concept of Socrates with Socrates in such a way that an apprehension of the concept of Socrates *causes* an apprehension of Socrates. Rather, on the objective-existence theory, the concept of Socrates is the objectively existent Socrates himself. And on the mental-act theory, the concept of Socrates *is* the apprehension of Socrates, the apprehension of which causes an apprehension of Socrates.

On Ockham's view, concepts are natural signs in the sense of being what "causes something to be cognized" for the first time.[19] And the natural relation that renders concepts signs in this sense is not one that can be made to obtain or not "at the pleasure of human beings," the way the causal relation between the apprehension of spoken and written signs and the apprehension of other things results from human conventions. The natural relation in question must be other than a causal relation that is within the power of human beings to establish or do away with.

As noted above, the so-called "intrinsic" relations of similarity, identity, and distinction meet this last requirement. And moderate realists and nominalists-conceptualists alike agree that concepts such as 'animal' and 'man' are related to their extensions by similarity relations. Thus, speaking of those general concepts that are determinate enough to be images, Ockham

19. *Ibid.*

concludes that such a concept can be the term of a proposition and can stand in a proposition for "all those things of which it is an image or likeness." And he comments that this is what it is for it "to be universal and common to them."[20] Even where concepts are too abstract to be images, however, they naturally signify what they resemble, since "every concept abstracted from a thing is equally related to everything that is maximally similar (*simillimum*) to it..."[21] Where concepts of particulars are concerned, he specifies the relation of identity or a combination of similarity and certain causal relations.

Since according to 8 similarity comes in degrees ranging from trivial to maximal, however, it is necessary to ask which degree of similarity constitutes the natural signification relation for abstract general concepts. At this point, the moderate realists may feel they have a decisive advantage in being able to appeal to their metaphysical analysis of similarity. For they maintain that just as the similarity of Socrates and Brownie or Socrates and Plato is to be analysed in terms of animal nature and human nature existing in as a metaphysical constituent of each, so they say the concept 'animal' or 'man' is animal nature or human nature existing in the intellect, so that the same animal nature or human nature that exists in the intellect as an abstract general concept exists in as a metaphysical constituent of each member of its extension. Thus, the natural signification relation for abstract general concepts such as 'animal' and 'man' is the intrinsic relation 'being a metaphysical constituent of' or, speaking loosely, "partial identity." Their charge against Ockham and other nominalists-conceptualists will be that without a metaphysical analysis of similarity in terms of unity, it will be impossible to specify any similarity relation as the natural signification relation.

In the next few sections I shall examine whether Ockham is able to meet this challenge, and conclude with some remarks on its relevance to the debate about universals.

(3.2) *Comparative Similarity and Natural Signification.*

20. *Ord.* I, d.2, q.8, (OTh II, 279); cf. (OTh II, 274).
21. *Ibid.*, q.9, (OTh II, 308).

Loosely speaking, Ockham's proposal is that general concepts such as 'animal' and 'man' naturally signify the things they resemble most; more precisely and schematically, a general concept C signifies a thing x, if and only if there is nothing else y which C resembles more than C resembles x. This is apparently what Ockham has in mind when he elaborates the objective-existence theory in *Ordinatio* I, d.2, q.8, saying that

> ...that *fictum*...can be called universal because it is indifferently related to all of the mind-independent particulars. And because of this likeness in objective existence, it can supposit for things that have a similar existence outside the understanding...[22]

And it is even more explicit in the following account of the mental-act theory:

> ...to have a confused act of understanding man is only to have a cognition by which one man is not more understood than another and nevertheless by such a cognition a man is cognized or understood more than a donkey is. And this is only to say that such a cognition is, by some sort of similarity, more similar to a man than to a donkey and not more similar to that man than to this one...[23]

This relation of comparative similarity—that of being that than which there is nothing more similar to the concept—is not one that holds trivially between a concept and anything else. Ockham maintains, for example, that while Socrates and Plato are so related to the concept 'man', Brownie the donkey is not. And like other similarity relations, it is an intrinsic, real relation. Can it really do the work of relating concepts to their significata, as Ockham claims?

(3.2.1.) *Comparative Similarity and the Objective-Existence Theory.* Whether or not comparative similarity will serve as an adequate criterion of the natural signification of general concepts on the objective-existence theory depends in part on what

22. (OTh II, 272); cf. *Expos. Periherm.* I, Prooemium, sec.7, (OPh II, 359–360).

23. *Ibid.*, sec.6, (OPh II, 355); cf. *Ord.* I, d.2, q.8, (OTh II, 270).

things are thought to enter into the comparison. In the above quoted passages where Ockham suggests this criterion, he speaks of concepts signifying mind-independent particulars. So we might start with the suggestion that only really existent things enter into comparison. The resultant criterion would be formulated as follows:

(T8) Letting 'C' range over concepts and 'x' and 'y' over real existents, for all x, C signifies x, if and only if there does not exist a y such that C resembles y more than C resembles x.

(T8) poses many difficulties. Decisive at this point is the fact that on the objective-existence theory, not all concepts signify real existents. For example, the concepts 'genus' and 'species'—and for that matter 'concept' and 'naturally significant name'—signify only concepts which the objective-existence theory identifies with things insofar as they have objective existence, not insofar as they have real existence.

It might seem that this difficulty with (T8) would be easily avoided simply by widening the universe of discourse as follows:

(T9) Letting 'C' range over concepts and 'x' and 'y' over both really existent and objectively existent things, for all x, C signifies x if and only if there does not exist a y such that C resembles y more than C resembles x.

(T9) might give us the result that some concepts signify only objectively existent things, since Ockham could say that concepts such as 'genus' and 'species' are more similar to objectively existent concepts such as 'animal' and 'man', respectively, than they are to really existent things.

Nevertheless, Ockham himself raises an objection that shows (T9) to be inadequate. Discussing the objective-existence theory in the *Expositio in librum Perihermenias Aristotelis*, he writes,

...such a *fictum* is more different from any real things than any real thing is from another, because a real being and a being of reason differ more than any two real things. Therefore, such a fictional being is less similar to a real thing. Therefore, how much less will it be able to supposit for a real thing than an act of intellect that is more similar to it. Consequently, a fictum will be less common to a mind-independent thing than an act of intellect and consequently will have the aspect of a universal less than an act of intellect...[24]

Ockham is suggesting that the gulf between the ontological statuses—that of being objectively existent and that of being really existent—is so great, that a being of reason is more similar to any other real being than to any being of reason. It would follow by (T9) that no concept signifies really existent things, since all concepts are objectively existent.

Ockham offers the following reply on behalf of the objective-existence theory:

> ...it can be said that such a *fictum* or idol is more distinct from a mind-independent real thing than any real thing is from another. Nevertheless, in intension existence, it is more similar to it, to the extent that if it could be produced in reality the way it can be imagined, it would genuinely be really similar to the mind-independent real thing. And this is why it is better able to supposit for a real thing and be common to it and be that in which a real thing is understood than an act of understanding or any other quality can...[25]

The move here is, in effect, to neutralize the similarities and differences between concepts and things that result from the mere fact that concepts are objectively existent, by excluding such similarities and differences from consideration in the calculation of comparative similarity. Thus (T9) would be replaced by

(T10) Letting 'C' range over concepts and 'x' and 'y' over both really existent and objectively existent things, for all x, C signifies x if and only if there does not exist a y such that C resembles y more than C resembles x, leaving aside any similarities between x and C and y and C that result from the fact that C is objectively existent.

24. I, Prooemium, sec.7, (OPh II, 360–61).
25. *Ibid.*, sec.10, (OPh II, 370–71).

Ockham would then allege that, leaving aside the fact of their objective (as opposed to real) existence, the concepts 'genus' and 'species' still resemble the concepts 'animal' and 'man', respectively, more than they resemble any really existent things; but the concept 'man' resembles particular men more than it resembles other concepts.

Unfortunately, not even this modification will suffice. For, leaving aside the fact that the concept 'man' has only objective existence, the concept 'man' will still resemble partially indeterminate, objectively existent things such as the concept 'australoid man' or 'negroid man' more than it resembles fully determinate particular men. Yet, the concept 'man' signifies the latter and not the former.

It might be thought that if Ockham could only find some other criterion for distinguishing concepts that signify only things that can really exist from those that signify only things that cannot really exist, his problems would be solved. For he could employ (T8) for determining what the first group signifies and (T9) for determining what the second group signifies.

Numerous obstacles stand in the way of this solution, however. One is that (T8) would force concepts that signify only things that can really exist, to signify some or other of the things that do really exist in fact. Consider a possible world whose only animals are human beings and donkeys and in which some human being has the general concept 'cow'. Applying (T8) in that world, we would have to conclude that the general concept 'cow' and at least one other thing will contain at least one cow. And on the objective-existence theory, according to which a concept can have objective existence only if there is a really existent act of thought, the latter condition will always be satisfied. (I assume that a thing is not similar to itself, but only to something else. But if a thing is similar to itself, the absurdity follows more easily.)

Notice, however, that (T10), with its universe of discourse including both real and objective existents, would not have this consequence. For even in a world with no real cows, all possible particular cows would have objective existence in God's mind. And the general concept 'cow' would be more similar to such objectively existent particular cows than to any particular donkeys. This brings us to a second difficulty with (T8): it implies that the signification of general concepts such as 'man', 'donkey', and 'cow' is exhausted by things that do in fact really exist. Ockham wants to say, however, that the concept 'man' signifies not only particular men that do actually exist, but—on one interpretation (see Part Two, chapter 11 below)—all of the unactualized possible men as well. (T10) makes such unactualized possible men available to be signified.

These observations suggest an alternative response to the difficulties with (T10). Divide concepts into those which signify only fully determinate particulars that can really exist and those that signify other things (whether instead of or in addition to fully determinate particulars). Use (T10) as it stands for the second group, and for the first use the following analogue:

(T11) Letting 'C' range over concepts and 'x' and 'y' over both objectively existent particulars, for all x, C signifies x if and only if there does not exist a y such that C resembles y more than C resembles x, leaving aside any similarities between x and C and y and C that result from the fact that C is objectively existent.

(T11) would allow general concepts such as 'man', 'donkey', and 'cow' to signify merely possible as well as actual particulars and even merely possible instead of any actual particulars. Once again, the obstacle to this solution is in finding some natural properties by means of which to discriminate concepts of one group from those of the other. We have seen that comparative similarity will not do this job, and I am at a loss to know what would.

(3.2.2) *Comparative Similarity and the Mental-Act Theory.* How does Ockham's proposal—that general concepts signify all of the things they resemble most—fare on the mental-act theory? Once again, it is necessary to ask what things figure into the calculation of comparative similarity. Given that the theory abandons the distinction between objective and real existents, only real existents seem to be left. The initially indicated criterion is thus

> (T8) Letting '*C*' range over concepts and '*x*' and '*y*' over both really and objectively existent things, for all *x*, *C* signifies *x*, if and only if there does not exist a *y* such that *C* resembles *y* more than *C* resembles *x*.

But we have already seen how (T8) poses difficulties that would necessitate at least some modifications in it. How, for example, would the mental-act theory cope with the problem that (T8) forces every concept to signify the really existent things it resembles most, no matter what really exists? So long as the mental-act theory restricts its ontological commitment to really existent particulars, the problem is insoluble. In the *Summa logicae*, however, Ockham writes from the viewpoint of the mental-quality theory and allows that in one sense a term '*F*' signifies not only all those things that are *F*, but also those that can be *F*;[26] further, he maintains that the term '*F*' signifies not only for those that are but also for those that can be in proposi- tions of the form '*x* can be *F*'. On one interpretation (whose merits will be examined in Part Two, chapter 11 below), Ockham can be seen there as extending the ontological com- mitments of the mental-act theory to unactualized possible par- ticulars as well, thereby opening the way to replacing (T10) with

> (T12) Letting '*C*' range over concepts and '*x*' and '*y*' over actual and possible real existents, for all *x*, *C* signifies *x* if and only if there does not exist a *y* such that *C* resembles *y* more than *C* resembles *x*.

(T12) brings difficulties of its own, however. For according to the mental-act theory, all concepts are mental qualities and as such would be essentially more similar to any other concept than to any extramental substance or quality. Ockham himself

---

26. I, c.33, (OPh I, 95).

cites an objection that invokes the premiss 'No accident can be similar to substance.'[27] It would follow by (T12) that no concepts could signify such extramental substances or qualities, but would signify other concepts—which is unacceptable.

Ockham could try to avoid this problem by removing (T12) and substituting the analogue of (T10) for the mental-act theory:

(T13)   Letting '*C*' range over concepts and '*x*' and '*y*' over actual and possible really existent things, for all *x*, *C* signifies *x* if and only if there does not exist a *y* such that *C* resembles *y* more than *C* resembles *x*, leaving aside any similarity between *x* and *C* and *y* and *C* that results from the fact that *C* is a mental quality.

I have not found a passage in which Ockham explicitly makes this move, but its necessity is acknowledged by the fifteenth century logician Paul of Venice. Facing a similar objection, he admits that where essences are concerned, "the resemblance between this intension [i.e., the intension of a man] and any other intension is greater than the resemblance between it and a man" and "the association between a man and a donkey or between Socrates and Plato is greater than the association between the intension of man and man or between the intension of Socrates and Socrates."[28] It is by virtue of accidental similarity, however, that an intension of the mind signifies what it signifies. Thus Paul writes,

> ...there is a greater accidental association between the intension 'man' and man than between it and another intension, because 'man' is caused by a man and not by some other intension.[29]

Just as it is the accidental arrangement of colors that makes what is essentially a piece of canvass a picture of a man rather than a

27. *Ord.* I, d.2, q.8, (OTh II, 282).

28. *Logica magna*, Part I, Tractatus de terminis, c.2, (Kretzmann ed. and trans., 67).

29. *Ibid.*, 67 and 69.

picture of a green house or a picture of a piece of canvass, so it is
the accidental features of a mental quality that make it a concept
of a man or the concept of man in general, rather than the concept of a green house or a concept of a concept.

Recall that according to the mental-act theory, my thought of
a green house is to be analysed in terms of the real existence of
an act of intellect that really has the property of being-of-a-
green-house. According to (T13), the property of being-of-a-
green-house would consist in the above mentioned accidental
features with respect to which my thought resembles a green
house more than it resembles anything else.

The question is, is it plausible to suppose that my thought of a
green house is similar to a green house, and indeed more similar
to a green house than to a man with respect to such accidental
features? For example, a color photograph of a green house
resembles green houses and resembles them more than it
resembles a man with respect to such accidental features. For
the picture's color will be more similar to that of the house than
to Socrates' coloring. Further, the shape of the green patch in
the picture will be (roughly) some two dimensional analogue of
the shape of part of the three dimensional green house, but will
presumably not be any two dimensional analogue of the shape
of Socrates. But an act of intellect that is of-a-green-house cannot resemble the green house in the same way that a color
photograph of a green house can. The reason is that the act of
intellect is an unextended mental quality and hence has no accidental features that can be green or a two dimensional
analogue of the shape of the house. This fact makes it highly
doubtful that an act of intellect should have any similarity to a
green house that it would not have to a man. If such similarity is
ruled out, then, on the mental-act theory, comparative similarity cannot be the relation that accounts for the signification of
material things by concepts.

(3.3) *Summary*. I do not see how Ockham can specify, either
on the objective-existence theory or on the mental-act theory, a
similarity relation that can constitute the natural signification
relation for general concepts such as 'animal' and 'man', but I
think this has no relevance whatever for deciding the issue be-

tween the nominalists-conceptualists, on the one hand, and the moderate realists on the other. For either my and/or Ockham's failure to identify such a relation results from limited imagination, or it comes from the fact that there is none. If the former, it has no tendency to reveal anything metaphysically pernicious in the nominalist-conceptualist refusal to ground similarity relations in common metaphysical constituents. If the latter, then both theories are equally mistaken about the natural signification of general concepts. For if there is no similarity relation that ties the concept 'man' to Socrates and Plato but not to Brownie the donkey and green houses, then there is no relation for the moderate realist to analyse by saying that the common human nature that exists in the mind as a concept is a metaphysical constituent of Socrates and Plato but not of Brownie and green houses. What the failure of (T8)–(T13) calls into question is at most the existence of the requisite similarity relation; but what moderate realists disagree with nominalists-conceptualists about, is the analysis of such relations, should they exist. Nevertheless, it is too early to conclude that Ockham's rebuttal of the objection in steps 1–6 is successful. For his account of what makes particulars co-generic and co-specific and of the natural signification of concepts such as 'animal' and 'man' avoids making these facts arbitrary and subjective, only if similarity relations are not arbitrary and subjective. Whether Ockham can consistently maintain that they are not, depends on his account of the signification of syncategorematic and connotative concepts, which will be the subject of chapter 9 below.

4.   APPENDIX: NATURAL SIGNIFICATION AND THOUGHTS OF PARTICULARS

Contemporary interest in the theory of proper names, makes it worthwhile to consider Ockham's account of the natural signification of thoughts of particulars. On the objective-existence theory, what makes an act of thought to be a thought or awareness of a given particular is that it is directed towards a certain objectively existent entity which naturally signifies the particular in question. On the mental-act theory, it is that the act of thought itself naturally signifies that particular.

What is the relation of natural signification between an objectively existent entity and a given particular, where thoughts of particulars are concerned? Our discussion above (chapter 3) indicates that the relation must be identity. Ockham says explicitly in the case of God's thoughts of particular creatures that "the same thing is an idea" insofar as it has objective existence in the mind of God "and is produced independently of the mind" by God.[30] And, since objectively existent entities are supposed to be the immediate objects of thought, saying that they are identical with the things they naturally signify is essential for reconciling the objective-existence theory with a direct realist position in theory of knowledge.

Obviously, the natural signification relation cannot be identity on the mental-act theory, since no mental act is identical with any material thing. Further, given Ockham's position that no mental act is an awareness of itself, it cannot naturally signify any mental act by identity either. An adherent of the mental-act theory might be expected to appeal again to

(T13) Letting 'x' and 'y' range over actual and possible real things, C signifies x, if and only if there does not exist a y such that C is more similar to y than to x, leaving aside any similarity between x and C and y and C that results from the fact that C is a mental quality,

noting that where we are dealing with thoughts of particulars, there is always one particular that is more similar to the thought or concept than any other particular is.

I have already questioned whether the appropriate similarity relations can obtain between mental acts and their mind-independent significata, even where abstract general concepts are concerned, and the same difficulty arises, a fortiori, in connection with thoughts of particulars. And Ockham himself

30. *Ord.* I, d.2, q.1, (OTh II, 25).

twice considers a related, although less sweeping, objection to defining the natural signification of thoughts in terms of (T13).[31] The argument begins with the observation that acts of cognition are "just as similar to one particular as to another maximally similar to it and represents one just as much as another."[32] If so, it follows from (T13) that no such cognitions are of single particulars but all are general, signifying numerically distinct particulars equally.

Ockham does not deny the premiss—that acts of cognition are equally similar to many, actual and/or possible, particulars—and in effect concedes the conclusion that (T13) needs amendment. His response is that "similarity is not the precise cause why it [an act of cognition] understands one thing and not another."[33] Rather a cognition

> is proper to one particular, not because it is more similar to one than to another, but because naturally it is caused by one and not by another, nor can it be caused by the other.[34]

When I look at a white patch, my cognition is equally similar to many whitenesses including this whiteness. But my cognition is of this whiteness rather than any of the others, because, unlike them, this whiteness stands in the requisite causal relation to that act. This suggests the replacement of (T13) by

> (T14) Letting 'C' range over concepts and 'x' and 'y' over actual and possible real things, for all x, C signifies x uniquely if and only if (i) there does not exist a y such that C is more similar to y than to x, leaving aside any similarity between x and C and y and C that results from the fact that C is a mental quality; and (ii) x stands in the appropriate causal relation to C.

Ockham does not give a precise specification of this causal rela-

---

31. *Rep.* II, q.12–13, (OTh V, 287) and *Quodl.* I, q.13, (OTh IX, 74, 76).
32. *Ibid.*, (OTh IX, 74).
33. *Rep.* II, q.12–13, (OTh V, 287).
34. *Quodl.* I, q.13, (OTh IX, 76).

tion here. In the Prologue to his commentary on the *Sentences*, however, he indicates that when I see an existent and present white patch, that whiteness is a partial efficient cause, whether mediate or immediate, of my awareness of it. In cases of human sensory cognitions, the angels' intellectual cognitions, and human intellectual cognitions of mental acts, it seems that the object is an immediate partial efficient cause of the act. And he speculates that this is the way it will be with our intellectual cognitions of material things when our souls are separated from our bodies. But he does not make clear whether the object acts immediately, or only by means of sensory cognitions, to cause intellectual acts of awareness in this life. Whatever the requisite causal relation, Ockham implies in *Quodlibeta* I, q.13, that it is one that does not obtain between particulars and cognitions of imagination and memory. Distinguishing between simple and composite concepts (the latter being composed of several concepts and the former not), he concludes that all simple cognitions of imagination and memory are general and none proper to a given particular.[35] Thus, Ockham seems to have in mind the relation of being an immediate partial efficient cause of the mental act and possibly that of being a mediate cause of the act by immediately causing a sensory cognition, which is an immediate cause of the intellectual act.

Ockham's reasons for replacing (T13) with (T14) invite comparison with the contemporary movement away from a Russellian analysis of proper names. Just as Ockham begins with an attempt to account for natural signification in terms of comparative similarity, so Russell maintained that ordinary proper names had a bearer only if one and only one thing had all of the concepts associated with the name. Some objected that the latter criterion was too stringent, and substituted the requirement that a thing have a sufficient number of those qualities. Others worried that the modified criterion was too permissive, in that several things might have all or a sufficient number of such qualities. Causal theorists do not deny that a collection of properties is usually associated with ordinary proper names.

35. (OTh IX, 76–77).

But they conclude that it is not the properties, but an appropriate causal relation between a thing and a speaker's use of the name, that picks out the name's bearer. Likewise, on reflection, Ockham concludes that comparative similarity "cannot be the precise cause" of a concept's signifying one thing to the exclusion of another. Conceivably, if he had dwelt longer on cases of misperception, he might have concluded that comparative similarity was not a necessary condition of a concept's signifying a thing either. Ockham overlooks these considerations, however, and invokes the causal relation to supplement rather than replace the similarity relation.

Nevertheless, the parallelism here should not be overstated. For it was the ordinary proper names of conventional language that Russell tried to expose as truncated descriptions. The proper names of Ockham's mental language are really more analogous to Russell's logically proper names. For they are the cognitions in which we apprehend particulars immediately and for the first time. In Russell's terminology, in such cognitions we know particulars "by acquaintance" and not "by description." Ockham allows that we can compound various simple cognitions of memory and imagination together to arrive at a composite concept that is proper to Socrates and by means of which we conceive of him as having a certain color, shape, location, etc.[36] The latter's composite concepts would be a closer analogue, in Ockham's theory, of Russell's alleged truncated descriptions. And, paralleling Russell, Ockham tacitly assumes that such a composite concept is proper, whereas its simple components are not, because many things may be equally similar to one simple concept, while one actual thing is more similar to the composite than any other actual thing.

Further, Ockham's theory appeals to different causal relations from contemporary causal theorists of proper names. The latter usually specify what counts as an appropriate causal connection by examples. P's witnessing x's being christened N would be a paradigm case of such a relation, but quite indirect connections—such as some fourth century divine's witnessing

36. *Ibid.*, (OTh IX, 77).

the christening and recording it in some official document which in turn is noted by successive historians including the one that P reads—are also held to qualify. Ockham, by contrast, calls only on causal connections that are comparatively direct. And, at least where memory cognitions are concerned, this requirement seems unduly restrictive. Suppose I have never seen anything white and see a white patch for the first time. Let us call the particular whiteness I see W_1. If I immediately close my eyes and remember what I saw, would we not be willing to say that I was remembering W_1 in particular, even if my memory cognitions were equally similar to many white patches that I have never seen? Suppose that in general R is the causal connection between a particular and the mental disposition D which Ockham thinks causes memory cognitions. Could not Ockham allow that a memory cognition signifies all of these particulars that meet condition (i) of (T14) and that are R to D? If there are many particulars of this sort, he could conclude that the memory cognition was common. But if there were only one such particular as in the example, he could say that the cognition was proper to it.

Given the range of causal connections that Ockham actually counts as appropriate, it is clear why he needs to retain condition (i) as well. For an act of thought or awareness may have more than one immediate partial cause. Ockham suggests, although he thinks it cannot be proved, that God is always an immediate partial efficient cause of any effect. If (T14) stipulated condition (ii) alone, it would follow as much from (T14) as (T13) that such acts were common to at least two things—to God and the creature. Adding condition (i) enables him to say that the above mentioned mental act is an awareness of whiteness and not of God, on the ground that the act resembles the whiteness more than it resembles God, but resembles nothing (besides other mental acts) more than it resembles the whiteness.

Nevertheless, difficulties with (T14) remain. As Ockham sees it, it is a consequence of divine omnipotence that whenever God acts together with a creature to produce some effect, He has the power to produce that same effect by acting alone. And in discussing the acts by which we are first aware of particulars, he explicitly concludes that God could act alone to produce a cognition that is of this whiteness in particular and not of anything else. (T14) does not allow for this possibility, since where God causes the cognition acting alone, nothing will satisfy both conditions (i) and (ii).

Ockham replies in *Reportatio* II, q.15 that

> ...any act of understanding a creature, which act is caused by God, can have a creature as a partial cause, although it is not caused [by that creature] in fact. Therefore, the act of the intellect cognizes that particular by which it would be determinately caused if it were caused by a creature. But one particular is of this sort and not of another. Therefore, etc.[37]

And in *Quodlibeta* I, q.13, he says that "such a vision is always apt to be caused by one created object and not by the other."[38] For an act of thought or awareness to have a single particular as its immediate object, it is not necessary that the particular should *actually* stand in the requisite causal relation, but only that it should be *apt* to do so. Thus, Ockham's proposal might be formulated as follows:

(T15)   Letting 'C' range over concepts and 'x' and 'y' over actual and possible real things, for all x, C signifies x uniquely, if and only if both (i) there does not exist a y such that C is more similar to y than to x, leaving aside any similarity between x and C and y and C that results from the fact that C is a mental quality; and (ii) either x is God and x stands in the appropriate causal relation to C, or x is the only creature that can stand in the appropriate causal relation to C.

Since, of the cognitions that he explicitly allows to be proper to a single particular, all are at least apt to have their objects as partial efficient causes, Ockham would probably have been willing

37. (OTh V, 289).
38. (OTh IX, 76).

to replace condition (ii) with

(ii′) either x is God and x stands in the appropriate causal relation to C, or x is the only creature that can be an immediate partial efficient cause of C.

Ockham's thoughts seems to be that being-caused-by-God-or-by-this-whiteness is an essential property of a cognition that is proper to this whiteness. That is, one could construe (T15) to mean that if C is a particular cognition that has this whiteness alone as its immediate object, it is impossible that anything actual or possible other than this whiteness or God should cause C to exist. It follows that for Ockham, there is a sense in which not all causal connections among creatures are contingent. For while 'C is caused by this whiteness' is contingent, since it is contingent that C exists at all and C could have been caused by God instead, 'If C is caused by a creature, C is caused by this whiteness' is necessary (see Part Four, chapter 18).

However these criteria fare as applied to created concepts, none of them adequately captures the relation between the divine conception and its particular objects. Neither (T14) nor (T15) do, because—as Ockham himself insists—God's act of thought neither is nor can be caused by anything. (T14) fails for an additional reason, because the divine essence is supposed by Ockham to be an act that at once has all actual and possible creatures as its immediate objects. This would be possible according to (T13), only if the divine essence were equally similar to everything—which it is not, because it is more similar to rational creatures made in God's image than to others.[39] And even if it were, (T13) could not explain why the divine cognition is hereby a distinct cognition of each particular rather than an abstract general concept of created being that is determinate only in those features had by all creatures and indeterminate and determinable with respect to the rest. Thus, the mental-act theory as Ockham develops it completely fails to explain what

39. *Ord.* I, d.3, q.10, (OTh II, 555–57).

makes God's thought a distinct cognition of all actual or possible creatures at once (see Part Five, chapter 24 below).

It might seem from this that the objective-existence theory would have a compelling advantage over the mental-act theory, when it comes to accounting for the direction of acts of thought to particulars. For the objective-existence theory says that a thought will be a thought *of* a particular x, if the thought is directed towards the objectively existent entity that is identical with x. Thus, God's thought will be a distinct thought of all possible particulars, if, for each such particular, His thought is directed towards the objectively existent entity that is identical with it. This advantage is only apparent, however. For, as we have already seen, what directs an act of thought towards a given objectively existent entity is its "content." And Ockham appears to identify the content of thoughts of particulars with the problematic relations mentioned in (T15). Thus, unless some more adequate account for such possible causal relations can be found, we shall have to conclude that neither the objective-existence theory nor the mental-act theory gives an adequate account of what makes a thought a thought *of* a given particular.

5

Ockham's Ontological Program

Ockham presents his own ontology as the conclusion to be drawn from his critique of the alleged mistakes of his predecessors and contemporaries. In chapters 1 and 2, we have seen how they assumed that Aristotle's ten categories were categories of common or universal things that somehow exist in reality in particulars. Ockham's program for refuting this thesis divides into two parts. The first, which we have already examined in chapter 2, consists in arguing that nothing but particulars can exist in reality. Ockham identifies universals primarily with naturally significant concepts and secondarily with conventionally significant general terms. And we will complete our measure of comparative ontological commitments of Ockham's objective-existence and mental act theories in Part Two, chapter 11 below.

Ockham's opponents were not, however, simply committed to the view that what is common or universal exists somehow in reality. They also held that there were at least ten, fundamentally different kinds of things—one for each of Aristotle's ten categories. The second part of Ockham's ontological program is aimed at showing that this contention is mistaken as well. Ockham argues that natural reason will support only a belief in particular substances and particular qualities, and doctrine requires us to add only the existence of certain relations.

Limitations of space prevent us from examining Ockham's whole defense of this selection. In the remainder of this chapter, I shall first sketch a composite of the views that Ockham is opposing and lay out the general strategy of his attack on them. Then, in chapters 6 and 7, I will turn to a detailed consideration of his arguments that nothing other than particular substances and particular qualities corresponds to the

categories of quantity and relation. His arguments regarding
motion and time will be postponed until Part Four below. In
chapter 8, I shall try to explain why Ockham did believe that
some qualities are things really distinct from substances.
Chapter 9 will deal with some general objections to the ontological program.

1. THE POSITION OF THE "MODERNS"

One can get a better feel for the sort of position Ockham was
set against by combining the various ontological theses he rejects in *Summa logicae*, Part I, chapters 42–62. Naturally, such
a composite ontology caricatures the views of some of his opponents, and some of these distortions will be corrected in the
detailed discussions of later chapters. For now, it will be useful
to have a general picture before us, so that we can appreciate
the general thrust of Ockham's arguments. Since Ockham often
refers to those he is criticizing generically as "moderns," I shall
label this view "the position of the moderns."[1]

According to this composite picture, then, trees and horses,
water and air, and even minds have a kind of layer-like structure. The core of each thing is its substance. And substance, by
virtue of its being one, is the subject of contraries of a fundamentally different kind—viz., substance is one by the inherence of discrete quantity, the accident of unity.[2] Even when
substance is thus made one by the inherence of discrete quantity, qualities do not inhere in substance directly, but in yet

1. This view is strongly suggested by the opening paragraphs of Peter of
Spain's *Tractatus suppositionum*: "Moreover, each noncomplex term
signifies either a substance, or a quality, or a quantity, or a relation, or an action, or a passion, or a place, or a time, or a situation, or a habit. Signification
is taken here for the conventional representation of a thing by a word.
Whence, since everything is either universal or particular, expressions that
do not signify only universal or particular are not significant..." (*Summulae
logicales*, (Mullally ed., 2)).

2. I infer that some of them thought this from the fact that Ockham
takes the trouble to argue against it in two places: his *Expos. Praedicam.*, c.2,
sec.15, (OPh II, 51–52) and *Summa logicae* I, c.44, (OPh I, 138).

another distinct thing, a continuous quantity that inheres in the substance directly.[3] Substance, quantity, and quality were conceived of as being distinct "absolute" things. Relations are things of a kind different from any of these and are not said to be "absolute" things but "respects" (*respectus*) or relative things (*res relativae*). These have their foundations in either the substance, quantity, or quality of a thing. Thus, if Socrates and Plato are both white, the foundation of Socrates' similarity to Plato is Socrates' whiteness and the foundation of Plato's similarity to Socrates is Plato's whiteness. Thus, a relative thing that is his relation of similarity inheres in Socrates or his whiteness and another one inheres in Plato or his whiteness. Again, if Socrates is the father of Plato a thing that is his fatherhood and that is distinct from Socrates' substance, quantity, and qualities inheres in Socrates or in his quantity or qualities. And a corresponding thing that is the relation of sonship inheres in Plato or in his quantity or qualities.[4] Again, if two boards are equal in length, there is a thing distinct from the substance, quantity, or qualities of the first board that inheres in it or its quantity and another distinct from the substance, quantity, and qualities of the second board that inheres in it or in its quanitity. Action is a respect or a relative thing said by some to exist in the agent and by others in the patient, while those of the former persuasion held that a passion is another relative thing that inheres in the patient.[5] Likewise, temporal location (*quando* or *quandalitas*) is a relative thing distinct from other relative things and from absolute things. Each one replaces and is replaced by other such relative things in succession, and other things exist first at one time and then another by virtue of their successive inherence.[6] Spatial location is still another kind of relative thing that has its foundation in the thing located and its term in the place.[7] Position is another respect existing in the

---

3. *Ibid.*, (OPh I, 132).
4. *Ibid.*, c.49, (OPh I, 154).
5. *Ibid.*, c.57, (OPh I, 186) and c.58, (OPh I, 188).
6. *Ibid.*, c.59, (OPh I, 190).
7. *Ibid.*, c.60, (OPh I, 191).

whole or in the parts of a substance; by virtue of it existing in the thing, the thing sits, rises, etc.[8] Finally, a having (*habitus*) is a relative thing that inheres in a body that is around or contained in another.[9] Aristotle had classified corporeity (three-dimensional extension and possibly impenetrability), surfaces, lines and (by reduction) points as falling under the division of continuous quantity. And some moderns had concluded that in a physical object, its corporeity is a thing really distinct from its substance; its surface, a thing really distinct from its substance; each of the infinity of lines on the surface, a thing really distinct from every other line and from the surface; and each of the points on the lines, a thing really distinct from every point and from the lines.[10]

The resultant ontology is rich both in the variety and the number of entities it assumes. An analysis of the metaphysical structure of a rolling billiard ball yields not only at least ten different kinds of things, but infinitely many of some of them. What sort of reasoning could lie behind such a surprising conclusion?

2.   SEMANTICS AND ONTOLOGY

Semantics, the science of how words are related to things, naturally has a close connection with metaphysics. A philosopher's firm ontological convictions are bound to affect what he allows words to stand for. Equally well, an overriding commitment to a general semantic thesis will influence his ontology. Ockham clearly believes that the "moderns" were led to make such extensive ontological commitments precisely because they endorsed one of a range of mistaken assumptions about how words are related to things.

(a) Of these, the crudest is attributed to them by Ockham in the *Summulae Physicorum*:

8. *Ibid.*, c.61, (OPh I, 192).
9. *Ibid.*, c.62, (OPh I, 193).
10. *Ibid.*, c.48, (OPh I, 152).

...This, therefore, is the basis of many errors in philosophy: [the assumption] that a distinct signification always corresponds to a distinct word, so that the distinction among things signified is just as great as that among names or significant words...[11]

Apparently, the thesis is that whatever else may be involved in the signification of a word, each token of a given word type signifies some entity distinctive to that word type and signifies it in such a way that that entity must exist if any affirmative categorical proposition in which it occurs is to be true. Ockham carps that if this rule were applied consistently, its adherents would not only be led to posit when-nesses (*quandalitates*) and where-nesses (*ubeitates*) corresponding to time and place words,[12] but also and-ness (*etitas*) and but-ness (*seditas*) corresponding to 'and' and 'but'! While scarcely anyone drew the latter conclusion (after all, conjunctions such as 'and' and 'but' are syncategorematic terms that are not thought to signify anything by themselves but only signify together with another term), Ockham was convinced that many of his opponents failed to appreciate the syncategorematic force included in the meaning of many terms.

(b) Less blatantly implausible was the assumption that the significations of every pair of concrete and abstract terms are related the way that of 'white' and 'whiteness' are. As Ockham explains in *Summa logicae* I, chapter 10, 'whiteness' is a merely absolute noun in that it does not signify one thing principally and something else or the same thing secondarily, but signifies whatever it signifies with equal primacy.[13] In this case, 'whiteness' signifies each and every particular whiteness and signifies one just as primarily as it signifies any other. By contrast, 'white' is a connotative term whose nominal definition is 'something informed by whiteness' or 'something having whiteness'. Accordingly, it signifies something primarily or directly, viz., the thing that is informed by or has the whiteness, and something obliquely, viz., the particular whiteness that in-

11. III, c.7, 55–56, (OPh VI).
12. *Quodl.* V, q.22, (OTh IX, 565).
13. (OPh I, 35).

heres in what has it.[14] If the significations of each pair of concrete and abstract terms were related in this way, then the abstract noun would always signify some entity or accident that inhered in the thing primarily signified by the concrete noun or adjective. Thus, paternity would be supposed to be some entity distinct from and inhering in the thing that is a father; similarity, an entity distinct from and inhering in the thing that is similar; quantity, an entity distinct from and inhering in the thing that is quantified; activity, an entity distinct from and inhering in the thing that acts, etc. Given the penchant of thirteenth and fourteenth century philosophers and theologians for inventing abstract nouns to correspond to concrete ones, this semantic assumption could prove ontologically permissive indeed!

Nevertheless, Ockham finds no compelling reason to endorse this thesis, and indeed brings arguments against its ontological consequences as we shall see in succeeding chapters. On the contrary, unaided natural reason would say that abstract and concrete terms in the category of substance are synonymous and are like merely absolute terms while abstract and concrete terms in all of the accidental categories except for certain species of quality are synonymous and are connotative terms that signify some substance or quality directly and some substance or quality obliquely.[15] Thus, 'horsehood' does not signify anything distinct from and inhering in a horse, but is a merely absolute term signifying particular horses, just as 'horse' is. And 'curvature' does not signify anything distinct from and inhering in what is curved, but signifies the curved object directly and obliquely signifies that its parts are arranged in a certain way.

(c) In the cases just mentioned, the abstract nouns do function as nouns, even if they are not merely absolute terms the

14. This analysis of the signification of 'white' and 'whiteness' presupposes that the quality whiteness is a thing really distinct from the substance that is white. Why Ockham believed this will be discussed in chapter 8 below.

15. *Quodl.* V, q.9, (OTh IX, 514–18); cf. *Summa logicae* I, c.6, (OPh I, 20–21) and *Expos. Praedicam.*, c.7, (OPh II, 316). For theological alterations in this thesis see Part Five, chapter 22 below.

way 'whiteness' is. Ockham cautions that this is not always so where the abstract nouns invented and used by philosophers and theologians are concerned. For often they use abstract nouns to abbreviate longer and more cumbersome expressions that contain syncategorematic terms, verbs, adverbs, etc. In such cases, it is not possible merely to replace the abstract noun with the complex expression it abbreviates without rendering the sentence ungrammatical. Rather the proposition must be expounded as a whole, sometimes in unobvious ways. In his first *Treatise on Quantity*, Ockham gives the following example:

> Thus, I maintain that the proposition 'Generation is in an instant' should not be understood as it sounds, as if one thing were in another, the way the proposition 'Water is in a vase' denotes that one thing is in another distinct thing. For it is clear by induction that it cannot be said that generation is in an instant in any of the ways of equivocally taking the preposition 'in' discussed by the Philosopher in Book IV of the *Physics*. Rather the proposition 'Generation is in an instant' should be understood as follows: when something is generated, it is not generated one part after another but all at once'. Thus, the short proposition 'Generation is in an instant' replaces the long expression 'When something is generated, it is not generated one part after another but all at once' for the sake of brevity. [16]

Likewise, 'Motion is in time' may be used to abbreviate 'When something is in motion, it acquires one part before another continuously'. Once introduced, these pseudo-nouns acquire a life of their own and may be used even when the resultant proposition is not shorter. For example, Ockham claims, Aristotle, Averroes, and other authorities may read 'A point is an indivisible thing' when they mean to say only 'A line is not further extended'. [17]

Here Ockham agrees with his opponents that if one takes the structure of the propositions 'Generation is in an instant' and 'Motion is in time' at face value, one will understand them to imply that there are such things as generation and motion, instants and time and that the former are in the latter, respective-

---

16. Q.1, (Birch ed., 54, 56).
17. *Ibid.*, (Birch ed., 41).

ly. But unlike the moderns, Ockham is not content to draw
these ontological conclusions. His strategy for avoiding them
recalls Bertrand Russell's treatment of definite descriptions. If
we suppose that definite descriptions always function as names
to denote an entity that satisfies the description, then we shall
have to conclude that the definite description in the true
proposition 'The present king of France does not exist' denotes
a nonexistent entity; for no existent entity satisfies the description. Wishing to avoid the resultant ontology of existent and
nonexistent entities, Russell proposed to give a contextual
definition of 'the present king of France' in that proposition,
analyzing it as 'It is not the case that there is one and only one x
such that x is presently king of France' where no term of the latter denotes anything but existent entities. Similarly with
Ockham's construal of 'Generation is in an instant'. When it is
replaced with 'When something is generated, it is not generated
one part after another but all at once', the impression that there
must be some such things as generation and as an instant to be
named by its terms is lost.

   Nevertheless, there is an important difference between
Ockham's and Russell's procedures here. For where Russell's
proposal is about how we are to understand the *literal* sense of
propositions containing definite descriptions, Ockham insists
that the above mentioned sentences represent a figurative use of
language by their authors and compares it to the license taken
with language by poets and rhetoricians. The reason for this
somewhat surprising move lies within Ockham's own logical
theory. He will say that a proposition is taken literally (*de virtute sermonis*, according to the force of the words), only when
it is analysed according to the rules he lays down in the *Summa
logicae*. But in these rules, grammar and syntax are a controlling factor in determining how a term functions in the proposition. If a noun in the proposition has a certain syntactical rela-
tionship to the copula and to quantifiers (if any) such as 'every',
'only', 'no', etc., then it must be taken as purportedly standing
for (denoting or suppositing for) some thing or things and as
standing for them in a certain way. If there is nothing that the
noun could appropriately stand for, then the proposition in

question is false taken literally (see Part Two, chapter 11 below). Thus, according to Ockham's logical theory, propositions with the same grammatical structure have the same logical structure; and taken literally 'Generation is in an instant' will imply that one thing is in another, just as much as 'Water is in a vase' does. Thus, he says that 'Generation is in an instant' and 'Motion is in time' are false taken literally, but they are true when they are understood figuratively, according to the intentions of their authors.

In appealing to the traditional rhetorical distinction[18] between how a proposition should be understood taken literally and how it should be understood according to the intention of the author, Ockham is promulgating an exegetical tool that he will use to explain away many passages in which Aristotle, Averroes, and various Saints and authorities seem to agree with the moderns' position. Thus, he writes,

> ...All propositions such as 'Action is in the thing acted upon', 'Motion is in what can be moved', 'Similarity is in the similar thing', 'Whiteness is the term of motion', 'Everything is produced by production', 'Fire heats by heating', and innumerable other propositions of this kind that are found in the sayings of the philosophers, the Saints, and even in Sacred Scripture, ought to be explained away as figurative by means of some grammatical figure. Nor is there any difficulty in granting that the philosophers and saints spoke figuratively in this way, since many such figures are found in Sacred Scripture, not [only] taking the claims of Sacred Scripture in their spiritual sense, but also in their literal sense.[19]

According to a long-standing tradition, when the literal meaning of a sacred text seems frivolous or unworthy, devout but intelligent men are hard pressed to justify claiming that the author's assertion is true. Even before the birth of Christ, pious Greeks, struggling with the texts of Homer, and rabbis interpreting the Bible found a solution: viz., regard the literal sense

18. *Boethius's 'De topicis differentiis'*, trans. E. Stump, (Ithaca, NY, 1978), 84.
19. *Treatise on Quantity* I, q.1, (Birch ed., 42, 44); cf. q.3, (Birch ed., 124–26).

of the unworthy passages as a stumbling block for the low-minded and hardhearted, and discover a deeper and true sense by means of allegorical interpretation. Some early fathers of the Christian church, including Clement of Alexandria and Augustine, would have found certain Biblical passages an insuperable obstacle to their conversion had this technique not been used to find Platonizing philosophy beneath the veil of the literal sense. Using this method of exegesis, certain Neoplatonists "discovered" that Plato and Aristotle really did not disagree at all. And in the hands of Ockham and his contemporaries, Aristotle comes to hold as many different views as he has differing interpreters.

(d) Ockham thinks that even when the moderns did recognize that various parts of a proposition may function as connotative terms, they failed to appreciate the full range of ways in which connotation can vary the signification. As we shall see, many of their arguments in favor of assuming a distinct kind of entity for each of Aristotle's ten categories rest on their construal of Aristotle's remark in *Categories*, 5, 4a22ff that there can be no passage from contradictory to contradictory apart from any change, assuming the change must be the generation or corruption of some thing (*res*). More precisely,

(A) Necessarily, if first p is true and then not-p is true, either something (*res*) has been produced in existence for the first time, or something that did exist has ceased to exist.

(B) makes two claims, the first of which is innocent:

(B) Necessarily, the circumstances in which p is true are different from the circumstances in which not-p is true.

As Scotus explains,

> ...There is never a passage from contradictory to contradictory apart from any change (*mutatio*). For if there were no change in anything, there would be no more reason why one contradictory should be truer than the other. Thus, either both are simultaneously false or both are simultaneously true.[20]

20. *Ord.* I, d.30, q.1–2, n.41, (Vaticana VI, 186–87).

But (C) stipulates further that

(C) The difference between the circumstances in which p is true and the circumstances in which not-p is true is a difference in which things exist.

And behind (C) lies yet another (in Ockham's mind) pernicious semantic assumption. The truth of affirmative, non-modal, categorical propositions presupposes the existence of at least one of the entities signified directly by each term and at least one of the entities signified indirectly (if any) by each term. Thus, 'A horse exists' can be true, only if there is at least one horse; 'An animal exists' can be true, only if there is at least one animal; 'A horse is an animal', only if there is at least one horse and at least one animal; and 'A horse is white', only if there is at least one horse, at least one whiteness, and at least one thing that has whiteness. (C) assumes that the negation sign invariably has the effect of denying that all of the existential presuppositions of such propositions have been satisfied. And the latter assumes in turn that propositions can never differ in meaning without carrying different existential presuppositions. Of course, many propositions do seem to differ in meaning in this way: 'Cicero exists' and 'Socrates exists' are not synonymous because the former can be true only if Cicero exists and whether or not Socrates exists, but the reverse is true for the latter. 'Socrates is white' and 'Socrates is black' differ in meaning at least partly because the former presupposes the existence of at least one whiteness but no blacknesses, while the latter presupposes the existence of at least one blackness but no whitenesses. Analogously, it would seem that modal propositions such as 'It is possible that Socrates is white' and 'It is possible that Socrates is black' differ in meaning because they presuppose existence of different things.

   Given this sort of analysis, it is easy to see how the moderns would conclude that 'Socrates exists' differs in meaning from 'Socrates is six feet tall' because the latter presupposes the existence of six-foot-tallness while the former does not; or that if this volume of gas is first five cubic feet and then six cubic feet, this is because five-cubic-foothood has been corrupted and six-cubic-foothood has been produced. Again, it might seem that 'Socrates is spatially proximate to Plato' differs in meaning from the conjunction 'Socrates exists and Plato exists' because the former presupposes the existence of spatial proximity, a relative thing really distinct from either Socrates or Plato, while the conjunction does not.

Ockham maintains, on the contrary, that while implying or presupposing the actual or possible existence of different things is sufficient for a difference in meaning, it is not necessary. In the *Summa logicae* I, chapter 6, he explains that

> ...those are called synonyms that signify absolutely the same thing in every way, so that nothing is in any way signified by one that is not signified *in the same way* by the other...[21]

On Ockham's view, expressions may fail to be synonymous either because they do not signify the same things or because they do not signify them in the same way. For example, 'man' and 'men' signify altogether the same things, but 'man' signifies them together with singular number and 'men' together with plural number. Likewise, 'This air occupies five cubic feet' and 'This air occupies six cubic feet' presuppose the existence of exactly the same things, but the predicate of the former connotes that the parts of the air are spatially separated, and the predicate of the latter connotes that they are even further apart. Similarly, for 'Socrates is spatially proximate to Plato' and 'Socrates is spatially remote from Plato'. And in general, if terms may fail to be synonymous because, while they signify the same things, they signify them to be in different ways, propositions may also fail to be synonymous without presupposing the existence of different things because they presuppose the same things to be in different ways. Ockham would accordingly replace (C) with

(C′) Either the circumstances in which *p* is true involve the

21. (OPh I, 19), (italics mine); cf. *Ord.* I, d.2, q.3, (OTh II, 88) and q.11, (OTh II, 365).

OCKHAM'S ONTOLOGICAL PROGRAM

> existence of different things from those in which not-p is
> true or the circumstances in which p is true involve the
> existence of the same things in a different way from that
> in which they exist when not-p is true,

where 'in a different way' has adverbial force and ways are not
to be reified.

Ockham grants (B) and concludes—with Aristotle in the
Categories, 5, 4a22ff—that the proposition cannot be first true
and then false without any change in reality. In *Categories*, 14,
15a13, however, Aristotle recognized six kinds of change:
generation, corruption, increase, diminution, alteration, and
locomotion. Having endorsed (C), the moderns conclude that
the last four involve one of the first two. Having replaced (C)
with (C'), Ockham denies that locomotion necessarily involves
either generation or corruption, but thinks that alteration does,
while increase and decrease reduce either to generation and
corruption or to locomotion. Thus, he thinks there are at least
three ways in which a proposition can change truth-value:
through the generation or corruption of some thing (*res*) or
through locomotion. He sometimes adds "or the actual or
potential passage of time."[22] But since the actual or potential
passage of time reduces, on Ockham's view, to the actual or
potential occurrence of a complicated set of locomotions (see
Part Four, chapter 19 below), we can represent his replacement
of (A) by

> (A') Necessarily, if first p is true and then not-p is true, than
> either some thing (*res*) has been produced in existence
> for the first time, or something that did exist has ceased
> to exist, or some locomotion has actually (or potentially)
> occurred.

Locomotion without the generation or corruption of any things
can, Ockham thinks, explain why this air first occupies five
cubic feet and then occupies six cubic feet and why Socrates is

22. *Rep.* IV, q.6, (OTh VII, 85); *Ord.* I, d.30, q.2, (OTh IV, 328).

first spatially remote from and then spatially proximate to Plato. And once (A') replaces (A) many of the moderns' arguments will lose their force.

3.   OCKHAM'S RAZOR

It is one thing to charge that the arguments in favor of a position are unsound; it is another to offer some positive reason that it is mistaken. Ockham's most famous attempts to refute the ontology of the moderns rest on the principle of parsimony better known now as "Ockham's razor." Frequently, he formulates it as

(D) It is futile to do with more what can be done with fewer,[23]

or as

(E) When a proposition comes out true for things, if two things suffice for its truth, it is superfluous to assume a third,[24]

or as

(F) Plurality should not be assumed without necessity;[25]

while in his most explicit version it becomes

(G) No plurality should be assumed unless it can be proved

---

23. "Frustra fit per plura quod potest fieri per pauciora." Cf. *Treatise on Quantity* I, q.3, (Birch ed., 104) and *Treatise on Quantity* II, c.28, (Birch ed., 318).

24. "Quando propositio verificatur pro rebus, si duae res sufficiunt ad eius veritatem, superfluum est ponere tertiam." E.g., *Quodl.* IV, q.24, (OTh IX, 413).

25. "Pluralitas non est ponenda sine necessitate." Cf. *Ord.* I, d.30, q.2, (OTh IV, 322) and *Rep.* II, q.18, (OTh V, 404).

(a) by reason, or (b) by experience, or (c) by some infallible authority.[26]

This last expansion stipulates that there are only three justifications for proliferating entities, causes, or whatever: (a) that there is some theoretical or a priori argument for doing so; (b) that one cannot account for the facts of experience without doing so; or (c) that the Bible, the Saints, or certain pronouncements of the Church require that one do so.[27]

There is some puzzle as to why any of (D)–(G) should have come to be known as *Ockham's* razor.[28] He did not invent the principle; versions of it are found in Aristotle. Further, Ockham's most explicit comments regarding its justification or status are frustratingly scant. He was not the only medieval to invoke it, and he clearly does not regard it as his principal weapon in the fight against ontological proliferation; rather the Law of Noncontradiction is. Nevertheless, the label has a certain appropriateness in that, in comparison with his predecessors, Ockham's metaphysical conclusions are what one would expect from a philosopher who let (D)–(G) be his guide.

Notice that none of (D)–(G) makes any categorical assertion about what pluralities do or do not exist in reality. (D) and (E) express a negative evaluation of an agent and secondarily (in this context) of a theory that does with more what could be done with fewer. (F) and (G) express what we might regard as precepts of prudence or hypothetical imperatives to the effect that if you want to formulate a good philosophical theory, you should not assume pluralities without necessity. In Ockham's terminology, since all of these principles have to do with what is effectible by us, they would, if sound, be the objects of prac-

26. "Nulla pluralitas est ponenda nisi per rationem vel experientiam vel auctoritatem illius, qui non potest falli nec errare, potest convinci." Cf. *Treatise on Quantity* II, c.28, (Birch ed., 318); *Ord.* I, d.30, q.1, (OTh IV, 290); *Rep.* III, q.9, (OTh VI, 281) and IV, q.3–5, (OTh VII, 51–52).

27. Cf. *Treatise on Quantity* I, q.1, (Birch ed., 6) and *Treatise on Quantity* II, Prologue, (Birch ed., 158–160).

28. See Armand Maurer, "Method in Ockham's Nominalism," *Monist* 61 (1978): 426–443, especially 427–431.

tical, not speculative knowledge.[29] They are, in the first instance, methodological principles, and it is not obvious how
they are related to truth or even to probability. As such, they
could serve as the basis of pragmatic arguments about what it
would be futile or superfluous to do, or what one ought to do,
but not of demonstrations in speculative metaphysics about
what entities really exist. In this, (D)–(G) contrast with

  (H) No plurality exists which cannot be proved from reason,
       experience, or infallible authority,

and

  (J) God never does with more what He could do with fewer,

which could serve as premisses in valid deductive arguments
concerning what entities really exist.

What reason could there be for adopting any of (D)–(G)? If
known to be true, (H) and/or (J) would provide excellent
grounds for doing so. If there are no unnecessary pluralities in
reality, then the most reasonable way for us to proceed is to
search for a theory that assumes only those pluralities demanded by our experience and the best arguments we can think of,
and to supplement it with any entities required by authorities
known to be infallible. But (H) is scarcely plausible, if the
experience in question is our experience. As subsequent
philosophers have eloquently explained, our experience is very
limited and for all we know unrepresentative. Why should
there not be, in some far-flung corner of the next galaxy,
pluralities of entities not known to exist by any a priori argument or necessary to explain our present experience? Ockham
himself denies (J). Discussing the order of salvation ordained by
God, Ockham asks whether the Holy Spirit Himself or only His
gifts are given to believers. An objector contends that only His
gifts are:

----

  29. *Ord.* I, Prologue, q.11, (OTh I, 315).

...it is futile to do with more what could be done with fewer. But it is sufficient for eternal life that the gifts of the Holy Spirit be given. Therefore, it is superfluous for the Holy Spirit Himself to be given.[30]

Ockham defends the opposite answer and replies that

...There are many things that God does with more that He could do with fewer. Nor should any other explanation be sought. And it follows from the fact that He wills it that it is fitting and not futile for it to be done. The matter is otherwise where natural and created voluntary causes are concerned. For these voluntary causes should conform themselves especially to right reason of the first [cause], and they do nothing justly or rightly otherwise.[31]

So far as the order of salvation is concerned, God does not abide by the principle of parsimony (see Part Five, chapters 30–31 below). And since whatever God wills is, for that reason alone, fitting, His action should not be called futile. Hence, (D) does not apply to God's actions and (J) is false.

Ockham's remarks in the last two sentences of the passage just quoted are terse, and it is not clear how much weight should be put on them. But they could be read as suggesting alternative reasons for endorsing (D)–(G). For Ockham comments that "the matter is otherwise where natural causes...are concerned." We may ask, what matter is otherwise? Not the conditions under which natural causes act rightly or justly, since as natural agents their actions are not the kind of thing that could be either just or unjust. The only alternative seems to be that whereas in the order of salvation God does with more what He could do with fewer, He has dealt otherwise with the order of natural causes, with the result that they never do with more what they could do with fewer. If these are God's policies, then it would be reasonable to try for the most economical theory regarding the natural order and rely on the authorities for information concerning the exceptions made in the order of salvation. Nevertheless, these claims about God's behavior could

30. *Ibid.*, d.14, q.2, (OTh III, 430).
31. *Ibid.*, (OTh III, 432).

provide us with a reason for endorsing (D)–(G), only if we could know or have good reason to believe that He has dealt with the world in this way, prior to having reason to endorse (D)–(G). But Ockham does not think that we could. Indeed, he thinks there is very little that unaided natural reason could prove about God's policies.

Ockham's comment about created voluntary causes is more ambiguous. He could simply be repeating a central tenet of his ethical theory: viz., that while whatever God wills is just or right simply because He wills it, the action of a created will is just or right only if it conforms to the standard laid down by God (see Part Five, chapter 30 below). On the other hand, he could be making a more specific claim: viz., that while God's action will be just and right even if He does with more what He could do with fewer, the action of a created will would not be just and right if it did so, because the action of a created will is right only if it conforms to the dictates of right reason and right reason stipulates that one should not do with more what one could do with fewer. On this latter, more speculative interpretation, Ockham would be claiming that it is a dictate of right reason that we should not do with more what we could do with fewer and that is why we should adopt (D)–(G). In any case, it should not be surprising if Ockham failed to provide any extensive justification for (D)–(G); contemporary philosophers of science are convinced that simplicity is a legitimate criterion against which to judge the adequacy of theories, but they are hard pressed to explain why or even to say what they mean by simplicity!

In at least one place, Ockham implies that (F)—and therefore, presumably, (D), (E), or (G)—cannot be the basis of a demonstration. For he contends that it cannot be demonstrated either that the matter of the heavens is or that it is not of the same kind as the matter of things here below. Nevertheless, he thinks the following "persuasive argument" can be given:

...plurality should never be assumed without necessity, as has often been said. But now there is no apparent necessity in supposing that the matter here and there are of different kinds. For whatever can be saved by different kinds of matter can be saved equally well or better by matter of the same kind.[32]

One reason why (F) cannot serve as the basis of a demonstration has already been mentioned: viz., that it is a principle of prudence expressing a hypothetical imperative about what one ought to do. A second reason is that demonstration requires premisses that are known to be necessary. But one premiss of the arguments based on (D)–(G) will assert that neither reason, nor experience, nor any infallible authority requires such and such a plurality. It is in principle possible to know which experiences we have had and what is required by the pronouncements of the Church. But it seems that we could not be certain that no reason required such a plurality unless we had discovered an independent demonstration that its existence was impossible.

Whether or not a plurality is necessary depends in part on what basic metaphysical principles are true. In arguing against the moderns' position, Ockham sometimes sets out to show that they have overestimated the ontological commitments required by their own basic tenets. Such an argument might well persuade them to give up an hypostatization, since it would cost them nothing in terms of the fundamental theses of their position. Other times, however, what Ockham actually shows is that it is possible to construct a consistent theory that is not contrary to experience or any infallible authorities and that avoids the hypostatization, if one relinquishes or replaces some part of their position. As we shall see in the next two chapters, Ockham does not always bother to distinguish the two sorts of arguments, probably because he thinks he has offered independent reasons for thinking his opponents' theses false or mutually incompatible.

32. *Rep.* II, q.18, (OTh V, 404).

4. NO ACTUAL INFINITY OF SIMULTANEOUSLY EXISTING THINGS

Not to be confused with arguments based on Ockham's razor, are his attempts to show that the opponents' theory commits them to an actual infinity of simultaneously existing things (*res*) that do not combine with one another to make something one *per se* (the way the infinitely many actual parts of a continuum do; see Part One, chapter 6 and Part Four, chapters 16, 19, and 20 below). For Ockham seems to have held that an actual infinity of simultaneously existing things was not only theoretically superfluous, but logically impossible. For example, in *Quodlibeta* III, q.1, Ockham considers the following purported proof that God's power (*virtus*) is intensively infinite (see Part Five, chapter 29 below): "that which *of itself* can produce infinitely many simultaneously is infinite; but God is of this sort; therefore, etc."[33] Ockham replies that the implication that something of itself could produce infinitely many simultaneously is false "because it involves a contradiction."[34] And he remarks that "if there were infinitely many that could be produced simultaneously, then God could produce them simultaneously. But the antecedent involves a contradiction."[35] Again in his proof that there is a first conserving cause (see Part Five, chapter 22 below), Ockham insists that there can be no infinite chain of simultaneously existing conserving causes, because "then there would be infinitely many actually existing —which is impossible."[36]

This thesis—that an actual infinity of simultaneously existing distinct things is impossible—was as commonplace among thirteenth and early fourteenth century Aristotelians as its motiva-

---

33. (OTh IX, 201).
34. *Ibid.*, (OTh IX, 204).
35. *Ibid.*
36. *Quaest. Physicorum*, q.136, in Boehner's edition in *Ockham: Philosophical Writings*, (Edinburgh and London, 1962), 123.

OCKHAM'S ONTOLOGICAL PROGRAM

tion is obscure. (a) One hypothesis focuses on an argument from Aristotle's *Physics*. Having identified number with the things numbered, Aristotle contends that it is impossible that there should actually be an infinite number on the ground that "every number is either actually numbered, or it is possible that it should be actually numbered": e.g., if there is a number of people in this room, either someone has actually counted them, or it is possible that someone should actually count them. Thus, "if there were an infinite number, it would be possible for an infinity to be actually numbered." But Aristotle denies that this is possible, because we could never finish counting infinitely many things.[37] But even if it were true by the Aristotelian definition of 'number' that any number is in principle countable and finite, it would not follow that there could not be infinitely many actually existing things at once. The most that would follow is that this would not count as *a number* of things. In any event, it would be infelicitous of Ockham to endorse such an argument. For if the alleged fact that infinitely many things could not be counted makes it impossible for them to exist simultaneously in reality, why should it not be enough to prevent them from all having objective existence at once as objects of God's thought? Yet, so long as he held the objective-existence theory, Ockham insisted that infinitely many do (see Part Five, chapter 24 below).

(b) Another suggestion comes from Anneliese Maier,[38] who claims that in denying the possibility of an actual infinity of simultaneously existing things, Ockham understands infinity as a maximum (*tantum quod non maius: tot quod non plures*). For example, in *Ordinatio* I, d.17, q.8, he comes out against not only an intensive infinity but also against an actual infinity of quantity and numbers, on the ground that God cannot make an

---

37. *Expos. Physicorum* III, t.41, (OPh IV).
38. "Diskussionen über das Aktuell Unendliche in der Ersten Hälfte des 14. Jahrhunderts," *Ausgehendes Mittelalter*, (Rome, 1964), vol.I, 41–85, especially 59–62.

infinitely great fire or infinitely many individuals of the same species, although no matter how great a fire He has made, He can make a greater; and no matter how many individuals of the same species He has made, He can make one more.[39] According to Maier, his underlying thought is that making infinitely many (i.e., the maximum possible) would exhaust God's power—which is impossible.

The whole question is muddied further by the fact that—his frequent appeal to the "no actual infinity" principle notwithstanding—in his disputed question,[40] Ockham joins some of his contemporaries in seeing no contradiction in an actual infinity of souls or *passiones animae* and freely admits that if the world were eternal, there would have been twelve times as many revolutions of the moon as of the sun, although infinitely many of each; that the time elapsed from eternity until this morning is less than that plus the time elapsed from yesterday until this evening; that there are twice as many parts in the whole line as in half the line, etc. Maier thinks this apparent contradiction is easily resolved on the assumption that Ockham is here conceiving of infinity not as a maximum, but as "transfinite" or "what exceeds anything finite beyond any determinate proportion," a conception which allows some infinities to be greater than others as modern mathematics claims.[41]

The textual picture is far more complicated than Maier lets on, however, and it is too much to say that Ockham anticipated the contributions of modern mathematics. Nevertheless, there are many passages in which Ockham denies all infinities are equal, but for different reasons in different places. (i) In his disputed question,[42] he allows not only that some infinities are

39. (OTh III, 550).
40. *Quaest. variae*, q.3, (OTh VIII, 68).
41. *Op. cit.*, 61–62.
42. *Quaest. variae*, q.3, (OTh VIII, 59–97).

unequal to others, but that there is a determinate proportion between them. Even if the world were eternal, there would be twelve times as many revolutions of the moon as of the sun and yet infinitely many of each. (ii) In *Quodlibeta* II, q.5, he reconsiders these two examples and explains that there are two ways in which 'more' and 'equal' can be taken. In one way x is said to be more than y because there are as many of x as of y and a determinate number more of x. Likewise, u is said to be equal to v because there is a determinate number in v and that number and not more are in u. Understood in this sense, it is not true that one infinity is either more than or equal to another, because no infinity constitutes a determinate number and none exceeds the other by a determinate number. Taken another way, x is said to be more than y because there are as many of x as of y and then some (but not a determinate number more); and u is said to be equal to v when u includes as many as v and no more. This way there would be more revolutions of the moon than of the sun, even if the world were eternal; and there are more parts in the whole of a line than in each half; and there are equally many parts in each of the halves. But in the former two cases, there is not a determinate number more; and in the last, not an equal number.[43]

(iii) In *Quaestiones in libros Physicorum*, q.70 and *Expositio in libros Physicorum* VI, t.79, Ockham does not distinguish senses of 'equal' but comments that equal and unequal are properties of finite numbers only, and concludes that the parts in half of a line are neither equal nor unequal to parts in the whole line. He allows that among infinities, "some are more than others when those from one part include those from another part and then some, and not vice versa," but denies that one infinity is more than another in the sense that "there is a certain number of these and a certain number of those" and the one is greater than the other.[44]

---

43. (OTh IX, 132–34).
44. *Ibid.*, (OPh VI and V).

(iv) In *Quaestiones in libros Physicorum,* q.7, Cod. Dom. 307, attributed to Ockham,[45] the author maintains that no multitude exceeds *infinities infinita*, and hence that it cannot be true to say that the parts of the whole line exceed those in part of the line; there are *infinities infinita* of both. He denies that the collection of couples exceeds the collection of unities, and denies that if the world were eternal, there would have been twelve times as many revolutions of the moon as of the sun—all of this on the ground that one infinity does not exceed another because they are beyond any determinate proportion. Nevertheless, the author allows[46] that part/whole relationships can obtain among infinities. For he allows that if God destroyed the parts in half of a line, He could not destroy more parts; but He could still destroy the parts in the other half. It is just that if He does, He will not have destroyed more by any determinate number.

It seems doubtful that Ockham's vacillation can be explained simply in terms of an equivocation on the word 'infinity', however. For in *Quodlibeta* II, q.5, he considers the objection that if the world were eternal, it would follow that "infinitely many can exist in act, as is clear if on each past day God had created one intellectual soul,"[47] and he offers two ways of responding: "first that it can be granted according to the way that infinitely many can exist in act. Otherwise, it can be said that this is not possible."[48] And he explains that the latter who deny the possibility of an actual infinity, can say that 'On each of infinitely many days God can produce a soul' is true in the sense of division, but not in the sense of composition; for each

---

45. F. Corvini, "Le 'Quaestiones in libros Physicorum' nella formazione del pensiero di Guglielmo d'Occam," *Rivista critica di storia della filosofia* XII (1957): 387–411.

46. Ockham does also in *Quodl.* II, q.5, (OTh IX, 132); *Quaest. Physicorum*, q.70, (OPh VI); and *Expos. Physicorum* VI, t.79, (OPh V).

47. (OTh IX, 129).

48. (OTh IX, 131).

day is a day on which He could have begun to produce intellectual souls.[49] If the alternative replies contradict one another,
they must mean the same thing by 'infinite'.

If Ockham's understanding of and reasons for the "no-ac-
tual-infinity" principles are unclear, its role in his arguments
against the moderns is prominent. And it is to a more detailed
examination of these that we now turn.

49. *Ibid.*

6

Quantity

1. ORIENTATION

When Descartes proclaimed that extension was the essence of body, he was advancing what was—from a medieval point of view—a radical reductionist position. Influenced by Aristotle, medievals thought the metaphysical structure of bodies much more complicated. First there was the substance which was composed of prime matter and substantial form (see Part Four, chapter 16 below); then there were various accidents, chief among which were quantity (including extension) and the sensible qualities such as color, flavor, odor, temperature, texture, etc. Descartes, in effect, eliminates prime matter and identifies the substantial form with one of the Aristotelian accidents, while explaining the other accidents away as unreal but apparent due to the confused ideas resulting from certain interactions between mind and body. His bodies are abstract mathematical images of their medieval predecessors.

For medievals, extension was merely an accident in the more inclusive Aristotelian category of quantity. Aristotle distinguished between continuous quantity, whose parts meet in a common boundary, and discrete quantity, whose parts do not meet in a common boundary. The former includes lines, whose parts meet in a point; surfaces, whose parts meet in a line; solids, whose parts meet in a line or surface; and time, whose past and future meet in the present instant. The latter includes number and, more surprisingly, speech, whose syllables are measured as long and short! I will pass over discrete quantity altogether and reserve the discussion of time for a later chapter. Here I will focus exclusively on the discussion of continuous permanent quantity—extension in one, two, or three dimensions. According to Aristotle and his medieval followers, some substances were by nature apt to have the accident of extension—viz., the ones we call bodies—and others such as angels were not. Ockham represents Aristotle as holding that whatever substance is apt to have this accident, necessarily has it, even though extension is not one of its defining properties.[1]

The most important feature extension has for Aristotle is that it is continuous, in the sense that it is composed of parts that meet in a common boundary, whose ends "touch" in the sense of being located in altogether the same place. Thus, line segment a is continuous with line segment b, because an end point of a (call it c) "touches" in the sense of existing in exactly the same place as an end point of b (call it d) —that is, because c and d exist in exactly the same place and hence are exactly the same point.[2] Given this definition of 'continuous', Aristotle finds it easy to argue that what is continuous cannot be composed of indivisible parts. For example, a given line segment could be made up of indivisible parts (in this case points), only if the points had ends that touched one another. But since points are indivisible, they do not have ends as distinct from other parts. If they "touch" one another, the whole of the point must be in exactly the same place as the whole of the other point. And no matter how many points we try to bring into contact with that point, we will never get the line extended beyond that point.[3] Analogously for surfaces and solids.[4] Consequently, Aristotle concludes that "anything continuous is divisible into parts infinitely divisible."[5] Medievals took over this doctrine from Aristotle, and Ockham makes a good deal of use of it in his arguments below.

When Locke examined the content of our idea of body, he found it to contain not only three-dimensional extension, but also impenetrablility, the tendency of a body to expel or prevent other bodies from entering or occupying the same space as

1. *Summulae Physicorum* I, c.19, 24, (OPh VI).
2. *Physics* V, 3, 227a10.
3. Cf. Ockham's *Expos. Physicorum* IV, t.1–3, (OPh V).
4. *Physics* V, 3, 227a10.
5. *Ibid*. VI, 1, 231b6–18.

it does. Impenetrability is supposed by Locke to be one of those features that distinguishes bodies from empty space, which is extended in three dimensions but not impenetrable. Aristotle, by contrast, had argued that a void is impossible.[6] And many medievals understood him to be asserting that impenetrability is a logically necessary side effect of the accident that extends bodies in three dimensions. Giles of Rome gives clear expression to this notion in his commentary on the *Physics*:

> ...a body does not occupy a place and resist another body because of its attributes, such as that it is hot or cold, heavy or light. Rather this pertains to a body because of its dimensions. For dimensions are incompatible with other dimensions through themselves, because dimensions cannot coincide with other dimensions. For if dimensions could coincide with other dimensions, it would be impossible to give a reason why two bodies could not coincide.[7]

A few dissented from this majority opinion and held that impenetrability was due to a distinct accident, which they referred to as the corpulence or the grossness (*grossities*) of a body.

Equally, many medievals thought that the accident which extends a body in three dimensions necessarily contains it in a single place. For they insisted that it was logically impossible for a single body to occupy discontinuous places simultaneously. This intuition lies behind Boethius's argument (see Part One, chapters 1 and 2 above) that genera and species cannot be numerically one, since each exists (or can exist) wholly and completely in numerically distinct things simultaneously. And combined with the above mentioned thesis—that two bodies cannot exist in the same place at once—it might seem to give

6. *Ibid*. IV, 7–9.
7. IV, t.76, (Venice, 1502), translated from the quote in Anneliese Maier, "Das Problem der Quantität oder Räumlichen Ausdehnung," *Metaphysische Hintergründe der spätscholastischen Naturphilosophie*, (Rome, 1955), 141–224; cf. 148. This excellent article outlines the history of the dispute about extension and impenetrability complete with extensive quotations. According to Maier, the above mentioned interpretation of Aristotle began with Averroes and was endorsed by Albert the Great, William of Ware, and Richard Middleton among others (147–152).

support to Aquinas's idea that matter signed by quantity is the principle of individuation for material substances (see Part One, chapter 2 above and Part Four, chapter 16 below). For reasons that we shall partly explore later, Ockham rejected both the claim that it is logically impossible for two bodies to be extended in the same place at once, and the assertion that it is logically impossible for a single body to exist in two discontinuous places at once.[8]

For medievals, it is not only the substance of body that is extended, however; so are many of its qualities. Scorates' whiteness is extended in exactly the same place at any given time as Socrates is. But if it is logically impossible for two sets of dimensions to coincide, as many of them believed, it must be that the dimensions of Socrates' qualities are the same as the dimensions of his substance. For this reason among others, many concluded that the quantity must inhere directly in the substance and the other accidents directly in the quantity.

The ontological question here is whether the accidents of continuous quantity by which bodies are extended are things (*res*) really distinct from substance and qualities. Aquinas and Scotus assumed that they were; while Peter Olivi (ca. 1248–1298) "recited" without explicitly asserting the opposite view, which Ockham later defended. Richard Middleton (fl. 1286) argued for Aquinas's position against Olivi, and Ockham's contemporaries Walter Burleigh. Franciscus de Marchia, and John Buridan joined forces against him.[9] In the remainder of this chapter, I will examine some of the issues—metaphysical, theological, and physical—that divided them on this ontological question. The problem is multifaceted; and the debate is not so conclusive as either side would have liked.

2.   THEORETICAL ARGUMENTS

Defenders of the thesis that continuous, permanent quantity

---

8. Cf. *Rep.* IV, q.6 (OTh VII, 97–98).
9. Cf. Maier, *op. cit.*

is a thing really distinct from substance and quality, respectively, thought that this could be established conclusively on the
basis of theoretical considerations in at least three ways. (2.1) In
one group of arguments, Richard Middleton contends that
the opposite would destroy the distinctions among Aristotle's ten categories. For to each distinct category, there corresponds a distinct sort of thing. But if quantity is not really
distinct from substance and quality, respectively, then it is really the same. Thus, one and the same individual would be *per
se* and essentially a substance and *per se* and essentially a
quality—both of which are impossible if substance, quantity,
and quality are three distinct categories as Aristotle says they
are. Alternatively, if quantity is really the same as substance and
quality, respectively, then, by the Indiscernibility of Identicals,
whatever is truly asserted about one is truly asserted about the
other. But the length and width of a volume of fire are of the
same species as the length and width of a volume of air, because
such lengths and widths fall under the same species of quantity.
If the length and width of fire is really the same as the fire, and
the length and width of the air is really the same as the air, it will
follow that air and fire are of the same species. On the other
hand, starting with the premiss that air and fire are elemental
substances of different species, we will have to conclude that
the length and width of the fire is of a different species from the
length and width of the air—which seems equally absurd.[10]

10. According to Maier, *op. cit.*, 157–58, Richard Middleton raises such
arguments against a position recited by Peter Olivi. She is convinced that
Ockham was conscious of the similarities between his and Olivi's positions
and his trying to defend his own theory by rebutting Middleton's criticisms of
Olivi (181–86). Ockham cites the arguments that "...No accident is the same
as substance. But every quantity is an accident, since it is in a category of accident..." (*Quodl.* IV, q.25, (OTh IX, 416)) and "Aristotle lays down nine
categories of accidents among which he numbers quantity. Therefore, quantity is a distinct category and consequently has its own individuals..." (*ibid.*,
q.27, (OTh IX, 434); cf. *Rep.* IV, q.6, (OTh VII, 81). Likewise, he lists the
argument that "...It is impossible for the same thing to be *per se* an individual
of substance and an individual of quality. Therefore, it is impossible for the
same thing to be *per se* an individual of substance and an individual of quantity. The premiss is true and the inference is clear, because quantity is just as

(2.2) A second sort of argument rests on the assumption discussed in chapter 5 above, that

(A) There can be no passage from contradictory to contradictory without the generation or corruption of some thing (*res*).

Focussing on the matter of the body of Christ that exists unextended in the Eucharist (see section 4 below), they reason that it is possible for matter to be first not extended and then extended apart from the generation or corruption of any substance, or any part of substance (whether of the matter or of the substantial form), or of any quality. Consequently, there must be some other thing—a quantity—that is really distinct from substance, the essential parts of substance, and quality, which is generated or corrupted when 'Matter is extended' or 'Matter is not extended' changes truth-value.[11] A similar argument could be given for changes in the truth-value of propositions such as 'This volume of fire occupies four cubic feet'.

(2.3) Some of Olivi's and Ockham's opponents held that it is logically impossible for two bodies to be extended in the same place at once. But all thought that this was naturally impossible, and regarded this consideration as an insurmountable objection to the view that quantity is nothing really distinct from extended substance and extended quality:

> ...It is impossible in the natural course of things for two bodies to exist in the same place at once. But substance and quality exist at the same place at once. Therefore, if each is a quantity and a body, then two bodies would exist in the same place at once. Indeed, as many bodies would exist naturally in the same place at once as there are natural

essentially predicted of its individuals as substance or quality of its individuals" (*Quodl.* IV, q.25, (OTh IX, 417–18)). According to Maier, this argument was also used by Richard Middleton against Peter Olivi (*op. cit.*, 157) and is cited together with Ockham's reply to it by Franciscus de Marchia (202).

11. *Rep.* IV, q.6, (OTh VII, 81).

qualities existing simultaneously together with substance—say flavor, color, odor, sweetness, heat, etc.[12]

Likewise, on Ockham's view, the prime matter and the substantial form of a substance would each have its own extension and be quantified. "...Therefore, either one thing cannot be made from them, or two quantified things will have one and the same place."[13]

Ockham's opposition to the *a priori* principles on which the first two sets of arguments rest runs as deep as any philosophical disagreement can go. (R2.1) Ockham is in sympathy with the desire to preserve the distinctions among Aristitle's ten categories. But where arguments of the first group assume that distinctions among the categories are at bottom distinctions among kinds of things, Ockham insists that they are distinctions among kinds of names and ways of signifying:

> ...I maintain that substance, quality, and quantity are distinct categories, although 'quantity' does not signify any absolute thing distinct from substance and quality. For they are distinct concepts and spoken sounds that signify the same things in different ways; and because they signify them in different ways, they are not synonymous names. For 'substance' signifies all of its significata in one way— namely, directly; 'quantity' signifies the same thing in a different way—namely, it signifies the whole directly and its parts obliquely, since it signifies the whole substance and connotes that it has one part at a distance from another. Likewise, for quality...[14]

If 'quantity' were an absolute term the way 'substance' and 'whiteness' are, then Middleton's arguments would pose serious

12. *Quodl.* IV, q.25, (OTh IX, 417); *Treatise on Quantity* I, q.3, (Birch ed., 118–19); *Treatise on Quantity* II, c.40, (Birch ed., 472–75). This objection was raised against Olivi by Richard Middleton; and it is repeated with Ockham's reply by Franciscus de Marchia; cf. Maier, *op. cit.*, 158, 163 and 203.

13. *Rep.* IV, q.6, (OTh VII, 82).

14. *Quodl.* IV, q.27, (OTh IX, 436); cf. V, q.22, (OTh IX, 566); *Rep.* IV, q.6, (OTh VII, 71–72, 84); *Summa logicae* I, c.44, (OPh I, 136–37); *Treatise on Quantity* I, q.3, (Birch ed., 94–96); *Treatise on Quantity* II, c.35, (Birch ed., 428–435).

difficulties. If the concept of *F* is an absolute concept, then it is true of any individual thing *x* that falls under the concept of *F*, that *x* is essentially *F*. Thus, if both the concept of substance and the concept of quantity were absolute concepts, then any individual thing *x* that simultaneously fell under both would be both essentially a substance and essentially a quantity. But where the concept of *F* is a connotative concept, it is not true in general that what in fact falls under the concept of *F* is essentially *F*. Ockham maintains that the concept of quantity is a connotative concept that signifies a substance or quality directly and connotes that their parts exist in a certain way; yet he disagrees with Aristotle in thinking that anything that falls under that concept could exist without falling under that concept.[15] Thus, Ockham's claim that quantity is not really distinct from substance or quality reduces to the thesis that really the same thing simultaneously falls, or is apt to fall, under the absolute concept of substance or quality and the connotative concept of quantity. And we can say that this thing is in two categories at once, if this is all we mean by it. But it will not follow further that one and the same individual *x* is both essentially a substance and essentially a quantity or both essentially a quality and essentially a quantity. Further, Ockham sees no difficulty in saying that while air and fire "are of different species in the genus of substance," "the length of the fire and the length of the air which are not distinct from the fire and the air, [respectively], are of the same species in the category of quantity."[16] For although the thing that is fire is of a different kind from the thing that is air, they have their respective parts at a distance from one another in the same sort of way.

(R2.2) Ockham's reasons for rejecting (A) and replacing it with

(A′) Necessarily, if first *p* is true and then not-*p* is true, then either some thing (*res*) has been produced in existence for the first time, or something that did exist has ceased

15. *Rep.* IV, q.6, (OTh VII, 78).
16. *Quodl.* IV, q.25, (OTh IX, 417).

to exist, or some locomotion has (potentially or actually) occurred

have already been examined in some detail in chapter 5 above. But while the importance of this move should not be underestimated, it will erode the opponents' present argument only if (A') does not sustain it as well as (A) does. Ockham argues that it will not. We can explain why 'Matter is not extended' is first false and then true by a locomotion of the parts of matter in which they come to be at a distance from one another after not being at a distance from one another. Likewise, 'This fire occupies four cubic feet' can be first true and then false if its parts are first at a certain distance from one another and they by locomotion come to be at a greater or lesser distance from one another.[17] This contention of Ockham's was contested in a lively debate over how to explain the phenomena of condensation and rarefaction, which will be examined in section 3 below.

(R2.3) Ockham finds it undiscriminating of his opponents to lump all the cases of extended things together under one general prohibition: that it is naturally impossible for two bodies to be extended in the same place at once. For "although any dimensions could exist in the same place by divine power," it is not even naturally "incompatible with all dimensions to exist in the same place at once."[18] It would be naturally impossible for "dimensions that can naturally subsist through themselves"—i.e., for two extended substances—to exist in the same place at once.[19] Likewise, it is naturally impossible for "...many accidents of the same species to exist in the same place" at once.[20] But where one extended thing is naturally apt to combine with the other extended thing in such a way as to make something one *per se*, as prime matter and substantial form are, or one *per accidens*, as a substance and its qualities are; or where a number of extended qualities are apt to

17. *Rep.* IV, q.6, (OTh VII, 78–79).
18. *Treatise on Quantity* II, c.40, (Birch ed., 472–74).
19. *Ibid*.
20. *Rep.* IV, q.6, (OTh VII, 87–88).

simultaneously inhere in the same substance, as the color, flavor, odor, temperature, etc. are, then it is not impossible for those really distinct things to be extended in the same place at once.[21]

3. THE DEBATE OVER CONDENSATION AND RAREFACTION

Richard Middleton not only thought that the real distinction of quantity from substance and quality could be proved *a priori*, he maintained that its denial is "contrary to our experience" of condensation and rarefaction.[22] Ockham records the following version of this argument from Pseudo-Campsall:

> ...experience teaches that something is lost in condensation. But not substance or quality, according to the Philosopher in Book IV of the *Physics*. Therefore, a quantity is corrupted and not the substance [or quality]. Therefore, they are really distinct...[23]

Ockham counters that "this experience tells in the opposite direction."[24] Thus, both parties purport to subject the other's metaphysical theory to an empirical test.

To speak of rarefaction and condensation in contrast to growth and decline, is to presuppose something that Ockham never makes explicit: viz., that we have some measure of the amount of a substance or quality that is independent of its extension. Franciscus de Marchia proposes to label the former "the quantity of the mass" (*quantitas molis*) of a substance or quality and to regard extension as a variable mode of that property.[25] Growth is a change in which new parts of the substance or quality are added to the so-called "quantity of its

21. *Ibid.*; *Quodl.* I, q.4, (OTh IX, 28); *Treatise on Quantity* I, q.3, (Birch ed., 140–43); *Treatise on Quantity* II, c.40, (Birch ed., 472–74).
22. Cf. Maier, *op. cit.*, 157.
23. *Quodl.* IV, q.25, (OTh IX, 417); cf. *Treatise on Quantity* I, q.3, (Birch ed., 116–19).
24. *Quodl.* IV, q.25, (OTh IX, 420).
25. Cf. Maier, *op. cit.*, 142, 206.

mass''; decline, one in which such parts of substance and quality are lost. By contrast, in rarefaction and condensation, "the
quantity of the mass" remains constant: parts of the substance
or quality are neither added nor lost. Rather the extension of
that quantity is increased or decreased, respectively. The question at issue is whether such a change in extension involves the
generation or corruption of any thing (*res*) that is really distinct
from substance and quality and that serves as a mean between
them, inhering directly in substance and having the qualities inhere in it.

Ockham argues that an affirmative answer combines with
two generally accepted principles to yield a result contrary to
experience. The first is the claim that

(B) Accidents do not migrate from subject to subject.

Ockham joined his predecessors and contemporaries in endorsing and attributing to Aristotle the belief that accidents as well as
substances are individuated. Thus, there are not only particular
shades of whiteness, but particular instances of a given shade.
Some, including Aquinas, took (B) to be a necessary truth,
"since the subject is the principle of individuation of the
accidents."[26] What makes the whiteness in this wall numerically distinct from the whiteness in that wall, is that the former inheres in this wall and the latter inheres in that wall. For Aquinas,
it is logically impossible that *numerically* the same whiteness
inhere in numerically distinct subjects simultaneously. And it is
also logically impossible that numerically the same whiteness
that now inheres in this wall should at any time "migrate" over
to that wall and inhere in it instead. Ockham, of course, could
not have had this reason for regarding (B) as a necessary truth.
For he denies that anything is individuated by something extrinsic to it (see Part One, chapter 2 above). And he thinks that
individual qualities could retain their individuation when
separated from any and every subject of inherence. But Ockham
does agree that it is naturally impossible that numerically the

26. *Summa theologiae* III, q.77, a.2; cf. a.1.

same thing should inhere in first one subject and then another.[27] And since condensation and rarefaction are natural phenomena, no adequate account of them will violate (B). (Of course, this does not mean that the whiteness that now inheres in a board and not in a table could not come to inhere in a table—say, when the board is used to make a table. But this apparent counterexample to (B) would be explained away by distinguishing the first subject of inherence—that in which the form inheres in the first instance—from the subject of inherence broadly speaking. In this case, the board or its surface is the first subject of inherence for the whiteness; the table is its subject of inherence only in an extended sense.)

The second principle assumes a distinction between two ways in which one thing may be in another: a thing is definitively in another if it is whole in the whole and whole in each part; circumscriptively in another, if it is whole in the whole and part in the parts.[28] It is then maintained that

(C) One thing exists circumscriptively in another, only if there is a proper proportion between them.

Scotus and Ockham take (C) to imply that in circumscriptive inherence the subject can be no more complex than what inheres is. Thus, a simple thing that has no parts can exist in a composite subject only definitively. (This is the way the intellectual soul exists in the body; see Part Four, chapter 15 below.) And where a form inheres circumscriptively in a complex subject, there must be at least one part of form for every part of the subject of inherence. Ockham thinks that if the form in question is of a property that can be had in more or less intense degree, then more than one part of the inherent form can exist in the same part of its first subject. For example, a physical object may be white in a less intense degree when one part of whiteness inheres in each part of the physical object, and white in a more intense degree when more than one part of whiteness inheres in

---

27. *Treatise on Quantity* II, c.18, (Birch ed., 254–55).
28. Cf. *Rep.* IV, q.6, (OTh VII, 65); *Quodl.* IV, q.21, (OTh IX, 400–401).

each part of that object. But since a thing cannot be more or less a man or any other sort of substance, there can be only one part of substantial form for each part of the matter in which it inheres.[29]

Given (B) and (C) and focussing on condensation and rarefaction, Ockham hopes to convince us of the absurdity of saying that quantity is a thing really distinct from substance and serves as a mean between them. I think we can readily grasp the strategy of these arguments by focussing on an example.[30] Suppose, for the sake of argument, that there are ten quarts of air to start with. According to the theory Ockham is opposing, the air is ten quarts full because there is something that is really distinct from the substance of the air—call it the form of ten-quart-hood—that inheres in the substance of the air and extends it throughout a ten quarter volume, and that serves as a mean between the substance of the air and its qualities. Now suppose that the air is rarified until it occupies an eleven quart volume. Either the whole of the form of ten-quarthood is corrupted in this process, or it is not. Ockham's opponents presumably wanted to say that when air is rarified from ten quarts to eleven quarts, the whole form of ten-quarthood is corrupted and a new form of eleven-quarthood is produced in the air. Ockham charges that this assumption has absurd consequences on their view. For they hold that the form of ten-quarthood is at first the subject in which the qualities of the air directly inhere. Given (B), however, it is impossible for numerically the same qualities to inhere first in the form of ten-quarthood and then in the form of eleven-quarthood. Consequently, if they say that the whole form of ten-quarthood is corrupted in the rarefaction of the air, they will have to admit that all of the qualities of the air are

29. *Ord.* I, d.17, q.7, (OTh III, 538).

30. Ockham offers such arguments as Aristotle's in *Summa logicae* I, c.44, (OPh I, 132–33) and on his own behalf in *Ord.* I, d.17, q.7, (OTh III, 538–39); *Treatise on Quantity* I, q.3, (Birch ed., 114, 132); *Treatise on Quantity* II, c.22, (Birch ed., 280–82) and c.34, (Birch ed., 408–414) and c.37, (Birch ed., 452–58); *Quodl.* IV, q.25, (OTh IX, 418–424) and q.28, (OTh IX, 441–45); *Summulae Physicorum* III, c.12, 62–63, (OPh VI).

destroyed as well. In fact, since the rarefaction of the air from a ten quart to an eleven quart volume is continuous, the air will successively assume infinitely many different volumes; and they will be committed to the consequence that infinitely many quantities and qualities are generated and corrupted during the interval in which the air is rarified from ten to eleven quarts. The same conclusion will follow if only part of the form of ten-quarthood is corrupted—say a one-quarthood part—and replaced with a new one—say a two-quarthood part.

The other possibility is that the form of ten-quarthood is not corrupted, whether wholly or partly, but a new part of quantity—a new one-quarthood—is added to the already quantified substance. Ockham asks what the first subject of this new one-quarthood could be. On the one hand, he reasons that there is no more reason why one part of the air should receive the new one-quarthood than the other. Therefore, either all would receive a new one-quarthood—which is impossible, in part for the reasons just given—or none would. Even leaving this objection aside, Ockham's opponents would be hard pressed to give a satisfactory answer. For each of the ten equal parts of the air already has a part of the quantity—say a one-quarthood—inhering in it. By (C), we cannot say that any part of the air comes to have two one-quarthoods inhering in it, because filling a one quart volume is not a property that can be had in more or less intense degrees. The only way for the new one-quarthood to inhere in the air would be for it to displace one of the old one-quarthoods. But this is doubly impossible. First, because then the qualities of the air that inhered in the old one-quarthood would be corrupted and new ones would be generated. Second, because then the old one-quarthood would exist without inhering in any subject—which is naturally impossible, while rarefaction as a natural phenomenon must be explained in terms of what is naturally possible. One cannot say that the new one-quarthood that is added exists without inhering in any part of the subject, for the same reason. Nor can one say that the displaced, old one-quarthood is simply corrupted, because then the air would occupy a ten quart volume at the end of the process as well as at the beginning.

Suppose instead that the air is condensed from ten quarts to nine quarts. This cannot simply involve the corruption of the whole form of ten-quarthood and its replacement with a newly produced form of nine-quarthood, for the reasons detailed above in connection with rarefaction. It would seem, then, that the only way to effect the reduction in volume, according to the opponents' theory, is by corrupting one of the one-quarthood parts of quantity, leaving the remaining nine to inhere in the substance. If a one-quarthood part of the quantity is corrupted, however, either the part of the air in which it inhered will remain unquantified, or it will acquire a part of quantity that inhered in one of the other parts of the air. But it is naturally impossible for any corporeal substance such as air to exist unquantified; and since condensation is a natural phenomenon, it must be explained in terms of what is naturally possible. The second alternative cannot be simply that the part of air that has lost its one-quarthood acquires the one-quarthood that used to inhere in another part of the air, for then the latter part would exist unquantified. The proposal must be that all of the parts of quantity "scoot over" so that the nine parts that used to inhere in nine parts of the air, now inhere in the ten parts. But this violates (B).

Given this ingenious argument, Ockham feels entitled to the following conclusion:

> ...Thus, on the basis of all of these things, I maintain that substance is condensed, because—by virtue of an efficient cause and apart from any quantity in between [substance and quality]—its parts are now spatially closer together and less distant from one another now than they were before. And they are that way apart from the loss of any substance or quantity...[31]

Likewise, simple locomotion explains why the parts of a rarified substance or quality are further apart than they were before, without the gain of any new parts of quantity really distinct

---

31. *Quodl.* IV, q.25, (OTh IX, 420–21); cf. *Treatise on Quantity* II, c.37, (Birch ed. 456–58); *Quaest. Physicorum*, q.99, quoted by Maier, *op. cit.*, 192–93.

from substance and quality.[32]

All Ockham really shows, however, is that his opponents cannot adequately explain the commonly experienced phenomena of condensation and rarefaction without accepting the consequence that infinitely many quantities and qualities are corrupted in the process of condensation and rarefaction. But Ockham cannot plausibly regard the latter as contrary to experience. For since the newly generated qualities would be of exactly the same kind as the ones destroyed, we would not be able to tell just by looking whether the qualities were numerically the same as before or not. Nor would this admission entail a simultaneously existing actual infinity. If there are finitely many qualities in the air to begin with, there will be finitely many qualities of the same kind at each instant in the condensing or rarefying process. And no one had said that an actual infinity of things through time was logically impossible. It remains for Ockham to resort to a slash with his famous razor: if neither reason nor any infallible authority requires us to assume such infinities, and if the experienced phenomena can be explained without them, then such a plurality would be assumed without any necessity.

Ockham's opponents did not see this appeal to Ockham's razor as settling the matter. For John Buridan renewed Middleton's charge that experience shows locomotion to be an inadequate explanation of condensation and rarefaction. And Buridan bolstered this contention with an appeal to experiments. He reports that he was able to rarify and condense air quite a lot if he heated and cooled it, respectively. But if he opened a pair of bellows as wide as they would go and then plugged the opening, he was unable to effect a noticeable decrease in the volume. Again, if he opened the bellows only half way and plugged the opening, he was unable to effect a noticeable increase in the volume. Buridan challenges those who, like Ockham, explain condensation and rarefaction in terms of locomotion, to account for these facts:

32. *Treatise on Quantity* II, c.34, (Birch ed., 414–420).

...I can move bodies by pushing or pulling them. What prevents me, then, from being able to compress the parts of air simultaneously, condensing them to obtain a smaller place? Matter is not the obstacle, since more matter could exist in a much smaller place. Nor is the substantial form of air the obstacle, since that whole form is made to exist in a smaller place when the air is condensed by cooling it, as has been said. Nor is heat the obstacle, according to them, for much more heat could exist in at least as small a place, since much more heat exists in a small, red hot piece of iron...[33]

Buridan thinks these experiments force us to conclude that there is something else in the air—really distinct from its matter, its substantial form, or its natural quality of heat—that resists his efforts to move the parts of the air closer together or further apart in these cases. He labels this thing "magnitude." Thus, Buridan meets the appeal to Ockham's razor by insisting that

...it is not useless to assume this sort of magnitude, since arguments have been found that force us to assume it. And it is clear from these arguments that this magnitude is just as much or more useful in nature than whiteness or blackness is.[34]

Once again, a really distinct accident of quantity is invoked to explain the impenetrability of a body.

Apparently Ockham's successors were in some degree swayed by Buridan's reasoning.[35] In my view, neither they nor Ockham should have been impressed. Buridan says that since I can move physical objects by pushing or pulling them, then, if condensation and rarefaction were merely the effects of locomotion, I could effect a noticeable condensation or rarefaction in the air. But Buridan has not observed that I can move any and every physical object by pushing it. In his experiments, he finds that he cannot move the parts of air by pushing or pulling them. And it hardly follows from the fact that I can move some physical objects—say chairs and dishes—by pushing them, that

33. *Quaestiones super octo libros Physicorum*, q.8, translated from Maier's quotation, *op. cit.*, 214–15.
34. *Ibid.*, translated from Maier's quotation, *op. cit.*, 217.
35. Cf. Maier, *op. cit.*, 218–222.

since I cannot move a house by pushing it, the house cannot be moved by pushing it but only by the generation or corruption of some form inhering in the house. A sufficiently large bulldozer or truck can move the house by pushing it. Nor does it follow from the fact that it is not impossible for the air to exist in a smaller place, that nothing about the substantial form of the air could account for my inability to move the air particles in such cases. It might be that the air is of such a nature that its particles are apt to be moved further apart only by heating or closer together only by cooling. The latter would explain Buridan's observations without assuming any dimensions or magnitudes really distinct from substance and quality.

In general, the assumption that an appeal to experience could settle this metaphysical dispute seems misguided. Experience confronts us with the phenomena—including condensation and rarefaction—that any adequate theory has to take account of. But what Middleton and Buridan do by adding quantitative forms to the ontology, Ockham manages by appeals to locomotion and the nature of the substantial and accidental forms already admitted. The former have not demonstrated any failure in Ockham's theory to account for condensation and rarefaction. And Ockham has not shown their theory to be in violation of experience of the principle of contradiction here, but only of Ockham's razor.

4.   THEOLOGICAL ARGUMENTS

Medieval Christians believed that when in the sacrament of the Eucharist or Holy Communion the priest repeats Jesus' words at his last supper with his disciples—"This is my body" and "This is my blood"—the bread and wine actually become the body and blood of Christ. The doctrine of transubstantiation was developed to explain how this happens. And, strange as it may seem to modern secular thinkers, medieval ideas about body were shaped as much by the constraints of this doctrine as by anything that Aristotle ever said. Indeed, philosophers continued to measure the adequacy of a philosophy of body in terms of its ability to make room for transubstantiation down to the seventeenth century when Descartes' theory is charged with a failure to do so.[36] According to the doctrine of transubstantiation, when the priest says the above mentioned formulae, the substance of the bread and wine are converted into the substance of the body and blood of Christ, respectively. The substances of bread and wine, both their matter and their substantial forms, cease to exist, but their accidents remain. And the body and blood of Christ are said to exist under those respective accidents and so to be present in the Eucharist. Nevertheless, these accidents do not come to inhere in the body and blood of Christ, but exist without being the accidents of any substance.

Prima facie, the doctrine of transubstantiation as summarized so far seems inconsistent with that medieval conception of body according to which it is logically impossible for two bodies to be extended in the same place at once and logically impossible for a single body to be extended in two discontinuous places at once. For if the accidents of bread and wine do not inhere in the body and blood of Christ, respectively, then it seems that two sets of dimensions—those of the accidents and those of the body and blood of Christ—exist together in the same place at once. Further, since it is assumed that the body and blood of Christ remain extended in heaven, and that they may come to exist simultaneously on different altars, it seems that a single body is simultaneously extended in many spatially discontinuous places.

Theologians who thought that extended bodies were necessarily impenetrable and necessarily contained in the place in which they are extended moved to resolve the difficulty by denying that the body and blood of Christ are present in the Eucharist in such a way as to be extended in the same place in which the accidents of the bread and wine are extended, respectively. That way, the body of Christ will be said to be extended in only one place, in heaven, and to be simultaneously

36. Arnauld's objections, *The Philosophical Works of Descartes*, ed. and trans. Haldane and Ross, (Cambridge, 1911–1912), vol.II, 95 and 116–122.

present, without being extended, on many spatially discontinuous altars. Aquinas says that by virtue of the conversion, the body of Christ exists in the Eucharist only "in the manner of substance"; that its quantity does not exist there by virtue of the conversion, but only "by natural concomitance"; and that, consequently, the body of Christ is not extended in the Eucharist but is only present to place mediately, by means of the accidents of the bread, which are extended in the place.[37] Scotus, on the other hand, tries to distinguish two senses of position—that which is a differentia of quantity and that which is a separate category. The first has to do with the order of the parts in the whole; the second with the order of the parts in place. Any body will have the former sort of position. But it may have the former without the latter. Given this distinction, Scotus thinks that he can formulate the doctrine of transubstantiation without contradicting the necessary impenetrability and necessary containment of extended bodies.[38]

Ockham's judgment is that both Aquinas's and Scotus's account of how the body of Christ can be present in the Eucharist without being extended in the same place as the accidents are extended, involve insurmountable difficulties.[39] But given the weight of theological opinion against saying that the body and blood of Christ are extended in the Eucharist, Ockham felt obliged to offer an alternative explanation, based on the above mentioned medieval distinction between a thing's being circumscriptively and definitively in place. A thing is circumscriptively in place, if it is whole in the whole place and part in each part of the place. This is the way bodies exist in a place when they are extended in it. By contrast, a thing exists definitively in place, if it is whole in the whole place and whole in each part of the place.[40] This is the way that an angel, which is an indivisible

37. *Summa theologiae* III, q.76, a.1 and ad 3; a.4 and ad 2–3; a.5 and ad 1.

38. See *Rep.* IV, q.6, (OTh VII, 65–66).

39. *Ibid.*, (OTh VII, 63–64, 67–70).

40. *Ibid.*, (OTh VII, 65); *Quodl.* I, q.4, (OTh IX, 25); IV, q.21, (OTh IX, 400–401).

incorporeal substance, exists in place.[41] Ockham says that in fact the body and blood of Christ do not exist circumscriptively in place in the Eucharist, but only definitively. Therefore, it is not the case either that the body and blood of Christ are extended in the same place as the accidents of the bread and wine are, or that the body and blood of Christ are simultaneously extended in discontinuous places.

Ockham considers the objection that angels can exist definitively in place because they are indivisible. But it does not follow that a material substance can exist definitively in place. For the latter is divisible into parts. If it exists definitively in place, that means all of its parts will exist at the same place—which might seem impossible if bodies are necessarily impenetrable. He replies that it is no less possible for a material than for a spiritual substance to exist definitively in place. Nor does he see any impossibility in two parts of a material substance simultaneously occupying the same place. After all, Ockham observes, this happens naturally every time something is condensed; for condensation is simply a process in which parts that earlier existed in different places come to exist in the same place. Further, Ockham contends, the gospels provide us with numerous examples of two whole bodies being simultaneously extended in the same place: e.g., the virgin birth of Christ in which His body is said to have passed through the closed womb of the Virgin, Christ's passing through a closed door after the resurrection, and His ascending through unopened clouds into heaven.[42] If the Bible says so, it must not be logically impossible for two whole bodies to be simultaneously extended in the same place at once; and a fortiori, numerically distinct parts of the same body will be able to do so.

On the other hand, Ockham reasons, there is no more difficulty in numerically the same body existing definitively in the same places at once than there is with the intellectual soul's being whole in the whole body and whole in its many parts, or in

41. *Ibid.* I, q.4, (OTh IX, 26).
42. *Rep.* IV, q.6, (OTh VII, 80, note 1); *Quodl.* IV, q.31, (OTh IX, 453); *Treatise on Quantity* II, c.6, (Birch ed., 192–93).

an angel's existing whole in the whole of a place and whole in its many parts.[43] If it is objected that intellectual souls and angels do not exist simultaneously in discontinuous places definitively, Ockham will reply that this is so in the natural course of things, but they can exist definitively in discontinuous places simultaneously by divine power.[44] In drawing his conclusion, Ockham moves beyond it to another:

> Therefore, I hold that the same body can exist in different places definitively. But the body of Christ coexists principally with the host and with each part of it. Therefore, likewise, how much more can it be present to distinct places in such a way that it is whole in the whole and part in the part—[i.e., how much more can it be circumscriptively in place].[45]

Let P_1 and P_2 be discontinuous places and B be a body; for the sake of simplicity, let a and b be the parts of P_1, c and d the parts of P_2, and e and f the parts of B (of course, each of P_1, P_2, and B and likewise a, b, c, d, e, and f is infinitely divisible on the Aristotelian assumption of continuity). If both of e and f can exist simultaneously in each of a, b, c, and d and hence if B can exist definitively in P_1 and P_2 at once, then it would be even easier for e to exist in a and c and f in b and d and hence for B to exist circumscriptively in P_1 and P_2 at once. To achieve the latter given the former, it is necessary only to take e away from b and d and f away from a and c. This being so, Ockham concludes that not only can a corporeal substance "exist in various places at once," "it can exist everywhere by divine power" though "not by any force of its own."[46] And even though the body and blood of Christ do exist in the Eucharist definitively, they could exist there circumscriptively without any logical difficulty.[47]

Even leaving aside disagreements about the impenetrabiity and containment of extended bodies, however, some thought

43. *Rep.* IV, q.6, (OTh VI, 79); *Quodl.* IV, q.31, (OTh IX, 453).

44. *Ibid.* I, q.4, (OTh IX, 28); q.12, (OTh IX, 70).

45. *Rep.* IV, q.6, (OTh VII, 80, note 1); cf. *Quodl.* IV, q.13, (OTh IX, 360–62).

46. *Rep.* IV, q.6, (OTh VII, 97).

47. *Ibid.*, q.8, (OTh VII, 147).

that the ontological question about quantity could be settled conclusively against Olivi and Ockham from the demands of the doctrine of transubstantiation. (4.1) First of all, they reasoned, if quantity is not a thing distinct from substance and quality, which inheres in the substance directly and is the immediate subject of the qualities, then when the substance of the bread is converted into the substance of the body of Christ, the qualities of the bread would exist without inhering in any subject at all. Aquinas thought this was impossible, in part because qualitites are individuated by their subjects (see section 3 above). If the qualities existed without any and every subject, then they would exist unindividuated—which is impossible.

On the other hand, if they inhere in a really distinct accident of quantity, that will suffice to individuate them, since the parts of dimensive quantity are individuated of themselves.[48]

(4.2) Second, the doctrine of transubstantiation requires them to hold that

(D) The *substance* of the bread and wine is converted into the *substance* of the body and blood of Christ, respectively.

But if quantity is nothing really distinct from the substance and qualities that are extended, it will be necessary to grant that

(E) The *quantity* of the bread and wine are converted into the substance of the body and blood of Christ, respectively,

and

(F) The substance of the bread and wine is converted into the *quantity* of the body and blood of Christ,

neither of which should be allowed.[49]

48. *Summa theologiae* III, q.77, a.2; cf. Part Four, chapter 6 below.
49. *Quodl.* IV, q.26, (OTh IX, 425–26); *Treatise on Quantity* I, q.3, (Birch ed., 118–121); *Treatise on Quantity* II, c.31, (Birch ed., 360–61).

(R4.1) Ockham does not regard the first argument as insurmountable. He merely points out that quantity is also an accident and as such depends on substance more than quality could
depend on quantity. Consequently, if God can preserve quantity in existence without the substance in which it inhered, a fortiori He can preserve qualitites in existence apart from any really distinct quantity. And if it is replied that this is not so, since
qualities depend on quantity for their individuation, but the
parts of dimensive quantity are individuated of themselves,
Ockham will reply that nothing is individuated by anything extrinsic to it, but everything is individuated in and of itself. Indeed, Ockham charges, his opponents' view is unphilosophical.
For if quantity is the immediate subject of the accidents,
then quantity would be subject to contraries; whereas the
Philosopher maintains that only substance is subject to contraries.[50] Similarly, this contention seems to be at odds with
various authorities in theology.[51]

(R4.2) To the second, Ockham replies that the allegedly objectionable claims in (E) and (F) can both be understood as true,
taken literally, although we can conceive of cases in which (D)
would be true and (E) and (F) false. For provided that the bread
exists extended somewhere,

> ...it should be granted that the quantity that is the substance of the
> bread is converted into the body of Christ, just as it is granted that the
> substance of the bread is converted into the body of Christ. Nor does
> the opposite appear to be found in any authoritative writing. Thus, in
> all such arguments the definition of quantity should be put in place of
> the noun to see what follows. For the definition of quantity is 'a thing
> that has one part situated at a distance from another part'. Therefore,
> just as 'The thing or substance of the bread that has one part at a
> distance from another is converted into the body of Christ' should be
> granted, so 'The quantity of the bread is converted into the body of
> Christ' should be granted, taken literally.[52]

50. Presented as Aristotle's argument in *Summa logicae* I, c.44, (OPh I,
132), as also found in *Treatise on Quantity* II, c.22, (Birch ed., 280) and
Treatise on Quantity I, q.3, (Birch ed., 114).

51. *Treatise on Quantity* II, c.21, (Birch ed., 266–279).

52. *Quodl.* IV, q.26, (OTh IX, 427–28); *Treatise on Quantity* I, q.3,
(Birch ed., 142–45); *Treatise on Quantity* II, c.31, (Birch ed., 364–371).

Analogously, if the body of Christ exists extended somewhere, then

> literally speaking, the proposition 'Substance is converted into the quantity of the body of Christ' should be granted, just as the proposition 'Bread is converted into the substance of the body of Christ' is. This is clear, putting the definition in place of the noun as before. For the proposition 'The bread is converted into the substance of the body of Christ that has one part at a distance from another—viz., in heaven' is true. Therefore, the other is equivalently true.[53]

On the other hand, if the bread existed only definitively and nowhere circumscriptively in place, (D) could be true when (E) was false; and if the body of Christ existed only definitively and nowhere circumscriptively in place, (D) could be true when (F) was false. For in those cases, the bread and the body of Christ would not have one part at a distance from another and so would not be signified by the term 'quantity'.

If it is objected that (F) entails that the body of Christ comes to exist under the host circumscriptively, Ockham denies it.

> ...For putting the definition of quantity in place of the noun, the proposition 'The quantity of the body of Christ begins to exist under the host or exists under the host' should be granted. ...But the proposition 'The body of Christ exists quantified and circumscriptively in place under the host by virtue of the conversion' is false, just as the proposition 'The body of Christ has one part outside another under the host by virtue of the conversion' is false.[54]

Thus, if one does the simple exercise of substituting his definition of quantity in place of the noun 'quantity', one will see that (E) and (F) are innocuous. In the *Treatise on Quantity* I, q.3, Ockham emphasizes that they are not only harmless, but

> their opposite is not found in the Bible or in the claims of the Saints or in canon law or in any authoritative book, although it is found in the writings of some who are condemned by many Catholics and solemn doctors. I do

---

53. *Quodl.* IV, q.26, (OTh IX, 429).

54. *Ibid.*, (OTh IX, 429–430); *Treatise on Quantity* I, q.3, (Birch ed., 148–151); *Treatise on Quantity* II, c.31, (Birch ed., 374–79).

not say that they condemn them as heretics but as holding false opinions. Thus, the Subtle Doctor condemns the Common and the Solemn Doctor and all those in whose writings the opposite is found, so far as many of their opinions are concerned. Likewise, many Catholic doctors condemn the Subtle Doctor in many of his theses. Therefore, although they are found to conclude the opposite of the [above propositions], one should not worry about it very much, since none of them is regarded as authoritative, although they should generally be referred to because when they have said something false, they stimulate our minds and offer us a greater occasion for discovering the truth.[55]

Like Olivi, Ockham thinks his opponents have made a natural mistake of confusing their own philosophical opinion with Catholic dogma.

(4.3) Since Ockham's teaching on quantity was challenged as theologically suspect, he found it prudent to join Olivi in retaliating with a theological defense. In at least five works,[56] Ockham offers the following *reductio ad absurdum* argument to show that his opponent's view of quantity is inconsistent with the doctrine of divine omnipotence.

Suppose 1. Quantity is an accident really distinct from substance, by virtue of which alone the substance in which it inheres is quantified. (Opponent's View)

2. God, as omnipotent, can conserve a substance while destroying all the accidents that are really distinct from it without changing the location or position of the substance.

---

55. *Treatise on Quantity* I, q.3, (Birch ed., 142–45) and *Treatise on Quantity* II, c.31, (Birch ed., 378–383).

56. *Presented by Ockham as valid in Summa logicae* I, c.44, (OPh I, 137), and as sound in *Rep.* IV, q.6, (OTh VII, 74–75); *Treatise on Quantity* I, q.3, (Birch ed., 96–98); *Treatise on Quantity* II, c.25, (Birch ed., 290); and *Quodl.* IV, q.22, (OTh IX, 404–405). Olivi had advanced a similar argument from theological considerations in his *Quodlibeta*; see David Burr, "Quantity and Eucharistic Presence: The Debate from Olivi through Ockham," *Collectanea Franciscana* XLIV (1974): 5–44; cf. 15.

Suppose 3. God does conserve a substance while destroying
all of its accidents that are really distinct from it,
without changing the location or position of the
substance. (2)

4. Either (a) the substance thus conserved is extended, or (b) the substance thus conserved is not
extended.

5. If 4b, then the substance has changed its place
—which is contrary to 3.

6. Therefore, 4a: The substance remains extended
even after all of the accidents that are really
distinct from it have been destroyed. (3, 4, and 5)

7. Therefore, substance is quantified without quantity—which is impossible by 1. (1 and 6)

8. Therefore, not-1. (7)

It is, of course, of premiss 2 that Ockham writes, "I base my proof
of this on the article of faith, 'I believe in God the Father
Almighty'..."[57] This doctrine was commonly held to entail the
following corollaries:

(G) Whatever God can produce by means of secondary causes,
He can produce and conserve immediately, by Himself,
without any secondary cause acting,

and

(H) God can produce or conserve what is naturally prior without what is naturally posterior.

Arguing in defense of 2 from (G), Ockham observes that there are

57. *Quodl.* IV, q.22, (OTh IX, 404).

cases in which God uses secondary causes to expel all of the absolute accidents from a patient and introduce new ones into it,
without that patient's changing place. Suppose, for example, that
a composite substance *A* is corrupted into a composite substance
B of the same size and shape and in the same place. By (C), the accidents of *A* will be numerically distinct from the accidents of *B*.
Consequently, the matter that persists through the change will
lose all of its absolute accidents without changing place.[58] If
God can produce this result by means of secondary causes,
then, by (G), He can bring it about without any secondary cause acting. Again, since substance is naturally prior to accidents, it follows from (H) that God can produce or conserve the
substance of a log without any of its absolute accidents. In that
case, either the log would change places or it would not. Ockham
asks, if it did, where would it go? Not up, because the log stripped
of its accidents has no more natural propensity to go up than it
had before; hence if it were going to go up, it would have gone up
before. Not down, for the same reason. Not backwards or for-
wards, because there is no more reason for it to go one way than
the other. Nor will its parts all collapse into a single point, because
there is no more reason why they should all locate at one point
than at any other. Ockham concludes that the substance of the log
would not change place at all, and hence that 2 is true.[59]

Ockham's opponents would hardly be convinced, however.
The most that the argument from (G) would show is that God can
destroy the quantity of a thing without changing its place, *if* He
replaces the destroyed quantity with another just like it. It does
not show that God can bring about this result, whether or not He
replaces the destroyed quantity. Likewise, Ockham's opponents
would grant (H) and the inference that God can produce or conserve a substance without the absolute accident that is its quantity. But when Ockham goes on to add in 2 "without changing the
location or position of the substance," he would seem to be begging the very point at issue. Ockham's contemporary and critic

---

58. For a fuller discussion of Ockham's hylomorphism and account of
substantial change, see Part Four, chapter 15 below.

59. *Quodl.* IV, q.22, arg.1 and 2, (OTh IX, 404–405).

Walter Burleigh contends that God can no more "conserve a substance in such a way that it has part outside part when its quantity is destroyed" than He could "make a white thing without whiteness or a man without a soul."[60] For not even God can do what is logically impossible (see Part Five, chapter 27 below). Burleigh thinks that (G) is advanced concerning secondary *efficient* causality, but not of secondary *formal* causality. And if a substance loses its location in place when its quantity is destroyed, it will not thereafter be able to move from one place to another, until its quantity is restored.

Ockham anticipates this objection and attacks it as theologically unacceptable:

> Nor does it hold good to say 'that substance exists in place only through quantity, which is an accident of that substance. Therefore, when the quantity is destroyed, the substance neither exists in place nor undergoes locomotion.' This assertion does not accord with Catholicism. For according to the Saints and authentic Doctors—and it is [clear] enough in the meaning of the canonical Scriptures—an angel exists in place and is transferred from one place to another, no matter how much it is not quantified but is indivisible and lacking in any parts that are apt to exist at a distance from one another. Therefore, how much more can it pertain to a substance that has parts that are apt to exist at a distance from one another to exist in place and change place, even if it lacks the quantity that is an absolute accident really distinct from and inhering in it.[61]

It was held that angels can genuinely have and change spatial location, where for an angel to be located in a place is *not* reducible to an angel's having perceptions of the sort a being literally located in the place would have or to an angel's being able to produce effects on things literally located in that place. Yet, if an angel can literally be located at a place apart from the inherence in it of any really distinct accident of quantity, why cannot a material substance be thus located apart from any really distinct accident of quantity?

It may be objected, however, that this argument from analogy does not force us to conclude that a material substance can be *ex-*

---

60. Translated from Maier's quotation, *op. cit.*, 190.
61. *Treatise on Quantity* II, c.25, (Birch ed., 296).

tended or exist circumscriptively in place, so that it has one part at a distance from another, apart from the inherence of a really distinct accident of quantity. For angels are simple substances and so can exist in place only definitively—i.e., whole in the whole and whole in each part. The analogy with the angels will show only that material substances can exist definitively in place without the inherence of a really distinct accident or quantity.

Of course, it does not follow from the fact that an angel exists definitively in place that an angel is extended. For what is extended has one part at a distance from another; and an angel has no parts. But Ockham thinks he can show by an argument similar to the one discussed at the beginning of this section, that if a material substance "exists in place definitively, it also exists in place circumscriptively" and therefore extended in place. Suppose that prior to the destruction of its accidents, a body B exists circumscriptively in place P. And suppose for the sake of simplicity, that P has parts a and b, while B has parts c and d; and that c exists in a and d exists in b. If after B's absolute accidents are destroyed, B exists definitively in P, then B is whole in the whole of P and whole in each part of P. This means that both c and d will exist in a, and both c and d will exist in b. But if so, c still exists in a and d still exists in b; and these parts are just as much at a distance from one another as they were before the absolute accidents of the substance were destroyed. Consequently, if, after B's absolute accidents are destroyed, B exists definitively in P, then, after B's absolute accidents are destroyed, B will exist circumscriptively in P and be extended as well.[62]

Perhaps it will be objected that when B exists definitively in P its parts will not be at a distance from one another. For c to be at a distance from d, it is not enough that c exist in a and d in b, where a and b are distinct places. It must be the case that c exists at a place at which d does not also exist, and vice versa.

Ockham obviously does not use the expression 'at a distance from one another' in this way; but he would not spend much time on a merely verbal dispute. Instead he would argue as above that if God can bring it about that both c and d exist in a and both c

62. Ibid., (Birch ed., 296–98); *Quodl.* IV, q.23, (OTh IX, 409).

and *d* exist in *b* apart from any really distinct accident of quantity, it will be even easier for Him to bring it about that *c* but not *d* exists in *a* and *d* but not *c* exists in *b* apart from any really distinct accident of quantity. For to obtain the latter given the former, He has only to take *d* away from *a* and *c* away from *b*. Surely an omnipotent God could do that!

Anyone who grants 2 should also concede Ockham's conclusion in 6: that substance can remain extended even after all of the absolute accidents that are really distinct from it have been destroyed. It does not follow from 6, however, that the quantity by which a substance is extended in three dimensions is *never* really distinct from that substance. One could hold that sometimes substances are extended by the activity of an efficient cause such as God who holds their parts at a distance from one another, but other times by a formal cause, a quantitative accident really distinct from and inhering in them.

Ockham rejects this "hybrid" position first on the ground that it is impossible:

> ...[quantity] is not the formal cause of the distance of parts the way something white is white through whiteness. For then it would be impossible for those that are now spatially distant from one another through quantity to exist in different places without such quantity (whether they are parts of a whole or separate from one another), the way it is impossible for any to be white without whiteness (whether they are separated from one another or parts of a whole)...[63]

But Ockham thinks he has just proved that it is not impossible for a thing to be extended without any such really distinct quantitative accident. Behind this reasoning lies the basic intuition that

(I) If any instance of an accident of a given kind is a thing really distinct from and inhering in the substance to which it belongs, every instance of that kind is.

Ockham does not see how accidents that are so different that one is really distinct from its substance and the other is not,

---

63. *Ibid.*, q.24, (OTh IX, 404).

could be accidents of the same kind, but he does nothing in the above passages to show why this intuition should be regarded as compelling. Elsewhere in the same question, Ockham implies that this position would violate Ockham's razor:

> ...When a proposition comes out true for things, if two things are suffi-cient for its truth, it is superfluous to assume a third. But the proposi-tions 'Material substance is quantified' and 'Material substance is cir-cumscriptively in place and has one part at a distance from another' come out true for things. A substance with its intrinsic parts and place are sufficient for the truth of such propositions, since it is impossible for a material substance to exist in a whole place and parts of the substance in parts of place without its being the case that all of these propositions would be true if they were formed. Therefore, it is superfluous to assume a third thing that is quantity, in order for these propositions to be true...[64]

If the substance with one part at a distance from another is sometimes enough to make the proposition 'Material substance is quantified' true, it is superfluous to suppose that quantitative things really distinct from the substance and its parts ever figure in the truth conditions.

Apparently, Franciscus de Marchia endorsed this hybrid position.[65] In his opinion, the fact that substances can be ex-tended apart from the inherence of any quantitative accidents really distinct from them does not show that such really distinct accidents are either superfluous or impossible. For the in-herence of such a quantitative accident has a double effect on its substance: viz., it extends the substance so that the latter has one part at a distance from the other, and it renders the substance impenetrable. Franciscus de Marchia concedes to Ockham that God can reproduce the first of these effects with-out any such formal cause, but not the second. When God holds the parts of substance at a distance from one another, they do not thereby acquire any tendency to exclude other parts from the place that they occupy. Thus, if such really distinct

---

64. *Ibid.*, (OTh IX, 413); *Treatise on Quantity* I, q.3, (Birch ed., 116–17).

65. Maier, *op. cit.*, 200–209.

qualities are not necessary for the extension of a substance, Franciscus de Marchia insists that they are required for its impenetrability. Turning to Ockham's argument, he would thus concede 6 but challenge the inference from 6 to 7, on the ground that a thing is positively quantified only if it is impenetrable. And using the term 'quantity' in this way, his point is well taken. For once the logical connection between extension and impenetrability is served—as it is by Ockham and Franciscus de Marchia alike—Ockham's premisses cannot be seen to entail anything about the conditions under which a thing will be impenetrable.

5.   POINTS, LINES, AND SURFACES

Many of Ockham's opponents thought that points were things (*res*) really distinct from lines; lines, things really distinct from surfaces; and surfaces, things really distinct from bodies. Further, they thought it possible to establish this conclusion on the basis of throughly uncontroversial principles: the Indiscernibility of Identicals (the principle that for any property F, if a is identical with b, a is F if and only if b is F) and some Aristotelian assumptions about the geometry of physical space. Ockham cites the following from their arguments in defense of the first part of their thesis—that points are things really distinct from lines.[66]

(a) A point is the limit of a line.
     A line is not the limit of a line.
     Therefore, a point is a thing really distinct from a line.

(b) A line is continuous through a point.
     The point through which the first half of a given line is continuous with the second half is continuous with the first.
     The first half of the line is not the same as the second half

66. *Treatise on Quantity* I, q.1, (Birch ed., 44–48); cf. *Expos. Physicorum* VI, t.3, (OPh V).

of the line; nor is any part of the one the same as any part
of the other.
Therefore, the point is a thing really distinct from the line
that is continuous through it.

(c) A point is the limit of a line.
The limits of two touching lines are the same.
Neither the lines nor any parts of the lines are the same.
Therefore, a point is a thing really distinct from a line.

(d) Points are indivisible.
Lines are divisible.
Therefore, points are things really distinct from lines.

Obvious parallels are available for the conclusions that lines are
things really distinct from surfaces, and surfaces things really
distinct from bodies.

Ockham's reaction is that these arguments are not nearly so
innocent as they might seem. For their proponents understand
the terms 'point', 'line', and 'surface' in them to function as absolute terms the way 'whiteness' does. And if their premises
were true on this interpretation, the arguments would be quite
conclusive. Nevertheless, Ockham insists that Aristotle and
other authoritative authors of such propositions as 'A point is
the limit of a line' or 'Points are indivisible' or 'Lines are divisible' did not understand them that way. Rather they took it that,
for example,

> ...the noun 'point' has the same signification as an expression com-
> pounded from a noun or a verb or a conjunction or an adverb together
> with the pronoun 'which', or compounded from a noun in an oblique
> case and a verb—which compound expression cannot, when taken
> literally, function as the grammatical subject of a verb. Consequently,
> no expression in which it occurs is a proper, but rather a figurative
> locution, and it can be reduced to a figure that grammarians call
> "hypallage," which they say is the changing of cases or of construc-
> tions or sometimes of the whole sentence.[67]

67. *Treatise on Quantity* I, q. 1, (Birch ed., 40).

According to the intention of their authors, 'A point is indivisible' means no more than 'A line is not further extended', and 'A
line is divisible' no more than 'Given any part of a line, it is
always possible to take another part', etc.[68] But on these con-
struals, the premises of (d) do not entail its conclusion that
points are things really distinct from lines.[69]

Ockham does not let his case against these opponents rest
here, however. He offers three types of arguments that their
theses—that points are things really distinct from lines; lines
from surfaces; and surfaces from bodies—are not only ill-
defended, but false: those of the first group try to show that
these theses commit them to a simultaneously existing actual infinity of things; the second, that there are no first subjects in
which such putative really distinct points, lines, and surfaces
could inhere; and third, that such really distinct accidents are
theoretically superfluous. I shall examine each in turn.

(5.1) *No Actual Infinity*. Ockham's attempt to show that if
points are things really distinct from lines, then there must be an
actual infinity of them, rests on the Aristotelian assumption that
whatever is extended is continuously extended and infinitely
divisible. He argues as follows:

> ...It is impossible that there should be infinitely many actually existing
> things such that (i) they are wholly distinct from one another, (ii) none
> is part of another, and (iii) they do not combine to make any one thing.
> But if points were such indivisible things, there would be infinitely
> many such things actually existing. For take a piece of wood. It is ob-
> vious that, according to them, there are infinitely many lines here,
> since however many there are, there are more. And each of these lines
> actually ends in a point, since otherwise no line would actually end in a
> point. And it is obvious that these points are wholly distinct from one
> another, since they are indivisible. Nor do they make anything one *per
> se*, since they are not parts of anything. Therefore, there will be in-
> finitely many of such actually existing things—which is impossible and
> contrary to all philosophy. It remains, then, that a point is not such an
> indivisible thing really distinct from every divisible thing...[70]

68. *Ibid.*, (Birch ed., 40–41).
69. Cf. *Expos. Physicorum* VI, t.3, (OPh V).
70. *Treatise on Quantity* I, q.1, (Birch ed., 26–28), and presented as

Ockham's opponents might reasonably respond, however, that he fails to take Aristotle's distinction between actual and potential infinities as seriously as they do. They would, of course, agree that since the piece of wood is actually finite in length, any lines that actually exist on it will actually end at a point—one at each end. Nor could they deny that if there were infinitely many lines actually existing on the piece of wood, there would be infinitely many actually existing points really and wholly distinct from one another—a consequence they would join Ockham in pronouncing unacceptable. Following Aristotle, they could hold that the piece of wood and/or its surface is infinitely divisible. And since a line is the limit of a surface, and a surface is infinitely divisible and thus potentially limited in infintely many ways, there is a potential infinity of lines on the piece of wood. But they could contend that the only actual lines there are, are the ones that represent the actual limits of surfaces. Since the piece of wood is not and cannot be infinitely *divided*, there are not and cannot be infinitely many lines on the log.

The premisses of two other arguments of Ockham's might seem to provide him with the materials of a reply. For he contends that no positive absolute thing (*res*) is either produced or destroyed by the mere division of a continuum into parts or by merely uniting parts that earlier existed separately. For example, he thinks that no new positive absolute things are produced by merely sawing a piece of wood in two. But if we assume that the only actual points, lines, or surfaces there are, are the ones that represent actual divisions of a continuum, we shall have to admit the opposite. Likewise, when two volumes of water are poured into one container, the points, lines, and surfaces that represented their earlier actual limits will be destroyed and new ones will be introduced.[71] This response is only as compelling as the causal principles on which it rests, however. And while

---

Aristotle's in *Expos. Praedicam.*, c.10, (OPh II, 209–210). A similar argument about lines is offered as valid in *Summa logicae* I, c.44, (OPh I, 135–36), and as sound in *Treatise on Quantity* I, q.2, (Birch ed., 82).

71. *Ibid.*, q.1, (Birch ed., 28) and q.2, (Birch ed., 82).

Ockham's claims seem the more plausible, they are not so over-whelmingly obvious as to change the mind of anyone who thought he had good theoretical reason for believing that points, lines, and surfaces are such really distinct accidents.

(5.2) *No First Subject.* Accidents by nature are apt to inhere in a substance. In the natural course of things, every real accident actually inheres in some substance. And even where, by divine intervention, accidents exist without actually inhering in a substance, it is at least possible that there should be a first subject in which it inheres. Ockham argues that points, lines, and surfaces cannot be really distinct accidents, because no such first subject is even conceivable where they are concerned. Once again his reply rests on the uncontroversial Aristotelian thesis that what is extended is continuously extended and consequently infinitely divisible and not composed of any indivisible parts. He also takes it for granted that there are only three ways in which one thing can exist in another—viz., circumscriptively, definitively, or an indivisible thing in an indivisible subject.

Ockham's argument that a point cannot inhere in a line as in a first subject goes as follows.[72] First, it is clear that a point cannot inhere in a line or any part of a line circumscriptively. For by (C) above, a point could exist in a line circumscriptively, only if there were a proper proportion between the point and the line: in particular, only if there were at least one part of the point for each part of the line. According to the theory under attack, however, a point is an indivisible thing and has no part, whereas a line is an infinitely divisible thing and divisible only into infinitely divisible parts. Consequently, a point cannot exist in a line or in any part of a line circumscriptively, because the requisite proper proportion is lacking.

Ockham argues that a point (call it *b*) cannot exist definitively in a line (call it *a*) either. For if it did, *b* would be whole in the whole of *a* and whole in each part of *a*. Since *a* is extended, it

---

72. Presented as Aristotle's in *Summa logicae* I, c.44, (OPh I, 133–34) and also in *Expos. Praedicam.*, c.10, (OPh II, 208), and offered in its most elaborate versions in the *Treatise on Quantity* I, q.1, (Birch ed., 8–23).

would follow that one and the same point *b* was located at a distance from itself—which his opponents would not admit. Further, suppose that *c* is one end of *a*. Then both *b* and *c* will be whole in the whole of *a* and whole in each part of *a*, with the result that numerically distinct points have exactly the same location and position—which his opponents would likewise deny. Nor, says Ockham, will it do any good to say that *b* and *c* do not exist definitively in the whole of *a*, but *b* exists definitively in one part of *a* (call it *d*) and *c* in another (call it *e*). For since *d*, like every part of *a*, is extended, it will still follow that *b* exists at a distance from itself. Further, let *f* be one end of *d*. If *f* exists definitively in *d*, then both *b* and *f* will exist in exactly the same place. Ockham's opponents object that in this last move Ockham is once again paying insufficient attention to the Aristotelian distinction between actual and potential infinities. For since *d* is not actually divided from *a*, *d* will not actually have an end and so *f* will not be an actual point. Ockham replies that it is enough if *d* is potentially divisible from *a*. For if that possibility were actualized, then *f* would be an actual point. And if points actually inhered in lines or parts of lines definitively, it would follow that both *f* and *b* would exist in the same place then. Since the impossible does not follow from the possible, and it is possible for *d* to be actually divided from *a*, it must be impossible that a point should inhere in a line definitively. The only way to avoid this conclusion would be to suppose that when *d* is actually divided from *a*, *b* moves and instead of inhering definitively in the whole of *d* comes to inhere only in a part of *d* and thus makes room for *f*. Should his opponents press this line, Ockham would fall back on his other charge—that if a point exists definitively in a line or in any part of a line, it will be at a distance from itself—which they would deny. Analogous arguments would show that a point cannot exist either circumscriptively or definitively in a surface or a body either.

There remains the third alternative that the indivisible point inheres in something indivisible as a first subject. Ockham asks what it would be? Either substance or accident. But if we say that it is an accident, then we will face the same problems all over again in determining what the subject of that indivisible accident is. Either there will be an infinite process, or we will have to say that there is an indivisible substance that is the first subject of the indivisible accident. But Ockham rejects this suggestion as well. According to his opponents, points, lines, and surfaces are only supposed to exist in material substances. But material substances in fact are, as they would agree, continuously extended and therefore divisible only into divisible parts. And their components—matter and form—are likewise continuously extended and infinitely divisible. Ockham does not see how any indivisible substance could combine with such matter and form to make something one *per se*, and so does not see how there could be any such indivisible substance in a material substance to serve as the first subject of the point.

It might be replied that substances are indivisible prior to their extension and that points inhere in them then. Ockham would reply that neither material substances nor their components of matter and form are indivisible prior to their extension. For a substance can be extended only if it has of itself parts that are by nature apt to exist at a distance from one another. A substance that does not have such parts is not apt to be extended. And since material substances have parts that are apt to be continuously extended, they have of themselves parts that are infinitely divisible into other parts, and they have them whether they are actually extended or not.

As we shall see in Part Four, chapter 16 below, Aquinas disagreed with Scotus and Ockham on this point. He believed that matter did not have parts of itself, but was only rendered divisible and divided by the inherence of quantity. Consequently, according to his view, substance is indivisible prior to the inherence of quantity and so could bear the proper proportion to an indivisible point. Could it be said that it is the first subject of points?

Even leaving aside his differences with Aquinas over the nature of matter and three-dimensional extension, Ockham would find this suggestion unpromising. For if points inhered in a substance prior to the inherence of any other accident of quantity, then either accidents of continuous quantity would be able to inhere in the substance afterwards or not. If they did, then each point would be whole in the whole of that continuous quantity; for there would be no more reason why it should be assigned to one part than to another. Consequently, many points would exist in exactly the same place—which both Ockham and his opponents deem impossible. Hence, if points inhered in the substance prior to the inherence of accidents of continuous quantity, it would be impossible for any accidents of continuous quantity to inhere in it thereafter and so impossible for that substance to be extended—which Ockham's opponents would also reject.

Analogous arguments would show that a point cannot inhere in a quality as in a first subject. But if a point cannot inhere in a line, a surface, a body, a substance, or a quality, then there is nothing in which it can inhere—which is impossible if it is an accident really distinct from lines, surfaces, bodies, substances, and qualities. The conclusion is that points are not such really distinct accidents.

Ockham thinks the same sort of argument will work for lines and surfaces.[73] For while lines are continuously extended in length, they have no width; and surfaces have no thickness.

(5.3) *Theological Arguments.* Ockham thinks that it follows from some further corollaries of the doctrine of divine omnipotence that his opponents' thesis is in violation of Ockham's razor. His strategy is to use the theological premises to show that God could produce a line without some or any points, and then to argue that the effects that such really distinct points are supposed to produce on lines would remain anyway. The conclusion is that since there is no theoretical work for which they are necessary, it is superfluous to assume that points, lines, and surfaces are really distinct accidents.

The first theological corollary is

(J) God can produce or conserve one thing (*res*) without another really distinct thing (*res*), if neither is the subject

---

73. *Expos. Praedicam.*, c.10, (OPh II, 209); *Summa logicae* I, c.44, (OPh I, 134); and *Treatise on Quantity* I, q.2, (Birch ed., 82).

or the cause of the other,

which Ockham defends by an appeal to the doctrine of the Eucharist:

> ...if divine power can separate what essentially depends on another either as an effect on a cause or an accident on a subject, from that other, how much more can he make what does not depend on another—whether as a whole or as an accident or as an effect—without that other. But an accident in the sacrament of the altar depends, before its separation, on the substance both as its cause and as its subject. Nevertheless, divine power makes the accident come to exist without the subject...[74]

Given (J), Ockham argues that according to the theory under attack, a point is really and wholly distinct from a line: for a line cannot be part of a point, since a point is indivisible and has no parts; and a point cannot be part of a line, since a line is infinitely divisible and so has no indivisible parts. Further, he has argued that a line cannot be the subject of a point (see section (5.2) above); and no one held that a point was the subject of a line. Nor is either the cause of the other. Consequently, "God can, in His absolute power, produce a line without any points."[75]

The same conclusion can be derived from another theological corollary

(K) When one absolute thing (*res*) can be naturally produced without each of many really distinct things taken one by one, that thing can be produced by divine power without any and all of them—especially where neither is part of the other, or the effect of the other, or an accident of the other,

which parallels claims we have encountered before (see Part One, chapters 2 and 3 above). Ockham says that if points were

74. *Ibid.*, q.1, (Birch ed., 32–35).
75. *Ibid.*, (Birch ed., 30–31).

things really distinct from lines, points and lines would be related in the requisite way. For given his opponents' commitment to the distinction between actual and potential infinities, only those points that are the actual limits of some line exist. But since any line is infinitely divisible, it is logically possible that a line be limited in any one of infinitely many ways to the exclusion of the others. Consequently, "the line can naturally exist without this point and without that point and so on for each [possible point]. Therefore, God can produce it without any point" at all.[76]

The first theoretical job of such putative really distinct points Ockham considers is the one mentioned in argument (a) above: viz., that of limiting or ending lines. He reasons that if God made or conserved a line without any points, then

> either the line is finite or infinite. If it is finite without any points, then it is useless to assume points for the purpose of ending lines. But those who assume them do not do so for any other reason. But if the line is not ended or finite, and it really exists according to the case assumed, then it is infinite—which is obviously false. For a line is not larger or longer because the point is separated from it or destroyed. Therefore, it will in no way be infinite, no matter to what extent every point is destroyed.[77]

Ockham's opponents might try to reject the second half of his argument, however, just as they initially denied that God could preserve a substance and destroy all of its absolute accidents without that thing's changing place. By (H) God can conserve a substance without its whiteness, but not without that substance losing its color; for whiteness was the formal cause of the substance's being white. Likewise, by (J) and (K), God can conserve a line while destroying every point, but not without making the line unlimited. For the point is the formal cause of the line's having an end.

Ockham would reject the analogy, however. For he has argued (see section (5.2) above) that a point cannot inhere in the

76. *Ibid.*
77. *Ibid.*

line as in its first subject—indeed that neither the point nor the line can inhere in anything as a first subject. In view of the latter, he doubts whether such really distinct points could fill the above mentioned theoretical rule at all. For he really does not see how the line can "be ended by a point in any other way than that in which water is limited by a solid body such as the ground."[78] No doubt Ockham would substitute an analogy of his own: that if God can hold the parts of a substance at a distance from one another while destroying all of its absolute accidents (see section 4 above), then He can hold the parts of the line in the same finite expanse as before while destroying all of the points. The latter seems as plausible as the former.

Second, Ockham focuses on the theoretical role mentioned in argument (b): that of being that through which a line is continuous. Ockham reasons,

> ...if God destroyed every point while conserving a line, I ask whether or not the line is continuous. If it is continuous and not through a point—since according to the assumed case, none exists—then the line is continuous without any point. Consequently, it is useless to assume a point there. If it is not continuous, I ask whether some part of it is continuous, and then I repeat the preceding argument; or no part of it is continuous, from which it follows that some line is not composed of continuous parts—which is impossible.[79]

Here Ockham's opponents cannot seize the second horn of the dilemma without accepting consequences that they find just as impossible as Ockham does. For in opting for it, they affirm that a line is only continuous through points that actually exist. If so, since a line is infinitely divisible, it will only be continuous when infinitely many points actually exist for it to be continuous through. On the other hand, when these points are destroyed, "each part is infinitely divided with respect to all of its parts." Thus, if they hold that a line is continuous only through a point that actually exists, they will be committed to a simultaneously existing actual infinity of things both when the

78. *Ibid.*, (Birch ed., 34–35).
79. *Ibid.*, (Birch ed., 30).

line is continuous and when it is not—which they would have regarded as impossible.

Ockham would offer analogous arguments to show that it is superfluous to assume lines really distinct from surfaces and surfaces really distinct from bodies or substances.[80]

6.   SUMMARY

The outcome of Ockham's attack on the thesis that quantity is a thing (res) really distinct from substance and quality is mixed. He argues persuasively that his opponents cannot consistently account for condensation and rarefaction without assuming that infinitely many quantitative and qualitative things are generated and corrupted in the process, and that since the changes in volume involved in condensation and rarefaction can be explained in terms of locomotion, it is superfluous to assume such infinities of things (in section 3 above). Likewise, he argues ingeniously from the doctrine of divine omnipotence that no such really distinct quantitative accident is needed to explain how bodies are extended in three dimensions. By themselves, these arguments do not show his opponents' position to be in violation of Ockham's razor, however, since they assume such really distinct quantities, not merely to explain how bodies are extended, but also to account for their impenetrability. Unlike some of his opponents, Ockham does not believe that three-dimensional extension is logically sufficient for impenetrability. And he thinks that his opponents even overestimate the natural impenetrability of things (argument (2.3) above). Nevertheless, he does hold that two substances or two qualities of the same kind are naturally impenetrable, and he scarcely addresses the question of what makes them so, beyond saying that experience makes it obvious that they are.

More telling are Ockham's arguments that points, lines, and surfaces are not things really distinct from one another or from substances and qualities. Given the Aristotelian assumptions

80. Cf. *ibid*., q.2, (Birch ed., 88–90).

that extension is continuous and therefore divisible only into divisible parts—which his opponents would have conceded—Ockham's proofs that there is nothing in a material substance for points, lines, and surfaces to inhere in as a first subject seem cogent. And if so, it follows that points, lines, and surfaces are not the really distinct accidents that his opponents take them to be. On the other hand, if points, lines, and surfaces were things other than accidents, they could not serve their assigned theoretical function of limiting lines, surfaces, or bodies in any way other than the ground serves the function of limiting water; neither could they function as that through which lines, surfaces, and bodies were continuous (see section (5.3) above). Ockham's initial attempt to convict his opponents of a simultaneously existing actual infinity of things (*res*), based on their thesis that points (lines, surfaces) are the limits of lines (surfaces, bodies), seems unsuccessful. For while they would admit the infinite divisiblity of lines, surfaces, and bodies, they would insist that there is only a potential infinity, not an actual infinity, of alternative limits (see section (5.1) above). This escape is available to them, however, only so long as they do not maintain that a line (surface, body) is continuous only through a point (line, surface) that actually exists. For when the latter is combined with the infinite divisibility of lines, surfaces, and bodies, it follows that there are infinitely many actual points, lines, and surfaces through which lines, surfaces, and bodies are actually continuous (see section (5.3) above). Finally, Ockham argues that even if such really distinct points, lines, and surfaces could fill the theoretical role of being that through which lines, surfaces, and bodies are continuous, they are not necessary for this purpose. For if there were such really distinct accidents, it would be logically possible that a line (surface, body) exist without any and every point (line, surface); nevertheless, his opponents cannot deny that the line (surface, body) would be continuous nonetheless, without admitting an actual infinity of simultaneously existing things (see section (5.3) above).

7

Relations

The category of relation is a subject about which Ockham thinks unaided natural reason will direct us to say one thing; the authority of Sacred Scripture and the Church another. For according to the latter, it is necessary to assume that some relations are real things really distinct from absolute things; but the former "will find it easier to deny than to sustain" such a thesis.[1] Some of Ockham's contemporaries and predecessors were of a different opinion, however. They thought it necessary to "suppose that relation is a thing (*res*) other than any absolute thing or things, not only because of authorities but also because of arguments."[2] In Ockham's view, the most distinguished among them was Duns Scotus; and it is his position that Ockham singles out for detailed refutation.[3] Some of these philosophers including Scotus thought not only that there were relative things really distinct from absolute things, but also relative beings of reason distinct from any and every absolute thing, real or unreal. Ockham likewise rejects this contention, denying that there are any relative entities—real or unreal —distinct from absolute entities.

In this chapter, I want to examine this discussion at closer range. I shall devote sections 1–6 below to Scotus's position and Ockham's attacks on it and section 7 to the alternative that Ockham proposes for unaided natural reason. In section 8, I

---

1. *Ord.* I, d.30, q.1, (OTh IV, 306).
2. *Ibid.*, (OTh IV, 283).
3. Ockham does bring up three other views—including that of Henry of Ghent—in *Reportatio* II, q.2, (OTh V, 28–30, 43–46). But his statement and refutations of the second and third are quite brief. And in dealing with Henry of Ghent, he largely confines himself to explaining how Scotus would have replied to the latter's arguments.

shall deal with Ockham's arguments that there are no relative beings of reason; and in section 9, his estimate of the theological commitment to relations really distinct from absolute things.

Before turning to Scotus's position, however, a few background remarks are in order. (a) The first is that Ockham's predecessors and contemporaries commonly contrasted real relations with relations of reason. We shall return to this distinction in section 8 below. For now it is enough to note that real relations are relations that obtain between things in reality and would obtain between these relata whether or not—*per impossibile*—anyone ever thought they did, while relations of reason obtain between their relata only by virtue of some mental activity. It was real relations that philosophers were tempted to regard as real things really or formally distinct from their relata; relations of reason with relative beings of reason.

(b) The appeal of identifying real relations with things really distinct from absolute things might seem obvious. If relations were real things, they could serve as a kind of metaphysical glue, sticking really distinct things together by inhering in both of them at once. While medievals did assign such real relations a unifying function, they would have rejected the latter development of their thesis as impossible. As we have seen in chapter 6, they believed that there had to be a proper proportion between the subject of inherence and that in which it inheres. When an accident inheres in a substance that has parts, the accident is whole in the substance and part in each part. If so, however, no single simple accident could simultaneously inhere in two, really distinct substances, whose combination could have no more unity than an aggregate has. Rather for two really distinct substances, there must be two really distinct accidents. Accordingly, they held that when an absolute thing a is related by such a real relation to an absolute thing b, and vice versa, two really distinct relative things are involved: one, R-ness, inheres in and has its foundation in a; the other, R'-ness, inheres in and has its foundation in b (where R-ness and R'-ness are corresponding or co-relations). The inherence of R'-ness in b makes b the term of a's relation of R-ness; and the inherence of R-ness in a makes a the term of b's relation of R'-ness. (The foundation or the subject in which the foundation inheres and the term of a relation, or the relata, are often referred to as "the extremes" of the relation.)

(c) Scotus drew a distinction between intrinsic and extrinsic relations, which Ockham explains as follows:

> ...[in intrinsic relations], given the extremes and the foundations of the two relations, the relation at once obtains; and so long as the extremes remain, the same relation will hold. But this is not the way it is with extrinsic relations. For if matter is separated from form and each is conserved in existence, the union does not remain. But given the father and the son, and that the father begat the son, paternity and filiation are always posited. And it is not thus understood that given the extremes, the relation immediately arises. For God can create the man who is begotten by Peter, and yet the man thus created would not be Peter's son because the later never begot him...[4]

Thus, a relation is said to be intrinsic, if it is logically impossible for the extremes to exist and the relation and/or its co-relation not to obtain. But a relation is extrinsic, if it is logically possible for the extremes to exist and the relation and its co-relation not to obtain.[5]

1.   SCOTUS'S POSITION

Scotus held that some real relations were things (*res*) really

---

4. *Ibid.*, (OTh V, 48–49).

5. This way of drawing the distinction admits of a difficulty that neither Scotus nor Ockham noticed. It is true *de dicto* that it is logically impossible for two white things to exist and not be similar, and this fact makes it plausible to identify similarity as an intrinsic relation. But it is not true *de re* that it is logically impossible for two white things to exist and not be similar, since it is logically possible for one of them to be white while the other is black. It is the *de dicto* impossibility that Scotus and Ockham relied on in classifying relations as intrinsic or extrinsic. But this criterion could be trivial unless some restriction is put on the sort of descriptions that occur in the *dictum*, since it is logically impossible *de dicto* for any two things related by *R*-ness not to be related by *R*-ness. On the other hand, it is clearly not the relata in themselves, but the relata considered insofar as they have certain accidental properties that are often related by the allegedly intrinsic relations of equality, similarity, doubleness, halfness, etc.

distinct from their foundations and others were not.[6] He offers a
number of arguments in favor of the first half of his thesis in his
Ordinatio II, d.1, q.4–5. (1.1) Ockham labels the first sort of
arguments offered by Scotus "separation" arguments, for reasons obvious from their form:

(i)   Nothing is realy the same as *a*, if it is not contradictory
      that *a* should exist without it.

(ii) There are many relations which are such that their foun-
      dations can exist without them apart from any con-
      tradiction.

(iii) Therefore, there are many relations that are really dis-
      tinct from their foundations.

(i) is uncontestable, and (ii) is illustrated by many examples. For
instance, if this white thing is similar to that white thing, it is
still logically possible that this white thing should exist and not
be similar to that white thing—say if that white thing did not
exist. Or again, a master can exist without being a master, and
he can be the master of slaves by acquiring them.[7]
   (1.2) A second group of arguments turns on the thesis that

(A) There can be no passage from contradictory to contradic-
     tory apart from the generation or corruption of some
     thing (*res*).

For if there could, then the same things would exist when *p* is

---

6. Ockham is somewhat misleading on this point in his *Ordinatio* I,
d.30 q.1, (OTh IV, 283), when he reports Scotus's view as being that "one
should suppose that a relation is a thing (*res*) other than any absolute thing or
things, not only because of authorities but also because of arguments." His
comment in *Reportatio* II, q.2, (OTh V, 31)—that according to Scotus,
"some relations are really distinct [from their foundations] and some are
not"—is closer to the mark. His discussion in both questions, however,
presupposes a familiarity with Scotus's arguments on both points.
   7. Ockham's *Ord.* I, d.30, q.1, (OTh IV, 283–84); Scotus's *Ord.* II, d.1,
q.4–5, n.200–205, (Vaticana VII, 101–104).

true as when not-*p* is true. And in that case,

> there would be no more reason why one contradictory should be truer
> than the other. Thus, either both are simultaneously false or both are
> simultaneously true.[8]

Applying this to the relation of composition,

> ...if *a* and *b* form the compound *ab*, and the union of these is not
> anything other than the absolute things *a* and *b* taken separately, then *a*
> and *b* will remain really united when they are separated...[9]

Again, Scotus invokes a conclusion of Aristotelian physics that

(B) Natural causes can act only within a determinate distance
     of the things they are acting upon.

If spatial proximity is not a thing really distinct from the proximate objects, then the same things may exist when they are
proximate and when they are not. And if spatial proximity does
not make any real difference in which things exist, it will not
make any real difference to whether or not a cause can produce
anything. But by (B), a cause cannot act when it is not spatially
proximate. Therefore, it will not be able to act when it is spatially proximate either.[10]
    Scotus considers the objection that "no relation is a distinct
thing, because it is not a thing (*res*), but exists only in the intellect."[11] In effect, the objection allows that contradictories
cannot be true successively without some difference in which
entities exist. But it emphasizes that the class of entities is
broader than the class of real things (*res*), since beings of reason

---

8. *Ibid*. I, d.30, q.1–2, n.41, (Vaticana VI, 186–87); cf. Part One,
chapter 5 above.
    9. Ockham's *Ord*. I, d.30, q.1, (OTh IV, 284); Scotus's *Ord*. II, d.1,
q.4–5, n.209, (Vaticana VII, 105).
    10. Ockham's *Ord*. I, d.30, q.1, (OTh IV, 284–85); Scotus's *Ord*. II, d.1,
q.4–5, n.210, (Vaticana VII, 105–106).
    11. Ockham's *Ord*. I, d.30, q.1, (OTh IV, 285–86); Scotus's *Ord*. II, d.1,
q.4–5, n.223, (Vaticana VII, 111).

that have a diminished mode of existence as objects of thought are also entities. (See Part One, chapters 2 and 3 above.) To reflect this more generous ontology, (A) should be replaced with

> (A″) There can be no passage from contradictory to contradictory apart from the generation or corruption of some entity.

If a statement of the form 'aRb' is first true and then false, or vice versa, and a and b exist throughout the process, then we can conclude either that the destroyed or produced relation was some real thing distinct from a and b, or that it was some being of reason distinct from a and b. The objector prefers the latter selection to the former.

Scotus would not really object to replacing (A) and (A″), but he thinks that metaphysical disaster will result if relations are invariably identified with beings of reason. Like Ockham, he insists that

> ...nothing real depends on what is only a being of reason (and chiefly a being of reason is caused by an act of our intellect)—at least no real thing that is not a mere artifact does...[12]

But some relations, e.g., the unity of the universe or the parts of a composite, the spatial proximity of a cause to its effect, and the relations of mathematics, must be thought of as real and as obtaining whether or not—*per impossibile*—anyone ever thinks about them. Consequently, they cannot be identified with any mind-dependent entities. Again, "the causation of a real effect does not require a being of reason in its cause." But by (B), natural causes cannot produce anything apart from a relation of spatial proximity; and according to the objector's proposal, spatial proximity is a mere being of reason. It follows that natural causes will not be really able to cause anything.[13]

12. Ockham's *Ord.* I, d.30, q.1, (OTh IV, 286); Scotus's *Ord.* II, d.1, q.4–5, n.225, (Vaticana VII, 112).

13. Ockham's *Ord.* I, d.30, q.1, (OTh IV, 286–87); Scotus's *Ord.* II, d.1, q.4–5, n.223–27, (Vaticana VII, 111–113).

Where the foundation of a relation can exist without the relation, there, Scotus says, the relation must be a thing really
distinct from its foundation. But where it is not even logically
possible that the foundation exist without the relation, there
they are really the same but only formally distinct. This contention rests on the general thesis that

(C) If *b* inheres, properly speaking, in *a*, and *a* cannot exist
without *b*, then *b* is really the same as *a*.

Scotus defends (C) by appeal to the Aristotelian notions of
natural priority, posteriority, and simultaneity. *a* is naturally
prior to *b* and *b* naturally posterior to *a*, if and only if *b* depends
on *a* for its existence but *a* does not depend on *b* for its
existence. And *a* and *b* are naturally simultaneous, if and only if
neither depends on the other for its existence or it is logically
impossible for one to exist without the other. Scotus reasons
that if *a* cannot exist without *b*, this is either because *b* is
naturally prior to *a*, or *b* is really the same as *a*. But what inheres is neither naturally prior to nor naturally simultaneous
with that in which it inheres. Therefore, if *b* inheres in *a*, and *a*
cannot exist without *b*, then *a* and *b* are really the same.[14] Now
real relations inhere in their foundations. Thus, if a foundation
cannot exist without a given relation, by (C), that relation will
be really the same as its foundation. On the other hand, Scotus
thinks, it follows obviously from his understanding of what it is
to be formally the same (see Part One, chapter 2 above), that the
relation is not formally the same as its foundation: "for the
aspect (*ratio*) of a relation does not include—formally and *per
se*—the aspect (*ratio*) of anything absolute; and, conversely, the
aspect (*ratio*) of an absolute does not include *per se* the formal
aspect (*ratio*) of a relation."[15] A paradigm case of this sort of
real relation is a creature's relation of depending upon or of being created by God. Thus, Scotus reasons on the basis of (C) that
"a relation to God inheres, properly speaking, in the stone and

14. *Ibid.*, n.262, (Vaticana VII, 129).
15. *Ibid.*, n.272, (Vaticana VII, 135).

it is contradictory for the stone to exist without it; therefore that relation is really the same as the stone" but formally distinct from it.[16]

2.   OCKHAM'S GENERAL ARGUMENTS AGAINST SCOTUS'S POSITION

Ockham wishes to refute Scotus's position by showing that the consequences of (A) are inconsistent with other principles accepted by Scotus himself. To this end, Ockham advances four general arguments, as well as several specific to certain kinds of relations. (2.1) Prominent among the former is Ockham's charge that Scotus's thesis entails the simultaneous existence of infinitely many things—something which both regarded as impossible (see Part One, chapter 5 above). Since Ockham offers rather different arguments on this point for various types of relations, I shall postpone consideration of them to succeeding sections. (2.2) Another of the general arguments rests on two tenets of epistemology: viz., that every thing (*res*) really distinct from and no part of another thing (*res*) can be really thought of when the other is not thought of; and that it is impossible for any thing (*res*) that is a relation to be thought of without another thing being thought of. This argument does have some force *ad hominem*, since Ockham argues plausibly for the first premise and Scotus follows Aristotle in accepting the second. I think that the argument fails because the second premise is false when the intentional contexts in it are construed *de re* as Ockham requires them to be. To see why would take us too far into Ockham's epistemology (see Part Three, chapter 13), however, and so I will pass over it for now.

(2.3) Ockham's third argument is that given (B), the view that real relations are things really distinct from each other and from absolute things, implies exceptions to the commonly accepted thesis that

(D) Co-relations are naturally simultaneous in that it is

16. *Ibid.*, n.261, (Vaticana VII, 129).

logically impossible for one of them to obtain without the other.

For example, it is logically impossible for Socrates to be similar to Plato without Plato's being similar to Socrates; logically impossible for x to be the double of y, unless y is the half of x; and logically impossible for Socrates to be the father of Plato unless Plato is the son of Socrates. As Ockham points out elsewhere, however, Aristotle endorses (D) for the above mentioned sorts of relations, but claims that it does not hold in certain cases.[17] Since Scotus follows Aristotle in this restriction, Ockham cannot consistently claim fully general application for his argument.

Ockham reasons as follows:

> ...For every sort of relatives and for every relative category, some extremes must be maximally separated in space. Therefore, some thing (*res*) can be produced in one of the extremes when no thing (*res*) is produced in the other. Therefore, if relations were things (*res*) distinct [from absolute things], then a relation could come to one of the extremes when nothing was produced in the other extreme.[18]

For example, a natural agent in Rome can act to make something in Rome white and therefore similar to something in London. But the natural agent in Rome is too far away to be able to produce anything in the white thing in London. If similarity is a relative thing really distinct from its foundation, then the natural agent in Rome can cause similarity to inhere in the thing in Rome but cannot cause similarity to inhere in the thing in London. And if it does not, neither will any other natural cause. Hence, it seems that the similarity of the white thing in Rome to the white thing in London can exist without the similarity of the white thing in London to the white thing in Rome—which (D) excludes as impossible.[19] This sort of argument can be repeated for other sorts of intrinsic relations. Contrary to Ockham's sug-

17. *Categories*, 7, 7b15ff; cf. Ockham's *Expos. Praedicam.*, c.13, (OPh II, 258–260) and *Ord.* I, d.30, q.2, (OTh IV, 334).

18. *Ibid.*, q.1, (OTh IV, 290–91); cf. *Expos. Praedicam.*, c.12, (OPh II, 241).

19. *Ord.* I, d.30, q.1, (OTh IV, 290–91); *Expos. Praedicam.*, c.12, (OPh II, 241); cf. *Rep.* II, q.2, (OTh V, 32–35).

gestion, it does not seem to work for all relations of power. Fire cannot produce a relation of causality in itself by heating water, unless it is close enough to the water to heat it and hence close enough to produce a relation of being an effect in it.

Ockham considers the objection that (B)

> ...the assumption about action at a certain distance is true where [the production of] absolute things is concerned, but not where relative things are concerned.[20]

That way an agent in Rome would not be able to produce whiteness in a thing in London, but would be able to produce similarity in it when it produces whiteness in the thing in Rome. Ockham responds,

> On the contrary, then it would follow that if God made a thousand worlds and one agent caused whiteness in one, that agent would cause similarity in a thousand worlds. For in every world whatever there can be some individual white thing.[21]

And this is to expand the power of natural agents to act at a distance to absurd limits.

(2.4) Again, Ockham charges that the thesis that relations are things really distinct from each other and from absolute things, is at odds with two other assumptions made by Scotus:

(E) Where relations are really distinct from their foundations, the relata are naturally prior to the relation,

and

(F) God can make the prior without anything naturally posterior to it.

If real relations of, for example, similarity were things really distinct from absolute things, then, by (E) and (F), God could make two white things without the similarity that is naturally

20. *Quodl.* VI, q.8, (OTh IX, 614).
21. *Ibid.*

posterior to them. Nevertheless, it is logically impossible that two white things exist without being similar. Ockham concludes that similarity must not be a thing really distinct from absolute things and naturally posterior to them.[22] The same argument can be repeated for other intrinsic relations, which cannot fail to obtain given the existence of their relata.

Causal relations are not intrinsic relations, however. According to Ockham, causal relations are contingent: even if x is the cause of y, it is logically possible that both x and y should have existed and not have been so related. Hence, the existence of x and y is not logically sufficient for the relation to obtain. Nevertheless, Ockham thinks the argument from (E) and (F) can be adapted to show that causal relations are not things really distinct from their relata either. Focussing on the case of paternity and filiation, he reasons that if paternity and filiation were things really distinct from absolute things, then

> ...it would follow that—given that Socrates is first the father of Plato and that Plato is the son of Socrates—God could conserve Socrates and Plato as before, and yet Socrates would not be the father of Plato. In that case, the inference 'Socrates begets Plato, and Socrates exists and Plato exists; therefore Socrates is the father of Plato' would not hold—which nevertheless seems awkward...[23]

On the other hand, if we insist that the latter inference does hold, and that once Socrates has begotten Plato, he remains the father of Plato so long as they both exist, no matter what else is produced or destroyed afterwards, then Ockham will conclude that paternity and filiation must not be relative things really distinct from and inhering in their relata.[24] Similarly for other causal relations.

In fact, such arguments prove only that the relata *can* remain related even after any such relative things inhering in them are destroyed. They do not yield Ockham's further conclusion that

22. *Ord.* I, d.30, q.1, (OTh IV, 291–92); *Rep.* II, q.2, (OTh V, 31–32); *Quodl.* VI, q.8, (OTh IX, 614).
23. *Ord.* I, d.30, q.4, (OTh IV, 368).
24. *Rep.* II, q.2, (OTh V, 48–49).

relations are never things really distinct from and inhering in their relata. Perhaps Socrates and Plato are sometimes similar, and sometimes father and son, by virtue of certain relative things inhering in each of them; and other times they are similar and father and son apart from the inherence of any such relative things.

Ockham rejects this suggestion:

> On the contrary, if similarity were a thing (*res*) distinct [from absolute things], then similarity and a similar thing will be related the way whiteness is related to a white thing. Therefore it will be impossible for anything to be similar without the similarity that is a thing (*res*) distinct [from absolute things], the way it is impossible for anything to be white without the whiteness that is a thing distinct [from its subject].[25]

Behind this reply is Ockham's basic intuition that

> (G) If any instance of a given relation is a thing really distinct from and inhering in its relata, then every instance of that relation is.

At the beginning of his next argument, Ockham advances the even more general thesis that

> (H) If one relation were a thing (*res*) really distinct from and inhering in its relata, by the same token, every other relation of any kind would be, too.

Thus, if similarity relations were things really distinct from and inhering in their relata, the relations of paternity and filiation would be as well.[26] In the text just quoted, Ockham suggests that it is *impossible* that things should be otherwise than as (G) stipulated, although he does nothing to show us why it would be impossible. In the next paragraph, he supports its application to similarity with an appeal to the famous razor:

25. *Ord.* I, d.30, q.1, (OTh IV, 292).
26. *Ibid.*

...it would be useful to suppose that similarity is a thing (*res*) really distinct [from absolute things] if some others could be similar without such a thing, the way it would be useless to suppose that whiteness is a thing distinct from its subject, if the subject could be white without any such thing (*res*).[27]

(G) and (H) are intuitively plausible and would contribute to the aesthetic value of uniformity in a metaphysical theory. Scotus thinks, however, that he has found reason in (A) and (C) to distinguish among real relations of the same and of different kinds those that are really distinct from and inhering in their relata and those that are not. But Ockham will reject both (A) and (C).

Ockham's attacks on (C) come in the context of his arguments that Scotus's theory entails an actual infinity of simultaneously existing things—a charge that I will examine in section 3. Then, in sections 4 and 5, I shall consider Ockham's attempt to establish the same conclusion for relations of power and quantitative relations, respectively. For each of the latter types, I shall discuss one additional argument that such relations cannot be things really distinct from their foundations.

3. NON-QUANTITATIVE INTRINSIC RELATIONS

Scotus uses the so-called separation arguments to prove that certain non-quantitative intrinsic relations of similarity, identity, and diversity are really distinct from their foundations. Ockham's principal objection to these conclusions is that it commits one to a simultaneously existing actual infinity of real things. For example, he argues that

...if distinction or diversity were a thing (*res*) distinct from absolute things, then the diversity is distinct from the absolute thing (*res*). Therefore, it is so related by another relation. Consequently, the second relation is really diverse from the first. Therefore, it is diverse by another relation. And I repeat the argument for it: it will be diverse by another relation, and there will be an infinite process, so that there will

27. *Ibid.*

be infinitely many really distinct things (*res*) in each thing—which is absurd.[28]

Again,

...if Socrates is similar to Plato, then this similarity is similar to that similarity. By the same token, the second similarity is similar to the other similarity. Thus, there will be an infinite process.[29]

But, as noted above (see Part One, chapter 5), an actual infinity of things (*res*) existing simultaneously was thought to be logically impossible.

Scotus had anticipated this sort of objection, however, and had in effect moved to halt such infinite processes by an appeal to (C)—the principle that if one thing inheres in another, and the latter cannot exist without the former, then they are really the same.[30] Consider first the case of diversity. Suppose that a and b are absolute things and c is a's relation of diversity from b and d is c's relation of diversity from a. Since a is the foundation of c, c cannot exist without a. And since it is also impossible that a and c should exist and not be diverse, it follows that c cannot exist without d existing. But d inheres in c, its foundation. Therefore, by (C), since d inheres in c and c cannot exist without d, d is really the same as c, and the infinite process is halted.[31] Likewise, with similarity. Let k be Socrates' similarity to Plato and l be Plato's similarity to Socrates; let m be k's similarity to l and n be l's similarity to m. Scotus will say that k is really distinct from Socrates and l from Plato, because in each case the latter can exist without the former. But k cannot exist without l, because they are co-relations and by (D) co-relations are naturally simultaneous in this sense. And it is impossible that both k and l exist without m's existing, because similarity is an intrinsic relation. Consequently, k cannot exist without m's existing. Therefore, since m inheres in its foundation k and k

28. *Ibid.*

29. *Ibid.*, (OTh IV, 293).

30. Cf. Scotus's *Ord.* II, d.1, q.4–5, n.198, (Vaticana VII, 100) and n.239, (Vaticana VII, 119).

31. Ockham's *Ord.* I, d.30, q.1, (OTh IV, 292–93).

cannot exist without m, m is really the same as k, and the infinite process is once again halted.[32]

Ockham's reactions to Scotus's reply are manifold and negative. (3.1) On the one hand, Ockham points out that even if one grants (C), an infinite process in relations of diversity can be generated another way. Suppose that Socrates and Plato both exist and that each is diverse from the other. Let Socrates' diversity from Plato be a and Plato's diversity from Socrates be b. Since Socrates can exist without Plato, who is the term of a, Socrates can exist without a. Hence, by Scotus's separation arguments, a must be really distinct from Socrates, and Socrates will be related by a relation of diversity—call it f—to a. Since Socrates can exist without a, which is the term of f, Socrates can exist without f. Consequently, according to Scotus's separation arguments, f will be really distinct from Socrates, too, and Socrates will be related by a relation of diversity to f... And so on to infinity. Thus, instead of arguing for an infinite process in relations of diversity by maintaining that each relation is related to another by another relation, Ockham argues that Socrates is related to each relation by yet another relation.[33]

It may be objected that this infinite process can be halted by an appeal to (C) as well. For

> ...although f is really distinct from Socrates, nevertheless, it is not really distinct from a, because a cannot exist without f. Thus, the process will stop with the second [relation].[34]

This reasoning will not hold good. For (C) allows one to infer that a and f are really the same, only if a cannot exist without f and f inheres in a. But this last condition is not satisfied, since a

---

32. Scotus spells out this reasoning in reply to an objection having to do with relations of identity in *Ordinatio* II, d.1, q.4–5, n.268–69, (Vaticana VII, 133–34), which Ockham quotes as a reply to his own argument about similarity in his *Ordinatio* I, d.30, q.1, (OTh IV, 293–94). I have changed the example to similarity and have used k, l, m, and n instead of a, b, c, and d to make the discussion less confusing.

33. *Ibid.*, (OTh IV, 295).

34. *Ibid.*

is the term of f and not its foundation. As Ockham comments,

> ...even though, according to this opinion, a relation could be the same as its foundation, nevertheless, a real relation cannot be really the same as its term. But the term of f is a. Therefore, f cannot be really the same as a.[35]

Thus, whether or not (C) is granted, it seems that Scotus will be forced to assume an actual infinity of simultaneously existing things.

(3.2) Ockham charges further that (C) halts the first two infinite processes only by allowing counter-instances to

(K) There is only one primary term for each primary relation,

a principle that Scotus himself accepts.[36] For in the first argument about diversity, Scotus claims that the relation c is related to its foundation through itself, and hence that the single relation c not only has b as its term insofar as it relates a to b, but also has a as its term insofar as it relates itself to a. In the argument about similarity, k is said to have Plato as its term insofar as it relates Socrates to Plato, but k is said to have l as its term insofar as it relates itself to l.[37]

Scotus might reply that he is not saying that what is in every way the same relation has distinct primary terms, but only that relations really the same but formally distinct do. Thus, in the first case, c has its term in b and d has its term in a, where c and d are really the same but formally distinct. In the second, k has its term in Plato and m has its term in l, where k and m are really the same but formally distinct. Hence, (C) does not lead to a violation of (K) properly understood.

The intelligiblity of this answer and of (C) itself turns on the

---

35. *Ibid.*

36. In fact, he endorses the more general claim that "it cannot be the same relation unless it is between the same extremes" in *Ordinatio* I, d.30, q.1–2, n.12, (Vaticana VI, 126).

37. *Ord.* I, d.30, q.1, (OTh IV, 292–94).

legitimacy of Scotus's formal distinction. For Ockham contends that "nothing can inhere in itself, properly speaking."[38] Scotus will agree that what is in every way the same as a thing cannot inhere in it, but will insist that if *b* is really the same as but formally distinct from *a*, then *b* can, properly speaking, inhere in *a*. Ockham, for his part, rejects any formal distinction in creatures on the ground that it leads to ontological paradox (see Part One, chapter 2 above), and concludes that if one creature inheres in another, it must be really distinct from it. Hence, from Ockham's point of view, Scotus's principle

(C) If *b* inheres in *a* and *a* cannot exist without *b*, then *b* is really the same as *a*

can be at most trivially true by virtue of the falsity of the antecedent; for the consequent cannot be true if the antecedent is.[39]

(3.3) The troublesome clause in (C) is the supposition that *b* inheres in *a*. Deleting it, Ockham acts on Scotus's behalf to replace (C) with

(L) If *a* cannot exist without *b* and vice versa, then *b* is really the same as *a*,

which combines with

(D) Co-relations are naturally simultaneous in that it is logically impossible for one of them to obtain without the other,

to yield the absurd conclusion that relations are neither substances nor accidents. For according to (D), it is impossible for any relation to exist without its co-relation. Thus, for example, it is logically impossible for Socrates' similarity to Plato to exist without Plato's similarity to Socrates, or vice versa. If so, by (L), the former relation of similarity is identical with the

38. *Ibid.*, (OTh IV, 297).
39. *Ibid.*, (OTh IV, 297–98).

latter. But Socrates' similarity to Plato cannot inhere in Plato, because Plato is not its foundation; therefore, by the Indiscernibility of Identicals, Plato's similarity to Socrates cannot inhere in Plato either. By the same token, Plato's similarity to Socrates cannot inhere in Socrates because Socrates is not its foundation. Therefore, neither can Socrates' similarity to Plato. So neither similarity inheres in anything. But neither is a substance, because each is a relative thing, while substances are absolute things. Therefore, some created things are neither substances nor accidents—which is absurd.[40]

Ockham's argument seems valid, but Scotus would deny that it tells against any view endorsed by him. For while he defends (C) he should have found in it an antidote to (A) and to his own separation arguments. For, Ockham contends, anyone who versa because *a* and *b* are naturally simultaneous, even though *a* and *b* are really distinct.

(3.4) Further, Ockham thinks that insofar as Scotus endorsed (C) he should have found in it an antidote to (A) and to his own separation arguments. For, Ockham contends, anyone who grants (C) in the singluar, should grant it in the plural. Proffering the analogous principle

> (M) If *c* inheres in *a* and *d* inheres in *b* and it is logically impossible for *a* and *b* to exist without *c* and *d*, then *c* and *d* are not really distinct from *a* and *b*,

Ockham argues that no intrinsic relations are really distinct from their relata. Since two white things cannot exist without being similar, even though one white thing can, the similarity of the one to the other and vice versa will not, by (M), be really distinct from the two white things. Likewise, since Socrates and Plato cannot both exist without being diverse from one another, even though each of them can exist without being diverse from the other, the diversity of one from the other and vice versa will not, by (M), be really distinct from Socrates and Plato.

Ingenious as Ockham's argument is, (M) does not seem to be

---

40. *Ibid.*, (OTh IV, 297); *Quodl.* VI, q.8, arg.4, (OTh IX, 615).

simply "(C) in the plural." Rather

> (N) If *c* inheres in *a* and *d* inheres in *b* and it is logically im-
> possible for *a* to exist without *c* and logically impossible
> for *b* to exist without *d*, then *c* is not really distinct from
> *a* and *d* is not really distinct from *b*,

is. But the above mentioned two white things or Socrates and
Plato do not satisfy the antecedent of (N), since each of them
could exist without the other and hence without its similarity to
or diversity from the other.[41]

(3.5) Having argued with mixed success that (C) is unacceptable and could not, in any event, have been consistently held by
Scotus, Ockham replaces it with

> (O) When some things are of the same kind, if one of them is
> related to another by a really distinct relation, the same
> thing is related to another of altogether the same kind by
> a distinct relation,

which can be used to reinforce his own argument for an infinite
process in relations of similarity. Scotus had tried to block this
regress by maintaining that Socrates' similarity to Plato was not
similar to Plato's similarity to Socrates by a third really distinct
similarity relation. But given Scotus's separation arguments, he
would have to grant that Socrates' similarity to Plato is similar
to John's similarity to Paul by a third really distinct similarity
relation. For since it is logically possible for Socrates and Plato
to exist when John and Paul do not, it is logically possible that
Socrates' similarity to Plato exists without being similar to
John's similarity to Paul. Therefore, by (O), since the similarity
of John to Paul is of the same kind as the similarity of Plato to
Socrates, the similarity of Socrates to Plato will be related to the
latter by a really distinct relation of similarity as well—contrary to Scotus's conclusion—and the infinite process will be
generated after all.

41. *Ord.* I, d.30, q.1, (OTh IV, 299–300).

4. RELATIONS OF POWER

Scotus claims that in creatures the relations of cause and effect are real things distinct from absolute things. In addition to his general arguments, Ockham offers three main arguments against this thesis, of which the second is *ad hominem*, the third theological, and the first an attempt to convict the theory of assuming a simultaneously existing, actual infinity of things.

(4.1) Ockham argues as follows that Scotus's thesis commits him to an actual infinity of simultaneously existing things:

> ...if causality were any such little thing, then any created agent would necessarily change with respect to some positive thing whenever it acted. Thus, whenever the sun heated these things here below, it would necessarily receive as many new things as it heated. In that case, if the sun heats a piece of wood, since there are infinitely many heated parts in the piece of wood, infinitely many such things are received in the sun.[42]

Here Ockham appeals to the Aristotelian doctrine, accepted by him and by Scotus, that extended bodies are infinitely divisible and continuous. If the sun is related to each of the infinitely many parts of the continuum by a relation of causing heat, and if such relations are things really distinct from absolute things, then infinitely many such things will come to exist in the sun every time it heats something extended.

It may be objected that Ockham misrepresents Aristotle's doctrine, however. For the Philosopher maintains that extended things are infinitely *divisible*, not that they are infinitely divided. Accordingly, he would assert that a continuous body is actually one thing that has infinitely many parts in potentiality only, but not in actuality. Thus,

> :...just as the piece of wood is one thing and has infinitely many parts of the same proportion only in potentiality, so the relation received in the sun is one thing extended in the sun that has infinitely many parts of

---

42. *Quodl.* VI, q.12, (OTh IX, 631); cf. *Ord.* I, d.30, q.1, (OTh IV, 301–302).

the same proportion only in potentiality.[43]

Ockham anticipated this objection and counters it with two ingenious arguments that even though such parts are not actually separated from one another still each must be regarded as a subject of inherence or property-bearer in its own right. The first argument runs as follows:

> ...On the contrary, no more actuality is required in something for being a term of different relations than for being the source that brings about some activity. But one part of a continuum, insofar as it is distinct from another and is in the whole, can be the source that brings about some activity. Proof: Take one large fire. One part of it can heat wood that is spatially proximate to it while another distant part does not heat the wood, as we see in the sense experience. Therefore, how much more can each part be the term of a relation...[44]

Again, Ockham observes that "one part of the thing acted upon can have one quality while another part can have the contrary quality."[45] Take any two mutually exclusive parts of a continuum p_1 and p_2. It is logically possible that p_1 be white when p_2 is black, and hence logically possible that p_1 has whiteness inhering in it and p_2 has blackness inhering in it at one and the same time. Again, it is logically possible that the sun should heat p_1 while not heating p_2, and hence logically possible both that p_1 should have heat inhering in it while p_2 does not, and logically possible that p_1 have the relation of being heated inhering in it while p_2 does not. But if the different parts of the continuum can have incompatible forms inhering in them simultaneously, it must be that each part is a property-bearer or subject of inherence in its own right.

It certainly follows from those arguments that if relations of causality and of being-an-effect-of are things really distinct from absolute things, there is an actual infinity of simultaneously existing things whenever a cause acts on a

43. Quodl. VI, q.12, (OTh IX, 631); Ord. I, d.30, q.1, (OTh IV, 301–302).

44. Rep. II, q.2, (OTh V, 34).

45. Quodl. VI, q.12, (OTh IX, 631); Ord. I, d.30, q.1, (OTh IV, 302).

continuum. Unfortunately for Ockham, his arguments have a further, more general consequence that he does not draw: viz., that anyone who allows that forms of any sort inhere in extended things is committed to an actual infinity of simultaneously existing things. If each part of the continuum is a property-bearer or subject of inherence in its own right and therefore must have its own relation of being-acted-upon even when the whole log is being acted upon, so also each part of the continuum must have its own form of whiteness even if the whole log is white. Since (as we shall see in chapter 8) Ockham himself believes that qualities such as whiteness are things really distinct from substance, and that an actual infinity of simultaneously existing things is impossible, he will have as much reason as Scotus to find a way around this argument.

It might be replied that Ockham's arguments still fail to take the idea of a potential infinity seriously. Of course, for any two parts of the continuum, it is logically possible that they be divided in actuality; for any two parts, it is logically possible that one act to produce an effect while the other does not; and for any two parts, it is logically possible that a form inhering in one is incompatible with a form inhering in the other. But so long as they are not actually divided, they are actually one thing and parts only in potentiality; so long as the whole causes, they are actually one cause and distinct causes only in potentiality; and so long as they do not actually have distinct, incompatible forms inhering in them, they are actually one but potentialy distinct property-bearers.

It is not clear that Scotus is in a position to rest his case with this reply, however. As we shall see in section 5, he admitted quantitative relations to be things really distinct from the absolute things in which they inhere. But even when the parts of a continuum are not actually divided, one part is the double or a fourth or a third of another, etc. Each part bears a different proportion of relation to the whole. Hence, if these relations of doubleness, halfness, fourthness, etc. are things really distinct from absolute things, then the parts of a continuum will always have incompatible forms inhering in them, and hence—even by the latter argument—be actually distinct property-bearers or subjects of inherence.

(4.2) To understand Ockham's second argument, we must briefly examine Scotus's doctrine of instants of nature, which is based on the Aristotelian notions of natural priority, natural posterity, and natural simultaneity explained above. Scotus suggests that just as there is—independently of anyone's thinking about it—a temporal order among things according to which some are before, others after, and still others simultaneous with a given thing; so there is—independently of anyone's thinking about it—a natural order among things according to which some are prior, others posterior, and still others simultaneous. Further, just as temporal relations can be specified by referring to instants of time, so natural relations could be marked by referring to earlier and later instants of nature. Thus, what is naturally prior to something else could be said to exist at an earlier instant of nature than it does; naturally simultaneous, the same instant of nature; and naturally posterior, a later instant of nature. And just as a thing may have different properties at different times, so also, Scotus contends, at earlier and later instances of nature. Consequently, Scotus concludes, it is just as appropriate to relativize predications to instants of nature as to instants of time; and he finds this device particularly fruitful in analyzing divine thought and volition. Although Ockham rejects Scotus's doctrine of instants of nature just as vehemently as his formal distinction (for reasons to be examined in Part Five, chapter 24 below), Ockham thinks it can be combined with Scotus's assertion that

(E) Where relations are really distinct from their foundations, the relata are naturally prior to the relation,

to show that being-the-cause-of and being-the-effect-of are not real things really distinct from absolute things. Ockham's two versions of this reasoning may be set out as follows:

(i)   If causality or production were a thing (res) distinct from absolute things, then either it would be (a) naturally prior, or (b) naturally simultaneous with, or (c) naturally posterior to the produced effect.

(ii)   A relation is essentially dependent on both its founda-
         tion and its term. (Scotus's equivalent to (E))

(iii)   Therefore, a relation is not naturally prior to either its
         foundation or to its term. (ii)

(iv)   The effect produced is the term of the relation of
         causality or production.

(v)   Therefore, not–(ia). (i, iii, and iv)

(vi)   Not-(ib). (ii)

(vii)   If (ic), then the effect would exist at an instant of nature
         prior to its production—which is absurd.

(viii)   Therefore, not-(ic). (vii)

(ix)   Therefore, causality or production is not a thing (res)
         distinct from absolute things. (i, v, vi, and viii)[46]

Everyone would agree that it is impossible that a and b both exist at t_1 and that t_2 is the first instance of b's existence (where t_2
is a later instant of time than t_1). Likewise, on Scotus's doctrine
of instants of nature, it is contradictory to assert that a and b
both exist at n_1 and n_2 is the first instant at which b exists
(where n_2 is a later instant of nature than n_1). But b is produced
in existence at the first instant (if any) at which b exists.
Therefore, if a thing were produced in existence only by virtue
of a really distinct relation of production inhering in its cause
and a really distinct relation of being-an-effect existing in it,
nothing could ever be produced in existence. For, by (E), the
first instant of inherence will be later than the first instant of b's
existence.

These arguments seem effective *ad hominem* against anyone
who grants (E) and the Scotistic doctrine of instants of nature.

---

46. *Ibid.*, (OTh IV, 300–301); cf. *Quodl.* VI, q.12, (OTh IX, 629–631).

Should anyone think to preserve the thesis that the relations of causality and of being-an-effect-of are things really distinct from absolute things by dropping the latter while retaining the former, Ockham will confront him with the argument in (2.4) above.

(4.3) The third argument is based on the doctrine of divine omnipotence, according to which God has the power to bring about anything logically possible and producible (with some exceptions not relevant here; see Part Five, chapter 28) and has the power to bring it about directly, without the assistance of any secondary causes.

(i)   Every thing (*res*) that God can make by means of a secondary cause that is efficient *per se*, He can make without any secondary efficient cause. (Doctrine of omnipotence)

(ii)   If relations of efficient causality are things really distinct from absolute things, and if God acts together with a given efficient cause to produce a relation of efficient causality in that cause, then God can produce that relation of efficient causality without a secondary cause. (instance of (i))

(iii)   Suppose God does produce that relation without a secondary cause.

(iv)   Anything can be denominated from any form existing in it.

(v)   Therefore, the thing in which that relation is produced is an efficient cause. (iii and iv)

(vi)   It effects only the relation.

(vii)   Therefore, God does not act alone to produce that relation. (v and vi)

(viii) (vii) and (iii) are contradictory.

(ix)   Therefore, the relation of efficient causality is not a thing to be caused. (viii and ii)[47]

Premise (i) is ambiguous between

(i′)   Everything (*res*) that God can make by means of a secondary cause that is efficient *per se*, He can make without any secondary efficient cause acting to produce that thing.

and

(i″)   Everything (*res*) that God can make by means of a secondary cause that is efficient *per se,* He can make without any secondary efficient cause acting to produce anything whatever.

If relations are things really distinct from absolute things, it seems obvious that (i″) is not true. For given (iv), God cannot produce a relation of efficient causality in anything x without x's being an efficient cause. And since given (E), no relation can exist without a term, it follows that God cannot produce such a relation in anything x without some secondary efficient cause (namely, x) acting to produce something or other.

All that is required by the doctrine of divine omnipotence, however, is (i′). The above argument derives a violation of (i′) from a violation of (i″) by means of premise (vi). But (vi) does not follow from (ii) and (iii) as they stand. Ockham probably intended some such assumption as

(iii′) Only God and a creature x exist, and God produces a relation of efficient causality in x without any secondary cause acting to produce that relation and God produces nothing else with or without the aid of any secondary cause.

47.   *Ibid.*, (OTh IX, 632); cf. *Summa logicae* I, c.57, (OPh I, 185) and *Quodl.* VII, q.3, (OTh IX, 710).

Since neither God nor x can be the term of x's relation of efficient causality, it follows that the relation of efficient causality itself must be.

Scotus might well question whether (iii') is a logically possible state of affairs, however. For it would seem to follow from (E) that a relation cannot be its own term, since a relation is naturally posterior to its term and is not naturally posterior to itself. Indeed, Ockham himself uses this claim against Scotus in *Ordinatio* I, d.30, q.1, when he is criticizing the latter's use of (C) to halt infinite processes in relations of diversity and similarity.[48] But if (iii') is contradictory, that will be enough to explain why we get a contradiction in step (viii) and we will not be able to draw any further conclusions about the ontological status of relations of efficient causality.

5.   INTRINSIC RELATIONS OF QUANTITY

Ockham gives two principal reasons for denying that intrinsic relations of quantity such as doubleness, halfness, equality, etc. are things really distinct from absolute things. There is the now familiar contention that such an assumption leads to an actual infinity of simultaneously existing things; and the further charge that such relations cannot be things because there could be no proper proportion between them and any subject of inherence. Since the first is easier to understand after the second, I shall reverse the order in discussing them here.

(5.1) Focussing on the relations of doubleness and halfness, Ockham argues as follows:[49]

(i)   Suppose doubleness (halfness) is some thing (*res*) really distinct from absolute things.

(ii)   Therefore, doubleness (halfness) is either (a) divisible or (b) indivisible. (i)

---

48. (OTh IV, 295).

49. *Ibid.*, (OTh IV, 303–304); *Quodl.* VI, q.9–10, (OTh IX, 620–22); cf. *Expos. Praedicam.*, c.12, (OPh II, 241–42) and *Summa logicae* I, c.50, (OPh I, 160–61).

(iii)   If (iib), the doubleness (halfness) would be whole in the whole subject and whole in each part.

(iv)   Anything can be denominated from any form existing in it.

(v)   Therefore, if (iib), then the same subject will be simultaneously double and half with respect to the same—which is absurd. (iii and iv)

(vi)   Therefore, not-(iib). (v)

(vii)   If (iia), then doubleness (halfness) would be divisible either (a) into parts of the same kind or (b) into parts of different kinds.

(viii)   If (viia), the part will still be double (half) the way the whole is and the same subject will be simultaneously both double and half—which is absurd.

(ix)   Therefore, not-(viia). (viii)

(x)   Not-(viib).

(xi)   Therefore, not-(iia). (vii, ix, and x)

(xii)   Therefore, not-(ii). (vi and xi)

(xiii)   Therefore, not-(i). (xii)

The disjunction in (ii) is logically exhaustive, and (iv) is a generally accepted thesis of hylomorphism. (iii) merely instantiates a general claim about the way indivisible accidents inhere in their subjects. And when an objector later suggests that an indivisible accident of doubleness might be whole in the whole subject but not exist in the parts at all, Ockham pours scorn on the idea:

> On the contrary, it is not imaginable that any accident should inform

a subject and nevertheless that neither the whole accident nor any of its parts is in any part of the subject.[50]

From an atomist's point of view, (x) might seem false, since for him a white thing is ultimately divisible into atoms none of which is white; a sweet thing into the atoms none of which is sweet; etc. But from an Aristotelian point of view, according to which a white thing is a composite of matter and substantial and accidental forms, (x) seems initially plausible where qualities are concerned: the form of whiteness seems divisible only into partial whitenesses; the form of sweetness, into partial sweetnesses; etc. On the other hand, it is far from obvious that doubleness (halfness) must be divisible into parts each of which is a doubleness (halfness). Ockham defends (x) by means of the following argument:

(a) Whenever parts are of a different kind, they form something that is one *per se* and they are related the way matter is related to substantial form and they are not distinct in place or subject.

(b) Therefore, if the parts of doubleness (halfness) were of different kinds from doubleness (halfness), they would not differ in place or subject.

(c) Therefore, if (viib), all of the parts of doubleness (halfness) would be in each part and so doubleness (halfness) would be in each part of the subject. (b)

(d) Therefore, if (viib), each part of the subject will be double and half with respect to the same — which is absurd. (c and iv)

(e) Therefore, not-(viib). (d)

This ingenious argument depends heavily on (a). Where matter and substantial form combine to make something *per se*, the

50. *Quodl.* VI, q.10, (OTh IX, 623); cf. *Ord.* I, d.30, q.1, (OTh IV, 305).

matter and the substantial form inhering in it occupy exactly the same place and constitute exactly the same subject in existence. (a) says that if parts of kinds other than doubleness (halfness) are essentially united to make doubleness (halfness), then all of those parts will be located in exactly the same subject.

An objector observes that (a) may admit of counterexamples: for "it is clear in anatomy that not every part of a human being is a human being, even where both matter and form go together."[51] This remark admits of a double interpretation. The objector may be alluding to the fact that the parts of a human being include hands, feet, arms, and legs, none of which is itself a human being. Yet, the accidents of the hands are in a different part of the matter from the accidents of the feet; and the matter in the hands is in a different place from the matter in the feet. Alternatively, the objector may refer to Ockham's own view (see Part Four, chapter 15 below) that a human being is a composite of matter, the form of corporeity, the form of sensory soul, and the form of intellectual soul; yet there is a sense in which these parts are distinct in place and subject. For while the forms of corporeity and sensory soul are extended in the matter, in such a way that the whole is in the whole and a part in each part, the form of intellectual soul is not extended and so is whole in the whole and whole in each part.

Ockham replies that

> ...this is inadequate, because whatever pertains to those that have different substantial forms, nevertheless, where there is only one substantial form and one matter, and where accidents are similar in all of the parts, there some parts and the whole must be of the same kind.[52]

He seems to be saying that he intended to restrict (a) to cases "where there is only one substantial form and one matter, and where accidents are similar in all of the parts," whereas a human being has a plurality of substantial forms and the hands and feet of the human body have different accidents. If so, the objector might still claim that (a) does not apply in the case at

51. *Ibid.*, (OTh IV, 304).
52. *Ibid.*

hand. For not only does he want to claim that the parts of doubleness are different in kind from doubleness, but also that they are different in kind from each other. Ockham acknowledges this suggestion:

> Suppose some heckler says that something quantified is the double of something else, and that this doubleness exists only in the whole, because it includes the halfness that exists in some part of it. For its fourth part is half of a part of which the whole is the double, and an intermediate part is equal to it, etc. For each part has some relation to that of which the whole is the double. But one has the relation of equality, the other, the relation of halfness, etc.[53]

Ockham replies that "it follows from this that there will be infinitely many things (*res*) of a different kind in this double."[54] For an extended body is infinitely divisible, and each of the infinitely many parts of the continuum will be related to the whole and to that of which the whole is the double, etc. Thus, doubleness will be composed of infinitely many such things, and there will be an actual infinity of simultaneously existing things—which was thought impossible.

A second objection rejects the inference of (v) from (iii) and (iv):

> Again, suppose a heckler says that doubleness exists in the whole and in each part. For no part of the double can be found, which is not double with respect to any part of the half. Thus, the whole doubleness is doubleness, certainly not with respect to the double, but with respect to a part of the double. For example, half of the double is double with respect to half of the first half. The same will hold true for equality and the like.[55]

Suppose the parts of doubleness (halfness) are doubleness (halfness), so that both doubleness and halfness exist in each part of the object. It does not follow that each part is double and half *with respect to the same part*. Rather each part is the double

53. *Ibid.*, (OTh IV, 304–305).
54. *Ibid.*
55. *Ibid.*, (OTh IV, 305).

of some smaller fraction of that of which the whole is the double; and each part other than the half is half of some smaller fraction than the half of the whole is. But the parts will be half with respect to one fraction and double with respect to a smaller fraction, etc.

Ockham charges that this is inadequate, because

> ...they assume that doubleness and halfness in numbers are like doubleness and halfness in a continuum. But where numbers are concerned, it is possible to take some double number, no part of which is the double of any part in the half—or at least not every part is. For four is the double of two, but three is the double of no part of two.[56]

This reply does not so much defend the inference of (v) from (iii) and (iv), as it challenges the adequacy of the objector's account of how doubleness is divided into parts. What the objector says may be plausible where the doubleness in a continuum is concerned, and it is on continua that discussion has focussed so far. But relations of doubleness and halfness are also to be found in numbers of discrete things. For example, suppose there is a group of four human beings. The whole group is the double of its half. But the subgroup of three men is not the double of any part of the whole. Hence, it seems that not all of the parts of doubleness can be doubleness after all.

Here the objector might respond that one should not give a uniform account of how doubleness is divided into parts. Rather one should say that where doubleness in a continuous body is concerned, the parts of doubleness are doubleness; but where doubleness in numbers of discrete entities is concerned, the parts of doubleness are of kinds other than doubleness. In Ockham's example, the doubleness in the group of four human beings is composed of fourthnesses, halfnesses, three-fourthnesses, etc.

No doubt Ockham would find himself unable to see how a thing that was divisible only into parts of the same kind and a thing that was divisible only into parts of different kinds, could be things of the very same kind. And plausibility would be on

56. *Ibid.*

Ockham's side here.

(5.2) Even if the inherence of doubleness, halfness, etc. could be explained, Scotus's view—that they are things really distinct from absolute things—would have to be rejected, according to Ockham. For it commits one to a simultaneously existing actual infinity of things. Thus, Ockham argues,

> ...If doubleness were some thing [distinct] from absolute things, then it follows that in [every] double there would be an infinity of small things, each of which differed in species from the others. For if one body (a) is the double with respect to another (b) separate from it, then the whole doubleness will be in the whole double. Therefore, just as the whole (of a) is double with respect to that body (b), so its (a's) half is equal to it (b); and the fourth part (of a) is half with respect to that body (b) of which its whole is the double. And so each part of the same proportion of the double body has some relation to that body of which its whole is the double: one has the relation of equality, another of halfness, etc. And no part (of a) has the same proportion to that body (b) as another has. Rather they are of different species. Consequently, there will be infinitely many relations of different species in this double, just as parts of the same proportion are infinitely many.[57]

So long as such quantitative relations are supposed to be things really distinct from absolute things, this conclusion seems inescapable.

6. SUMMARY OF OCKHAM'S ATTACK ON SCOTUS'S THEORY OF REAL RELATIONS

Although Ockham's critique of Scotus's theory of real relations is not entirely successful, it nevertheless inflicts considerable damage on the latter's position. Using the separation arguments and

(A) There can be no passage from contradictory to contradictory apart from the generation or corruption of some thing (*res*),

57. *Quodl.* VI, q.10, (OTh IX, 622–23).

Scotus infers that many intrinsic relations and relations of power are things really distinct from and inhering in absolute things. Ockham tries to show that these principles commit Scotus to simultaneously existing actual infinities of such relations, which both regard as logically impossible. Scotus seeks to fight off these consequences with

> (C) If b inheres, properly speaking, in a, and a cannot exist without b, then b is really the same as a.

Some of Ockham's proofs of actual infinities are unaffected by (C), however: viz., one argument for an infinite process in relations of diversity, and the arguments concerning intrinsic relations of quantity, such as doubleness, halfness, etc. Further, (C) is only as intelligible as Scotus's formal distinction, which Ockham has argued is a bogus notion (see Part One, chapter 2 above).

Ockham also tries to detail other ways in which Scotus's position can be reduced to contradiction. In (2.4), Ockham argues that Scotus's theory also combines with

> (E) Where relations are really distinct from their foundations, the relata are naturally prior to the relation,

and

> (F) God can make the prior without anything naturally posterior to it,

to yield a contradiction. For if similarity were a thing really distinct from its foundation, God could, by (E) and (F), make two white things apart from any such real relations of similarity; yet they would still be similar. And if paternity and filiation were things really distinct from their foundations, God could preserve Socrates and Plato in existence after Socrates begot Plato without the things that are their paternity and filiation; yet Socrates would still be the father of Plato and Plato the son of Socrates. This reasoning would be telling against Scotus if he had claimed that all such intrinsic and causal relations are things really distinct from their relata. But Scotus has made a point of distinguishing cases in which they are from those in which they are not by means of (C). Having shown that (C) is unacceptable, Ockham replaces it with

(G) If any instance of a given relation is a thing really distinct from and inhering in its relata, then every instance of that relation is,

and

(H) If one relation were a thing (*res*) really distinct from and inhering in its relata, by the same token, every other relation of any kind would be, too,

and

(O) When some things are of the same kind, if one of them is related to another by a really distinct relation, the same thing is related to another of altogether the same kind of a distinct relation,

to show that the consequences of (A) and the separation arguments are inconsistent with (E) and (F).

In (2.3) Ockham successfully shows Scotus's assumption that some intrinsic relations are things really distinct from their relata to be incompatible with

(B) Natural causes can act only within a determinate distance of the things they are acting upon,

and

(D) Co-relations are naturally simultaneous in that it is logically impossible for one of them to obtain without the other.

both of which are endorsed by Scotus for relevant instances. Again, in (4.2), Ockham successfully combines Scotus's doctrine of instants of nature with (E) to infer that created relations of causality and of being-an-effect-of cannot be things really distinct from absolute things, contrary to Scotus's contention. And in (5.1) he urges with some plausibility that if quantitative relations such as doubleness, halfness, etc. were things really distinct from absolute things, some uniform account would have to be given of how those accidents can be divided into parts, whereas no such account can be found.

7.   THE POSITION OF UNAIDED NATURAL REASON REGARDING REAL RELATIONS

Ockham thinks that his arguments against Scotus's theory provide substantial grounds for denying that any real relations are things really distinct from their relata.[58] The question remains whether Scotus's arguments in favor of this thesis are even weightier. For example, if unaided natural reason denies that any real relations are things really distinct from their relata, will it not be forced to identify them with beings of reason and hence face the seemingly insurmountable difficulties raised by Scotus against such an alternative? Ockham is convinced that it will not. Accepting (A) or (A''), Scotus and his opponent agree that statements of the form 'aRb' entail statements of the form 'R-ness exists', where substitutions for 'R-ness' function as merely absolute terms to name some entity. Their ontology offers them two alternatives: either substitutions for 'R-ness' name a real being or they name a being of reason. Ockham concedes that Scotus has reduced the second alternative to an absurdity.[59] But he thinks that the latter arguments combine

58. *Ord.* I, d.30, q.1, (OTh IV, 306).
59. A concession not made by Ockham's older contemporary Peter Aureol, who tries to defend such a view in his commentary on the *Sentences* I, d.30, p.2, a.l, (Rome, 1596, vol.I, 698–700). There is also one passage in which Ockham takes a more tolerant attitude towards such a viewpoint. While considering what sort of relation God's eternal thought of creatures is, Ockham spells out answers given both (i) by those who hold that a and b are related only if a and b are actually denoted by a conventional or natural relative sign; and (ii) by those who maintain that a and b are related if they are of the sort that a conventional or natural relative sign would signify, if

with his own against Scotus's theory, to show that statements of
the form '*aRb*' do not entail statements of the form '*R*-ness exists' (where substitutions for '*R*-ness' function as merely absolute terms) and hence that (A) and (A″) are false. According to
Ockham, those who are guided by unaided natural reason
would replace (A) and (A″) with

(A′) Necessarily, if first *p* is true and then not-*p* is true, then
either something has been produced in existence for the
first time, or something that did exist has ceased to exist,
or some locomotion has occurred,

which will not sustain the arguments of Scotus and his opponents.

According to Ockham, unaided natural reason would hold
that relation terms are connotative terms that signify both
relata, or signify one primarily and connote the other, and connote that the relata exist in a certain way. Considering some of
Scotus's examples, adherents of unaided natural reason would
say that

> ...'composition' does not signify precisely two absolute things—say
> matter and form—but signifies them together with the fact that nothing
> corporeal comes between them...[60]

Similarly,

> They would reply...that 'spatial proximity' signifies not only those two
> absolute things but also signifies that no impediment lies in between
> them...[61]

As for 'similarity', they would say that it "signifies two white
things immediately, apart from any intermediate relation, or it

such a sign existed. And he refers to the difference between their answers as
posing "more of a verbal than a logical or real difficulty" (*Ord.* I, d.35, q.4,
(OTh IV, 474)).
    60. *Ibid.*, d.30, q.1, (OTh IV, 312).
    61. *Ibid.*

signifies one principally and the other connotatively."[62] Turning to causal relations, they would say that

> a cause and its effect, a producer and its product can really exist apart from any relation of reason, since 'cause' and 'active production' signify the absolute nature of the cause and connote the effect; the other way around for 'effect' and 'passive production', since they signify the effect principally and connote the cause apart from any relation of reason.[63]

Or again, "...'Socrates is the father of Plato' signifies only that Socrates has begotten Plato and both actually exist...."[64] And in general, they would say that statements of the form '*aRb*' assert no more than that *a* and *b* exist in a certain way, without implying the existence of a relation in any way distinct from the relata.

Ockham thinks that this treatment of relation terms as connotative terms provides the followers of unaided natural reason with a reply to Scotus's arguments based on (A) and to the "separation" arguments. They would distinguish two sorts of cases in which a foundation can, or first does and then does not, exist without being related in a given way. Sometimes the latter fact is to be explained by the fact that the other relatum can, or first does and then does not, fail to exist.

> ...the argument from separation does not hold good. For when a name signifies one thing principally and another connotatively, then when only the thing connoted and nothing real in the principal significatum is destroyed, that name will not denominate its principal significatum. For it does not signify the principal significatum unless the thing connoted exists together with it. Therefore, when the connoted object is destroyed, the denomination does not pertain to it. And given that the connoted object exists together with the principal significatum of that name or concept, immediately, without anything real being acquired by the principal significatum, that name or concept denominates both, in such a way that there has been a passage from one contradictory to another because of a mere change in the connoted object. The same

---

62. *Rep.* II, q.1, (OTh V, 16); cf. (OTh V, 9).
63. *Ibid.*, (OTh V, 26).
64. *Ord.* I, d.30, q.4, (OTh IV, 368).

holds if the principal significatum is destroyed and the connoted object remains...[65]

Since 'Socrates is similar to Plato' entails the existence of both Socrates and Plato, it may be first true and then false either because Plato first does and then does not exist or because Socrates first does and then does not exist. Likewise, one rod may first be and then not be the double of the other, because the second rod first does and then does not exist, or because the first rod first does and then does not exist. No relative entities—whether real things or beings of reason—need to be assumed to explain the change of truth value in such cases.

Sometimes things may both exist and first be unrelated and then related, or vice versa, because they first exist in one way and then in another.

> ...Thus, when the cause becomes spatially proximate, it has nothing positive then that it did not have before, but only that negation—viz., that there are not as many in between the spatially proximate cause and the thing acted upon as there are between a cause that is not spatially proximate and the thing acted upon. Thus, the relation is not that through which the cause is formally denominated cause or the product formally denominated cause...[66]

Rather it is the fact that they now exist in such a way as to have fewer things in between them. Again, they would say that the generation or corruption of some entity is not required to explain a change of truth-value in such cases:

> ...where the same absolute things remain in existence and there is locomotion between them, it is never necessary to assume such relations, but everything is saved through negations. For example, fire cannot act on water unless it is spatially proximate to it; and when it is spatially proximate, it can act. This spatial proximity is not a real relation. But the contradictories 'able to act' are successively true of fire because of locomotion by which one negation is acquired in fire that earlier was not in fire—viz., that when fire is spatially proximate, there are not as many things in between fire and water as when they are

---

65. *Rep.* II, q.2, (OTh V, 38–39).
66. *Ibid.*, (OTh V, 36).

not spatially proximate. Thus, the negation of many intermediate
things is acquired by fire through locomotion, and for this reason it can
act now and could not act before...[67]

When Ockham speaks of a negation being acquired in the fire,
he does not, of course, mean to imply that negations are entities
that inhere in things. Rather he means that a negative proposition becomes true about the fire, and that it does so is to be explained in the case by locomotion without the generation or
corruption of any entities.

Further, on this analysis, the truth-value of many statements
of the form 'aRb' will be independent of whether or not—*per
impossibile*—anyone ever thinks about it. 'Fire is spatially proximate to water' does not entail the existence of any being of
reason, and neither does 'Socrates is similar to Plato', 'Matter
and form make a composite', or 'This line is the double of that
one'. Rather they assert the existence of states of affairs that do
or do not obtain, whether or not—*per impossibile*—anyone
ever thinks they do. Hence, this analysis of relation statements
will not destroy the unity of the universe, the causality of secondary causes, or the reality of the mathematical sciences, the way
that of Scotus's opponent does.

It is one thing to ask what it is for things to be related—i.e.,
what the truth conditions for statements of the form 'aRb' are;
another to inquire what relations are—i.e., what the truth conditions for statements of the form 'R-ness exists' are. Scotus has
answered the latter by saying that for some statements of the
form 'R-ness exists', the statement will be true, if and only if
some thing (*res*) really distinct from its relata exists. And corresponding statements of the form 'aRb' will be true, if and only
if a exists and b exists and R-ness exists and R-ness inheres in a.
By contrast, Scotus's opponent has claimed that statements of
the form 'R-ness exists' are true, if and only if some being of
reason exists; and statements of the form 'aRb' exist and will be
true, only if such a being of reason exists. Ockham has offered
unaided natural reason a single answer to the first question: viz.,

67. *Ibid.*, (OTh V, 45).

that statements of the form '*aRb*' are true if and only if both *a* and *b* exist in the way connoted by the substitution for '*R*'. So far as Ockham can see, however, adherents of unaided natural reason have a choice between two principal answers to the second question: (i) they can say that 'relation' is a term of first intention, in that it has personal supposition[68] for extramental things other than signs, in addition to anything else it may have personal supposition for; or (ii) they can hold that 'relation is a term of second intention that has personal supposition for concepts only.'[69] In his various discussions, Ockham indicates that the first alternative could be developed in a number of ways. (ia) First, one could allow that 'relation' and particular relation terms—whether concrete or abstract—can be predicated of par-

68. A term has personal supposition in a proposition when it stands in the proposition for those things it has been imposed to signify—e.g., both terms have personal supposition in the proposition 'A man is an animal'; material supposition, when it stands in proposition for tokens of the sound or mark type—e.g., the subject has material supposition in 'Man is a spoken monosyllable'; and simple supposition when it stands for its concept—e.g., the subject has simple supposition in 'Man is a species', according to Ockham. See Part Two, chapter 10 below.

69. In his article "Zur Relationslehre Wilhelms von Ockham," *Franziskanische Studien* XLIX (1967): 248–258, Hermann Grieve tends not to take this first alternative seriously, in the course of defending his conclusion that "Doncoeur schreibt somit zu Recht, dass die Beziehungen für Ockham eine Sache des Verstands geworden sind" (251). But twice at *Ordinatio* I, d.30, q.1, Ockham offers two choices. He says that "a relation is not its foundation, but only an intention and concept in the mind that signifies many absolute things. Or it is many absolute things the way a people is many human beings..." (OTh IV, 314). And again, "'similarity', taken in its abstract form can stand only for an intention in the mind, or for many things each of which is similar; just as 'people' can stand only for many" (OTh IV, 315). Hermann Grieve refers to these passages on p.250, note 12, and simply omits the second disjunct. Later, on p.253, he quotes both and explains, "...Der zweite Teil: 'Vel est plura absolute,' besagt: Die Wirklichkeit, für die eine Beziehung steht, ist die Wirklichkeit mehrerer Absoluta." In fact, Ockham is fairly persistent about posing this choice, and I see no reason to suppose that he favored the one rather than the other. For him, it would not have been a matter of much importance, since, as Grieve notes, "Die Wirklichkeit, um die es geht, ist in beiden Fallen dieselbe" (253).

ticular absolute things. Thus, one could grant 'A quality is a relation',[70] 'Socrates is a relation', 'Whiteness is a relation',[71] 'Socrates is a similarity' and 'Socrates is paternity'.[72] (ib) One could hold that while *concrete* relation terms such as 'similar' and 'equal' can be truly predicated about *a single* absolute thing, the abstract terms 'similarity' and 'equality' signify only *many* absolute things together, so that 'Socrates is similar' and 'Socrates is dissimilar' are true, but 'Socrates is similarity' and 'Socrates is dissimilarity' are false.[73] But 'Socrates and Plato are similarity or equality' may be true.[74] Ockham comments that the latter suggestion is plausible where the relation and co-relation are the same (as with similarity and equality) but not otherwise: he finds 'God and a creature are active creation' odd. (ic) Finally, Ockham takes note of a peculiar common usage according to which 'Whiteness is similarity' and 'Two white things are similarity' are false, while 'Similarity is two white things' would be true.[75] Each of these alternatives seems to imply that statements of the form '*R*-ness exists' are true if and only if both relata exist and exist in the way connoted by substitutions for '*R*-ness'; but they disagree about just what syncategorematic force is built into the meaning of abstract relation terms.

Ockham thinks that Aristotle endorsed (ii).[76] If 'relation' is a term of second intention, it has personal supposition only for the concepts 'similarity', 'equality', 'paternity', etc. Accordingly, 'Socrates is a relation' and 'Whiteness is a relation' would be false,[77] while 'No substance is a relation' would be true and immediate.[78] Likewise 'Similarity is a relation', 'Equality is a relation', etc. would be true. But there is an ambiguity in this

70. *Quodl.* VI, q.17, (OTh IX, 648).
71. *Ibid.*, q.22, (OTh IX, 666).
72. *Ibid.*, q.25, (OTh IX, 680).
73. *Ord.* I, d.30, q.1, (OTh IV, 314).
74. *Quodl.* VI, q.25, (OTh IX, 681–82); cf. *Summa logicae* I, c.6, (OPh I, 21).
75. *Quodl.* VI, q.25, (OTh IX, 681).
76. *Ibid.*, q.22, (OTh IX, 667).
77. *Ibid.*, (OTh IX, 669).
78. *Ibid.*, q.17, (OTh IX, 648).

position. (iia) It could mean that 'Similarity is a relation' is true where 'similarity' is taken to have personal supposition. (iib) Alternatively, it could mean that 'Similarity is a relation' is true where 'similarity' is taken to have simple supposition. There are a few passages in which (iia) may be suggested. For example, in *Ordinatio* I, d.30, q.1, Ockham writes,

> In reply to another argument, I grant the major, but I reply to the minor that the foundation does not contain such relations—either simultaneous or successively—by being identical with them. For the proposition 'Socrates really is similarity' and the proposition 'Socrates really is dissimilarity' are false. Therefore, I do not assume that a relation is really the same as its foundation. Rather I maintain that a relation is not its foundation, but only an intention or concept in the mind that signifies many absolute things. Or it is many absolute things the way a people is many human beings. But which of these theses represents the more proper use of speech is more relevant to a discussion of logic than of theology.[79]

And again in *Quodlibeta* VI, q.15,

> I reply to the principal argument that whiteness does not For whiteness is not similarity or dissimilarity. But I say that either similarity is a relative concept that signifies many taken together or it signifies many taken together; just as a people is many men and no man is a people, so similarity is many white things and no white thing is similarity...[80]

These texts seem to say that there are two alternatives: we can say that similarity is many white things, or we can say that it is a concept signifying many white things. If all Ockham means here is that we can take 'similarity' in personal supposition, and then the proposition 'Similarity is many white things' is true, or we can take it in simple supposition and then 'Similarity is a concept signifying many white things' is true, he would not seem to have presented any significant option. All terms can be construed as having either personal or simple supposition, and we can just as well say that either a man is an animal (personal sup-

79. (OTh IV, 314).
80. (OTh IX, 638–39).

position) or that a man is a concept that signifies an animal (simple supposition). There is no theoretical choice between these two. Insofar as Ockham purports to be confronting us with a genuine theoretical alternative in these passages, he must be taken as saying that where 'similarity' has personal supposition, we can say either that similarity is many white things, or we could say that similarity is a concept signifying many white things. On the latter option, the adherent of unaided natural reason would agree with Scotus's opponent in maintaining that a statement of the form '*R*-ness exists' is true, if and only if the relevant concept exists.

On the other hand, Ockham clearly represents Aristotle as opting for (iib) in the following passage from *Quodlibeta* VI, q.22:

> ...Therefore, I maintain that, according to the Philosopher's opinion, all of the following propositions, 'Socrates is a relation', 'Whiteness is a relation', 'A man is relative' and 'Whiteness is relative', should be denied. But the propositions 'Father is a relation', 'The Son is relative' and likewise 'Similarity is a relation' should be granted, and this where the subjects have *simple* supposition and the predicates personal supposition...[81]

Again, in *Ordinatio* I, d.30, q.3, Ockham assigns Aristotle the view that

> ...a relative name signifies in relation to something—i.e., it signifies various things of which one is similar or equal to another, etc. In that case, such names do not signify things other than substances and qualities, but signify substances and qualities...[82]

And he goes on to add that according to this view 'Two similar things are similarity' is a true proposition. But if 'similarity' signifies similar substances such as Socrates and Plato, it cannot be that it has personal supposition for concepts only. Rather the view ascribed to Aristotle here is that abstract relation terms have personal supposition for the relata and only simple sup-

81. (OTh IX, 669).
82. (OTh IV, 355).

position for the relation concepts. On this interpretation, the truth conditions for propositions of the form '*R*-ness exists' will vary as the substitutions for '*R*-ness' are taken to have personal or simple supposition. Where personal supposition, the proposition would be true if and only if the relata *a* and *b* both exist and exist in the way connoted by substitutions for '*R*' and '*R*-ness'; where simple supposition, the proposition would be true if and only if the concept corresponding to the substitution for '*R*-ness' existed.

8.   RELATIONS OF REASON

Just as Scotus held that real relations were relative things (*res*) really or formally distinct from absolute things, so some—including Scotus—thought that relations of reason were relative beings of reason distinct from and inhering in absolute things in the non-real mode of objective or intelligible existence.[83] As Ockham describes it, their view is that

> ...so far as a relation of reason is concerned, the intellect compares one thing (*res*) to another, which is in no way compared in reality, and understands such a comparison to exist in one as in a foundation and the other as a term, and thereby causes a relation of reason between some that are not related in reality.[84]

And they maintain that "just as a real relation is founded on a thing in real existence, so a relation of reason is founded on a cognized thing."[85] Further, they defend the supposed distinction between the relation and its relata by an appeal to separation arguments. Focussing, for example on the relations of being-a-subject and being-a-predicate, they reason that

> ...the subject of a proposition can be cognized as far as everything ab-

---

83. Thus, Scotus writes that "a relation of reason is a different being of reason from its foundation" (*Ord.* II, d.1, q.4, n.215, (Vaticana VII, 108)).

84. *Rep.* II, q.1, (OTh V, 10).

85. *Ibid.*, (OTh V, 12).

solute in it is concerned, and so can the predicate; and yet the one no more has the aspect of a subject and the other of a predicate than the other way around. For example, I can distinctly think of a man so far as everything intrinsic to him is concerned, by a simple and non-complex cognition; likewise an animal, whether by the same cognition or by another; and yet not think that a man is a subject with respect to animal. Therefore, it is clear that for man to be a subject and animal a predicate more is required than a cognition of them. But clearly nothing absolute. Therefore, relative. Not a real relation. Therefore, a relation of reason...[86]

And they offer analogous proofs in other cases.

Ockham's response is that "no relation of reason exists," where relations of reason are conceived of as relative entities distinct from and inhering in the relata.[87] Ockham contends that

> ...if we should assume such a relative of reason, this will be especially because of the intentions 'genus', 'species', 'subject', and 'predicate'. But I can understand any of these apart from any relation of reason, since I can understand the concept of genus and species which have only objective existence absolutely, apart from any relation of reason. The same is true of subject and predicate.[88]

As for the separation argument that subject and predicate cannot be understood apart from some relation of reason, Ockham grants the assumption that man and animal can each be thought of without either's having the aspect of a subject or a predicate. Indeed, he admits that both man and animal might be thought of without either's being a subject or a predicate, and he concedes

86. *Ibid*.

87. *Ibid*., q.1, (OTh V, 8). This claim seems inconsistent with his own objective-existence theory, however. According to it, if certain philosophers think of relations of reason as relative entities distinct from and inhering in their relata, then, in the mode of objective existence, there are such relative entities. Otherwise, these philosophers would be thinking of nothing (see Part One, chapter 3 above). What Ockham could maintain—consistent with his objective-existence theory—is that such relative entities do not figure in the truth conditions for various relation statements the way their sponsors suppose they do. On the mental-act theory, his original statement that there are no such relative entities could be sustained.

88. *Ibid*., q.1, (OTh V, 7).

that something else is required for them to be related. But he rejects their contention that it must be something relative.

> Suppose you say that the extremes are united in a proposition now and earlier were not. Therefore, something must be acquired for the first time. [I reply that] it is true—something absolute or relative. For when they are united, the absolute concept of the copula that did not exist earlier comes to exist there, and it is because of this absolute thing that they are now said to be united and earlier were not.[89]

Returning to their example,

> ...a man can be thought of and so can an animal; and yet it is not necessary that a man is a subject or that animal is a predicate, since a certain absolute concept indicated by the verb 'is' is lacking. But given this concept, together with the concepts of man and animal, whether they are thought of by a single act or by distinct acts, it is necessary that 'man' is the subject and 'animal' the predicate, apart from any relation of reason in between.[90]

It may be objected that if the concept of the copula is merely another absolute concept, distinct from and additional to the concepts of man and animal, it will do nothing to link the latter together in a proposition. Ockham rejects this objection:

> I reply that [the concept of the copula] is a common concept distinct from the concepts of the extremes, the way one being of reason is distinct from another or from a real being. I maintain that if I had only a concept of the copula and no concept of the extremes, then I would not have [a concept of] either subject or predicate. But if I had a concept of the copula and also a concept of the extremes, whether by one act or by three—one of which has the term that is the subject as its object, the other the copula, and a third the term that is the predicate—I would necessarily have a subject and a predicate, apart from any relation of reason.[91]

Just as the existence of one white thing does not suffice to make the proposition 'This white thing is similar to that' true but the

89. *Ibid.*, (OTh V, 19).
90. *Ibid.*, (OTh V, 17–18).
91. *Ibid.*, (OTh V, 18–19).

existence of two white things does, apart from any real relative thing distinct from them; so neither the objective existence of the concept of the copula nor the objective existence of one or both extremes suffices to make 'Man is subject' or 'Animal is predicate' true, but the objective existence of all three does, apart from any relative being of reason distinct from them.

The adequacy of Ockham's reply may be questioned, however. For it seems logically possible that the concepts of man, animal, and the copula all have the objective existence in my mind without 'man' being a subject and 'animal' a predicate: e.g., if I think the proposition 'An oak is a tree' and think the concepts of man and animal, without thinking the proposition 'A man is an animal'. Again, the objective existence of the concepts of man, animal, and the copula cannot suffice for 'man' to be a subject and animal a predicate, since they would all have objective existence when I think the proposition 'An animal is man' and think no other propositions. If Ockham denies that the objective existence of any further entities is required, he should at least stipulate that the extremes and the copula must not only have objective existence, but also that they must exist in a certain way in the mode of objective existence, and that they exist in a different way when 'man' is subject and 'animal' predicate than when 'animal' is subject and 'man' predicate. How to specify this difference is a problem that Ockham confronts briefly in his commentary on Aristotle's *Perihermenias* and finds difficult to resolve (see Part Two, chapter 11 below).

As Ockham sees it, unaided natural reason would give real relations and relations of reason a uniform treatment. It would deny that they are entities distinct from absolute entities, on the ground that no possible entity is. Nevertheless, it would acknowledge that some connotative names or concepts may be called relative because of the way they signify; and relations may be identified either with such names or concepts or with the absolute thing or things signified by them.[92]

92. For his account of real relations, see section 7 above. As for the analogous treatment of relations of reason, he writes that "relations are not the sort of things that others imagine them to be. Nor are relations—whether

If so, it may be asked how unaided natural reason could preserve the distinction between the two sorts of relations? On the view Ockham has rejected, they are easily distinguished in terms of their ontological status: real relations are real things (*res*); relations of reason, beings of reason.

Ockham replies first that it is not all that important for unaided natural reason to retain this distinction, since 'relation of reason' is not a philosophical term; Ockham cannot remember ever finding it in the works of Aristotle.[93] Nevertheless, it is possible to preserve the distinction for the sake of common usage. Ockham proposes that it is a necessary[94] and a sufficient condition[95] of a term's being or signifying a relation of reason that things would not be of the sort that the term denotes to be apart from any act of intellect:

> (P) A term is or signifies a relation of reason as opposed to a real relation, if and only if (a) it is or signifies a relation and (b) things would not be of the sort that the term denotes to be apart from any act of intellect.

(P) seems to make two sorts of cases relations of reason. One sort of case occurs when a statement of the form '*aRb*' is true, but one or both of *a* and *b* is an act of intellect or a concept. Since a concept would not exist— whether objectively or in reality—apart from any act of intelligence, a fortiori it would not be of the sort signified to be by any relation term apart from any act of the intellect. Another sort of case is one in which *a* and *b* both exist in reality apart from any act of intellect, but are

---

real relations or relations of reason—even caused the way some imagine that they are. Rather, besides the signs that are, in themselves, certain absolute things, and the absolute things they signify, there is nothing. Therefore, even a relation of reason is either those absolute things or the sign that is absolute in itself, and yet the sign is called relative because it signifies something while connoting something else or the same thing in some other way" (*Ord.* I, d.35, q.4, (OTh IV, 477); cf. *Rep.* II, q.1, (OTh V, 12)).

93. *Ord.* I, d.30, q.5, (OTh IV, 385); *Quodl.* VI, q.30, (OTh IX, 699).
94. *Ord.* I, d.31, q.1, (OTh IV, 396); *Rep.* II, q.1, (OTh V, 15–16).
95. *Ord.* I, d.30, q.5, (OTh IV, 385–86); *Quodl.* VI, q.30, (OTh IX, 699).

not of the sort the relation term signifies to be apart from any
act of the intellect.

Ockham seems to acknowledge a significant difference between the two sorts of cases when he takes the trouble to
distinguish a broader and a stricter way of understanding 'relation of reason' in *Ordinatio* I, d.35, q.4.[96] Broadly,

> (Q) A term is or signifies a relation of reason if and only if (a)
> it is or signifies a relation and (b) things cannot be of the
> sort expressed by the relative name apart from some ra-
> tional act or power.

(Q) is in fact broader than (P), since (Q) allows the relation to depend either on some act of intellect or on some rational power.
And Ockham comments that this way being thought of, being
intelligible, being a subject and being a predicate are all relations
of reason.[97] And God's eternal relation of thinking of creatures
is a relation of reason "because the divine essence itself"— i.e.,
one of the relata—"is a single cognition."[98] In the strictest
sense, however,

> (R) A term is or signifies a relation of reason, if and only if (a)
> it is or signifies a relation, and (b) if *a* and *b* exist together
> with a certain (other) act of intellect or will, then they
> are of the sort the relation term denotes to be, and (c) if *a*
> and *b* exist without a certain (other) act of intellect or
> will, then they will not be of the sort the relation term
> denotes to be.[99]

Ockham says that God's relation of thinking of creatures from
eternity is not a relation of reason, according to (R),[100] because
it is not logically possible that God's act of thought should exist
and the creatures exist (in reality or objectively) and not be so

96. (OTh IV, 472).
97. *Ibid.*
98. (OTh IV, 476).
99. *Ibid.*; cf. (OTh IV, 472).
100. (OTh IV, 476).

related, no matter what acts of intellect or will besides God's thought fail to exist. Presumably, the natural signification of concepts will not be a relation of reason in this strictest sense either; for it is not logically possible that the concept of man and Socrates should both exist and the latter not be signified by the former, no matter what other acts of intellect or will exist or fail to exist. On the other hand, the conventional signification of a spoken sound and the value of money are relations of reason, according to Ockham:

> ...For a spoken sound is a sign and money is precious only by a previous act of the intellect or will by which we will to sue the spoken sound or the money this way. And given that there is or at one time was such a volition in us, and that there was no contrary volition, immediately, apart from the addition of anything else, a spoken sound is a sign and money is precious...[101]

Likewise, the relations of being-a-master and being-a-slave between creatures are relations of reason because they depend upon conventionally established property laws, etc.[102] Thus, it is clear that relations of reason may obtain, not only between beings of reason, but between real things.[103]

101. (OTh IV, 472); cf. *Quodl.* VI, q.30, (OTh IX, 699).
102. *Ord.* I, d.35, q.4, (OTh IV, 472).
103. Contrary to what Hermann Grieve says in his article "Zur Relationslehre Wilhelms von Ockham," *Franziskanische Studien* XLIX (1967): 248–258. For example, he explains that for Ockham, "Sind die Extrema einer Beziehung, genauer: die Absoluta für die ein Bezeihungsbegriff steht, von der Verstandestätigkeit unabhängige wirkliche Dinge, so handelt es sich um eine reale Beziehung. Diese wird jedoch nur zu Recht ausgesagt, wenn die Dinge die die Beziehung supponiert bzw. supponieren soll, ganz bestimmter Beschaffenheit sind. Geht es um eine Ahnlichkeitsbeziehung, so müssen sie zum Beispiel wirklich weiss sein. Ist dagegen zumindest eines der Extrema nur auf Grund einer vorgangigen Verstandestätigkeit der Beschaffenheit, dass zu Recht von einer Beziehung gesprochen werden kann, so handelt es sich um eine Vernunftbeziehung..." (252). And again, he comments, "...Dazu, dass eine Beziehung real genannt werden kann, ist es nicht erforderlich, dass sie etwas Wirkliches (reale) ist. Es genügt, dass sie für wirklich Dinge, die freilich als solche weder Beziehungen sind noch Beziehungen enthalten, supponieren kann" (253). But 'conventional sign' supposits for really existent spoken sounds and connotes what they signify—in many cases, real things.

On the other hand, Ockham suggests that it is both a necessary[104] and a sufficient condition[105] of a relation term's being
or signifying a real relation that things are of the sort the term
denotes to be apart from any activity of the intellect:

> (S) A term is or signifies a real relation, if and only if (a) the
> term is or signifies a relation, and (b) things are of the sort
> that the term denotes to be apart from any activity of the
> intellect, so that the activity of the intellect does nothing
> to bring it about that things are of this sort.

Taken at face value, (b) would have the consequences that no
concept or act of thought can have a real relation to anything.
But Ockham evidently understands (b) to refer to activity of the
intellect other than any that may be required for the mere existence of one or both of the extremes; for he allows that God's
thought of creatures is a real relation.[106] Ockham's contemporaries noticed another difficulty with (S)—viz., that it seems
to allow that

> ...something has a real relation to a non-being: e.g., that matter has a
> real relation to the form with respect to which it is in potentiality,
> since—leaving aside any activity of the intellect—matter is genuinely in
> potentiality to form.[107]

This consequence would be absurd on the view that real relations are real things distinct from and inhering in their relata;
for a real thing cannot inhere in something that does not
exist. On the theory Ockham has proposed for unaided natural

Again, 'master' and 'slave' supposit for real things: and so does 'precious'
in 'Money is precious'. Nevertheless, in the passage cited by Grieve
himself—*Ord.* I, d.30, q.5, (OTh IV, 385–86)—in note 26, p.252, Ockham
identifies these as relations of reason.

104. *Quodl.* VI, q.25, (OTh IX, 678).

105. *Ord.* I, d.30, q.5, (OTh IV, 386); cf. (OTh IV, 384) and *Quodl.* VI,
q.30, (OTh IX, 700).

106. *Ord.* I, d.35, q.4, (OTh IV, 476–77).

107. *Ibid.*, d.30, q.5, (OTh IV, 387); cf. *Quodl.* VI, q.25, (OTh IX, 679).

reason, however, it becomes "more a verbal than a real difficulty."[108] One could stipulate that

(T) A term is or signifies a real relation, only if both relata actually exist in reality.[109]

And in *Ordinatio* I, d.35, q.4, Ockham says that (T) is true when 'real relation' is taken strictly and draws the conclusion that, strictly speaking, God's relation of understanding creatures from eternity is not a real relation because creatures do not really exist from eternity.[110] On this understanding, matter's relation of being in potentiality to some form will not be a real relation either.[111] And the division between real relations as defined by (T) and relations of reason as defined by (Q) and (R) will not be exhaustive. In *Ordinatio* I, d.30, q.5, Ockham concludes that given (T), "it is necessary to assume something in between real relation and relation of reason, which some call a potential or aptitudinal relation, although perhaps not properly speaking."[112] But this suggestion is omitted from the discussion in *Quodlibeta* VI, q.25. On the other hand, one could retain (S) as the criterion for real relations and understand it to apply whether the relata actually exist in reality or only potentially. That way, matter's potentiality to forms will count as a real relation;[113] and God's thought of creatures not yet actual as well as His thought of those that actually exist, will be a real relation in this broad sense.[114]

9. OCKHAM'S OWN VIEW

Ockham thinks that we should assume the existence of relative entities distinct from absolute entities, only if we are

108. *Ord.* I, d.30, q.5, (OTh IV, 387); cf. *Quodl.* VI, q.25, (OTh IX, 680).
109. *Ord.* I, d.30, q.5, (OTh IV, 387); *Quodl.* VI, q.25, (OTh IX, 680).
110. (OTh IV, 476).
111. *Ibid.*, d.30, q.5, (OTh IV, 387); *Quodl.* VI, q.25, (OTh IX, 680).
112. (OTh IV, 387).
113. *Ord.* I, d.30, q.5, (OTh IV, 387); *Quodl.* VI, q.25, (OTh IX, 680).
114. *Ord.* I, d.35, q.4, (OTh IV, 476).

forced to do so by experience, theoretical arguments, or the authority of the Scriptures and the Church. Where real relations are concerned, no experience could lead us to this conclusion. And Ockham has argued at length that unaided natural reason will find it easier to deny than to hold that there are any such relative things (*res*) really or formally distinct from absolute things. Nor does any authority require us to admit any exceptions to this conclusion where intrinsic relations—such as similarity and dissimilarity, double and half, identity and distinction[115]—or the extrinsic relations of causality, paternity, and filiation in creatures are concerned. Finally, Ockham has insisted—contrary to his own objective-existence theory—that neither reason nor experience forces us to concede the existence of relative beings of reason distinct from absolute entities, whether real or unreal. Nevertheless, Ockham concludes, there is theological motivation to assume the existence of some real relations really distinct from absolute things. (a) First, the doctrine of the Trinity requires us to say that the Father is not Father by that by which He is God; likewise for the Son and Holy Spirit. Further, Augustine has argued that the Father is called Father only in relation to another; likewise for the Son and Holy Spirit. But not in relation to creatures. The theological conclusion was that there must be some distinction in reality between the divine essence and that by which the persons are constituted. Ockham's predecessors and contemporaries felt bound by the Fourth Lateran Council to maintain that Paternity, Filiation, and Spiration are three relative things that are really distinct from each other but really the same as the divine essence.

(b) Second, the doctrines of the Incarnation and Transubstantiation seem to demand the assumption of still more relative things. In the Incarnation, the Divine Word unites itself to human nature in such a way as to become the same person as a particular human being. In Transubstantiation, God brings it about that the accidents of the bread exist in the same place as the body of Christ without inhering in it. Further, God can bring

115. *Ibid.*, d.30, q.4, (OTh IV, 367); *Rep.* II, q.1, (OTh V, 15–17).

it about that all of the parts of the body of Christ exist at a single point; yet the part of the substantial form that exists in His foot exists in the same place as the matter of His hand without the former inhering in the latter.

Ockham comments that "there is only one argument for all of these cases," based on (A'): "It is impossible for contradictories to be successively true about the same thing unless because of the locomotion of something, or because of the passage of time, or because of the production or destruction of something." Its application may be schematically set out as follows:

1.1 It is possible for human nature first to be united and then not be united to the Divine Word, or vice versa, apart from any locomotion.

1.2 This change cannot be explained by the mere passage of time.

1.3 Therefore, this change is to be explained in terms of the production or destruction of some thing (*res*). ((A'), 1.1, and 1.2)

1.4 Not any absolute thing.

1.5 Therefore, this change is to be explained in terms of the production or destruction of some real relation of union really distinct from absolute things. (1.3 and 1.4)

2.1 God can bring it about that a form equally present to the same matter first did not and then did inform the matter, or vice versa.

2.2 This change cannot be explained by the mere passage of time.

2.3 Therefore, this change is to be explained in terms of the production or destruction of some thing (*res*). ((A'), 2.1, and 2.2)

2.4 Not any absolute thing.

2.5 This change is to be explained in terms of the production or destruction of a real relation of inherence distinct from absolute things. (2.3 and 2.4).

3.1 God can bring it about that an accident is equally present to the same substance and yet first does and then does not inhere in it, or vice versa.

3.2 This change cannot be explained in terms of the passage of time.

3.3 Therefore, this change is to be explained in terms of the production or destruction of some thing (*res*). ((A'), 3.1, and 3.2)

3.4 Not any absolute thing.

3.5 Therefore, this change is to be explained in terms of the production or destruction of a real relation of inherence distinct from absolute things. (3.3 and 3.4)[116]

Ockham remarks that the above arguments would not convince the Philosopher, "because he would deny all of the minor premises. Nor could these minor premises be proved by reason."[117] The Philosopher would say that it is logically impossible that matter and form, subject and accident should exist in altogether the same place and yet the latter not inhere in the former, and hence that 2.1 and 3.1 are false. Presumably, one who took his lead from unaided natural reason would say that 'inherence' principally signifies the form or the accident and connotes the matter or the substance and connotes that the form or accident is in altogether the same place as the matter or substance, respectively. On this account, the fact that this form and this matter (this accident and this substance) exist from t_1-t_{10} and the former first does and then does not inhere in the latter, has to be explained in terms of the fact that they first are and then are not in altogether the same place. And the latter fact can be explained in terms of the locomotion of one or both of them. Thus, Ockham remarks that "if it were impossible for an acci-

116. *Ord.* I, d.30, q.4, (OTh IV, 369–370); *Rep.* II, q.1, (OTh V, 14–16); q.2, (OTh V, 38–40). In *Reportatio* II, q.1, (OTh V, 15), he adds an argument for spatial proximity; but later on in the same question (at (OTh V, 24)), he reverts to the line taken in *Ordinatio* I, d.30, q.1, that it can be accounted for in terms of locomotion. And the latter view is repeated at *Reportatio* II, q.2 (OTh V, 35–36). He alludes to the first two arguments in *Reportatio* IV, q.2, (OTh VII, 29–31) and to the last in *Quodlibeta* IV, q.28, (OTh IX, 411) where he affirms 3.5.

117. *Ord.* I, d.30, q.4, (OTh IV, 370); cf. (OTh IV, 372).

dent to be separated from its subject or a form from its matter without their being in different places, I would not assume any relation there, since I would save by locomotion whatever you save by relation.''[118] Given the denial of 2.1 and 3.1, (A') will not require us to assume any relative thing really distinct from absolute things.[119]

118. *Rep.* II, q.2, (OTh V, 40).
119. Despite Ockham's apparent appreciation of this approach in *Ordinatio* I, d.30, q.4, (OTh IV, 369–370) and *Reportatio* II, q.2, (OTh V, 38ff), he is surprisingly uncomprehending of and unsympathetic to a similar suggestion raised in *Reportatio* II, q.1. Thus, he writes,

> Suppose you say that, by the same token, it is not necessary to assume the existence of the other extrinsic relations. For the union of parts in a whole does not signify the parts absolutely, but signifies it insofar as they are in the whole. Likewise, the inherence of an accident does not signify the accident absolutely, but signifies it insofar as it is in a subject. Therefore, when it is not in a subject, 'inherence' cannot be predicated of it—and this apart from any relation in between (OTh V, 16–17).

Ockham's reaction is decidedly negative:

> On the contrary, when you say that 'inherence' signifies the accident in a subject, I ask whether 'inherence' signifies precisely the absolute accident, or signifies the absolute accident while connoting the subject, or signifies a relation. Not the first or second way, because whenever an absolute accident and subject existed, 'inherence' would be predicated of the accident the way 'similarity' is predicated of other things—which is obviously false, if God were to separate an accident from its subject while conserving both in existence. Therefore, the third alternative remains and my contention is established. Likewise, if it signified an accident insofar as it is in a subject, what does 'accident insofar as it is in a subject' add beyond 'accident' taken absolutely? Either nothing or something. If something, either it is absolute or relative, and the argument goes as before. And so it is clear, therefore, that it is not necessary to suppose that there are any real relations in the genus of relation and distinct from their foundations or any relations of reason in God. But it must necessarily be supposed that there are some extrinsic relations (*ibid.*).

Neither argument seems to give the suggestion that 'inherence' is a connotative term that signifies the accident *insofar as it is in the subject* a fair hearing. In both Ockham takes the suggestion to be merely that 'inherence' principally signifies the accident and connotes the subject, and draws the conclusion that in that case the accident would inhere in the subject

The rejection of 2.1 and 3.1—an option excluded by the authority of the Church—permits Aristotle to explain why form or an accident first does and then does not inhere in matter or a subject, without assuming the existence of anything besides the form and matter or the accident and subject, respectively. Another way to avoid the conclusion that there are relative things really distinct from absolute things, is to suppose that the additional things are distinct absolute things. Ockham has argued in *Ordinatio* I, d.30, q.1, that from the point of view of unaided natural reason, there is no criterion for distinguishing some of the things that there are as relative rather than absolute things.[120] Ockham can think of only three criteria

whenever both existed. Presumably, however, the thought was that 'inherence' principally signifies the accident and connotes not only the subject but also that the accident is in the subject. The last condition will not always be satisfied whenever both subject and accident exist.

Perhaps the thrust of Ockham's argument is that this account is circular. We are trying to explain what it means for an accident to inhere in a subject; we are in effect being told that it is for both the accident and the subject to exist and for the accident to be in the subject. But precisely what we wanted to know is what 'to be in the subject' adds to 'accident'. On the other hand, it is not circular to explain that 'inherence' principally signifies the accident and connotes both the subject and that the accident and subject are in altogether the same place.

A similarly obtuse remark occurs a little earlier. Speaking of the arguments laid out above, Ockham warns that "these conclusions cannot be avoided by an appeal to grammatical or logical modes. For if no intellect existed, and hence no grammatical or logical modes, still the extremes of a contradiction could be successively true about some things, as is clear in the examples already given" (*ibid.*, (OTh V, 15–16)). This comment seems to misrepresent the general strategy that Ockham himself has proposed on behalf of those who follow unaided natural reason, however. For according to them, 'inherence' does not principally signify or connote any being of reason for whose existence the existence and activity of some intellect is required. So far as they understand the term 'inherence', things may first not be and then be of such a sort as to be signified by that term apart from any activity of the intellect, because it may first be and then not be the case that they are not in altogether the same place. And, as noted above, this can be explained in terms of the locomotion of one or both of them apart from any activity of the intellect.

120. (OTh IV, 306–307).

that have any initial plausibility. One might say that some thing (*res*) *a* is not an absolute but a relative thing because either (i) *a* is essentially dependent on some other thing *b*; or (ii) *a* cannot exist unless some other thing *b* exists, although *b* can exist without *a*'s existing; or (iii) *a* cannot exist unless *b* exists, and *b* cannot exist unless *a* exists. But (i) does not provide a sufficient condition for saying *a* is not an absolute but a relative thing; for every effect is essentially dependent upon its cause, but no one says that every effect is a relative thing. All creatures are effects, but Socrates and his whiteness are paradigm cases of absolute things. (ii) does not provide a sufficient condition for identifying *a* as a relative thing either. For

> ...necessarily, if a man exists, he exists together with God. Indeed, it is a contradiction that a man exists without God. Nevertheless, a man is genuinely an absolute thing.[121]

Nor, from the point of view of unaided natural reason, is (iii) a sufficient condition.

> ...For following natural reason, it should be said that no accident can exist without its subject and no subject without its accidents. Yet, each is genuinely an absolute thing. Thus, I may just as easily say that whiteness is a relation to something else as that any other imaginable thing (*res*) is...[122]

Thus, "it cannot be shown by reason that any thing (*res*) really distinct from another thing (*res*) is not just as absolute as any other..."

Thus, Ockham notes, the distinction of divine persons from one another could be preserved by supposing that

> ...three really distinct absolute things, none of which is formally the divine essence, exist in God; and that one of them is the Father and not the Son, and one of the absolute things is really the Son and not the Father—nevertheless in such a way that 'the Father' would not signify anything in reality in addition to that absolute thing, any more than

121. (OTh IV, 307).
122. (OTh IV, 308).

'creator' signifies anything in reality in addition to God who creates.[123]

Similarly,

> So far as the second difficulty about the union of the human nature to the divine word is concerned, some would perhaps say that just as, according to others, it is only because a relation informs human nature that it can be said that God is a man; so perhaps they would say that it is because an absolute form—that is much more perfect than such a relation would be and much more consonant with the divine nature—informs the human nature, that it can be said that God is truly a man. And this would only be to say that human nature is united to the Word or to God.[124]

Thus, the conclusion 1.5 is avoided by denying 1.4. It would seem that the same approach would be available in dealing with the second and third arguments—viz., that of denying 2.4 and 3.4 and maintaining that inherence is not a relative but an absolute thing really distinct from the form and the matter or the accident and the substance, respectively. For some unexpressed reason, Ockham does not think so; he writes,

> It might be more difficult to reply to the other two difficulties, however, unless someone were to say that God could not bring it about that a form is intimately present to matter without informing it, or that an accident is altogether in the same place as its subject without informing it.[125]

This remark is the stranger in view of Ockham's arguments in *Ordinatio* I, d.30, q.1.[126] But whether the appeal to additional absolute things rather than relative things would be in principle available in all or only in some of the doctrinal cases, Ockham does not personally endorse it for any. Rather he follows the tradition of the Saints in supposing that there are really distinct relative things in each case. On examination, Ockham's conces-

123. *Ibid.*, q.4, (OTh IV, 370–71).
124. *Ibid.*, (OTh IV, 371).
125. *Ibid.*, (OTh IV, 372).
126. (OTh IV, 306–308).

sions to the thing-theory of real relation are quite substantial. Ockham concentrates on the cases specifically involved in the doctrine—those involving the body of Christ and the accidents of the bread. But the body of Christ is part of Christ's human nature and hence a creature. What God can do to it and to the accidents of bread, he can presumably do to other created substances and accidents. Thus, if God can bring it about that the accidents of the bread exist in exactly the same place as the substance of the body of Christ without inhering in it, he could bring it about that the accidents of any substance, while remaining in exactly the same place as the substance, first did and then did not inhere in that substance. And if He can bring it about that the matter of Christ's hand exists in exactly the same place as the substantial form of His foot without the latter form inhering in the former, then God can bring it about that any substantial form inhering in some matter, while remaining in exactly the same place as the matter, first inheres in it and then does not. If these are genuine logical possibilities, it must be that inherence is a relative thing really distinct from accident and substance, form and matter, and that such a relative thing is present in every genuine case of an accident's inhering in a substance or a form's inhering in matter. Ockham himself seems to concede this extension of his conclusion to other creatures when he says that

> ...in the proposition 'Whiteness inheres in Socrates' it is better to say that the copula signifies the actual inherence,[127]

where it is clear in the context that such a relation is supposed to be a thing really distinct from Socrates and his whiteness.

Oddly, Ockham does not acknowledge this consequence. In *Ordinatio* I, d.30, q.4, he concludes that

> ...we can save everything without any relation in the genus of relation and without any action and passion of that sort and without when, where, position, and habit. Nevertheless, we cannot save everything without Paternity in God or a relation of union.[128]

127. *Rep.* II, q.1, (OTh V, 22–23).
128. (OTh IV, 373–74).

And in *Reportatio* II, q.1, Ockham remarks that while "it is necessary to assume some extrinsic relations that do not formally pertain to any genus,"[129] "it is not necessary to assume any relation in the genus of relation distinct from its foundation..."[130] And the same point is repeated in *Quodlibeta* VI, q.27;

> ...'relative' cannot supposit for the thing which is not a sign, but only supposits for signs, at least according to the intention of the Philosopher. According to Truth, it can supposit for no extramental created thing...[131]

The divine relations of Paternity, Filiation, and Spiration are not in the genus of relation, because they are really the same as the divine essence, which does not fall under any of the ten categories. Perhaps the relation of union that inheres in human nature and related it to the Divine Word is not said to be in the genus of relation because—while it inheres in a creature—it relates a creature to God. But the relations of inherence of form in matter and of accident in substance relate one creature to another. And even if Ockham had limited such relations to the body of Christ alone— a move that lacks rationale—that body is still a creature and real relations among its parts should, accordingly, fall under the genus of relation. Probably the explanation lies in the fact that inherence—the relation between any putative accident-thing and its substance—is not included under any of the species of relation or other accidents recognized by Aristotle in the *Categories*.

129. (OTh V, 14).
130. (OTh V, 16).
131. (OTh IX, 689).

8

Quality

Ockham thinks that distinct real things (*res*) correspond to the category of substance and the category of quality. He never defends his conviction that there are any such things as substances or his choice of substance as the basic ontological category. It is not the only possible selection. More recent philosophers have fixed instead on processes, events, or space-time slices as ontologically fundamental. But Ockham's regard for substance is hardly surprising in view of the dominance of Aristotelian philosophy in the late thirteenth and fourteenth century metaphysics.

More striking in view of his general program of ontological reduction is his contention that qualities are things really distinct from substance. After all, Ockham has argued that when 'This air occupies four cubic feet' and 'This air occupies five cubic feet' are true successively, there are no such really distinct quantity-things as four-cubic foothood and five-cubic foothood which inhere successively in the air; rather the air and its parts exist first one way and then another (see chapter 6 above). Again, for 'Socrates is spatially proximate to Plato' to be first false and then true does not involve the successive inherence of any such really distinct relation-things as spatial distance and spatial proximity in Socrates and Plato, but only Socrates and Plato existing first one way, with many things in between them, and then another way, with few things in between them (see chapter 7 above). Why should not Ockham also maintain that for Socrates to be first white and then black, is not for things really distinct from Socrates—viz., whiteness and blackness—to inhere in him successively, but for Socrates himself to exist first one way and then another? Again, if God can bring it about that air is extended through four cubic feet without any quantity really distinct from and inhering in the air, and bring it about that Socrates and Plato are spatially proximate without any really distinct relations of spatial proximity, why can He not bring it about that Socrates is white without any really distinct whiteness? And if He can, is it not superfluous to suppose that there are any such really distinct whitenesses?

Nor was the thesis—that no quality is a thing (*res*) really distinct from substances—entirely overlooked by fourteenth century philosophers. The author of an anonymous *Physics*-commentary in the second half of the fourteenth century opines that "it is indeed possible that neither heat nor cold are things distinct from their subjects" and that "when fire heats water, it produces nothing but makes something to be otherwise (*aliter se habere*)."[1] And John Mirecourt allows as rationally defensible the view that acts of thought, sensation, and volition are not things (*res*) really distinct from the thinking, sensing, or willing substance.[2] The general thesis was condemned by the bishop of Paris in 1347, no doubt in part because it seemed to contradict the doctrine of transubstantiation (see chapter 6 above). John Buridan explains this reasoning clearly in the following passage:

> This goes against those things that we hold concerning the sacrament of the altar. For there the accidents remain without the subject. Therefore, the bread, which was white, large, and of a certain shape, was not the whiteness, largeness, or the shape which remain in the sacrament. For these remain when the substance of the bread does not remain. Thus, the syllogism 'This substance of bread will not remain and this whiteness will remain; therefore, this whiteness is not the substance of the bread' holds good.[3]

We can see that the sensible qualities of the bread and wine —their color, flavor, odor, temperature, etc.—remain after the consecration. According to the doctrine of transubstantia-

---

1. Translated from quotes in Anneliese Maier, *Zwischen Philosophie und Mechanik*, (Rome, 1958), 330. This interesting essay is primarily concerned with issues about locomotion.
2. Translated from Maier, *op. cit.*, 333.
3. *De anima* III, q.11, translated from Maier's quote, *op. cit.*, 335.

tion, the substances do not remain. Therefore, by the Indiscernibility of Identicals, such qualities must be distinct from the substances. And since they really exist, they must be really distinct things (*res*).

Perhaps projecting this later drama back onto Ockham, some commentators have suspected that it was primarily for theological reasons that he conceded any qualities to be things really distinct from substances. Initially plausible as this hypothesis may seem, I think an examination of the texts will suggest that, on the contrary, Ockham found the category of quality to be a topic about which faith and reason were in full agreement. For one thing, when Ockham explicitly turns his attention to the question of whether qualities are things really distinct from substances, he does not invoke theological dogmas to decide the issue but the now familiar

(A′) Necessarily, if first *p* is true and then not-*p* is true, then either some thing (*res*) has been produced in existence for the first time, or something that did exist has ceased to exist, or some locomotion has actually (or potentially) occurred.

And the view that he endorses as his own in *Quodlibeta* VII, q.2, is almost *verbatim* the same as the one he assigns to Aristotle in *Summa logicae* I, c.55, and identical in substance with that outlined as Aristotle's in his *Commentary on the Categories,* c.14. Where Ockham thinks that faith and natural reason lead to different conclusions—as, for example, with the category of relation (see chapter 7 above) and with future contingents (see Part Five, chapter 27 below)—he does not hesitate to distinguish what must be said "by those who follow unaided natural reason" or "from the Philosopher's point of view" and what must be held according to "Truth" and "the Faith." That Ockham makes no such contrast here is strong presumptive evidence that he regarded the thesis that some qualities are really distinct from substances as not only theologically necessary but indicated by unaided natural reason as well.

Indeed, in examining the ontological question about qualities, Ockham scarcely considers the possibility that *no* quality is a thing really distinct from substance, but thinks his main opponents are the moderns who hold that *every* quality is.[4] In chapter 8 of the *Categories*, Aristotle divides the genus of quality into four principal sorts (*modi*) or species. The first includes longer-term (*habitus*) and shorter-term dispositional properties (*dispositiones*), such as virtue and health; the second species is that of natural capacities or incapacities; the third, affective qualities (*passiones*) including the Lockean secondary qualities of color, flavor, odor, temperature, etc; and the fourth, the shape and external form of a thing, straightness, curvature, etc.[5] And some moderns had argued on the basis of

(A)   There can be no passage from contradictory to contradictory apart from the generation or corruption of some thing (*res*),

for the conclusion that "each quality is a thing really distinct from substance and quantity and relative things," and that the contents of the four species of qualities "are really distinct from one another."[6] Thus, by (A), 'Socrates is sick' and 'Socrates is healthy' could not be successively true unless something really distinct from Socrates—say, a really distinct quality of health— were produced; likewise 'Cleopatra is beautiful' and 'Cleopatra is ugly' could not be successively true unless a really distinct thing—say the quality of beauty—first inhered in Cleopatra and then was corrupted.

Once again, Ockham charges that the moderns have been ontologically too permissive. And he uses (A') together with the razor to argue that some qualities are things (*res*) really distinct from substance while some are not. Thus he writes that

...it is convenient to use this method for knowing when a quality should be assumed to be a thing other than a substance and when not:

4. *Summa logicae* I, c.56, (OPh I, 182–83).
5. Cf. *ibid.*, c.55, (OPh I, 181); *Expos. Praedicam.*, c.14, (OPh II, 269, 274, 276, 282).
6. *Summa logicae* I, c.56, (OPh I, 182–83).

when some predicables can be truly asssserted of the same thing successively but not simultaneously because of locomotion alone, it is not
necessary for these predicables to signify distinct things...7

And since by Ockham's razor "when a proposition comes out
true for things (*res*), if one thing (*res*) is enough for its truth, it is
superfluous to assume two," such really distinct qualities
should not be assumed. On the other hand, if locomotion is
insufficient to accout for this, they should be assumed. And
Ockham reasons that

> ...qualities of the third species are really different from substance.
> Proof: It is impossible for anything to pass from contradictory to con-
> tradictory without acquiring or losing anything where this is not saved
> by the passage of time or by locomotion. But a man is first not white
> and then white, and this transition is not saved by locomotion or the
> passage of time. Therefore, whiteness is really distinct from a man.8

But "qualities of the fourth species, such as figure, curvature,
density rareness, etc., are not things distinct from substance and
other sensible qualities,"9 because

> ...such predicables as 'curved' and 'straight' could be successively true
> of the same thing because of locomotion alone. For when something is
> straight, if the parts are brought closer together, so that they are less
> distant than before, by locomotion without any other thing coming to
> it, it is called 'curved'. For this reason, 'curvature' and 'straightness' do
> not signify things (*res*) other than the straight or curved things.
> Likewise for 'figure', since by the mere locomotion of some of its parts
> a thing can come to have different figures...10

Likewise, Ockham maintains that some dispositional properties
are not things really distinct from substances and other
qualities. For example, "health is not a quality distinct from

7. Proposed for Aristotle in *ibid.*, c.55, (OPh I, 180) and on his own
behalf in *Quodl.* VII, q.2, (OTh IX, 708).
8. *Ibid.*, (OTh IX, 707); cf. *Summa logicae* I, c.55, (OPh I, 180–81).
9. *Quodl.* VII, q.2, (OTh IX, 707); cf. *Summulae Physicorum* III, c.15,
65–67, (OPh VI).
10. *Summa logicae* I, c.55, (OPh I, 180); *Quodl.* VII, q.2, (OTh IX, 708).

other qualities, because it is only a required or determinate proportion of the humors.'' Again, 'beauty' ''does not signify
anything besides the size of the parts, their color, and other
qualities required for beauty.''[11] On the other hand, he argues
that knowledge and virtue are such distinct things:

> ...everything that has the power to do an action that it did not have the
> power to do earlier—where there is no difference in the thing acted
> upon—has an absolute thing that it did not have earlier or lacks an ab-
> solute thing that it had earlier. But the intellect and will that have these
> dispositions (*habitus*) have the power to do something that they could
> not do earlier, as is clear from experience. There is no difference in the
> thing changed—say in the intellect or will—since neither locomotion
> or any other act is an obstacle to its receiving these dispositions.[12]

And as a general rule, where the act by which a disposition is exercised is a thing really distinct from substance and other
qualities, so is the disposition.[13] Again, Ockham uses (A′) to
argue for the existence of other, really distinct mental qualities.
Thus,

> ...a disposition (*habitus*) sometimes inclines the intellect and some-
> times not. For when one is asleep, one does not experience one-
> self as being inclined to think. But as soon as one wakes up, on ex-
> periences oneself as inclined to think. Therefore, since there is such a
> passage from contradictory to contradictory, something exists in the
> intellect when it is awake that does not exist in it when it is asleep. This
> can only be an act, because the disposition is the same in someone
> asleep and awake.[14]

And he takes for granted that locomotion could play no role in
accounting for this difference. Similarly, Ockham thinks that
happiness is a real distinct mental quality; for

> ...the soul passes from contradictory to contradictory, because it is first
> not happy and then happy. This transition could not be brought about

11. *Expos. Praedicam.*, c.14, (OPh II, 271).
12. *Quodl.* I, q.18, (OTh IX, 93–94).
13. *Ibid.* VII, q.2, (OTh IX, 708); *Summa logicae* I, c.55, (OPh I, 181);
Rep. III, q.7, (OTh VI, 197–98).
14. *Quodl.* I, q.18, (OTh IX, 94).

by locomotion or the passage of time or the loss of anything. Therefore, something is acquired. Not a relation, because this presupposes that something absolute is acquired. Therefore, something absolute is acquired.[15]

—an absolute thing, really distinct from the soul. And Ockham's psychological discussions assume that similar arguments would show that acts of thought (*intellectiones*) and volitions are things really distinct from the soul and other qualities (see Part Three, chapter 13 below).

Those who believe that no quality is a thing (*res*) really distinct from substances might challenge Ockham's reasoning on one or both of two grounds: (a) First, they might take issue with Ockham's claim that while "a thing can come to be shaped differently by the mere locomotion of some ot its parts," "it is not the case that a thing changes from whiteness to blackness or likewise from being hot to being cold by the mere locomotion of some of its parts"[16] and not the case that the soul first thinks one thought and then another, wills one thing and then another, is not virtuous or knowledgeable and then is virtuous or knowledgeable, is not happy and then happy through the mere locomotion of its parts. Such an objection might arise from the viewpoint of Democritean atomism, according to which all that exists is atoms, whose primary qualities are size and shape, and the void; and all changes are to be accounted for in terms of the locomotion of atoms. Consequently, the fact that composites appear to have first one color, flavor, or temperature and then another, is to be accounted for in terms of the locomotion of atoms.[17] Similarly, the soul is thought to be composed of very small atoms, and changes in it will be accounted for in terms of locomotion as well. Thus, an atomist would contend that once Ockham had replaced (A) with (A'), he should have used (A') and the razor to eliminate all really distinct qualities from his ontology.

15. *Ibid.*
16. *Ibid.* VII, q.2, (OTh IX, 708).
17. *The Pre-Socratic Philosophers*, eds. G. S. Kirk and J. E. Raven, (Cambridge, 1957), chap.17, 414–424.

Ockham would, of course, have known of Democritus' views from Aristotle's discussions of pre-Socratic natural philosophy. But while Ockham does argue for his own positive position that substances are composites of matter and substantial form (see Part Four, chapter 15 below), he apparently regards Aristotle's critique of atomism as so conclusive as not to need any supplementation. So great was Aristotle's influence, that most late thirteenth and fourteenth century philosophers would have joined Ockham in rejecting atomism as a live philosophical option. John Buridan, for example, denounces the rejection of hylomorphism in favor of atomism as "obscure and dangerous."[18]

(b) On the other hand, someone might question why—having rejected (A)—Ockham feels compelled to replace it with (A'). Even if the change from being white to being black, from being hot to being cold, or from being ignorant to being knowledgeable could not be accounted for in terms of locomotion, why should a metaphysician not still say that these changes are a function of a substance existing first one way and then another and not of the successive inherence of really distinct qualities?

While Ockham does not explicitly address himself to such a query, I think he would give the following reply: To be responsible in proposing ontological reductions, it is not enough to say that the difference between a proposition p's being true and its being false is not a difference in which things (res) exist but in how things exist. It is necessary to make some proposal regarding how things would change from existing one way to existing another way. Otherwise the proposal that things might be one way and then another is not fully intelligible. Ockham's opponents would, of course, reply that Socrates changes from being white to being black by qualitative change or alteration. But he would deny that this answer casts any light on the issue. For Ockham recognizes only three basic sorts of change: generation, corruption, and locomotion. We can understand how the production or destruction of a thing might change the truth-value

18. Maier, op. cit., 336.

of a proposition. And we can literally see how things change size and shape in locomotion. But Ockham would contend that he has no conception of alteration as a distinct kind of change in its own right. And without one, anyone who wants to be responsible about ontological reduction should adopt (A') as Ockham himself does.

9

Evaluation of Ockham's Ontological Program

Ockham's notorious ontological program is supposed to "turn things (*res*) into names." In the first and more famous half (examined in chapters 1–4 above), he argues that universals are nothing other than names—primarily concepts that naturally signify many particulars indifferently. Then, turning to the logically independent issue of how many fundamentally different kinds of things there are, he argues that—from the viewpoint of natural reason—nothing created is a thing (*res*) really distinct from substances and qualities. His own thesis is that Aristotle's ten categories classify not things, but names and represent ten fundamentally distinct ways of signifying particular substances and qualities. Now that considerations for and against distinct quantity-, relation-, and quality-things have been examined and weighed (in chapters 5–8 above), it is time to consider two general objections to Ockham's program and its resultant ontology: the first, to the effect that its difficulties are insuperable; the second that it carries no compensating advantages. I shall argue that Ockham need not accept either charge.

1. THE CHARGE OF ARBITRARINESS AND SUBJECTIVITY REVIVED

The first objection contends that by "turning accident-things into names" Ockham renders all claims that things are somehow quantified, related, active or passive, spatially or temporally located, etc. arbitrary and subjective. It relies on the following analogue of the argument examined in chapter 4 above:

1. No distinct things (*res*) correspond to quantity-concepts, relation-concepts, action- or passion-concepts, place- or time-concepts, etc.

2. Therefore, the extension of quantity-, relation-, action-, passion-, place-, and time-concepts is fixed partly by convention.

3. Convention or use depends in part on contingent human free choice.

4. Therefore, convention or use is arbitrary and subjective. (3)

5. Therefore, the extension of quantity-, relation-, action-, passion-, place-, and time-concepts is arbitrary and subjective. (2 and 4)

6. Therefore, it is an arbitrary and subjective matter whether or not things are somewhat quantified, related, active, passive, located in space and time, etc. (5)

The picture behind the above argument is this: The basic scientific language (*Begriffschrift*) for describing reality contains names only for the primitive entities of the ontology. If Ockham's ontology were correct, the true theory formulated in the basic language would make reference to substances and qualities only and exclude any statements about how they are quantified or related, whether they are active or passive, where or when they exist, etc. Rather quantity-, relation-, action- or passion-, place- or time-terms would be invented as alternative ways of talking about or signifying (*modi significandi*) the substance and qualities that could be more fundamentally described without them. Such "shorthand" terms would be in principle eliminable; and, dictated by changing human interests, they would be arbitrary and subjective and replaceable by others. Furthermore, the consequences of 6 reach back into the first half of Ockham's ontological program. For as we saw in chapter 4, similarity relations determine which things are co-generic or co-specific, which concepts are generic or specific. If whether or how things are related is arbitrary and subjective, the matter of which things are co-generic or co-specific, which concepts genus- or species-concepts, will be arbitrary and subjective after all.

How would Ockham respond to these charges? (1.1) *Does Ockham Agree that Quantity-Terms, Relation-Terms, Etc. Are in Principle Eliminable?* The answer is that he should have. (a) Ockham would have admitted the notion of a basic scientific language ideally suited for describing the way things are, and would have identified it with the mental language.[1] But while he regards the mental language as semantically primary, in that spoken and written words acquire significance by being conventionally related to concepts, he finds spoken and written language epistemologically more accessible. And he sets out to describe the structure of the mental language by considering which features of spoken and written language should be mapped onto it. Ockham's principal criterion in this sorting out procedure is

(T1) A feature of or distinction among spoken or written signs has a counterpart in mental signs if and only if the feature or distinction is necessary for signifying or expressing the way things are.[2]

He recognizes that conventional languages contain many features that do not satisfy the right-hand side of (T1). Among them, some are introduced merely for the ornamentation of speech and make rhetorical eloquence, literary flourish, and poetry possible. Others, such as abbreviating expressions, facilitate conversation. But while such features improve conventional languages for some purposes, they can get in the way

1. As John Trentman notes in "Ockham on Mental," *Mind* N.S. LXXIX (1970): 588.
2. Ockham clearly regards the right-hand side of (T1) as both a necessary and a sufficient condition of the truth of the left-hand side in *Summa logicae* I, c.3, (OPh I, 11–14) and *Quodlibeta* V, q.8, (OTh IX, 509–510, 513).

when it comes to giving a full, clear, and accurate account of the ways things are. In proferring (T1), Ockham refuses to transfer such supposed liability to the mental language. Ockham regards the principal that

(T2) No distinction of concepts corresponds to a distinction among synonymous expressions in spoken and written language,

as an obvious corollary of (T1), since "whatever is signified and expressed by all" of the synoymous expressions "could be adequately expressed by one of them."[3] And in considering which of the grammatical accidents—e.g., case, number, being of one declension or conjugation rather than another—that characterize conventional signs are found among mental signs, he appeals to another corollary of (T1):

(T3) If a and b are spoken or written signs that vary with respect to a certain grammatical accident and yet a and b are synonyms, then that grammatical accident does not pertain to mental signs.

His thought is that if a and b remain synonymous, while differing with respect to some grammatical accident, then the difference with respect to that grammatical accident must not have any effect on their signification. And what has no effect on signification cannot be necessary for signifying the way things are.

In discussing which grammatical accidents transfer to the mental language. Ockham also makes use of the following criterion:

(T4) An element of a spoken or written proposition has a counterpart in the corresponding mental proposition, if and only if a variation of that element alone can pro-

---

3. *Ibid.*, (OTh IX, 513).

duce a variation in the truth value of some proposition in which it occurs.[4]

Like (T1), (T4) seeks to project onto the mental language only those features of spoken or written language that pertain to its speculative use to make assertions that are either true or false. But Ockham was mistaken if he regarded (T1) and (T4) as equivalent. The mere fact that an element is such that a variation in it alone produces a variation in the truth-value of some proposition in which it occurs, does not insure that such an element is necessary for signifying things as they are, because spoken and written languages may well have numerous equivalent features that satisfied the right-hand side of (T4). (T4) as it stands is a more liberal criterion than (T1) is, but

(T5) An element of a spoken or written proposition has a counterpart in the corresponding mental proposition, if and only if (i) a variation in that element alone can produce a variation in the truth-value of the proposition in which it occurs, and (ii) it is not the case that this element is a member of a set of equivalent features some other member of which set is preserved in the mental language,

does seem equivalent to (T1).[5]

(T1)–(T4) are not free from difficulties, however. First, one might question whether (T2) and (T3) are genuine corollaries of

4. Invoked in *Summa logicae* I, c.3, (OPh I, 13) and *Quodl.* V, q.8, (OTh IX, 509–511).

5. If (T1)–(T4) are the criteria that Ockham employs, then Peter Geach is clearly wrong to suggest that Ockham's sole or even his principal criterion for distinguishing concepts is synonymy or lack thereof on the part of Latin words. Likewise, Geach is mistaken in contending that Ockham first maps the structure of Latin onto the mental language and then uses the structure of the mental language to *justify* the structure of Latin. Ockham has no interest in justifying or explaining the grammatical features of Latin as such, since for Ockham the primary language is the mental language. See Peter Geach, *Mental Acts*, (London, 1957), chap.23, 101–103. Trentman elaborates these criticisms in his article, "Ockham on Mental," 586–590.

(T1). Someone might believe, for example, that bachelors are not married males, but not believe that unmarried males are not unmarried males. Since merely changing 'bachelor' to 'unmarried male' can result in a proposition of different truth-value, it follows by (T4) that the distinction between 'bachelor' and 'unmarried male' must be reflected in the mental languages. And this conclusion will also be supported by (T1), since the distinction will be necessary for describing the ways things are—in particular, what people believe.[6]

Ockham would reply that in the above mentioned case, the belief loosely described as "the belief that bachelors are not unmarried males" is at bottom a belief about how spoken and written signs are used. Someone who did not know English very well might not realize that the noise pattern or inscription pattern 'bachelor' had exactly the same signification as 'unmarried male'; but no one would question whether the term 'unmarried male' signified the same thing as itself. On this construal, the objector's case shows only that there must be distinct concepts of the noise patterns or inscriptions 'bachelor' and 'unmarried male'—something that Ockham would freely admit.

Second, it may be alleged that Ockham's criteria in (T1)–(T4) are insufficient. (T2) and (T3) tell us that distinctions among features of equivalent expressive power will not be preserved in the mental language. But suppose that we have isolated a set of features each of which satisfies criterion (T4) and such that something equivalent in expressive power to each of the members of the set is necessary for signifying the way things are. Where these features have different grammatical structures, how are we to tell which structure (if any) the mental language has? None of (T1)–(T4) sheds any light on this point.

One supplementary criterion would be

(T6) The mental language has the same structure as that of the most fully articulated spoken or written language.

Other things being equal, (T6) would lead us to prefer 'walks

6. This objection was suggested to me by Tyler Burge.

about idly' to 'saunters' and '*est currens*' ('is a runner') to '*currit*' ('runs'). At least two arguments could be given in favor of (T6): (i) First, the components of the more fully articulated expression have roles to fill in other contexts. If their counterparts must be preserved to fill these other roles, there is no need—indeed, it is contrary to (T2)—to retain the less fully articulated expressions in addition. For example, 'saunter' is equivalent to 'walks about idly'; and 'walks' also occurs in 'walks heavily' or 'walks in a jaunty manner'. Thus, if we are retaining 'walks' anyway, we may as well drop 'saunter'. Analogous reasoning might lead us to drop 'walks' in favor of 'is a walker', etc. (ii) Another argument is that the more fully articulated form enables us to preserve more of the logical relations between the component parts of the complex expression. Thus, I can infer that 'walks about idly' entails 'x walks' on the basis of the structure alone; but I cannot infer that 'x saunters' entails 'x walks' without knowing the meaning of the word 'saunters'. Retaining the more complex in preference to the less complex structure makes the logical relations among the parts explicit and therefore preserves more inferences solely on the basis of logical form than retaining the less fully articulated expression will.

Even the conjunction of (T1)–(T6) will be insufficient, however. For it will not enable us to choose between equally articulated alternative conventional languages. Compare, for example, the languages of *Principia Mathematica* and Polish notation. One might say that 'Kpg' and 'p q' are inter-translatable and equally articulate; yet their grammatical structures are different. To which does the structure of the mental language correspond? Since it is conceivable that no spoken or written language makes the logical form of an expression fully explicit, it seems (T6) might lead us astray and should be replaced with

(T7) The mental language has a structure that makes the logical form of an expression fully explicit.

If we are able to discover the structure of the mental language only by reference to conventional language, however, we will be able to test the explictness of a given formulation only by comparing it with others in the same or different spoken or written languages. Clearly, Ockham has undertaken no such investigations in comparative grammar. And this fact, together with his use of the more liberal criterion (T4), leads him to project more features of Latin onto the mental language than he should have.

What conclusions does Ockham draw from (T1)–(T4)? (i) Beginning with the most obvious case, he thinks it follows from (T1) that the distinction between nouns or name-like expressions (including adjectives) and verbs is preserved in the mental language. In this he follows Aristotle's contention that every statement or proposition that can be true or false contains both a noun and a verb, or else what is elliptical for such an expression.[7] It seems to Ockham that to describe the ways things are, one needs at least the copula. But Ockham explicitly notices that verbs other than the copula are equivalent in signification to the copula plus a participle—e.g., *currens* ('is a runner').[8] It follows by (T2) that the distinction between such verbs and the conjunction of the copula with their participles is not preserved in the mental language.[9] Although it is not warranted by any of the criteria Ockham actually enunciates, he concludes—contrary to (T6) and (T7)—that the mental language contains verbs and not participles.

Each of these contentions could be challenged, however. Why should we suppose that the mental language mirrors the structure of 'A man is a runner' or 'A man runs' rather than that of the artificial language of *Principia Mathematica*, where the copula and other verbs are dropped in favor of predicates and parentheses? (T6) or (T7) might provide a reason, but Ockham does not have either of them in mind when he puts verbs rather than participles in the mental language.

---

7. *Expos. Periherm.* I, c.4, sec.6, (OPh II, 395); cf. Prooemium, (OPh II, 374).

8. *Summa logicae* I, c.3, (OPh I, 11).

9. *Ibid.*; *Quodl.* V, q.8, (OTh IX, 512–13).

Again, Ockham's claim that mental propositions contain name-like expressions seems reasonable. But, focussing no doubt on propositions such as 'Socrates is running and he is engaging in disputation', which contain what Peter Geach has called "pronouns of idleness" that can be eliminated in favor of nouns, Ockham doubts whether the distinction between nouns and pronouns will be preserved among concepts—by (T2)—and seems to suggest that pronouns should be eliminated in favor of nouns. Even without studying the comparative grammar of spoken and written languages, it is clear that such a move would not be warranted by (T1) and (T2). For replacing pronouns with nouns does not preserve the sense of general propositions such as 'A man is running and he is engaging in disputation', as Ockham elsewhere recognizes.[10]

(ii) Again, Ockham contends that "since it is impossible to express everything through verbs and nouns alone,"[11] distinctions between them and adverbs, conjunctions, and prepositions will likewise be preserved in the mental language. Something corresponding to conjunctions such as 'and', 'or', 'if', and 'not' etc. is clearly needed. Whether the distinctions between verbs, adverbs, and prepositions would all appear in the mental language is unclear, however. After all, adverbial force is built into the meaning of some verbs—to saunter is to walk about *idly*—or adjectives—to be delicious is to be *very* tasty. If Ockham retains the verbs and adjectives, the abverbs might be superfluous. On the other hand (T6) and (T7) would prima facie tell in favor of keeping the adverbs. Again, if the mental language has verbs and adverbs, will it also have prepositions? Some prepositional force is already included in the meaning of some verbs—to approach something is to move *towards* it. And it seems as if adverbial prepositional phrases are often equivalent to single adverbs. But once again, retaining the prepositions might make the mental language more analytical.

(iii) If there are name-like expressions and at least one verb

10. See *Summa logicae* I, c.76, (OPh I, 234) and Geach, *Reference and Generality*, (Ithaca, NY, 1962), 124–25.
11. *Quodl.* V, q.8, (OTh IX, 509).

(the copula) in mental propositions, it is natural to ask which of the grammatical accidents that pertain to nouns and verbs in conventional languages, characterize those in the mental language as well? In Latin, nouns have cases. And applying (T4), Ockham concludes that since '*Sortes est homo*' ('Socrates is a man') and '*Sortes est hominis*' ('Socrates is a man's') differ only with respect to the case of the predicate noun, and since that difference alone can account for a difference in truth-value between the two statements, mental nouns must have case. Similarly, '*Homo est animal*' ('A man is an animal') is true when '*Homo est animalia*' ('A man is animals') is false, even though they differ only with respect to the number of the predicate term. Hence, by (T4), mental nouns are singular or plural.[12] In the *Summa logicae*, Ockham remains agnostic as to whether degree of comparision found among adjectives—e.g. between 'white', 'whiter', and 'whitest'—carries over to mental terms.[13] But in *Quodlibeta* V, q.8, he applies (T4) to conclude that it does.[14] On the other hand, there is a double basis for thinking that differences of gender and declension will not be preserved. First, the truth-values of '*Lapis est*' and '*Petra est*' (both 'A stone exists') cannot differ, given present coventions, even though '*lapis*' is third declension masculine and '*petra*' is first declension feminine. It follows by (T4) that such distinctions do not transfer to the mental language.[15] Applying the same two criteria will show that distinctions of conjugation are not found amoung mental verbs. Again, '*Tu legis*' ('you are reading') and '*Tu legisti*' ('You have read') differ only in the tense of their verbs but may have different truth-values as a result. Hence, by (T4), mental verbs should have tense; and similar arguments are constructed to infer that distinctions between number, person, mood, and active and passive voice are preserved in mental verbs.[16]

12. *Ibid.*, (OTh IX, 510); cf. *Summa logicae* I, c.3, (OPh I, 12).
13. I, c.3, (OPh I, 12).
14. (OTh IX, 510).
15. *Ibid.*; *Summa logicae* I, c.3, (OPh I, 12).
16. *Quodl.* V, q.8, (OTh IX, 511–12).

While distinction of case or tense may satisfy the right-hand side of (T4), it is not clear that either satisfies the right-hand side of (T1). If the cases of a noun indicate various relations of the thing principally signified by the noun to other things, why could not cases be eliminated in favor of prepositional phrases in the mental language? Again, if the mental language includes nouns and prepositions and adverbs, why are tenses needed as well? Granted that we would want to be able to express the difference between Socrates' reading today and his having read 2300 years ago, why could not that be done with tenseless verbs and prepositions and dates or with temporal adverbs such as 'now' and 'then'? Similarly, if the mental language contains numbers such as 'one', 'two', etc., it is not clear that number need be indicated in nouns and adverbs as well. Thus, Ockham's use of (T4) in addition to (T1) has led him to transfer more grammatical accidents from Latin to mental language than would be necessary to signify the way things are.

(b) Returning to the case at hand, we have seen (in chapters 5–8 above) how Ockham treats both abstract and concrete terms in the eight categories other than substance and quality as connotative and not absolute terms. Does he think that both connotative and absolute terms are to be found in the mental language?

Ockham explicitly considers this question in *Quodlibeta* V, q.9, and replies in effect that where corresponding concrete and abstract terms are synonymous, then the distinction between them is not preserved in the mental language,[17] but where they are non-synonymous the way 'just' and 'justice', 'white' and 'whiteness' are, both concrete and abstract terms are found in the mental language as well,[18] since truth is not preserved when one is substituted for the other.

Ockham's application of (T2) and (T4) seems over-hasty, however. For to decide whether both the concrete term 'white' and the abstract term 'whiteness' are included in the mental language, he needs to consider not only whether 'white' is

17. (OTh IX, 518).
18. (OTh IX, 517).

synonymous with 'whiteness', but whether or not either is synonymous with some other term or complex of terms found in the mental language: e.g., with 'something having whiteness'. Ockham maintains that all connotative terms are susceptible of nominal definitions the way 'white' is. And a development of his logic along the lines suggested by (T6) and (T7) would conclude that all connotative terms are synonymous with complexes of primitive syncategorematics and absolute terms that name substances or qualities (see Part Two, chapter 10 below). If so, Ockham should have, by (T2), regarded all connotative terms and hence all terms in the categories other than substance and quality as in principle eliminable in favor of such complexes.

(1.2) *Would Ockham Accept Sub-Conclusions 2 and 5?* Steps 2 and 5 are ambiguous. They could mean merely that there is something arbitrary and subjective about a complex of concepts being grouped together as the nominal definition of a single term in spoken or written language and hence about that complex being singled out and labelled as a "quantity-concept" or "relation-concept." Alternatively, they could be claiming further that it is partly a matter of convention and hence arbitrary and subjective that the concepts, which are in fact thus labelled, signify what and as they do. If Ockham should have granted the first, would he concede the second as well?

To be entitled to reject 2, Ockham would have to deny that any simple concept included in the complex nominal definition of quantity-terms, relation-terms, etc. signifies partly by convention. We saw in chapter 4 how he maintains that the absolute names of substances and qualities signify naturally. And he has insisted in the *Summa logicae* and the *Quodlibeta* that various syncategorematics are necessary for signifying things as they are, or for making any statements at all, true or false, since every statement involves a noun and a verb. It might seem obvious, therefore, that Ockham intended his doctrine of natural signification to apply to syncategorematics as well.

Surprisingly, the texts show Ockham to have vacillated on this point. For, in at least two places, he implies that the syncategorematic force of concepts is merely conventional. (a) In

Ordinatio I, d.2, q.8, Ockham considers the question of how—on the theory that concepts are objectively existent objects of thought—we derive syncategorematic, connotative, and negative concepts?

> ...If precisely from things, it is not clear how they can be distinguished from other absolute "concepts" such as 'man' and 'animal'. But it is clear that there are such concepts, since there can be a mental proposition corresponding to every spoken proposition. Therefore, distinct mental propositions correspond to the propositions 'Every man is an animal' and 'Some man is an animal'. Therefore, something corresponds to the sign in one proposition that does not correspond to the sign in the other.[19]

Ockham replies that on the objective-existence theory,

> A concept is syncategorematic, or connotative, or negative only by convention, the way all such terms [i.e., 'syncategorematic', 'connotative', and 'negative'] are predicated of the spoken word and other signs by convention. And in general, grammatical and logical modes of themselves can pertain no more to these concepts than to those, but only by convention. Rather such concepts can be imposed or abstracted from spoken words. This is the way it happens in fact— whether always or commonly. For example, a grammatical mode pertains to the spoken word 'man' so that it is singular in number, nominative in case, masculine in gender, etc. And other grammatical modes pertain to the spoken word 'man's'. Likewise, it belongs to the spoken word 'man' to signify a thing determinately through itself, but not to the spoken word 'every'; rather the latter signifies together with another. Likewise, the spoken word 'not' and the spoken words *'per se'*, 'insofar as', 'if', and syncategorematics of this sort. Then from all of these spoken words signifying this way, the intellect abstracts common concepts predicable of them and imposes these concepts to signify the same as the extramental spoken words signify. And just as one could institute such concepts to signify this way, so one can institute those concepts abstracted from things to signify under the same grammatical modes that spoken words signify under...[20]

The view is that abstraction from things produces a universal in objective existence, which signifies particulars naturally by a

19. (OTh II, 282).
20. (OTh II, 285–86).

comparative similarity relation. But these objectively existent universals do not, by their very natures, signify according to one grammatical or logical mode rather than another. For example, the objectively existent universal man is not, of itself, either singular or plural, nominative or genitive, masculine or feminine. Rather such grammatical or logical modes first pertain to words by convention. From them, we can abstract the general concepts of singular number, nominative case, masculine gender, etc. and add these to the objectively existent universals abstracted from things. Combination with some such concepts yields the nominative, singular, masculine term '*homo*', while others give the genitive, singular, masculine term '*hominis*', etc. Other syncategorematics are similarly abstracted and may be combined with objectively existent universals to produce connotative or negative mental terms. And the occurrence of different conventionally significant syncategorematics in categorical propositions accounts for the difference between 'Every man is an animal' and 'Some man is an animal' in the mental language.

(b) According to the conventions of spoken and written language, the copula is a syncategorematic that functions to render the categorematic term that occurs (temporally or spatially) before it a subject and the one that occurs (temporally or spatially) after it a predicate. But what in the mental language performs the function of making one term of a proposition into the subject as opposed to the other: i.e., what in the mental language determines whether we have 'Every animal is white' rather than 'Every white is an animal'? In elaborating the mental-quality theory, Ockham proposes several solutions, one of which is the following:

> ...a proposition can be an act of understanding that is equivalent to a whole proposition composed of really distinct acts of understanding [as they would be] if they had the kind of order that spoken terms have. In that case, propositions will be distinct insofar as the corresponding propositions would be distinct if their terms or their parts were ordered differently...[21]

21. *Expos. Periherm.* I, Prooemium, sec.6, (OPh II, 356).

We are to imagine a case in which the conventions of spoken and written language about which term counts as subject and which as predicate applied to concepts: i.e., that the concepts are not thought of simultaneously but first one categorematic term, then the copula, then the other; or that—*per impossibile*—the concepts were arranged in spatial order. The subject and predicate are then identified by the conventions usual for spoken and written language. Ockham says that single mental acts differ by virtue of being equivalent to different complexes of this sort. This proposal makes the syncategorematic force that binds terms into the subject and predicate position of a proposition derivative from that of conventional language. And both passages imply that mental propositions signify in part by convention.

Apparently focussing on *Ordinatio* I, d.2, q.8, Ockham's critic and confrere Walter Chatton finds its conclusions without justification; he reports,

> ....Here they say that many of them—for example, grammatical concepts—signify by convention and presuppose voluntary conventions regarding spoken sounds and do not proceed from things.
>
> It seems to me that the opposite is true, however, for the concept of perseity is no more a product of voluntary conventions than the concept of man is. I argue for this as follows: Leaving aside all voluntary convention, the mental proposition 'Man is man *per se*' is just as true as the proposition 'Man is man' is. Therefore, since the truth of the second arises from the fact that the concepts signify the extramental thing only, so does the truth of the first.
>
> Nor does the analogy with grammatical concepts hold good. For the conditions of concepts depend on the will no more than the mooing of a cow does. Therefore, the proposition 'Man is man' is precisely *per se* because the nature of the extramental thing and the nature of the concepts that are natural signs of things, are of the sorts they are. For although it is voluntary that the definition exists in the mind, nevertheless, the fact that it *per se* signifies a thing if it is posited in the mind, is not voluntary.[22]

22. Gideon Gál, "Gualteri de Chatton et Guillelmi de Ockham Controversia de Natura Conceptus Universalis," *Franciscan Studies* N.S. XXVII (1967): 211.

Restricting the notion of a grammatical feature to spoken (and presumably written) words, Chatton says that grammatical features do depend on voluntary conventions that could change, but the conditions of concepts to which they correspond do not. Chatton's view is that the existence of any concept—whether absolute such as 'man', connotative such as 'white', negative such as 'immortal', or syncategorematic such as 'if' or '*per se*'—depends on the thinker's will to think, just as the existence of spoken sounds or inscriptions depends on his will to speak or write. But given that any of these concepts exists, what it signifies does not depend further on human choices, the way the signification of spoken sounds and inscription does. And this goes for concepts of syncategorematics and whatever syncategorematic force is exercised by the grammatical accidents of conventional language. For how man is related to being man or rational and to being white—man is man and rational *per se* and white *per accidens*—is just as much a feature of reality apart from any and every system of conventions, as man's being man, rational, and white are. Indeed, given that 'is', 'have', and 'inhere' are among the primitive syncategorematics, he might well have said that a man's being white or having whiteness and whiteness' inhering in him are convention-independent features of reality, just as much as human nature and whiteness themselves are. Hence, the former features are there to be naturally signified by concepts, just as much as the latter.

Although Ockham nowhere explicitly acknowledges Chatton's criticism, he doubtless knew of it and had taken it to heart by the time he wrote the *Summa logicae*. (c) For example, in the opening chapter of that work, Ockham relates that

> just as Boethius says in the *Perihermenias*, Book I, that expressions (*orationes*) are of three sorts—written, spoken, and conceived that exist in the intellect alone—so there are three sorts of terms—written. spoken, and conceived...[23]

and goes on to explain that

23. I, c.1, (OPh I, 7).

a conceived term is a mental intention or *passio* that naturally *signifies or consignifies* something and that is apt to be part of a mental proposition and supposit for the thing...[24]

Since only syncategorematics, and by extension connotative and negative terms, consignify, he apparently means to assert that syncategorematic, connotative, and negative concepts signify and/or consignify naturally just as absolute concepts do. Continuing the same discussion, without any intervening restriction of the reader's attention to absolute categorematic terms, Ockham notes that

> There are some differences among these terms, however. One is that a concept or mental *passio* naturally signifies whatever it signifies, but a spoken or written term signifies only by convention. Another difference follows from this: that a spoken or written term can change its signification at the pleasure [of the language users], while a conceived term does not change its signification at the pleasure of anyone.[25]

(Should anyone have doubts about the scope of 'term' in *Summa logicae* I, c.1, Ockham explicitly sets out what he means in the next chapter, where he distinguishes three ways in which 'term' can be taken—most broadly for whatever can be the copula, the subject, or the predicate of a proposition (including propositions as well as non-complexes); a narrower sense that excludes propositions but includes everything else covered by the first sense; and the narrowest which excludes complexes and syncategorematics but includes absolute, connotative, and negative categorematic terms. Ockham says that he used 'term' the second way in chapter 1.)[26]

(d) Ockham had already paved the way for these conclusions in *Expositio in librum Perihermenias Aristotelis*, Book I, Prooemium, section 6, where he allows the following as defensible on the mental-quality theory of concepts:

> ...to each spoken significant term—whether categorematic or syn-

24. *Ibid.*, (italics mine).
25. *Ibid.*, (OPh I, 8).
26. (OPh I, 9).

categorematic—corresponds or can correspond an act of understanding that naturally signifies the same thing the same way as the conventional spoken expression. And just as the groans and cries of the sick and many such spoken sounds naturally signify the same as conventionally significant spoken sounds do, so the soul's acts of understanding, which the Philosopher here calls mental *passiones,* can naturally signify what conventionally significant spoken sounds signify. Not only that, but a single intention can *naturally* signify the same and the same way as a composite of *categorematic and syncategorematic* spoken words do...[27]

On this proposal, categorematic and syncategorematic concepts are alike naturally significant. And this conclusion is taken for granted in his discussion in *Quodlibeta* V, q.8. His considered opinion would thus be that 2 and 5 are false.

(1.3) *Would Ockham Accept the Inference from 5 to 6?* Chatton seems to take the inference from 5 to 6 for granted when he apparently equates 'Leaving aside all voluntary conventions, "Man is man" is true' with '"Man is man" is true solely by virtue of the extramental things signified'. It is the extramental fact that a man is a man that makes the proposition true, and this is a fact apart from any voluntary conventions. But if the concepts are signified by convention, he reasons, the truth of the mental proposition 'Man is man' would depend partly on such conventions. Likewise, for 'Man is *per se* man'.

Although Ockham does not address himself to this issue directly, I think it is a fundamental presupposition of his ontology that the inference from 5 to 6 does not hold. He agrees with his opponents that

(T8)   things are co-specific, co-generic, quantified, related, active or passive, have spatiotemporal location, etc. prior to and independently of their being signified, whether naturally or by convention.

In advancing the argument in steps 1–6, however, Ockham's adversaries assume that

27. (OPh II, 335–37), (italics mine).

(T9)   it is only which things (*res*) exist that is thus prior to signification, whether natural or conventional.

But just as Ockham thinks differences in truth-values may reflect differences not merely in which things (*res*) are signified to exist, but also in how the same or different things exist (see chapters 5–8 above), so he would contend that, contrary to (T9),

(T10) it is not only which things (*res*) exist, but how they exist that [may be—in many cases—prior to their being signified, whether] naturally or by convention.

And (T10) applies to whether and how things are co-specific, co-generic, quantified, related, active or passive, spatiotemporally located, etc. By insisting on (T9), Ockham would charge, his opponents have once again begged the question against him.

2.   DOES OCKHAM'S ONTOLOGICAL PROGRAM REPRESENT ANY GENUINE ONTOLOGICAL ECONOMY?

Ockham's aim in ontology is to admit nothing real other than particulars in the categories of substance and quality. For him, general terms do not signify universal things but particulars "confusedly," while abstract terms in the last eight categories do not signify distinct quantity-things, relation-things, action-things, etc., but substances and qualities in different ways. And we have seen (in chapter 8 above) how some who came after Ockham thought that the second half of his program could be extended even further to eliminate qualities as well. Other difficulties aside, we may ask whether the economies of Ockham's strategy are genuine or merely apparent.

(2.1) *Do Syncategorematics Name?* It will do little good to treat abstract nouns in categories other than substance and quality as connotatives, if syncategorematics themselves function as names. But we have already seen (in chapter 5 above) how Ockham ridicules the crude semantic thesis that assigns a distinct signification to each distinct word, even to conjunctions such as 'and' or 'but', and we shall see (in chapter 10 below) how he makes the failure to name on their own a distinguishing mark between syncategorematic and categorematic terms.

Nevertheless, philosophers—medieval and modern—have doubted the success of his strategy for cutting off further ontological commitments, and this on several grounds.

(2.2) *Modes versus Things*. Buridan argued that as an economy measure this strategy—of replacing talk about distinct kinds of things with talk about substances and qualities existing otherwise (*aliter et aliter se habere*)—is ineffective, because it merely substitutes an ontology of modes for one of things. Focussing on the question of whether opinions are qualities really distinct from and inhering in the soul, he argues as follows:

> Again, 'to be otherwise and otherwise' (*aliter et aliter se habere*) signifies the same as 'to exist in one way and another' (*alio et alio modo se habere*). Therefore, if our intellect existing in one way and another is now one opinion and tomorrow will be a contrary opinion, the latter way/mode is not the former way/mode, from which it follows that different modes are posited. Therefore, if there are many modes that are distinct from one another, and the intellect is not and will not be different but is always the same, it is necessary for the intellect to be distinct from those modes and from each of them. And in that case, all of the difficulties that arose about the difference and identity of opinions come back with more force about modes. Therefore, it is better to stop immediately with the differences of opinions...[28]

So far as Buridan is concerned, one may continue to speak of modes, but one should acknowledge after all that they are accidents and hence things really distinct from the subject of inherence.

It is true that Olivi before and Mirecourt after Ockham did

---

28. Quoted by Maier, *Zwischen Philosophie und Mechanik*, (Rome, 1958), chap.6, 337.

speak about ways or modes of being (*modi se habendi*) in the nominative case[29] and thus invite Buridan's charge that in dodging an ontological commitment to things (*res*) they have accepted one to entities of another sort. And some later philosophers did wish to define a new ontological category distinct from that of Aristotelian substance and accidents. Fourteenth century philosophers had reasoned that since substance and accidents were distinct things, it was both logically possible for substance to exist without accidents and logically possible for accidents to exist without substance. By contrast, the new ontology held that the subject of a mode could exist without being thus modified, but a mode could not exist without the modified subject.[30]

Ockham would have denied any implicit ontological commitment to modes, however. He favors the oblique-case expressions '*aliquo modo*' and '*alio et alio modo*' and rarely uses the nominative case '*modus*' or '*modi*'. Ockham would agree with Buridan that '*aliter et aliter se habere*' and '*alio et alio modo se habere*' are synonymous. But whereas Buridan assimilates the former to the latter and treats them both as phrases including expressions that name modes, Ockham takes the adverbial form as canonical. The expression '*alio et alio modo*' is thus misleading as to its logical form, because it contains expressions that purport to name something. And had he regarded Olivi and/or Mirecourt as fellow-travellers, he might have explained his and their use of 'mode' in the nominative case as shorthand for adverbial circumlocutions.

(2.3) *Quantification over "Hows"*. It may be argued that replacing nouns with adverbs is not so decisive as Ockham imagines, however. For the criterion of ontological commitment is quantification: a theory has an ontological commitment to the entities that must be taken to be values of the variables if the theory is to be true; and a philosopher has an ontological commitment to those entities if he accepts the theory. If the

29. *Ibid.*, 328–338.
30. Cf. Paul of Venice, *Logica magna*, Part II, Tractatus de significato propositionis, first opinion, (Del Punta and Adams ed., 82–85).

philosophers who renounce distinct things in favor of the same things existing differently, proceed to quantify over these "hows," they will be as guilty of ontological proliferation as if they had used noun phrases in the nominative case.

What is more, it seems that Ockham and those who have extended his ontological program have done just that. (i) Buridan may have this in mind: to speak of something existing first one way and then another (*alio et alio modo*) in the oblique case, is still to count. (ii) Again, Ockham seems to quantify over modes explicitly. For example, in *Ordinatio* I, d.2, q.1, he asks "whether as much and every mode (*omnis modus*) of identity that obtains between the divine essence and the divine essence, obtains between the divine essence and the attributal perfections in reality."[31] He answers that "divine wisdom is the same as the divine essence in every way (*omnibus modis*) that the divine essense is the same as the divine essence."[32] Again, in *Ordinatio* I, d.26, q.2, Ockham sets out to show that "origin and relation are in no way (*nullo modo*) distinct in reality...Rather everything that is saved by assuming a distinction between generation and the relation can be saved by positing them to be every way identical (*omnimodam*)."[33] Further, he cites the rule that "whenever something is absolutely (*simpliciter*) the same and no way distinct, it is impossible to truly affirm and truly deny the same of it."[34] Again, Ockham holds that "the property that is generation and paternity is the same in every way (*omnibus modis*), nor is it in any way (*aliquo modo*) distinct in reality."[35] (iii) Later on, Paul of Venice draws inferences that seem to amount to existential generalization and universal instantiation, respectively. He argues that since x and y are distinct formally, in signification, and in origin, they are *somehow* distinct.[36] And he moves from the conjunction of

31. (OTh II, 3).
32. (OTh II, 17–18).
33. (OTh IV, 176).
34. (OTh IV, 178).
35. *Ord.* I, d.27, q.1, (OTh IV, 193).
36. *Op. cit.*, Part II, Tractatus de significato propositionis, c.7, 157–59.

'However x-or-y is' and 'x is this way'.[37] How can Ockham and
the others pretend metaphysical economies when they permit
such quantification?

Medieval ontologists could give one of two answers to our
Quinean query. First, they might deny, appearances to the contrary, that any genuine quantification is involved. Paul of
Venice classifies the inference 'x and y are distinct formally;
therefore x and y are distinct somehow' as an inference from inferior to superior of the sort instanced by 'x is a man; therefore
x is an animal.' His assumption—that there is an order of subordination among adverbs analogous to that among nouns in
the category of substance—has some plausibility. After all,
if 'animal' is generic relative to 'man', 'horse', 'cow', and
'pig', why is not 'wickedly' generic relative to 'cruelly' and
'dishonestly' or 'intelligently' to 'insightfully' and 'cleverly'?
Paul's thought must be that the subordination of 'formally', 'in
signification', and 'in origin' to 'somehow' is of the same sort.
Perhaps he would also construe the putative universal instantiation involved in 'x is whatever way y is and y is this way;
therefore x is this way' on analogy with 'x is whatever sort of
animal y is and y is a man; therefore x is a man'. But it looks as if
'man' is inferior to 'animal' or 'sort of animal' and not to
'whatever sort of animal' and hence that the last example includes quantification over sorts. Analogously, 'this way' would
be inferior to 'way' and not to 'whatever way' and quantification over ways or modes would stand.

Alternatively, they might contend that it is not mere quantification that carries ontological commitment. "To be" is not
"to be the value of a variable"; it is to be a property-bearer. But
the quantification in 'x is in every way the same as y', 'x is in no
way distinct from y', and 'x is whatever way y is' does not involve attributing any properties to the ways or the "hows."
Hence, this usage carries no ontological commitment to ways or
"hows" after all.

It might be objected that in an artificial language, one may
treat any element of the ordinary-language sentence as the sub-

37. *Ibid.*, c.5, 126–28.

ject and the rest as the predicate. Thus, one could hold that '*x* is whatever...*y* is' is an open sentence satisfied by ways, and hence that the whole sentence attributes a property to a way. If we are generous enough to allow logicians to stipulate any rules they like for analyzing sentences of ordinary language, nevertheless, we will be able to assess the ontological commitments of a given author only by reference to the rules he in fact lays down. Nothing could be clearer than that Ockham would not countenance the above analysis. For he refuses to allow adverbs to supposit, while insisting that expressions such as '*aliquo modo*' and '*nullo modo*' are equivalent to adverbs, where the adverbial form is clearly canonical. I conclude that *his* use of such phrases does not saddle him with an unwanted ontological commitment to modes or ways.

(2.4) *The Adequate Significatum of the Whole Proposition.* Granted that syncategorematics such as adverbs do not stand for entities on their own, one might still hold that they do so 'together with another' — in fact that the proposition as a whole stands for its own adequate significatum. But what is (*quid sit*) the adequate significatum of the whole proposition?[38]

Investigating this question, Ockham's youngest contemporary Gregory Rimini agreed with him that it is not merely *which* things exist, but *how* they exist that determines the truth-value of a proposition:

> ...The proposition 'A man is a donkey' is not false because a man is not or a donkey is not, but because a man is not a donkey. Nor is the proposition 'A man is white' true because a man exists or because whiteness exists, or even because a man and whiteness exist, but because a man is white...[39]

Strictly speaking, the adequate significatum of a proposition is not some things or things (*res*), but things being this way (*res sic esse*) or existing somehow (*aliqualiter esse*). Nevertheless,

---

38. This issue occupies the lion's share of discussion in Paul of Venice's *Tractatus de significato propositionis*.

39. *Super primum et secundum Sententiarum* I, d.1, q.1, a.1, (reprint of the Venice, 1522 edition, fol.1 Q).

Gregory allows that the terms 'something' (*aliquid*), 'thing' (*res*), or 'being' (*ens*) can be taken three ways: (i) in the broadest sense for whatever can be signified by a proposition or by a term, whether truly or falsely; (ii) less broadly, for whatever can be signified by a proposition or a term, but truly; and (iii) strictly, for an essence or existing thing that can be signified by a complex by itself.[40] Thus, the adequate significatum of proposition may be something the first or second way, but not the third way. And a false proposition such as 'some dodos are pink' signifies some thing$_i$—that dodos are pink, or dodos being pink—even though there are no things$_{iii}$ for the subject term 'dodo' to signify. And since some things$_i$ and things$_{ii}$ are objects of scientific knowledge, they must be—by Aristotelian standards—necessary and eternal.

It is necessary to ask, however, what the relation of things$_i$ and things$_{ii}$ are to things$_{iii}$ (things, strictly speaking). Either necessary and eternal things$_i$ and things$_{ii}$ exist independently of any things$_{iii}$ or they do not. If they do, then some things$_i$ and things$_{ii}$ will be necessary and eternal, and hence states of affairs will be necessary and eternal independently of God, the only necessary and eternal thing$_{iii}$—which seems contrary to the Christian doctrine of creation. On the other hand, if necessary and eternal things$_i$ and things$_{ii}$ depend on God, what sort of dependence is it? As Paul of Venice contends at length, they are not simply identical with God, because different propositions are true of them and of Him.[41] And if some less straightforward reduction is envisaged, what is it?

Ockham occasionally alludes to what is denoted by a proposition as a whole, but he does not enter into the debate about the ontological status of its adequate significatum. In my judgment, if he had, he would have joined his secretary Adam Wodeham in rejecting the question of its quiddity as ill-formed and ridiculous. Adam admits that the proposition 'A man is an animal' signifies that a man is an animal, and turns to consider some objections:

40. *Ibid.*, fol. 1 Q–fol. 2 A.
41. *Op. cit.*, Part II, Tractatus de significato propositionis, c.3, 102–104.

Suppose you say that for a man to be an animal is either something or nothing.

I say that neither should be granted. Instead, it should be held that it is not something, but is for a man to be something, as was said. Thus, I may ask you, whether people is a man or a non-man? Neither should be granted; rather it is not a man but men.

Suppose you say that if it is not nothing, then it is something. I may argue this way from the other part: if people is not a non-man, then it is a man. You deny both consequences.

Suppose you say, what then is it (*quid igitur est*)? It must be replied that it is for a rational animal to be a sensitive animate substance. Nevertheless, a more proper response is that for a man to be an animal is not a what (*quid*), but for it to be something (*esse quid*). Therefore, the question is ill-formed the way it would be ungrammatical and perverse to ask, what is a man is an animal? For a man is an animal in reality, every proposition left aside. It should not be granted that a man is an animal is a substance or accident, neither what is something nor what is nothing, because none of these answers would be intelligible or anything to say...[42]

Understood that way, Wodeham's concession—later taken up by Peter of Ailly—that the adequate significatum of a proposition is *res sic esse* or *res sic non esse*, is fully compatible with Ockham's ontological program and its contention that only substances and qualities existing somehow or otherwise are real.

3.   CONCLUSION

If Ockham was a nominalist-conceptualist, he does not make metaphysics arbitrary and subjective; nor does he replace ontologies that proliferate things with an equally luxuriant ontology of modes. Contrary to modern pragmatists and verificationists, he joins his "realist" opponents in affirming that certain things exist and are co-specific, co-generic, quantified, related, etc. prior to and independently of their being signified

42. Gideon Gál, "Adam of Wodeham's Question on the 'Complexe Significabile' as the Immediate Object of Scientific Knowledge," *Franciscan Studies* N.S. XXXVII (1977): 66–102, at 89.

by anyone or anything. And he held that disputes about which ontology corresponds to things as they are could be settled both in principle and often in practice by appeal to indisputable first principles. He argues at great length and repeatedly that more generous ontologies cannot be true, because somewhere or other they run afoul of the Principle of Contradiction, etc.

On the whole, Ockham's own positive proposal—to treat all terms in categories other than substances and qualities as connotatives that signify particular substances and/or particular qualities existing one way or another—remains essentially programmatic. A full development of it would require him to state truth conditions for statements about how things are related, quantified, active, etc. using absolute terms that name only substances and qualities. Here Ockham provides us with only the barest hints: for example, he suggests that occurrences of the word 'point', which appears to name a quantity-thing, can be replaced with 'a line is not further extended'. But 'line', too, is a putative quantity-name and would have to be eliminated, and Ockham never pursues the exposition to its end. In spilling more ink refuting others than in elaborating his own view, Ockham may merit the title "critical philosopher" hurled at him by hostile opponents. On the other hand, how many nominalists have gone further, and by how much and how recently? In Ockham's view, the realists' program is demonstrably impossible; how much less an evil, if his own is merely incomplete.

Part Two

Logic

10

The Properties of Terms

When presenting a formal system, contemporary logicians begin by listing the vocabulary and grammatical rules for constructing sentences in the language. Similarly, Ockham devotes Part I of the *Summa logicae*, his principal work on logic, to the properties of terms. In the broadest sense, a term is anything that is or can be part of a proposition.[1] Yet, he observes, "not all terms are of the same nature," inasmuch as they have different semantic functions. The first sixty-one chapters discuss how terms differ with respect to their signification; while the last sixteen treat the different but related property of supposition. Inevitably, some of the divisions among terms have been examined or alluded to already and others can be passed over for our purposes. In what follows, I shall first review the distinction between syncategorematic and categorematic, between absolute and connotative terms. Then I shall turn to one of the most discussed but highly perplexing parts of medieval logic: the theory of supposition.

1. SYNCATEGOREMATIC VERSUS CATEGOREMATIC TERMS

The distinction between syncategorematic and categorematic terms corresponds roughly to that in contemporary logic between logical and non-logical constants, respectively. Sometimes it is misleadingly put by saying that for Ockham and other medievals, categorematics signify or have signification, while syncategorematics do not. But while Ockham does hold

---

1. *Summa logicae* I, c.1, (OPh I, 7).

that syncategorematics do not have signification, strictly speaking,[2] he does not intend thereby to suggest that syncategorematics are meaningless, but only that they have a different logical function from categorematic terms. Recall that for Ockham, strictly speaking, to signify is to bring to mind or make understood (see Part One, chapter 4 above). His contention is that categorematics—such as 'man', 'animal', and 'whiteness'—have "a finite and determinate signification" because 'man' brings to mind all men and no horses, 'animal' all animals but no trees, 'whiteness' all whitenesses and no substances or other qualities.[3] By contrast, "syncategorematic terms such as 'every', 'no', 'some', 'whole', 'except', 'only', 'insofar as', etc. lack a finite and determinate signification,"[4] "because they do not make any determinate thing understood except when they are put together with another term or terms."[5] Unlike 'man', 'animal', and 'whiteness', 'except' and 'insofar as' do not suffice by themselves to bring any determinate thing to mind. Rather the copula 'is' and negation 'not' function to join or divide terms to form propositions.[6] Other syncategorematics—viz., 'every', 'no', 'some', 'whole', 'only', 'except'— are quantifiers that operate on a term "to make it signify something or make it supposit in a determinate way for some thing or things."[7] Still others—viz., 'and', 'or', 'if', 'since', 'when', 'while'—correspond to sentential connectives and join propositions into "hypothetical" or molecular propositions.[8] Thus, syncategorematics function to form propositions, and which syncategorematics are present affects the truth-value of the resultant proposition. For example, propositions of the form 'Every A is B' and 'Some A is not B', 'No A is B' and 'Some A is B' are contradictory; and 'If giraffes are plants, the moon is

2. *Ibid.*, c.4, (OPh I, 15); *Expos. Periherm.* I, c.1, sec.1, (OPh II, 378–79).
3. *Summa logicae* I, c.4, (OPh I, 15).
4. *Ibid.*
5. *Expos. Periherm.* I, c.1, sec.1, (OPh II, 378–79).
6. *Quodl.* IV, q.35, (OTh IX, 470).
7. *Summa logicae* I, c.4, (OPh I, 15).
8. *Ibid.* II, c.1, (OPh I, 241–42); III–4, c.5, (OPh I, 768–770).

made of green cheese' and 'Giraffes are plants and the moon is made of green cheese' differ in truth-value, while differing only in sentential connectives. Because they have these genuine semantic functions, Ockham allows that syncategorematics have signification in a broad sense.[9]

2. ABSOLUTE VERSUS CONNOTATIVE TERMS

As we have already seen, a fundamental division among categorematics is that between absolute terms which do and connotative terms which do not signify whatever they signify the same way ("with equal primacy").[10] A realist about universals would say that absolute terms name universal kinds or natures the same way proper names name particulars. Roughly speaking, a proper name signifies only one thing per imposition.[11] Thus, although the name 'Socrates' is given to

9. *Expos. Periherm.* I, c.1, sec.1, (OPh II, 378–79). Michael J. Loux ("The Ontology of William of Ockham," in *Ockham's Theory of Terms: Part I of the 'Summa logicae'*, (Notre Dame, 1974), 1–21) and Alfred J. Freddoso ("Ockham's Theory of Truth Conditions" in *Ockham's Theory of Propositions: Part II of the 'Summa logicae'*, (Notre Dame, 1980), 1–76) suggest that Ockham includes demonstrative pronouns among the categorematics. I know of no passage in which he says so explicitly. The closest he comes is his remark that "discrete supposition is the supposition a proper name or demonstrative pronoun has when taken as significant" (*Summa logicae* I, c.70, (OPh I, 209)). If a demonstrative pronoun is taken as significant, then it must have some signification and thus be categorematic. This reasoning is undercut by Ockham's example, however—'This man is a man'—whose subject includes the categorematic term 'man' as well (*ibid.*). In conventional language, demonstrative pronouns seem to be hybrids: on the one hand they take the place of categorematic terms in propositions—e.g., 'This is white'—but on the other hand they signify nothing except when taken together with a context. Often the mental language correlate will not be a pronoun but a proper name—an intuitive cognition of some particular or some other uniquely significant concept. Further, Ockham does not speak of a demonstrative pronoun taken by itself as suppositing but rather as "demonstrating" or "indicating" (*demonstrare*) something.

10. *Summa logicae* I, c.10, (OPh I, 35–36).

11. Strictly speaking, it does not, because even Socrates is a composite of many things—of his prime matter and of several substantial forms, although they unite to make something that is one *per se* (see Part Four, chapter 15

many men, each christening imposes it to signify or name a single man. The same way, the term 'man' is conventionally instituted to signify human nature; 'whiteness' the nature of whiteness, etc.[12] Ockham agrees that general terms such as 'man' and 'whiteness' signify things and that they are related to their significata the way proper names are related to their bearers. But he denies that there are any universal or common things (see Part One, chapter 2 above). Thus, he concludes that every such term signifies (or can signify) many particulars, but is related to each just as directly and primarily as a proper name is related to its bearer, and hence signifies each in exactly the same way as it signifies any other. As we have seen, Ockham recognizes abstract and concrete substance terms—such as 'man' and 'animal'—and abstract terms in certain species of quality—such as 'whiteness' and 'heat'—as absolute terms (see Part One, chapters 5–8 above).

Of course, any general term contrasts with a proper name in that it can signify many with equal primacy. But where absolute terms signify *whatever* they signify the same way, connotative terms signify some of their significata one way and others another way. Ockham often says that they signify some primarily and others *secondarily*, or that they *signify* some and *consignify* or connote others. Such connotative terms have a nominal definition (*definitio exprimens quid nominis*), which "explains what is signified by the word— viz., what we ought to understand by the word."[13] Ockham's favorite example is the

---

below). Likewise, nations and cities, which are aggregates of things, receive proper names.

12. See William of Sherwood, *Introduction to Logic*, chap.5, sec.1, (Kretzmann trans., 105–106); also Walter Burleigh, *De puritate artis logicae*, Tractatus longior, Prima pars, c.1 and 3, (Boehner ed., 1–3, 6–9).

13. *Summa logicae* III–3, c.23, (OPh I, 682); III–2, c.28, (OPh I, 556); III–3, c.26, (OPh I, 690). In *Summa logicae* III–2, c.33, Ockham alludes to a tradition that imposes the division between real and nominal definitions on Aristotle's distinction between material and formal definitions. Thus, the formal/nominal definition of 'saw' is 'something by which we can divide wood', while the material/real definition of 'saw' is 'iron of a sort that we can divide wood with'. Ockham thinks that this is a loose way of speaking about real definitions, however, and holds that strictly speaking connotative terms do

concrete quality term 'white' that has as its nominal definition 'something having whiteness' or 'something informed by whiteness'.[14] He contends that all concrete and some abstract quality terms, as well as all terms in the other eight accidental categories are connotative (See Part One, chapter 5–8 above). But fiction terms such as—according to medieval science—'vacuum', 'infinite', and 'goat-stag' also receive nominal definitions.[15] Further, other parts of speech may be connotative and accordingly receive a nominal definition.[16] Thus, a verb such as 'runs' breaks down into a primitive syncategorematic 'is' and a partially categorematic component 'runner', which can be further analyzed. Similarly, for many other verbs, participles, adverbs, etc.

Since such nominal definitions often involve putting something in the nominative case (*in recto*) and something in an inflected case (*in obliquo*), Ockham often says that connotatives signify something directly (which he identifies as the primary significatum) and something obliquely (which he identifies with the secondary significatum).[17] But this grammatical criterion is inadequate to distinguish primary from secondary significata in every case, as Ockham acknowledges implicitly, when he observes that "often (*frequenter*)"—not "always (*semper*)"—"it is necessary to put one term of the definition in the nominative and another in an oblique case."[18] In *Summa logicae* II, c.12, he says that even "negative, privative, and infinite terms are genuinely connotative because in their nominal definitions something should be put in the nominative case and something in an oblique case *or* in the nominative case with a preceding negation."[19] It seems that things signified negatively albeit by nominative case expressions in the nominal definition

---

not have any real definition (OPh I, 568–570).

14. *Ibid*. I, c.10, (OPh I, 36–37); III–2, c.22, (OPh I, 556).

15. *Ibid*. I, c.26, (OPh I, 88); III–2, c.33, (OPh I, 568); III–3, c.26, (OPh I, 690).

16. *Ibid*. I, c.26, (OPh I, 89).

17. E.g., *ibid*., c.10, (OPh I, 36–37); II, c.11, (OPh I, 279–280).

18. *Ibid*. I, c.10, (OPh I, 36).

19. (OPh I, 283), (italics mine).

are to be counted among the secondary significata of the term defined. Ockham's combined remarks thus suggest that a *term* signifies a thing *x primarily*, if and only if *x* is signified affirmatively and by a nominative case expression in *t*'s nominal definition, while a term *t* signifies *x secondarily*, if and only if either *x* is signified by an oblique case expression in *t*'s nominal definition or *x* is signified negatively. But might not other modifications of a nominative case expression render the term thereby defined connotative rather than absolute and the things thereby signified secondary rather than primary significata? Without extensive knowledge of the mental language correlates of connotative terms, Ockham is really in no position to recognize any grammatical criterion as adequate to the task of distinguishing primary from secondary significata, and neither are we.[20]

Strictly speaking, a nominal definition not only identifies the extension of a term—this it would do if it were truly predicable and hence directly signified all and only those things about which the term was truly predicable—but also is *synonymous* with it, and hence subordinated to the same concept or concepts in the mental language. For one term or phrase to be synonymous with another, not only their primary but also their secondary significata must be the same; and they must signify their secondary significata the same way.[21] Ockham's examples

20. Paul Vincent Spade ("Ockham's Distinctions between Absolute and Connotative Terms," *Vivarium* XIII (1975): 55–76, at 72–73) offers the following formula for identifying the secondary significata of a term: "(16) A term *t* secondarily signifies a thing *x* if and only if either (a) *t* obliquely signifies *x* or else (b) *t* signifies *x* but not primarily." But this is not a criterion for distinguishing the primary from the secondary significata in the first place. Rather he assumes that we have identified all of the significata of a term, and have further determined which ones are the primary significata (by seeing which ones the term is truly predicable of); we derive the secondary significata by subtraction. Since for Ockham a term is predicated about something only if the term signifies it directly and affirmatively, Ockham's grammatical criterion includes whatever Spade's includes, but it may take in more besides.

21. *Summa logicae* I, c.6, (OPh I, 16): "Broadly speaking, synonymous terms are those that signify absolutely the same in every way, so that nothing

of nominal definitions, as well as his lumping together of syn-categorematics, connotatives, and negatives in *Ordinatio* I, d.2, q.8, make attractive the thesis that on his view, a fully expanded nominal definition of connotatives would include only absolute terms and primitive syncategorematics not capable of further definition themselves. Insofar as he holds to his claim that there is no synonym in the mental language, Ockham will be commit-ted to the view that connotative terms in conventional language are subordinated to arrays of primitive syncategorematics and absolute terms in the mental language.[22] And the conventional language explanation of what the terms signifies, that counts as a nominal definition of that term will be subordinate to the same array.

Corresponding to each absolute general term, there is a real definition that expresses the nature of the thing in its exten-sion.[23] Strictly speaking, a real definition is ''a succinct phrase that expresses the whole nature of the thing and does not men-tion anything extrinsic to the thing defined.''[24] Such definitions are of two kinds: *Metaphysical* definitions include only terms in the nominative case—whether genus and differentia or terms that express or connote the essential parts of what is defined. For example, 'Man is a rational animal' and 'Man is sensible ra-tional animate substance', where all the terms occur in the

is in any way signified by one that is not signified the same way by another.'' Later on, he considers a quibble about modes of signifying. Literally, a thing would be signified in altogether the same way only if the second term were of the same declension etc. as the first. Ockham rejects this broad interpretation of 'signify in the same way' (*ibid.*, c.72, (OPh I, 223–24)) and recognizes as relevant only differences in grammatical accidents that would be reflected in the mental language (see Part One, chapter 3 above).

22. Paul Spade makes this his central thesis in ''Ockham's Distinctions between Absolute and Connotative Terms;'' as he puts it, ''the paper argues for the claim that connotation-theory, or at least that part of it presented here, requires no new primitive notions beyond those already required for the theory of absolute terms'' (55). The relation between a connotative term and the thing connoted reduces the relation between an absolute term in an oblique case and its significatum.

23. *Summa logicae* III–3, c.23, (OPh I, 682); III–2, c.28, (OPh I, 556).

24. *Ibid.* I, c.26, (OPh I, 85).

nominative case and signify particular men directly, but connote their essential parts. Thus, 'sensible' connotes the sensory
soul, which is really distinct from the intellectual soul connoted
by 'rational'. A *natural* definition is one that includes oblique
case expressions, but only those that express the essential parts
of a thing. For example, 'Man is a substance composed of body
and soul'.[25] Following Aristotelian empiricism (see Part Three,
chapter 13 below), Ockham thinks that the natures of things can
be discovered only by experience. Only someone who has had
an intuitive cognition of a lion will have a simple absolute concept proper to lions or a concept of the differentia needed to
formulate the real definition. Those who, like Ockham, have
never seen lions, can "know what the name 'lion' signifies" —
i.e., can fix the extension of the term—because such persons
can have the absolute concept 'animal' and other non-complex
connotative and negative concepts none of which is proper to
lions and use these to form a composite concept that is
equivalent to, in the sense of being necessarily coextensive
with, the concept 'lion'.[26] Similarly for the concepts of color
and whiteness formed by someone blind from birth. Since
(almost) no one sees angels, the latter is the only sort of concept
we have to correlate with the conventional language term
'angel' "by addition" (*per additamentum*).[27] As a rule, the extension of such substance and quality terms can be fixed by one
or more such phrases including connotative and negative terms.
For example, the name 'angel' is equally well explained by 'an
intellectual and incorruptible substance that does not form a
compound with anything else',[28] each of which is necessarily
coextensive with the term 'angel' and defines it by addition.

25. *Ibid*.
26. *Ibid*. III–2, c.29, (OPh I, 558–560).
27. *Ibid*., c.32, (OPh I, 566): "A definition by addition not only mentions the essence of the thing, but also at the same time mentions something
other than the thing, whether affirmatively or negatively. Therefore, such a
definition is composed not only of terms predicable *per se* in the first way,
but also of terms predicable *per se* in the second way, which are the passions
of the term defined."
28. *Ibid*. I, c.10, (OPh I, 36).

Nevertheless, these phrases are not synonymous, because their parts signify different things and the same things differently. 'Matter' in 'a substance that exists independently of matter' signifies matter directly and affirmatively, whereas 'incorruptible' in 'an intellectual and incorruptible substance' signifies it obliquely and negatively. Ockham concludes that since what absolute terms signify can be explained equally well by many non-synonymous if necessarily co-extensional phrases, absolute terms do not have nominal definitions strictly speaking.[29]

Whether or not Ockham's criteria of primary and secondary signification are adequate, his predecessors and contemporaries thought that Ockham had the priorities exactly reversed. For example, in *De grammatico*, Anselm says that the *per se* signification of 'literate' is literacy, while 'literate' appellates, or signifies *per aliud*, one who is literate. Since the name 'literate' is imposed on Socrates through something else—viz., literacy—Anselm suggests that literacy is the primary and the one who is literate the secondary signification of 'literate', and not vice versa.[30] Burleigh takes a similar line in *De puritate artis logicae*.[31] An echo of this debate is found in *Summa logicae* I, c.33, where Ockham explains that "logicians take 'signify' many ways."[32] (i) The signification of a term is sometimes understood to include all and only those things about which it can be truly predicated. (a) One use restricts it to those about which it can be truly predicated in present tense propositions; and (b) a broader use expands it to include that about which it can be truly predicated in a singular categorical proposition, whether of the past, present, or future tense, whether assertoric or modal. Thus, the term 'man' would be said to signify all presently existing men the first way, all possible men the second way; the term 'white' all presently existing or possible white things.[33] But the term 'white' does not signify whiteness in

29. *Ibid.*, (OPh I, 35–36).
30. D. P. Henry dwells on this point at length in section 3 of *The Logic of St. Anselm*, (Oxford, 1967).
31. Tractatus primus, De proprietatibus terminorum, c.3, 7–10.
32. (OPh I, 95).
33. *Ibid.*

either way, because the proposition 'Whiteness is (was, will be, can be) white' is false. (ii) Alternatively, a term can be said to signify that from which the word is imposed, or what is signified the first way (in sense (i)) by the principal concept or word occurring in its nominal definition. This way 'white' signifies whiteness. For things are called white, because whiteness inheres in them, and whiteness is what is signified the first way by 'whiteness', the principal concept in the nominal definition of 'white'.[34] (iii) Finally, logicians sometimes take the term 'signify' comprehensively, so that a term is significant if "it is apt to be part of a proposition or to be a proposition or an expression indicating something, whether principally or secondarily, whether directly or obliquely, whether it makes something understood or connotes it, or is in any other way significant, whether it signifies it affirmatively or negatively."[35] This way, 'white' signifies both whitenesses and white things, and negative terms such as 'blind' signify vision. And syncategorematics combine with categorematics to signify various things in various ways. Where connotatives are concerned Ockham has fixed on what they signify in sense (i) as their primary significata, what they signify in sense (ii) their secondary significata.

Behind this apparently verbal dispute lurks the problem of universals. Most of us think that the meaning of general terms such as 'man' or 'white' does not change when particular men come into or go out of existence or when particular bodies change colors. Burleigh contends that Ockham's position has precisely this consequence, however, since it identifies a term's primary signification with its extension.

> ...If this were true, assuming that Socrates if first white and later black, the name 'white' would signify Socrates first and the name 'black' would signify Socrates later. Thus, assuming that whatever is white today became black tomorrow, then whatever 'white' signifies today 'black' would signify tomorrow. Thus, words would continuously lose their significata. No one could even move a finger without a word's

---

34. *Ibid.*; cf. II, c.11, (OPh I, 280).
35. (OPh I, 96).

thereby losing its significatum. For when the finger is at rest, the word 'rest' signifies the finger and not when the finger has moved—which seems absurd.[36]

By contrast, human nature and the nature of whiteness remain the same while particulars change. That is why Burleigh identifies whiteness as the primary significatum of 'white'.

This move would not be much use to Ockham, whose rejection of really existent universal things makes whitenesses just as particular as white things are. Anticipating this objection, he makes the different reply that while the extension identified for 'white' by (ia) does change as the particulars do, that picked out by (ib) does not because it includes whatever can be white.[37]

3. SUPPOSITION

Whereas the terms have signification even when taken by themselves, supposition is a property of terms as they occur in propositions. Roughly speaking, it corresponds to the relation of satisfaction in modern logic, and Ockham concurs with other medieval logicians when he explains supposition as "being put in the place of something else."[38] Supposition Theory is a

36. *Op. cit.*, Tractatus primus, De proprietatibus terminorum, c.3, 9.

37. *Summa logicae* I, c.33, (OPh I, 95). This interchange between Burleigh and Ockham is highlighted by Calvin B. Normore in his dissertation, *The Logic of Time and Modality in the Later Middle Ages: the Contribution of William Ockham*, (University of Toronto, 1976), chap.1, 27–28. A hint that Ockham was once willing to say that 'white' primarily signified whiteness is found in *Reportatio* II, q.10, (OTh V, 227): "Notice that where accident terms are concerned, the concrete term can have a fourfold supposition—viz., personal, simple, material, and significative. For example, 'white' supposits the first way for its subject, the second way for its concept, the third way for a spoken word, and the fourth way *for its significatum*. But where substance terms are concerned, personal and significative supposition are the same, because their significatum is the same as their suppositum—e.g., 'man'." Here 'white' is allowed not only to *signify* whiteness as opposed to the subject of whiteness, but to supposit for it. This last idea drops out of Ockham's mature works entirely. I am indebted to Gedeon Gál for calling my attention to this passage.

38. *Summa logicae* I, c.63, (OPh I, 193). Peter of Spain says that sup-

theory about what things a term may stand for and how it stands for them in various sorts of propositions. Anticipated by the twelfth century work of Peter Abelard,[39] its full development came in the thirteenth and fourteenth centuries and constituted one of the genuine novelties of medieval logic.[40] Nevertheless, its origins and motivation remain obscure, and attempts in the secondary literature to assimilate it to one or another part(s) of contemporary logic have not yet provided a satisfactory solution to this puzzle.[41] Ockham's discussion breaks into two principal parts: first, a general division of supposition into personal, material, and simple supposition; and then the subdivisions of personal supposition itself. We shall consider each in turn and along the way examine the considerable controversy that has arisen over the second half.

(3.1) *The Threefold Division.* The threefold division of supposition into personal, material, and simple was developed to

position is "the taking of a substantival term for something. Moreover, supposition and signification differ, because signification is produced by imposing the spoken sound to signify the thing, but supposition is the taking of a term that already signifies a thing for something..." (*Summulae logicales*, Tractatus suppositionum, translated from Mullally's edition, 2–4). And Walter Burleigh says that "generally speaking, supposition is the taking of a term for something—viz., for a thing or a spoken sound or a concept" (*op. cit.*, Tractatus primus, De proprietatibus terminorum, c.1, 2). But Peter of Spain restricts supposition to substantival nouns such as 'man' as opposed to adjectives such as 'white' or verbs, which are said to copulate (*copulare*) (*op. cit.*, (Mullally ed., 2–4)). And this distinction is likewise repeated by William of Sherwood, (*op. cit.*, chap.5, sec.1, 105); and exemplified by Burleigh, who says that strictly speaking only the subject term has supposition, while the predicate term has appellation (*op. cit.*, Tractatus primus, De proprietatibus terminorum, c.1, 1–2). But Burleigh was willing to use the term 'supposition' broadly to cover both; and after mentioning this distinction, Ockham announces his intention to follow the broader use (*Summa logicae* I, c.63, (OPh I, 193)).

39. William and Martha Kneale, *The Development of Logic*, (Oxford, 1962), Part IV, sec.2, 209–212. The most important of Abelard's works in this connection is his *Dialectica*, ed. L. M. De Rijk, (Assen, 1956).

40. See I. M. Bochenski, *A History of Formal Logic*, trans. and ed. Ivo Thomas, (Notre Dame, 1961), Part III, sec.I, "Semiotic Foundations," 153–177. See also Kneale, *op. cit.*, Part IV, sec.5, 246–273.

41. See sections 5–6 below.

deal with the fact that in medieval Latin, the true propositions *'Homo est albus'* ('Man is white'), *'Homo est nomen'* ('Man is a noun'), *'Homo est vox disyllabus'* ('Man is a spoken monosyllable'), *'Homo est dictio scripta'* ('Man is a written expression'), and *'Homo est species'* ('Man is a species') all have the same subject term, but yet are about very different sorts of things. The first but none of the others is about particular human beings; the second and third but none of the others are about the spoken sound; only the second and fourth about written inscriptions; and only the fifth about human nature. Medieval logicians described this fact by saying that the same term can have different sorts of supposition in different propositional contexts: *personal* supposition for particular men; *material* supposition for the sounds and inscriptions; and *simple* supposition for human nature.[42] Ockham draws this distinction for spoken words first. He makes it clear that

(R1) The division among personal, material, and simple supposition applies equally to spoken, written, and mental terms.[43]

For each of the three divisions, Ockham provides a characterization in terms of the sort of thing thereby stood for, and identification rules for determining when a given term can have that sort of supposition.

(3.1.1) *Material Supposition*. According to Ockham,

42. While most medieval logicians would accept this assignment of types of supposition for the cases at hand, not all would make this tripartite division the first one. William of Sherwood (*op. cit.*, chap.5, sec.2, 107) and Walter Burleigh (*op. cit.*, Tractatus primus, De proprietatibus terminorum, c.1, 2–3) first distinguish formal and material, and then under formal divide simple from personal. This division is a good one for realists like them, who believe that simple supposition is for a universal thing and personal supposition for the particulars that have or exemplify it, while material supposition is for signs. By contrast, since Ockham thinks that natures are concepts, he would have more incentive to assimilate simple and material supposition the way Buridan did. See section (3.1.3) below. Peter of Spain, a realist, (*Tractatus* IV, (De Rijk ed., 80–88)) omits to discuss material supposition entirely.

43. *Summa logicae* I, c.64, (OPh I, 196–97); III–4, c.4, (OPh I, 761–62).

(C1) A term has material supposition "when the term does not supposit for what it signifies but supposits for a spoken or written word."[44]

It is not—as the label might suggest—supposition for matter.[45] Although, strictly speaking, all he offers is a sufficient condition, his actual discussion shows that he regards it as a necessary condition as well. In a more detailed treatment, Walter Burleigh distinguishes five sorts of cases, four of which would have been admitted by Ockham: (i) when a spoken term supposits for itself or (as we would say) other spoken tokens of the same type, (ii) or a written term for itself or other written tokens of the same type—e.g., 'man' in the spoken proposition 'Man is a spoken word'; (iii) when a term supposits for some other spoken or written word that it does not signify—e.g., in Latin, when a spoken or written word in one case supposits for a different inflection of the same word, or when a clause in indirect discourse supposits for its direct discourse counterpart; and (iv) when a term taken with one supposition supposits for another of the same type taken with a different supposition—e.g., the first occurrence of 'man' in "man has personal supposition in 'Every man is an animal'."[46] Given (R1), Ockham would add a corresponding array of cases in which mental terms supposit for spoken and written terms of the same or different cases etc.[47] Spoken and written nonsense syllables such as 'bu' and 'ba' can have material supposition the first two ways. A fortiori, Ockham notes that not only nouns, but any part of speech can have material supposition, as for example in the following propositions: 'Well is an adverb', 'Reads is a verb', 'This is a pronoun', 'If is a conjunction', 'From is a preposition', and 'Ouch is an interjection'.[48]

When can a term or marks of any of these sorts have material

---

44. *Ibid.* I, c.64, (OPh I, 196); *Expos. Elench.* I, c.2, sec.9, (OPh III, 25).
45. *Summa logicae* I, c.64, (OPh I, 197).
46. *Op. cit.*, Tractatus primus, De proprietatibus terminorum, c.2, 4–5.
47. *Summa logicae* I, c.67, (OPh I, 206).
48. *Ibid.*

supposition? At first Ockham proposes

(R2) A term can have material supposition in a proposition in which it is matched with another extreme that signifies spoken or written words.[49]

Hence, the subject terms of the above mentioned propositions can have material supposition, because their predicate terms—'adverb', 'verb', 'pronoun', 'conjunction', 'preposition', and 'interjection'—signify conventional signs. Nevertheless, Ockham elsewhere acknowledges that not just every proposition containing such a term as subject or predicate is one in which the other extreme can have material supposition. Later on, distinguishing names of second imposition, which are "names of names" (narrowly speaking of conventional names only and broadly speaking of natural signs as well), from names of first imposition such as 'man' that do not signify names, Ockham substitutes

(R3) A term can have material supposition in a proposition if it is a term of first imposition that is not determined by a universal or particular sign and if it is matched with a term of second imposition,[50]

where Ockham treats what is stated as a sufficient condition as both necessary and sufficient. Thus, by (R3), the term 'noun' cannot have material supposition in the proposition 'Noun is a part of speech'. For although 'part of speech' is a term of second imposition, 'noun' is also a term of second imposition and is indeed one of its own significata. Hence it has personal supposition for itself in that proposition (see section (3.1.3) below). The stipulation in (R3) that only terms that are not names of names can have material supposition, seems too restrictive, however. For both subject and predicate in 'Verb is a term of second im-

49. *Ibid.*, c.64, (OPh I, 197).
50. *Ibid.* III–4, c.4, (OPh I, 761); *Expos. Elench.* I, c.2, sec.9, (OPh III, 26).

position' are terms of second imposition. Yet, 'verb' is not one of its own significata and cannot have personal supposition for itself. It seems that we should be able to use the sentence 'Verb is a term of second imposition', just as much as we can use 'Man is a term of first imposition' to say that the term 'man' is a term of first imposition. Ockham could make room for such cases by replacing (R3) with

> (R4) A term can have material supposition in a proposition, if and only if it is a term of first imposition or a term of second imposition that does not signify itself and if it is not determined by a universal or particular sign and if it is matched with a term of second imposition.[51]

Perhaps it will be objected that (R4) is too permissive, because it will allow 'verbs' to have material supposition for itself in the proposition 'Verbs are tensed'. But so interpreted, that proposition is false, because the noun 'verbs' is not tensed. On the other hand, nothing has been said to suggest that a term cannot have material supposition in false propositions. For example, the term 'man' does in 'Man is a spoken disyllable'. So Ockham might consent to (R4) nonetheless.

Ockham's second restriction is more puzzling. He seems to imply that no term can have material supposition in propositions of the form 'Every ____ is ____' or 'Some ... is ...'.[52] Thus, (R3) and (R4) exclude 'noun' from having material sup-

---

51. In his article "Ockham's Rule of Supposition: Two Conflicts in His Theory," *Vivarium* XII (1974): 63–73, Paul Spade points out the incompatibility between (R2) and Ockham's declaration in (C5) below that when a term stands for one of its significata, the supposition is personal supposition (sec.III, 69–70). But Spade does not consider (R3). In his lecture "Supposition: The Theory of Reference," Council for Philosophical Studies, Summer Institute, 1980, 8, Spade sees the inconsistency resolved in another way: by stipulating that a term that signifies itself has personal supposition for itself only when it supposits for all of its significata and not itself alone. This will not do, however, because terms do not supposit for *all* of their significata in most tensed and modal propositions (see chapter 11 below).

52. *Summa logicae* II, c.3, (OPh I, 257); *Expos. Elench.* I, c.2, sec.9, (OPh III, 26).

position in 'Every noun is a part of speech' or 'Some noun is a part of speech' twice over. In one place, Ockham appears to renege on this restriction, suggesting that the subject term in a proposition such as 'Every man is composed of a general term and a universal sign' can have material supposition.[53] What he has in mind, however, is not the assertion that every token of the word type 'man' is thus composed, but the claim that 'every man' is a written expression. Ockham includes a parallel restriction in the identification rule for simple supposition (see section (3.1.2) below). Yet, we may wonder why, if we can use 'Man is a written expression' to assert of a written token that it is a written expression, we may not then use 'Every man is a written expression' to say the same about every such token; and why if we may use 'Man is a concept' to assert of a concept token that it is a concept, we may not use 'Every man is a concept' to say the same about every such token. Ockham never makes his motive explicit. Perhaps he thinks that since scarcely anyone would use quantified sentences this way, there is no need to accommodate such a possibility in the regimentation of Latin for scientific purposes. Alternatively, he may think that there is no point in using quantified sentences here, because of his habit of treating linguistic units as if they were types rather than tokens. For example, in considering whether God can know more than He knows, Ockham takes for granted that the number of propositions is always constant and that there is always an equal number of true and false ones—an assumption that will not hold up if the propositions in questions are tokens rather than types (See Part Five, chapter 26 below). If conventional or natural linguistic units are tokens then there is reason to specify whether a feature is had or lacked by some or all of them. Since there is only one type, however, such quantification loses its point in talk about types.

Most scholars[54] regard the division of material from personal

53. *Summa logicae* II, c.1, (OPh I, 248).
54. For example, Ernest A. Moody, *Truth and Consequence in Mediaeval Logic*, (Amsterdam, 1953), sec.II.6, 24, and Calvin Normore, *op. cit.*, chap.1 and 2, 38–44.

334 PART TWO: LOGIC

supposition as a medieval attempt to distinguish the use of a term from its mention. Contemporary logicians have largely followed Frege's suggestion that we not use a term to stand for itself, but create a name of the term by enclosing it within quotation marks. This solution was not the first to occur to medieval logicians, however, because quotation marks were not included in the repertoire of medieval Latin punctuation marks. By Ockham's time, their probable ancestor 'li' was sometimes prefixed to a term or sentence to signal its mention. But Ockham uses it infrequently, and even then he does not think of it as creating a new term that has personal supposition for the first one, but rather as making explicit the fact that the same term is occurring in material supposition. It is worth noting that at least one modern logician, Alonzo Church, has abandoned Frege's quote-convention in favor of the medieval practice of using a term to name itself.[55]

(3.1.2) *Simple Supposition.* In the category of simple sup-position, logic once again makes contact with the problem of universals (see Part One, chapters 2–4 above). For a philos-opher's view of what the term 'man' stands for in the true proposition 'Man is a species', depends on what he thinks species are. Realists who contend that natures are mind-independent common or universal things (*res*), will say that simple supposition is for such things; and since they are what common terms such as 'man' or 'animal' primarily signify,

(C2) Simple supposition is the supposition of a term for its primary significatum.

Thus, having asserted that general terms such as 'man' signify universal things,[56] Peter of Spain declares that

...accidental simple supposition is the taking of common term for a

55. *Introduction to Mathematical Logic*, vol. I, (Princeton, 1956), In-troduction, sec.8, 61–62.
56. *Summulae logicales*, Tractatus suppositionum, (Mullally ed., 2).

universal thing signified by the term, as when one says 'Man is a species' and 'Animal is a genus'. There the term 'man' supposits for man-in-general and not for anything subordinate to it, and the term 'animal' supposits for animal-in-general and not for anything subordinate to it. The same should be said about any general term, as in 'Risible is a proprium', 'Rational is a differentia', 'White is an accident'...[57]

William of Sherwood takes the same line, defining 'signification' as 'the presentation of some form to the understanding' and distinguishing simple and personal supposition as follows:

...It is simple when a word supposits what it signifies for what it signifies, as in 'man is a species'. It is personal, however, when a word supposits what it signifies but for a thing that is subordinate to it, as in 'a man is running'; for running is in man because of some individual....[58]

According to Sherwood, 'man' has material supposition in 'Man is a species'.[59] He elaborates further as follows:

...This is unlike the preceding supposition since the predicate is not ascribed to the abstract species itself but to the species insofar as it is in things. Thus such a predicate can be ascribed to any of the things belonging to the species insofar as it shares the nature of the species; and so one can say 'this man, insofar as he is a man, is the noblest of creatures'...[60]

By contrast, Burleigh says that in this case 'man' has "absolute simple supposition" which occurs "when a common term supposits for its significatum absolutely and not in relation to its supposita, whether those that it exists in or those that it is said of."[61] He explains, "the sense is that among corruptible creatures, man is the noblest of creatures."[62] Ockham objects that on Burleigh's view it should be false that universal human

57. *Ibid.*, (Mullally ed., 4–6).
58. *Op. cit.*, chap.5, sec.2, 107.
59. *Ibid.*, sec.7–7.1, 111.
60. *Ibid.*, sec.7.2, 111.
61. *Op. cit.*, Tractatus primus, De proprietatibus terminorum, c.3, 11.
62. *Ibid.*, 14.

nature is the noblest of creatures. For he will say that Socrates is a composite of universal human nature together with some individuating principles. If he agrees with others that these individuating principles have some perfection, Socrates' total perfection will be greater than that of universal human nature by itself. Hence, Socrates will be a nobler creature than it is.[63] Burleigh replies that it is not true "that Socrates is a nobler creature than man-in-general, because while Socrates includes the perfection of man, nevertheless, he includes it not necessarily but contingently; for when Socrates ceases to exist, Socrates is not a man."[64]

Facing the example 'Pepper is sold here and in Rome', Sherwood distinguishes a third type of simple supposition in which the term supposits "for the significatum connected with things insofar as it is related to anything generally, in an unfixed way, and is not identified with anything in a determinate way."[65] He explains,

> ...This supposition is unlike the first, since the species itself is not sold, and unlike the second, since 'pepper' is not used here for instance of pepper insofar as it is pepper. Instead 'pepper' here supposits for it [as] related in a general, unfixed way to supposition. A term having this third mode of simple supposition supposits for a species insofar as it does so through individuals belonging to the species, but undesignated. It is as if someone asked 'what animal is useful for plowing?' and one answered 'the ox'. In answering one does not intend to speak of a particular ox, but simply of ox. Likewise, whoever says 'pepper is sold here and in Rome' does not intend to speak of some pepper in particular, but simply of pepper.[66]

Both Burleigh and Ockham reject this treatment of 'Pepper is sold here and in Rome'. In similar discussions, they insist that 'pepper' has personal supposition. Burleigh writes,

> ...It must be said that the proposition 'Pepper is sold here and in Rome'

63. *Summa logicae* I, c.66, (OPh I, 200–201).
64. *Op. cit.*, Tractatus primus, De proprietatibus terminorum, c.3, 14.
65. *Op. cit.*, chap.5, sec.7, 111.
66. *Ibid.*, 112–13.

is multiplex with respect to composition and division. Taken in the sense of composition it is false, because it is an indefinite proposition, each of whose corresponding singulars is false. Taken in the sense of division, it is true and denotes that pepper is sold here and pepper is sold in Rome. This way it is a conjunction of two indefinite propositions, one of which is true about one singular and the other for another. Nor does its truth require some one singular, but it is enough that one part is true about one and another about another.[67]

In a less clear sighted treatment, Peter of Spain finds still other instances of simple supposition. For example, in the proposition 'Every animal but man is irrational', "the term 'man' has simple supposition." He reasons that if it had personal supposition, then it would have to be true with respect to some particular man that every animal but this man is irrational. At least where there is more than one man, this is not true.[68] Then there is the case of

> common terms in the predicate position of an affirmative proposition such as 'Every man is an animal'. There the term 'animal' in the predicate position has simple supposition, because it supposits only for the nature of the genus.[69]

Once again, he reasons that 'animal' cannot have personal supposition there, because it is not true of any particular animal that every man is this animal. Sherwood,[70] Burleigh,[71] and Ockham[72] concur against Peter, however, insisting that 'animal' has merely confused supposition for many particular animals under disjunction (see section (4.2) below). Peter struggles with this suggestion but in the end abides by his original claim.[73]

Although Ockham agrees that 'man' has simple supposition for human nature in 'Man is a species', he rejects

---

67. *Op. cit.*, Tractatus primus, De proprietatibus terminorum, c.4, 21.
68. *Summulae logicales*, Tractatus suppositionum, (Mullally ed., 6).
69. *Ibid.*
70. *Op. cit.*, chap.5, sec.2, 108.
71. *Op. cit.*, Tractatus primus, De proprietatibus terminorum, c.4, 21.
72. *Summa logicae* I, c.70, (OPh I, 211).
73. *Summulae logicales*, Tractatus suppositionum, (Mullally ed., 10–16).

> (C2) Simple supposition is the supposition of a term for its
>   primary significatum.

For he is as sure as he is of anything that human nature is a concept and not any mind-independent universal or common thing
(see Part One, chapters 2–4 above). And he agrees with Burleigh
that words such as 'man' primarily signify things, not the concept 'man'. Hence, if 'man' has a simple supposition for the
concept 'man', it does not thereby supposit for its primary
significata, which are—as we have seen in section 2 above—
particular human beings. Rather Ockham explains that

> (C3) A term has simple supposition when it "supposits for a
>   mental intension and is not taken insofar as it is signifi-
>   cant."[74]

And although (C3) explicitly states only a sufficient condition,
Ockham treats it as necessary and sufficient. Simple supposition
is not to be characterized as supposition for simples, although
concepts are neither composed of matter and form nor divisible
into spatial parts. If it were, then no term could ever have personal supposition for God.[75]

Ockham's identification rules for when a term can have simple supposition are analogous to those he gives for material
supposition. At first, he proposes

> (R6) A term can have simple supposition in a proposition in
>   which it is matched with another extreme that signifies
>   mental intensions,[76]

where he treats the sufficient condition as necessary as well.
Ockham has defined 'first intension' as a sign that does not

---

74. *Summa logicae* I, c.66, (OPh I, 205–206); *Expos. Elench.* I, c.2,
sec.9, (OPh III, 25).

75. *Summa logicae* I, c.64, (OPh I, 197).

76. *Ibid*. III–4, c.4, (OPh I, 760); *Expos. Elench.* I, c.2, sec.9, (OPh III,
26).

signify concepts or signs only, while 'second intension' was explained as a sign of first intensions.[77] Thus, the new rule still allows 'man' to have simple supposition for the concept 'man' in 'Man is a species', because 'man' is a first intension and 'species' is a second intension. Given these definitions of 'first intension' and 'second intension' however, (R6) is both too permissive and too restrictive. It is too permissive because it allows 'being' to have simple supposition for the concept 'being' in 'Being is a first intention'. Yet, by (C3) 'being' cannot have simple supposition there, because the concept 'being' is itself a being and hence one of the things signified by 'being'.[78] On the other hand, (R6) is too restrictive because it prevents 'species' from suppositing for the concept 'species' in the proposition 'Species is a second intension' on the double ground that 'species' is not a first intension and 'second intension' is not a second intension because it does not signify any first intensions. The latter half of the difficulty could be removed by widening the scope of 'second intension' to include names of concepts generally. But (R6) would still leave us unable to use the proposition 'Species is a concept' to assert of the concept 'species' that it is a concept, where we are able to use 'Man is a concept' to assert of the concept 'man' that it is a concept. Perhaps Ockham could handle such cases by replacing (R6) with

(R7) A term can have simple supposition in a proposition if and only if it is a term of first intension or a term of second intension that does not signify itself and it is not determined by a universal or particular sign and it is matched with a term of second intension.

As in the substitution of (R4) for (R3), (R7) allows terms to have material supposition on false readings of the proposition in question: e.g., 'Species is a first intension'. But Ockham may not

77. *Summa logicae* I, c.12, (OPh I, 43).
78. Spade gives an example of this sort—'Being is a participle'—and notes such a conflict of (C3) with (R5) ("Ockham's Rule of Supposition: Two Conflicts in His Theory," sec.III, 70).

find this objectionable.

Given his alternative characterization of simple supposition, Ockham does not further subdivide the category of simple supposition the way his realist opponents did. As for the proposition 'Man is the noblest of creatures', Ockham says it is false, whether the supposition is taken to be personal or simple. For contrary to Burleigh, not only is no particular man the noblest of creatures, "what is common or a species is never nobler than its particulars" either, since the species is merely a concept. What people usually mean when they use the spoken proposition 'Man is the noblest of creatures' is correctly expressed by 'Man is nobler than any creature that is not a man'.[79] Again, Ockham underscores Sherwood's putative mistake in claiming that 'pepper' has simple supposition in 'Pepper is sold here and in Rome', noting that "taken as having simple supposition it is false, because no one wants to buy pepper-in-general, whether it exists as a mind-independent reality or in the mind, but anyone intends to buy a particular thing that he lacks."[80] Even if simple supposition is for concepts, however, it seems that Ockham might have had a use for Burleigh's distinction between generic and specific simple supposition to allow 'substance' to stand for the concept 'substance' and not the concepts 'man', 'animal', etc. on the true reading of 'Substance is a genus of the highest generality', and yet to stand for those ordered under it on a true reading of 'Substance is second substance' and 'Substance is properly defined'.

Ockham's characterization of simple supposition, not as the supposition of a common term for the corresponding nature, but as supposition for a mental intension, opens up the category to a range of cases excluded by his opponents' classification. For while he does not explicitly say so, it seems that Ockham must allow 'man' to have simple supposition for the concept 'man' in 'Man is a concept' and 'Man is a mental quality' as well as in 'Man is a species', given that the term 'man' does not signify the concept 'man' but particular men. Further, Ockham

79. *Summa logicae* I, c.66, (OPh I, 200–201).
80. *Ibid.*, (OPh I, 205).

allows that "any significant non-complex that can have material supposition can have simple supposition."[81] Thus, since 'man' can have material supposition in 'Man is a noun' for spoken and written words, it can have simple supposition in 'Man is a noun' for mental nouns. And just as the nominative case 'man' in "Man has personal supposition in 'A man is a donkey'" has material supposition for a spoken or written counterpart in the genitive case, so also may it have simple supposition for its mental counterpart of a different case. Likewise, since the that-clause in 'That a man is an animal, is true' does not signify propositions, but signifies that a man is an animal (see Part One, chapter 3 above), it may be taken to have simple supposition in that proposition for the corresponding mental proposition.[82]

We can now begin to see how Ockham's alternative characterization of simple supposition in (C3) undermines the rationale for distinguishing simple from material supposition in the first place. For simple supposition is supposition for concepts and concepts are natural signs. But much material supposition is supposition for signs (see section (3.1.1) above). Ockham himself must have been aware of this overlap when he observed that terms such as 'universal', 'common', 'predicate', 'subject', and 'noun' signify both conventional and natural signs.[83] Nevertheless, he never considers dropping simple supposition as a separate division.

It was left to John Buridan, Ockham's younger contemporary, to draw the consequence that the division of simple supposition was a vestigial organ in a nominalist's logic. Having announced that "supposition is divided into material and personal supposition," he observes that

> Some, who believed that universal natures were extramental things distinct from particulars, laid down a third division, which they call simple supposition. Therefore, they said that a common term supposits personally when it supposits for the particulars and simply when it supposits for the universal nature and materially when it supposits for

81. *Ibid.*, c.68, (OPh I, 207).
82. *Ibid.*, (OPh I, 208).
83. *Ibid.* III–4, c.4, (OPh I, 762).

itself. But I believe that Aristotle did a good job of destroying that opinion in Book VII of the *Metaphysics*. Therefore, such simple supposition should be done away with, at least according to this explanation.

Nominalists like Ockham, who think that universal natures are concepts, sometimes

> call it simple supposition when a spoken word supposits for the concept with which it is conventionally associated and material when it supposits for itself and those equiform with it...

And Buridan thinks that "while this can be permitted," the division is superfluous: he declares, "I do not care about this sort, because I call both material supposition."[84]

(3.1.3) *Personal Supposition*. As noted above, everyone agreed that 'man' in the proposition 'Every man is an animal' has personal supposition for particular men, which would suggest the following, noncontroversial characterization of personal supposition:

(C4)   A term *'T'* has personal supposition for a thing x in a proposition p, if and only if *'T'* occurs in p and x is one of the particulars that falls under *'T'*.

Thus, Peter of Spain explains, "personal supposition is the taking of a common term for those that fall under it; for example, when one says 'A man runs', the term 'man' supposits for those that fall under it."[85] And Burleigh could assent to this characterization.[86] Nevertheless, Ockham foregoes such consensus. Against these realist opponents, who identified the primary significatum of absolute terms such as 'man' with universal or common natures, he has insisted that 'man' primarily signifies particular men and signifies whatever it

84. Translated from Tractatus de suppositionibus in *Summulae de dialectica* in Maria Elena Reina, "Giovanni Buridano, Tractatus de suppositionibus," *Rivista critica di storia della filosofia* XII (1957): 201–202.

85. *Summulae logicales*, Tractatus suppositionum, (Mullally ed., 8).

86. *Op. cit.*, Tractatus primus, De proprietatibus terminorum, c.1, 3.

signifies primarily. And he offers the following polemical characterization:

(C5) Generally speaking, a term has personal supposition when it supposits for its own significata,[87]

where once again what is stated as a sufficient condition is treated as both necessary and sufficient. Since only categorematic terms have significata, strictly speaking it follows that only categormatic terms can have personal supposition.[88] And since not all categorematic terms signify persons, personal supposition should not be characterized as supposition for persons.[89] Rather 'donkey' has personal supposition for donkeys and 'whiteness' for whitenesses.

As for when a term can have personal supposition, Ockham maintains that "a term can always have personal supposition, no matter what proposition it is put in."[90] Later on, Ockham notes that strictly speaking only the whole subject or whole predicate and not part of it can supposit. The suggested identification rule is thus

(R8) A term 'T' can have personal supposition in a proposition p, if and only if 'T' is a categorematic term that occurs in p either as the whole subject or the whole predicate.

Thus, "in the proposition 'A white man is an animal', neither 'man' nor 'white' supposits, but the whole extreme supposits."[91] Sometimes he allows that there is a broader sense "in which part of an extreme can supposit"—e.g., 'horse' can supposit in this extended sense in 'I promise you a horse'; but many

87. *Summa logicae* I, c.64, (OPh I, 195); *Expos. Elench.* I, c.2, sec.9, (OPh III, 24).
88. *Summa logicae* I, c.69, (OPh I, 208).
89. *Ibid.*, c.64, (OPh I, 197).
90. *Ibid.*
91. *Ibid.*, c.69, (OPh I, 208).

of his rules hold good only when applied to whole extremes.[92]

If (C5) is motivated by Ockham's debate with realists over the signification of absolute natural kind terms that signify whatever they signify the same way, it is too vague to handle connotatives such as 'white' that signify some things one way and others another. For which of its significata does a connotative term stand when it has personal supposition? Ockham seems to clarify this point when he explains that among logicians, 'signify' is used one way so that 'a sign signifies something when it supposits or is apt to supposit for that thing—evidently, in such a way that the name is predicated of a pronoun indicating that thing by means of the verb 'is'.''[93] And it is used more broadly, when the predication can occur either through the verb 'is', 'was', 'will be', or 'can be'.[94] This suggests the following equivalences:

(E1) A term *'T'* signifies x, if and only if *'T'* is apt to supposit for x, if and only if 'This is T' (where 'this' indicates x) is (was, will be, can be) true.

This explanation is repeated in *Summa logicae* I, c.63:

> Moreover, 'supposition' means, as it were, being put in place of something else. Thus, when a term stands for something else in a proposition, in such a way that we use that term in place of something of which, or of a pronoun indicating which the term (or the nominative case of that term, if it is in an oblique case) is truly predicated, the term supposits for that thing. This is true at least where the term is taken to

    92. *Ibid.*, c.72, (OPh I, 219–220); see section 4 below. Spade notes that nothing in Ockham's definition of supposition—in terms of being put in place of a thing in a proposition—rules out the supposition by parts of extremes, and even speculates that "the theory of descent to singulars is included in supposition-theory *only* because the parts of extremes have supposition" ("Priority of Analysis and the Predicates of 'O'-Form Sentences," *Franciscan Studies* N.S. XXXVI (1976): 263–270, at 267, note 14)—an assumption needed to give an account of the truth conditions of such sentences as this.
    93. *Summa logicae* I, c.33, (OPh I, 95).
    94. *Ibid.*; see section 2 above.

supposit significantly.[95]

Ockham sets out to say in general when a term supposits for something, but he qualifies his remark to cover only those cases in which the term is taken as significant—i.e., cases of personal supposition. Thus, he claims

(E2) A term 'T' has personal supposition for x in p, if and on-
      ly if 'T' occurs in p and 'This is T' (where 'this' indicates
      x) is (was, will be, can be) true.

(E2) seems to say that a term has personal supposition for the things about which it can be truly predicated; and we have seen how Ockham identifies the primary significata of a term with those of which it can be truly predicated. If it held good, (E2) would help us decide that 'white' has personal supposition for white things and not for whitenesses. For everyone agrees that 'white' cannot be truly predicated of whitenesses, no matter what suppositon 'white' is taken to have.

Nevertheless, (E2) does not seem true as it stands, since the right-hand side could be true when the left-hand side was false. In assessing the truth-value of 'This is T' (where 'this' indicates x), we have to ask what sort of supposition 'T' has in that proposition—material, simple, or personal? It might seem ob-vious that it must have personal supposition, for it is matched there with the demonstrative pronoun 'this', which is neither a term of second imposition nor a term of second intension, and by (R4) and (R7) only such can have material and simple supposition, respectively. Doubtless Ockham was forgetting singular sentences with demonstrative pronouns as subjects when he formulated (R3) and (R6). The natural extension of the rules would allow a term to have material or simple supposition when it is matched with a demonstrative pronoun that indicates a conventional or natural sign, respectively. Assuming such an amendment, it could be true that 'man' occurs in 'Every man is an animal' and true that 'This is man' (where 'this' indicates the

95. (OPh I, 193).

term 'man' and the term 'man' in the proposition has material supposition), and yet be false that 'man' has personal supposition for the term 'man' in 'Every man is an animal'. To avoid this difficulty, (E2) would have to be replaced with

> (E3) A term '*T*' has personal supposition for x in p, if and only if '*T*' occurs in p and 'This is *T*' (where 'this' indicates x, and where '*T*' has personal supposition) is (was, will be, can be) true.

(E3) says that a term supposits personally for those things that it can be truly predicated of when it is taken to have personal supposition. And it will do as well as (E2) would for informing us which of its significata the term 'white' has personal suppositon for. It is worth noting, however, that the true biconditional in (E3) cannot serve as a non-circular definition of personal supposition the way some scholars have taken the biconditional in (E2) to do.[96]

(3.1.4) *Rules and Biases.* Ockham holds that the division between personal, material, and simple supposition is exhaustive. By (R4) and (R7), a term can have material or simple supposition only in certain propositional contexts—those in which it is matched with a term that signifies signs. It follows that

> (R9) A term must have personal supposition if it is matched with a term that does not signify signs.

96. Spade understands Ockham to be offering a definition of personal supposition in the above quoted passage from *Summa logicae* I, c.63 (''Priority of Analysis and the Predicates of 'O'-Form Sentences''; cf. 266, note 9.) For a fuller discussion of why (E2) cannot constitute a successful definition of supposition in general or of any particular type of supposition, see my article ''What Does Ockham Mean by 'Supposition'?'' *Notre Dame Journal of Formal Logic* XVII (1976): 375–391. For different reflections on how this formula should be treated, see Alfred J. Freddoso, ''Ockham's Theory of Truth Conditions,'' in *Ockham's Theory of Propositions*, 1–76. Sherwood defines 'appellation' as ''the present correct application of a term, i.e., the property with respect to which what the term signifies can be [only] said of something through the use of the verb 'is''' (*op. cit.,* chap.5, sec.1, 106).

According to Ockham, however,

(R8)   A term can have personal supposition in any proposition in which it occurs.

Hence, there are no propositional contexts in which a term must be taken to have material or simple supposition. Rather in contexts in which it can, the resultant proposition is equivocal the third way, and different readings of it must be distinguished according to the following rules:

(R10)   In those contexts in which a term can have material supposition, it is necessary to distinguish one reading on which it has personal supposition, another material supposition, and another simple supposition.[97]

Further, since (R4), (R7), and (R9) stipulate that the supposition of one term is determined by the signification of the other, it follows that according to these rules at least one extreme of a categorical proposition must be taken as significant and hence taken to have personal supposition.[98]

This bias in favor of personal supposition was traditional. Sherwood defends it on the ground that

> Words considered in themselves always present what they signify; and if they present their utterance they do so not in themselves but as a result of adjunction to a predicate. For one predicate is disposed to have reference to only the utterance or the word but another to what is signified...[99]

And Burleigh also endorses (R9)–(R11).[100] To a logician engaged

---

97. *Summa logicae* III–4, c.4, (OPh I, 760–62); *Expos. Elench.* I, c.2, sec.9, (OPh III, 26).

98. John Swiniarski makes this last observation in "A New Presentation of Ockham's Theory of Supposition with an Evaluation of Some Contemporary Criticisms," *Franciscan Studies* N.S. XXX (1970): 181–217, especially 189.

99. *Op. cit.*, chap.5, sec.4, 109–110.

100. *Op. cit.*, Tractatus primus, De proprietatibus terminorum, c.3, 9–10.

in the regimentation of Latin for scientific purposes, however, this bias in favor of personal supposition does not have much to recommend it. Why should we be allowed, by (R10), to use 'Man is a spoken monosyllable' to say that a particular man is a spoken monosyllable and not, by (R9), to use 'Man is an animal' to assert that the spoken word 'man' is an animal? Would Ockham not have done better to exhibit a bias in favor of the sensible by stipulating, with some contemporaries and successors[101]

(R13) In those contexts in which a term can have material (simple) supposition, it does have material (simple) supposition?

Further, why must we regard propositions such as 'Man is a noun' whose predicates signify both mental and conventional signs, as equivocal? Is it not a good policy to keep equivocation to a minimum, and would it be better to stipulate that

(R14) In those contexts in which a term can have either simple or material supposition, it supposits both for the supposita it has in simple and those it has in material supposition?

(3.1.5) *Equivocation in the Mental Language.* As we have seen, Ockham endorses

(R1) The division among personal, material, and simple supposition applies equally to spoken, written, and mental terms,

which implies that different tokens of the same sign type—whether spoken, written, or mental—stand in propositions for quite different things. His further commitment to

101. Spade cites Richard Lavenham and Paul of Pergula ("Ockham's Rule of Supposition: Two Conflicts in His Theory," *Vivarium* XII (1974), sec.IV, 70–73).

(R10)–(R12) implies that the same token of a given sign type—whether spoken, written, or mental—may be equivocal the third way as between standing for its significata, for itself, or for the corresponding conventional or mental sign.

These consequences seem wrongheaded, however, because they are incompatible with Ockham's original conception of mental language as the ideal language. Whereas conventional language contains synonymous and equivocal expressions due to the ornamentation of speech and variations in usage, mental language was to include neither. Ockham even defines an equivocal sign as "one that signifies many and is not subordinate to one concept but is a single sign subordinate to many concepts or mental intentions"[102] and remarks that

> only a spoken word or some other conventional sign is equivocal or univocal, and therefore a mental intension is neither equivocal nor univocal, properly speaking.[103]

Indeed if the division between personal and material supposition is a medieval attempt to distinguish use from mention, it is an accident of medieval punctuation that the same conventional sign stands for itself and its significata. But the concept of the spoken word 'man' is distinct from the concept of human nature and from the concepts of Socrates, Plato, etc. Thus, the different readings of the conventional propositions distinguished by (R10) and (R12) must correspond to different mental propositions. Likewise, different mental propositions must correspond to the conventional language proposition 'Man is a species' read to assert that a particular man is a species, and read to assert that the abstract general concept 'man' is a species, respectively. There is thus no need to assert that a particular man is a species, respectively. There is thus no need for the third sort of equivocation among conventional signs to be replicated in the mental language. Should we not regard Ockham's endorsement of (R1) as a careless blunder and offer him

102. *Summa logicae* I, c.13, (OPh I, 45).
103. *Ibid.*, (OPh I, 44).

(R15) The division among personal, material, and simple
supposition applies equally to spoken and written
terms, but not to mental terms,

by way of reconstruction? Yet, how can his adherence to (R1)
be simply careless, when he repeated it in such widely spaced
passages of the *Summa logicae*?

Is there a method behind Ockham's apparent madness in proposing (R1)? There would be if he thought the following: just
as every mental term naturally presents all of its significata,
and every conventional sign conventionally presents all of its
significata, so every mental or conventional sign naturally presents itself, and every mental or conventional sign conventionally presents the sign(s) with which it is conventionally
associated. Therefore, just as we must appeal to propositional
context to determine which of the things it presents a conventional sign stands for in a proposition, so also with mental signs.
Hence, (R1) is true and (R4), (R7), and (R8) apply to mental as
well as conventional signs.

There are at least three objections to attributing this rationale
to Ockham, however. (i) First, if this were his motive for extending the divisions of material and simple supposition to the
mental language, we would not expect him to have a bias in
favor of personal supposition. For if a term always presents
itself and the signs with which it is conventionally associated, as
well as its significata, it should be able to have material or simple
supposition in any context in which it occurs the way it is able
to have personal supposition in any context; e.g., 'man' should
be just as apt to have material supposition in 'Man is an animal'
as personal in 'Man is a spoken monosyllable'; to have simple
supposition in 'Man is an animal' as personal in 'Man is a
species'. And, as we have seen, Sherwood defends the bias in
favor of personal supposition on the ground that whereas a
term always presents it significata, it does not always present
itself or the signs conventionally associated with it. Insofar as
Ockham is following this tradition, there is some reason to see
him as endorsing Sherwood's justification.

(ii) Second, it is unclear whether Ockham would really agree that a mental term *presents itself*, or brings itself to mind. As we shall see below (see Part Three, chapter 13), Ockham denies that any mental act is an awareness of itself (is a "reflex" act). If I am aware of my act of thinking of Socrates, it is by a distinct mental act.

(iii) A third objection is that this proposal would render all mental language systematically ambiguous. For suppose that mental terms do always present themselves, the signs conventionally associated with them, and their significata, and it is this fact that makes a mental term able to have personal, material, or simple supposition in appropriate propositional contexts. If so, what makes it the case that a mental proposition corresponding to 'Man is a species' is the assertion of the concept 'man' that it is a species rather than the assertion of a particular man that he is a species? And since entertaining the thesis that man is a species is merely having such a mental proposition in mind, what makes it the case that I am having the one thought rather than the other? Something must; yet the above proposal does not explain what could.[104]

These objections are powerful. On the other hand, what better explanation is there of why Ockham transferred the tripartite division of supposition from spoken to mental language? Is it incredible that he sometimes found it obvious that anything presents itself by being present, and that one kind of term presents those with which it is conventionally associated just as much as its significata, and was thus moved to assign mental terms material and simple as well as personal supposition?

---

104. Paul Spade raises a related objection in his paper "Synonymy and Equivocation in Ockham's Mental Language," *Journal of the History of Philosophy* XVIII (1980): 9–22: "if mental terms may have simple or material supposition we do not always know what we are asserting in a mental sentence..." (21). But the issue is not really whether or not one of our thoughts could be about something (in the sense of a term's standing for some particular) without our knowing it. Ockham allows that when I think 'Every man is an animal', the term 'man' supposits for lots of things without my knowing that it does, since I have no awareness of those particular men. Rather the question is whether on the above proposal anything would make it the case that the term was suppositing for these things rather than those.

4. DIVISIONS OF PERSONAL SUPPOSITION

Although some of his predecessors gave detailed breakdowns of all three categories of supposition, Ockham reserves detailed consideration for the category of personal supposition. He first contrasts the personal supposition of singular terms such as 'Socrates' and 'this man', which he labels "discrete personal supposition," with that of general terms, which he labels "common personal supposition,"[105] and then proceeds to lay out the species of the latter. If the original division between personal, material, and simple supposition was based on a difference among the kinds of things a given term can stand for in a proposition, the divisions of common personal supposition are based on variations in how a general term stands for things it signifies.[106]

In particular, medieval logicians distinguished various kinds of common personal supposition on the basis of the possible descents to and ascents from the singulars under a general term in a propositional context. What they had in mind was this. If a nonempty general term supposits in a proposition for something it signifies, it should be possible in principle to indicate its supposita by singular terms, and the latter would constitute the singulars under a general term. Ockham contended that whenever a nonempty and multi-referential general term

105. *Summa logicae* I, c.70, (OPh I, 209–210).

106. In his lecture, "The Logic of the Categorical: The Theory of Modes of Personal Supposition," Council for Philosophical Studies, Summer Institute, 1980, Spade suggests that originally, whereas the division into personal, material, and simple supposition was supposed to answer the question *"What* does a term supposit for?" the modes of common personal supposition are to answer the question "How many does it supposit for?" (10–12). He cites Lambert of Auxerre who contrasts determinate supposition in which a common term supposits indifferently for one thing or several and confused supposition in which a common term of necessity is taken for all of its supposita or for several. But this was not Ockham's way of drawing the distinction. For him, a common term in personal supposition has supposition for all of its—present, past, future, or possible, depending on the verb or modal context—significata, but in different ways, e.g., conjunctively, disjunctively, etc.

occurs in a proposition, that proposition implies one or more propositions in which the general term is replaced by its singulars. For categorical propositions consisting of a subject, predicate, the copula, and sometimes quantifiers (such as 'every' and 'some') and negation signs (such as 'no' and 'not'), two such descents are possible: one under the subject and another under the predicate term. Sometimes it is also possible to ascend from the singular(s) to the proposition that contains the general term. Which propositions are implied in each descent depends on the syntactical relations of the general term to the syncategorematics in the proposition.

Accordingly, Ockham offers two sets of rules for each division: those which characterize the type of common personal supposition in terms of permitted descents and ascents, and those for identifying when a term has that type of common personal supposition. (4.1) *Common Determinate Supposition*. He characterizes common determinate supposition as follows:

> (C6) A general term has common determinate supposition in a proposition when if (a) it has many singulars under it, then (b) it is possible to descend under the general term to its singulars by means of a disjunctive proposition without changing the other extreme; and (c) it is possible to infer the proposition containing the general term from each singular,

where in practice he treats (a)–(c) as both necessary and sufficient.[107] As for when a term has it, Ockham stipulates,

> (R16) A common term has determinate personal supposition in a categorical proposition if (i) it does not fall within the scope of a universal sign (or its equivalent) which

---

107. *Summa logicae* I, c.70, (OPh I, 210). Condition (a) is not explicitly stated for determinate supposition, but it is for confused and distributive supposition, and the same rationale would apply in each case: there cannot be a conjunction or a disjunction of singulars if there are no singulars or there is only one singular.

distributes the whole extreme of which it is a part, or
(ii) it does not fall within the scope of a negation sign
(or its equivalent),

where for a term to fall within the scope of a universal sign is for
it to be "mediately or immediately governed by it"—i.e., for the
universal sign to be added to the same extreme or to the
preceding extreme—and for a term to fall within the scope of a
negation sign is for it to come after it in the proposition.[108]
Ockham treats conditions (i) and (ii) as both necessary and
sufficient where the whole subject or whole predicate of a
categorical proposition is concerned. Thus, he infers by condition (i) that neither the subject nor the predicate of 'Every man
is an animal' nor the predicate of 'An animal is every man' has
common determinate supposition, because each falls within the
scope of the universal sign 'every'.[109] Likewise, condition (ii)
excludes both the subject and the predicate of 'No man is an
animal' and the predicate of 'A man is not an animal' because
each falls within the scope of a negation sign. Ockham even
treats conditions (i) and (ii) as necessary conditions when he excludes the partial extreme 'man' in 'Socrates is different from a
man', on the ground that 'is different' is equivalent to a negation
sign.[110] On the other hand, (R16) assigns common determinate
supposition to both the subject and the predicate terms of 'A
man is an animal' and 'Some man is an animal'.[111] And in accordance with (C6), it is possible to descend under the subject
term, inferring 'A man is an animal; therefore this man is an
animal or that man is an animal and so on for the other
singulars' and to ascend from the singulars, inferring 'A man is
this animal; therefore a man is an animal'.[112]

(4.2) *Merely Confused Supposition.* Ockham characterizes
common merely confused supposition as follows:

108. *Ibid.*, c.71, (OPh I, 212–13).
109. *Ibid.*, (OPh I, 213).
110. *Ibid.*, (OPh I, 213–14).
111. *Ibid.*, (OPh I, 213).
112. *Ibid.*, c.70, (OPh I, 210).

(C7) A general term has common merely confused supposition in a proposition when if (a) it has many singulars, then (b) it is not possible to descend under the general term to its singulars by means of a disjunctive proposition without changing the other extreme, and (c) it is possible to descend under the general term to its singulars by means of a disjunctive predicate; and (d) it is possible to ascend from any singular to the proposition containing the general term.[113]

And he offers a list of identification rules that does not purport to be complete. First,

(R17) A general term has merely confused supposition in a proposition when it falls within the scope of a universal affirmative sign (or its equivalent) that governs the whole of the other extreme.[114]

Thus, the predicate term of a universal affirmative proposition has merely confused supposition by (R17); and by (C7b) the inference 'Every man is an animal; therefore either every man is this animal or every man is that animal or...' fails, but by (C7c) the inference 'Every man is an animal; therefore every man is either this animal or that animal or...' holds, as by (C7d) does the inference 'Every man is this animal; therefore every man is an animal'.[115] Since Ockham holds that 'Every man is an animal' and 'Only an animal is a man' convert, he likewise proposes

(R18) The subject of an affirmative exclusive proposition always has merely confused supposition.[116]

Again, Ockham holds that

(R19) A general term has merely confused supposition when

113. *Ibid.*, (OPh I, 211).
114. *Ibid.*, c.73, (OPh I, 226).
115. *Ibid.*
116. *Ibid.*, (OPh I, 228).

it is part of the subject term and follows a universal sign that immediately governs another part but not the whole of the subject.[117]

Thus, 'man' in 'At every time after Adam some man existed' has merely confused supposition by (R19), because the universal sign 'every' immediately governs 'time' but not the rest of what follows it and precedes 'existed'. And by (C7b) the inference 'At every time after Adam some man existed; therefore at every time after Adam this man existed or at every time after Adam that man existed or...' fails, but by (C7c) the inference 'At every time after Adam either this man or that man or...existed' holds, as by (C7d) does 'At every time after Adam this man existed; therefore at every time after Adam some man existed'.[118]

(4.3) *Confused and Distributive Supposition.* Ockham characterizes confused and distributive supposition as follows:

(C8) A general term has confused and distributive supposition when (a) if it has many singulars, (b) it is possible to descend in some way under the general term to its singulars in a conjunction; and (c) there is no formal inference from any singular to the proposition containing the general term.[119]

Condition (C8b) covers two subdivisions: Mobile Confused and Distributive Supposition in which

(bi) it is possible to descent under the general term to its singulars in a conjunction without making any other change in the proposition.

and Immobile Confused and Distributive Supposition in which

117. *Ibid.*, (OPh I, 226).
118. *Ibid.*, (OPh I, 227).
119. *Ibid.*, c.70, (OPh I, 211).

(bii) it is possible to descend under the general term to its singulars in a conjunction only where some change is made in addition to the replacement of the general term by its singulars—viz., something is left out.[120]

Without purporting to be exhaustive, Ockham offers several identification rules for Mobile Confused and Distributive Supposition:

(R20) The subject of any universal propostion—whether affirmative or negative—that is not exclusive or exceptive has mobile confused and distributive supposition

and

(R21) The predicate of a universal negative proposition that is not exclusive or exceptive has mobile confused and distributive supposition.[121]

Thus, the subject of 'Every man is an animal' and both subject and predicate of 'No man is an animal' have this type of common personal supposition. These examples show (bi) to be inaccurate where descent under subject terms is concerned, however. For the prescribed descent is from 'Every man is an animal' to 'This man is an animal and that man is an animal and....' and from 'No man is an animal' to 'This man is not an animal and that man is not an animal and...' But in both cases, descent under the subject term involves dropping the initial quantifier, and in the second case inserting a negation sign governing the copula.[122] It does cover descent under the

120. *Ibid.*, (OPh I, 211–12).
121. *Ibid.*, c.74, (OPh I, 228–29).
122. Ockham seems to abide by (bi) as it stands when he argues that the subject term of 'Only a man runs' does not have Mobile Confused and Distributive Supposition, because 'Only a man runs; therefore only this man runs and only that man runs and...' is not a good inference, where 'only' remains prefixed to each conjunct (*ibid.* II, c.17, (OPh I, 303); cf. (OPh I, 304–305)).

predicate term from 'No man is an animal' to 'No man is this animal and no man is that animal and...', however. Further, Ockham holds that

> (R22) The predicate of a proposition whose principal copula is governed by a negation sign has mobile confused and distributive supposition.

For example, the predicate of 'A man is not an animal', which implied the conjunction 'A man is not this animal and a man is not that animal and...' by (C8bi), while 'A man is not this animal; therefore a man is not an animal' is not a formal inference by (C8c).[123] Again, Ockham proposes that

> (R23) A term that immediately follows the verb 'differs' or the verb 'is distinct from' or the corresponding participles or the noun 'other than' or their equivalent, has mobile confused and distributive supposition.

Thus, Ockham claims, the inference 'Socrates is other than a man; therefore Socrates is other than this man and Socrates is other than that man and...' holds by (C8bi), while the inference 'Socrates is other than this man; therefore Socrates is other than a man' does not.[124] His corresponding claims about 'Socrates differs from a man' and 'Socrates is distinct from a man' accord less well with ordinary English usage.[125]

As for Immobile Confused and Distributive Supposition, Ockham offers the following identification rule:

> (R24) The subject of an exceptive proposition always has immobile confused and distributive supposition.

For example, one cannot descend to the singulars under the subject term of 'Every man but Socrates is running' to 'This man but Socrates is running and that man but Socrates is running and...'

123. *Ibid.* I, c.74, (OPh I, 229).
124. *Ibid.*
125. *Ibid.*

Rather one must leave the 'but Socrates' out (an instance of (C8bii)) and descend to 'Socrates does not run and this man runs and that man runs and so on for all the men other than Socrates'.[126] Further, because the descent is limited to all of the singulars other than Socrates, Ockham sometimes says it has "limited confused and distributive supposition."[127]

(4.4) *Difficulties*. If these divisions of common personal supposition are intended to chart the descents and ascents between general terms and their singulars, they seem to be something of hodgepodge. Ockham's focus has been principally on general terms that constitute the whole extreme of indefinite and the standard *A, I, E,* and *O*-form categorical propositions. His consideration of propositions including verbs other than the copula—such as '*A* differs from *B*'—and his treatment of the supposition of partial extremes is neither systematic nor exhaustive. His discussion of what is left out in descents under terms with Immobile Confused and Distributive Supposition remain unacceptably vague.

Some commentators have argued that his divisions do not even provide an adequate treatment of the examples that he does bring up. (4.4.1) *Not All of the Divisions Are Necessary*. First, it is charged that the division of Merely Confused Supposition is superfluous. Logically, the most obvious ways to descend to singulars under a general term would be in a disjunction (Determinate Supposition) or conjunction (Confused and Distributive Supposition) of singulars. The division of Merely Confused Supposition was introduced to cover cases in which such descents were "immobilized" or blocked. Thus, Burleigh writes,

> Merely confused supposition occurs when a common term supposits for many in such a way that it is inferred from each of the terms and it is impossible to descend to any of them either in a conjunction or in a disjunction. This is the way the predicate supposits in 'Every man is an animal', because the term 'animal' supposits for many, since the proposition would be false if the term supposited for any determinate

126. *Ibid.*, (OPh I, 230).
127. *Ibid.* II, c.18, (OPh I, 308).

one. And it is inferred from each singular, since the inference 'Every man is this animal; therefore every man is an animal' holds. And it is impossible to descend under 'animal' either in a disjunction or a conjunction. For neither the inferences 'Every man is an animal; therefore every man is this animal or every man is that animal...' nor the inference 'Every man is an animal; therefore every man is this animal and every man is that animal etc.' holds.[128]

Peter of Spain ultimately concludes that where this happens the term does not have personal supposition after all, but simple supposition.[129] Sherwood characterizes merely confused supposition in terms of the impossibility of descent to singulars.[130] Ockham's characterization mentions the impossibility of descent to singulars in a disjunction (C7b), but he omits the impossibility of descent to a conjunctive. Perhaps he thought the latter condition would be redundant, since where it is impossible to descent to a disjunction it is likewise impossible to descend to a conjunction. On the other hand, Ockham introduces the idea of non-truth-functional descent to a disjunctive predicate (condition (C7a)), which is cautiously mentioned by Buridan ("although perhaps the singulars follow in a proposition with a disjunctive extreme").[131]

Some historians of logic have argued that the two divisions of (Mobile) Confused and Distributive Supposition and Determinate Supposition are really enough. The former corresponds to universal and the latter to existential quantification;[132] the permitted descents under conjunction (C8bi) and disjunction (C6b) roughly parallel universal and existential instantiation; the prohibited (C8c) and permitted (C6c) ascents, universal and ex-

128. *Op. cit.*, Tractatus primus, De proprietatibus terminorum, 21.

129. *Summulae logicales*, Tractatus suppositionum, (Mullally ed., 8–16).

130. *Op. cit.*, chap.5, sec.2, 108–109 and 119.

131. *Tractatus de suppositionibus*, 40, in a reprint (Florence, 1957) of Maria Elena Reina, "Giovanni Buridano, Tractatus de suppositionibus," *Rivista critica di storia della filosofia* XII (1957).

132. Peter Thomas Geach, *Reference and Generality*, (Ithaca, NY, 1962), 175–76. John Swiniarski, "A New Presentation of Ockham's Theory of Supposition with an Evaluation of Some Contemporary Criticisms," *Franciscan Studies* N.S. XXX (1970): 209–210.

istential generalization, respectively. The "problem" cases can be handled simply by laying down a priority of analysis rule, telling us to descend under the other term first.

Would medieval logicians have welcomed such a suggestion? The answer depends in part on what the proposed rule looks like. One suggestion is

(R25) In categorical propositions whose subjects and predicates are both general terms, always descend under the subject term first and then descend under the predicates of the resultant propositions.[133]

This rule would allegedly eliminate the need to assign Merely Confused Supposition to the predicate of 'Every man is an animal' (and the cases of Merely Confused Supposition posited by (R17) generally). For descending first under the subject, we get 'This is an animal and that man is an animal and...', and (R16) assigns determinate supposition to the predicate of each conjunct. (R25) would be counterproductive for dealing with the subject terms of exclusive propositions (the range of cases postulated by (R18)), however, and with the partial extremes mentioned in (R19). We might try to remedy this defect by substituting a more specific rule:

(R26) In categorical propositions whose subject and predicate are both general terms, (i) if the proposition is universal and affirmative, descend first under the subject term; (ii) if the proposition is exclusive but affirmative, descend first under the predicate; and (iii) if the proposition contains a universal sign that determines only part of the extreme, descend under the part so governed first.

Thus, from 'Only an animal is a man' we would infer 'Only an animal is this man and only an animal is that man and...' The subject term of each conjunct could then be assigned deter-

---

133. Swiniarski, *op. cit.*, 209.

minate supposition. Again, from 'At every time after Adam some man existed' we could infer 'At this time after Adam some man existed and at that time after Adam some man existed and...', and 'man' in each conjunct could be assigned determinate supposition. But even (R26) would be inapplicable to propositions such as 'I promise you a horse,' where Ockham proposes a descent to a disjunctive term under the partial extreme 'horse'.[134] Thus, it seems doubtful that any general priority of analysis rule could cover all of the cases. The most we could hope for would be an ad hoc list.

Even if it is replied that Ockham's identification rules represent an ad hoc list already, there will still be reason to doubt whether medieval logicians would have looked favorably on such priority of analysis rules. For the latter assume that the interest in identifying kinds of common personal supposition is always one that is served by descending under both extremes at once. Medieval discussions including Ockham's make no such interest explicit, however. On the contrary, they—to my knowledge invariably—treat descent under each term separately and purport to offer rules that are indifferent to the order of "analysis." We shall return to this issue in section 5 below.

(4.4.2) *Ockham's Divisions Require Supplementation.* On the other side, it seems easy to argue that Ockham's divisions are insufficient to cover all of the cases he mentions. (a) At first he seems to concede this himself in his discussion of propositions containing verbs such as 'begins' and 'ceases'. He denies that 'literate' has determinate, merely confused, or confused and distributive supposition, on the ground that it is impossible to descend under 'literate' in the relevant ways. The last is clear enough, since where many people are literate, Socrates does not begin to be each and every one of them. But Ockham also declares that

---

134. *Summa logicae* I, c.72, (OPh I, 219–221). Spade emphasizes the last case in his article "Priority of Analysis and the Predicates of 'O'-Form Sentences," *Franciscan Studies* N.S. XXXVI (1976): 263–270, at 265–68, where he concludes that "The 'priority of analysis' rule is a red herring."

The inference 'Socrates begins to be literate; therefore Socrates begins to be this or Socrates begins to be that or...' (where all of those for which the predicate supposits are indicated) does not hold, because the premiss can be true when each part of the conclusion is false.[135]

Suppose that after Socrates has learned to read, only Socrates, Plato, and Aristotle are literate. Ockham's thought is that Socrates does not begin to be Socrates, because he has been Socrates throughout his existence and the proposition 'Socrates begins to be literate' does not imply the proposition 'Socrates begins to exist'.[136] Nor does Socrates begin to be Plato or Aristotle, since it is impossible that he should be either of them. Hence he does not begin to be any of the persons who are literate, and the disjunctive proposition is false. The same considerations make the proposition with the disjunctive predicate false as well. Ockham's conclusion is that "it can be said that the predicate term in such propositions—whether what follows the verb is a substantive expression or even an adjective—...has another kind of supposition for which we lack a name."[137]   It is characterized by

(C7d)   It is possible to ascend from any singular to the proposition containing the general term

—since 'Socrates begins to be this (where any literate person is indicated); therefore Socrates begins to be literate' holds; but by the negation of

(C7a&c) If it has many singulars under it, it is possible to descend under the general term to its singulars by means of a disjunctive predicate

and

(C6a–b) If it has many singulars under it, then it is possible to

135. *Summa logicae* I, c.75, (OPh I, 231).
136. Cf. *ibid*. II, c.19, (OPh I, 315).
137. *Ibid*. I, c.75, (OPh I, 231).

> descend under the general term to its singulars by
> means of a disjunctive proposition without chang-
> ing the other extreme.

Nevertheless, Ockham does not think this sort of case is so
damaging to his theory of common personal supposition,
because the anomaly can be readily explained in terms of the
fact that 'Socrates begins to be literate' is exponible into
'Socrates is literate now for the first time and was not literate
before', and 'literate' occurs with determinate supposition in
the first exponent and with confused and distributive supposition in the second. The predicate of the exponible proposition
somehow conflates the two and so does not have common personal supposition of any of the ordinary types.[138]

The latter attempt to explain away this range of counterexamples suggests an appeal to the general thesis that where a
proposition is exponible, we should not apply the identification
rules to its terms directly but only to those of its exponents.
Ockham does not follow this practice, however. For he thinks
that any categorical proposition containing a connotative term,
e.g., 'Socrates is white', is exponible, e.g., into 'Socrates exists
and whiteness inheres in Socrates'.[139] Likewise, affirmative exclusive propositions such as 'Only an animal is a man' are exponible by 'An animal is a man and nothing other than an animal
is a man'.[140] Yet Ockham offers identification rules that apply
directly to them. What difference does he see between the latter
cases and propositions containing 'begins' and 'ceases'?
Ockham replies that

> The subject of an affirmative exclusive proposition has merely con-
> fused supposition. For although its exponents have subjects with dif-
> ferent suppositions, nevertheless their subjects are not the same as the
> subject of the exclusive proposition, since the negative exponent has a
> different subject from the affirmative. Therefore, the subject of the ex-
> clusive proposition will be able to have one of the above mentioned

138. *Ibid.*, (OPh I, 232).
139. *Ibid.* II, c.11, (OPh I, 281).
140. *Ibid.*, c.17, (OPh I, 296).

three suppositions. Now in such propositions as 'Socrates begins to be literate', 'Socrates ceases to be white', 'Socrates was black twice', the subject of exponents is the same as the subject of expounded proposition, however,[141]

and so is the predicate.

By the time he wrote *Summa logicae* II, however, Ockham had thought of a way to handle such propositions without positing another principle division of common personal suppostion. He distinguished descents in which the singular descended to is a proper name or demonstrative pronoun taken by itself—e.g., Socrates begins to be literate; therefore Socrates begins to be this or Socrates begins to be that or...'—from those in which it is a demonstrative pronoun taken together with an adjective—e.g., 'Socrates begins to be literate; therefore Socrates begins to be this literate or Socrates begins to be that literate or...'. The first sort of descent is impossible, but the second sort is possible under the predicate term of propositions containing such verbs. For although Socrates does not begin to be Socrates or begin to be Plato or begin to be Aristotle, he does begin to be white Socrates because he is white Socrates and was not white Socrates before. Hence he begins to be white Socrates or he begins to be white Plato or he begins to be white Aristotle etc.

Ockham notes further that his characterization of determinate supposition in *Summa logicae* I, c.70, did not distinguish the two sorts of singulars, since it makes no difference for the propositions he was concentrating on there —simple categoricals whose main verb is the present tense copula. But this characterization will not hold good in general where singulars are understood the second way, since

(C6c) it is possible to infer the proposition containing the general term from each singular

will sometimes fail. For while one can—in accordance with

141. *Ibid.* I, c.75, (OPh I, 232–33).

(C6a–b)—descend from 'Socrates begins to be colored' to 'Socrates begins to be white or Socrates begins to be black or...', one cannot ascend from 'Socrates begins to be white' to 'Socrates begins to be colored'.[142] These reservations do not really require a new division of common personal supposition, however. For what must be preserved for determinate supposition is the possibility of ascent from the proposition containing the singular term 'this *A*' to the proposition containing '*A*', not ascent to the proposition containing '*B*', where '*B*' is a general term to which '*A*' is subordinate.

Thus, Ockham suggests that

> (R27) If the predicate of a singular categorical proposition whose main verb is 'begins' or 'ceases' is a general term, it has determinate supposition, where determinate supposition is defined by the second sort of descent,

and

> (R28) If the predicate of a universal affirmative categorical proposition whose main verb is 'begins' or 'ceases' is a general term, it has merely confused supposition, where merely confused supposition is defined by the second sort of descent[143]

(b) In giving identification rules, Ockham brings up the proposition 'An animal is every man' and assigns its subject term determinate supposition.[144] But what sort of supposition does the predicate term of 'No animal is every man' have? Not confused and distributive, because the inference 'No animal is every man; therefore no animal is this man and no animal is that man and...' does not hold good. Not determinate because the inference 'No animal is every man; therefore no animal is this man

---

142. *Ibid.* II, c.19, (OPh I, 314–15).
143. *Ibid.*, (OPh I, 313–315).
144. *Ibid.* I, c.71, (OPh I, 213).

or no animal is that man or...' fails. Not merely confused, because the inference 'No animal is every man; therefore no animal is either this man or that man or...' is likewise to be rejected.[145]

One solution to this difficulty would be to appeal to the priority of analysis rule (R25). Descending first under the subject of 'No animal is every man' by (Cbi), we get 'This animal is not every man and that animal is not every man and...' Determinate supposition can then be assigned to the predicate term of each conjunct. This proposal inherits all of the above mentioned difficulties, however.

Alternatively, one could assume a further division of common personal supposition, parallel to Merely Confused Supposition and characterized by a descent to singulars not in a conjunction or disjunction and not in a disjunctive extreme, but in a proposition with a *conjunctive* extreme. Thus, descending under the predicate of 'No animal is every man,' we get 'No animal is this man and that man and...'[146]

5. IS THE THEORY OF COMMON PERSONAL SUPPOSITION A THEORY OF QUANTIFICATION?

If the divisions of common personal supposition constitute a theory, what is it a theory about? Searching for an analogue in modern logic, much of the secondary literature assigns it the ambitious role of a theory of quantification. But is it a theory of quantification? And/or was it so intended by Ockham? The very question has an anachronistic air about it. What is meant by

145. Alfred J. Freddoso focuses on propositions with a universal quantifier before the predicate in arguing that Ockham did not intend his divisions of common personal supposition as a theory of quantification ("Ockham's Theory of Truth Conditions," in *Ockham's Theory of Propositions*, 16–28). See section 5 below.

146. Freddoso, *op. cit.*, 22–23, discusses both proposals. Swiniarski mentions this new division of common personal supposition, which he calls "Impurely Confused" supposition, as a solution to a problem about O-form propositions, and rejects it for that purpose (*op. cit.*, 212–13). See section 5 below.

'theory of quantification' in this context? A set of axioms and rules of inference that would be adequate to prove all of the valid formulae containing quantifiers in a given language? Ockham never conceived of such a program, and his divisions of common personal supposition are obviously inadequate to that task. But the doctrine of descent to and ascent from singulars can suggest an attempt at a Ramsey-style contextual definition of quantifiers and/or the more modest proposal to give truth conditions for sentences containing general terms and quantifiers in terms of propositions whose subjects and predicates are singular terms.

Commentators who find this idea attractive begin by suggesting that where first order predicate calculus quantifies over individuals, medieval logic quantifies over terms.[147] According to Ockham, in simple *A*, *I*, *E*, and *O*-form propositions, the quantifiers affect both terms—the subject immediately and the predicate term mediately. Hence, each sentence frame—'Every ____ is ____', 'Some ____ is ____', 'No ____ is ____', and 'Some ____ is not ____'—in effect involves two quantifications. Thinking that this amounts to saying that each implicitly contains two quantifiers,[148] they are drawn to the idea that Ockham's doctrine of descents and ascents under the subject and predicate terms is intended to map the effect of such quantifiers.

In developing their case, these commentators put a certain construction on the metalinguistic characterizations of the various divisions of common personal supposition in (C6)–(C8). (i) First, they assume that the descents described in (C6a–b), (C7a&c), and (C8a–bi) are intended by Ockham to be reversible. Hence, he is taken to assert that a proposition with a general term in Determinate Supposition *is equivalent to* a disjunction

---

147. Gareth B. Matthews makes this point in "Ockham's Supposition Theory and Modern Logic," *Philosophical Review* LXXIII (1964): 91–99.

148. Matthews worries about the fact that no quantifiers are explicitly stated immediately in front of the predicate term in *A*, *I*, *E*, and *O* propositions ("*Suppositio* and Quantification in Ockham," *Nous* VII (1973): 13–24, especially 16). But Ockham doubtless thinks this unnecessary: the initial quantifier together with position in the sentence does the job.

of propositions in which the general term is replaced by one of its singulars, a proposition with a general term is replaced by a distinction of its singulars; and a proposition with a general term in Confused and Distributive Supposition *is equivalent to* a conjunction of propositions in which the general term is replaced by one of its singulars.

(ii) Second, they assume that the metalinguistic rules are intended by Ockham to describe object-language equivalences, and so can be restated as such. Let substitutions for 'A' and 'B' be general terms, for 'A_i' and 'B_j' singulars falling under those general terms. Suppose further that there are n A's and m B's where n and m are both greater than zero. They apply Ockham's identification and characterization rules to derive the following equivalences:

(E4) Every A is B if and only if (A_1 is B and A_2 is B and ... A_n is B)

(E5) Every A is B if and only if (Every A is B_1 or B_2 or ... B_m)

(E6) Some A is B if and only if (A_1 is B or A_2 is B or ... A_n is B)

(E7) Some A is B if and only if (Some A is B_1 or some A is B_2 or ... some A is B_m)

(E8) No A is B if and only if (A_1 is not B and A_2 is not B and ... A_n is not B)

(E9) No A is B if and only if (No A is B_1 and No A is B_2 and ... No A is B_m)

(E10) Some A is not B if and only if (A_1 is not B or A_2 is not B or ... A_n is not B)

(E11) Some A is not B if and only if (Some A is not B_1 and some A is not B_2 and ... some A is not B_m)

Given (E4)–(E11), some find it inviting to compare Ockham's doctrine of descents and ascents with the claim by Ramsey, Johnson, and Wittgenstein that

(x) Fx

is equivalent to

Fa & Fb & Fc & Fd & ...

while

(Ex) Fx

is equivalent to

Fa v Fb v Fc v Fd v ...

and to see in them a contextual definition of quantifiers.[149] Perhaps Ockham's theory of Common Personal Supposition is an attempt at such a contextual definition as well. Alternatively, whether or not those equivalences constitute *definitions*, they can still be regarded as stating the truth conditions for propositions with quantified general terms by means of conjunctions and disjunctions that replace quantified general terms with singulars.[150]

149. Matthews makes this comparison in *"Suppositio* and Quantification in Ockham," 13–14. Actually Ramsey regarded it "only as a contribution to the analysis of 'I believe that all (or some)'" (*The Foundations of Mathematics and Other Logical Essays*, (New York, 1950), 153).

150. This weaker hypothesis was advanced by Ernest A. Moody, in *Truth and Consequence in Mediaeval Logic*, sec.I.2, 10–11 and 15; II.5, 23; II.8, 32; III.11, 48. William Kneale assumes that descent is to a logically equivalent statement (*The Development of Logic*, 268). In his article "A New Presentation of Ockham's Theory of Supposition with an Evaluation of Some Contemporary Criticisms," John Swiniarski speaks of Ockham's *analyzing* the propositions in which the general term occurs in terms of singulars (191–92) and assumes that the propositions are equivalent (211–13). The weaker hypothesis has been taken up by Michael Loux, "Ockham on Generality," in

Nevertheless, some temptations are to be resisted. And some commentators have defended the following argument:

1. If Ockham's theory of Common Personal Supposition were taken as a theory of quantification, it would be a very bad theory of quantification for reasons $r_1, r_2, r_3, \ldots$

2. The Principle of Charity forbids us to attribute such a bad theory to Ockham, the More than Subtle Doctor.

3. Therefore, we should not suppose that Ockham intended his theory of Common Personal Supposition as a theory of quantification.

Various reasons are supplied for premiss 1 against the stronger and the weaker of the above mentioned hypotheses.

(5.1) *First Objection: Ockham's Descents Are Not Uniformly Reversible.* The above attempt to find a theory of quantification—whether in the form of a contextual definition of quantifiers, or a statement of truth conditions for quantified propositions—in Ockham's theory of Common Personal Supposition can succeed only if all of the prescribed descents are reversible. (E11) is an obvious howler, however. For where Socrates and Plato are the only men, 'Some man is not an animal' (an instance of the left-hand side of (E11)) is false, while it is true that some man, viz., Socrates, is not the animal that Plato is and some man, viz., Plato, is not the animal that Socrates is (an instance of the right-hand side of (E11)). The Principle of Charity thus requires us to deny that Ockham intended to assert (E11) or saw himself as providing a theory of quantification.[151]

Ockham's Theory of Terms, 28ff, and Paul Spade, "Priority of Analysis and the Predicates of 'O'-Form Sentences," 265, where he declares that "While Matthews is certainly right in saying that Ockham never claims equivalence explicitly, I for one find it hard to imagine that he means anything else. For if equivalence fails, the elaborate distinction of various kinds of personal supposition cannot be used in an account of truth-conditions. What then is the distinction for? Is it simply an idle decoration in the theory of supposition?"

151. Matthews argues this way in "*Suppositio* and Quantification in Ockham," 20.

Other commentators, unwilling to abandon this interpretive hypothesis, have refused to go so far with charity. They assume that even a logician of Ockham's stature could let (E11) slip by in haste, and suggest that the difficulty it causes is easily mended in one of two ways. (a) One could modify Ockham's identification rules to assign the predicate of O-form propositions Merely Confused Supposition instead of Mobile Confused and Distributive Supposition, and replace (E11) with

> (E12) Some A is B if and only if some A is not B_1 or B_2 or ... B_m.[152]

(b) Alternatively, one could adopt (R25) which would require us first to resolve the O-form proposition according to (E10). And (R22) assigns Mobile Confused and Distributive Supposition to the predicate of each conjunct. And

> (E13) Some A is not B if and only if ((A_1 is not B_1 and A_1 is not B_2 and ... A_1 is not B_m) or (A_2 is not B_1 and A_2 is not B_2 and ... A_2 is not B_m) or ... (A_n is not B_1 and A_n is not B_2 ... A_n is not B_m))

does hold good.[153] (E13) displays the effect of 'some' and 'not' on both general terms at once. And this result inspires the thought that, by abiding by (R25), A, I, and E propositions can be reduced to expansions of singulars the same way:

> (E14) Every A is B if and only if ((A_1 is B_1 or A_1 is B_2 or ... A_1 is B_m) and (A_2 is B_1 or A_2 is B_2 or ... A_2 is B_m) and ... (A_n is B_1 or A_n is B_2 or ... A_n is B_m));

---

152. This proposal is made by Spade, "Priority of Analysis and the Predicates of 'O'-Form Sentences," 269–270, and also by Graham Priest and Stephen Read, "The Formalization of Ockham's Theory of Supposition," *Mind* N.S. LXXXVI (1977): 109–113, especially 109, 111–12.

153. The adoption of this priority of analysis rule is the suggestion preferred by Swiniarski, *op. cit.*, 211–12. Spade rejects it in "Priority of Analysis and the Predicates of 'O'-Form Sentences," 265–68.

(E15) Some A is B if and only if ((A_1 is B_1 or A_1 is B_2 or ... A_1 is B_m) or (A_2 is B_1 or A_2 is B_2 or ... A_2 is B_m) or ... (A_n is B_1 or A_n is B_2 or ... A_n is B_m));

(E16) No A is B if and only if ((A_1 is not B_1 and A_1 is not B_2 and ... A_1 is not B_m) and (A_2 is not B_1 and A_2 is not B_2 and ... A_2 is not B_m) and ... (A_n is not B_1 and A_n is not B_2 and ... A_n is not B_m)).

(E13)–(E16) make the comparison with Ramsey-style contextual definitions even more inviting. A fortiori, they could be regarded as stating truth conditions.[154]

(5.2) *Second Objection: A Contextual Definition of Quantifiers?* It may be argued from Charity that Ockham did not intend either (E4)–(E11) or (E12), (E13)–(E16) as contextual definitions of quantifiers in terms of expansions of singulars because they would be unsuccessful definitions. One reason is that —even leaving (E11) out of account—the expansions of singulars on the right-hand side are not logically equivalent to the quantified statements on the left-hand side. (a) 'Every literate is Greek' will not be equivalent to 'Socrates is this Greek and Plato is that Greek and Aristotle is the other Greek'. We need at least to add that Socrates, Plato, and Aristotle are all the literate persons there are. Likewise, the stipulation that there are n A's and m B's, where both n and m are greater than one, strictly speaking, should be included on the right-hand sides—in which case the right-hand sides will no longer be free either of quantifiers or of general terms.[155]

(b) Again, (E4)–(E10), (E12), and/or (E13)–(E16) cannot be regarded as successful contextual definitions of quantifiers,

154. Loux prefers this version of the weaker thesis in "Ockham on Generality," 30.

155. Ramsey makes a parallel observation, *op. cit.*, 154. Matthews mentions this consideration as a reason why Ockham might not have claimed equivalence but only the possibility of descent to singulars in "*Suppositio* and Quantification in Ockham," 20.

because such expansions of singulars as are found on their right-hand sides are inapplicable where the general term in question is mono-referential or empty. Yet, according to Ockham, *E* and *O* propositions can be true even if either or both categorematic terms are empty,[156] while *A* and *I* propositions can be true where one or both of the categorematic terms is mono-referential.[157] And Ockham does not want to admit that quantifiers such as 'every', 'some', and 'no' function differently depending on whether the categorematic terms are poly-referential, mono-referential, or empty.[158]

(c) If empty terms pose a problem, so do general terms with infinite domains. For a successful definition must make the meaning of the *definiendum* clear. But where there are infinitely many singulars, (E13)–(E16) resolve quantified propositions into infinitely many conjunctions and/or disjunctions. And we cannot understand such infinitely long propositions.

(5.3) *Objection Three: The Equivalences Cannot Provide Truth Conditions Either.* The considerations raised in (5.2a) and (5.2b) above seem to block an object-language statement of truth conditions for *A*, *I*, *E*, and *O*-form categoricals in terms of quantifier-free expansions of singulars alone. But they do not show that the modified equivalences could not serve this

---

156. *Summa logicae* I, c.72, (OPh I, 218–19).

157. *Ibid*. II, c.4, (OPh I, 260–61).

158. Matthews in "*Suppositio* and Quantification in Ockham" raises this issue and concludes: "But now it becomes absurd to consider the doctrine of descent as an embryo quantification theory. A doctrine that applies to propositions of the logical forms 'No *S* is *P*' and 'Some *S* is not *P*', only in case their terms are nonempty (perhaps only in case they are poly-referential) is not a quantification theory at all, not even a rudimentary one" (22). In the course of elaborating this point, Matthews worries about how the distinctions among the various types of common personal supposition can be drawn from mono-referential and empty terms, since there can be no conjunction or disjunctions of different singulars, where there is only one or there are no singulars (21–22). This concern seems misguided, however, since Ockham relies on his identification rules for determining that 'god' has Determinate Supposition in 'Some god is omnipotent', not the characterization rules. Where the metalinguistically described descents cannot be made to true propositions, the original proposition is deemed false.

purpose. At least one commentator thinks that the problem about infinite domains mentioned in (5.2c) would exclude them, however, since the truth conditions should be just as intelligible to us as definitions must be.[159]

(5.4) *Evaluation*. Although Ockham does not, in my opinion, intend his divisions of common personal supposition as a theory of quantification, the above objections do not provide uniformly good reasons for thinking so. We have seen how some commentators argue that the first, in (5.1), is inconclusive. As for the second, in (5.2), the fact that a Ramsey-style contextual definition of quantifiers is impossible would not, by itself, support an argument from Charity that Ockham did not attempt it. After all, if Ramsey, Wittgenstein, and Johnson seriously considered such a proposal, it would not be all that uncharitable to attribute it to another fine logician!

The biggest objection to supposing that Ockham saw his divisions as a theory of quantification is that he never claims equivalence between A, I, E, and O propositions, on the one hand, and quantifier-free expansions of singulars, on the other. Nor do we need an argument from Charity to show that he did not regard all of the proposed descents as reversible. For in outlining the divisions of Common Personal Supposition, Ockham never asserts that *any* of them is reversible. Where Determinate Supposition is concerned, he notes in (C6c) that one can ascend from one singular to the proposition containing the quantified general term (e.g., in 'Socrates is an animal; therefore some man is an animal') but does not comment on the possibility of ascending from the disjunction (as in 'This man is an animal or that man is an animal or...; therefore some man is an animal'). Again, with Merely Confused Supposition, Ockham tells us in (C7d) that we can infer 'Every man is an animal' from 'Every man is this animal', but does not mention the inference 'Every man is this animal or that animal or...; therefore every man is an animal' there. Finally, with Mobile Confused and Distributive Supposition, he explicitly rejects the inference

159. Alfred J. Freddoso, "Ockham's Theory of Truth Conditions," 24–26.

'Socrates is white; therefore every man is white' in (C8c), but has nothing to say about whether the conjunction of all of the singulars implies the propositions with quantified general terms. If Ockham had wished to present his theory of common personal supposition as a theory of quantification based on equivalences between propositions containing quantified general terms and expansions of singulars, surely he would not have remained silent on this point.

Likewise, it is not the argument from Charity, but the fact that Ockham never asserts the relevant equivalences, which undermines the hypothesis that he intended the divisions of Common Personal Supposition to serve as Ramsey-style contextual definitions of quantifiers.

Nor will the points raised in (5.2) and (5.3) support an argument from Charity that while Ockham did not propose object-language equivalences, he did intend to offer object-language inference rules. For these considerations can be marshalled with equal success or failure against both claims. Paralleling (5.2a), it is clear that the inference 'Some literate is Greek, therefore either Socrates is Greek or Plato is Greek or Aristotle is Greek' does not hold without the addition 'Socrates, Plato, and Aristotle are all the literates there are' to the consequent.[160] On the other hand, it is not clear that Ockham regarded descent as a move to quantifier-free propositions. For, implicitly recognizing the difficulty posed by (5.2a), his examples of conjunctions and disjunctions end with the clause "and so on for the singulars" (*et sic de singulis*).[161]

Again, if Ockham had been aiming to state inference rules in the object-language, he would have had to worry about the empty-term (5.2b) and infinite domain (5.2c) objections as much for one direction descents as for equivalences. (Mono-referential terms would have posed no special problem for descents assigned for Determinate and Mobile Confused and

---

160. Matthews notes this fact in "*Suppositio* and Quantification in Ockham," 19–20.

161. For example, *Summa logicae* I, c.70, (OPh I, 210, lines 20–21, 33–34, 35–37); (OPh I, 211, lines 50–52, 54–57).

Distributive Supposition, since both hold even though each reduces to descent to one singular proposition. Following (C8c), 'Aristotle is Greek' does not imply 'Every literate is Greek', but 'Aristotle is Greek and Aristotle is every literate person' does. And the contrast between descent to a disjunction of singulars (C7a–b) and descent to a disjunctive extreme (C7a–c) collapses.) But Ockham does not assert equivalences at all, and all of his characterizations of the divisions of common personal supposition are metalinguistic. If we cannot understand or formulate (except recursively) an infinitely long conjunction or disjunction, Ockham's metalinguistic characterizations are intelligible nonetheless.

6. FALLACY DETECTION

Commentators come closer to the truth when they relegate Ockham's division among types of common personal supposition to his theory of inference.[162] After all, descents and ascents are inferences, whether or not they are reversible. But what role do they play in a theory of inference? Ockham's characterizations obviously do not catalog all of the permissible and tempting-but-prohibited inferences to be drawn from or among the standard types of categorical propositions. They do not even do this job where inferences between quantified their singulars are concerned. For, as we have seen, Ockham has nothing to say in this context about the reversibility of descents. Even if his views about the latter can be extrapolated from his remarks elsewhere in the *Summa logicae*, this uniform omission makes it highly implausible that he intended his treatment of the divisions of common personal supposition to supply such a list.

If we want to assess the role of supposition theory in medi-

---

162. Calvin G. Normore, in his unpublished reply to Alfred J. Freddoso's "*O*-Propositions and Ockham's Theory of Supposition," read at the Eastern Division APA, 1979. Freddoso accepts this diagnosis in "Ockham's Theory of Truth Conditions," 28.

eval theories of inference, we will do better to look—for at least part of our answer—at where its divisions are *explicitly* appealed to. When we do, we find that it is in the context of rules for identifying and avoiding fallacies. The very organization of William of Sherwood's *Introduction to Logic* suggests this intent: chapter 1 deals with statements and corresponds to Aristotle's *De interpretatione*; chapter 2, with predicables and parallels Porphyry's *Isagoge*; chapter 3, with syllogisms as covered by Aristotle's *Prior Analytics*; chapter 4, with the dialectical reasoning of the *Topics*; and chapter 6, with fallacies of the *Sophistical Refutations*. The properties of terms are treated, not at the beginning, before the statements of which they are parts, but in chapter 5 after the discussion of dialectical reasoning and before the catalog of fallacies! Peter of Spain follows the same order in his *Summulae logicales* and sandwiches the properties of terms between the material of the *Topics* and that of the *Sophistical Refutations*.[163] Within the chapter itself, Sherwood first defines 'supposition' and lays out the division between material and formal, simple and personal supposition, offering characterizations for subdivisions under the last two.[164] He then turns to rules having to do with supposition, and offers first the identification rule

Rule I...every distributive sign confuses the term immediately adjoining it confusedly...

...an affirmative [distributive] sign confuses the remote term merely confusedly...

...a negative [distributive] sign confuses the remote term confusedly and distributively,[165]

163. Boehner finds this arrangement "peculiar and hardly understandable"; he expected "the *Tractatus de suppositionibus* after the tract on Fallacies" since he views it as a medieval addendum to an Aristotelian syllabus (*Medieval Logic*, (Manchester, 1966), chap.3, 78–79) and sees Ockham's integration of the discussion of supposition into the properties of terms as an advance (82). On my hypothesis, the actual arrangement of Sherwood and Peter of Spain has a rationale.

164. Sec.2–12, 107–117.

165. Sec.13, 117.

and then four to regulate inferences from general terms with one sort of personal supposition to the same term with another sort:

> Rule II: An argument from merely confused to distributive confused supposition does not follow...
>
> Rule III: An argument from many cases of determinate supposition to one of determinate supposition does not follow, but [only] to one of confused supposition...
>
> Rule IV: An argument from determinate supposition to distributive confused supposition does follow, but not from merely confused supposition...
>
> Rule V: An argument from determinate supposition to distributive confused supposition does follow, but not from merely confused supposition...[166]

It is as if Sherwood's principal interest in the move from a general term embedded in one context of quantifiers and/or negations to the same general term embedded in a different context of quantifiers and/or negations. He thought that to map the latter, as he partially does in Rules II–V, it would be necessary to determine the relation between a general term embedded in one context of quantifiers and/or negations and expansions of singulars. His characterizations of types of common personal supposition, together with Rule I were meant to accomplish that task.

Although it is not so obvious from the table of contents, I suggest that Ockham's own interest in the divisions of supposition generally, and not just of the divisions of common personal supposition in particular, lies in their utility for labelling fallacies—especially of equivocation, figure of speech, and the consequent. Having made the original tripartite division among the sorts of things a term can stand for in material, simple, and personal supposition, respectively, Ockham identifies a third type of equivocation, which occurs when a term is used with one supposition in one part of the argument and another in

166. Sec.13.2–13.5, 118–19.

another part. What amounts for Ockham, to slippage between use and mention "occurs frequently in the various sciences and deceives many."[167] It is to aid in identifying such fallacies that Ockham offers identification rules for when a proposition can have material and simple supposition, respectively.[168] Ockham tries to dissolve the Liar Paradox in terms of an equivocation of this sort.[169] And he repeatedly notes how certain sorts of inference rules will hold good only if the terms are taken to have personal supposition throughout.[170] Similarly, for equivocations in supposition produced by past or future tense verbs or modal operations.[171] Finally, he turns his attention to fallacies that result when one moves from a general term with one type of common personal supposition to the same general term with another type. Not every such transition is fallacious; for example,

> (R29) The inference from a term with Determinate Supposition to a term with Merely Confused Supposition (with no variation made in the other terms) is a good inference,

"because"—by (C7d)—"it is possible to ascend to the term with Merely Confused Supposition" from the singular and hence from the indefinite or particular proposition whose subject term has, by (R16), Determinate Supposition.[172] But some involve a

167. *Expos. Elench.* I, c.2, sec.9, (OPh III, 24–27); *Summa logicae* III–4, c.4, (OPh I, 759–763).

168. (R3) and (R6) in *ibid.*, (OPh 1, 760–61); *Expos. Elench.* 1, c.2, sec9, (OPh III, 26).

169. *Summa logicae* III–3, c.46, (OPh I, 744–46); *Expos. Elench.* II, c.10, sec.5, (OPh III, 268).

170. *Summa logicae* III–3, c.2, (OPh I, 593, 595); c.6, (OPh I, 601–606, 608); c.9, (OPh I, 630); c.13, (OPh I, 642).

171. See chapter 11 below; *Summa logicae* III–4, c.4, (OPh I, 762–63); II, c.22, (OPh I, 321–25); *Expos. Elench.* I, c.2, sec.9, (OPh III, 28–29); II, c.7, sec.2, (OPh III, 190).

172. *Summa logicae* III–4, c.12, (OPh I, 828).

fallacy of figure of speech (one arising from similarity of expressions):[173]

> (R30) In general, when a term has Merely confused Supposition in the antecedent of any enthymeme and Determinate Supposition in the consequent, there is a fallacy of figure of speech,

as in 'For any part of the continuum, some part is less; therefore some part is less than any part of the continuum'.[174] Again,

> (R13) The argument from a term with Determinate or Merely Confused Supposition to a term with Confused and Distributive Supposition commits a fallacy of figure of speech,

as in 'Every man is risible; therefore every man is every risible' and 'Socrates is not every man; therefore every man is not Socrates'.[175] (R31) follows from the various characterization rules. (C7a–b) makes it characteristic of Merely Confused Supposition that the descent definitive of Confused and Distributive Supposition (C8a–bi) is impossible. Likewise, by (C8c), the singular cannot yield the general term in Confused and Distributive Supposition. Since the singular entails the indefinite or particular proposition whose subject term has, by (R16), Determinate Supposition, it follows that the general term in Determinate Supposition cannot yield that in Confused and Distributive Supposition either. It is not generally true either that one singular or an exhaustive disjunction of them implies an exhaustive conjunction of the same. Similarly, for the fallacy of the consequent, which arises when the antecedent is believed to follow from the consequent the way the consequent follows from the antecedent:[176]

173. *Ibid.*, c.10, (OPh I, 792).
174. *Ibid.*, (OPh I, 799); *Expos. Elench.* II, c.7, sec.2, (OPh III, 190–91).
175. *Summa logicae* III–4, c.10, (OPh I, 800); *Expos. Elench.* II, c.7, sec.2, (OPh III, 191–92).
176. *Summa logicae* III–4, c.12, (OPh I, 826).

(R32) The argument from a term with Merely Confused Supposition to the same term with Determinate Supposition (with no variation made in the other terms) commits a fallacy of the consequent,

as in 'Every man is an animal; therefore an animal is every
man',[177] where by (R29) the reverse move—'An animal is every
man; therefore every man is an animal'—holds. Likewise,

(R33) The argument from a term with Determinate or Merely
Confused Supposition to a term with Confused and
Distributive Supposition commits a fallacy of the con-
sequent.[178]

I conclude that the divisions of common personal supposition are not the means to the end of giving a contextual definition of quantifiers nor for stating the truth conditions for
propositions containing quantified general terms. Rather the
divisions of supposition generally were marshalled into service
for the task of identifying fallacies. In Ockham's hands, the two
parts of Supposition Theory are not disjointed the way a
use/mention distinction and a theory of quantification are, but
are united under the rubric "aspects of the way words stand in
propositions for things, useful in fallacy detection." Thus, he
employs the principal tripartite division to locate equivocations
between use (personal supposition) and mention (material and
simple supposition), which he thought were plentiful in
metaphysics and theology. (R30) and (R32) fix on a fallacy like
our notorious quantifier-interchange—the illicit move from '(x)
(Ey) Rxy' to '(Ey) (x) Rxy'—while (R31) and (R33) note that
neither of the two forms of existential generalization recognized
by the theory (Determinate or Merely Confused Supposition)
yields a universal generalization. Even the greatest philosophers
are occasionally caught in such mistakes. It is small wonder if
medieval logicians found some way to point them out.

177. *Ibid.*, (OPh I, 828).
178. *Ibid.*, (OPh I, 829).

11

The Logic of Propositions

Having examined the divisions and properties of terms, Ockham has the tools to deal with the next larger unit of logical interest, the proposition. Procedurally, Ockham informs us,

> it is necessary first to lay down some divisions; second, to see what is necessary and sufficient for the truth of propositions; and third, to treat some aspects of the conversion of propositions.[1]

In the *Summa logicae*, Ockham never gives a general definition of 'proposition', but makes clear what linguistic units count as such by cataloging and describing their kinds. The principal division is between categorical propositions, which "have a subject, a predicate, and a copula and do not include many propositions," and molecular propositions, which "are composed of many categorical propositions."[2] The latter category subdivides into six types—conjunctions, disjunctions, conditional, causal, temporal, and local propositions, depending on the connective that joins the categoricals together.[3]

Ockham's characterization of categorical propositions analyzes them into three principal parts: the subject, which is "the part of the proposition that comes before the copula and of which something is predicated";[4] the predicate, which is "the part of the proposition that follows the copula";[5] and the copula, which is "the verb that joins the predicate to the subject."[6] Features of these components indicate further

1. *Summa logicae* II, c.1, (OPh I, 240–41).
2. *Ibid.*, (OPh I, 241).
3. *Ibid.*; also, c.30–36, (OPh I, 345–354).
4. *Ibid.* I, c.30, (OPh I, 92).
5. *Ibid.*, c.31, (OPh I, 93).
6. *Ibid.*, (OPh I, 94).

breakdowns in the division of categorical propositions. For example, the categorematic terms that occupy the subject or predicate position may be of the *nominative* or of an *oblique* case (e.g., 'A man is an animal' and 'A man's is an animal').[7] Again, the copula that joins them may be of the past, present, or future *tense*; and it may be assertoric (e.g., 'is') or *modal* (e.g., 'can be'). Again, a categorical proposition may be modal because a mode (e.g., 'necessary', 'possible', 'contingent', or 'impossible') occurs as its subject or predicate.[8] Further classifications arise from other components which may be added or omitted. For example, categorical propositions with an assertoric copula may turn modal with the addition of an adverbial modifier (e.g., 'necessarily', 'impossibly', 'contingently', or 'possibly'). Again, categorical propositions vary as to *quality* (affirmative or negative), depending on whether or not a negation sign is added (e.g., '*A* is *B* ' or '*A* is not *B* ').[9] And they differ as to *quantity*, depending on whether the subject term is singular or general, whether or not a quanitifer is added, which quantifer it is, and where it is put in the proposition. When no quantifier is added and the subject is a singular term, the proposition is a singular proposition; where a general term, an indefinite proposition equivalent to a particular proposition to whose subject term a sign of particularity has been added (i.e., '*A* is *B* ' is equivalent to 'Some *A* is *B* '; '*A* is not *B* ' to 'Some *A* is not *B* ' or 'No *A* is *B* ').[10] Again, some categorical propositions are not *equivalent to molecular propositions* (e.g. affirmative existentials such as 'God exists' and predications to which no sign has been added and whose categorematic terms are absolute such as 'A man is an animal'), while others are. Thus, any categorical whose subject or predicate is a connotative term is equivalent to a molecular proposition.[11] Others are equivalent to molecular propositions because of the addition of an exclu-

7. *Ibid.* II, c.2, (OPh I, 249).
8. *Ibid.*, c.1, (OPh I, 242).
9. *Ibid.*, (OPh I, 244).
10. *Ibid.*
11. *Ibid.*, c.11, (OPh I, 279).

sion sign (e.g., 'Only *B* is *A*') or an exceptive clause ('Every *A* but this *A* is *B* ') or a reduplicative clause ('*A* qua *A* is *B* ').[12]

After identifying various types of propositions, Ockham makes it his first business to state truth conditions for them. Beginning with the easiest sorts—viz., present tense assertoric propositions that are not equivalent to molecular propositions and that have both subject and predicate in the nominative case[13]—Ockham extends his account to past and future tense propositions[14] and modal propositions.[15] He then turns to standard types of categorical propositions that *are* equivalent to molecular propositions and shows how the former can be expounded in terms of categorical propositions whose truth conditions have already been discussed. These expositions also facilitate the second major part of Ockham's project in *Summa logicae* II—that of mapping conversion relations. Ockham closes with a discussion of truth conditions, equivalences, and inference rules for the principal types of molecular propositions.

Metaphysical considerations lie behind the first and fundamental parts of Ockham's enterprise. I shall first set out his account of truth conditions for present tense assertoric propositions, contrasting them with some alternative proposals. His extension of it to past tense, future tense, and modal propositions brings us face to face with the question of whether he accepted an ontological commitment to merely past, merely future, or merely possible entities; and I shall examine this issue at some length. Ockham's expositions of standard types of categoricals equivalent to molecular propositions and his chart of conversion relations will be dealt with more briefly, and his treatment of molecular propositions will conclude the chapter.

1. TRUTH CONDITIONS FOR THE "EASIEST" CASES

Focussing on present tense assertoric propositions whose

12. *Ibid.*, c.1, (OPh I, 243).   14. *Ibid.*, c.7.
13. *Ibid.*, c.2–6.   15. *Ibid.*, c.9–10.

categorematic terms are both in the nominative case and which are not equivalent to molecular propositions, Ockham divides them as to quantity and quality and offers truth conditions for a number of principal types. (1.1) *Singular Propositions*. Under what circumstances are propositions such as 'Socrates is a man' and 'He is an angel' true? Ockham rejects the views that

> (T1) It is necessary for the truth of a singular proposition that is not equivalent to a molecular proposition that its subject and predicate be really the same,[16]

or, put schematically, where singular terms substitute for 'N' and absolute terms for 'P',

> (T1′) 'N is P' is true only if 'N' and 'P' are really the same;

and

> (T2) It is necessary for the truth of a singular proposition that is not equivalent to a molecular proposition that the predicate really inhere in the subject,[17]

or, put schematically,

> (T2′) 'N is P' is true only if 'P' really inheres in 'N'.

Why does Ockham even bring up (T1) and (T2), when (T1′) and (T2′) make their conflation of use and mention so flagrant? A partial answer is that a tradition going back to Porphyry and Boethius used the terms 'subject' and 'predicate' ambiguously for linguistic units, on the one hand, and for really existent subjects of inherence and inherent properties, on the other.[18]

16. *Ibid.*, c.2, (OPh I, 249).
17. *Ibid.*
18. As Ockham notes, *Expos. Praedicam.*, c.8, (OPh II, 170).

Traces of this conflation can be found in Ockham's own objective-existence theory, according to which mental propositions are compounded out of objectively existent objects of thought (see Part One, chapter 3 above). Corresponding to the conventional proposition 'God is a being', there may be in the mind of the Blessed a mental proposition whose subject and predicate term alike are the divine essence itself. And where I have an intuitive cognition of Socrates and his whiteness, I may form the mental proposition 'Socrates is white (i.e., a haver of whiteness)' in which the objectively existent Socrates is the subject and the predicate includes the objectively existent whiteness that really inheres in him (see Part Three, chapter 13 below). When Ockham abandoned the objective-existence theory in favor of the mental-quality theory, however, he gave up the idea that the real things the proposition is about (except where the subject term is a mental quality that signifies itself) could be the subjects or predicates of mental propositions.

Even where such use/mention confusions are avoided, however, it is tempting to propose that

(T3)   A singular proposition that is not equivalent to a molecular proposition is true if and only if what the predicate signifies is had by or inheres in what the subject signifies,

or, put schematically,

(T3′) N is P if and only if N has P-ness or P-ness inheres in N

For example, 'Socrates is a man' is true, if and only if Socrates has humanity or humanity inheres in Socrates. The object-language equivalence in (T3′) is compatible with a variety of semantic analyses of propositions of the form 'N is P', however. (i) One could hold that in such propositions 'N' supposits for the particular it names while 'P' supposits for the really existent property P-ness, and 'is' stands for a real relation between them. (ii) Or one could say that both 'N' and 'P' supposit for particulars, but '*P* ' supposits for particulars only by virtue of the inherence of *P*-ness in them. (iii) Or one could claim with Frege that it is not '*P* ' but 'is *P* ' that is the predicate in '*N* is *P* ', and insist that 'is *P* ' does not function to supposit for anything but to characterize what the subject '*N* ' supposits for. Hints of each view can be found in medieval authors, especially those who were realists about universals. For Peter of Spain held that 'animal' has simple supposition for animal nature in 'Every man is an animal', and thought that natures were individuated by the matter in which they inhered.[19] Burleigh insisted that it supposited for particulars, but only for those that fell under the universal.[20] Again, taking off from Aristotle's discussion in the *Perihermenias*, William of Sherwood offered a two part analysis of categorical propositions into the noun and the verb:

> The integral parts of the statement are, therefore, the subject and the predicate. The subject is what the discourse is about. The predicate, however, is what is proclaimed or predicated about something other than itself. For example, in 'Socrates runs' the term 'Socrates' is the subject, because the discourse is about him, and the predicate is 'runs', because it is said about something other than itself.[21]

As we shall see, Ockham would be sympathetic to (T3) where connotative terms substituted for '*P* '. But accepting (T3) as a general analysis of singular propositions would be tantamount to regarding all general terms as connotative, whereas he has metaphysical reasons for insisting that substance terms are absolute terms. (T3′) fails for 'Socrates is a man' because the latter is true when 'Socrates has humanity' or 'Humanity exists in Socrates' is false. For either 'humanity' would stand for something extrinsic to Socrates, for Socrates himself, or for one of his parts. But Socrates does not have and is not in himself.

---

19. *Summulae logicales*, Tractatus suppositionum, (Mullally ed., 8–12, 18).

20. *De puritate artis logicae*, Tractatus primus, De proprietatibus terminorum, c.4, (Boehner ed., 19–21).

21. *Introduction to Logic*, chap.1, sec.11, (Kretzmann trans., 26).

Contrary to the Platonists, nothing extrinsic to Socrates is his humanity. And against the moderate realists, it is wrong to think of Socrates as composed of parts one of which is his humanity and the other some thisness or individuating principle (see Part One, chapter 2 above). Even if humanity is thought of as a particular thing (see Part One, chapter 5 above), it is not one part of Socrates as distinct from others.[22] Thus, Ockham rejects (i) and (ii) on metaphysical grounds. As the quotation from Sherwood makes clear, the plausibility of Aristotle's analysis arises from examples such as 'Socrates runs' that have verbs other than the copula. Noticing such cases, Ockham writes in his own *Perihermenias*-commentary that

> every categorical statement includes a subject, a predicate, and a copula, or there is a verb equivalent to the predicate and the copula —which has to be added because of propositions such as 'A man runs', 'Socrates disputes', etc.[23]

thereby suggesting that 'A man is a runner' and 'Socrates is a disputer' would be more canonical—contrary to his own preference for verbs over the copula plus participle in the mental language (see Part One, chapter 3 above). Burleigh notes how existential propositions such as 'God exists' can be reduced to Ockham's canonical tripartite form the same way, yielding 'God is a being'.[24] And although Ockham does not comment on this point explicitly, there is no reason to suppose that he would disagree. Hence, dismissing (iii) on semantical grounds, Ockham proposes

(T4) A singular proposition that is not equivalent to a molecular proposition is true if and only if its subject and predicate supposit for the same thing.[25]

or, put schematically,

22. *Summa logicae* II, c.2, (OPh I, 250–54); cf. I, c.7, (OPh I, 23–29).
23. I, c.4, sec.7, (OPh II, 396).
24. *Op. cit.*, Tertia pars, (Boehner ed., 54).
25. *Summa logicae* II, c.2, (OPh I, 250).

(T4′) '*N* is *P* ' is true if and only if there is something for which '*N* ' and '*P* ' both supposit in the proposition '*N* is *P* '.

So 'Socrates is a man' is true because there is something for which 'Socrates' and 'man' both supposit in that proposition—viz., Socrates.

(1.2) *Indefinite, Particular, and Universal Present Tense Propositions*. If the subject of a categorical proposition is a general term with personal supposition, then the proposition is indefinite, particular, or universal.[26] On one view.

(C1) An indefinite proposition is one whose subject is a general term that stands in personal supposition and is not governed by a universal or particular sign.[27]

For example, '*Homo est animal*' and '*Animal currit*' (literally, 'Man is animal' and 'Animal runs'; there are no articles in Latin). But

(C2) A particular proposition is one whose subject is a general term governed by a particular sign.

For example, 'Some man runs', 'A certain man runs', etc. Given (C1) and (C2), it follows that indefinite and particular propositions always convert—e.g., 'Man runs' with 'Some man runs', 'Animal is man' with 'Some animal is man', 'Animal is not man' with 'Some animal is not man'.[28] Ockham then stipulates that

26. For Ockham's stipulation that terms preceded by a particular or universal sign can have only personal supposition, see (R4) and (R6) in chapter 10 above. Ockham recognizes two opinions about propositions of the form '*A* is *B*'. One could hold that they are invariably indefinite, whether the subject term has personal, material, or simple supposition; or that they are indefinite only where the general term has personal supposition but singular otherwise (*Summa logicae* II, c.3, (OPh I, 255–57)). Ockham does not commit himself, but I shall focus on the latter option here.

27. *Ibid.*, c.1, (OPh I, 244); c.3, (OPh I, 255–57).

28. *Ibid.*, c.3, (OPh I, 255).

(T5) It is sufficient for the truth of an indefinite or particular affirmative proposition, whose predicate is not governed by a universal sign, that there is something for which its subject and predicate both supposit,

or, put schematically,

(T5′) '(Some) *A* is *B*' is true if there is something for which '*A*' and '*B*' both supposit.[29]

On the other hand,

(T6) It is necessary for the truth of an indefinite or particular negative proposition whose predicate is not governed by a universal sign that either its subject does not supposite for anything or its subject supposits for something the predicate does not supposit for,

or, put schematically,

(T6′) '(Some) *A* is not *B*' is true only if either '*A*' does not supposit for anything or '*A*' supposits for something that '*B*' does not supposit for.[30]

Although Ockham does not say so here, he presumably regards the right-hand side of (T5′) as necessary as well as sufficient; the right-hand side of (T6′) as sufficient as well as necessary.

Turning to universal propositions, Ockham explains that

(C3) A universal proposition is one whose subject is a general term that is governed by an affirmative or negative universal sign.

For example, 'Every man is an animal', 'No man is an animal', 'Each of them runs', etc.[31] After classifying various universal

29. *Ibid.*
30. *Ibid.*, (OPh I, 255–56).
31. *Ibid.*, c.1, (OPh I, 244).

signs as to what they distribute, Ockham focuses on those such as 'every' and 'no' that can function indifferently to distribute substances and/or accidents, individuals or their integral parts, and rejects

(T7) It is necessary for the truth of a universal affirmative proposition that its subject and predicate be really the same,

for reasons discussed above in connection with (T1) and (T2), but maintains

(T8) It is necessary for the truth of a universal affirmative proposition that its predicate supposits for everything its subject suppostis for,

or, put schematically,

(T8′) 'Every A is B' is true only if 'B' supposits for everything that 'A' supposits for.

Ockham adds, "if this is so, the universal proposition is true unless this is prevented by some special cause," which he does not identify.[32] The most likely candidate would be an empty subject term, since 'Every man is an animal' is false when there are no men. If this is what Ockham had in mind, he would be seen as endorsing

(T9) 'Every A is B' is true if and only if (i) 'A' supposits for something and (ii) 'B' supposits for everything that 'A' supposits for.

Ockham neglects to comment on E-propositions, but judging from the fact that they are contradictory to I-propositions, and assuming he regards the conditional in (T5′) as reversible, we may supply

32. *Ibid.*, c.4, (OPh I, 260).

(T10) 'No *A* is *B* ' is true if and only if either (i) '*A*' does not supposit for anything, or (ii) '*B* ' does not supposit for anything, or (iii) '*B* ' does not supposit for anything that '*A*' supposits for,

on his behalf.

(1.3) *A Charge of Circularity*. So far, then, in handling the "easiest" cases, Ockham does seem to advance a "two-name" theory of predication,[33] and to account for the truth of singular, indefinite, particular, and universal propositions in terms of whether or not their subjects and predicates supposit for anything and whether or not for some or all of the same things. This approach lay open to objection and misunderstanding from the beginning, however. Thus, Peter of Ailly, writing against some logicians of the next generation, contends

> The second conclusion: *A sentence is not true or false because its subject and predicate supposit for the same, or because they do not supposit for the same, whether it is an affirmative or a negative sentence.*
>
> *Proof*: Those who define a true or false sentence in terms of suppositing or not suppositing for the same...also give the definition of supposition in which it is said that [supposition] is the taking of a term in a sentence for its significate or significates, of which the term is verified by means of the copula of the sentence in which it occurs. Thus, they define supposition in terms of verification or in terms of a sentence. They should not, therefore, define the verification of a sentence conversely in terms of supposition or of suppositing or not suppositing for the same. For circularity should not occur in the case of definitions. Neither should the same thing be defined by the same...[34]

In advancing

(E2) A term '*T* ' has personal supposition for *x* in *p*, if and only if '*T*' occurs in *p* and 'This is *T* ' (where 'this' indicates *x*) is true

33. A theory much reviled by Peter T. Geach, who writes from a Fregean bias, in *Reference and Generality*, (Ithaca, NY, 1962), chap.2, sec.28, 34–36.

34. *Concepts and Insolubles*, trans. Paul Vincent Spade, (Dordrecht, 1980), 45–46.

(see chapter 10 above), along with (T4), (T5), (T6), and (T8), is not Ockham following into the same fallacy?

The answer is that he is not.[35] For he does not intend (E2) as a *definition* of 'supposition' or even of 'personal supposition'. Nor does he regard (T4), (T5), (T6), and (T8) as *definitions* of truth. Rather Ockham's closest approach to defining 'truth' comes in the following remark from his *Categories*-commentary:

> ...an expression is said to be true, because it signifies things to be as they are in reality. Therefore, an expression is said to be first true and afterwards false without any change in the expression itself, because it first signifies things as they are in reality and then—because things change—signifies things as they are not in reality...[36]

And even here, Ockham's focus is on metaphysics rather than semantics. He is trying to refute the view that truth and falsity are things really distinct from and inhering in the proposition, and defend his own view that 'truth' and 'falsity', like 'true' and 'false', are connotative terms that signify the proposition directly and connote that it signifies things to be as they are or are not, respectively. Ockham does not anticipate his successor's interest in refining this formulation of the correspondence theory of truth in the face of various objections, whether pedantic or formidable, the most notable of the latter being the semantic paradoxes.[37]

With Ailly's objection thus deflected, another rises in its place. For if Ockham intended his remarks in the above quoted

35. I used the above objection and some of the following arguments in my article, "What Does Ockham Mean by 'Supposition'?" *Notre Dame Journal of Formal Logic* XVII (1976): 375–391, where I was concerned to argue that equivalences like (E2) did not constitute a definition of 'supposition', 'personal supposition', or any other kind. Freddoso considers this question with particular attention to the issue of what (T4), (T5), (T6), (T8) or the like are intended by Ockham to do ("Ockham's Theory of Truth Conditions" in *Ockham's Theory of Propositions*, 15–16).

36. C.9, sec.13, (OPh II, 201).

37. See Paul of Venice, *Logica magna*, Part II, Tractatus de veritate et falsitate propositionis, (Del Punta and Adams ed. and trans., 4–77).

passage to suggest his nominal definitions of 'true' and 'false', respectively, he must have seen (T4), (T5), (T6), and (T8) as criteria by means of which we can come to know whether quantified categorical propositions are true or false.[38] But they can serve this function only if the propositions on the right-hand side are epistemologically prior to the propositions on the left. To test whether this is so, consider the proposition 'Socrates is a man'. (T4) tells us it is true, if and only if 'Socrates' and 'man' supposit for the same thing. But (E2) tells us that 'man' supposits for Socrates in the proposition 'Socrates is a man' if and only if the proposition 'This is a man' (where 'this' indicates Socrates) is true. And it seems doubtful whether knowledge of the latter (T4) is to be a viable criterion of truth.

The reply here is that Ockham does not regard (T4), (T5), (T6), and (T8) as criteria either. Rather at the outset of *Summa logicae* II, Ockham sets himself the more manageable task of discovering what is necessary and sufficient for the truth of propositions. This objective will be met if he identifies true biconditionals. (We have seen that in practice he is not always careful to claim that the conditionals are reversible.) He need not maintain that the right-hand side defines or is epistemologically prior to the left. Hence, niether charge of circulairty vitiates Ockham's intent.

It is worth noting that while Ockham offers all of (T4), (T5), (T6), (T8), and (T9) under the rubric of considering categorical propositions not equivalent to molecular propositions, he in fact thinks that the conditionals hold for a wider range of cases—viz., not only for categorical propositions whose subject and predicate are both absolute terms, but for those whose subject and/or predicate are connotative as well. Thus, in discussing indefinite and particular propositions, he mentions not only 'Man is animal', but also 'White man is animal', 'Man runs', and

---

38. Freddoso notes this construal of the conditionals. I advanced epistemological considerations as reasons for thinking (E2) not a *definition* of 'supposition'; I did not consider the separate hypothesis that (T4), (T5), (T6), and (T8) are not definitions but criteria (*op. cit.*, 15–16).

'God begets God'.[39] Likewise, for universals, he cites 'Every man is risible'.[40]

2.   TENSE AND TRUTH CONDITIONS

So far, Ockham has given truth conditions for quantified categorical propositions in terms of whether the subject and predicate do or do not supposit for all or some of the same things. What affects the supposition of subject and predicate terms in a proposition will vary its truth conditions accordingly. We have already examined in chapter 10 how a term's supposition is a function of various features of its propositional context—viz., the categorematic term with which it is matched and its relation to quantifiers or negation signs in the proposition. It is now time to map the effect that the tense and mode of the verb have on supposition and hence the truth conditions of such categorical propositions.

Ockham's initial discussion of personal supposition focuses exclusively on present tense propositions in which a term stands for its presently existing significata (those that are its significata in the first and narrower of Ockham's preferred senses in *Summa logicae* I, c.33, (OPh I, 95); cf. chapter 10 section 2 above). Then, facing the question of 'How terms supposit in past and future tense propositions, in propositions of possibility and other modal propositions,' he replies that

> ...the terms supposit personally in all such propositions. In connection with this, it should be understood that a term supposits personally when it supposits for its significata, or for those which were its significata or for those that will be or those that can be. This is the way my earlier claim should be understood, since it was said earlier that this was one way to take 'signify'...[41]

Where 'signify' is taken in the broader of Ockham's preferred

---

39. *Summa logicae* II, c.3, (OPh I, 255–56).
40. *Ibid.*, (OPh I, 258).
41. *Ibid.* I, c.72, (OPh I, 215).

senses, the significata of the term '*F*' may sort themselves into several groups—those that are *F*'s, those that were *F*'s, those that will be *F*'s, and those that can be *F*'s. And hence

(C5) Generally speaking, a term has personal supposition when it supposits for its own significata[42]

allows '*F*' to have personal supposition for any of these. But not in any context whatever. Rather

(R1) A term can have personal supposition for its presently existing significata (if any) in any proposition in which it occurs as subject, no matter what its tense or mode;[43]

but

(R2) A subject term "can supposit for *those that were* its significata only in relation to a verb about the past" or its equivalent

and

(R3) A subject term "can supposit for *those that will be* only in relation to a verb about the future" or its equivalent

and

(R4) A subject term "can supposit for *those that can be* and are not its significata only in relation to a verb of possibility or contingency" or its equivalent.[44]

Given these rules, Ockham concludes that tensed and modal propositions are equivocal in the third way:

(R5) ...when a common term has personal supposition and is

42. *Ibid.*, c.64, (OPh I, 195); see chapter 10, section (3.1.2) above.
43. *Ibid.*, c.72, (OPh I, 215).
44. *Ibid.*, (OPh I, 216).

subject in relation to a verb about the past, the proposition should be distinguished because of the fact that the
subject term can supposit for those that are or for *those
that were*...

(R6) ...when a common term supposits personally and is subject in relation to a verb about the future, the proposition should be distinguished according to the third
mode of equivocation, because the subject can supposit
for those that are or for *those that will be*.

(R7) ...when a common term supposits personally and is subject in relation to a verb of possibility or contingency,
the proposition should be distinguished because the
subject term can stand for those that are or for *those
that can be* or for *those that can be and can not be*...,[45]

depending upon whether the subject-term is taken to fall inside
or outside the scope of the tense or mode. "But this distinction
does not arise in connection with the predicate," which is une-
quivocally governed by it.[46]

Difficulties arise over these rules and their interpretation,
however. (2.1) *The Rule of Three*. It follows from (R1)–(R4)
that the subject term of a present tense proposition that is
not equivalent to a past tense, future tense, or modal proposition can supposit only for its presently existing significata.
Straightforward as this suggestion seems, however, it was not
universally accepted among Ockham's predecessors. For example, William of Sherwood proposes the alternative rule

(R8) An unrestricted common term that has sufficient appellata and supposita in connection with a present
tense verb that has no ampliating force supposits only
for those things subordinate to it that do exist.[47]

45. *Ibid*. III–4, c.4, (OPh I, 762–63).
46. *Ibid*. I, c.72, (OPh I, 216).
47. *Op. cit*., chap.5, sec.16.1, (Kretzmann trans., 123–24).

Sherwood cautions that "sufficient appellata amount to at least three: therefore if there are not that many appellata a term can supposit for something that does not exist."[48] Therefore, where there are fewer than three men,

> 'every man exists' is false and its contradictory 'some man does not exist' is true. Therefore a man does not exist. But nonexistence is not predicated of something that exists; therefore 'man' supposits for something that does not exist.[49]

Again, where there are fewer than three men, "this does not follow: 'every animal exists; therefore every man exists' because the term 'animal' does have sufficient appellata"—say because one horse, one cow, and one man exists—"and so supposits only for what exists, while 'man' does not"— because only one man exists—"and so supposits for something that does not exist."[50] Likewise Sherwood rejects the inference 'every animal is; every man is an animal; therefore every man is', as involving an equivocation on the verb 'is'. In the first premiss and the conclusion, he says, it signifies actual existence (*esse actuale*), but in the second premiss relational being (*esse habituale*).[51]

Ockham has no sympathy and little patience with this position, dismissing its suggestions as "frivolous" and its adherents as "incapable of perceiving any truth."[52] He insists that where there are singulars, a universal proposition is true whenever all of its singulars are true—a condition that can be satisfied if there is at least one singular. Thus, where there is only one angel and no man 'Every intelligent creature is an angel' is true, and so is 'Every man is white' where there are only two men and each is white.[53] As for the suggestion that where there are only two men—say Socrates and Plato—'Every man exists' is false and

48. *Ibid.*, sec.16.2, 124.
49. *Ibid.*, 125.
50. *Ibid.*
51. *Ibid.*, 125–26.
52. *Summa logicae* II, c.4, (OPh I, 263).
53. *Ibid.*, (OPh I, 260–61).

'Some man does not exist' is true, Ockham denies it, saying that the latter has no true singulars—evidently because 'Socrates does not exist' and 'Plato does not exist' are both false.

Defenders of the Rule of Three would say that Ockham is begging the question. They have insisted that where there are only two men, 'man' supposits for something besides presently existing things, and hence that 'Some man does not exist' has singulars besides 'Socrates exists' and 'Plato exists'—say, 'The Antichrist exists'—which are false. Similarly, they diagnose a fallacy of equivocation between actual and relational being where some of the categorematic terms in a syllogism have fewer than three actually existing significata.

Ockham's fundamental objection to the Rule of Three is that it makes it impossible to give purely formal criteria for valid inferences. Aristotle, he takes it, was out to identify argument forms that held good no matter what categorematic terms they contained; a fortiori, no matter whether their categorematic terms were empty, monoreferential, or polyreferential. Chief among such forms are 'Every B is C; every A is B; therefore Every A is C' and 'Every A is; every B is A; therefore every B is'.[54] By making the validity of such inferences depend on whether or not terms substituted for 'A' and 'B' have three presently existing significata, Sherwood and company abort this whole project.

(2.2) *Tense, Modes, and Ontological Commitment.* A second difficulty arises over the interpretation of the italicized phrases of (R2)–(R7). On the face of it, Ockham appears to be operating with a universe of discourse that includes whatever the term can supposit for in some context or other; and the universe of discourse includes those that are, those that were, those that will be, and those that can be. Thus, on the first reading licensed by the rules, 'Some A was (will be, can be) B' appears to say of some presently existing thing that it was (will be, can be) B; while on the second of some (merely) past (future, possible) thing that it was (will be, can be) B. Yet, this interpretation

54. *Ibid.*, (OPh I, 263).

seems to commit Ockham to a more generous ontology than one might have expected of him. Recall that for Quine, a theory has an ontological committment to those entities that must be taken to be values of the variables if the theory is to be true; and a philosopher has an ontological commitment to those entities if he accepts the theory. The natural way to map this notion onto Ockham's logic is to say that a theory has an ontological commitment to entities of a certain sort if, in order for the theory to be true, a term must be taken to supposit or stand for such entities in a proposition included in the theory. On the above construal, Ockham is allowing subject terms to supposit for non-present temporalia in past and future tense propositions; for unactualized possibles in propositions of possibility. Given the proposed criterion, he will accept an ontological commitment to non-present temporalia and unactualized possibles if he admits any such propositions to be true on the relevant readings.[55] Does the evidence really require us to see Ockham as that ontologically permissive?

The textual picture is complicated. I shall first consider some difficulties with the first interpretation and then assess alternative readings. (2.2.1) *Objections to a Wider Ontological Commitment.* Evidence can be brought that an ontological commitment to non-present temporalia and unactualized possibles is incompatible with the rest of Ockham's philosophy and theology. I reserve detailed discussion of the latter for Part Five, chapters 24–26 below, where I shall argue that the wider ontological commitment need not bring additional difficulties to his position. For now it is important to evaluate two pieces of evidence that he actually rejected it on philosophical grounds.

(a) First, it seems that an ontological commitment to non-pres-

55. I interpreted Ockham this way in my articles "Ockham's Nominalism and Unreal Entities," *Philosophical Review* LXXXVI (1977): 144–176, and "Ockham's Theory of Natural Signification," *Monist* LXI (1978): 444–459. It has been rejected by Alfred J. Freddoso, "Ockham's Theory of Truth Conditions," 37ff, and Elizabeth Karger in her unpublished Ph.D. dissertation, *A Study in William of Ockham's Modal Logic*, (University of California at Berkeley, 1976). My reassessment is found below.

ent temporalia and unactualized possibles involves the notion
that *there are* merely past, merely future, or merely possible entities or beings. Walter Burleigh does this boldly in the following passages from *De puritate artis logicae*:

> ...'being' can be taken three ways. One way, so that it has maximum ex-
> tension and is common to all intelligibles. This way it is the adequate
> object of the intellect, and the inference 'This is a being; therefore this
> is' does not follow. The second way, it is taken for anything to which
> being is not prohibited. This way whatever can be is a being and this
> way, too, the inference 'This is a being; therefore this is' does not
> follow. The third way, it is taken for an actually existing being and is
> thus a participle derived from the verb 'is'. This third way the inference
> 'This is being; therefore this is' does hold...,[56]

although his added comment that being taken the second way
exists in its cause seems to imply a reduction of unactualized
possibles to the power to produce them.[57]

By contrast, Ockham seems to reject any such ontological
commitment, reduced or otherwise. For example, in *Summa
logicae* I, c.38, he writes,

> ...Similarly, being is divided into being in potency and being in act.
> This should not be understood to mean that something which does not
> actually exist but possibly exists is truly a being, and that something
> else which actually exists is also a being. Rather, in dividing being into
> potency and act in *Metaphysics* V, Aristotle meant that the term 'being'
> is predicated of some term by means of the word 'is' in a proposition
> that is absolutely assertoric and not equivalent to a proposition of
> possibility, e.g., 'Socrates is a being' and 'A whiteness is a being'; but of
> other terms it is predicated only in a proposition of possibility, e.g.,
> 'The Antichrist is possibly a being' or 'The Antichrist is a being in
> potency'. Hence in the passage in question he wants to say that 'being',
> like 'knowing' and 'resting' is predicable both potentially and actual-
> ly — and yet nothing knows or rests unless it actually knows or rests.[58]

And in *Summa logicae* III-1, c.31, Ockham says that "the
proposition 'Every being exists in act' is necessary."[59] As for
temporalia, Ockham notoriously argues with Aristotle that no

56. Tertia pars, 59.   58. (OPh I, 108).
57. *Ibid*.   59. (OPh I, 442).

part of time exists, because neither the past nor the future exists; instead they are pure nothing (see Part Four, chapter 20 below). But if Ockham would say about non-present temporalia what he says about time, he would be committed to the thesis that they are purely nothing as well. This projection seems confirmed by his remark in *Summa logicae* I, c.59, that although 'The Antichrist will exist before Judgment Day' is true now, nevertheless, the Antichrist "is nothing."[60] If Ockham had an ontological commitment to merely future entities, he would surely not say that the Antichrist is nothing and hence presumably neither a primitive item in his ontology nor reducible to any.[61]

(R2.2.1a) If a philosopher's ontological commitment is to be measured in terms of what *beings* or *entities* he says there *are*, as the above adaptation of the Quinean criterion suggests, Ockham will have to be seen as rejecting one in the above cited passages. But his remarks seem less than decisive in view of his adherence to the Aristotelian thesis that verbs connote time and hence cannot be tenseless. 'Is' and 'exists' are present tense verbs, so that to say that x is or exists is to imply that x is or exists in the present. If 'being' or 'entity' or 'existent' are nouns deriving from such present tense verbs, Ockham will take them to signify only presently existing things. When he says in the *Summa logicae* and in his *Physics*-commentaries that the parts of time—the past and the future—do not exist (present tense), he may simply be asserting that they are not present. And he may think 'Every being exists in act' is necessary because it reduces to 'Every actually existing thing exists in act'; and 'That is a non-being' is necessarily false, because it is expounded by the obviously contradictory conjunction "That is (present tense) something and it is not (present tense) a being."[62]

60. (OPh I, 190).

61. The contrast with Burleigh is noted by Calvin Normore in his dissertation, *The Logic of Time and Modality in the Later Middle Ages: The Contribution of William of Ockham*, chap.2, 52. Freddoso makes most of this case against my earlier contention that Ockham did retain such an ontological commitment (op. *cit.*, 35–36).

62. *Summa logicae* II, c.12, 13, (OPh I, 283, 287).

When he says that the Antichrist is nothing, he may simply be claiming that it is not a presently existing entity. And when he denies that "something which does not actually exist but possibly exists is truly a being," he may be repeating what is analytically true, that an unactualized possible does not actually exist at the present.

This explanation finds support in Ockham's remarks about 'nothing' in *Ordinatio* I, d.36, q.1, which appears to have been written from the viewpoint of the mental-act theory. He distinguishes there three ways of taking the term 'nothing': (i) First, syncategorematically as a negative universal that includes the term distributed—viz., 'being'. Alternatively, 'nothing' can be taken categorematically either (ii) insofar as it "signifies what does not really exist or have any real existence," or (iii) insofar as it "is taken for what lacks not only real existence, but also in such a way that real existence is incompatible with it." Thus, he holds, impossibles such as chimeras were nothing from eternity the second way. And they were thus nothing even though they were understood by God from eternity (see Part Five, chapter 24 below). All of these claims are so noncontroversial as to be fully acceptable to the objective-existence theorist, however. For when the objective-existence theorist argues that neither chimeras nor creatures before their creation are nothing, because only being can be thought of and God thought of chimeras and creatures from eternity, he is not denying the obvious fact that chimeras are nothing in senses (i)–(iii) or that before their creation creatures are nothing in sense (ii). Instead, he is using 'being' equivocally to cover not only things that actually exist in reality in the present, but objectively existent things that cannot really exist as well (see Part One, chapters 3–4).

Thus, the fact that Ockham denies in the *Summa logicae* that unactualized possibles and non-present temporalia *are* (present tense) *beings* or *entities* does not prove that he had abandoned an ontological commitment to them. But given his restriction on the use of 'being' and 'is', some other term would have to be used to express it. Ockham does not explicitly use any, but we might draft the noun 'item' and the verb '*datur*' (is-given). We could say that an item is-given (present tense) in the ontology even if not presently existing. And the criterion for whether or not an item is-given in the ontology would be the above stated criterion for ontological commitment.

(b) Again, one might argue that Ockham cannot have intended an ontological commitment to non-present temporalia and unactualized possibles, because this would be incompatible with his position regarding future contingencies. Peter Aureol and other alleged Aristotelians had argued that present determinate truth-value for a proposition requires that something about the way things are (present tense) or were in the past settled it that things would be in the future as the proposition signifies that they will be. Assuming that no proposition about future contingents could have its truth-value fixed in this way, they concluded that such propositions have (present tense) no determinate truth-value. Ockham maintained, on the contrary, that propositions about future contingents must have determinate truth-value in the present, since one part of every contradiction (either p or not-p) is known by God in the present and only what is true is knowable. Rejecting their thesis that present determinate truth requires that things are or were such as to settle the matter of how they will be in the future, Ockham held that it is enough if things will be in the future as the proposition signifies that they will be (see Part Five, chapter 7). Ockham's claim seems tantamount to saying that future states of affairs are not reducible to any past or present state of affairs, in such a way that the truth of propositions about the former could be settled by the latter. Is this not inconsistent with admitting merely future things into one's ontology?

(R2.2.1b) The answer to this question is "no," because it does not follow from the proposition that Ockham accepts—viz., that future states of affairs are not reducible to past or present states of affairs—that merely future things are not given in the ontology either as primitive items or as reducible to such. Since only what is possible can be past, present, or future, an ontological commitment to things that were or will be but are not, is subsumed under an ontological commitment to actual and unactualized possibles. The mere fact that things are included in the ontology does not, by itself, settle the question of whether or how they were or will be, or which (if any) past or future states of affairs they will enter into. Thus, their mere status as items presently included in the ontology does not settle the truth value of future contingents, and is thus not inconsistent with Ockham's position on future contingents.

(2.2.2) *First Alternative Construal.* It may be argued that if the above considerations do not prove that Ockham rejected a wider ontological commitment, the italicized phrases in (R2)–(R7) do not conclusively show that he accepted one either. For Ockham does not say there that a term may supposit for those that were *simpliciter*, will be *simpliciter*, or can be *simpliciter*; but rather for those that were *F*, will be *F*, or can be *F*. And the latter phrases ambiguously pick out either those past (future, possible) things that were (will be, can be) *F*, or those presently existing things that were (will be, can be) *F*, where only the former construal involves a putative ontological commitment to non-present temporalia or unactualized possibles. Thus, when Ockham says in *Summa logicae* I, c.72 that

> assuming that no man is now white, but that there were many white men before, then the predicate in the proposition 'A man was white' cannot supposit for those that are, but only for those that were,[63]

he need not be saying that 'white' cannot supposit for those that exist now, but only for those that existed in the past. He may instead be saying of those that exist now, 'white' supposits only for those that were white in the past. Similarly for other cases.

(R2.2.2) If this were what Ockham meant, his theory would be inadequate to deal with his own examples of tensed and modal propositions. Consider 'Socrates existed' (where Socrates no longer exists), 'The Antichrist will exist', and 'The Antichrist can exist' (where the Antichrist does not exist yet). Ockham would say that no presently existing individual who is not Socrates or the Antichrist could be, have been, or be going to be Socrates or the Antichrist, respectively. Therefore, these

---

63. (OPh I, 218).

true statements should not be taken as asserting of some presently existing thing that it is Socrates or that it will or can be the Antichrist. Likewise, where Socrates exists no longer, 'Socrates was a man' and 'Socrates was white' should not be seen as asserting that some presently existing thing was a man or was white. For Ockham will say that these propositions are true only if their subjects and predicates supposit for the same thing, and no presently existing thing could have been Socrates. Again, 'Dinosaurs once existed' and 'Dinosaurs can exist' are true, but —so far as unaided natural reason is concerned—no presently existing thing can be or have been a dinosaur. For dinosaurs are now extinct, and whatever was, will be, or can be a dinosaur could not exist without being a dinosaur.

Again, in the introduction to his *Perihermenias*-commentary, Ockham considers the following objection to the mental-act theory's claim that the general concept 'man' is an act of understanding by which each and every man is understood, but no one man more than any other:

> ...some man is understood and one no more than another, a man who is no more than a man who can be, since [the concept] 'man' supposits for those who can be men, just as it supposits for those who are men. And those who can be men are infinitely many. Therefore, infinitely many would be understood by such an act of understanding.[64]

Ockham says that a mental-act theorist would grant the conclusion and agree that the general concept 'man' does not enable us to conceive of infinitely many particulars distinctly, while insisting that we can thereby conceive of infinitely many confusedly.[65] Even after Ockham had adopted the mental-act theory, he would have denied that infinitely many created substances actually exist in the present and held that only created substances, the divine essence, or the divine persons can be a man.[66] Hence, he would not take 'Those who can be

64. Prooemium, sec.6, (OPh II, 353).
65. *Ibid.*, (OPh II, 355).
66. For discussion of how non-human created substances, the divine essence, or the divine persons can be a man, see Part Five, chapter 22 below.

men are infinitely many' to say of actually existing things that each of infinitely many of them can be men. He must have thought it compatible with the mental-act theory that the general concept 'man' supposits for infinitely many that can exist but do not.

(2.2.3) *Another Alternative*. There are other ways to read Ockham's logic without assigning him an ontological commitment to unactualized possibles or non-present temporalia, however. If the initial interpretation says that the terms of the presently existing proposition '*A* was (will be, can be) *B* ' may bear (in the present) the semantic relation of supposition to merely past (future, possible) things, and the second holds that they have semantic relations to presently existing things only, a third maintains that the truth of '*A* was (will be, can be) *B* ' implies that certain semantic relations held in the past (will hold in the future, can hold) between the terms of the corresponding present tense proposition and things contemporaneous with it.[67] A closer look at what Ockham says about the predicates of past and future tense propositions and propositions of possibility positively suggests the last construal in preference to the first two. He writes,

> ...such a proposition denotes that the proposition in which the predicate itself, under its own form—i.e., that very predicate and not another—is predicated of that for which the subject supposits, or of a pronoun indicating (*demonstrante*) precisely that for which the subject supposits, was true, if such a proposition [i.e., the first mentioned one] is about the past; or will be true, if such a proposition is about the future; or is possible, if the first proposition is a proposition of possibility; ... and so on for other modal propositions...[68]

The same account of what it is for a predicate to supposit for those that were, those that will be, or those that can be is given

---

67. This interpretation is advocated by Freddoso, *op. cit.*, 28–43. He wants to claim both that it is a plausible reading of the text of the *Summa logicae* II, and that Ockham's logic can in any event best be reconstructed along these lines.

68. *Summa logicae* II, c.72, (OPh I, 216).

in *Summa logicae* II, chapters 7 and 10.[69] Ockham's idea can be represented schematically as follows: In propositions of the form '*A* was *B* ', '*B* ' supposits for those that were in the sense that '*A* was *B* ' denotes that 'This is *B* ' (where 'this' indicates something that '*A*' supposits for in '*A* was *B*') was true. Again, in propositions of the form '*A* will be *B* ', '*B* ' supposits for those that will be in the sense that '*A* will be *B* ' denotes that 'This is *B* ' (where 'this' indicates something that '*A*' supposits for in the proposition '*A* will be *B* ') will be true. Finally, in propositions of the form '*A* can be *B* ', '*B* ' supposits for those that can be in the sense that '*A* can be *B* ' denotes that 'This is *B* ' (where 'this indicates something that '*A*' supposits for in '*A* can be *B* ') can be true. Hence the assertion that a presently existing term '*B* ' bears (present tense) the semantic relation of supposition to those that were, those that will be, or those that can be gets analyzed in terms of the past, future, or possible truth of a present tense proposition containing '*B* ' and hence ultimately in terms of the past, future, or possible obtaining of a semantic relation between simultaneously existing terms and things. Ockham almost says this in so many words in *Summa logica* I, c.72, when he remarks that in past and future tense propositions and modal proposition "terms with personal supposition supposit for those that are or were or will be or can be supposita."[70]

(R2.2.3) Two sets of difficulties arise for this interpretation, however. (a) First, the text cited in its favor still implies that a presently existing term bears (present tense) a semantic relation to non-actual things. Take the true proposition 'Socrates was white', where Socrates no longer exists. According to Ockham, 'Socrates was white' denotes that the proposition 'This is white' (where 'this' *indicates* Socrates) was true. Hence the demonstrative pronoun 'this' is said to bear the semantic relation of indicating to the merely past object, Socrates; and it is said to bear the relation in the present, since Ockham uses the present active participle '*demonstrante*'. Second, Ockham says

69. (OPh I, 269, 276).
70. (OPh I, 217).

that '*A* was (will be, can be) *B* ' denotes that the predicate supposited, will supposit, or can supposit for what the subject supposits for. But Ockham has also said that the subject may supposit for those that were, those that will be, and those that can
be. When the subject is taken to supposit for merely past, merely future, or merely possible items (as it does in the proposition
'Socrates was white' or 'Some animal can be a dodo' or 'Some
man will be the Antichrist') the predicate will do the same, and
will once again be left with semantic relations between presently existing terms and merely past, merely future, or merely
possible items.[71]

This obstacle may seem easily surmountable, however. After
all, it is the *past* truth of 'This is white' that is at issue. Hence
the relation of indication between 'this' and Socrates should be
presumed to be past, too. Ockham should have said that
'Socrates was white' denotes that 'This is white' (where 'this'
indicated Socrates) was true. And in at least one place he does
use the perfect passive participle '*demonstrato*'.[72]

Nevertheless, Ockham's account of how the subject term
functions in such propositions seems to raise the problem all
over again; he writes,

> ...any proposal about the past and about the future whose subject is a
> common term must be distinguished with respect to the third mode of
> equivocation, because the subject can supposit for what is or for what
> was, if the proposition is about the past. That is, because the subject
> can supposit for what it is truly predicated of by means of a verb about
> the past. For example, the proposition 'A white was Socrates' must be
> distinguished because 'white' can supposit for what is or for what will
> be. That is, for what the subject is truly predicated of by means of a
> verb about the present or for what the subject is truly predicated of by

---

71. Calvin Normore notes this point in his thesis, *op. cit.*, chap.2, 50.
And he thinks it combines with Ockham's broader use of 'signify' to show
that Ockham did think terms bore semantic relations to nonexistents. But
Ockham's restriction of the word 'being' or 'entity' to presently existing
things and lack of explicit alternative vocabulary, make him sceptical about
saying Ockham shared the Quinean conception of ontological commitment.

72. *Summa logicae* II, c.10, (OPh I, 276).

means of a verb about the future. And this rule should be understood to hold where the subject supposits personally, that is significantly.[73]

The term '*A*' supposits for those that are in '*A* was *B* ' when it stands for all those of which 'This is *A*' is true; for those that were, when it stands for all those of which 'This was *A*' is true. Likewise, '*A*' stands for those that are in '*A* will be *B* ' when it stands for those of which 'This is *A*' is true; for those that will be, when it stands for those of which 'This will be *A*' is true. But if the past and future tensed singular propositions 'This was *A*' and 'This will be *A*' are true now, then the truth-conferring semantic relations between their parts and things must obtain now. Thus, the above formulation seems to recommit Ockham to the thesis that the semantic relation of indication does obtain between the demonstrative pronoun 'this' and merely past or merely future entities, respectively. Likewise, for the parallel formula regarding propositions of possibility.

Ockham could avoid this difficulty, too, if he endorsed the following equivalences, where singular terms or demonstrative pronouns substitute for '*N* ' and general terms for '*A*':

(E17) '*N* was *A*' is true if and only if '*N* is *A*' was true,

(E18) '*N* will be *A*' is true if and only if '*N* is *A*' will be true,

and

(E19) '*N* is possibly *A*' is true if and only if '*N* is *A*' is possibly true;

and held that the right-hand side is the more basic in each case. Ockham asserts the last at least once,[74] and there seems to be no reason why he should hold (E19) and not (E17) and (E18).

(b) *The Existence Problem*. This proposal is supposed to have the merit of attributing to Ockham an ontology restricted to

73. *Ibid.*, c.22, (OPh I, 321–22).
74. *Expos. Periherm.* II, c.5, (OPh II, 467).

presently existing things only. As always, the question is, are there (were there, will there be) enough of them to do all of the theoretical jobs, especially given Ockham's rejection of abstract entities and inherent universals?

It may be argued that there are not (were not, will not be) enough to permit Ockham to state truth conditions of past tense and future tense propositions without positing merely past or merely future entities. For if only presently existing things can have semantic properties, it follows that

(A) Nothing is true unless it exists.

Ockham endorses this thesis in *Summa logicae* II, c.9, when he says of the proposition 'God exists' that "if it does not exist, it is not true."[75] And in *Quaestiones in libros Physicorum*, q.115, he implies it again when he comments that

> if no intellect existed, still man would not be a stone and yet the proposition 'man is not a stone' would not be true then, because no proposition would exist then.[76]

And what holds for the mode 'true' ought to hold for the other modes—'false', 'possible', 'necessary', 'impossible'—as well.[77]

On the interpretation under consideration, however, (E17)–(E19) state truth conditions for such tensed and modal singular propositions, and hence are supposed to be necessary truth. But (E17)–(E19) make the present truth of the past and future tense propositions depend on the past and future truth of the corresponding present tense proposition; and the present truth of the proposition of possibility on the possible truth of the assertoric proposition. By (A) and its analogues for other modes, it follows that the present truth of the past tense proposition, the future tense proposition, and the proposition of possibility requires the past, future, and present existence of

    75. (OPh I, 275).
    76. (OPh VI).
    77. *Summa logicae* II, c.1, (OPh I, 242–43); *Expos. Periherm.* II, c.5, (OPh II, 457–468).

the corresponding present tense proposition. Yet, is it logically necessary that if the past tense (future tense, modal) proposition is true now, the corresponding present tense proposition existed in the past (will exist in the future, does exist in the present)? There is a problem about how Ockham can say so without changing his mind. For from the point of view of his mental-act theory, all propositions are creatures—really existent inscriptions or sounds and really existent mental qualities. And God can make, have made, or be going to make one without making, having made, or being going to make any other.[78]

Ockham was not totally oblivious to this difficulty and occasionally responds to it in passing. Thus, in *Summa logicae* I, c.63, he writes that

> the proposition 'A man is an animal' denotes that Socrates is truly an animal in such a way that the proposition 'This is an animal; (where 'this' indicates Socrates) *would be true if it were formed*...[79]

And in *Summa logicae* II, c.7, he explains that since 'The creator was God from eternity' is true now,

> the proposition 'This is God' (where 'this' indicates what 'creator' supposits for in the proposition 'The creator was God from eternity') was true from eternity, or *would have been true, if it had been formed*.[80]

Again, he remarks that

> the truth of the proposition 'The Apostles preached, while Christ was preaching' requires the truth of each part and that they were true at the same time, *if they were formed*.[81]

Such passages suggest a reformulation of (E17)–(E19) as follows:

(E20) '*N* was *P* ' is true if and only if '*N* is *P* ' was true or

---

78. For a more thorough discussion of these issues, see Part Five, chapter 26 below.
79. (OPh I, 194).
80. (OPh I, 270).
81. *Ibid.*, c.35, (OPh I, 352).

would have been true if it had been formed;

(E21) '*N* will be *P* ' is true if and only if '*N* is *P* ' will be true or would be true in the future if it were formed in the future;

(E22) '*N* can be *P* ' is true if and only if '*N* is *P* ' is possible or would be possible if it were formed.

These revisions are insufficient, however. For the right-hand side of each of (E20)–(E22) can be satisfied without the actual past, future, or present existence of the present tense proposition; a fortiori without the present existence of the past tense, future tense, or modal proposition. But by (A), the left-hand side of each of (E20)–(E22) will be false unless the existence condition is satisfied. To escape the existence problem entirely, it seems necessary to conditionalize both sides:

(E23) '*N* was *P* ' is true or would be true if it were formed, if and only if '*N* is *P* ' was true or would have been true if it had been formed;

(E24) '*N* will be *P* ' is true or would be true if it were formed, if and only if '*N* is *P* ' will be true or would be true in the future if it were formed in the future;

and

(E25) '*N* is possibly *P* ' is true or would be true if it were formed, if and only if '*N* is *P* ' is possible or would be possible if it were formed.

If the biconditionals in (E23)–(E25) are necessary, they seem ill-suited to the original task. For the truth conditions of subjunctive conditionals remain among the most elusive. Although Ockham surveys a variety of conditional propositions and inferences, including causal, temporal, and local propositions (see section 5 and chapter 12 below), he never singles out subjunctive conditionals for special treatment. Of course, this could be because he anticipated one modern view—that subjunctive conditionals are primitive and do not admit of analysis. But I find incredible the notion that Ockham actually thought through the difficult and currently controversial issues regarding subjunctive conditionals, drew the conclusion that they did not admit of analysis, and therefore passed over them without comment in the *Summa logicae*. A logician who takes time to spell out truth conditions for propositions of the form '*N* is *P*' and '*A* is *B*' (see (T4) and (T5) above) would surely not have concealed such fruitful reflections about subjunctive conditionals from his readers. Rather I suspect that since such propositions had not yet become a standard part of the syllabus, Ockham did not think the matter through at all, and employs such propositions in passing in an unreflective way. Accordingly, I find it difficult to believe that if pressed, Ockham would not have discarded (E20)–(E22) for (E23)–(E25) on the ground that they expound the clear in terms of the opaque, and have preferred the explanation of tenses and modes in terms of quanitification over non-present temporalia and unactualized possibles.[82]

Alternatively, Ockham could have regarded the biconditionals in (E17)–(E19) as necessary, if he had identified propositions with necessarily existent, mind-independent, eternal abstract objects; for then he could have claimed that every proposition exists eternally and necessarily. Or he could have granted this if he had reduced the necessary existence of each and every proposition to God's necessary act of thinking of them. I shall explain below how the former is as inimical to his theology as it is to his philosophy, while the latter could be accomodated with no less and no greater ease than non-present temporalia and unactualized possibles (see Part Five, chapters 24–26). Drawing on that promissory note, I may say that, where facility of integration into the major lines of Ockham's

82. Freddoso notes the existence problem and the need to replace (E20)–(E22) with (E23)–(E25), but passes the more benign judgment that the latter are "enormously complicated" (*op. cit.*, 46–47).

philosophy and theology are concerned, the present proposal does not enjoy any advantage over the initial reading with its wider ontological commitment. The fact remains, however, that Ockham neither envisions nor makes a clear choice between them and so never gives a full development to either.

3. EXPONIBLE CATEGORICAL PROPOSITIONS

Having dealt with simple categorical propositions, their tenses and modes, Ockham turns to those that are "equivalent to molecular propositions." The latter description is scarcely perspicuous, however, since any categorical proposition is trivially equivalent to a molecular proposition: viz., to the conjunction or disjunction of itself with itself. Ockham's intent is to focus on what medieval logicians called "exponibles": propositions that imply a number of categorical propositions that express "what the proposition signifies by virtue of its form."[83] He means to exclude categoricals of the form 'N is P' or 'A is B' whose categorematic terms are either singular terms or absolute terms (see chapter 10, section 1 above), because he thinks there are no propositions whose truth-value is easier to assess than these. But where some clause involving syncategorematics is inserted as happens with reduplicatives, exclusives, and exceptions (e.g., 'A qua A is B', and 'Every A but this A is B'), it is possible to find molecular propositions the truth-value of whose components is easier to evaluate. Likewise, where one or more of the categorematic terms is connotative, infinite, or privative and hence partly syncategorematic in force. Without being exhaustive, Ockham provides expositions for important cases which he will later draw on in mapping their conversion relations and formulating inference rules.[84]

(3.1) *Reduplicatives*. Frequent in discussions of medieval metaphysics were reduplicative propositions of which Ockham

83. *Summa logicae* II, c.11, (OPh I, 279).
84. *Ibid*. III–1, c.5, (OPh I, 377–381); c.65, (OPh I, 497).

gives the following, uninformative characterization:

> (C6) a reduplicative proposition is one that includes the expression 'qua' or its equivalent, where the expression is taken to have a reduplicative function.[85]

Paradigm among reduplicatives are propositions of the following forms, which vary in where the reduplicative clause falls in relation to the negation sign: '*A* qua *B* is *C* ', '*A* qua *B* is not *C* ' and '*A* is not *C* qua *B*'.[86] The reduplicative clause has a *reduplicative* function, when the proposition is taken to imply that the principal predicate is affirmed (denied) of the reduplicated predicate in a universal proposition: e.g., 'qua *B*' has a reduplicative function in '*A* qua *B* is *C* ' if the latter is taken to imply 'Every *B* is *C* '. It has a *specifying* function when the latter universal proposition is not asserted to be true, but the reduplicated predicate expresses the reason why the principal predicate is affirmed (denied) of the subject. Thus, someone might say 'The fire, insofar as it is hot, heats' without claiming that everything hot actually heats, but only that the reason this fire heats is that it is hot.[87] Further, among genuine reduplicatives, Ockham distinguishes *causal* reduplicatives in which the reduplicated predicate expresses the cause why the principal predicate pertains to the subject, from *concomitant* reduplicatives in which this is not asserted to be so.

Turning to truth conditions, let us focus on those for singular or indefinite concomitant reduplicatives of the above three forms: '*N* qua *B* is *C* '/'*A* qua *B* is *C* ', '*N* qua *B* is not *C* '/'*A* qua *B* is not *C* ', and '*N* is not *B* qua *C* '/'*A* is not *B* qua *C* '. Ockham offers the following rule for expounding the first:

> (E26) An affirmative singular or indefinite concomitant reduplicative proposition has the following four exponents: (i) one in which the principal predicate is truly predicated of the principal subject; (ii) one in which

---

85. *Ibid*. II, c.16, (OPh I, 289).   87. *Ibid*., (OPh I, 290, 295).
86. *Ibid*., (OPh I, 290).

the reduplicated term is predicated of the principal
subject; (iii) one in which the principal predicate is
predicated of the reduplicated term in a universal
proposition; and (iv) a true conditional from the
reduplicated term to the principal predicate,

from which the following truth conditions can be derived:

(T11) 'N qua B is C' is true if and only if 'N is C and N is B
and every B is C and if something is B, then it is C' is
true

and

(T12) 'A qua B is C' is true if and only if 'A is C and A is B
and every B is C and if something is B, then it is C' is
true.

These form the basis of many of Ockham's criticisms of many
opposing positions in philosophy and theology. For from it he
easily derives

(R9) The inference from an affirmative singular or indefinite
concomitant reduplicative proposition to its prejacent
is a formal inference,

or, put schematically,

(R9′) 'N qua B is C; therefore N is C' is a formal inference,

and

(R9″) 'A qua B is C; therefore A is C' is a formal inference,

"because its prejacent is always one of the exponents."[88] By
contrast, others had thought that adding a reduplicative clause

88. *Ibid.*, (OPh I, 291).

to a term could distract or diminish its supposition so that '*A* qua *B* ' could take predicates that '*A simpliciter* ' could not and vice versa. For example, we saw in Part One, chapter 2 above, how some asserted 'Socrates conceived one way is particular and conceived another way is universal', while denying 'Socrates *simpliciter* is universal'. Appealing to (R9′), Ockham rejects the position as contradictory.

Corresponding to such affirmative propositions, there are two sorts of negations: one in which only the principal predicate is governed by the negation sign and the other in which both the principal and reduplicated predicates are so governed. Concerning the former, Ockham stipulates

(E27) A singular or indefinite concomitant reduplicative proposition whose principal predicate but not its reduplicative predicate is governed by a negation sign has the following four exponents: (i) an affirmative proposition in which the reduplicated term is truly asserted of the principal subject; (ii) a negative one in which the principal predicate is denied of the reduplicated term in a universal proposition; (iii) a negative proposition in which the principal predicate is denied of the principal subject; and (iv) a conditional proposition from the reduplicated term to the negation of the principal predicate,

from which the following truth conditions can be derived:

(T13) '*N* qua *B* is not *C* ' is true, if and only if '*N* is *B* and *N* is not *C* and no *B* is *C* and if anything is *B*, it is not *C* ' is true

and

(T14) '*A* qua *B* is not *C* ' is true, if and only if '*A* is *B* and *A* is not *C* and no *B* is *C* and if anything is *B*, it is not *C* ' is true.[89]

89. *Ibid.*, (OPh I, 293).

Nevertheless, this first sort of negation is not the contradictory opposite of the corresponding affirmative proposition, since both could be false at once: viz., in case neither 'Every *B* is *C* ' nor 'No *B* is *C* ' is true. Rather the contradictory opposite of '*N* qua *B* is *C* '/ '*A* qua *B* is *C* ' is '*N* is not *C* qua *B* '/'*A* is not *C* qua *B* '. Thus Ockham stipulates

> (E28) A singular or indefinite concomitant reduplicative proposition whose principal predicate and reduplicated predicate both fall within the scope of the negation sign is true if and only if any one of the exponents of the corresponding affirmative singular or indefinite concomitant reduplicative proposition is false.[90]

Thus, neither 'Socrates qua man is white' nor 'Socrates qua man is not white', but 'Socrates is not white qua man' is true.

(3.2) *Exclusive Propositions*. Ockham identifies exclusive propositions by reference to an exclusion sign:

> (C7) An exclusive proposition is one that includes the expressions 'only' or 'alone' taken syncategorematically.[91]

The qualification 'taken syncategorematically' is inserted to cover an ambiguity that may have been more striking in Latin; yet, even in English, we may say 'Socrates runs alone' and mean either that he runs in a place where no else is running (although others may be running elsewhere), or that he is the only one running at all. Ockham identifies the latter use as syncategorematic; the former as categorematic. Construed syncategorematically, 'only' and 'alone' are equivalent and in Latin may govern the subject, the predicate, or the copula.[92] Further, he observes that even taken syncategorematically, 'only' and 'alone' have a primary use and a secondary use.

Looking at their primary use, Ockham stipulates that

90. *Ibid.*, (OPh I, 294).   92. *Ibid.*, (OPh I, 297).
91. *Ibid.*, c.17, (OPh I, 296–97).

(E29) whenever an exclusion sign taken according to its primary use is put in the subject position of an affirmative categorical proposition, the proposition always denotes that the predicate is truly predicated of the subject and denied of everything of which the subject is not truly predicated. Therefore, any [such] exclusive proposition has any two exponents: one affirmative and one negative,[93]

from which the following truth conditions can be derived:

(T15) 'Only A is B ' is true if any only if 'A is B and no non-A is B ' is true.

The right-hand side of (T15) contains an infinite term 'non-A' (Ockham sometimes says 'other than A'), and Ockham's rule for expounding propositions including such terms is recorded in (T22) below. On the other hand,

(E30) Whenever an exclusion sign taken according to its primary use is put in the subject position of a negative categorical proposition, "the proposition denotes that the predicate is truly denied of the subject and holds of everything that the subject is truly denied of. Thus, it has two exponents: viz., its negative prejacent and an affirmative one,"[94]

from which the following truth conditions may be derived:

(T16) 'Only A is not B ' is true if and only if 'A is not B and every non-A is B ' is true.

According to this primary usage, 'non-A' in the exposition of exclusive propositions includes the parts of A at least where the parts of A are not A's in their own right. Thus, 'Only man is white' will be false on this use, because if a man is white, his arm

93. *Ibid.*   94. *Ibid.*

is white, even though his arm is not a man in its own right. So will 'Only man is rational', since a man's soul is rational, even though it is not a man in its own right.[95] Broadly speaking, the exclusion sign can be taken to rule out everything extrinsic to that of which the subject is predicated, but not the parts of those of which it is predicated.[96]

Turning to cases in which the exclusion sign is put in the predicate position, Ockham says that properly speaking

> (E31) When an exclusion sign is put in the predicate of an affirmative categorical proposition, the proposition denotes that the predicate is said of the subject and that everything that the predicate is not true of is denied of it.[97]

Thus,

> (T17) '*A* is only *B* ' is true if and only if '*A* is *B* and *A* is not non-*B* '.

And once again, recourse must be had to Ockham's rule for expounding propositions containing infinite terms, if one is to be in a position to assess the truth conditions.

(3.3) *Exceptives*. Ockham informs us that

> (C8)   syncategorematics such as 'but' (*praeter*) and 'except' (*nisi*) when they function as exceptives make the propositions in which they occur exceptives.[98]

Ockham notes that besides their use as exceptives, '*praeter*' has a diminutive use in Latin in expressing the subtraction of one number from another, and '*nisi*' serves as a propositional connective (as when it is translated 'unless'); and these occurrences do not turn the propositions of which they are a part into exceptives.[99] As for truth conditions, Ockham stipulates that

---

95. *Ibid.*, (OPh I, 298).   98. *Ibid.*, c.18, (OPh I, 307).
96. *Ibid.*, (OPh I, 299).   99. *Ibid.*
97. *Ibid.*, (OPh I, 302).

(T18) An affirmative exceptive is true if and only if "the predicate is denied of the part taken out and pertains to everything else contained under the subject,"

or, put schematically,

(T18') 'Every *A* but this *A* is *B*' is true if and only if 'This *A* is not *B*' and 'Everything other than this *A* is *B* are true,

where the right-hand side is thought to expound the left.[100] On the other hand,

(T19) A negative exceptive is true if and only if the predicate is affirmed of the part taken out and denied of everything else that is contained under the subject,

or, put schematically,

(T19') 'No *A* but this *A* is *B*' is true if and only if 'this *A* is *B*' and 'Everything other than this *A* is not *B*' are true,

where the right-hand side expounds the left.[101]

(3.4) *Propositions Containing Connotative and Relative Terms*. When Ockham says that a proposition is exponible if a molecular proposition expresses what it signifies by virtue of its form (*ex forma sua*), he is using the notion of form broadly to cover not only the implications a proposition has by virtue of the presence and arrangement of explicit syncategorematics, but also those implicit in its categorematic terms. He says that "all propositions that include connotative and relative terms are exponible"[102] because such terms signify something primarily and something secondarily by virtue of syncategorematics in the nominal definitions. The replacement of such terms by their nominal definitions makes the logical form of propositions

100. *Ibid*.
101. *Ibid*., (OPh I, 307–308).

102. *Ibid*., c.11, (OPh I, 279).

containing them more fully explicit. Hence, "any proposition that includes such a term has exponents that express what that proposition implies."[103]

We have seen how for Ockham connotative and relative terms are sorted through nine of the ten Aristotelian categories, and it is therefore impossible to give a general formula that covers all cases. Properly speaking, it is the business of metaphysics, not logic, to pursue such analyses, and the completion of this task would constitute the full realization of Ockham's ontological program (see Part One, chapters 5 and 9 above). Nevertheless, it is worthwhile for now to look at one important case—viz., that of concrete inherence terms. He explains that

(E32) Any proposition that includes a concrete term whose corresponding abstract term signifies a thing that informs another thing, has two exponents—one with both terms in the nominative case and the other with a term in an oblique case.[104]

Letting such concrete inherence terms substitute for 'F', the corresponding abstract terms for 'F-ness', singular terms for 'N', and any general term for 'B', he stipulates the following:

(T20) 'N is F' is true if and only if 'N exists and F-ness inheres in N' is true

and

(T21) 'F is B' is true if and only if 'Something is B and F-ness inheres in it' is true.[105]

For example, 'Socrates is white' is expounded by 'Socrates exists' and 'Whiteness inheres in Socrates', where the former has only nominative case terms, while the latter has one oblique

103. *Ibid.*, (OPh I, 280–81).   105. *Ibid.*
104. *Ibid.*, (OPh I, 281).

case term.

Initially, it is puzzling why Ockham should have thought it necessary or advisable to propose (T20) and (T21), when he already had

(T4') 'N is P' is true if and only if there is something for which 'N' and 'P' both supposit in 'N is P'

and

(T5') '(Some) A is B' is true if there is something for which 'A' and 'B' both supposit.

The latter pair seems more perspicuous than the former, since the two-name theory is easy to apply and Ockham never gives comparable directions for evaluating oblique case propositions such as 'F-ness inheres in N'. And we have seen how Ockham originally proposes (T4') and (T5') for propositions with absolute categorematic terms, but frequently gives examples that include one or more connotative terms.

Ockham would doubtless reply that (T20) and (T21) only spell out what is implicit in applying (T4') and (T5') to propositions containing concrete inherence terms. For by

(E2) A term 'T' has personal supposition for x is p, if and only if 'T' occurs in p and 'This is T' (where 'this' indicates x) is true,

there is something for which 'Socrates' and 'white' both supposit in 'Socrates is white'; only if 'This is white' (where 'this' indicates Socrates) is true; and (T20) tells us that the latter is true only if 'Whiteness inheres in Socrates'. In short, in determining that 'white' supposits for Socrates, we recognize what we need to know to evaluate the oblique case proposition 'Whiteness inheres in Socrates'.

In *Reportatio* II, q.1, where Ockham gives theological reasons for holding that inherence is a thing really distinct from the subject and the inhering form, he contrasts the role of the copula in categorical propositions containing only absolute terms with that in oblique case propositions or in those contain-

ing concrete inherence terms. In the first case, the copula is
said to be "common by union" because it joins one term to
another.[106] In the second case, it is both "common by union"
and "common by predication." For 'inheres' in 'Whiteness inheres in a man' signifies real relations of inherence in such a way
that it can be predicated of and supposit for them.[107] On this
view, the oblique case proposition involves not two names, but
three! In *Summa logicae* I, c.51, however, Ockham notes how
Aristotle would reject this view[108] and makes no mention of his
own endorsement of it for theological reasons (see Part One,
chapter 7 above).

(3.5) *Negative Terms*. Of negative terms, the most systematically well-behaved are infinite terms of the form 'non-A'.
Ockham explains vaguely that

(E33) Any proposition containing an infinite term has two
      exponents—an affirmative one with 'something' or
      'some things' or their equivalent as subject or pred-
      icate.

For example,

(T22) 'A is non-B ' is true if and only if 'A is something and A
      is not B '.[109]

The affirmative exponent makes any proposition of the form 'A
is non-B ', where 'A' is an empty term, false. It also explains
why 'White man is man' and 'White man is non-man' can both
be false—viz., when no man is white.[110]

The exposition of privative terms such as 'blind' and 'foolish'
that are not equivalent to infinite terms varies so much that only
the following can be said in general:

(E34) Affirmative propositions containing privative terms

106. *Ibid.*, (OTh V, 21).   109. *Ibid.* II, c.12, (OPh I, 283–84).
107. *Ibid.*, (OTh V, 21–22).   110. *Ibid.*, (OPh I, 285).
108. (OPh I, 169–170).

not equivalent to infinite terms have more than two exponents,[111]

which can be easily derived by examining the nominal definition of the term in question.[112]

4.   MOLECULAR PROPOSITIONS

Molecular propositions are composed of categorical propositions joined by propositional connectives. Perhaps because it was involved in the regimentation of a natural language and not in the construction of artificial ones, medieval logic did not share the modern preoccupation with truth-functional connectives and examined the more difficult logical relations apart from any systematic effort to minimize their number or reduce them to truth-functional ones. Thus, Ockham sorts molecular propositions as conjunction, disjunctions, or conditionals, as causal, temporal, or local propositions, depending on the kind of propositional connective employed. He explains that conditionals are equivalent to inferences and defers full-scale treatment of them to *Summa Logicae* III;[113] they will be the subject of chapter 12 below. For each type he attempts to supply identification rules, truth conditions and sometimes necessity, possibility, and impossibility conditions, equivalences and inference rules.

(4.1) *Truth-Functional Connectives*. Of the five remaining types, conjunction and disjunction are the only truth-functional connectives. Regarding the first, Ockham explains that

(C9) A conjunction is a proposition composed of many categorical propositions joined by the conjunction 'and' or one equivalent to it.

Thus, 'Socrates runs and Plato disputes' is a conjunction. But so

111. *Ibid.*, c.13, (OPh I, 285).
112. *Ibid.*, (OPh I, 286).
113. *Summa logicae* II, c.31, (OPh I, 347).

428 PART TWO: LOGIC

are 'Socrates is neither white nor black' and 'Socrates is both white and hot', because they are equivalent to 'Socrates is not white and Socrates is not black' and 'Socrates is white and Socrates is hot', respectively.[114] As for the truth and necessity of conjunctions, Ockham stipulates that

> (T23) it is necessary for the truth of a conjunction that each part be true

and

> (T24) it is necessary for the necessity of a conjunction that each part be necessary.[115]

In relation to truth and necessity, a conjunction follows its weakest member. Although he does not say so explicitly, the conditions just mentioned are sufficient as well as required for truth and necessity in such propositions. The matter is different where possibility and impossibility are concerned. For while

> (T25) it is necessary for the possibility of a conjunction that each part be possible,

this is not sufficient. For example, each part of 'Socrates is sitting and he is not sitting' is possible, but the conjunction is impossible because the parts are incompossible. Thus,

> (T26) it is necessary for the impossibility of a conjunction that one part be impossible or incompossible with another part,

where either is sufficient.[116] Given the truth conditions in (T23), Ockham derives the following rule:

> (R10) the inference from a conjunction to each part is always

---

114. *Ibid.*, c.32, (OPh I, 347).   116. *Ibid.*
115. *Ibid.*, (OPh I, 348).

a good inference...but the reverse commits a fallacy of the consequent...,

although "sometimes the inference from one part of a conjunction to the conjunction can be good inference by virtue of the matter, as if one part of the conjunction implies the other."[117]
On the other hand, Ockham explains that

(C19) a disjunction is a proposition composed of many categorical propositions joined by the conjunction 'or' or one equivalent to it;

for example, the proposition 'You are a man or a donkey' and likewise the proposition 'You are a man or Socrates disputes' are disjunctions.[118] Truth conditions for disjunctives were a matter of some controversy. Normally we would suppose that

(T27) A disjunction is true, if and only if one of its parts is true.

Ockham follows the medieval interpretation of Aristotle, however, when he notes that Aristotle would restrict

(T28) it is necessary for the truth of a disjunction that one part be true

to propositions about the present and deny it for propositions about the future or those equivalent to propositions about the future. Where future contingents were concerned, Aristotle allegedly claimed that the disjunctive of contradictory opposites was true, although each part lacked truth-value. As we shall see in Part Five, chapter 27 below, Ockham thought the doctrine of omniscience required his unqualified endorsement of the principle of bivalence, and so maintained that "in truth a proposition about the future is either true or false, although

117. *Ibid.*, (OPh I, 348–49).
118. *Ibid.*, c.33, (OPh I, 349).

avoidably so."[119]

As for the other modalities, Ockham observes that

> (T29) it is necessary for the necessity of a disjunction that either one part is necessary, or the parts are mutually contradictory, or are equivalent to contradictories, or are convertible with contradictories.

Thus 'Socrates runs or God exists' is necessary, because one part is necessary, but 'God creates or does not create' is necessary, because its parts are contradictory.[120] Further,

> (T30) It is sufficient for the possibility of a disjunction that one part be possible,

where this condition is likewise necessary; while

> (T31) It is necessary for the impossibility of a disjunction that each part be impossible,

where this condition is also sufficient.[121]

From the above truth conditions, Ockham easily reads off the following inference rule:

> (R11) The inference "from one part of a disjunction to the whole disjunction is a good argument, and the reverse is a fallacy of the consequent" except in special cases,[122]

and likewise

> (R12) The "inference from a disjunction together with the negation of one part, to the other part is a good inference;

for example, 'Socrates is a man or a donkey; Socrates is not a

119. *Ibid.*
120. *Ibid.*
121. *Ibid.*
122. *Ibid.*, (OPh I, 350).

donkey; therefore Socrates is a man' does follow.''[123]

Further, comparing the truth conditions for conjunctions and disjunctions, Ockham anticipates the De Morgan laws:

(R13) the contradictory opposite of a conjunction is a disjunction composed of the contradictories of the parts of the conjunction.

For example, the contradictory opposite of 'Socrates is white and Plato is black' is not 'Socrates is not white and Plato is not black' but 'Socrates is not white or Plato is not black', since the falsity of one conjunct is sufficient for the falsity of the conjunction.[124] Likewise,

(R14) the contradictory opposite of a disjunction is a conjunction composed of the contradictories of the parts of the disjunction.[125]

For example, the contradictory opposite of 'Socrates is not white or Plato is not black' is 'Socrates is white and Plato is black', since the latter implies that neither part of the former is true.

(4.2) *Non-Truth-Functional Connectives*. Ockham deals with the non-truth-functional connectives more briefly. (4.2.1) *Causal Propositions*. Among molecular propositions, the most important of these is the causal relation. Ockham explains that

(C11) A causal proposition is one composed of many categorical propositions by means of the conjunction 'since' or 'because' ('*quia*') or its equivalent.

For example, 'Since Socrates is a man, Socrates is an animal' is a causal proposition. So are 'Socrates works in order to be healthy' and 'Socrates takes a walk after dinner lest he get sick' because they are equivalent to 'Socrates works, because he

123. *Ibid*.
124. *Ibid*., c.32, (OPh I, 348).

125. *Ibid*., c.33, (OPh I, 349).

wants to be healthy' and 'Socrates takes a walk after dinner, because he does not want to get sick'. Likewise, so is 'Socrates becomes hot inasmuch as he is in motion' because it is equivalent to 'Socrates becomes hot because he is in motion'.[126]

As for truth conditions, Ockham stipulates that

> (T32) It is necessary for the truth of a causal proposition that (i) each part be true and that (ii) the antecedent express a cause required for the truth of the consequent.

Thus, 'Socrates is white, because Plato is white' is false even where 'Socrates is white and Plato is white' is true, because 'Plato is white' does not express any cause necessary for the truth of 'Socrates is white'.[127] 'Cause' here is taken broadly to cover logical relations such as that between 'man' and 'animal' in the true causal proposition 'Since Socrates is a man, Socrates is an animal'; or the priority and posteriority with which a predicate applies to its first subject and those subordinate to it as in the true causal proposition 'An isosceles has three..., because a triangle has three...'; or for an efficient cause—whether *per se* or *per accidens*, natural or voluntary—as in the true causal proposition 'The wood gets hot, because it is near the fire' (see Part Four, chapter 18 below).

Turning to the other modalities, Ockham explains that

> (T33) It is necessary for the necessity of a causal proposition that each part be necessary

since otherwise condition (T32i) would not be necessarily satisfied. Nevertheless, this is not sufficient, since (T32ii) must be necessarily satisfied as well. Likewise,

> (T34) "it is necessary for the possibility of a causal proposition that each part be possible,

---

126. *Ibid.*, c.34, (OPh I, 350).
127. *Ibid.*

but this is not sufficient, any more than the necessity of each part is sufficient for its necessity."[128] It is also required that it be possible for what the antecedent expresses to be the cause of the truth of the conclusion. For this reason, "neither the impossibility nor falsity of any part is required for the impossibility of a causal proposition; rather

(T35) it is sufficient that the antecedent could not be a cause of the consequent."[129]

The same considerations yield the following inference rules:

(R15) the inference from a causal proposition to one part holds good, but not the other way around

and

(R16) the inference from a causal proposition to the conjunction of its parts holds good but not the other way around.

Thus, 'Every man sins because he has free will; therefore every man sins and every man has free will' holds good, but the reverse does not follow.[130]

(4.2.2) *Temporal Propositions.* First offering an identification rule, Ockham says

(C12) A temporal proposition is one composed of many categorical propositions by means of a temporal adverb.

For example, 'Socrates runs while Plato disputes', 'Socrates was white, when Plato was black', 'Socrates was white, when Plato was not running'.[131] As with causal propositions, a temporal proposition is not true unless both parts are true. But this is not

128. *Ibid.*, (OPh I, 351).
129. *Ibid.*
130. *Ibid.*
131. *Ibid.*, c.35, (OPh I, 352).

sufficient; they must be true about the relevant times. Since different temporal adverbs—e.g., 'while', 'when', 'before', 'after'—indicate different temporal relations, only the following general statement is possible:

> (T36) It is necessary for the truth of a temporal proposition (i) that each part be true, and (ii) that they be true about the same or different times as indicated by the temporal adverb connecting them.[132]

The necessity of a temporal proposition requires the necessity of both (T36i) and (T36ii); the possibility of a temporal proposition, the possibility of both; but the impossibility requires the impossibility of only one and for this it is enough if the parts are incompossible.[133]

Turning to inference rules, Ockham maintains that

> (R17) the inference from a temporal proposition to one part holds good but not vice versa

and

> (R18) from a temporal proposition, the conjunction of its parts follows but not vice versa,

since the satisfaction of (T36i) does not in general guarantee the satisfaction of (T36ii).[134]

(4.2.3) *Local Propositions*. Predictably, Ockham explains that

> (C13) a local molecular proposition...is one that is composed of many categorical propositions joined by an adverb of place or its equivalent;

for example, 'An accident is where its subject is' and 'Christ suf-

132. *Ibid.*
133. *Ibid.*, (OPh I, 352–53).
134. *Ibid.*, (OPh I, 353).

fered where he preached'.[135] And paralleling temporal propositions,

    (T37) It is necessary for the truth of a local proposition that (i) each part be true, and that (ii) they be true about places related the way the adverb of place indicates,

and analogous inference rules hold as well.[136]

135. *Ibid.*, c.36, (OPh I, 354).
136. *Ibid.*

12

Arguments

Ockham's treatment of arguments, the principal subject matter of logic, in *Summa logicae* III and IV is a mixture of tradition and innovation. His syllabus is largely conservative. In identifying and commending good argument-forms, he embraces Aristotle's program in the *Analytics*, declaring the syllogism to be the prince of arguments (III–1) and demonstration the noblest of syllogisms (III–2). He then turns to dialectical or topical arguments (III–3) and in chapters 1–9 treats the subject matter of Boethius's *De topicis differentiis,* before dealing with the legacy of Aristotle's *Topics* in chapters 17–30. He concludes (in III–4) with an extensive discussion of fallacies that parallels Aristotle's *Sophistical Refutations.* Yet, no part of this discussion fails to bear the stamp of Ockham's distinctive contribution. The completeness of his coverage of valid syllogistic forms is unprecedented in its attention to syllogisms with singular propositions and its consideration of "mixed" syllogisms with some propositions assertoric and some modal or some of one mode and some of another. His discussion of demonstration reflects his appreciation of the contingency of creation and the importance of intuitive cognitions of sensible particulars as the source of all knowledge (see Part Three, chapter 13 below). Finally, whatever had been learned in the traditional study of topics is diverted by Ockham to his theory of inference.

In its focus on the logic of terms, Ockham's theory of inference contrasts with that of modern logic.[1] The latter begins with the propositional calculus and develops as much of a

---

1. As noted by Otto Bird in his excellent article "The Tradition of the Logical Topics: Aristotle to Ockham," *Journal of the History of Ideas* XXIII (1962): 307–323, especially 320–21.

theory of inference as possible within that framework. Predicate calculus is parasitic on propositional calculus in that, roughly speaking, instantiation is applied to quantified formulae to yield concatenations that can be handled within the propositional calculus and generalization is applied to the derived formulae to restore a quantified conclusion. By contrast, Ockham follows Aristotle in beginning with syllogisms, which hold good by virtue of relations among quantified terms. After more than one hundred chapters on syllogisms and demonstration, he tries—as I shall argue—to explain the validity of as many non-syllogistic inferences as possible in terms of available reductions to syllogisms. The inference rules of our propositional calculus are not completely ignored but receive comparatively short shrift in one chapter.[2]

In modern logic, the principal division among inferences is that between material and strict implication—i.e., between inferences whose premisses *are not* and those whose premisses *cannot* be true without their conclusions being true—where the division is not exclusive but instances of the latter are included among those of the former. In medieval logic, the driving wedge is between those that hold good for any subject matter and those that do not—that between "formal" and "material" inferences. Aristotle's syllogistic was seen to focus on formal inferences, which could be instantiated with equal legitimacy in any of the sciences. Since the division between formal and material inferences is exclusive, it is not equivalent to the modern one between material and strict implication. It might be thought at least that all formal inferences would be instances of strict implication, since all formal inferences would hold good by virtue of the syncategorematic terms in the premiss(es) and conclusion and so would be among those whose premiss(es) cannot be true when the conclusion is false. We shall see that Ockham's program to assimilate as many good inferences as possible to the syllogism so complicates the pattern of his divisions that any neat mapping is out of the question.

An exhaustive survey of Ockham's treatment of arguments is

2. *Summa logicae* III–3, c.38, (OPh I, 727–731).

the subject matter for many books[3] and beyond the scope of this one. In what follows, I shall say as much about the syllogism and demonstration as will be useful elsewhere in our discussion and conclude with an examination of Ockham's division among inferences.

1. SYLLOGISMS

According to customary definition, "a syllogism is discourse in which a conclusion follows necessarily from two premisses disposed in mood and figure."[4] It follows that no invalid argument counts as a syllogism, but no stipulation is made regarding the truth or falsity of the premisses.[5] Syllogisms are distinguished from other valid arguments in having two and only two premisses; categorical syllogisms, in having three and only three categorematic terms: the major term, which occurs in the first premiss and as the predicate of the conclusion; the minor term, which occurs in the second premiss and as the subject of the conclusion; and the middle term, which occurs in both premisses but not in the conclusion at all.[6]

The *figure* of a categorical syllogism is determined by whether the middle term occupies the subject or predicate position in the major and minor premisses, respectively. Ockham distinguishes three figures for syllogisms:

> ...The first figure is that in which the middle term is subject in the first proposition and predicate in the second. The second figure occurs when the middle term is predicate in both. The third figure, when the middle term is subject in both...[7]

These can be represented schematically as follows, where '*P*'

3. For example, Damascene Webering, *Theory of Demonstration According to William Ockham*, (St. Bonaventure, NY, 1953), and Calvin Normore, *The Logic of Time and Modality in the Later Middle Ages: The Contribution of William Ockham*, an unpublished Ph.D. dissertation.

4. *Summa logicae* III–1, c.1, (OPh I, 361).

5. *Ibid.*

6. *Ibid.*, c.2, (OPh I, 362).

7. *Ibid.*

stands for the major term, '*S*' for the minor, and '*M*' for the middle; and where all syncategorematic terms except the copula are omitted:

	1st figure	*2nd figure*	*3rd figure*
Major Premiss:	*M* is *P*	*P* is *M*	*M* is *P*
Minor Premiss:	*S* is *M*	*S* is *M*	*M* is *S*
Conclusion:	*S* is *P*	*S* is *P*	*S* is *P*

It might seem obvious that one possible combination has been omitted: viz., that in which the major term is a subject and the minor is a predicate:

	4th figure
Major Premiss:	*P* is *M*
Minor Premiss:	*M* is *S*
Conclusion:	*S* is *P*

Ockham follows Aristotle in maintaining that in fact no argument of this fourth figure is valid and hence that none is a syllogism. If the premisses are transposed, however, the middle terms will be arranged as they are in the first figure, and it will be possible to draw a valid inference to the conclusion '*P* is *S*' but not to the conclusion '*S* is *P*'.[8] For example, the fourth figure inference 'Every man is an animal; every animal is a substance; therefore every substance is a man' is invalid, but the first figure inference resulting from transposing the premisses—'Every animal is a substance; every man is an animal; therefore every man is a substance'—is valid.[9]

8. *Ibid.*
9. *Ibid.*

The *mood* of a categorical syllogism depends upon whether its premisses are universal or particular (on their quantity), negative or affirmative (on their quality). Ockham calculates that "taking the combinations for two propositions through universal and particular, affirmative and negative, there will be sixteen combinations" for each figure.[10] Not all of these are valid or syllogistic, however. And Ockham's program in the rest of *Summa logicae* III–1 is to catalog the valid syllogistic forms for each figure, beginning with the easiest cases (those with present tense assertoric propositions), moving on to those with one or more propositions in the past or future tense, and finally considering those with modal propositions. For present purposes, it will be enough to look at syllogisms whose propositions are present tense and assertoric in the nominative case only.

Of sixteen possible combinations for each figure, syllogistic theory allows only those regulated by the *dici de omni* or the *dici de nullo* to count as valid or syllogistic. *Dici de omni* occurs in a proposition that denotes or signifies that nothing is taken under the subject that the predicate is not asserted of, the paradigm being a universal affirmative proposition. *Dici de nullo* occurs in a proposition that denotes or signifies that the predicate is denied of whatever the subject is affirmed of, the paradigm being the universal negative proposition.[11] Accordingly, every valid syllogistic mood contains at least one universal or singular premiss which includes (excludes) everything contained under the major or the minor in (from) what is included under the middle, or vice versa. Apparently, more is involved, because Ockham remarks that valid moods in the first figure are so regulated *immediately*, while those of the second and third figure *mediately*, insofar as they are reducible to arguments in the first figure.[12] He does not say explicitly what it is, however, but instead offers rules to use in distinguishing

10. *Ibid.*, c.3, (OPh I, 364); cf. c.10, (OPh I, 388–89) and c.14, (OPh I, 398).
11. *Ibid.*, c.2, (OPh I, 363).
12. *Ibid.*, c.4, (OPh I, 371).

arguments so regulated from those that are not.[13] Ockham emphasizes that such styles of argument hold good regardless of which three categorematic terms occur as subject and predicate—whether they are from the category of substance or the categories of accident—and so can be legitimately instantiated in any science.[14]

To be thus regulated and so count as syllogistic, moods in the *first figure* must have a universal major and an affirmative minor. The following four qualify—

	"Barbara"	"Celarent"	"Darii"	"Ferio"
Major Premiss:	A All M is P	E No M is P	A All M is P	E No M is P
Minor Premiss:	A All S is M	A All S is M	I Some S is M	I Some S is M
Conclusion:	A All S is P	E No S is P	I Some S is P	O Some S is not P

—and received the quoted traditional nicknames, whose vowels give the quantity and quality of the premisses and conclusion in order. Ockham scarcely mentions these mnemonic devices, but Sherwood makes a good deal of them and may have authored a verse summarizing the moods and their reduction relations.[15] (Ockham says that all four moods of the first figure are "self-evident,"[16] but Sherwood gives priority to Barbara and Celarent whose respective regulation by *dici de omni* and *dici de nullo* he finds more obvious.[17] Arguments in the *second figure* (except those whose middle terms are discrete terms or are

13. E.g., *ibid.*, c.5, (OPh I, 377–381), apparently for arguments in the first figure.
14. *Ibid.*, c.4, (OPh I, 376).
15. *Introduction to Logic*, chap.4, sec.9, (Kretzmann trans., 66–67); cf. Peter of Spain, *Tractatus* IV, (De Rijk ed., 52–53).
16. *Summa logicae* III–1, c.4, (OPh I, 371).
17. *Op. cit.*, chap.4, sec.6, 61–62.

categorematics taken together with a universal sign[18]) must have a universal major and one negative premiss;[19] the following moods hold good:[20]

	"Camestres"	"Baroco"	"Festino"	"Cesare"
Major Premiss:	*A* All *P* is *M*	*A* All *P* is *M*	*E* No *P* is *M*	*E* No *P* is *M*
Minor Premiss:	*E* No *S* is *M*	*O* Some *S* is not *M*	*I* Some *S* is *M*	*A* All *S* is *M*
Conclusion:	*E* No *S* is *P*	*O* Some *S* is not *P*	*O* Some *S* is not *P*	*E* No *S* is *P*

Finally, valid moods in the *third figure* always have a universal or singular premiss, an affirmative minor, and never a universal conclusion;[21] the following six are acceptable:

	"Datisi"	"Ferison"	"Disamis"	"Bocardo"
Major Premiss:	*A* All *M* is *P*	*E* No *M* is *P*	*I* Some *M* is *P*	*O* Some *M* is not *P*
Minor Premiss:	*I* Some *M* is *S*	*I* Some *M* is *S*	*A* All *M* is *S*	*A* All *M* is *S*
Conclusion:	*I* Some *S* is *P*	*O* Some *S* is *P*	*I* Some *S* is *P*	*O* Some *S* is not *P*

	"Darapti"	"Felapton"
Major Premiss:	*A* All *M* is *P*	*E* No *M* is *P*
Minor Premiss:	*A* All *M* is *S*	*A* All *M* is *S*
Conclusion:	*I* Some *S* is *P*	*O* Some *S* is not *P*

18. Cf. *Summa logicae* III–1, c.13, (OPh I, 396).
19. *Ibid.*, c.10, (OPh I, 387–88).
20. *Ibid.*, (OPh I, 389).
21. *Ibid.*, c.14, (OPh I, 397–98).

Ockham indicates how syllogisms of the second and third figures can be reduced to syllogisms of the first figure by some combination of converting premisses or conclusion, transposing the order of the premisses, or by arguments *ad impossibile* that derive from one premiss and the opposite of the conclusion the opposite of the other premiss.[22] Since 'No *P* is *M* ' and 'No *M* is *P* ' convert simply, "Festino" in the second figure reduces to "Ferio" in the first figure by converting its major premiss. Likewise, "Cesare" converts to "Celarent". Again, if we convert the minor premiss and conclusion of "Camestres" and transpose the premisses, yielding 'No *M* is *S*, All *P* is *M*; therefore no *P* is *S* ', we get "Celarent" in the first figure.[23] But "Baroco" is reduced to "Barbara" by an argument *ad impossibile*: for the contradictory of the conclusion 'Some *S* is not *P* ' is the *A* proposition 'All *S* is *P* ', which combines with the premiss 'All *P* is *M* ' to yield 'All *S* is *M* ', the contradictory of the other premiss 'Some *S* is not *M* '.[24]

Turning to moods of the third figure, Ockham says that these, too, can be reduced to some in the first figure by conversion and by arguments *ad impossibile*. Thus, since 'Some *M* is *S* ' converts simply with 'Some *S* is *M* ', "Datisi" in the third figure is reduced to "Darii" in the first figure by converting its minor. Likewise, "Ferison" to "Ferio". "Disamis" reduces to "Darii" by converting its major and conclusion and transposing its premisses to yield 'All *M* is *S*; some *P* is *M*; therefore some *P* is *S* '. "Darapti" reduces to "Darii" by the conversion *per accidens* of its minor—'All *M* is *S* ' to 'Some *S* is *M* '. Likewise "Felapton" to "Ferio". "Bocardo" cannot be reduced by converting its minor, because the resultant argument would lack a universal premiss and hence be invalid. But it can be reduced to "Barbara" by an argument *ad impossibile*: for the contradictory opposite of the conclusion—'All *S* is *P* '—combines with the minor 'All *M* is *S* ' to yield 'All *M* is *P* ', which is the con-

---

22. *Ibid.*, c.11, (OPh I, 393); c.14, (OPh I, 400–401).
23. *Ibid.*, c.11, (OPh I, 393).
24. *Ibid.*

tradictory opposite of the major.[25]

Sherwood defends the primacy of "Barbara" and "Celarent" over all others on the ground that "Darii" can be reduced *ad impossibile* to "Camestres", which in turn reduces to "Celarent", while "Ferio" reduces to "Cesare", which in turn reduces to "Celarent".[26]

In sum, then, syllogistic proper purports to elaborate a theory of two-premiss inferences that hold good for any subject matter. In addition, the reductions of second and third figure arguments to first figure arguments and that of first figure arguments to each other call on conversion rules for one premiss inferences and/or the general rule

(R1) In a good inference with two premisses, the opposite of the consequent together with one premiss implies the opposite of the other premiss.[27]

2. DEMONSTRATION

When Aristotle formulated his conception of an ideal science in the *Posterior Analytics*, he singled out a special type of syllogism—viz., the demonstration—as its vehicle of inferential knowledge. He defines 'demonstration' as 'a knowledge-producing syllogism', but the operative conception of knowledge has Platonic roots. In the middle dialogues at least, Plato held that spatiotemporal particulars that come to be and pass away and change constantly are proper objects of belief, while knowledge was only of the Forms, which are what they are in an unqualified sense and which exist eternally and immutably, separated from particulars and independently of any thought about them. Aristotle concedes that Plato's theory of knowledge is right on several points: First, the notion that knowledge properly speaking is of essences, their definitions,

25. *Ibid.*, c.14, (OPh I, 400–401).
26. *Op. cit.*, chap.4, sec.9, 67.
27. *Summa logicae* III–3, c.38, (OPh I, 728).

and relations among them. Second, that such knowledge is of causes. Third, that because essential connections are necessary, knowledge properly speaking is of what cannot be otherwise than it is. Fourth, since what pertains to man essentially, pertains to every man, knowledge properly speaking is universal.[28] Aristotle's model of a developed science was Euclidean geometry, which proceeds from axioms, postulates, and definitions to theorems by means of demonstrations. But he hoped to extend this paradigm to astronomy, physics, and biology as well. Rejecting separately existing Platonic Forms, Aristotle insisted that natures had a mind-independent existence in reality in particulars. If Socrates and Brownie come into being and pass away, are contingent and changing, nevertheless, the species will exist in some particulars or other eternally; and what it is to be a man or a donkey cannot be otherwise than it is. We have noted the conclusion of moderate realists like Burleigh and Scotus that if astronomy, physics, and biology are to be about what is real, natures must be universal or common in reality (Part One, chapter 2).

If any demonstration is a *knowledge-producing* syllogism, it follows that the conclusion must not be so obvious that anyone who formulates it cannot help assenting to it (i.e., it cannot be a proposition known *per se*; see Part Three, chapter 13 below) the way 'If a man exists, an animal exists' is. In Ockham's terms, the conclusion must be "susceptible of doubt" (*dubitabilis*) and "a question."[29] Not that the conclusion must actually be doubted by anyone who has not considered the premises. For there may be more than one way to demonstrate a given proposition, and some demonstrable propositions can be known from experience. A person who knows it one way will not hold the conclusion in doubt until he learns it another way. But the conclusion must be such that a person ignorant of any such demonstration could both formulate the conclusion and doubt it. Further, it must be possible that someone should be

28. *Posterior Analytics* I, 2, 71b10; 6, 74b5–17, 75a13–17.
29. *Summa logicae* III-2, c.9, (OPh I, 521–22); *Ord.*, Prologue, q.2, (OTh I, 76).

caused to know it for the first time and do so through knowing the premisses.[30] Hence, it must not be the case that knowledge of the conclusion is necessary for knowledge of the premisses.[31]

Since knowledge properly speaking is of causes, the ideal demonstration (called the "*demonstratio potissima*") will be one whose premisses explain the truth of the conclusion by signifying the cause of what the conclusion signifies.[32] Because such demonstrations not only prove the fact (*quia est*) but also give the explanation (*propter quid est*), they are called "demonstrations *propter quid*"; and because the cause is prior to the effect, they are said to be *a priori*.[33] Aristotle maintains that since these explanations will be in terms of essential connections, and since the essence is both universal and affirmative, the most scientific form of demonstration will be Barbara:[34]

"Barbara"

Major Premiss:	A	Every *M* is *P*
Minor Premiss:	A	Every *S* is *M*
Conclusion:	A	Every *S* is *P*

And he holds that the explanation will be best provided when the major term '*P*' is a *passio* of the minor '*S*' and the middle '*M*', while the middle '*M*' is a definition of the minor '*S*'.[35]

Ockham notes that by 'definition', Aristotle does not mean 'nominal definition' (even in the broad sense according to which both absolute and connotative terms have nominal

30. *Summa logicae* III–2, c.11, (OPh I, 524–25); *Ord.*, Prologue, q.2, (OTh I, 77).
31. *Summa logicae* III–2, c.16, (OPh I, 531–32).
32. *Ibid.*, c.15, (OPh I, 530).
33. *Ibid.*, c.17, (OPh I, 533).
34. *Posterior Analytics* I, 14, 79a17–33; cf. Ockham, *Ord.*, Prologue, q.5, (OTh I, 165).
35. *Summa logicae* III–2, c.2, (OPh I, 507).

definitions; see Part Two, chapter 10 above). For where the minor premiss states the nominal definition of the minor term, the same mental proposition will correspond to the major premiss and the conclusion, and the argument will beg the question. Likewise, if the major expresses the nominal definition of the *passio* the same mental proposition will correspond to the minor premiss and the conclusion, and the question will again be begged. Rather in affirmative categorical demonstrations, knowledge that the nominal definitions of all three terms are consistent is presupposed for the demonstration.[36] What Aristotle intends is that the middle 'M' should be (all or part of) the real definition of 'S', which expresses the essential parts of the things signified by 'S'.[37]

Ockham emphasizes that so far as logic is concerned, "a *passio* is not an extramental thing inherent in the subject " but "only something predicable of its subject *per se* the second way."[38] Aristotle had distinguished two ways in which one term may be predicated *per se* of another: "one when the predicate occurs in the definition of the subject; the other when the subject occurs in the definition of the predicate."[39] His examples are from mathematics: 'line' is predicated of 'triangle' *per se* the first way because the former occurs in the defintion of the latter; but 'straight' or 'curved' is predicated of 'line' *per se* the second way because the latter occurs in the definition of the former. Similarly, 'odd' and 'even' are predicated of 'number' *per se* the second way. In *Summa logicae* III–2, c.7, Ockham recognizes a broader sense, according to which terms are predicable *per se* not only of the terms they define or the terms that define them, but also of terms inferior to the latter.[40] Thus,

---

36. *Ibid.*, c.12, (OPh I, 525); c.3, (OPh I, 508–509).

37. *Ord.*, Prologue, q.5, (OTh I, 166).

38. *Summa logicae* I, c.37, (OPh I, 105); cf. III–2, c.2, (OPh I, 507–508) and *Ord.*, Prologue, q.3, (OTh I, 133–36).

39. *Summa logicae* III–2, c.7, (OPh I, 515); cf. *Posterior Analytics* I, 4, 73a34–73b1.

40. Recall that one term 'F' is inferior to another 'G' if and only if 'x is F; therefore x is G' is a good formal inference, but 'x is G; therefore x is F' is not.

'substance' will be predicable *per se* the first way not only of 'body' but also of 'man'. Likewise, 'susceptible of contraries' is predicable *per se* the second way not merely of 'substance' but also of 'man'.[41] But the defined and defining terms are the "first subjects" of the predicates in question.

According to Aristotle's idealized picture of scientific inquiry, then, we begin by wondering whether (*si est*) and if so for what reason (*propter quid est*) every S is P. The best way to answer both questions is to find some feature 'M' that either is mentioned in the real definition of 'S', or something superior to 'S', or 'M' is superior to (follows by a formal inference from) something that is and that either occurs in the definition of 'P' or something inferior to 'P', or is inferior to something that does (something that does follow by a formal inference from it). Where these conditions are satisfied, the fact that every S is P will be explained in terms of an essential connection between being S and being M, and being P and being M. And the explanation will be even better if 'M' is the first subject of 'P', because in that case being M will be that without which nothing is P and with which anything is P.[42]

Ockham finds this picture oversimple and attributes it to Aristotle's focus on mathematical models. In fact, the Philosopher did not really mean to say that the definition of the subject is always the middle term. For the class of secondary subjects is even wider than has been thus far suggested. In the Prologue to the *Ordinatio*, Ockham recognizes them to include not only terms inferior to the first subject, but also terms superior to it (so that 'isosceles' can be predicated not only of 'isoceles triangle' but also of 'triangle'), terms that signify a whole of which the first subject signifies a part (e.g., 'intellectual soul' is the first subject of 'capable of instruction', while 'man' is a secondary subject), and terms that signify something that sustains as an inherent form what is signified by the first subject (e.g., 'heat' is the first subject of 'calefactive', while 'fire'

41. (OPh I, 517).
42. *Ord.*, Prologue, q.4, (OTh I, 144–45).

is a secondary subject).[43] Thus, when 'capable of instruction' is demonstrated of 'man', it is not the definition of 'man', but the definition of 'intellectual soul' that occurs as the middle term, since the latter is the first subject of *passio* 'capable of instruction'.[44]

Further, according to Ockham, Aristotle did not mean to suggest that every *passio* is demonstrable of its first subject. For while *passiones* are alike connotative terms that signify directly what their subjects signify, they divide into four groups on the basis of their oblique signification. (i) Those in the first group signify obliquely a form that really inheres in what the subject signifies. For example, 'colorable' has the nominal definition 'something that can have color' and obliquely signifies really inherent color qualities. Such *passiones* can be known to pertain to their first subjects only by experience.[45] (ii) The second group obliquely signify things that are neither essential parts of nor really inherent in what their first subjects signify. For example, 'God is creative' asserts this sort of *passio* of 'God', because 'creative' obliquely signifies neither an essential part of God nor any accident inhering in Him, but the really distinct things that He makes out of nothing. These *passiones* cannot be demonstrated of their first subjects either but can be known to pertain to them only through experience.[46] (iii) *Passiones* of the third type obliquely signify parts of what the subject signifies and something that does not inhere in it. For example 'what has three angles equal to two right angles' signifies a triangle directly and obliquely signifies its parts and other angles (viz., the two right angles) that are not part of it.[47] And (iv) *passiones* of the fourth type signify the parts of what the subject signifies negatively and obliquely. For example, 'corruptible' has the nominal definition 'something whose parts can not exist or one

43. Q.4, (OTh I, 148).
44. *Ibid.*, q.5, (OTh I, 165–66); *Summa logicae* III–2, c.12, (OPh I, 527).
45. *Ibid.*, (OPh I, 526–27); *Ord.*, Prologue, q.4, (OTh I, 144).
46. *Summa logicae* III–2, c.12, (OPh I, 526–27); c.35, (OPh I, 573–74); *Ord.*, Prologue, q.1, (OTh I, 50–51); q.4, (OTh I, 150–51).
47. *Summa logicae* III–2, c.12, (OPh I, 526).

of whose parts can be separate from the other' and so signifies substance directly and its parts negatively and obliquely.[48] Ockham says that *passiones* of the last two types can be demonstrated of their first subjects. It is these that are involved in mathematical demonstrations, and in such cases the definition of the subject is always or frequently the middle term,[49] as Aristotle says. Further, whether or not *passiones* can be demonstrated of their first subjects, they can be demonstrated of secondary subjects, using the first subject or a concrete term corresponding to the first subject as the middle. For example, 'Every being is one; God is a being; therefore God is one' can be a demonstration[50] and "perhaps" 'Every being is good; God is a being; therefore God is good'.[51] Again, 'heat' is the first subject of 'calefactive' and from 'Every heat is calefactive' we can derive 'Every hot is a calefactive' to which we can add 'Every fire is hot' as the minor to conclude 'Every fire is calefactive'.[52] And 'Every triangle has three; and isosceles is a triangle; therefore an isosceles has three',[53] and 'Everyone having an intellectual soul is capable of instruction; every man has an intellectual soul; therefore every man is capable of instruction'.[54]

According to Aristotle, knowledge properly speaking is of what cannot be otherwise than it is. Hence the conclusion of my demonstration must be necessary. And although "you can in fact infer the necessary even from a non-necessary premiss, just as you can infer the true from the not true,"[55] still the premisses of a demonstration must be necessary. For they are supposed to be a basis not only for knowing some proposition which is necessary, but for knowing that it is necessary. In the case of a demonstration *propter quid*, they are supposed to explain not

48. *Ibid.*
49. *Ibid.*, (OPh I, 527); *Ord.*, Prologue, q.4, (OTh I, 150–51).
50. *Summa logicae* III–2, c.37, (OPh I, 576).
51. *Ord.*, Prologue, q.2, (OTh I, 115).
52. *Summa logicae* III–2, c.38, (OPh I, 577–78).
53. *Ord.*, Prologue, q.2, (OTh I, 120); q.4, (OTh I, 148).
54. *Ibid.*, q.2, (OTh I, 120).
55. *Posterior Analytics* I, 6, 75a2–4.

only why what the conclusion signifies is a fact, but why it is a necessary fact.[56] Because he believed that species really exist eternally and necessarily, Aristotle saw no difficulty in the categorical assertoric propositions of 'Every M is P, every S is M; therefore every S is P ' meeting this condition.

The possibility of any "Aristotelian" science about created things seemed challenged by the Christian doctrine of creation, however. For according to it,

(A) God exists necessarily and everything else exists by His free and contingent volition.

Hence, that any creatures of a given species really exist is a matter of God's free and contingent choice. If propositions of the form 'Every S is M ' entail propositions of the form 'S 's exist' and 'M 's exist', then the A-proposition cannot be necessary unless the existential assertions are. It seems to follow that none of the propositions in Aristotle's paradigm scientific syllogism is necessary, where the names of created natures, their definitions and *passiones* are substituted for 'S ', 'M ', and 'P '.

Ockham noticed this problem and admits that no assertoric syllogism in Barbara—or for that matter any that includes an affirmative premiss or conclusion—could count as a demonstration about corruptible things. He writes,

> ...although it is incompatible with Aristotle's claims, it is nevertheless true that no proposition formed from [terms] that signify corruptible things only and that is merely affirmative and merely categorical and merely present tense, can be the premiss or conclusion of a demonstration, since any such proposition is contingent...[57]

Nor is Ockham willing to revise his truth conditions and construe 'Man is a rational animal' as a covert conditional equivalent to 'If a man exists, a man is a rational animal', since this would obliterate the distinction between categoricals

56. *Ibid.*, 75a13–18, cited by Ockham, *Summa logicae* III–2, c.5, (OPh I, 512).
57. *Summa logicae* III–2, c.5, (OPh I, 512–13).

and conditionals.[58] Nevertheless, he refuses to conclude that physics and biology cannot be Aristotelian sciences, since

> ...many propositions composed from such terms can be the premisses or conclusions of a demonstration. For the conditional propositions or their equivalents can be necessary. For the proposition 'If a man exists, an animal exists' and the proposition 'If a man laughs, an animal laughs', and the proposition 'Every man can laugh', where the subject stands for those that can be, and propositions likewise equivalent to them are necessary.[59]

Thus, "the propositions formed from terms that signify such contingent things and that enter into a demonstration are necessary and not merely present tense and assertoric, categorical and affirmative, but are either negative or molecular or *de possibile* or some other mode or equivalent."[60]

Unfortunately, Ockham does not pursue any of these proposals systematically or in detail. Given his extensive treatment of modal syllogisms in *Summa logicae* III–1 (44 chapters), one might expect him to favor the modal approach, replacing the present tense assertoric syllogism

> Every hot thing is calefactive.
> Every fire is hot.
> Therefore, every fire is calefactive,

whose premisses and conclusions are contingent, because it is contingent that any fire or hot things exist and contingent that any heat inheres in fire, with the *de possible* syllogism

> It is possible that every hot thing is calefactive.
> It is possible that every fire is hot.
> Therefore, it is possible that every fire is calefactive,

58. *Ibid.*, (OPh I, 513).
59. *Ibid*.
60. *Ibid.*, (OPh I, 513–14).

whose premises and conclusion are necessary but still about things that are by nature susceptible to generation and corruption.

Nevertheless, this proposal carries heavy costs. For the premises and conclusion of the *de possibile* syllogism have to be distinguished with respect to composition and division. Where all are taken in the sense of composition, the inference is not formally valid (as can be seen by substituting 'man' for 'S', 'white thing' for 'M', and 'donkey' for 'P' in 'It is possible that every M is P; it is possible that every S is M; therefore it is possible that every S is P'.[61] If the propositions are taken uniformly in the sense of division, they must once again be distinguished as to whether their subject terms supposit for those that are for those that can be (see Part Two, chapter 11 above). And only the second construal removes the originally troublesome implication that generable and corruptible things actually exist. The resultant inference *is* formally valid,[62] but the conclusion tells us rather less than we wanted to know. Cast anachronistically into possible worlds semantics, it asserts only that there is a possible world w in which fire exists, and every fire in w is such that in some possible world w' (which may or may not be identical with w) it is calefactive, whereas the natural scientist had hoped to show that every fire (if any) *in the actual world* has the power (*virtus*) to produce heat (is calefactive) *in the actual world*. The necessity of the premises and conclusion has thus been bought at the price of considerable information!

To be sure, Ockham has the resources to extract more from such conclusions. For (as we shall see in detail in Part Four, chapter 18 below) if he denies that any created nature is necessarily instantiated, he retains the Aristotelian assumption that being of a certain species is what makes a thing to be a certain causal power (*virtus*). Hence, if heat is capable of producing heat and so is the power (*virtus*) to produce heat, it is so by its

61. Cf. *ibid*. III–1, c.23, (OPh I, 419).
62. *Ibid*., (OPh I, 420).

very nature. And by the Uniformity of Nature Principle, if this
heat is the power (*virtus*) to produce heat, so is every other. But
since what is of a given species cannot exist without being a
member of that species, the causal powers of a given thing will
not vary from possible world to possible world. Thus, given the
de possible proposition 'It is possible that every hot is calefactive', we can derive 'Necessarily, if something is a hot thing, it is
calefactive', and further 'Necessarily, if fire is a hot thing, it
is calefactive'. Nevertheless, such repairs will not restore the
Aristotelian ideal of a demonstration that will display the desired ultimate conclusion together with its explanation in a
single valid syllogism.

These observations suggest that Ockham could better reha-
bilitate demonstrations *propter quid* with conditional than
with *de possibile* propositions, since the former can assert
essential connections as well as assertoric categorical propositions, while the latter cannot. Thus, 'Every hot thing is calefactive, and every fire is hot; therefore every fire is calefactive'
could be replaced with 'If something is hot, it is calefactive, and
if fire has heat, it is hot; therefore, if fire has heat, it is calefactive', all of whose propositions are necessary. Likewise 'Every
substance is susceptible of contraries, and evey man is a substance; therefore every man is susceptible of contraries' can
be replaced with 'If anything is a substance, it is susceptible
of contraries, and if anything is a man, it is a substance; therefore if anything is a man it is susceptible of contraries', and
'Everything that has an intellectual soul is capable of instruction, and every man has an intellectual soul; therefore every
man is capable of instruction' with 'If anything has an intellectual soul, it is capable of instruction, and if anything is a man, it
has an intellectual soul; therefore if anything is a man, it
is capable of instruction'. Sometimes Ockham does mention
syllogisms involving temporal conditions—e.g., 'Whenever the
earth is in between the sun and the moon, the moon is eclipsed;
and whenever the sun is in such and such a position and the
moon in such and such a position, then the earth is in between

the sun and the moon; therefore, then the moon is eclipsed'.[63] But following Aristotle, his focus there is on phenomena that happen sometimes and not others and so are not universal with respect to time. Clearly, he does not envision conditional syllogisms as the paradigms of demonstrations *propter quid* when he devotes over 54 chapters to categorical syllogisms and allots only sixteen lines to syllogisms involving molecular propositions,[64] leaving it to the reader to adapt his remarks about categoricals to conditionals.

After examining ideal demonstrations (demonstrations *propter quid* and *a priori*) that give knowledge of a necessary truth together with its explanation, Aristotle recognizes other demonstrations (demonstrations *quia*) which give knowledge of the fact only.[65] Ockham explains that "a demonstration *propter quid*" is one "which is from necessary and prior propositions and which puts a stop to every doubt and every question about the conclusion," while "a demonstration that either does not proceed from prior premises or does not put a stop to every question about the conclusion."[66] Borrowing from Aristotle's illustrations, Ockham offers 'When the moon is in such and such a position, then the moon is eclipsed; the moon is now in such and such a position; therefore the moon is eclipsed now' as an argument *propter quid* and *a priori*, from cause to effect, whereas 'When the moon is eclipsed, the earth is in between the sun and the moon; the moon is eclipsed now; therefore the earth is in between the sun and the moon' as an argument *a posteriori*, from effect to cause.[67] (Ockham warns that neither is it strictly speaking a demonstration, because 'The moon is eclipsed now' is a contingent premiss; the examples are taken merely because they illustrate the contrast between *a*

---

63. *Ord.*, Prologue, q.4, (OTh I, 154–55); cf. *Summa logicae* III–2, c.15, (OPh I, 530–31); c.17, (OPh I, 532–34); c.19, (OPh I, 536–37).
64. *Ibid*. III–1, c.68, (OPh I, 501–502).
65. *Posterior Analytics* I, 13, 78a22ff.
66. *Summa logicae* III–2, c.19, (OPh I, 536).
67. *Ibid.*, c.17, (OPh I, 533).

priori and *a posteriori*.[68] On the other hand, the syllogism 'No non-animal breathes; a plant is a non-animal; therefore a plant does not breathe' is *a priori*, since it is from cause to effect. But it is not *propter quid*, because it does not give the immediate positive cause why a plant does not breathe.[69]

3. DIVISIONS AMONG INFERENCES

Ockham's acceptance of the traditional syllabus has introduced an apparent disorganization into his discussion of arguments. For Part III plunges us immediately into extensive treatments of the syllogism (III–1) and demonstration (III–2). To find general remarks about the relation of inference, we have to turn back to his sketch chapter on conditional propositions (II, c.31), and his ninefold division among inferences in general is postponed until the outset of III–3. In the first of these passages, Ockham makes it clear that he regards conditional propositions of the form 'if p, then q' 'not p unless q' as equivalent to inferences of the form 'p; therefore q'. Accordingly, he says that 'a conditional proposition is true, when the antecedent implies (*infert*) the consequent, and not otherwise',[70] so that the conditions under which inferences do or do not hold good are the same as those under which conditional propositions are true or false. In the chapter on conditional propositions, he says something about what is *not* necessary for the truth of a conditional proposition: viz.,

...neither the truth of the antecedent nor the truth of the consequent is required for the truth of a conditional. In fact, sometimes the conditional is necessary, and each of its parts is impossible. For example, the proposition 'if Socrates is a donkey, Socrates is capable of braying'.[71]

And at the end of his discussion of inferences, he lays down the

68. *Ibid.*
69. *Ibid.*, c.19, (OPh I, 537); c.20 (OPh I, 538).
70. *Ibid.* II, c.31, (OPh I, 347).
71. *Ibid.*

general rule that

> The false never follows from the true, and therefore whenever the antecedent is true and the consequent false, the inference does not hold good,[72]

thereby making it necessary for the truth of a conditional proposition or validity of an inference that

(A) It is not the case that the antecedent is true and the consequent false.

An attractive hypothesis[73] sees Ockham as making (A) *definitive* of the fundamental relation of inference and distinguishing subordinate "species" under this "genus" by the stipulation of other, non-truth functional criteria.[74] Difficulties in making out this contention will be examined below.

As for their divisions, Ockham classifies inferences on the basis of their terms—whether they are first or second intentions[75] and whether they have personal, simple, or material supposition[76]—and on the basis of the quantity,[77] quality[78] and modality[79] of the propositions. And while the latter help to articulate Ockham's discussion in succeeding chapters,[80] the first three—between inferences that hold good by intrinsic or by extrinsic means, between formal and material inferences, and between simple and as-of-now inferences—are the most important.

72. *Ibid*. III–3, c.38, (OPh I, 727).

73. This claim was first made by Boehner in "Does Ockham Know of Material Implication?" in *Collected Articles of Ockham*, #19, 319–351, and later defended by me in "Did Ockham Know of Material and Strict Implication? A Reconsideration," *Franciscan Studies* N.S. XXXIII (1973): 5–37.

74. Eleonore Stump summarizes my position this way in her 1980 lectures to the Council for Philosophical Studies Seminar on Medieval Logic.

75. Fourth distinction, *Summa logicae* III–3, c.1, (OPh I, 590).

76. Fifth distinction, *ibid*.

77. Sixth distinction, *ibid*.

78. Seventh and eighth distinctions, *ibid*.

79. Ninth distinction, *ibid*.

80. *Ibid*., c.2–9.

I suggest that the controlling interest between Ockham's deviant and untidy versions of them is his desire to subsume enthymemes under the rubric of formal inferences by indicating how they can be reduced to syllogisms. Let us test these hypotheses by examining each division in turn.

(3.1) *Intrinsic versus Extrinsic Means.* The division between intrinsic and extrinsic means has its historical roots in discussions of the topics. Boethius and Cicero divided the art of discourse into dialectic, the art of finding arguments, and logic, the art of judging them.[81] Aristotle's *Topics* had dealt with the former and constituted an attempt to systematize the method of dialectic in Plato's dialogues.[82] And in *De topicis differentiis*, Boethius summarizes the efforts of Themistius and Cicero at further simplification. Begin with the question, "Is *S P*?" or "Is it the case that *S* is *P*?" In debate one must give an affirmative or negative answer and defend it with arguments. Themistius undertook to aid the disputant by providing a convenient catalogue of places (*topoi*; *loci*) where such arguments might be sought. In trying to prove a connection (lack of connection) betwen *S*'s and *P*'s, one may look either to "the substance, of the terms" '*S*' and '*P*' for "intrinsic grounds" or to what is outside and separated from them for "extrinsic grounds." Primary among intrinsic grounds would be the *definition* or *description* of absolute terms (see Part Two, chapter 10 above) or the *interpretation of the name* for connotative terms. For example, if the question is whether whiteness is a substance, the disputant may appeal to the maxim "whatever the definition/description/interpretation is predicated of (denied of) the term defined/described/interpreted is predicated of (denied of)" and, recalling that substance is described as that which can be the substance of any accident, conclude that since whiteness is the

81. For this point and for otherwise helpful discussions of the topics, see Otto Bird, "The Tradition of the Logical Topics: Aristotle to Ockham," *Journal of the History of Ideas* XXIII (1962): 307–323, and Eleonore Stump, *Boethius's 'De topicis differentiis'*, Book I, 29.

82. See Stump, *op. cit.*, 13–26.

subject of no accident, whiteness is not a substance.[83] Other intrinsic grounds are taken not from the substance but from things that go together with it. For example, the disputant may consider whether S 's are (universal, integral, quantitative, modal, spatial, or temporal) *wholes* of which P 's are *parts*, or vice versa. If the question is whether God exists here and now, the disputant can appeal to the maxim "what suits the whole fits the part" and reason that since God exists everywhere and always, He exists here and now.[84] Again, the disputant may inquire about the *causes* or *effects* of S 's and P 's to see if they somehow connect or exclude one from another. If the question is whether the Moors have weapons, the disputant may recall that weapons are made of iron and appealing to the maxim "if the material cause is lacking, the thing made from it is also lacking," conclude that since the Moors lack iron, they lack weapons.[85] Finally, other intrinsic grounds are taken from *concomitant accidents*, *uses*, the *generation* and the *corruption* of substance, yielding maxims "if the use/generation of a thing is good (bad), the thing is good (bad)" and "if the destruction of a thing is good (bad), the thing is bad (good)."[86]

Extrinsic grounds comprise a still more diverse collection. For they include (contrary, relative, privative, and contradictory) *opposites* that lie so far outside the substance of the terms as to be incompatible with it. As an illustration, a disputant asked whether virtue is praised, might appeal to the maxim "contraries are suited to contraries," and argue that since virtue is contrary to vice and vice is reviled, virtue is praised. Likewise, faced with whether seeing is a proprium of those who have eyes, he might conclude that it is not, calling on the maxim "where the privation can be present, the possession is not a proprium" and observing that the blind have eyes and do not see.[87] Then there is a group of strategies that yield what might, broad-

---

83. *De topicis differentiis*, Book II, (Stump ed., 50).
84. *Ibid.*, 52–53.
85. *Ibid.*, 53.
86. *Ibid.*, 53–54.
87. *Ibid.*, 56.

ly speaking, be called arguments from analogy.[88] For a disputant might argue from *the more/greater* to *the less/lesser*, using the maxims "if what seems more to inhere does not inhere, what seems less to inhere does not inhere" (e.g., if a king cannot take the castle, neither can a knight) and "if what seems less to inhere does inhere, so does what seems more to inhere" (e.g., if the knight can take the castle, so can the king). Again, there are arguments from *proportion*: e.g., asked whether the ruler of a city should be chosen by lot, a disputant might argue that they should not, given that even pilots of ships should not be chosen by lot.[89] Again, their are arguments *from* quantitative or qualitative *similarity*. Again, there is an argument *from transumption* when the question is transferred from what is less known to what is more known. Transumption from one thing to another occurs in the *Republic* when Socrates approaches the question of justice in the republic by looking at justice in the individual. Transumption from one word to another occurs when an obscure term is replaced with a familiar one: e.g., if you ask whether a philosopher is envious, the question is replaced with whether a wise man is envious.[90] Finally, there are arguments from *authority* or *judgment* which appeal to the maxim "what seems true to everyone or the many or the wise should not be gainsaid."[91]

Not finding the division between intrinsic and extrinsic grounds entirely exhaustive, Themistius also lists some *intermediate grounds*. First, there is a "*case*" or the inflection of a principal name into an adverb. For example, 'justice' is inflected into 'justly', and one can legitimately reason that since justice is good, what is done justly is good. Similarly, *conjugates* are drawn from the same thing in different ways—e.g., 'justly' and 'just' from justice. And the argument 'if what is done justly is good, what is just is good' holds good. Finally, there are arguments from *division* or exclusive disjunction, which form

88. As Bird notices, *op. cit.*, 316.
89. Boethius, *De topicis differentiis*, Book II, 55.
90. *Ibid.*, 56–57.
91. *Ibid.*, 54.

the basis of disjunctive syllogisms.[92]

Boethius calls 'description', 'whole', 'cause', 'generation', 'contraries', 'authority', 'cases', and the like the "differences of the topics," whereas the self-evident propositions such as 'whatever the description is predicated of, the described term is predicated of' and 'contraries are suited to contraries' are called "maximal propositions."[93] At first, emphasis was put on their use in *finding* arguments, but gradually maximal propositions came to be treated more as warrants for inferences, usually one-premiss inferences. Thus, Peter of Spain gives substantially the same catalogue of topics as Themistius does, but the context of looking for arguments in a debate has disappeared.[94] Further, Peter of Spain is more concerned to list topical maxims than Boethius; he states 81 where Boethius offered 25.[95] William of Sherwood repeats the tabulation in his discussion of dialectical syllogisms. While he does identify the differentiae and maximal propositions as sources of arguments to settle questions, he also indicates—in every case but definition, description, and the interpretation of a name—how the one-premiss inference in question could be reduced to a syllogism.[96] And he even construes the division between intrinsic, extrinsic, and intermediate topics as one among the sorts of middle terms involved in such reductions. Thus, he writes that the topics

> are also divided into intrinsic, extrinsic, and mediate grounds, [a division] which is understood the following way. When there is some doubt about a proposition, we first put it in the form of a question; then we find a middle term; and then we syllogize it, either affirmatively or negatively. So when the argument is extracted from an internal property of one of the terms in question, the ground is called intrinsic; when from an extrinsic property the grounds are called extrinsic; when from a mediate property, the ground is called mediate.[97]

92. *Ibid.*, 57–58.
93. *Ibid.*, 47–48.
94. *Tractatus* V, (De Rijk ed., 55–78), as Stump notes, *op. cit.*, 235–36.
95. As Bird says, *op. cit.*, 313.
96. *Introduction to Logic*, chap.4, 69–102.
97. *Ibid.*, sec.2, 71.

Topical maxims serve as inference warrants because such middles are available for syllogistic reductions.

Ockham has so reworked these materials from the Boethian topics in *Summa logicae* III–3, c.2–9, that their traditional source is easy to miss.[98] To begin with, some traditional labels are entirely missing. Unlike both his predecessors—Peter of Spain and William of Sherwood—and his successors—Albert of Saxony,[99] John Buridan,[100] and the authors of the *Tractatus logicae minor*[101] and *Elementarium logicae*[102]—Ockham never mentions "topics" by name but incorporates the entire discussion as a subdivision of nonsyllogistic inferences.[103] Further, he does not speak in the traditional way of "maximal propositions" or "maxims" but offers "rules" of inference instead. Interestingly, some of his successors combine both usages, as when the author of the *Tractatus logicae minor* describes a topic as "*a maximal proposition*, that is *a rule* from which an argument is drawn and holds and can be proved"[104] and when Albert of Saxony declares that "*a topical maxim* is

98. I did in my article "Did Ockham Know of Material and Strict Implication? A Reconsideration," 15–21, when I dismissed the distinction between intrinsic and extrinsic means as "of interest, not so much for its own sake, but because it is the basis for Ockham's third distinction between formal and material inferences" (15). Bird remarks on the transformation of the materials from the topics by Ockham in "The Tradition of the Logical Topics: Aristotle to Ockham," 317, and in "Topic and Consequence in Ockham's Logic," *Notre Dame Journal of Formal Logic* II (1961): 65–78, especially 68–69.

99. *Perutilis logicae*, (Venice, 1522; repr. Hildesheim, 1974), Tractatus quartus, c.19–24, fol.32vb–37rb.

100. *Compendium totius logicae*, (Venice, 1499), Tractatus sextus, unpaginated and unfoliated.

101. Eligius M. Buytaert, "The *Tractatus logicae minor* of Ockham," *Franciscan Studies* N.S. XXIV (1964): 34–100, Liber V, 'De locis et regulis consequentiarum,' 77–81.

102. Eligius M. Buytaert, "The *Elementarium logicae* of Ockham," *Franciscan Studies* N.S. XXV (1965): 151–276, Liber VI, 'De locis,' 253–276.

103. *Summa logicae* III–3, c.1, (OPh I, 587).

104. Liber V, 'De locis et regulis consequentiarum,' (Buytaert ed., 77).

said to be *a rule* that can confirm and prove an inference."[105]

More importantly, Ockham's presentation of the rules is organized in a completely different way. Where earlier authors followed the syllabus of the Boethian topical differences and listed all the maxims of a given topical difference together, Ockham's focus is on types of inferences, and he catalogues inference rules in accordance with the above mentioned ninefold distinction. Thus, he first lists rules for inferences with affirmative premises and universal conclusions that hold for all[106] or for only some[107] predicates; then those for inferences with a universal negative conclusion that hold for all[108] or for only some[109] predicates; then those for inferences involving particular or indefinite propositions;[110] then rules for inferring an affirmative from an affirmative by an extrinsic mean;[111] those for inferring negatives from negatives;[112] and finally for inferring a negative from an affirmative or vice versa.[113] In this presentation, for example, rules for the intrinsic topic relatives and the intrinsic topics whole and part and the intermediate topic of conjugates get classified together under rules for inferences with universal affirmative conclusions that hold for some predicates only[114] and rules for the intrinsic topics definition, description, and interpretation are scattered among the chapters on different quantities and qualities.[115]

Given all these changes, it is not suprising that Ockham's distinction between intrinsic and extrinsic means has shifted considerably from the traditional division among intrinsic, extrinsic, and intermediate topics. His explicit account of it in

---

105. *Op. cit.*, Tractatus quartus, c.19, fol.33ra.
106. *Summa logicae* III–3, c.2.
107. *Ibid.*, c.3.
108. *Ibid.*, c.4.
109. *Ibid.*, c.5.
110. *Ibid.*, c.6.
111. *Ibid.*, c.7.
112. *Ibid.*, c.8.
113. *Ibid.*, c.9.
114. *Ibid.*, c.3, (OPh I, 596–98).
115. *Ibid.*, c.2, 4, 6, 8.

Summa logicae III–3, c.1, runs as follows:

> ...the inference holds by intrinsic means when it holds by virtue of a proposition formed from the same terms. For example, the inference 'Socrates does not run; therefore a man does not run' holds good by virtue of the mean 'Socrates is a man'. Thus, if the proposition 'Socrates is a man' were not true, the inference would not hold good. An inference holds by extrinsic means, however, when it holds by a general rule that has no more to do with these terms than with others. For example, the inference 'Only a man is a donkey; therefore every donkey is a man' does not hold by means of a true proposition formed from the terms 'man' and 'donkey' but by the general rule 'The exclusive and universal from transposed terms signify the same and convert'. And all syllogisms hold through such means.[116]

Responding to the objection that

> the inference 'Socrates does not run; therefore a man does not run' holds through the extrinsic mean 'The inference from the singular to the indefinite with a negation afterwards hold good'...,

Ockham grants that

> it does hold through the extrinsic mean remotely, mediately, and inadequately, since besides this general rule more is required—viz., that Socrates is a man. Therefore, it holds more immediately and more adequately through the mean 'Socrates is a man', which is an intrinsic mean.[117]

Whereas traditionally, the adjectives 'intrinsic', 'extrinsic', and 'intermediate' modified 'topics' and alternatively classified differentiae or metalinguistically stated maximal propositions, Ockham uses the term 'intrinsic mean' to refer to the object-language proposition 'Socrates is a man' in which a term from the conclusion is predicated of a term from the premiss of the original inference 'Socrates does not run; therefore a man does not run', while 'extrinsic mean' stands for general metalinguistic rules such as 'The exclusive and universal from

116. (OPh I, 588).
117. (OPh I, 588–89).

transposed terms signify the same and convert' and 'The inference from the singular to the indefinite with a negation afterwards' holds good.

One commentator[118] maps Ockham's procedure onto traditional discussions by seeing extrinsic means as analogous to topical maxims and intrinsic means as roughly analogous to topical differences. Consider the inference 'No animal is running; therefore no donkey is running'. On Peter of Spain's scheme, we see that it holds good by realizing that 'animal' is the *genus* of 'donkey' and locating the maxim 'Whatever is removed from the genus is removed from the species' under the topical difference genus; so that there are three factors involved:

> *The Inference*: 'No animal is running; therefore no donkey is running'

> *Topical Difference:* Genus—'Animal' is the genus of 'donkey'

> *Topical Maxim*: Whatever is removed from the genus is removed from the species.

Ockham cites this inference as an example under the rule 'Negatively from a distributed superior to a distributed interior there is a simple inference'.[119] The suggestion is that for Ockham the latter general rule is an extrinsic mean, and we are informed that it applies—that 'animal' is *superior* to 'donkey'—by the intrinsic mean 'Every donkey is an animal'. Once again, three factors are involved:

> *The Inference:*   'No animal is running; therefore no don-

---

118. Otto Bird makes this proposal in "The Tradition of the Logical Topics: Aristotle to Ockham," 318–320, and also in "Topic and Consequence in Ockham's Logic," 70–73.

119. *Summa logicae* III–3, c.4, (OPh I, 598).

key is running'

Intrinsic Mean: 'Every donkey is an animal'

Extrinsic Mean: 'Negatively from a distributed superior to a distributed inferior there is a single inference'.

Applying this analysis to Ockham's example in *Summa logicae* III–3, c.1, we get

The Inference: 'Socrates is not running; therefore a man is not running'

Intrinsic Mean: 'Socrates is a man'

Extrinsic Mean: 'The inference from a singular to an indefinite with the negation afterwards holds good'.

The inference does not hold good by the extrinsic mean immediately or adequately, because without the intrinsic mean we do not know that the extrinsic mean applies to the inference in question.

This proposal faces several difficulties, however. First, it fails to explain the anomalous identification of intrinsic means with object-language propositions "formed from the same terms" as the premiss and conclusion of the original inference. If Ockham intended intrinsic means to inform us of which general rule might apply to the original inference, would he not have identified them with metalinguistic statements such as 'Socrates is a singular of man' in which the terms of the original inference occur in simple rather than personal supposition?[120]

Second, it appears from the treatment of the first example

---

120. Bird acknowledges this difficulty, but does not seem to think it undermines the gist of his analysis, "The Tradition of the Logical Topics: Aristotle to Ockham," 320, and "Topic and Consequence in Ockham's Logic," 73.

that this interpretation would count as extrinsic means all of the general rules for non-syllogistic inferences mentioned in *Summa logicae* III–3, c.2–9. Every inference that holds good immediately by an intrinsic mean, holds good mediately by some general rule under which it falls. As general and metalinguistic, none could count as an intrinsic mean for Ockham. But this proposal divides his extrinsic means into two classes: those containing terms that signify the terms of the original inference—e.g., 'Negatively from a distributed superior to a distributed inferior there is a simple inference'—and those that fix on something else—e.g. 'The exclusive and universal from transposed terms signify the same and convert'. Hence, all of the traditional topical maxims—whether intrinsic, extrinsic, or intermediate—would be lumped by Ockham into the category of extrinsic means.

The trouble is that with one exception, Ockham never so labels the general rules taken from the traditional intrinsic topics, or even those taken from the traditional extrinsic topics of opposites. *Summa logicae* III–3, c.7 is the only chapter explicitly announced as having to do with extrinsic means.[121] Its list includes one rule from the traditional intermediate topics of Conjugates and Cases:

(R2) If the abstract is true of the abstract, the concrete is true of the concrete and the adverb of the adverb,

on which Ockham imposes numerous qualifications; one rule corresponding to Peter of Spain's intrinsic topic Whole in Mode:

(R3) If an inference is good, it will hold good when the same addition is made to the premiss and the conclusion,

so that since 'A man runs; therefore an animal runs' holds, 'A white man runs; therefore a white animal runs' holds, too;[122]

121. (OPh I, 610).
122. (OPh I, 613).

several rules not listed by Peter of Spain and William of Sherwood, which license a kind of analogical reasoning and would fit with their extrinsic topics of More, Less, and Proportion, although they do not hold good in general:

(R4) If the simple is predicated of the simple, then the comparative of the comparative, and the superlative of the superlative,

as in 'A sinner is evil; therefore a worse sinner is more evil',

(R5) If the singular is true of the singular, the plural is true of the plural,

and

(R6) If the plural is true of the plural, the singular is true of the singular;[123]

and finally the extrinsic topic of authority:

(R7) What a wise man says is true,

which Ockham says "is not a general rule unless the author is one who cannot err or one whose words are instructed by someone who cannot"—viz., God or those instructed by Him.[124]

The other principal class of rules explicitly identified as extrinsic means by Ockham fix on relations among the syncategorematic words in the premiss(es) and conclusion. His examples of rules governing one-premiss inferences are

(R8) The inference from the universal to the exclusive with the terms transposed holds good,[125]

and

123. (OPh I, 615–17).
124. (OPh I, 614).
125. *Ibid*., c.1, (OPh I, 588); *Expos. Elench*. II, c.7, (OPh III, 204–205).

(R9) The inference from a singular to an indefinite with the
      negation afterwards holds good.[126]

Regarding two-premiss inferences, Ockham twice says that all
syllogisms hold good through extrinsic means,[127] and gives the
example of

(R10) From a *de necessario* major and an assertoric minor, a
       necessary conclusion follows[128]

And he remarks that (R9) and (R10) both have to do with the
form of a proposition.[129] But no rules of this kind were ever included among the traditional lists of topical maxims—whether
intrinsic, extrinsic, or intermediate—presumably because they
were concerned with form directly and so not primarily part of
the subject matter of dialectical reasoning. Hence, if Ockham's
class of extrinsic means pirates, it does not do so in the way required by the above interpretation.

Focussing on one-premiss inferences, I am inclined to identify intrinsic means with the premisses that would have to be
added to the original arguments to reduce them to valid syllogisms. The general metalinguistic inference rules offered by
Ockham and not explicitly identified as extrinsic means would
be rules to inform us—usually by reference to the comparative
extensions of the categorematic terms in the orginal inference—when an inference can be so reduced. Thus, Ockham
tells us that, given appropriate quantities and qualities in
the premiss and conclusion, an intrinsic mean will always
(sometimes) be available when the categorematic terms are
related as defined term to definition, described term to description, interpreted name to its interpretation and vice versa—i.e.,
where they are coextensive;[130] as inferior to superior[131] or su-

126. *Summa logicae* III–3, c.1, (OPh I, 589).
127. *Ibid.*, (OPh I, 588); *Expos. Elench.* II, c.7, (OPh III, 205).
128. *Summa logicae* III–3, c.1, (OPh I, 589).
129. *Ibid.*
130. *Ibid.*, c.2, (OPh I, 591–92, 595).
131. *Ibid.*, (OPh I, 591).

perior to inferior[132] or part to whole or whole to part[133] —i.e., where the extension of one includes the extension of the other; as contraries, as privations and havings, as infinite to finite[134] as co-generic species[135]—i.e., where the extension of one is excluded from the extension of the other; or as correlatives[136]—i.e., where one cannot have extension unless the other does. The fact that such a reduction is available is what stands behind an extrinsic mean such as (R8), and that is why Ockham says the inference 'Socrates does not run; therefore a man does not run' holds not only more immediately, but also more adequately by the intrinsic mean 'Socrates is a man'. Thus, on this reading of *Summa logicae* III–3, c.2–9, most of the rules offered there for non-syllogistic inferences fit into a program of assimilating as many good inferences as possible to paradigm syllogisms.[137]

Support for this contention is found in a parallel discussion in Ockham's *Expositio super libros Elenchorum*:

> ...it must be said that (i) just as some inferences are formal because of *complexes*, so (ii) some because of *noncomplexes*. That is, (ii) some hold by an *intrinsic mean* and (i) some by an *extrinsic mean*. For the inference 'Every man runs; therefore Socrates runs' does not hold by reason of complexes, since if it did whenever the antecedent was universal and the consequent singular, the inference would hold good. Thus, the inference 'Every animal is a substance' would hold good. Therefore, the inference does not hold good because of *complexes* or through an *extrinsic mean*, but because of *noncomplexes* and through an *intrinsic mean*. For since Socrates is a man, *the mean* 'Socrates is a man' is true. Therefore, the above mentioned inference is good. Moreover, it is called an intrinsic mean, when adding that mean to the antecedent makes a good syllogism. For example, when one argues

132. *Ibid.*, c.4, (OPh I, 598).
133. *Ibid.*, c.3, (OPh I, 596–97).
134. *Ibid.*, c.9, (OPh I, 632–35).
135. *Ibid.*, (OPh I, 628–630).
136. *Ibid.*, c.3, (OPh I, 596).
137. I took this line in "Did Ockham Know of Material and Strict Implication? A Reconsideration," 18–19. Calvin Normore also suggests this approach in *The Logic of Time and Modality in the Later Middle Ages: The Contribution of William Ockham*, chap.5.

'Every man runs; therefore Socrates runs', the addition of the premiss 'Socrates is a man' will make a good syllogism that argues thus: Every man runs, Socrates is a man; therefore Socrates runs.

But some inferences hold (i) because of *complexes* and by *an extrinsic* mean. For example, the inference 'Only Socrates is a man; therefore every man is Socrates' holds good, and does so *because of complexes*, since evidently the argument is from an exclusive to a universal with the terms transposed. And it holds by an *extrinsic mean*—viz., through 'From an exclusive to a universal with the terms transposed is a good inference'. Moreover, it is called an extrinsic mean because when this added is to the antecedent, it does not make a syllogism. For there is no syllogistic form in the following: Only Socrates is a man; from the exclusive to the universal with the terms transposed is a good inference; therefore every man is Socrates...[138]

A non-syllogistic inference holds by an intrinsic mean when the noncomplexes or categorematic terms in its premiss and conclusion are such that a proposition may be formed from them and added to the premisses to yield a syllogism. In the *Ordinatio*, he adds the further stipulation that the resultant proposition be true:

> when such a proposition through which the inference should be reduced to a syllogism is true, then it is a good inference. When it is not true, then the inference does not hold good.[139]

But surely Ockham does not think that any proposition formed from the terms of the premiss and conclusion that meets these additional conditions suffices as an intrinsic mean. If it did, then every inference that has either a false premiss or a true conclusion could be seen to hold good by intrinsic means. For any such inference ('*p*; therefore *q*') can be cast into a valid disjunctive syllogism by adding a disjunctive premiss formed from the consequent and the denial of the antecedent ('-*p* v *q*'). In every case this additional premiss will have a true disjunct and will therefore be true. On the other hand, Ockham's inclusion of the traditional intrinsic topics of generation and corruption suggests he would not want to restrict the resultant syllogisms to

138. II, c.7, (OPh III, 204–205).
139. I, d.4, q.1, (OTh III, 15).

categorical syllogisms. And his further remark in the *Elenchi* —that a multi-premiss argument can be seen to hold "as it were" (in a broad sense) through an intrinsic mean when the addition of a true premiss formed from its terms yields a good argument—suggests that he does not want to restrict the resultant arguments to syllogisms either.[140] Unfortunately, Ockham does not bother to make his proposal precise in either work.

On the other hand, an argument is said to hold good by an extrinsic mean, when it holds by complexes—i.e., by a general rule having to do with the syncategorematics in its component propositions; and such a general rule having to do with syncategorematics cannot be added as a premiss to reduce the original argument to a syllogism. Here Ockham focuses exclusively on the second class of extrinsic means mentioned in the *Summa logicae*, and passes over the rules drawn from traditional topical maxims—such as (R1)—(R6)—entirely.

This text notwithstanding, my interpretation might be challenged. After all, if Ockham had intended the general rules for intrinsic means as reduction rules, would they not be of the form

(B) To reduce an inference whose terms are related as ____ to . . . to a syllogism, add a premiss in which ____ is predicated of . . . or vice versa,

where '____' and '. . .' take substitutions such as 'defined'/ 'definition'. Yet almost all of the rules Ockham states are variations on the following form

(C) There is a good inference from ____ to . . . and/or vice versa;

and none instantiates (B). Further, if Ockham had intended (C)-form rules to be applied in reductions, one might expect him to indicate this as he went along. After all, William of Sherwood, whose topical maxims often take the form

140. II, c.7, (OPh III, 205).

(D) Whatever is predicated of (removed from) ____ is
    predicated of (removed from) . . .

or

(E) ____ is predicated of whatever . . . is predicated of,

and not (B), regularly indicates in all cases except the intrinsic
topics drawn from substance—viz., definition, description, and
interpretation of a name—that and how such reductions can be
made.[141] But Ockham lists his rules for inferences involving
universal affirmatives and negatives[142] without once mentioning how they could supply the premiss for such reductions.
Surely these considerations make it extremely doubtful that
Ockham had a program of reducing enthymemes to syllogisms
explicitly in mind when he catalogued these rules.

In spite of these objections, I think the balance of evidence
suggests that the second interpretation is closer to Ockham's
meaning. After all, in both of his explicit accounts of what it is
for an argument to hold by an intrinsic mean, Ockham identifies
the intrinsic mean with the premiss that could be used to reduce
the original inference to a syllogism. Many of the rules in *Summa logicae* III–3, chapters 2 and 4 that are not explicitly so
applied correspond to maxims from the intrinsic topic of
substance for which Sherwood does not bother to spell out
reductions either. Further, commenting on variations of the rule

(R11) There is a good inference from something taken with a
      determination to the same term without it,

Ockham remarks

> ...for all such enthymemes can be reduced to a syllogism by assuming
> the proposition that is the intrinsic mean of such an inference. Thus,
> just as the inference 'Every man runs; therefore Socrates runs' holds
> good, because it is reduced to a syllogism by assuming the mean

141. *Introduction to Logic*, chap.4, 72–104.
142. *Summa logicae* III–3, c.2–5.

'Socrates is a man'; and arguing 'Every man runs, Socrates is a man; therefore Socrates runs'; so the inference 'Socrates runs quickly; therefore Socrates runs' holds good because the syllogism 'Everyone who runs quickly is a runner; Socrates runs quickly; therefore Socrates runs' holds good. And so on for the others...[143]

This passage has the air of saying that such rules hold good because syllogistic reductions that stand behind the other inference rules already listed are available for (R11) as well. And elsewhere he further classifies the original enthymemes on the basis of whether the added premiss would be necessary or contingent.[144] Finally, this interpretation explains the imperialism of Ockham's division of formal inferences, to which we now turn.

(3.2) *Formal versus Material Inferences*. Behind the division between formal and material inferences, lies the distinction between the *form* of a proposition or argument—which is determined by the arrangement of its syncategorematic components—and its *matter* or categorematic terms. Thus, we might expect a formal inference to be one whose validity could be established solely from the arrangement of its syncategorematics, while that of a material inference could be determined only by recourse to the particular categorematic terms it contains. But Ockham widens the class of formal inferences to include enthymemes as well. Thus, in *Summa logicae* III–3, c.1, he writes,

...Formal inferences are of two sorts. For some hold by extrinsic means that have to do with the form of propositions. Examples are rules such as 'From the exclusive to the universal formed from transposed terms, is a good inference', 'For a *de necessario* major premiss and an assertoric minor premiss, a *de necessario* conclusion follows', etc. Some hold by intrinsic means immediately, and mediately by extrinsic means having to do with the general conditions of propositions, not truth or falsity, necessity or impossibility. The inference 'Socrates is not running; therefore a man is not running' is an inference of this sort.[145]

143. *Ibid.*, c.6, (OPh I, 605).
144. *Ibid.*, c.8, (OPh I, 618).
145. (OPh I, 589).

And he concludes the above quoted passage from the *Elen-chi*-commentary by saying, "and so some inferences are formal because of complexes and through an extrinsic mean, some formal because of noncomplexes and through an intrinsic mean."[146] Some of the original intuition is preserved because—even on this broadened understanding—all formal inferences *ultimately* hold good by virtue of the arrangement of the syncategorematics in their premiss(es) and conclusion.

On the other hand, Ockham says,

> ...An inference is called 'material' when it holds precisely because of the terms and not because of some extrinsic mean having to do precisely with the general conditions of propositions. Inferences such as 'A man runs; therefore God exists' and 'A man is a donkey; therefore God does not exist' etc. are inferences of this sort.[147]

Ockham's sample material inferences do fall under the general rules 'The necessary follows from anything' and 'Anything follows from the impossible', respectively.[148] But the necessity of the conclusion and impossibility of the premiss in those inferences does not arise out of their logical form alone, but depends on the particular categorematic terms they contain. What Ockham explicitly rules out is that material inferences hold even mediately by extrinsic means having to do solely with the arrangements of syncategorematics in the premiss(es) and conclusion. Thus 'A man is a donkey; therefore a man is capable of braying' is not a material inference even though it can be seen to hold by means of the rule 'Anything follows from the impossible'. For it can also be seen to hold good immediately by the intrinsic mean 'Every donkey is capable of braying' and mediately by some extrinsic mean—e.g., that 'An *A* is *B* and every *B* is *C*; therefore an *A* is *C* ' is a good inference. Inferences that hold immediately by intrinsic means but mediately by extrinsic means are formal, not material inferences.[149] Likewise,

146. II, c.7, (OPh III, 205).
147. *Summa logicae* III–3, c.1, (OPh I, 589).
148. *Ibid.*, c.38, (OPh I, 730–31).
149. Given this characterization of material inferences, it follows that Ockham's favorite examples of material inferences would not be material in-

although Ockham does not explicitly consider examples with molecular premisses or conclusions, it seems that inferences of the form 'q; therefore p or not-p' and 'p & not-p; therefore q' would not count as material inferences for Ockham. The reason is that the necessity of the conclusion and impossibility of the premiss can be determined from their logical form alone apart from any consideration of their categorematic terms, and the inferences can thus be seen to hold by extrinsic means.

The examples Ockham gives are of an inference with a necessary conclusion and an inference with an impossible premiss, although as just noted not all such inferences are material. Presumably, the inferences 'Dodos are not extinct; therefore there are pink giraffes' and 'There are no pink giraffes; therefore dodos are extinct' would count as material inferences, too, because the falsity of the premiss and the truth of the conclusion, respectively, depends on their categorematic terms and is not determined solely by their logical form.

The author of the *Elementarium logicae* gives a different kind of example:

> A material inference is one which does not hold good by virtue of the mode of argument, but by virtue of the terms from which it is composed. For example, this follows—'An animal is disputing; therefore a man is disputing'—not because the inference from the superior to the inferior holds good, but because the predicate 'to dispute' cannot pertain to any animal other than man...[150]

Disputation is an activity in which only rational creatures can engage. Consequently, if it is true that an animal is disputing, it is true that a rational animal is disputing; and man is the only rational animal. This inference can thus be reduced to one that holds good by virtue of its logical form by the addition of two

ferences if Ockham allowed molecular propositions as intrinsic means. For as indicated in section (3.1) above, every inference with a false premiss and/or true conclusion could be seen to hold good immediately by intrinsic means, if a disjunction of the denial of the premiss and the conclusion were supplied as a premiss.

150. (Buytaert ed., 255).

premisses to the antecedent: viz., 'Every disputant is rational' and 'Every rational animal is a man'. It seems, therefore, that Ockham would class it among inferences that hold good by intrinsic means in the broad sense and hence as a formal inference of the second type. Perhaps the author of the *Elementarium* does not for two reasons: (i) that although the addition of these two true premisses does yield an argument that holds good by virtue of its logical form, it does not yield a valid *syllogism*; and (ii) the original inference is seen to hold good simply by considering the meaning of its categorematic terms, since 'Every disputant is rational' and 'Every rational animal is a man' are true by virtue of the definitions—nominal and real—of the categorematic terms.

(3.3) *Simple versus "As of Now" Inferences*. The last distinction we will discuss but the first explained by Ockham is that between simple inferences and inferences which hold good "as-of-now." He writes,

> ...There is an inference as-of-now when at some time the antecedent can be true without the consequent, but not at this time. For example, the inference 'Every animal runs; therefore Socrates runs' is good as of now, since at the time at which Socrates is an animal, the antecedent cannot be true without the consequent. Nevertheless, at some time it will be possible for the antecedent to be true without the consequent, because when Socrates will be dead, it will be possible for the antecedent to be true and the consequent false. There is a simple inference when at no time will it be possible for the antecedent to be true without the consequent. For example, the inference 'No animal runs; therefore no man runs' is simple, because it never will be possible for the proposition 'No animal runs' to be true without the proposition 'No man runs' being true, if it were formed.[151]

Put schematically,

(F)   An inference holds good as-of-now if and only if (i) it is not possible now for its antecedent to be true and its consequent false and (ii) at some time it will be possible for

---

151. *Summa logicae* III–3, c.1, (OPh I, 587–88).

the antecedent to be true and the consequent false,

whereas

(G) An inference is a simple inference if and only if (i) it is not possible now for its antecedent to be true and its consequent false, and (iii) at no time will it be possible for the antecedent to be true and the consequent false.

(F) and (G) add to condition

(A) It is not the case that the antecedent is true and the consequent false

further determinations of time and modality, and the division is between inferences that can fail to hold good at some future time and those which cannot.

Ockham brings in the notion of time because in his logic all propositions are tensed and thereby contain indexical temporal indicators (see chapters 10–11 above). As the times to which they refer change, so their truth-values may change. Thus, he has already contrasted as-of-now and simply assertoric (*de inesse ut nunc* and *de inesse simpliciter*) propositions as follows:

(H) A proposition is an as-of-now assertoric proposition if and only if the predicate can be truly affirmed of the subject at one time and not at another,

for example, 'Socrates is white', while

(J) A proposition is a simply assertoric proposition if and only if the predicate cannot pertain to the subject at one time and not at another but is always related to it the same way—either always truly predicated of it or never.[152]

152. *Ibid*. III–1, c.31, (OPh I, 441).

Ockham reads condition (A) as equivalent to

(A′) It is (present tense) not the case that the antecedent is (present tense) true and the consequent false,

and not as

(A″) It is (tenselessly) not the case that the antecedent is (tenselessly) true and the consequent false.

Since whether or not an inference holds good thus depends on the relative truth-values of its antecedent and consequent, the possiblity is opened that some inferences may hold good at one time and not at another.

Nevertheless, not even this possibility would arise in Ockham's logic, if he had restricted good inferences to those that are formally valid the first way. For they hold—i.e., satisfy condition (A)—by virtue of the arrangement of their syncategorematics alone; the relative truth-values of premiss and conclusion is constant regardless of the categorematic terms and of changes in their extensions. But Ockham has insisted on including others whose premiss(es) and conclusion have the relevant truth-values—and hence satisfy (A)—only by virtue of having certain categorematics rather than others and/or by virtue of those terms having certain extensions and not others—viz., material inferences and those that hold good immediately by intrinsic means. And in the above quoted passage, he notes that the enthymeme 'Every animal runs; therefore Socrates runs' holds good as of now, because the truth-value of the intrinsic mean 'Socrates is an animal' can and will change while the inference 'No animal runs; therefore no man runs' depends on a necessary premiss 'If something is a man, it is an animal' to be reduced to an argument formally valid the first way. Similarly, presumably the material inference 'Dodos are not extinct; therefore pink giraffes exist' holds good as of now, when dodos are extinct, but did not hold good in the past when there were dodos but no pink giraffes. It is in connection with such inferences that the distinction between simple and as-of-now inferences comes prominently into play.

What does Ockham mean when he says that "at some time the antecedent" of an as-of-now inference such as 'Every animal runs; therefore Socrates runs' "can be true without the consequent, but not at this time"? The answer is far from clear. (a) Surely not that it would be *contradictory* to suppose that the antecedent of such an inference is true now, while its consequent is false now. For there is no contradiction involved in supposing that 'Every animal is running' is true now, while 'Socrates is running' is false now. Indeed, this may happen now (1980) when Socrates is dead. And Ockham is too good a logician to have thought otherwise.[153]

(b) Medieval logicians including Ockham often contrasted absolute necessity (*necessitas absoluta*) or being absolutely necessary (*simpliciter necessarium*) "in such a way that it is contradictory for its opposite to be true"[154] and hence "in such a way that it neither can nor will be able to be false,"[155] with necessity *per accidens* which pertained to all true propositions about the past (see Part Five, chapters 27 and 28 below). Beginning with the assumption that not even God can alter the past, they reasoned that there are propositions such as 'Judas betrayed Christ', whose denials are not contradictory, but which are nevertheless such that nothing could happen now or

153. Stump does not think so. She maintains that "the denial of the consequence 'Every animal is running; therefore Socrates is running'" "is contradictory when Socrates is alive" but "is not contradictory when he is dead" (Lectures to the Council for Philosophical Studies Seminar on Medieval Logic (1980), 22). I do not see how this can be right unless it means merely that 'Every animal is running and Socrates is an animal and Socrates is not running' is contradictory, while 'Every animal is running and Socrates is not an animal and Socrates is not running' is not—in which case her comment is not relevant. For the issue is what Ockham means by saying that it is not possible that the antecedent 'Every animal is running' be true and the consequent 'Socrates is running' false, but this will be possible at some time; and whether he means that it is now contradictory that 'Every animal is running' be true and 'Socrates is running' false, although this will not be contradictory at another time.

154. *Quodl.* VI, q.2, (OTh IX, 590).

155. *Summa logicae* III–2, c.7, (OPh I, 526).

in the future that would make them false. They are necessary *per accidens*, since it is only because the facts were as they were (and in many cases there was a time at which something could have made them otherwise) that such propositions cannot now be false. Their corresponding denials are impossible *per accidens*.

(c) Some have suggested that Ockham understood the modalities in (F) and (G) in terms of time, equating 'possible' with 'true at some time', 'impossible' with 'true at no time', and 'necessary' with 'true at all times'.[156] On this reading, Ockham is seen as falling in with Aristotle's putative conflation of natural necessity and omnitemporality[157] and the temporal interpretation of modalities by the Stoics.[158] True, Ockham seems to say the opposite in *Summa logicae* II, c.9, where he remarks that

> ...this mental proposition 'God exists' is necessary—not because it is always true—because if it does not exist it is not true. But if it exists, it is true and cannot be false...[159]

But his concern here is with the fact that necessary propositions are not thereby necessary or perpetual beings and hence are not always true merely because they do not always exist (see Part Five, chapter 25 below). This focus is explicit in his remark that the necessary, perpetual, and incorruptible propositions required for demonstration are not necessary beings but "cannot be false" and are true in such a way that if formed they would not be false but only true and hence "cannot be false but only true."[160] But the last remark can be rendered temporally as the

156. Moody wanted to read Ockham this way; see *Truth and Consequence in Medieval Logic*, (Amsterdam, 1953), sec.IV.14, 74, and "Medieval Logic," in "History of Logic," *The Encyclopedia of Philosophy*, vol.4, (New York, 1967), 528–534, at 532.

157. See Jaakko Hintikka, "Aristotle and the 'Master Argument' of Diodorus," *American Philosophical Quarterly* I (1964): 101–114.

158. This comparison is made by Moody, *Truth and Consequence in Medieval Logic*, sec.IV.14, 74–75.

159. (OPh I, 275).

160. *Ibid*. III–2, c.5, (OPh I, 512).

assertion that it is never the case that a necessary proposition exists and is false. Likewise, a temporal interpretation of the modalities appears to explain Ockham's remark that "if a proposition is simply assertoric and true, it is necessary;"[161] since it does follow from the claim that the predicate cannot be first true and then false about its subject but is always true about its subject, that it is always true about its subject and hence necessarily true (in the sense of always true) about its subject.

Nevertheless, the results of substituting this temporal understanding of modalities in (F)–(J) are not easy to interpret. For (F) becomes equivalent to

(F') 'p; therefore q' is an as-of-now inference, if and only if (i) now there is no time at which the conjunction 'p & not-q' is true, although (ii) there will be some time at which there is some time at which 'p & not-q' is true.

If 'now there is not time at which' means 'neither the present time nor any time future relative to it is one at which', then Ockham clearly does not accept (F'). For he does not think that if 'Every animal runs; therefore Socrates runs' is an as-of-now inference, then it is true now that there is no time at which 'Every animal runs and it is not the case that Socrates runs' is true. Instead he thinks that there is a time future relative to now at which the conjunction is true—viz., when Socrates dies. Alternatively, we could take the present tense of 'now there is no time' at face value. Since there is only one time at a time, so to speak, that expression becomes equivalent to 'now is not a time' and condition (ii') is equivalent to (A'). Likewise, 'there will be some time at which there is a time' will be equivalent to 'there will be a time'. This construal fits Ockham's example. For where Socrates is now an animal, now is not a time at which 'Every animal runs' is true and 'Socrates runs' is false. But there will be such a time when Socrates dies. Likewise, substituting in (G), (iii) becomes

161. *Ibid*. III–1, c.31, (OPh I, 444).

(iii′) at no time will there be a time at which the antecedent is true and the consequent false,

which reduces to 'there will not be a time at which the antecedent is true and the consequent false'.

Does Ockham also think that there never was a time at which the antecedent of a simple inference was true and its consequent false? If he did, then the resultant contrast would be between inferences which always hold and those which hold now but now always. And this is similar to that found in the *Tractatus logicae minor*, formerly but mistakenly attributed to Ockham, between "an as-of-now inference" "which does not hold at every but only at determinate time"—the present time not explicitly specified—and a simple inference "which holds at every time..."[162] Ockham's example here—'No animal runs; therefore no man runs'—whose antecedent contradicts the denial of its consequent, suggests an affirmative answer. But elsewhere he admits as simple inferences those whose antecedents and consequents are merely necessary *per accidens*.[163] Thus, 'The Word of God existed from eternity; therefore an incarnate existed from eternity', where 'incarnate' supposits for that which was, is a simple inference guaranteed by the proposition 'The Word of God was incarnate', which is now and always will be necessary *per accidens*, but was always false if formed prior to the incarnation. Thus, even if a temporal interpretation of modalities were attributed to Ockham, he could not be read as supposing that good simple inferences hold good at all times, past, present, and future.[164]

On this interpretation, conditions (ii) and (iii′) are contradictories. Hence, every inference must satisfy either one or the other and none can meet both. Since on this reading (i′) is

162. Eligius Buytaert, "The *Tractatus logicae minor* of Ockham," *Franciscan Studies* N.S. XXIV (1964): 34–100; cf. 77. For a discussion of its authorship, see *Summa logicae*, Intro., c.6, (OPh I, 62*–66*).

163. *Summa logicae* III–3, c.6, (OPh I, 608).

164. The importance of Ockham's notion of necessity *per accidens* in his modal logic is emphasized by Calvin Normore in *op. cit.*, chap.7–8.

equivalent to (A′), which characterizes every good inference, it follows that the resultant division between simple and as-of-now inferences would be both exclusive and exhaustive of good inferences. A further consequence would be that (A′) is not only necessary but also sufficient for an inference to count as a good inference. For if it is a necessary truth that every inference satisfies (ii) or (iii′), all one needs to determine in order to establish which inferences hold good is whether (A′) is satisfied.

Yet, the temporal interpretations do not fit so easily with (H) and (J). For there is no single time at which there is (present tense) one time at which the predication holds and is (present tense) a time at which it first holds and then does not. To get the distinction between as-of-now and simply assertoric true statements to be one between those that are sometimes true and sometimes false and those that are always true, one will have to regard the 'can' and 'cannot' as redundant and replaceable by 'is' and 'is not', respectively. Further, while Ockham does make regular use of the first two interpretations of necessity elsewhere in his philosophy, the temporal interpretation does not recur. In theology and natural philosophy, as well as in metaphysics and epistemology, Ockham often supposes that it is possible for God to do things that He never does or will do.

(d) Medieval theologians also followed Aristotle in contrasting absolute with hypothetical necessity. As before, a proposition is absolutely necessary if its opposite involves a contradiction. But a contingent proposition p can be hypothetically necessary if and only if there is a true proposition q such that 'if q then p' is necessary.[165] On this way of drawing the distinction, only contingent propositions can be hypothetically necessary. Originally, the contrast was supposed to be between propositions or states of affairs the source of whose necessity was somehow intrinsic to them, and those that derive their necessity from another already given. Nevertheless, the requirement of contingency can be abstracted from the conditions of hypothetical necessity to yield

165. *Quodl.* VI, q.2, (OTh IX, 590).

(K) A proposition p is hypothetically necessary, if and only if there is a true proposition q such that 'if q then p' is necessary.

Now suppose that p is itself a conditional proposition. By (F) the corresponding inference would be an as-of-now inference if and only if (i″) p is hypothetically necessary now but (ii″) at some other time p will not be hypothetically necessary, because there is now a true proposition q such that 'if q then p' is necessary, but at some time there will be no such true proposition. On the other hand, by (G), the corresponding inference would be simple if and only if (i″) there is and (iii″) always will be a true proposition q such that 'if q then p' is a necessary statement. Likewise, according to (H) and (J), a true as-of-now assertoric statement is one that is hypothetically necessary at one time and not at another, whereas a true simple assertoric statement is one that is always hypothetically necessary.

This interpretation fits well with Ockham's example of an as-of-now inference: 'If every animal runs, Socrates runs' is not hypothetically necessary—because 'Socrates is an animal' is true now and 'If Socrates is an animal, then if every animal runs, Socrates runs' is absolutely necessary; but it will not be hypothetically necessary later—when Socrates dies and 'Socrates is an animal' becomes false. And without employing the label 'hypothetically necessary', the author of the *Elementarium logicae*, also formerly but mistakenly attributed to Ockham, gives substantially the same account of as-of-now inference:

> ...For those who say that an inference is good as-of-now intend to say only that the antecedent cannot be true without the consequent while something is or is situated in some determinate way. For example, when they say that the inference 'Every man is running; therefore Socrates is running' is good as-of-now, they intend to say only that while Socrates exists, as he does now, it is impossible that 'Every man is running' should be true unless the proposition 'Socrates is running' is true...[166]

166. Eligius Buytaert, "The *Elementarium logicae* of Ockham," *Fran-*

Likewise, Albert Saxony explains that

> these inferences are called as-of-now inferences that are not good ab-
> solutely speaking, because it is impossible for things to be as their
> antecedent signifies without being as their consequent signifies, but are
> good as-of-now because it is impossible that things be altogether the
> way they are as-of-now and be the way the antecedent signifies without
> being the way the consequent signifies...[167]

And John Buridan follows suit.[168]

Even so, it may be doubted whether the present interpretation really captures Ockham's understanding of simple inference. After all, 'If no animal runs, then no man runs' is not
merely always true and hence hypothetically necessary at all
times; it is absolutely necessary. And 'If each divine person
existed from eternity, a creator existed from eternity', where
'creator' supposits for those that were, is not only true and
hypothetically necessary now and forever afterwards; it is
necessary *per accidens*. Would we not come closer to Ockham's genuine opinion, if we assigned him

(A″) An inference '*p*; therefore *q*' is a simple inference if and
       only 'if *p* than *q*' is absolutely necessary or necessary *per
       accidens*,

which accords more closely with the streamlined formulations
of Albert of Saxony[169] and John Buridan?[170]

(3.4) *Comparison of Ockham's Divisions with Material and
Strict Implication*. Assuming that (A) defined the modern notion of material implication, I once argued that satisfying (A) is
also necessary and sufficient in Ockham's logic for an inference
to count as a good inference. My reason was that for Ockham
the division between simple and as-of-now inferences is both an

ciscan Studies N.S. XXV (1965): 151–276; cf. 254. On the authorship of the
Elementarium, see *Summa logicae*, Intro., c.6, (OPh I, 62*–66*).

167. *Op. cit.*, Tractatus quartus, c.1, fol.24rb.
168. *Tractatus de consequentiis* I, c.4, (Hubien ed., 23–24).
169. *Op. cit.*, fol.24rb.
170. *Tractatus de consequentiis* I, c.4, 23.

exclusive and an exhaustive division among good inferences, while satisfying (A) is necessary for satisfying each and sufficient for satisfying one or the other. My conclusion was, in effect, that for Ockham material implication is the "genus" of good inference under which formal and material, simple and as-of-now divide as species.[171]

The soundness of this argument depends on Ockham's definitions of simple and as-of-now inference. If we accept

(F'') The inference 'p; therefore q' is an as-of-now inference, if and only if (i'') 'if p then q' is hypothetically necessary now, but (ii'') at some other time 'if p then q' will not be hypothetically necessary,

and

(G'') The inference 'p; therefore q' is a simple inference if and only if (i'') 'if p then q' is hypothetically necessary now, and (iii'') 'if p then q' always will be hypothetically necessary,

then the first part of the argument holds. For given the above understanding of hypothetical necessity, a proposition satisfies (i'') if and only if it satisfies (A'); no inference can satisfy both (ii'') and (iii'') because they are contradictory; and every good inference must satisfy one or the other of (ii'') and (iii''). So the division will be exclusive and exhaustive of good inferences; and satisfying (A') will be necessary and sufficient for being one or the other kinds of good inference. It will not follow further that Ockham's "genus" of good inference is material implication, however, since the modern notion of material implication is identified with

(A'') It is (tenselessly) not the case that the antecedent is (tenselessly) true and the consequent false

171. "Did Ockham Know of Material and Strict Implication? A Reconsideration," 35–37.

and not with

(A′) it is (present tense) not the case that the antecedent is (present tense) true and the consequent false.

The most that could be concluded is that since (A′) is the analogue of (A″) for a logic whose propositions are tensed and able to change truth-value, all of Ockham's good inferences fall under an analogue of the modern division of material implication.[172]

What if we replace (G″) with

(G‴) An inference 'p; therefore q' is a simple inference if and only if 'if p then q' is absolutely necessary or necessary *per accidens*?

The division will still be exclusive. For where a condition is absolutely necessary or necessary *per accidens*, it is and always will be hypothetically necessary. Hence, any inference that satisfies (G‴) does and always will satisfy (G″). But the division fixed by (F″) and (G‴) will not be exhaustive. For if there always will be men in the future, the conditional 'if an animal exists, a man exists' is and always will be trivially true and hypothetically necessary—and so will fail to satisfy (F″). Yet it is neither absolutely necessary nor necessary *per accidens*—and so will fail to satisfy (G‴) as well.

Even passing over the differences between (A′) and (A″), it would be wrong to equate Ockham's division of material inference with modern material implication, since the latter includes and the former excludes all of Ockham's formal inferences. If Ockham had restricted simple inferences to those whose corresponding conditional proposition is absolutely necessary, his division would be equivalent to modern strict im-

172. That material implication is equivalent to (A″) and not (A′) is urged by Eleonore Stump in her criticism of my article in her lectures at the summer institute, Council for Philosophical Studies, 1980.

plication.[173] But this identification collapses as well when a disjunctive interpretation of the modalities is introduced into (G'').

In view of our examination of Ockham's motivations, however, this result of general non-coincidence should no longer seem surprising.

(3.5) *Formal Logic and the Doctrine of the Trinity.* Aristotle's project in the *Analytics* was seen as that of identifying argument forms that hold good regardless of the matter. Thus, Barbara ('Every B is C; every A is B; therefore every A is C ') is supposed to hold good regardless of which categorematic terms are substituted for 'A', 'B ' and 'C ', provided that the substitution is univocal and uniform throughout. Similarly for inferences governed immediately by extrinsic means (e.g., those of the form 'Every A is B; therefore only B is A'). By the early fourteenth century, however, theologians had begun to question whether Aristotle's logic could accomodate the truths of faith.[174]

Suppose that 'N_1' and 'N_2' are proper names and that 'N_1' stands for a distinct thing from 'N_2'. It follows from the truth conditions laid down by Ockham that 'This A is N_1' (where 'this A' indicates x) is true if and only if 'This A is N_2' (where 'this A' indicates x) is false. Likewise, 'Every A is N_1' is true if and only if 'Only N_1 is A' is true, and if and only if 'Every A is N_2' and 'N_2 is A' are false. Conversely, if each of 'This A is N_1' and 'This A is N_3', 'Every A is N_1' and 'N_3 is A' is true, it follows that 'N_1' and 'N_3' name the same thing. Thus, arguments of the form 'This A is N_1, this A is N_3; therefore N_1 is N_3'—so-called "expository syllogisms"—hold good. So do arguments of the form 'Every A is N_1, N_3 is A; therefore N_3 is N_1' and 'No N_1 is N_2, this A is N_1; therefore this A is not N_2', regulated as they are by *dici de omni* and *dici de nullo*.

173. As Ernest Moody (*Truth and Consequence in Medieval Logic*, sec.IV.14, 78) and I (*op. cit.*, 27) have noted.

174. For a thorough examination of late thirteenth and early fourteenth century attempts to deal with this problem, see Hester Goodenough Gelber, *Logic and the Trinity: A Clash of Values in Scholastic Thought, 1300–1335*, an unpublished Ph.D. dissertation.

Such truth conditions and argument-forms would fail, however, if it were possible for one thing (*res*) to be really identical with many distinct things (*res*). Ockham labels this relation 'formal distinction' and finds it to be instanced by the relation between the divine essence and the divine persons on their personal properties. Thus, for Ockham, a formal distinction, by its very definition, involves the violation of some self-evident logical principles—viz., the Transitivity and Symmetry of Identity and the Principle of Contradiction. And such formal distinctions and resultant logically anomalous signification patterns make it impossible to substitute the names of persons of the Trinity or their personal properties or 'divine essence' or 'God' in some Aristotelian argument-schemata, while preserving validity. Thus, the arguments 'This essence is the Father; this essence is the Son; therefore the Son is the Father',[175] 'This Spiration is Paternity; this Spiration is Filiation; therefore Filiation is Paternity',[176] 'Every divine essence is the Father; the Son is the divine essence; therefore the Son is the Father',[177] and 'No Father is the Son; the divine essence is the Father; therefore the divine essence is not the Son',[178] fail. Ockham adds a new category of fallacy of accident to classify them.[179] It follows that the argument schema 'This A is N_1, this A is N_2; therefore N_2 is N_1', 'Every A is N_1, N_2 is A; therefore N_2 is N_1', and 'No N_1 is N_2, this A is N_1; therefore this A is not N_2' do not hold good regardless of what categorematic terms are substituted for 'A', 'N_1', and 'N_2', but only where the categorematic term 'A' does not signify one thing that is really the same as distinct things signified by 'N_1' and 'N_2'.

Some theologians concluded that the expository syllogism was not a formally valid argument, and that the *dici de omni*

175. *Summa logicae* III-4, c.11, (OPh I, 820–22); II, c.27, (OPh I, 336–38).
176. *Ibid.* III-4, c.11, (OPh I, 821–22).
177. *Ibid.*
178. *Ibid.* III-1, c.4, (OPh I, 370).
179. *Ibid.* III-4, c.11, (OPh I, 820–21).

and *dici de nullo* were not formally valid rules.[180] By contrast,
Ockham insists that the expository syllogism holds good for any
matter, but stipulates that arguments of the form 'This A is N_1,
this A is N_2; therefore N_2 is N_1' will not count as an expository
syllogism, if the term substituted for 'A' signifies one thing that
is really the same as the really distinct things signified by the
terms substituted for 'N_1' and 'N_2'.[181] Again, he insists that
every argument regulated by *dici de omni* or *dici de nullo* holds
good, but an argument of the form 'Every A is N_1; N_2 is A;
therefore N_2 is N_1' or 'No N_1 is N_2; this A is N_1; therefore this A
is not N_2' is so regulated only if its categorematic terms are not
related that way.[182]

Once restrictions are admitted on the categorematic terms for
which such argument schema hold good, the project of identifying valid arguments by attention to form alone has been
compromised.[183] That Ockham did not simply abandon it, or
start over to develop a comprehensive logical system that
would accomodate the doctrine of the Trinity as well, is a
reflection of his theological method, which will be the topic of
Part Five, chapter 22 below.

180. E.g., the author of the *Centiloquium*; Philotheus Boehner, "The
Medieval Crisis of Logic and the Author of the *Centiloquium*," *Franciscan
Studies* IV (1944): 151–170, repr. in *Collected Articles on Ockham*, #20,
351–372.
    181. *Summa logicae* II, c.27, (OPh I, 336–38); III–1, c.16, (OPh I, 403).
    182. *Summa logicae* III–1, c.4–5, (OPh I, 370, 379–380).
    183. Boehner seems to think, mistakenly in my judgment, that Ockham
escapes this difficulty by building the material restrictions into the criteria for
what counts as an expository syllogism ("The Medieval Crisis of Logic and
the Author of the *Centiloquium*," 359–363).

Part Three

Theory of Knowledge

13

Conceptual Empiricism
and Direct Realism

The questions—where do our concepts come from? what are the immediate objects of our thought? and what, if anything, can we know with certainty and how can we know it?—lie at the heart of theories of knowledge, both ancient and modern. Hence, it is not surprising that they puzzled medievals as well. The first divides philosophers into conceptual empiricists and those who believe that some of our concepts are *a priori*; the second, into representationalists and direct realists; and the third, into sceptics and those who insist that certain knowledge is possible.

In accounting for the origin of our concepts, Ockham agrees with Aquinas,[1] Henry of Ghent,[2] and Duns Scotus[3] in the Aristotelian thesis that the human mind begins its existence as a *tabula rasa*:[4] in order for it to engage in any activity at all (and, in particular, in order for it to know anything), it must first be furnished with concepts all of which have to be acquired after birth. Aquinas begins his theory of knowledge with the axiom that a thing is knowable only insofar as it is actual.[5] Accepting Aristotle's arguments against Plato, Aquinas believed that forms that are the genera and species of physical objects do not exist separated from particular physical objects;[6] it follows that such

1. *Summa theologiae* I, q.75, a.2.
2. *Quodlibeta* IV, q.8, (Venice, 1613, T.I, fol.151va–b).
3. *Quaest. subtil. Metaphysicorum* II, q.1, n.2, (Wadding IV, 3).
4. *De anima* III, 9, 432b5.
5. *De ente et essentia*, c.2, (Roland-Gosselin ed., 7).
6. *Ibid.*, c.3, (Roland-Gosselin ed., 23); *Summa theologiae* I, q.75, a.4 and 7.

forms never really exist in separation from matter. Influenced by Arab interpretations of Aristotle, however, Aquinas affirmed that a thing is actual only insofar as it is formal, and that matter in itself is not actual at all, but merely potential.[7] Concluding that

> forms are not actually intelligible unless they are separated from matter and material conditions; nor are they rendered actually intelligible except through the power of intelligent substance which receives them within itself and produces them...,[8]

Aquinas devotes his attention to explaining the mechanism by which the intellect extracts the intelligible form from the unintelligible matter with which it is mixed.[9] But the processes which he postulates turn out to be almost impossible to identify in experience. And he has considerable difficulty explaining how on this scheme the intellect ever thinks of particulars.[10]

Given that what principally motivates Aquinas's psychological analysis is his metaphysical conviction that matter is unintelligible in itself, it is easy to see how philosophers would lose interest in his analysis as soon as they came to doubt its metaphysical underpinnings. Convinced that matter was not, as Aquinas had maintained, pure potentiality (see Part Four, chapter 15 below), Ockham looked for a fresh analysis of the psychological processes involved in our coming to know the world. Alternative psychologies combined with different metaphysical assumptions to yield varying answers to the second question—what are the immediate objects of our thought?—as well.

In this chapter, I shall concentrate on Ockham's answers to the first two questions: on his analysis of the mental acts involved in our coming to know true propositions, and his account of the relations among such acts and between them and extramental things. Then, in the following chapter, I shall ex-

---

7. *De ente et essentia*, c.2, (Roland-Gosselin ed., 7).
8. *Ibid.*, c.4, (Roland-Gosselin ed., 31).
9. *Summa theologiae* I, q.79, 84, and 85.
10. *Ibid.*, q.86, a.1.

amine his answer to the third question—what, if anything, can we know with certainty and how can we know it?—together with the charge that Ockham's theory of knowledge leads to scepticism.

1.   THE DISTINCTION BETWEEN ACTS OF APPREHENSION AND ACTS OF JUDGMENT

Ockham begins his psychological account by distinguishing acts of apprehension from acts of judgment.[11] There are numerous parallels between Ockham's acts of apprehension and Lockean ideas, which might mislead the modern reader into assimilating the former to the latter: (a) Locke says that our mental activity begins when particular mind-independent physical objects cause us to have simple ideas of sensation.[12] Ockham says that it begins when such physical objects cause us to apprehend themselves by our senses. (b) Locke thinks that we have ideas of reflection[13] as well as ideas of sensation, but that the latter are temporally prior to and presupposed by the former.[14] Ockham allows that we do apprehend our own mental acts, but insists that this would be causally impossible if we did not first apprehend physical objects. (c) Locke thinks that from ideas of particulars, we can form abstract general ideas.[15] Ockham supposes that given acts of apprehending particulars, we can form abstract general concepts.

Despite such comparisons, it is clear that Ockham does not conceive of acts of apprehension the way Locke conceives of ideas. Locke explicitly states that ideas are objects, indeed the immediate objects, of thought.[16] By contrast, according to Ockham, acts of apprehension are not primarily or merely ob-

11. *Ord.* I, Prologue, q.1, a.1, (OTh I, 17–18).
12. *An Essay Concerning Human Understanding* II.1.20, 23; cf. II.1.2, 4–5.
13. *Ibid.*, II.1.2, 4–5.
14. *Ibid.*, II.1.23.
15. *Ibid.*, III.3.6–9, 13; II.11–12.
16. *Ibid.*, Intro., sec.8; II.8.8.

jects of thought, but rather mental acts of awareness in which the mind apprehends such objects. As already indicated, Ockham does allow that some acts of apprehension have mental acts for their objects. But, unlike Lockean ideas, acts of apprehension are not that by being aware of which the mind can be aware of physical objects and other mental acts.[17] They are the acts in which the mind is aware of such objects immediately or directly.

Among acts of apprehension, Ockham distinguishes noncomplex from complex cognitions. This distinction must not be conflated with Locke's distinction between simple and complex ideas, however. Locke says that a simple idea is one which "contains in it nothing but one simple uniform appearance."[18] It is one within whose content no distinctions are possible. But Ockham allows that a single noncomplex cognition can have two, really distinct things—viz., Socrates and his whiteness—as an object.[19] By 'complex' Ockham means a complex of terms.[20] Not just any plurality of terms is a complex, however, but only those that form a proposition which is either true or false. Thus 'A white man is running' is a complex of terms; 'white man' and 'man' are noncomplexes. A noncomplex cognition is, then, an act of apprehending one or more terms that do not form a proposition, whereas a complex cognition is an act of apprehending a proposition.[21]

Ockham seems to regard this distinction as exhaustive. For he says that there are acts of apprehension "of *anything* that can be an object of the intellectual power, *whether it is complex or noncomplex...*"[22] This remark is surprising at first, since we seem to be aware of something other than propositions and their terms. Nevertheless, Ockham's claim is easily explained in

17. *Rep.* II, d.12–13, (OTh V, 273–75).
18. *Op. cit.*, II.2.1.
19. *Rep.* II, q.12–13, (OTh V, 279–281).
20. See, e.g., *Ord.* I, Prologue, q.1, a.1, (OTh I, 21, lines 8–10).
21. Cf. *Expos. Periherm.* I, Prooemium, sec.12, (OPh II, 372–73); *Expos. Praedicam.*, c.4, (OPh II, 148).
22. *Ord.* I, Prologue, q.1, a.1, (OTh I, 16, lines 8–9).

terms of his objective-existence theory, according to which concepts are identified, not with acts of apprehension, but with their objectively existent objects. On the objective-existence theory, any object of a noncomplex act of apprehension is a conceived object (*conceptum*) and thus can be a term in a mental proposition. Ockham apparently wrote the above quoted sentence when he still subscribed to his early view and neglected to change it later to allow for the mental-act theory. In numerous places, Ockham has altered the text to make room for his later contention that concepts (and hence the terms of mental propositions) are to be identified with acts of apprehension. For example, he speaks of cognizing "the extremes [of a proposition] or the things signified by the extremes."[23] Thus, Ockham's final view is that an act of apprehension is a complex cognition when its object is a proposition, and that all other acts of apprehension—whether they are of the terms of a proposition or of the things signified by such terms—are noncomplex cognitions.

Closer to Locke's division between simple and complex ideas is Ockham's distinction between simple concepts "which do not include many concepts" and composite concepts "which are not simple and which include many concepts in their own way."[24] On the objective-existence theory, which identifies concepts with the objects and not with the acts of thought, this would amount to a distinction among the contents of acts of thought. Even after he has clearly abandoned the objective-existence theory and come to identify concepts with acts of thought, he continues to employ the distinction as a content distinction.[25] Thus, both an intuitive cognition of whiteness alone and an intuitive cognition of both Socrates and his whiteness would be noncomplex cognitions, but the former would be a simple and the latter a composite cognition.

When Ockham speaks of *acts* of apprehension, he does not mean to signify that they are voluntary or that the mind is not

23. *Ibid.*, (OTh I, 24, lines 13–14, 18–19).
24. *Ibid.*, d.3, q.5, (OTh II, 472–73).
25. *Quodl.* I, q.13, (OTh IX, 73).

caused to have them by something other than itself. Acts of apprehension are acts of the senses or intellect, not acts of will. Ockham confesses that if it were not for the authority of the saints and philosophers, he would say that the intellect is purely passive.[26] And, although the knower's volition is sometimes the partial cause of an act of apprehension, Ockham thinks that in many cases such acts have a total efficient cause other than the mind. He speaks of *acts* of apprehension to indicate a condition in which the mind is *actually*, as opposed to merely *potentially*, aware of something.

Acts of judgment are those by which one assents to or dissents from a proposition.[27] On Ockham's view, such acts are neither acts of the senses[28] nor acts of will, but acts of the intellect. Some acts of judgment, like some acts of apprehension, have volitions as partial efficient causes, while some do not.[29]

Ockham thinks that both kinds of mental acts are involved in knowing a proposition.[30] It is not logically possible that anyone should know a proposition that he never formulates or thinks of.[31] Further, it is impossible that anyone should formulate a proposition whose terms he never thinks of.[32] Yet, it is possible that one should entertain a proposition without knowing it or believing it. For there to be knowledge, there must not only be an act of apprehending the terms of the proposition and the proposition itself, but also an act of judgment by which one assents to the proposition. Ockham admits the possibility that in some cases there might be a single complex cognition which was an act of apprehending the proposition and at the same time an act of apprehending its terms, rather than distinct non-complex cognitions of single terms and a complex cognition of the proposition. Similarly, there might be an act of assent that

26. *Rep.* II, q.20, (OTh V, 425, 443).
27. *Ord.* I, Prologue, q.1, a.1, (OTh I, 16).
28. *Rep.* III, q.2, (OTh VI, 85–86).
29. *Quaest. variae*, q.5, (OTh VIII, 171–73).
30. *Ord.* I, Prologue, q.1, a.1, (OTh I, 16).
31. *Ibid.*, (OTh I, 17); a.6, (OTh I, 59).
32. *Ibid.*, a.1, (OTh I, 21).

was at one and the same time an act of apprehending the complex of terms, rather than two distinct acts, one of apprehension and one of judgment.[33] Nevertheless, numerically distinct acts are often involved; and either way an act of judgment logically presupposes an act of apprehension but not vice versa.

2.   DISTINCTION BETWEEN INTUITIVE AND ABSTRACTIVE COGNITIONS

According to Ockham, acts of apprehension are mental acts of awareness. But experience makes us aware of differences among our acts of apprehension. My awareness of the chair that I see is different from my awareness of the chair that I imagine. Again, my awareness of my present pain is different from my awareness of the pain I had yesterday. Where sensible things are concerned, this may be the difference Hume was trying to mark when he distinguished impressions from ideas.[34] Duns Scotus had tried to capture it by distinguishing intuitive from abstractive cognitions. According to Scotus, intuitive cognitions are those which (i) are of the object as existing and present, and (ii) are caused in the perceiver directly by the existing and present object; whereas abstractive cognitions are those which (iii) either are not of the object as existing and present but abstract from the existence and presence of the object, or are of an object which is in fact not existing or present, and (iv) are not caused by the existing and present object directly, but rather indirectly by means of a species or *likeness of the object*.[35]

Ockham is confident that he can identify in experience those acts of apprehension that Scotus called intuitive cognitions. According to Ockham, experience "certifies" that we can have an

33. *Ibid.*, a.6, (OTh I, 59).
34. *A Treatise of Human Nature*, Book I, Part I, sec.1.
35. Scotus elaborates this distinction in discussions in his *Quodlibeta* and in his commentaries on the *Sentences*. For a review of the relevant texts, see Sebastian Day's *Intuitive Cognition: A Key to the Significance of the Later Scholastics*. (St. Bonaventure, NY, 1947). For Ockham's critique of Scotus, see *Ord*. I, Prologue, q.1, a.1, (OTh I, 33–38).

intuitive cognition of Socrates and his whiteness.[36] He even suggests that we can know from experience that we do not, by any natural cause, have intuitive cognitions of absent things.[37] Nevertheless, Ockham rejects Scotus's attempt to distinguish intuitive from abstractive cognitions on the basis of their content or of their causes. First Ockham insists that "if a thing is an object of an intuitive cognition, then the same thing under the same aspect can be the object of an abstractive cognition."[38] Nor is it right to say that intuitive cognition is possible only of existing objects. Even though in the natural order of things we have intuitive cognitions only of existing things, still it would be possible for God to cause us to have an act of apprehension of this sort, even when the object does not exist.[39] For "whatever God can do through an intermediate efficient cause, He can do all by Himself immediately."[40] Therefore, God could directly produce acts that possess the distinctive feature that makes them intuitive.[41]

What is Ockham's criterion for distinguishing intuitive from abstractive cognitions? According to Ockham, an intuitive cognition of a thing is that by virtue of which one can have evident knowledge of whether or not a thing exists, or more broadly, of whether or not a contingent proposition about the present is true.[42] By contrast, abstractive cognition in this sense[43] is a noncomplex apprehension of terms by virtue of

36. *Ord.* I, Prologue, q.1, a.1, (OTh I, 23).
37. *Rep.* II, q.12–13, (OTh V, 269).
38. *Ord.* I, Prologue, q.1, a.1, (OTh I, 36–37); cf. d.27, q.3, (OTh IV, 242).
39. *Ibid.*, Prologue, q.1, a.1, (OTh I, 35–36).
40. *Ibid.*, (OTh I, 35).
41. *Ibid.*, (OTh I, 37).
42. *Ibid.*, (OTh I, 31–32); *Rep.* II, q.12–13, (OTh V, 256–57); cf. *Quodl.* V, q.5, (OTh IX, 496).
43. In the *Ordinatio* I, Prologue, q.1, a.1, (OTh I, 30–31), Ockham notes that 'abstractive cognition' can be taken in two ways: one way for the cognition of a universal that can be abstracted from many particulars; and another way as contrasting with intuitive cognitions. The first way, the content of the cognition is more abstract than that of the cognition of a particular; the second way, the content is no more abstract than that of an intuitive cogni-

which it is not possible to have evident knowledge of whether or not a thing exists, or whether or not a contingent proposition about the present is true.[44]

By 'evident knowledge of a proposition' Ockham does not mean knowledge based on grounds or evidence from which the proposition is inferred. Instead, Ockham defines 'evident cognition' as the cognition of a true complex of terms or proposition, a sufficient mediate or immediate efficient cause for which is a noncomplex cognition of its terms.[45] (According to Ockham, the intellect itself is the material cause of such acts.)[46] Any apprehension of the terms will suffice to give us evident knowledge of simple analytic propositions. But where contingent propositions are concerned, only intuitive, not abstractive cognition naturally suffices to produce evident knowledge. In fact, according to Ockham, this is the definitive difference between intuitive and abstractive cognition.[47]

Ockham makes it clear that 'by virtue of which' (*virtute*) or

tion, according to Ockham, but the cognition is not the sort that can cause an evident judgment about the existence or nonexistence of the particular. Ockham modifies the latter claim in *Quodlibeta* I, q.13, (OTh IX, 74, 77), when he concedes that no abstractive cognition is proper to a particular (see section 7 below). Every cognition that is abstractive in either of the above two senses is a noncomplex cognition. In *Reportatio* II, q.12–13, (OTh V, 257), however, Ockham recognizes a broad sense of 'abstractive cognition', according to which every cognition other than an intuitive cognition is an abstract cognition. This way, not only the above mentioned noncomplex cognitions, but also every complex cognition will count as an abstractive cognition. But Ockham almost never uses the term 'abstractive cognition' in this broad sense.

    44. *Ord.* I, Prologue, q.1, a.1, (OTh I, 32); *Quodl.* V, q.5, (OTh IX, 496).

    45. *Ord.* I, Prologue, q.1, (OTh I, 5).

    46. See *Quaest. variae*, q.5, (OTh VIII, 166–67).

    47. In *Quaestione variae*, q.5, (OTh VIII, 183–89), Ockham adds to the list of evident cognitions the cognition of the conclusion of an argument caused by an evident cognition of its premisses. And he notes that in this case "the evidence of the object is not taken precisely from the terms..." (OTh VIII, 186). Normally, however, Ockham restricts the class of evident cognitions for those by which we have non-inferential knowledge of true propositions.

'by means of which' (*mediante qua*)[48] expresses a causal notion,[49] and hence that cognitions—like other things—are
sorted into species by means of their causal powers (see Part
Four, chapter 18 below). Ockham holds that God is an immediate partial cause of every act of understanding as well as of
every other effect because of "his general influence" in up-
holding or maintaining the causal order.[50] And he thinks that
the causal powers in this world are naturally so distributed that
the existing and present object is a mediate or immediate cause
both of the existence and conservation of an intuitive cognition.[51] Further, the causal powers are such that—barring any
obstacle to their action[52]—an intuitive cognition together with
the existing and present object suffices to cause the intellect to
judge that the object exists. Likewise, an intuitive cognition of
Socrates and his whiteness will act together with Socrates and
his whiteness to cause the judgment that Socrates is white.[53]
Nor can this process be naturally obstructed by a simple act of
will on the part of the one who has the intuitive cognition.
Arguments or persuasion would be needed to make the opposite
judgment causally possible.[54] Ockham thinks that all of the intuitive cognitions that we actually have are caused by the existing and present objects of those cognitions and that therefore
in every actual case of intuitive cognition we are caused to judge

48. In *Rep.* II, q.12–13, (OTh V, 256).

49. For example, in *Ordinatio*, Prologue, q.1, a.6, (OTh I, 71, lines 4–9),
he writes: "Therefore, the intuitive cognition of the thing and the thing
cause the judgment that the thing exists. But when the thing does not exist,
the intuitive cognition without the thing will cause the opposite judgment.
Therefore, I grant that the cause of the judgments is not the same, because the
cause of the one is the cognition without the thing and the cause of the other
is the cognition acting together with the thing as a partial cause" (italics
mine; cf. *Rep.* II, q.12–13, (OTh V, 276).

50. *Quaest. variae*, q.5, (OTh VIII, 162–63).

51. *Ord.* I, Prologue, q.1, a.1, (OTh I, 38); cf. *Rep.* II, q.12–13, (OTh V,
258–260, 268).

52. *Ord.* I, Prologue, q.1, a.1, (OTh I, 31, lines 22–23); a.1, (OTh I, 33);
a.6, (OTh I, 70).

53. *Ibid.*, q.1, (OTh I, 6).

54. *Ibid.*, q.7, (OTh I, 192).

that the object exists.

Nevertheless, God could withdraw "his general influence" and act alone to conserve acts of intuitive cognition. Ockham suggests, for example, that God could conserve one's intuitive cognition of a star, while bringing it about that the star no longer existed.[55] But he thinks the intuitive cognition, taken by itself, has causal efficacy only to produce judgments of nonexistence.[56] In such a case one would be caused by one's intuitive cognition of the star to judge that the star did not exist. Further, Ockham says that God could act alone to cause one to have an intuitive cognition of an existing but absent object. In that case, one would be caused to judge that the object exists.[57] It is clear that an intuitive cognition of an existing but absent object could serve as a partial cause only of a judgment of existence, since any judgment of which an intuitive cognition is a total or partial cause is an evident and therefore true judgment. But the intuitive cognition without the object naturally suffices only to cause judgments of nonexistence, not judgments of existence. Ockham does not say what would act together with the intuitive cognition to produce the judgment of existence in this case, but most probably he would say that it is God Himself. Finally, Ockham says that God could act alone to prevent an intuitive cognition from causing any judgment at all.[58]

---

55. *Ibid.*, q.1, a.1, (OTh I, 38–39; cf. *Quodl.* VI, q.6, (OTh IX, 605).

56. *Ord.* I, Prologue, q.1, a.1, (OTh I, 31); cf. a.6, (OTh I, 71).

57. *Rep.* II, q.12–13, (OTh V, 258).

58. *Ord.* I, Prologue, q.1, a.6, (OTh I, 70); cf. *Quodl.* V, q.5, (OTh IX, 499). In reply to one objection, Ockham speculates that "perhaps there is no difficulty in a thing's being intuitively seen and nevertheless the intellect believes that the thing does not exist, although this could not happen naturally. It is enough for a cognition to be intuitive that it is in itself sufficient for producing a correct judgment of existence or nonexistence" (*Ord.* I, Prologue, q.1, a.6, (OTh I, 70)). Presumably, Ockham has in mind a case in which God prevents the intuitive cognition from causing any judgment and in which God or something else acts to produce a false judgment about the existence or nonexistence of the thing. This would not run contrary to Ockham's contention in other passages that it is a logically necessary condition of a cognition's being intuitive that any judgments *it* causes are true ones.

In sum, then, Ockham thinks that an intuitive cognition is naturally produced only by the existing and present object, and that the intuitive cognition, together with the existing and present object, naturally suffices to produce a judgment of existence. Further, he thinks that the intuitive cognition alone naturally suffices only to produce a judgment of nonexistence. Thus, intuitive cognitions are acts of apprehension which have the causal efficacy to produce an evident judgment of existence when the object exists, and of nonexistence when the object does not exist. Since any natural cause can be obstructed, it is not logically or metaphysically necessary for a cognition to be intuitive that it cause a judgment. But it is logically or metaphysically as impossible for an intuitive cognition to cause a false judgment as it is for heat to cool (see Part Four, chapter 18 below). An abstractive cognition is an act that by nature lacks this power.[59]

3. SENSORY AND INTELLECTUAL INTUITIVE COGNITIONS OF SENSIBLE PARTICULARS

Ockham thinks that the objects of such acts of apprehension include sensible particulars and particular mental acts;[60] and that both the senses and the intellect are capable of intuitive and

---

59. Thus, Ockham's remark in *Ord.* I, Prologue, q.1, a.1, (OTh I, 38)—"Therefore, I maintain that intuitive and abstractive cognitions differ of themselves and not at all with respect to their objects or any of their causes"—can be misleading, if the 'of themselves' is stressed out of context (the way it appears to be in Gilson's discussion in his *History of Christian Philosophy in the Middle Ages*, (New York, 1955), 490 and 784, note 8). For five pages prior to the above remark, Ockham has been attacking Scotus's attempt to distinguish intuitive from abstractive cognition (OTh I, 33–38). When Ockham says that intuitive and abstractive cognitions differ in themselves, this claim is to be contrasted with Scotus's contention that they differ as regards their objects and what causes them. Ockham does not mean that there is no difference as regards the causal relations into which they can enter. For on his full account, intuitive cognitions differ from abstractive cognitions precisely in the fact that they cannot be the cause of any false judgments, while abstractive cognitions can.

60. *Ord.* I, Prologue, q.1, a.6, (OTh I, 69).

abstractive cognition.[61]

Ockham maintains that when a human being is aware of a sensible particular and thereby acquires evident knowledge of its existence and/or of some contingent proposition about it, both sensory and intellectual intuitive cognitions are involved. When, for example, I look at a sensible particular, it causes me to have a sensory intuitive cognition of itself under those aspects (namely, color and shape) that can be perceived by vision. But Ockham does not see how the senses could apprehend a complex (such as 'Socrates is white') and proceed to pass judgment on it themselves.[62] Nor is the sensory intuitive cognition "an immediate proximate cause—whether partial or total—of an act of judgment by the intellect."[63] For "every act of judgment presupposes an act of apprehension in the same power."[64] Therefore, the intellect could not formulate any singular propositions or pass judgment upon them unless it apprehended particulars. Indeed, Ockham insists that without intellectual intuitive cognition of particulars, the intellect could not have any knowledge of any contingent propositions.[65] Consequently, it must be an intellectual act of apprehension, not a sensory one, that is an immediate and proximate partial cause of an act of judgment. And the immediate and proximate cause of evident knowledge of such a proposition would be an intellectual intuitive cognition of its terms.

Why does Ockham hold that "every act of judgment presupposes an act of apprehension *in the same power*"?[66] It seems clear that my intellect cannot judge that Socrates is white, unless I am somehow aware of Socrates and whiteness. But my soul has many powers. Why does Ockham deny that my sensory awareness of Socrates and his whiteness is enough for this

61. *Ibid.*, (OTh I, 63–65).
62. *Rep.* III, q.2, (OTh VI, 85–86).
63. *Ord.* I, Prologue, q.1, a.1, (OTh I, 22).
64. *Ibid.*, (OTh I, 21); cf. (OTh I, 25, line 15)–(OTh I, 26, line 10).
65. *Ibid.*, d.3, q.6, (OTh II, 494); cf. Prologue, q.1, a.1, (OTh I, 43, line 10–11).
66. *Ibid.*, (OTh I, 21).

purpose?

Ockham's secretary Adam Wodeham remarks that this conclusion "follows necessarily from one of his tenets with which
I disagree—viz., that the intellectual and sensory souls are
distinct forms in man..."[67] This explanation fits well with
Ockham's remarks in *Reportatio* III, q.3, (OTh VI, 125), where
he acknowledges that some of the principles laid down in the
Prologue of his *Sentence*-commentary—viz., those to the effect
that an act of type *A* in a power presupposes an act of type *B* in
the *same* power—need revision. For since the sensory soul in
man is a single form that has many powers, one sensory power
may have an act of type *A* provided only that some sensory
power or other—not necessarily the same one—has an act
of type *B*. Thus, my intuitive cognition of Socrates and his
whiteness can be a partial cause of my abstractive imagining of
Socrates and his whiteness, because my visual and imaginative
powers are powers of numerically the same substantial form,
while my vision of Socrates and his whiteness cannot be a partial cause of your imagining them, because your sensory soul
is a numerically distinct substantial form from mine. Given
Ockham's belief that my sensory soul and my intellectual soul
are really distinct substantial forms (see Part Four, chapter 15),
my sensory apprehension of Socrates and his whiteness is of no
more use to my intellectual soul in formulating the propositon
'Socrates is white' and passing judgment on it, then your apprehension of these things is. Thus, he concludes that an act of
judgment presupposes an intellectual as well as a sensory
apprehension.

Nevertheless, the sensory intuitive cognition is not causally
superfluous. For where souls are connected with bodies as
human souls are in this life, having a sensory intuitive cognition
is a causally necessary condition of having an intellectual intuitive cognition of a sensible particular.[68] At one point, Ockham

---

67. *Quaestiones in I librum Sententiarum*, Prologue, q.1, fol.105va; I
translate from a transcription lent to me by Father Gedeon Gál, who called
my attention to this question.

68. *Ord.* I, Prologue, q.1, a.1, (OTh I, 27, lines 10–18); a.6, (OTh I, 67,
lines 11–15); *Rep.* II, q.12–13, (OTh V, 302–303).

suggests that this fact is a consequence of the first sin.[69] And he allows that angels and souls separated from bodies can naturally have intellectual intuitive cognitions without prior sensory intuitive cognitions.[70] The sensory intuitive cognition of a given object under a given aspect causes an intellectual intuitive cognition of the same object under the same aspect.[71] It is the latter act that is the immediate partial cause of the act of judgment. But the sensory intuitive cognition of the object is a *mediate* partial cause of that judgment, since it is an immediate partial cause of the intellectual intuitive cognition.

4.   OUR AWARENESS OF IMMATERIAL THINGS

Aquinas argued that the human mind was designed to abstract the natural forms of material things. But he thought that material and immaterial things had no natural forms in common. Consequently, the concepts abstracted by the human mind do not apply univocally, but only analogically to immaterial things.[72] We cannot understand immaterial things as they are in themselves.[73]

Scotus and Ockham both reject Aquinas's view.[74] Appealing to Augustine for support, Ockham insists that we have both intuitive and abstractive cognition of intelligibles that are in no way sensible. Thus he writes,

> ...it is clear that our intellect in this life not only cognizes sensible things, but also has intuitive cognitions of some intelligible things that do not fall under the senses and cognizes them as particulars...For example, acts of intellect, acts of will, the consequent delight and sorrow,

69. *Rep.* IV, q.14, (OTh VII, 316).

70. *Ibid.*

71. *Ord.* I, Prologue, q.1, a.6, (OTh I, 64, line 22)–(OTh I, 65, line 4); cf. q.8, (OTh I, 208–209); d.3, q.5, (OTh II, 474); d.3, q.6, (OTh II, 496–97).

72. *Summa theologiae* I, q.88, a.2.

73. *Ibid.*, a.1.

74. Scotus, *Opus oxon.* IV, d.45, q.3, n.12–18, (Wadding X, 200–208), noted by Ockham, *Ord.* I, Prologue, q.1, a.1, (OTh I, 45–46).

etc. that a man can experience to exist in himself and that nevertheless do not fall under any sense...[75]

If we had no intuitive cognition of such intelligibles, we could not have evident knowledge of propositions such as 'I understand', 'I love Socrates',[76] 'I am alive', 'I want to be happy', 'I do not want to make mistakes'.[77] But our knowledge of these propositions is the most evident that we have.[78] Ockham apparently understands all of these propositions to be about occurrent mental acts or momentary states. For he thinks that experience shows that "in this life [we do not have] intuitive cognitions of all intelligibles, even of those equally present to our intellects, since [we have them] of acts and not of dispositions (*habitus*)."[79] We know of the latter only by reasoning and inference.[80] Thus, "no one can have an intuitive vision of faith and charity that are dispositions in us, although one could have an intuitive vision of the acts of believing and loving that are elicited when these dispositions exist."[81] Ockham appears to have been genuinely unable to decide whether or not we can have naturally produced intuitive cognitions of our own souls in this life. For he raises the issue at least twice in *Ordinatio* I, d.3 alone—viz., at q.2, (OTh II, 274) and at q.8, (OTh II, 541)—and both times refuses to say one way or the other.

By contrast with modern classical philosophers, Ockham shows only marginal interest in the problem of our knowledge of other minds. In replying to an objection, he does say that we cannot have intuitive cognition of the mental acts of others.[82] In fact, he maintains that we cannot even have an abstractive cognition (in the sense defined above) of Socrates' particular act of loving Plato. Ockham thinks that just as we can think of

---

75. *Ord.* I, Prologue, q.1, a.1, (OTh I, 39–40).
76. *Ibid.*, (OTh I, 40–41).
77. *Ibid.*, (OTh I, 43).
78. *Ibid.*, (OTh I, 43, lines 7–13, 25–26)–(OTh I, 44, line 6).
79. *Ibid.*, a.6, (OTh I, 69).
80. *Ibid.*
81. *Ibid.*
82. *Ord.* I, Prologue, q.1, a.1, (OTh I, 42, lines 4–7).

physical objects that we have never experienced only by compounding various abstract general concepts, so we can conceive of the particular mental acts of another only by compounding such abstract general concepts. He does not argue for this claim, but apparently thinks it is obvious from experience. Nor does he discuss in any detail whether we have or how we acquire any knowledge or well-grounded beliefs about them. In *Reportatio* II, q.3–4, he does observe that we cannot prove that anything is a human being from the effects we are able to observe, because such observable bodily movements as eating and drinking could be produced by an angel just as easily as by a human soul.[83] On the other hand, unlike modern classical philosophers, Ockham does not see any logical impossibility in one mind's having an intuitive cognition of another or of the mental acts of another. God, of course, has such cognitions of all created minds and mental acts.[84] And in *Quodlibeta* IV, q. 9, he allows that it is possible for the angels to see (intellectually apprehend) our intellects and argues that "since any power can have an intuitive cognition of a subject, it can also have an intuitive cognition of any of its accidents which is apt to be the object of that power. But an angel can see our intellect, and hence can see thoughts."[85] Nevertheless, they do not in fact do so "except when God wills that they do."[86] Hence, for Ockham, it is in principle possible for us and the angels to verify that other minds exist, even though we do not do so in this life.

Ockham maintains that all that is required for us to have intellectual intuitive cognitions of a sensible particular is the existing and present object, together with the intellect and (in this life) the sensory powers of the soul. One might suppose that, by parity of reasoning, only the mental act and the intellect would be required for us to have an intuitive cognition of our own mental acts. Nevertheless, this turns out to be an issue on which Ockham vacillates considerably. In *Reportatio* II, q.12–13, he

83. (OTh V, 73).
84. *Ord.* I, d.35, q.5, (OTh IV, 493).
85. (OTh IX, 342).
86. (OTh IX, 343).

takes the expected line, commenting that "just as the power and the object without any species are required for a corporeal intuitive cognition, so the object together with the intellect suffices for an intellectual intuitive cognition."[87] And at one point in the Prologue, Ockham declares that "every act of intellect is evidently known to [the intellect] itself."[88] Nevertheless, Ockham is led in the Prologue to qualify this claim by considering the following objection raised by Walter Chatton:

> ...In that case, infinitely many acts of intellect would exist in the intellect simultaneously. For if there is an intuitive vision of the first act of intellect, this is only because it is sufficiently present to the intellect. But that intuitive cognition of the first intuitive cognition is equally present. Therefore it will be seen by a third act of intellect; and by parity of reasoning, the third, since it is sufficiently present, will be seen by a fourth, and so on.[89]

Ockham agrees that if I can be aware of the first mental act, I can be aware of the second, and so on.[90] Nevertheless, it does not follow that whenever I have one intellectual intuitive cognition, I have infinitely many intuitive cognitions. For

> ...The first act of intellect will be seen by an intuitive cognition and the latter intuition in the present life prevents the second intuition, not absolutely, but because the mere presence of the first act of intellect does not suffice for the second intuition. But the reason why it does not suffice cannot be given except in the nature of the thing which we now know by experience...[91]

Thus, my intellectual intuitive cognition of Socrates together with the intellect suffices to cause an intuitive cognition of that intuitive cognition. But experience shows the causal order

---

87. (OTh V, 302).

88. *Ord.* I, Prologue, q.7, (OTh I, 191).

89. *Ibid.*, q.1, a.6, (OTh I, 53, lines 13–19); cf. Jeremiah O'Callaghan, "The Second Question of the Prologue to Walter Catton's Commentary on the *Sentences*: On Intuitive and Abstractive Knowledge," *Nine Medieval Thinkers*, ed. J. Reginald O'Donnell, (Toronto, 1955), 233–269, at 257.

90. *Ord.* I, Prologue, q.1, a.6, (OTh I, 65, line 22)–(OTh I, 66, line 3).

91. *Ibid.*, (OTh I, 66, lines 8–13).

simply to be such that the second intuitive cognition, together with the intellect, is not a sufficient cause of the third. Why God has ordered the causes this way, we simply do not know. Nor does Ockham explain in the Prologue what the other partial causes of the third and fourth acts of apprehension might be. In *Quodlibeta* I, q.14, Ockham repeats the answer that the infinite process is avoided because at some point there is a natural obstacle to further intuitive cognitions of intuitive cognitions, but he does not make clear whether this obstacle is a positive obstacle or merely the lack of some necessary partial cause.[92]

In *Quaestiones variae*, q.5, (OTh VIII, 177–78), Ockham offers an alternative, and in my opinion, a better solution to this difficulty. There he maintains that the mental act alone is never a sufficient cause of an intuitive cognition of itself, but rather the mental act taken together with a volition to be aware of it. It is "in the power of the will to reflect on its own act or on an act of intellect" or not.[93] And it is the presence or absence of volitions to be aware of such acts that explains why we are sometimes aware of them and sometimes not, and why we have one intellectual intuitive cognition without having infinitely many of them.

Apparently, Chatton was unconvinced. For while acknowledging that we do have evident knowledge of propositions such as 'I understand a stone', he explains that

> ...the soul experiences something in two ways, since it experiences something as an object and something the way a subject experiences its own act...Therefore, although the experiences by which the soul experiences something as an object require an intuitive cognition..., the experiences by which it experiences something as its act and not its object do not require such an intuitive cognition. And for this experience to occur, is only for a subject to receive its act.[94]

Assent to 'I understand a stone' is caused when an intuitive cognition of a stone is received into the soul. Since sensible

92. (OTh IX, 79–82).
93. (OTh VIII, 178).
94. *Lectura in Sententias*, Prologue, q.2, (O'Callaghan ed., 257).

things are the only particulars that can be objects of thought, the infinite regress of intuitive cognitions of intuitive cognitions cannot get started.

Even though Ockham thinks that we can have intuitive cognitions of intelligibles that are in no way sensible, he follows Aristotle in saying that

> nothing can be understood without phantasms, because every intellectual intuitive cognition in this life necessarily presupposes a sensory cognition of both the external and internal senses.[95]

As indicated above, where awareness of sensible particulars is concerned, sensory intuitive cognition is a causally necessary condition of intellectual intuitive cognition. As for our awareness of our own mental acts, Ockham says,

> ...likewise, an intuitive cognition of an act of intellect or an affection or delight etc. Nevertheless, if it were possible for love to exist in the will without any previous cognition, the intuitive cognition of that love would not presuppose another. But this is impossible in this life...[96]

To be sure, an act of intellect or will presupposes some awareness of its object. But that fact by itself does not show that every intellectual intuitive cognition presupposes a sensory cognition. As Ockham himself has insisted, not every intuitive cognition has a sensible particular for its object. Ockham's remarks in the last two sentences are likewise puzzling. For he indicates that it is not possible in this life that an act of love should exist apart from every previous cognition of its object. The "in this life" might suggest that on Ockham's view, this will be possible in the next life. Perhaps all Ockham means to say is that it is in principle possible for an act of love to exist without any numerically distinct, temporally prior cognition of its object; but not that it is logically possible for an act of love to exist without any awareness of its object.

I suspect Ockham's position was this. In this life, all intellec-

---

95. *Ord.* I, Prologue, q.1, a.6, (OTh I, 67, lines 8–10).
96. *Ibid.*, (OTh I, 67, lines 15–20).

tual cognition begins with the intuitive cognition of sensible particulars. Thus, if we single out some awareness of a mental act, we will, if we trace the chain of awareness back to its starting point, eventually come to an act whose object is a sensible particular. What will be possible in the next life is not to have an act of love apart from any and every awareness of an object, but to have an act of love without a preceding intuitive cognition.

5.   ABSTRACTIVE COGNITIONS AND OCKHAM'S THEORY OF MEMORY

Ockham has contrasted intuitive cognition through which we can naturally have evident knowledge of contingent truths, with "abstractive cognition...through which we do not judge a thing to be when it is and not be when it is not."[97] If in the natural course of things we have intuitive cognitions when we are aware of existing and present objects, we presumably have abstractive cognitions when we imagine, remember, anticipate, or hallucinate things. Ockham quite obviously did not develop a fully comprehensive theory about how abstractive cognitions are produced. Instead, having noted a general dependence of abstractive cognitions on prior intuitive cognitions, he concentrates on the production of "recordative" or memory cognitions. Later, in *Reportatio* III, q.6, he sketches an account of sensory imagination.

In general, then, Ockham thinks that just as every naturally acquired intellectual intuitive cognition presupposes sensory intuitive cognition, so

> ...every naturally acquired abstractive cognition of a thing presupposes an intuitive cognition of the *same* thing. The reason for this is that no intellect can naturally acquire a cognition of a thing unless by means of that thing acting as a partial efficient cause. But every cognition for which the coexistence of the thing is necessary is an intuitive cognition. Therefore, the first cognition of a thing is intuitive. Nevertheless, God can cause an abstractive cognition both of deity and of

97. *Rep.* II, q.12–13, (OTh V, 261).

other things without any previous intuitive cognition...[98]

As it stands, Ockham's claim here has the consequence that someone who has not had an intuitive cognition of a purple cow cannot imagine a purple cow—which is contrary to experience. No doubt, he intended this remark to be understood in the light of his distinction between simple and composite concepts, as the assertion that we have no simple abstractive cognitions—e.g., no abstractive cognition of purple—without having a simple intuitive cognition of the same thing. So understood, Ockham's principle anticipates the Humean dogma that we have no simple ideas without prior corresponding simple impressions. And in *Ordinatio* I, d.3, q.2, he defends it by appealing to Aristotle's observation (in *Physics*, II, 1, 193a6–9) that "otherwise a man blind from birth could thus have an abstractive cognition of colors, just as anyone else can—which is obviously false."[99]

If Ockham thinks that intuitive cognitions are causally necessary for having an abstractive cogntion of a given object at some other time, he does not think that they are causally sufficient. He maintains that "in order to have an abstractive cognition, one must necessarily suppose something prior besides the object and the intellect."[100] The reason is that "every power that is now able to issue in some act which it was not able to issue in earlier, now has something that it did not have earlier." But, according to Ockham, an abstractive cognition of a given object is naturally possible only after intuitive cognitions, not before. Therefore, intuitive cognition must, directly or indirectly, cause something to exist in the intellect that did not exist there prior to the intuitive cognition. Ockham argues against Aquinas and Scotus that what the intuitive cognition leaves behind is not a species, but a disposition or habit inclining one to have the abstractive cognition,[101] but I shall not

98. *Ord.* I, Prologue, q.1, a.6, (OTh I, 72, lines 3–8); d.3, q.9, (OTh II, 544).

99. (OTh II, 410).

100. *Rep.* II, q.12–13, (OTh V, 269).

101. *Ibid.*, (OTh V, 271–76).

discuss these arguments here.

Ockham begins his discussion of recordative or memory cognitions in particular by introducing them as a subdivision of intuitive cognition: they are "imperfect intuitive cognitions" whereas those discussed in the preceding sections are "perfect intuitive cognitions."[102] But in numerous places he refers to them as abstractive[103] and even as "absolutely abstractive."[104] According to his initial description, recordative cognition is "that by which we judge that a thing was, or was not, at some time."[105] For example, he says that "when I see a thing intuitively, there is generated a habit that inclines me to have an abstractive cognition, by means of which I judge an assent that such a thing was at some time, because I saw it at some time."[106] He does not at first specify that the judgment about the past must be evident, in order for the cognition to be recordative. But he asserts this qualification later in the section[107] and again when he draws the distinction between perfect and imperfect intuitive cognitions at *Reportatio* IV, q.14. This requirement fits with our ordinary refusal to say that someone remembers a past situation *p* unless *p* was the case. Thus, recordative cognition is similar to perfect intuitive cognition in that it is naturally a partial cause of evident judgments about contingent propositions.[108] Unlike perfect intuitive cognition, recordative cognition can occur naturally even when its object no longer exists.[109] Further, it is not a partial cause of evident judgments of contingent truths about the present, but only about the past.[110] In at least two places, Ockham widens the scope of imperfect intuitive cognition to include cognitions

102. *Ibid.*, (OTh V, 261–62).
103. *Ibid.*, (OTh V, 261, 265, 277, 302); q.14, (OTh V, 334–35).
104. *Ibid.*, q.12–13, (OTh V, 262).
105. *Ibid.*, (OTh V, 261).
106. *Ibid.*
107. *Ibid.*, (OTh V, 262).
108. *Ibid.* II, q.12–13, (OTh V, 262).
109. *Ibid.*
110. *Ibid.*, q.16, (OTh V, 363).

that are partial causes of evident judgments about the future.[111] But he does not discuss such anticipatory or premonitory cognitions or the psychological mechanisms involved in producing them. Probably he was thinking of proper predictions which are caused naturally.

Ockham discusses two theories of how recordative cognitions are naturally produced, and his words do not make unambiguously clear which of the two he preferred. According to Philotheus Boehner, an examination of the manuscripts and text tradition shows that the theory presented first at *Reportatio* II, q.12–13, (OTh V, 261–65) and repeatedly alluded to[112] represents Ockham's considered opinion, while the theory discussed at *Reportatio* II, q.12–13, (OTh V, 263–64, 266–67) is Ockham's original but later discarded view.[113] I am in no position to evaluate Boehner's arguments based on the text tradition. But the fact that Ockham repeatedly alludes to the former rather than the latter theory supports Boehner's conclusion. If he is right, however, it seems to me that Ockham discarded the better as well as the simpler of the two theories.

According to Boehner, Ockham's final view is that

> ...while there is an intuitive cognition of some thing, I have at one and the same time an abstractive cognition of the same thing. And that abstractive cognition is a partial cause that acts together with the intellect to produce a habit that inclines me to have an imperfect intuitive cognition, through which I judge that a thing was at some time...[114]

Ockham's motive for saying that at one and the same time there is in the intellect both an intuitive and an abstractive cognition of the same object is an Aristotelian principle to which Ockham often appeals in his psychology: viz., "that a habit is always produced by acts that incline one to have similar acts of the same species."[115] But "an imperfect intuitive cognition is absolutely

---

111. *Ibid.*, q.14, (OTh V, 334–35); q.16, (OTh V, 363).

112. E.g., at *ibid.*, (OTh V, 276, 302); *Ord.* I, d.27, q.3, (OTh IV, 242).

113. "The Notitia Intuitiva of Non-Existents according to William Ockham," *Collected Articles on Ockham*, #17, 268–300, at 273–74.

114. *Rep.* II, q.12–13, (OTh V, 261–65).

115. *Ibid.*, (OTh V, 262).

an abstractive cognition" and "a perfect intuitive cognition and an abstractive cognition are of different kinds."[116] Therefore, the disposition for having a recordative cognition must be caused by an abstractive cognition. But it is possible that we should have a recordative cognition of an object immediately after we have ceased to have an intuitive cognition of it. Therefore, the abstractive cognition that causes the disposition must be simultaneous with the intuitive cognition.[117] Elsewhere, Ockham says that this abstractive cognition "immediately follows the intuitive cognition"[118] or that it "always followed the intuitive cognition,"[119] although it does not continue to exist after the intuitive cognition ceases to exist. Ockham's thought in these passages may be that the intuitive cognition exists a short interval, that the abstractive cognition is produced at some time after the first instant,[120] and that a recordative cognition is possible only after the intuitive cognition has ceased to exist.

Thus, according to this theory, the object, the intellect, and the intuitive cognition act as partial causes to produce an abstractive cognition simultaneous with or immediately following the intuitive cognition. This abstractive cognition has exactly the same content as the intuitive cognition[121] but is not apt to cause any judgment—whether "that a thing exists or that it does not exist, nor even according to any differentia of time"[122]—but it does cause a disposition or habit in the intellect inclining it to have a recordative cognition. The recordative cognition is naturally apt to cause an evident judgment concerning a contingent truth about the past.[123]

Ockham offers a parallel account of sensory imagination in

116. *Ibid.*
117. *Ibid.*, (OTh V, 262–63) and q.14, (OTh V, 333).
118. *Ibid.*, q.12–13, (OTh V, 274); *Ord.* I, d.27, q.3, (OTh IV, 242).
119. *Rep.* II, q.12–13, (OTh V, 277).
120. *Ibid.* III, q.2, (OTh VI, 65).
121. *Ord.* I, d.27, q.3, (OTh IV, 242).
122. *Rep.* II, q.14, (OTh V, 335); cf. q.12–13, (OTh V, 292).
123. *Ibid.*, q.12–13, (OTh V, 266–67); q.14, (OTh V, 334–35).

Reportatio III, q.6. My sensory intuitive cognition of Socrates' whiteness acts on my sensory power of imagination to produce my first act of imagining Socrates' whiteness.[124] The latter is an abstractive cognition and—since causes are simultaneous with their effects (see Part Four, chapter 18 below)—comes into existence while the sensory intuitive cognition still exists.[125] The first act of imagination then produces in the power of sensory imagination a habit that is a partial cause inclining the power to elicit similar acts of imagining Socrates' whiteness when it and the sensory intuitive cognition are absent or nonexistent.[126]

The Aristotelian principle—that a disposition to *A* can be used only by an act of the same species as acts of *A*-ing—does explain why Ockham assumes an abstractive sensory cognition simultaneous with the intuitive cognition. But it will force us to posit an abstractive *intellectual* cognition in addition to an intuitive one, only on the assumption that recordative cognitions are of the same species as the abstractive cognition but of a different species from the original intuitive cognition. And while Ockham does claim this, a consideration of the similarities and differences among these three types of acts makes this classification seem arbitrary. According to the theory as developed so far, none of the three cognitions differs from the others in content. Ockham has said that perfect and imperfect intuitive cognitions differ into two respects: (i) perfect intuitive cognitions are naturally apt to cause an evident judgment regarding a contingent truth about the present while imperfect intuitive cognitions are naturally apt to cause evident judgments regarding only a contingent truth about the past or future, and (ii) perfect intuitive cognitions are naturally produced only when the object exists and is present, while imperfect intuitive cognitions can be naturally produced even when the object does not exist. According to the theory, however, the abstractive cognition that is assumed to be simultaneous with or immediately consequent upon the intuitive cognition resembles imperfect intuitive cognitions with respect to the second fea-

124. (OTh VI, 123–24).   126. (OTh VI, 120–21).
125. (OTh VI, 124–25).

ture only. Ockham has even argued that it cannot resemble imperfect intuitive cognitions with respect to the first feature. For if it did, it would itself be an imperfect intuitive cognition, and there would be some imperfect intuitive cognition caused directly by a perfect intuitive cognition—which is contrary to the theory.[127] It would seem as reasonable to classify recordative cognitions as intuitive cognitions as to regard them as abstractive cognitions, and even more reasonable to say that they constitute a species of their own, distinct from that of perfect intuitive cognitions and from that of abstractive cognitions that are not apt to cause evident judgments. In either case, it would then be a violation of the Aristotelian principle invoked by Ockham to say that the abstractive cognition that is simultaneous with or immediately following the intuitive cognition and that is apt to cause no evident judgments, is the cause of a disposition or habit inclining one to have a recordative cognition. On the former classification, the perfect intuitive cognition could cause the habit directly and it would be superfluous to assume an abstractive cognition simultaneous with it. On the latter, neither of these supposed cognitions could cause the habit, and Ockham would either have to abandon the Aristotelian principle or give up his claim that a habit is involved in the production of the first recordative cognition. Ockham was not oblivious to this difficulty. In *Reportatio* II, q.14, he spells it out in full, then remarks that "the reply to this is clear from what was said above."[128] Presumably, it consists in his insistence that imperfect intuitive cognitions are of the same species as the first abstractive cognition, even though the latter is not apt to cause any evident judgment.

According to Ockham's earlier theory, "a habit is produced by an intuitive cognition [acting] as its partial cause and the abstractive cognition that is assumed to be simultaneous with the intuitive cognition can be denied."[129] In defense of this, Ockham notes that "no one experiences that he at one and the

---

127. *Ibid.* II, q.14, (OTh V, 336–37).
128. (OTh V, 337).
129. *Ibid.*, q.12–13, (OTh V, 265).

same time cognizes the same thing both intuitively and abstrac-
tively...but rather a man experiences the opposite."[130] Ockham
judged that fewer undesirable consequences would arise from
compromising the Aristotelian principle in this case than from
advancing a theory that was openly contrary to experience.[131]
He tried to soften his disagreement with the principle by asserting that a qualified version of it is true: viz., where the act in
question is the total cause of the habit, but not where the act is
only a partial cause. In this case, the intuitive cognition is not
the total cause but acts together with the intellect and the object
to produce the habit inclining one to have a recordative
cognition. This theory seems to be the more satisfactory of the
two. Nevertheless, Ockham apparently came to feel that the unqualified version of the Aristotelian principle was so central to
his psychology that he could not consistently violate it here.
And he upholds the unqualified version of it in one of his latest
works.[132]

In *Reportatio* II, q.12–13, Ockham concentrates on defending his claim that the intuitive cognition leaves behind a habit,
not a species, and on explaining how the habit is produced from
the intuitive cognition. He does not say how the recordative
cognition is produced from the habit. In *Quaestiones variae*,
q.5, (OTh VIII, 161), he notes an objection that the habit alone
cannot be a sufficient cause of our thinking of absent or past
things. For at any given time, the intellect has dispositions to
think of more such objects than it actually thinks of. Ockham
grants the objection and indicates that in addition to the habit,
"an act of will is the immediate cause of one such object being
cognized rather than another, since, evidently, the will wills
that one such object be cognized and not another..."[133]

The account in *Reportatio* II, q.12–13, (OTh V, 261–67) suggests that once we have the imperfect intuitive cognition, it acts
together with the intellect to produce the judgment that the

130. *Ibid.*
131. *Ibid.*, (OTh V, 266).
132. *Quodl.* II, q.18, (OTh IX, 189–192).
133. (OTh VIII, 191).

thing in question was or was not; just as the perfect intuitive cognition acts together with the intellect and the object to produce the judgment that the thing is, or with the intellect alone to produce a judgment that the thing is not. As stated there, the theory is perfectly general—applying equally to imperfect intuitive cognitions of sensible things and to those of mental acts and passions. For instance, having yesterday had a perfect intuitive cognition of a book on the table, I today have an imperfect intuitive cognition of the same book on the table and am thereby caused to judge that there was a book on the table yesterday. Likewise, I yesterday had a perfect intuitive cognition of my act of seeing the book on the table and today have an imperfect intuitive cognition of that act and am caused to judge that I saw a book on the table.

Ockham's extended discussion of memory in *Reportatio* IV, q.14, (OTh VII, 292–93), offers a different analysis, however. He focuses there on "acts of recording," which he confusingly identifies, not with imperfect intuitive cognitions, but rather with complex acts of apprehending and passing judgment on propositions about the past. And he insists that "...an act of recording has primarily as its immediate object, a past act insofar as it is past..."[134] Ockham emphasizes that the acts in question must be none other than the thinker's own past mental acts and

> ...not the act of someone other than the recorder—i.e., another man's act of speaking or disputing or writing. For I record such only to the extent that I record that I heard or saw him do such things, so that the act of mine which I am recording sometimes has as its term those acts of disputing, reading, etc.[135]

Presumably, he would say the same thing about the past existence of mind-independent states of affairs. Ockham considers the objection that I have acts of recording with respect to propositions about things other than my own past mental acts—e.g., "I record that the master read in the schools then and disputed etc., in such a way that I have an evident cognition

---

134. (OTh VII, 295).   135. *Ibid.*

of such complexes."[136] And he agrees that we have evident cognitions of propositions about such states of affairs. But he thinks that such evident cognitions insofar as they are produced naturally, invariably *follow from* acts of recording the past existence of our own mental acts. Thus, he writes,

> ...I have one act whose term is the complex 'I have heard the master dispute then'; the term of the other is 'The master shouted in disputing and sat in the chair'. The first cognition is recordative properly speaking. The second is an evident cognition that follows from a recordative cognition. For I do not have an evident cognition that the master shouted except because I heard him dispute and shout then and saw him then etc....[137]

Presumably, when Ockham says that the evident cognition of 'The master was disputing then' follows from the act of recording, he is using 'evident' in its broader sense, according to which propositions validly inferred by a simple inference from evident propositions are known by an evident cognition. And this account assumes an asymmetry between our memories of our own past mental acts and our memories of other past states of affairs, which asymmetry he did not assume in the account in *Reportatio* II, q.12–13 and which he does not find among our cognitions of present states of affairs.

Ockham's remarks in *Reportatio* IV, q.14 also complicate the analysis of how acts of recording are produced. So far as *Reportatio* II, q.12–13 is concerned, the imperfect intuitive cognition acts together with the intellect to cause the formulation of and assent to the past tense proposition. In *Reportatio* IV, q.14, (OTh VII, 293), however, Ockham declares that "a habit produced by abstractive acts, which acts are the partial object of the habit of recording, and the intellect and God" are a sufficient cause of an act of recording. This comment is somewhat puzzling, since one should have thought that the partial object of an act of recording was not the abstractive cognition that (on the later account) is the immediate cause of the habit, but rather the perfect intuitive cognition. Later on, in *Reportatio* IV, q.14,

136. (OTh VII, 296).   137. (OTh VII, 296–97).

(OTh VII, 297–98), Ockham introduces the notion that the complex act of assenting to the present tense proposition—e.g., to 'I hear the master disputing now'—causes a habit that inclines one thereafter to assent to the corresponding past tense proposition. When it is objected that a noncomplex abstractive act could, by the above mentioned Aristotelian principle, cause only a habit inclining one to noncomplex acts of apprehension and not to acts of assent, Ockham grants this and explains that

> ...the habit produced by a past act of the recorder together with many other noncomplex habits inclines partially to an act of recording, and besides this there are some complex habits that incline to an act of recording immediately...A noncomplex habit does not incline one to a complex act—i.e., an act of recording—immediately, but only by means of its own act...[138]

Ockham does not make himself entirely clear, but perhaps he has the following causal chain in mind: The noncomplex cognition—whether the original perfect intuitive cognition or the first abstractive cognition—causes a noncomplex habit that inclines one to have an imperfect intuitive cognition of the same thing. And the acts of formulating and assenting to the present tense proposition cause a habit that inclines one to assent to the past tense proposition. But the latter habit cannot be activated unless the former one is. Thus, the noncomplex habit mediately causes the act of recording by causing the imperfect intuitive cognition, which acts together with the complex habit and the intellect and God to cause the formulation of and assent to the past tense proposition.

6.   THE PRODUCTION OF ABSTRACT GENERAL CONCEPTS AND JUDGMENTS INVOLVING THEM

Once the intellect has acquired concepts of particulars in intuitive and abstractive cognition, it is able to form concepts whose content is more abstract than the content of any sensa-

138. (OTh VII, 310).

tion can be.[139] Since Ockham identifies universals with such abstract general concepts, the intellect can be said, by such activity of abstraction, to produce universals.[140]

Just how is this abstraction accomplished? Ockham does not say in much detail. Indeed, he shows much more interest in what and how such abstract general concepts signify and what their ontological status is, than in the psychological mechanisms by which they are produced. Nevertheless, his account in *Summa logicae* III–2, c.29, of how we come to have evident knowledge of propositions formed from abstract general concepts sheds some light on the matter:

> The first part of the definition—viz., the genus—cannot be demonstrated of the defined term either *a priori* or *a posteriori*; for example, it cannot be demonstrated that a man is an animal. But knowledge of such a proposition is acquired without a syllogism by means of intuitive cognition. Thus, when these concepts 'man' and 'animal' exist in the intellect and some man is seen, immediately one knows that a man is an animal. Not that these concepts precede the intuitive cognition of a man. Rather this is the process: first, a man is cognized by some particular sense. Then the same man is cognized by the intellect. Given this [intellectual] cognition of that man, [the intellect] comes to have a cognition that is general and common to every man. That cognition which is common to every man is called a concept, intention, or affection (*passio*). When this concept exists in the intellect, immediately the intellect knows, without any discursive reasoning, that a man is something. Then, when it has apprehended an animal or animals other than man, a general cognition common to every animal is produced. This general cognition is common to every animal and is called an affection (*passio*) or mental intention or concept common to every animal. When this concept exists in the mind, the intellect can compound it with the previous concept. When they are mutually compounded by means of the verb 'is', immediately the intellect assents to that complex without any syllogism...[141]

From the above passage, it is clear that an intuitive cognition of a particular is a partial cause of an abstract general concept.

139. *Ord.* I, Prologue, q.1, a.6, (OTh I, 65, lines 4–6).
140. *Rep.* II, q.12–13, (OTh V, 304).
141. (OPh I, 557).

Three points are left obscure, however.

(i) This passage does not make it clear whether Ockham thinks that such an intuitive cognition, together with the intellect, can serve as a total cause of the abstract general concept, or whether some other act of intellect is required. In *Quaestiones variae,* q.5, (OTh VIII, 175), however, he insists that noncomplex cognitions—say of "a whiteness or two whitenesses"—suffice as a natural cause of an abstract general concept of whiteness, just as much as fire suffices as a natural cause of heat. No further activity of the intellect or any act of will is required. This claim is not very plausible. For it seems that we have intuitive cognitions of many things, a concept of whose most specific specific species we should find difficult to abstract. We would not experience this difficulty, if the intuitive cognition, together with the intellect, were a total cause of the abstract general concept.

(ii) Similarly, Ockham does not state unambiguously whether or not he thinks that an intuitive cognition of *one* particular always suffices, or whether it is sometimes necessary to have intuitive cognitions of more than one particular. The wording of the long passage quoted above suggests that we can abstract a general concept of man on the basis of an intuitive cognition of one particular man. On the other hand, he does not say that we can abstract a general concept of animal on the basis of a single animal, but suggests that we must first apprehend at least one animal of a different species as well. Likewise, in *Ordinatio* I, d.3, q.6, Ockham says that

> a cognition of whiteness and of blackness suffices for a cognition of color, and similarly, [a cognition] of two other species [of color] between [black and white] suffice for a cognition of color. And universally, any two species of color suffice for a cognition of color...[142]

Ockham holds here that a cognition of colors of two species is sufficient, not necessary to produce a general concept of color. But if he had thought that a cognition of one species would suffice, one wonders why he did not say so. On the other hand,

142. (OTh II, 501).

in *Quaestiones variae,* q.5, (OTh VIII, 175), Ockham speaks indifferently of "someone who sees a whiteness or two whitenesses" abstracting a concept of whiteness in general—which suggests that an intuitive cogntion of one whiteness would suffice. Perhaps Ockham's view was that an intuitive cognition of one particular is enough to produce an abstract general concept of the most specific species, but that intuitive cognition of particulars from more than one species are required to abstract a general concept of the genus. This conjecture is at least partially confirmed by Ockham's remark in *Quodlibeta* I, q.13 that "...the concept of genus is never abstracted from one individual..."[143] But he adds that the most general concept of being can be derived from the experience of any particular whatever!

Although Ockham thinks that every abstract general concept presupposes for its production, the cognition of some particular or other, he explicitly says that it does not require the cognition of all of them or of any one in particular.

> ...Nevertheless, in any man, the cognition of any universal presupposes the cognition of some particular or particulars. But in different human beings it is sometimes not the cognition of the same particulars that precedes, but of different ones, although the universal concept (*ratio*) known is the same.[144]

Or again,

> In different human beings, however, the cognition of universals begins from cognition of different particulars of different species. For example, a student in Greece begins with a cognition of the particular animals that are found there, and perhaps many of them are not found in Italy. Conversely, for the students in Italy or France or England, and so on for the other regions...[145]

If this were not so, we would not be able to formulate general

143. (OTh IX, 75).
144. *Ord.* I, d.3, q.6, (OTh II, 502).
145. *Ibid.*

propositions such as 'Every man is an animal' without first having an intuitive cognition of every particular human being.

(iii) Ockham does not say in the above passage whether intuitive cognitions are always required for abstraction, or whether abstractive cognitions of particulars are sometimes enough. In *Quaestiones variae* q.5, (OTh VIII, 175), however, he explicitly says that either intuitive or abstractive cognitions of particulars may serve as a basis for making the abstraction.

7. THE CAUSES OF PROPOSITION-FORMATION AND ACTS OF JUDGMENT

Ockham says that intuitive cognition is that "noncomplex cognition of a term or terms by virtue of which one can have evident cognition of a contingent truth."[146] His remarks in the Prologue and *Reportatio* II, q.12–13 fill out the causal chain that culminates in assent to a contingent truth. Where judgments about sensible particulars are concerned, the chain starts with the object's causing one to have a sensory intuitive cognition of itself under some aspect. For example, when I look at the existent and present Socrates, if there is no interference with the natural order of causes I will be caused to have a sensory intuitive cognition of Socrates and his whiteness.[147] The sensory intuitive cognition will then cause an intellectual intuitive cognition of the same object under the same aspect. In the above case, I might apprehend Socrates and his whiteness by two distinct intellectual intuitive cognitions or possibly by a single noncomplex cognition.[148] The intellectual intuitive cognition or cognitions, acting together with Socrates and his whiteness, then cause an act of apprehending the copula. But, as Aristotle says, the copula cannot be understood without extremes. Thus,

146. *Ord.* I, Prologue, q.1, a.1, (OTh I, 31).
147. *Ord.* I, Prologue, q.1, (OTh I, 6–7).
148. *Rep.* II, q.12–13, (OTh V, 280–81).

> an act whose term is the copula or the concept of the copula does not
> have this as its term absolutely, but also has at the same time the subject
> and predicate as its term. The acts whose terms are only the subject and
> predicate are noncomplex, but the act whose term is the copula is com-
> plex insofar as it has the whole complex as its immediate term...[149]

Since by definition intuitive cognitions can cause only evident
cognitions, and since evident cognitions are of true propositions only, the complex thus apprehended must be a true one.
And the apprehension of it causes an act of assent. (As noted
above, Ockham does allow that there could be complex acts of
apprehension without prior and distinct noncomplex acts, and
acts of judgment without prior and distinct acts of apprehension.[150] But this is apparently not the natural case.) The complex act of apprehension is also a partial cause of disposition
(*habitus*) to understand the whole proposition by one act.[151]
An analogous causal chain would be involved in producing
judgments about our own mental acts.

In the case just described—where I have an intuitive cognition of Socrates and his whiteness and thereby formulate
the judgment 'Socrates is white'—the intuitive cognition of
Socrates and whiteness themselves serve as the subject and
predicate terms of the mental proposition. No abstract general
concept of whiteness is needed. But Socrates is also an animal
and a substance. Thus, when I have an intuitive cognition of
Socrates, I thereby have an intuitive cognition of an animal and
a substance. Can I use my intuitive cognition as both the subject
and the predicate terms in the mental propositions 'Socrates is
an animal' and 'Socrates is a substance'? It would seem that I
cannot. For if I did, the result would be 'Socrates is Socrates',
not 'Socrates is an animal' or 'Socrates is a substance'. To formulate the latter, I should have to use abstract general concepts
of animal and substance, respectively. Ockham's remarks in
Quodlibeta I, q.13 confirm this suspicion. Focussing on the case
in which I see an object approaching in the distance and judge it

---

149. *Ibid.*, (OTh V, 280).
150. *Ord.* I, Prologue, q.1, a.6, (OTh I, 59, lines 14–23).
151. *Rep.* II, q.12–13, (OTh V, 280).

to be an animal, he says,

> ...I judge it to be an animal because I have the concept of animal, which is the concept of a genus, earlier...Thus, if I did not have the concept of the genus animal earlier, I would have to judge only that the thing seen was something.[152]

The second sentence seems to allude to Ockham's contention that we cannot abstract the general concept of a genus from the experience of only one member of that genus. The most that would follow from this alone, however, is that I cannot judge that Socrates is an animal if Socrates is the only animal I have ever seen. Ockham here suggests that even if he is the second or third animal I have seen, I must have abstracted the general concept 'animal' prior to this occasion of seeing him, if I am to use this concept in formulating a judgment.

Two singular categorical propositions can be formed from the concept of Socrates and the concept of his whiteness—viz., 'Socrates is white' and 'Socrates is not white'. According to what Ockham says in *Reportatio* II, q.12–13, (OTh V, 256–57), an intuitive cognition of Socrates and his whiteness, together with the existing and present Socrates and his whiteness, are sufficient cause of the intellect's forming and apprehending the true one, 'Socrates is white'. In *Quaestiones variae,* q.5, however, Ockham maintains that a volition is a partial efficient cause of proposition-formation in every case. He argues that

> noncomplex cognitions of the terms and the intellect, if it is active, are natural agents and are no more inclined to form a true proposition than a false one, an affirmative than a negative one...[153]

Hence, they cannot be a sufficient cause of our forming one proposition rather than another. Ockham concludes that

> ...Therefore, I say that the cause of a true proposition's being formed rather than a false one, an affirmative rather than a negative one, is the will. For the will wills to form one and not the other. Therefore, the act that is apprehended after the complex, is formed from a noncomplex

152. (OTh IX, 77–78).   153. (OTh VIII, 169).

cognition of the terms of the proposition and by an act of will, and this
is general...[154]

Thus, it is the noncomplex cognitions of the terms, together
with a volition to form one proposition rather than the other,
that is the sufficient cause of the intellect's forming a certain
proposition.

> ...For, having assumed the act of will by which it wills that such a com-
> plex be formed, and having assumed the noncomplex cognitions of the
> terms of that complex, an act of apprehending or forming that complex
> necessarily follows, just as an effect necessarily follows its cause.[155]

The inconsistency between Ockham's accounts might be resolved if we supposed that in *Quaestiones variae*, q.5, (OTh
VIII, 169–70), he was concentrating on the cases where the
noncomplex cognitions are either abstractive cognitions or
abstract general concepts rather than intuitive cognitions. But
so far as I know, Ockham never removes the inconsistency
himself.

Further, just as he claims in *Questiones variae* q.5, (OTh VIII,
169–70), that violations play an essential role in proposition
formation, so in *Questiones variae*, q.5, (OTh VIII, 174–75), he
assigns them an essential role in our syllogistic reasoning. For he
claims that volitions are a necessary partial cause of our formulating syllogisms.

> ...I say that these acts—viz., of producing a syllogism, forming proposi-
> tions disposed according to mood and figure—have, as their sufficient
> causes, noncomplex cognitions of the terms and an act of will by which
> the will wills to form such complexes. Thus, these noncomplex cogni-
> tions of the terms and the volition combine with God to make a total
> cause of such acts. For given the above mentioned cognitions and voli-
> tions, the act of syllogizing follows immediately as an effect without
> any activity of the intellect...

Where acts of assent or dissent are concerned. Ockham observes that no single reason can be given why assent or dis-

154. (OTh VIII, 170).   155. *Ibid*.

sent to all propositions is caused.''[156] But he does try to account for a number of cases. First of all, evident assent, by definition, has a noncomplex cognition of the terms as a sufficient mediate or immediate cause. When evident assent is given to contingent propositions, the noncomplex cognitions of the terms must be intuitive cognitions. Sometimes a person assents to a contingent proposition because of an authority. In that case, ''assent to the authority,'' presumably together with acts of apprehending the proposition and its terms, ''cause assent to that proposition.''[157] Sometimes a person assents to a contingent proposition ''because he wants to believe it...In that case, the volition, together with noncomplex cognitions and an act of apprehending the complex, causes the assent.''[158] Again, a person sometimes assents to a proposition that he has inferred from other propositions. Ockham says that in such cases, assent to the premiss(es), together with acts of apprehending the conclusion and its term, causes assent to the conclusion. Ockham never explictly mentions as one of the causes a belief that the conclusion follows from the premisses, although such a belief would seem to be involved in many cases. He does say, however, that if assent to the premiss(es) is evident, and if the inference is necessary and *very evident*, then assent to the conclusion will be certain and evident; and if one has doubts about the premiss(es), and if the inference is necessary and *very evident*, then one may be led to dissent from the conclusion. By including the stipulation that the inference must be very evident, Ockham seems implicitly to acknowledge that whether or not the inference was clear to someone might make a difference as to whether or not he would assent to the conclusion. Again, omitting this proviso, Ockham says that an act of faith with respect to the premisses, together with acts of apprehending the conclusion and its terms, suffice to cause an act of faith with respect to the conclusion.[159] ''...Sometimes someone assents to a false proposition or dissents from a true one, and sometimes

156. (OTh VIII, 171–73).

157. (OTh VIII, 173).

158. *Ibid*.

159. (OTh VIII, 185).

the other way around..."[160] In some cases, this happens because some causally necessary condition of dissent or assent, respectively, is lacking. Again, having assented to some false propositions or dissented from some true ones, someone may be led to assent to and dissent from propositions that evidently follow from them. Finally, one may assent to false propositions, respectively, by fallacious inferences.

8.   COMPLICATIONS AND DIFFICULTIES

The theory Ockham offers in the Prologue to his commentary on the *Sentences* and in *Reportatio* II, q.12–13, seems fairly simple and straightforward. In the natural course of things, when Socrates exists and is present before me, I am caused to have a sensory intuitive cognition of Socrates and his whiteness, which in turn causes me to have an intellectual intuitive cognition of those same objects. And the latter is an immediate partial cause of my judgment that Socrates is white. Simultaneously or immediately thereafter, I have an abstractive cognition of Socrates and his whiteness whose content is exactly the same as that of the intuitive cognition which is a partial cause of habit inclining me to have an imperfect intuitive cognition of these objects. And if I have such an imperfect intuitive cognition later, it will act as a partial cause of my forming the evident judgment that Socrates was white. Thus, Ockham's view seems to be that I have intuitive cognitions of sensible substances and sensible qualities (as well as of my own mental acts and passions) and abstractive cognitions of exactly the same things.

Ockham's further reflections seem to call various aspects of this account into question, however. (8.1) First, Ockham appears to back off from his claim—insisted on in his criticism of Scotus—that our initial abstractive cognitions are of the same object under the same aspect as our intuitive cognitions are. For, as already discussed in Part One, chapter 4, Ockham comes to believe that what makes an act of thought proper to and

160. (OTh VIII, 172).

determinately of one particular rather than others equally similar to it is the fact that the act stands or can stand in the appropriate causal relation to the former and not the latter. But Ockham specifies the appropriate causal relation in such a way that no abstractive cognition bears that relation to any mind-independent particular. And he concludes in *Quodlibeta* I, q.13, that

> the first simple and abstractive cognition by the primacy of generation is not proper to any particular, but sometimes—indeed always—a common cognition.[161]

As if realizing that this would be contrary to his earlier explanation, Ockham notes the following objection:

> ...it seems that the first abstractive cognition is proper—especially when the object is close enough. For through the first abstractive cognition, I can have a recordative cognition concerning the same thing seen earlier—which I could not do unless I had a proper abstractive cognition of the thing seen earlier.[162]

He replies that

> ...as a result of seeing something, I do have a proper abstractive cognition, but it is not simple but composed of simples. And this composite cognition is a principle of recording, since through it I record concerning Socrates that I saw him so formed and so figured, so colored, of such a height and breadth, and in such a place. And through that composite, I record that I have seen Socrates...[163]

Ockham does not claim that no abstractive cognitions are proper, but only that no simple ones are. Apparently, when I see Socrates and his whiteness, I have an intuitive cognition that is equally similar to many whitenesses but is proper to Socrates' whiteness. But this intuitive cognition causes an abstractive cognition that is equally similar to many whitenesses and proper to none. This consequence is at odds with the account discussed

161. (OTh IX, 74).   163. (OTh IX, 77).
162. (OTh IX, 75).

above, according to which the first abstractive cognition caused by an intuitive cognition of Socrates' whiteness would be one that was proper to that same whiteness. Ockham seems to suppose that the composite concept may be proper because Socrates may be the only thing that has all of the properties conceived of by it. The difficulties with this suggestion parallel those involved with Russell's treatment of ordinary proper names as truncated descriptions, and would cast doubt on whether Ockham's theory ever or often allows us a proper abstractive cognition of anything.

(8.2) Ockham has insisted that all of our mental activity begins with sensory and intellectual intuitive cognitions of particulars. But Ockham's predecessors had appealed to familiar perceptual phenomena in arguing that universals, not particulars, are the first objects of intellect. For example, there is the (alleged) fact that children at first call all men father and all women mother. Again, there is the experience of watching an object approach from the distance. At first, we have a cognition whose content is such that we are able to judge only that the approaching thing is a being; then, only that it is an animal; then, only that it is a man; and finally, that it is Socrates. Ockham's predecessors explained that we are first aware of things under their more universal aspect and then under their more particular aspect.[164] To sustain his own viewpoint, Ockham must provide an alternative explanation of these phenomena.

The examples cited both involve failures of perceptual discrimination. And neither seems to be a case in which the perceiver takes himself to be aware of a universal rather than a particular. We do not think that there is a universal approaching from a distance. Rather we judge that it is some particular or other, although our conception of it does not enable us to tell which particular it is.

So far as the mental-act theory is concerned, Ockham's analysis of what makes a cognition proper to a particular seems to account for these facts. When I see an object approaching in

164. For Ockham's discussion of their views, see *Ordinatio* I, d.3, q.5–7, (OTh II, 442–523).

the distance and my cognition enables me to judge only that it is an animal, this is because my cognition is equally similar to all animals, leaving aside similarities resulting from the fact that my cognition is a mental quality. Nevertheless, the cognition is of one animal rather than another because it was or could have been caused only by that one and not others (see Part One, chapter 4 above).

On the objective-existence theory, however, the fact that a thought is of a particular is analysed in terms of the direction of the mental act towards an objectively existent particular. And if my thought is so directed, when I watch an object approaching from the distance, how can its content be sufficient to enable me to judge only that it is a being or an animal?

Ockham's reply is, basically, that merely thinking of things that are distinct and under the aspect by virtue of which they are distinct does not necessarily enable the thinker to discriminate one from the other.[165] It is essential to Ockham's metaphysics that things are numerically distinct in and of themselves and not by virtue of any individuating principle's combining with a common nature. In particular, numerically distinct things are not made numerically distinct by some difference in properties that could be substituted in a nontrivial

165. Ockham makes these points quite explicitly in commenting on our sensory awareness of things:

> ...I say that the object of one sensation is numerically one. When it is said that 'a power that cognizes the object this way—viz., insofar as it is one by this unity—cognizes it insofar as it is distinct from every other', I say that it cognizes what is distinct from every other and cognizes it under that aspect (ratio) through which it is distinct from every other. For that aspect, which is the thing itself, is the immediate term of the act of cognition. Nevertheless, it is not necessary that because of this, it could discern or distinguish it from everything else, since more is required for discrete cognition than for an apprehending cognition. For there is never actually a discrete cognition except with respect to distinct things. Nor is it even sufficient that distinct things are apprehended unless they are dissimilar in themselves or distinct in place or situation...(Ord. I, d.2, q.6, (OTh II, 208–209)).

Similar points are made about both sensory and intellectual cognition in Ordinatio I, d.3, q.6, (OTh II, 496–99).

version of the Identity of Indiscernibles. Ockham is committed
to the claim that it is in principle possible that numerically
distinct things should not differ with respect to any such
properties. Thus, if things are numerically distinct in and of
themselves, one who is aware of those things is aware of that by
virtue of which they are distinct. Nevertheless, Ockham insists
that "a created power of apprehension can discriminate one
thing from another only because of some dissimiliarity..."[166] If
a and b are numerically distinct but not dissimilar, no creature
who apprehends them will be able to distinguish between them.
Even where a and b do differ with respect to properties that
could be substituted in a nontrivial formulation of Identity of
Indiscernibles, Ockham does not think it follows from the fact
that one is aware of both a and b that one is aware that they differ in a and b, respectively, as the immediate objects of one's
thought and another to know all of the properties that can be
truly predicated of a and b, respectively. Creatures are capable
of the former. But since infinitely many properties can be truly
predicated of each actual or possible thing, only God is capable
of the latter.[167]

Sometimes a thinker fails to be aware of dissimilarities be-

---

166. *Ibid.*, d.3, q.6, (OTh II, 498).

167. For example, Ockham writes in *Ordinatio* I, d.3, q.7:
...I say that 'comprehension' is taken in many ways. (i) In one way for
every cognition, and so understood it means the same as 'apprehension'...(ii) Otherwise, it is taken for the apprehension of whatever is
essential to the thing cognized and so is the same as a distinct cognition
of a thing when nothing is hidden but everything intrinsic to the thing
is clear. (iii) In the third way, it is taken for the clearest and most
perfect cognition that there can be of a thing. (iv) In the fourth way, it
is taken for the cognition of a thing under everything predicable of the
thing. (v) In the fifth way, it is taken for a distinct cognition of a thing
and for such perfection in the act of cognition as there is in the object
cognized.

God and creatures are comprehended by the intellect in the first and
second way. In the third and fourth way, neither God nor creatures can
be comprehended by creatures...In the fifth way a creature can be comprehended by a creature, but God cannot (OTh II, 522–23).
The second sort of comprehension does not imply the fourth. Similar points
are made in *Reportatio* IV, q.5, (OTh VII, 319).

tween things he has apprehended, because he is aware of only some of their parts and not others, and the parts he is aware of are maximally similar to each other. Ockham distinguishes distinct from confused cognitions as follows:

> ...A distinct cognition of a thing is that by which anything essential to the thing cognized is clear to the power, so that nothing essential or intrinsic is hidden from the power...A confused cognition of the object is that by which something of the object is clear to the power and something of the object is hidden from the power...[168]

And the suggestion is that when I watch an object approaching from a distance, my initial cognitions of it are confused.

Thus, Ockham's view is that when I see an object approaching from the distance, and my cognition is such that I am able to judge only that it is an animal, this is not because the object of my thought is a universal rather than a particular. Rather it is because I have only a confused cognition of the thing, and the particular parts I am aware of are dissimilar to plants but maximally similar to some parts of any animal. Again, when I am able to judge only that it is a man approaching, this is because the particular parts I am aware of are maximally similar to those of other men. It seems more doubtful whether I am—as the example suggests—ever able to judge of the approaching object only that it is a being. For it would seem that the parts that I am aware of by sight are always more similar to physical objects and/or physical phenomena (such as rainbows) than to incorporeal substances. I would thus be able to judge that the approaching being was a physical object or physical phenomenon of some sort.

(iii) Ockham's remarks in the Prologue imply that we can have naturally produced intuitive cognitions of particular corporeal substances. For he says that we have intuitive cognitions of Socrates and his whiteness, and Socrates is a particular substance compounded out of particular matter and a plurality of particular substantial forms.[169] And from what has been said

168. *Ord.* I, d.3, q.5, (OTh II, 471–72).
169. Cf. Part One, chapter 2 above. For a full discussion of Ockham's hylomorphism, see Part Four, chapter 15 below.

so far, one might guess that Ockham thought we could have distinct cognitions of Socrates when he is close at hand, if we can have only confused cognitions of him when he is far away. Ockham's assertions elsewhere contradict both claims, however.

First, Ockham does not allow that we can have distinct cognitions of any corporeal substances in this life for the simple reason that matter is an essential part of any such substance, and we cannot have any intuitive cognitions of matter in this life.[170]

Not only that: we cannot have any confused cognitions of such substances either. For matter and substantial form are their only essential parts. But in *Summulae Physicorum*, where he is discussing corporeal substances that can be generated and corrupted, he insists we do not have any noncomplex cognitions either of matter or of substantial form. Rather the term 'matter' is shorthand for a complex such as 'something is deprived of something and afterwards can stand under it' or 'there is something in reality which is first deprived of form and afterwards does not lack it and that is called matter'; and the term 'substantial form' for 'a thing is apt to inform another'.[171] It follows that we have no intuitive cognitions either of matter or of the substantial form that inheres in it and hence no confused intuitive cognitions of corporeal substances.

Again, Ockham's discussion in *Ordinatio* I, d.3, q.8, implies that we cannot have any naturally produced intuitive cognitions of corporeal substances at all. For he maintains (i) that "it is necessary for an intuitive cognition that the very thing that is in-

---

170. For example, *Reportatio* IV, q.2:
In reply to another, I say that just as there is no difficulty in the fact that some natural matter is extended and nevertheless could not be apprehended by any sense or by the intellect in this life, nor be understood by an intuitive cognition and never by a sensory intuitive cognition; so there can be a quality that can be cognized by an intellectual intuitive cognition, although not in this life and nevertheless never could be cognized by any sense (OTh VII, 37–38).
Cf. *Summulae Physicorum* I, c.15, (Rome, 1637, 19); c.20, (Rome, 1637, 25).
171. I, c.20, 25.

tuitively cognized cause the act of understanding, since otherwise that thing could not be intuitively cognized naturally..."[172] This claim was part of the theory originally presented. But in the very next reply Ockham goes on to say (ii) that

> in the present life...nothing can move the intellect to have a cognition of it except mind-independent sensible qualities, or at least what is sensible through itself, and some things within the soul—viz., acts and passions—and perhaps the intellectual soul itself (this would be the case if it were intuitively seen by itself in this life)...[173]

From premises (i) and (ii), it follows (iii) that in this life we can have a naturally produced intellectual intuitive cognition only of sensible qualities, or what is sensible through itself, and of the acts and passions of our own soul, and perhaps of our own intellectual soul itself. Omitted from the lists are mind-independent corporeal substances. And in *Ordinatio* I, d.3, q.2, Ockham explicitly declares that

> ...no exterior corporeal substance can be cognized by us naturally in itself, whatever is [true] of the intellectual soul or any substance that pertains to the essence of the knower...[174]

This claim is not equivalent to (iii), since it leaves open the possibility not only that we might have an intuitive cognition of our own intellectual soul, but of any substance that pertains to our own essence. Ockham in fact thinks that each particular human being contains three substantial forms—the intellectual soul, the sensory soul, and the form of the body— of which the first is the dominant substantial form that places a man in a species. Nevertheless, he does not think that this conclusion can be adequately proved (see Part Four, chapter 15 below). Accordingly, Ockham may here be leaving open the possibility that we might have—in which case we would be able to have an intuitive cognition of at least one corporeal substance, our own body—or merely acknowledging that for all natural reason can

172. (OTh II, 540).   174. (OTh II, 474).
173. (OTh II, 541).

demonstrate, it is not the intellectual soul but some other substance that pertains to our essence. Either way, his claim is that we cannot have an intuitive cognition of any corporeal substance that is "exterior" to ourselves in the sense of not belonging to us essentially.

Why does Ockham deny that exterior corporeal substances can act on our intellects to produce intuitive cognitions of themselves? Scotus had given a theological argument based on the doctrine of Transubstantiation. According to this doctrine, in the sacrament of Holy Communion or the Eucharist, the host starts out as the substance bread with accidents inhering in it. When the priest says the words of consecration, the substance of the bread disappears and the substance of the body of Christ becomes present. The accidents that formerly inhered in the bread do not come to inhere in the body of Christ, however. Rather they do not inhere in anything. Scotus says that if we were able to have intuitive cognitions of substances, this change of substance would be evident to us in our experience—which it is not. Hence, it must be that substances cannot act on our intellects to produce intuitive cognitions.[175] Scotus draws a general conclusion about all substances, but the most ex-periences during the Mass would support is the conclusion that exterior corporeal substances cannot cause intuitive cognitions of themselves in our intellects. Ockham would have rejected this argument, however, maintaining that there are two pos-sible explanations of our failure to experience the change of substances: the one offered by Scotus—that we are naturally unable to apprehend corporeal substances; and the other—that God intervenes to prevent us from exercising our natural ability to apprehend them on this occasion. In Ockham's opinion, it is the divine will obstructing our natural ability to apprehend sen-sible accidents that explains our failure to detect Christ's ac-cidents under the consecrated host.[176] Perhaps Ockham merely bases his claim—that we do not naturally have intuitive cogni-tions of mind-independent corporeal substances—on the results

175. *Ord.* I, d.3, p.1, q.3, n.140, (Vaticana III, 87–88).
176. *Rep.* IV, q.7, (OTh VII, 120); cf. Part One, chapter 6 above.

of introspection.

Replying to the suggestion that "substance is cognized by us in itself and nevertheless not by an intuitive cognition,"[177] Ockham denies it, saying

> ...that no one can naturally have an abstractive cognition of anything in itself unless he previously had an intuitive cognition of the same thing, since otherwise a man blind from birth could thus have an abstractive cognition of colors, just as anyone else can—which is obviously false.[178]

He does allow that we can have connotative and negative concepts of substance in general, such as that of a being that subsists through itself, a being that is not in another, or a being that is the subject of all accidents.[179]

If we cannot naturally have intuitive cognition of substances, how do we come to conceive of substances at all? Ockham's answer is that we do so through accidents. Thus, he writes at *Ordinatio* I, d.8, q.3, that

> ...according to Truth, the differentiae of substances are unknown to us—indeed, they are more unknown to us than accidents, since they do not become known to us except through accidents...[180]

And in *Quodlibeta* III, q.6, he twice remarks to the effect that "...we have no other experience of substance than through accidents."[181] And he adds that since there is no necessary correlation between producing similar or different accidents and being of the same species given that we know substance only through the accident, we have no way of proving with certainty that things differ in substance.

Ockham's assumption that we could acquire the above mentioned connotative and negative concepts of substance in general on the basis of our experience of accident is not

177. *Ord.* I, d.3, q.2, (OTh II, 406).
178. *Ibid.*, (OTh II, 410).
179. *Ibid.*, (OTh II, 416–17).
180. (OTh III, 206).
181. (OTh IX, 227).

surprising. But how we should conceive of or come to know the existence of particular substances or kinds of substances (such as animal or man) through accidents is left unclear. As we have seen in Part One, chapter 8, Ockham thinks that certain qualities are really distinct from substances. Hence there is no logically necessary connection between the existence of, e.g., a color quality and the existence of something in which it inheres. And Ockham explicitly denies that there is any necessary connection between accidents of a certain kind and substances of a certain kind. Further, if in this life we cannot naturally have any intuitive cognitions of particular corporeal substances, we will never be able to observe any constant conjunction between the existence of accidents and the existence of substances, on which to base an inference of the latter from the former. Ockham admits that we have no way of telling with certainty whether substances of the same or of different kinds are associated with various collections of accidents. But it seems that he should have added that we have no way of knowing with certainty whether or not any substance is associated with a given collection of accidents.

In his article "Ockham on Evidence, Necessity, and Intuition," T. K. Scott tries to show that Ockham is not really saddled with this conclusion.[182] He admits that

> ...if Ockham had held that only accidents are seen, he would indeed have left himself an insuperable problem, since his repeatedly stated view is that knowledge of one thing never yields knowledge of another, unless the latter is already known as associated with the former (see, e.g., *Sentences*, Prologue, q.9 F...)...[183]

But Scott appeals to Ockham's remark in *Quodlibeta* I, q.13, that

> ...I record concerning Socrates that I saw him so formed and so colored, of such a height, of such a breadth, and in such a place. And through that composite I record that I have seen Socrates...[184]

182. *Journal of the History of Philosophy*, VII (1969): 27–49.
183. 33, note 22.
184. (OTh IX, 77).

as evidence that

> Ockham holds no such position...What is seen is Socrates shaped, not Socrates' shape. What is intuited is a substance as subject of an accident, not merely an accident (see *Sentences,* Prologue, q.1 X; (*Quodlibeta* I, q.8; *Quodlibeta* VII, q.7, for just a few examples). Furthermore, as the quotation above again illustrates, it could not be the case that only accidents are seen, since shape, length, breadth, and location are not 'real' accidents at all, but are only ways of conceiving a substance and its parts (see e.g., *Summa logicae* I, c.47 & 61).[185]

And he asserts that at least where typical, non-miraculous cases are concerned, Ockham would without doubt agree with Buridan's account in his *Questions on the Eight Books of Physics* I, q.4, where he says that

> I first have a concept that confusedly and simultaneously represents substance and accident, as when I perceive a white thing (*album*). I do not see the whiteness alone, but the white thing.[186]

Unfortunately, not all of the passages Scott cites bear on the issue at hand. For instance, *Quodlibeta* I, q.8 deals exclusively with the cognitions of angels, whereas the present concern is with what human beings can naturally apprehend in this life. Again, *Quodlibeta* VII, q. 7 (now VIII, q. 2, (OTh IX, 706–708)) contains Ockham's views about which qualities are really distinct from substances and says nothing about our cognitions of them. The remaining two do suggest that we can have intuitive cognitions of substances as well as accidents. *Ordinatio*, Prologue, q.1 X is a familiar passage in which Ockham speaks of our having intuitive cognition of Socrates and his whiteness. And the wording of the above quoted passage from the *Quodlibeta* I, q.13 does lend support to Scott's interpretation and is suggestive of the line Buridan appears to take. Even so, the unqualified assertion—that Ockham thought we have

185. 33–34, note 22.
186. Translated from Scott's quotation of the Paris, 1509 edition on 34, note 22.

naturally produced intuitive cognitions of mind-independent corporeal substances—would not thereby be warranted. For there are the passages in *Ordinatio* I, d.3, q.2 and q.8, as well as those in *Summulae Physicorum*, which imply the opposite. And in any event two problems remain with Scott's handling of the *Quodlibeta* I, q.13 passage and with his confidence that Ockham is anticipating Buridan. (a) First, Scott is mistaken when he infers that substances must be seen because shape, length, breadth, and location are seen and are not real accidents. As we have seen in Part One, chapter 6, Ockham contends that the latter accidents are not things (*res*) really distinct from substances *and qualities*. And he thinks that whiteness and other sensible qualities that are really distinct from substances have shape, length, breadth, and location *of themselves*.[187] Thus, he could hold that what one sees is not Socrates so shaped, so located, etc. but Socrates' whiteness so shaped, so located, etc.—although this is not the literal interpretation of *Quodlibeta* I, q.13. (b) Second, some clarification is needed of Buridan's suggestion that we first have a concept which confusedly represents the substance and accident simultaneously. Ockham distinguishes two senses in which something can be cognized confusedly. According to the first and proper sense, an object is cognized confusedly "when something is cognized and not everything whatever intrinsic to it is clear to the power..." According to the second and improper sense, a thing is conceived confusedly by means of a general concept that is common to it and to others—e.g., Socrates and Plato are confusedly conceived of by means of the abstract general concept 'man'.[188] The wording of Buridan's statement suggests that he may have something more like the latter in mind. On Ockham's view, the suggestion would be that just as my concept 'man' is equally similar to Socrates and Plato, so the concept I first get of corporeal things is equally similar to whiteness and the substance. If we add that the latter concept

187. E.g., *Rep.* IV, q.4, (OTh VII, 77); cf. Part One, chapter 6, section 2 above

188. *Ord.* I, d.3, q.5, (OTh II, 472).

has both the substance and the whiteness as partial efficient causes, it follows that it is equally of both of them. In the second sense, we have a confused cognition of a whole when we cognize some of its intrinsic or essential parts and not others. It follows, on Ockham's definition, that we have a confused cognition of a whole only if we have a distinct cognition of one or more of its intrinsic or essential parts. Thus, to have a confused intuitive cognition of substance in this sense, we should have to have a distinct intuitive cognition of matter or of substantial form—both of which Ockham elsewhere denies.

So far as I know, Ockham nowhere abandons his claim that we can have intuitive cognitions of mind-independent sensible qualities such as whiteness. And it is presumably such particular sensible qualities that Ockham has in mind when he says that we sometimes do have distinct intuitive cognitions of sensible particulars.[189]

9.   CONCEPTUAL EMPIRICSM AND DIRECT REALISM

It is clear.from the above discussion how, for Ockham, intuitive cognition is the starting point of our mental activity in this life. According to the natural order of causes, human mental acitvity begins with sensory intuitive cognitions of particular physical objects. Ockham's discussion in the Prologue would suggest that these include physical substances as well as qualities, but elsewhere he implies that in this life we have no intuitive cognitions of corporeal substances—at least of none other than our own bodies. Such acts of the sensory soul, together with the existing and present object, naturally suffice to cause an intellectual intuitive cognition of the same object under the same aspect. Given one or more intellectual intuitive cognitions of such things, the intellect compounds them by means of the copula or the copula with a negation sign, thus producing a complex act of apprehending a contingent proposi-

189. *Ibid.*, (OTh II, 476); cf. q.6, (OTh II, 497–98).

tion. Once the proposition is formed from such intuitive cognitions, the intellect immediately assents if the proposition is true and dissents if the proposition is false. Such intuitive cognitions of particular physical objects are likewise presupposed for volitions having particular physical objects as their intentional objects.

Given that there are some mental acts that have particular physical objects as their intentional objects, Ockham thinks that we can and do have intellectual intuitive cognitions of mental acts. Sometimes he says that an existing and present intuitive cognition of a particular physical object suffices, together with the intellect, to produce an intuitive cognition of that intuitive cognition. Other times, he says that a volition is required in addition. Either way, according to the natural order of causes, the second intuitive cognition does not suffice, together with the intellect, to cause an intuitive cognition of itself. Such intellectual intuitive cognitions of mental acts are naturally apt to cause evident judgments with respect to contingent propositions about them.

Ockham claims that sensory and intellectual intuitive cognitions of particulars are, according to the natural order of causes, necessary for the production of abstractive cognitions. Intellectual intuitive cognitions are also at least mediate and partial causes of abstract general concepts. In the Prologue and *Reportatio* II, q.12–13, Ockham claims that we cannot have a naturally produced abstractive cognition of something without having an intuitive cognition of the same thing and probably intends it to apply only to simple intuitive and abstractive cognition. And even in *Quodlibeta* I, q.13, where he denies that any simple abstractive cognition is proper to a particular, he would still retain the claim that we cannot have a simple abstractive cognition of whiteness unless we have had an intuitive cognition of some particular whiteness or other. That we have never had a simple intuitive cognition of something does not, in Ockham's view, mean that we cannot conceive of it at all. Ockham suggests that we can conceive of particulars by means of composite abstractive cognitions. Again, we think of God, of whom we never have an intuitive cognition in this life, by means of a composite abstract general concept (see Part Five, chapter 21 below) and of matter by means of a complex act of apprehending a proposition (see Part Four, chapter 15 below). Intellectual intuitive cognitions are also at least mediate and partial causes of abstract general concepts.

Thus, all naturally acquired noncomplex cognitions that are not themselves intuitive cognitions have intuitive cognitions at least as a mediate and partial cause. All complex acts of apprehension are either propositions formed from intuitive cognitions, propositions formed at least in part from abstractive cognitions, or propositions formed at least in part from abstract general concepts. The first group obviously involve intuitive cognitions as partial causes. Therefore, on Ockham's view, it is not naturally possible that we should be aware of anything without having intuitive cognitions. And without acts of apprehension, no acts of judgment or volitions are possible. In this life all our mental activity depends upon intuitive cognitions.

Although Ockham shares Locke's conceptual empiricism, he would reject—at least so far as present qualitative states of the physical world are concerned—Locke's claims that (i) we are aware of physical objects indirectly, by being aware of something mental; and (ii) that all of knowledge of the physical world is inferred for propositions about our own mental acts and passions. If Ockham had agreed with these claims, he would have given the following account of how we come to know a proposition such as 'Socrates is white': first, Socrates and his whiteness cause us to have sensory intuitive cognitions of Socrates and his whiteness, which in turn causes an intellectual intuitive cognition of Socrates and his whiteness; and the latter intuitive cognition causes an intuitive cognition of itself. The intellect then judges that the intellectual intuitive cognition of Socrates and his whiteness exists and infers that probably Socrates exists and is white. It is clear from the above summary, however, that Ockham does not endorse such a representationalist position. He, of course, allows that sensory cognitions often cause intellectual intuitive cognitions of themselves. But he is adamant that the intellect's awareness of acts of sensation or of its own acts is not the only or the primary means by which the intellect is aware of physical objects, and that such an awareness does not invariably play any causal role in producing the judgment that Socrates is white. Rather the sensory intuitive cognition of Socrates and his whiteness cause an intellectual intuitive cognition of the same; and the latter act, which is the immediate proximate cause of the judgment that Socrates is white, is one in which the intellect is aware of Socrates and his whiteness, not indirectly, but directly. Thus, he says that in intuitive cognition "the thing itself is seen and apprehended immediately, without any intermediary between it and the act,"[190] and again that "in intuitive cognition nothing other than the object and the act is required to represent the object..."[191] Thus, in these passages, Ockham clearly intends to endorse a direct realist position in the theory of knowledge.

Further, although Ockham would not deny that some of our beliefs about contingent states of affairs in the physical world are inferred from other beliefs, he insists that not all of our beliefs about such contingent states of affairs are of this sort. Since we cannot know infinitely many propositions, if we know any contingent propositions, we must know some contingent proposition non-inferentially.[192] And although Ockham does at one point (where he is discussing passages from Augustine) say that our knowledge of our own mental acts is the most evident that we have,[193] he never suggests that all of our beliefs about present states of affairs in the physical world must be inferred from them. His considered opinion is that intuitive cognitions of physical objects cause evident judgments, just as much as intuitive cognitions of mental acts do. So far as Ockham's theory of memory in *Reportatio* II, q.12–13 is concerned, the same is true of our memories of past states of affairs in the physical world. But in *Reportatio* IV, q.14, he takes a step in the Lockean direction, contending that our memories of such past states of affairs invariably "follow from" our memories of our own past mental acts.

190. *Ord.* I, d.26, q.3, (OTh IV, 241).
191. *Rep.* II, q.12–13, (OTh V, 273–74).
192. *Ord.* I, Prologue, q.1, a.1, (OTh I, 43).
193. *Ibid.*, (OTh I, 43–44).

14

Certainty and Scepticism
in Ockham's Epistemology

The question of whether certain and infallible knowledge is possible for human beings is one of the perennial questions of epistemology. And repeatedly, the debate about its answer has been seen to depend on what standards of certainity have been adopted. Some philosophers have maintained that a belief that p is true counts as knowledge of p, only if (i) p is true and (ii) the believer has some infallible sign by means of which he can distinguish, among instances of belief that p is true, genuine from merely apparent cases of true belief. And they have argued that while—for all we know—some of our beliefs may satisfy condition (i), it is impossible that any of our beliefs should satisfy condition (ii). These philosophers are known as sceptics, because they conclude that certain and infallible knowledge is impossible for human beings.

Historically, the sceptics' contentions have met with a threefold response: (1) The most ambitious of their opponents accept the sceptics' standards for certain and infallible knowledge and argue that these standards are sometimes met. (2) Others report that no rational person should accept the sceptics' demand for an infallible sign by means of which to distinguish genuine from merely apparent instances of true belief. And they substitute "lower" alternative standards for certain knowledge. These philosophers reply, in effect, by changing the subject. For the sceptics have not denied that it is impossible for us to have certain knowledge as measured by these "lower" standards, and often have allowed that—for all we know—we do have it. (3) Still other philosophers, of stronger constitution, have accepted the sceptics' standards and granted their conclusions.

In the present chapter, I want to consider this drama as it is played out on the stage of late 13th and early 14th century epistemology. Since the whole play would constitute a book in itself, I shall turn the spotlight on Henry of Ghent, Duns Scotus, William Ockham, and Nicolas of Autrecourt. Many reviews in the secondary literature bill Ockham as the chief of the medieval sceptics. But, constrasting Ockham with these other characters, I shall argue that it is wrong to cast him in that role.

1.   THE PROBLEM AS POSED BY HENRY OF GHENT

Although Henry's *Summae quaestionum ordinariarum* is primarily a theological work, it begins with the question of whether knowledge or certain cognition of anything is possible,[1] and if so, to what extent it is possible for human beings by their purely natural powers. On the one hand, Henry cites arguments that it must be possible: (i) For example, Aristotelians maintain that knowledge is the natural activity and end of man and accordingly that for which each human being has a natural desire. But everything must be able to attain its end by purely natural powers, and it is impossible that any natural desire should be frustrated.[2] (ii) Again, Augustine contends that one who doubts whether he knows, knows at least one thing—that he doubts.[3] On the other hand, Henry presents a rich collection of arguments from ancient and Augustinian sources, that knowledge is altogether impossible for human beings. (iii) Among these, there is the argument of the Academics that knowledge is impossible, because there are no infallible signs by means of which to discriminate the true from the false.[4] (iv) Another group maintains that knowledge is impossible for human beings, because all human perception begins with the senses, and the senses cannot be a source of certain cognition.

1. A.1, q.1; a.2, q.1.
2. A.1, q.1, (Paris, 1520, fol.1va); a.1, q.2, fol.4r A.
3. A.1, q.1, fol.1v.
4. A.1, q.1, fol.2r C; a.2, q.1, fol.23v A.

For one thing, knowledge of the unadulterated truth—i.e., a clear, stable, infallible grasp of the truth—is not to be expected from the senses.[5] Again, the senses perceive at most the sensible qualities of things, not their essences.[6] Worse still, sensible things appeared differently to the same perceiver at different times and circumstances or to different perceivers at the same time.[7] Hence, the intellect forced to rely on the senses would not even acquire certainty about the sensible qualities of things. (v) Still another group finds knowledge impossible for human beings, not because of defects in our faculties of cognition, but because mind-independent sensible things are unknowable. Some held that such things have no determinate properties.[8] Others asserted that only what is immutable is knowable, but sensible things change.[9]

Henry's defense of the possibility of human knowledge concedes something to many of these arguments. As if sensing that disagreements in this matter can often be traced back to varying standards of certainty, Henry identifies four certainty-making features of cognitions: (a) freedom from doubt and error; (b) stability of the known object and knowing subject; (c) infallibility; and (d) clarity. He then distinguishes four ways in which knowledge may be taken, the degrees of certainty corresponding to each, and how it is possible for human beings.

2. KNOWLEDGE IN THE BROAD SENSE

Henry's first main distinction is between knowledge in the broad sense which includes "every certain cognition by which a thing is cognized as it is, apart from every fallacy and deception"[10] from knowledge properly speaking by which the conformity of a thing with its exemplar is recognized.[11] From this description and a comment he makes in the next article.[12]

5. A.1, q.1, fol.1r A.
6. A.1, q.1, fol.1v A.
7. A.1, q.1, fol.1r A.
8. A.1, q.1, fol.2r–v C.

9. A.1, q.1, fol.1r–v A.
10. A.1, q.1, fol.1v B.
11. A.1, q.2, fol.4v C, D.
12. A.2, q.1, fol.23v B.

it would seem that every error-free cognition counted as knowledge in the broad sense. But other remarks and examples suggest that only error-free cognitions that we do not, cannot, or should not doubt are included,[13] and indeed only cognitions that have certainty-making feature (a) and not (b), (c), and (d). A further restriction still is implied by the fact that Henry regards the above division between knowledge in the broad sense and knowledge properly speaking as exclusive.

Henry thinks that knowledge in the broad sense is clearly possible for human beings in this life by their purely natural powers, and he gives two sorts of cases in which we in fact have it: (a) The first is "by exterior or alien testimony"—i.e., by taking someone else's word for it. Following Augustine's lead in *Contra Academicos*, Henry stresses the importance of such knowledge. Without it, he says, we should be ignorant of the ocean and of many celebrated lands and cities, which we have never seen for ourselves. We also depend upon the testimony of others for our knowledge of the past—e.g., that human beings existed in the past.[14] (2) The second is the testimony of our own senses and intellect. Henry insists that both we and the lower animals[15] sometimes perceive things as they are apart from any fallacy or deception, by means of our senses. In defending this, Henry seems to concede the Aristotelian claim that all natural things have a proper activity in which they engage unless they are prevented from doing so by something else. He argues that

> ...it is proper to a sense to have a very certain cognition of its proper object, unless it is prevented from doing so either by itself or by the medium or by something else. And when every impediment ceases, it cannot err or apprehend its proper object otherwise than as it is, although such an apprehension does not remain, whether because of the thing or because of the mutability of the sense...[16]

But, of course, we may doubt error-free sensory cognitions, if,

13. A.1, q.1, fol.1v B; a.2, q.1, fol.23v B.
14. A.1, q.1, fol.1v B.
15. A.1, q.2, fol.4v C.
16. A.1, q.1, ad 2, fol.2v F.

for example, we doubt whether or not the sense faculty is impeded in its natural operation. Henry offers the following criterion of the reliability of the senses:

> ...In sensory cognition, that sense truly perceives a thing as it is apart from any deception and fallacy, which is not contradicted in its proper action of sensing its proper object by a truer sensation or by an act of understanding taken from a truer sensation, whether in the same one or in another...[17]

When a given deliverance of my sense of sight is not contradicted by other truer deliverances of the sense of sight or of some other sense (whether in me or someone else) or by an act of understanding based on other truer deliverances of the senses, then I am to take it that my sense of sight represents things to be as they are on this occasion. "Nor," Henry adds, "should it be doubted that what we perceive in this way we perceive to be as it is. Nor is it necessary to seek any further cause of certainty."[18]

The latter criterion would, in at least some cases, be easy to apply: viz., in those cases in which the deliverance of a given sense is not contradicted at all, either by other sensations or by intellectual cognitions. As one of the arguments against the possibility of knowledge points out, however, the deliverances of one's senses very often contradict each other and/or those of another person's senses. And even where this is not actually so, it is potentially so. Hence, if we are to make much use of Henry's criterion, we must be able to determine when the deliverances of one sense are *truer* than those of another. Arguments against the possibility of human knowledge assume that where the senses contradict one another, the senses themselves provide us with no criterion for choosing among them.

Henry's view is that in such cases, the truer sensation is the one that is produced in a faculty whose operation is unimpeded in relation to the other faculties. And it is the job of the intellect to judge on the basis of repeated past experience, what those

17. A.1, q.1, fol.1v B.   18. *Ibid.*

circumstances are in which a faculty of sensation is apt to be impeded.[19] For example, he thinks that experience shows that the
taste of a healthy person ought to be trusted more than the taste
of a sick person, and the vision of someone who looks at this
from nearby more than the vision of someone who looks at it
from a distance, of one who looks through a uniform medium
more than of one who looks through a medium that is not
uniform, etc.[20] Henry is probably correct in thinking that we ordinarily do appeal to such criteria and doubt or trust our senses
accordingly, but he is wrong to suggest, as he does at one point,
that these are the infallible signs demanded by the Academic
sceptics in their arguments that knowledge is impossible.[21]

In the same way, we may have knowledge in the broad sense
by intellectual cognition. Thus, Henry writes,

> ...that intellect truly perceives a thing as it is without any fallacy or
> deception, which is not contradicted in its proper act of understanding
> by a truer act of intellect or by one taken from a truer sense. Nor should
> such an act of understanding be doubted any more than one from the
> senses should...[22]

Among such intellectual cognitions, Henry includes what
Ockham calls acts of apprehension and what Henry himself
labels acts of simple intelligence (simple by contrast with acts
that involve compounding and dividing). Where such intellectual acts of apprehension are concerned, Henry says that intellect "follows sense," in that we do not have an intellectual
cognition of a given thing unless we first have a sensory cognition of it.[23] But intellectual knowledge in the broad sense also
includes knowledge of some propositions. All of the knowledge
that we get "by exterior or alien testimony" seems to be of this
sort. And in discussing intellectual knowledge in the broad
sense, Henry notes with apparent approval Cicero's comment
that the sense cannot apprehend propositions such as 'This is
white'; rather it is left to the intellect to do so.

19. A.1, q.1, ad 3, fol.3r G.   22. A.1, q.1, fol.2r B.
20. A.1, q.1, ad 2, fol.3r F.   23. A.1, q.2, fol.4v C.
21. A.1, q.1, ad 3, fol.3r G.

In maintaining that human beings can have knowledge in the broad sense of sensible things, Henry is disagreeing with all of those ancient philosophers who argued that sensible things have no determinate properties. If there is no determinate way that sensible things are, one cannot be said to apprehend them as they *are* apart from any fallacy or deception. On the other hand, he is not asserting anything that the Academic sceptics could have conscientiously denied. Arguing, as they do, that all things are uncertain, they do not deny that there is some determinate way that sensible things are, nor that we sometimes apprehend them as they are. What they argue is that if we ever do apprehend the determinate properties of sensible things as they are, we are in no position to identify such occasions with certainty, by their standards of certainty which include not only feature (a) but also feature (c). Nor would they be impressed with Henry's criteria for doing so. For in determining whether we have knowledge in the broad sense, Henry advises us to presume that the deliverances of a given faculty are reliable unless they are shown to be contradicted by a truer one. And it may be that by following his advice we should arrive at a cognition that is free from doubt and error, that a given sensation or act of intellect is reliable. But if we are after Academic certainty that we have knowledge in the broad sense, we cannot rely on such presumptions but only on some infallible sign. Similarly, applying Henry's maxim that the taste faculty of a healthy person is more reliable than that of a sick person, we may often arrive at knowledge in the broad sense that a given taste sensation is reliable. But we could thereby acquire Academic certainty that this is so only if on numerous occasions we had certified, by some infallible sign, that a given person is sick and that another is well and then determined by an infallible sign which person had the veridicial and which the erroneous taste sensations. And this we could do only if we had already identified, by some infallible signs, some cases in which our intellect and senses perceived things as they were. In general, to identify any cognition as veridical, we should have identified with certainty that another is verdical, and so on to infinity. Medieval philosophers generally agreed, however, that our minds are not capable of carrying out an infinite number of operations.

3.   KNOWLEDGE PROPERLY SPEAKING

According to Henry, knowledge properly speaking is cognition "by which the truth of a thing is cognized."[24] He explains that it is one thing to cognize a thing or "that which is true in it" and another to cognize its truth.[25] Henry has in mind the transcendental sense of 'true' according to which every being is true. Thus, any error-free cognition of a thing will count as a cognition of that which is true in it. But the truth of a thing consists of its conformity with an exemplar.[26] Therefore, knowledge properly speaking involves grasping not only the thing itself, but also its relation to something else—which can not be done by a simple act of apprehension, but only by the intellectual activity of compounding and dividing.[27] Sometimes he says that the latter activity results in a judgment—e.g., the judgment concerning a man that he is a true man, concerning a color that it is a true color.[28] Other times he says that it results in a concept of the thing.[29] Still other times, in a word.[30] Further, Henry explains that there is a double truth of things, inasmuch as each thing had a double exemplar: (i) its created exemplar which is a species produced on the basis of sensations; and (ii) the uncreated exemplar which is the idea of it in the mind of God.[31] And there are two ways in which either of these exemplars might figure in our coming to know things: either the exemplar might serve as an object of knowledge or it might play some causal role (be a *ratio cognoscendi*) in our coming to apprehend the truth of things. And depending on which exemplar

24. A.1, q.2, fol.4v C.
25. *Ibid.*
26. A.1, q.2, fol.4v D.
27. A.1, q.2, fol.4v C, D.
28. *Ibid.*
29. A.1, q.2, fol.5r E, fol.7r–v L, and fol.8r S.
30. A.1, q.3, fol.10r G.
31. A.1, q.2, fol.5r E.

is involved and how that exemplar functions, different degrees of certainty will attach to our knowledge—properly speaking.

4. KNOWLEDGE OF THE TRUTH OF THINGS BASED ON A CREATED EXEMPLAR

Henry thinks that unaided natural human powers suffice to provide human beings with knowledge properly speaking, based on a created exemplar. And in this process, the created exemplar serves, not as the object, but as a cause of such knowledge. His account of just how this happens is obscured by his failure to make clear just what sort of species the created exemplar is, however. Sometimes, he suggests that the created exemplar is an image of the sort we are aware of in dreams and imagination and which we mistake for real sensible things—i.e., a particular, determinate sense image.32 His more considered

32. A.1, q.2, fol.5r–v E. In criticizing the argument in which this statement occurs, Scotus implies that Henry rejects the idea that we know things by means of intelligible species and that he has to explain how we know things by means of sense images alone (*Ord.* I, d.3, p.1, q.4, n.252, (Vaticana III, 153)). This is puzzling because Henry speaks of our having intelligible species later on in *Summae*, a.1, q.2. Wolter refers us to Henry's *Quodlibeta* IV, q.7, 8 and 23; V, q.4 (*Duns Scotus: Philosophical Writings*, (Edinburgh, 1962), notes to sec.5, 183). In *Quodlibeta* IV, q.7, however, Henry is not primarily concerned with our knowledge of God in the next life. He attacks a theory according to which the only way we have of ever knowing anything—whether in this life or the next—is by means of intelligible species. He argues that an intellect can know something either by means of intelligible species or through the thing's essence itself. He admits that in this life we know physical objects by means of intelligible species which they cause in us (Venice, 1613, fol.148va). But it is an imperfection in an intellect to be able to understand only by means of intelligible species (fol.150ra). And Henry insists that in the next life the Blessed will know God not by means of His causing an intelligible species in them, but through the presence of the divine essence itself (fol.149ra–b).

I have not found Henry categorically rejecting intelligible species in the other questions cited by Wolter either. In setting out Henry's position, however, I have concentrated on his account in the *Summae quaestionum ordinariarum*. There may be a place in some other work in which Henry contradicts this account and rejects intelligible species altogether.

view seems to be that the created exemplar is "a *universal* species existing in the mind through which the mind acquires a cognition of all of its supposita"[33] or that it is "a species abstracted from the thing through sense," "purified and made universal."[34] Some of Henry's discussion suggests an account along Aristotelian lines: when we have sensations of particular animals, their images are stored in memory. Repeated experiences of different kinds of animals results in the production of a phantasm from which we abstract a universal species (the created exemplar). We then form a universal concept of animal that is conformed to that exemplar, and on the basis of this concept judge concerning anything we run across whether or not it is an animal.[35] Presumably when we thus judge of Socrates that he is an animal, we grasp the truth of Socrates, in that we perceive his conformity to the created exemplar.

Henry realizes that those who deny the possibility of human knowledge will raise an objection at this point:

> ...But perhaps you will say that the sensible species is received from sense. Therefore, since it is an accident and a likeness of accidents only, it will not lead to a cognition of what the thing is, or to a cognition of its substance...[36]

Sense images represent only the sensible qualities of a thing. It would seem, therefore, that the species abstracted from the phantasm they produce and the concept conformed to that species could be of sensible qualities only, which are accidental and do not pertain to the essence of the things that have them. How even on the basis of universal and abstract species of sensible qualities, could we arrive at a concept of man as a rational mortal animal? Henry's reply seems to concede that the species we have been speaking of so far are of sensible qualities only.

> ...It must be replied to this that even if the intellect first receives in-

33. *Summa quaestionum ordinariarum*, a.1, q.2, fol.5v E.
34. A.1, q.2, fol.5v E, F.
35. A.1, q.2, fol.5r–v E.
36. A.1, q.1, ad 7, fol.3v L.

telligible species of sensible things and of corporeal things insofar as they are sensible and first understands those things through those species, nevertheless, secondarily, under those species of sensible things and by the investigation of natural reason it conceives through itself the cognitions of things that are not sensible, such as the quiddities of substance and other things of the same sort that do not have their own species in the intellect...[37]

Henry explains how the mind conceives things that are not sensible *through itself* by comparing it to the way in which

...a sheep, by natural instinct, appraises things not sensed through species that are sensed, e.g., by imagining or seeing through the sensible species of a wolf, it appraises the wolf to be harmful and unfriendly...[38]

Harmfulness and unfriendliness are not sensible qualities and therefore are not represented in sensible species. The gray coat, pointed-shaped teeth, and large jaws can be represented by sensible species, however. Henry seems to be saying that the soul of a sheep is by nature so constructed that when a sensible species of a wolf occurs in it, this triggers (''by natural instinct'') in it the thought that the wolf is harmful or unfriendly. In the same way, Henry is suggesting, the human mind is by nature so constructed that the occurrence in us of the created exemplar of man (which represents, although abstractly, only the sensible qualities of men) and perhaps the resultant universal concept of the sensible qualities of man, causes the mind ''by the investigation of natural reason'' to form a concept of the substance or quiddity of man. Henry does not explain here what sort of investigation natural reason has to engage in to form this concept (his attributing it to natural reason implies that it does not involve any special divine illumination). Nor does he clarify in what sense (if any) this concept of the quiddity (as opposed to the first mentioned one of the sensible qualities) conforms to the created exemplar. It is perhaps more likely that he thinks it conforms vaguely and imperfectly to the uncreated exemplar, which does represent the substance or quiddity of things.

37. *Ibid.*   38. *Ibid.*

At first, Henry suggests that we use the latter, naturally acquired concepts, not only in forming judgments such as 'Socrates is a man' or 'This is triangular', but also in formulating and coming to have certain knowledge of simple analytic propositions such as 'Human beings are animals' and 'Animals are substances', which are the first principles of the speculative sciences. For he says that we can cognize such simple analytic propositions accurately and in such a way that we could not doubt them "by the precise action *of the natural powers* of the soul by looking to the created exemplar abstracted from the thing" (italics mine). But he immediately adds "if nevertheless that exemplar suffices for this apart from the illumination of the eternal exemplar.[39]

5.   HOW CERTAIN IS KNOWLEDGE PROPERLY SPEAKING BASED ON THE CREATED EXEMPLAR?

According to Henry, knowledge of the truth of things based on the created exemplar possesses the certainty of freedom from error and actual doubt. Yet this is not to contradict the objector who denies unaided human powers of any "knowledge of the unadulterated truth"[40]—i.e., any stable, infallible, and clear vision of the truth of things. For Henry himself insists that knowledge properly speaking based on the created exemplar does not possess these certainty-making features. And Scotus points out that Henry's arguments have even readier application to sensory apprehension of things as they are, which Henry classifies as knowledge in the broad sense.

Henry's first two arguments contend that such knowledge falls short of the higher degree of certainty, because the created exemplar is mutable. (1) "The first reason is that such an exemplar, since it is abstracted from a mutable thing, necessarily has some principle of mutability in itself..."[41] The suggestion is

---

39. A.2, q.1, fol.23v B.
40. A.1, q.2, fol.5v E; cf. a.2, q.1, fol.23v B.
41. A.1, q.2, fol.5v E.

that a mutable thing cannot be the cause of an immutable effect. But sensible things are mutable. Hence the images and species of which they are, directly or indirectly, the cause must also be mutable. The same would obviously be true of sensory apprehensions. (2) Secondly, Henry contends that

> ...the human soul, because it is mutable and capable of being affected by error, cannot be set right in such a way that it avoids error and persists in the rightness of truth, by anything that is as mutable as or more mutable than it is. Thus, every exemplar that it receives from natural things, since that exemplar is of a degree inferior to it, is necessarily as mutable or more mutable than it is. Therefore, such an exemplar cannot set the soul right in such a way that it persists in the infallible truth...[42]

The suggestion seems to be that even if an image or a species provided us with an accurate cognition of things as they are or of their truth, it would not provide us with a stable grasp of them. For, as mutable, such an image or species is apt to go out of existence at any time and to be replaced by another that might perhaps misrepresent things. Again, even if an image represents sensible things as they are at a given time, the sensible things themselves may change at any time and hence come to be no longer accurately represented by the image.

Scotus, examining Henry's discussion, raises a double objection to this reasoning. First, Scotus singles this out as one of the places in which Henry fails to distinguish the characteristics of sense images from those of intelligible species and knowledge derived from intelligible species. Scotus considers that physical objects have both a mutable and an immutable aspect. It is by virtue of their mutable aspect—viz., their sensible qualities—that we are caused to have sense images of them. And it is quite true that a change in the sensible qualities of a physical object might render a veridical sense image non-verdical. But, on Scotus's view, it is by virtue of their immutable aspect—viz., their nature—that we have intelligible species. Even if the sensible qualities of physical objects change, and even if particulars

---

42. *Ibid*.

come into being and pass away, what it is to be a man, what it is to be a horse, or what it is to be an animal, does not change. Neither do the relations among natures vary from one time to another. Consequently, the ability of an intelligible species to represent a nature accurately is unaffected by the above mentioned changes in physical objects.[43]

Secondly, so far as the other source of instability is concerned, Scotus would grant that intelligible species are just as liable to cease to exist in the mind as sense images are. But he observes that

> ...if the mutability of the exemplar in our soul makes certitude impossible, then since anything that exists in the soul as in a subject is mutable—even the act of understanding itself—it follows that the soul cannot be prevented from erring by anything...[44]

whether it is produced in the soul by the natural activity of a creature or by special divine illumination. Once Henry regards the fact that the existence of accidents in a mutable substance is unstable, as a barrier to certain knowledge in the highest degree, he will be forced to conclude that such knowledge is entirely beyond human reach—which is the conclusion of the sceptics.[45]

Henry can reply here by granting that divine action cannot alter the fact that an effect produced in the soul has the ontological status of being an accident inhering in a mutable substance. But he can maintain that it is only as a result of the natural order of causes that the existence of such accidents in the soul is less stable than the existence of the soul itself. Hence, the latter fact can be altered by divine intervention: if God wills an accident to have uninterrupted existence in the soul, that accident will so persist. Nevertheless, Scotus's objection calls to our attention at least one thing divine illumination must do, if it is to remove the defect of instability from our knowledge.

(3) Henry's third argument concedes some legitimacy to the

---

43. *Ord.* I, d.3, p.1, q.4, a.2, n.246, (Vaticana III, 150–51).
44. *Ibid.*, n.220, (Vaticana III, 134).
45. *Ibid.*, n.222, (Vaticana III, 134–35).

demand of the later Academics for an infallible criterion of truth and argues that the created exemplar does not provide such a criterion:

> ...This sort of exemplar, since it is an intention and species of a sensible thing abstracted from the phantasm, bears a likeness to the false as well as to the true, so that they cannot be distinguished by considering the exemplar. For through the same images, in dreams and madness we judge the images to be the things themselves, and when we are awake and sane we make judgments about the things themselves. Therefore, it is impossible to have certain knowledge and a certain cognition of the truth through such an exemplar...[46]

Henry here concedes the Academics' point that exactly similar images may occur in dreams and madness as in healthful waking life, in non-verdical as in veridical perception. By the Academics' criterion, it would follow that we cannot have certain knowledge of the existence and sensible properties of physical objects by means of such sense images alone.

Responding to Henry's reasoning, Scotus once again seems to grant that it has validity where sense images are concerned. He does not object to the ancient theory according to which in dreams, madness, or hallucination, what happens is that we mistake the sense images for the physical objects themselves. And he admits that if we had to rely on sense images alone for acquiring knowledge, the Academics would be right in drawing their negative conclusion about the possibility of certain knowledge. Nevertheless, what is true of sense images is not true of intelligible species. For no one would want to say that we mistake the intelligibile species, which are abstracted from phantasms, for the physical objects themselves.[47]

If one is willing to give a generous interpretation, however, one can regard Henry as drawing a different point from the Academics' observation. He may be suggesting that since exactly similar sense images may occur in dreams and madness as in sane wakefulness, the phantasm and the species abstracted from

46. A.1, q.2, fol.5v E.
47. *Ord.* I, d.3, p.1, q.4, n.251, (Vaticana III, 153).

it will be as much like the non-veridical as like the veridical images, and hence will be no more a sign of the true than of the false. From this, he may be concluding that certain knowledge of the truth cannot be had on the basis of such a species either.

To evaluate this reasoning, we need to reconsider Henry's account of how we base knowledge on the created exemplar. He has claimed that on the basis of such a species we form a universal concept of the sensible qualities of things and that the existence of the species together with this latter concept may cause the mind to form a universal concept of their quiddities. Either of these may be used in formulating judgments about particulars of which we have sense images (e.g., 'That is a man', 'That is color'). Since we may receive images of things that do not exist, we may be misled into a non-verdical cognition of such things and mistakenly come to believe that they exist. Thus believing, we may take the further step of applying either of the above concepts to the putative things and hence formulate false judgments of the form 'That is a man' or 'That is color'. The fact that the created exemplar, from which these concepts are derived, is equally similar to the veridical and non-veridical sense images might thus seem to be connected with some mistakes of judgment. And if there is nothing in the images that would enable us to distinguish the one case from the other to the Academics' satisfaction, one might conclude that we cannot in this way have knowledge that is certain according to the Academics' standard.

It will follow further that we can have no certain knowledge on the basis of the created exemplar, only if this is the only way in which we use it. Scotus maintains that it is not. For he claims that the universal concepts formed on the basis of the species can be used to formulate the first principles of the various speculative sciences and that the truth of such principles in no way depends either upon the existence or nonexistence of sensible things, or upon their contingent sensible properties.[48] The fact that the created exemplar is equally similar to verdical and non-veridical exemplars would thus be irrelevant to our

48. *Ibid.*, n.246, (Vaticana III, 150–51); n.250, (Vaticana III, 152–53).

knowledge of first principles. In the passage noted above, Henry appears uncertain about whether or not to say that it is the concepts acquired through the created exemplar apart from divine illumination that we use to formulate and come to know first principles. Of course, if it is not these concepts, Scotus's counterexample fails, at least *ad hominem*. On the other hand, Henry considers in a.2, q.2, an argument similar to his own argument here, and makes the same response to it as Scotus makes to him.[49]

The third principal defect Henry identifies in knowledge based on the created exemplar alone has to do with its content. He says that everything "impressed by any exemplar abstracted from the thing itself is imperfect, obscure, and nebulous"[50] and again that all cognition acquired through phantasms is somehow obscure.[51] In the same vein, he reasons that since the created exemplar is an incomplete likeness of the thing, the mind, by its purely natural powers, is able to conceive through it only the incomplete truth of that thing.[52] It is clear why Henry should think that the first concept formed on the basis of the created exemplar should provide only an imperfect apprehension of the truth of things: for by it, we conceive of things only in terms of their sensible qualities and not in terms of their substance or quiddity. Henry is suggesting further that while we do conceive of the substance or quiddity of things by means of the second concept, we are not thereby furnished with a clear and distinct cognition of it.

Thus, while knowledge properly speaking based on the created exemplar may possess the certainty of freedom from error and actual doubt, Henry thinks it does not possess the higher degrees of certainty that come with stability, infallibility, and clarity. The latter are possible for us only by divine illumination.

49. Ad 1, fol.24r G.
50. A.1, q.2, fol.7v L.
51. A.2, q.1, fol.23v B.
52. A.1, q.3, fol.10v G.

6.   KNOWLEDGE ACQUIRED BY DIVINE ILLUMINATION

So far, Henry has agreed with the Aristotelians that know-ledge is the natural activity of man, and has conceded that knowledge that is free from doubt and error lies within the scope of purely natural human powers. In saying this, Henry does not mean that such knowledge is entirely within our control, however. We have not been endowed with a natural power to see-things-at-will or to hear-sounds-at-will. Rather what we have a natural power to do is to-see-things-when-our-faculty-of-vision-is-acted-upon-by-visible-things and to-hear-sounds-when-our-faculty-of-hearing-is-acted-upon-by-sound-waves. Again, our minds are so constructed that we are able to have an incomplete conception of the truth of things when the requisite species have been produced in our minds. Never-theless, Henry thinks that sensible things are by their natures so constructed that when they get sufficiently close to a sense faculty, and when the appropriate medium is present, in short, when the standard conditions of perception obtain, they act on the sense faculty by natural necessity to produce images and in-directly phantasms and species in the mind of the perceiver.

Yet, Henry thinks the Aristotelians are wrong if they think that the perfection of knowledge—the attainment of the higher degrees of certainty—lies within the scope of our natural powers. For he thinks we have not been endowed with the natural power to have these higher degrees of certainty either at will or when acted upon by some natural object. Rather what we have the natural power to do is to-have-these-higher-degrees-of-certainty-when-specially-illuminated-by-the-divine-exemplar.[53] There is no psychological state producible in man by creatures alone which divine illumination follows with a law-like regularity. Rather God reveals the eternal rules to whomever He wishes.[54]

As noted above, there are two ways in which Henry thinks the divine exemplar may illuminate the human mind: (1) one

53. A.1, q.2, fol.8v T.
54. A.1, q.2, fol.7v M, fol.8r M; a.1, q.4, fol.11v D.

way—and the only way that is made available to us in this life—is by serving as a *cause* of the intellect's apprehending the truth of things with a higher degree of certainty. Henry's account of how this happens is marked more by metaphor than by precision. Briefly, he reasons that in order for the soul to cognize a thing, it must become like that thing. But the created exemplar furnishes it only with an imperfect and incomplete likeness of the thing and the concept formed on the basis of it is likewise imperfect and incomplete. The divine exemplar repairs this defect by causing a more perfect likeness in the intellect.[55] Nevertheless, it performs such a service for us in this life only with regard to those things of which we already have a created exemplar.[56] The uncreated truth is said to complement the created exemplar and to act together with it as one cause of cognition,[57] and so "impresses itself in our concept and transforms our concept to its own character,"[58] just as a signet ring impresses its image into the wax.[59] By means of the resultant transformed concept, we can have clear knowledge of the unadulterated truth of a thing. Since God is not bound by any necessity to provide such aids to our knowledge, He offers it to whomever He wills. Most of the time, God wills to make it available to each according to his disposition or capacity, although it is a gift of grace.[60] Sometimes, however, He may have reason to reveal the truth of things to the evil—perhaps even to the devil himself[61]—and to hide it from the good.[62] Alternatively, He may altogether deprive someone of such illumination because of some serious misdeed.[63]

The advantage of this knowledge of the truth of things over that produced by the unaided created exemplar, is one of in-

55. A.1, q.2, fol.7r L.
56. A.1, q.3, fol.10r F; a.1, q.4, fol.12v E.
57. A.1, q.3, fol.10v G.
58. A.1, q.2, fol.7r L.
59. A.1, q.3, fol.10r F.
60. A.1, q.2, fol.8v S.
61. A.1, q.3, fol.9r A.
62. A.1, q.2, fol.8r M.
63. A.1, q.2, fol.8v S.

creased clarity. (i) Nevertheless, it is not clear in the highest degree.[64] A human being may know some of the things he knows in this fashion with greater clarity than others: first principles, with greater clarity than those of natural science; and the latter with greater clarity than the tenets of theology.[65] Perfect clarity is reserved for the beatific vision in which the divine exemplar is not merely a cause but the object of cognition, in the next life. (ii) Further, this knowledge does not possess perfect stability. For while one of its causes, viz., the divine exemplar, is immutable, another, viz., the created exemplar, is mutable. And Henry does not include among the effects of divine illumination in this life, any special intervention to make the existence of the species more stable. (iii) Finally, Henry seems to deny that this knowledge is self-certifying. For while endorsing Augustine's claim that in the next life "we shall see the truth without any difficulty and thoroughly enjoy that most clear and certain truth," he adds that "because of the overshadowing of this present life, it frequently happens that one who knows with certainty does not know to what extent he knows with certainty..."[66] And on the other hand, he approves Aristotle's comment that some who hold opinions do not doubt them but mistake them for certain knowledge. Henry thus seems to be admitting that there are no infallible signs by means of which we can identify such knowledge of the truth and distinguish it from mistaken opinion about the natures of things.

(2) The second way the divine exemplar can illuminate the human mind is by serving as an object of cognition. Henry says that the angels see the truth of creatures better in such an unobstructed vision of the divine essence than they do in a direct vision of the creatures themselves. He suggests that just as "we cognize that an image of Hercules is a true image of him by seeing Hercules and thus noticing the correspondence of the image to the exemplar," so we would be able to judge, e.g., that Socrates is a true man by seeing the divine exemplar and noticing the correspondence of Socrates (the image) to his ex-

64. A.2, q.1, fol.23v B.   66. A.2, q.1, fol.23v B.
65. A.2, q.3, fol.24v M.

emplar.[67] The divine exemplar, unlike the created exemplar, is stable and immutable. Further, knowledge based on it would be clear and distinct in content.[68] Finally, following Augustine, Henry thinks that such knowledge would be self-certifying—i.e., that there are infallible signs by which it may be distinguished from false cognitions[69]—although he does not explain how it is or can be so. Such an unobstructed vision of the divine exemplar is not generally available to human beings in this life. It has perhaps been granted to a few Saints by a very special privilege, but it is for the most part reserved for the Blessed in the next life.[70]

7. SUMMARY OF HENRY'S POSITION

Henry's response to the question of whether certain knowledge is possible is, on the whole, positive. But how far it is possible for human beings by their purely natural powers, depends upon what standards of certainty are employed. He admits that the certainty of freedom from doubt and error characterizes several kinds of cognitions naturally produced in human beings: viz., some sensory and intellectual apprehensions of things, some knowledge of a thing's conformity to its created exemplar, and some second hand information. Nevertheless, cognitions produced by purely natural powers never attain to the certainty of stability, infallibility, and clarity. Cognitions caused by the divine exemplar acting together with the created exemplar, may, in addition to being free from doubt and error, possess increased clarity, but not clarity in the highest degree. And only cognitions in which the divine exemplar is the object, and not merely the cause, of a cognition, possess the highest degree of certainty; and these are for the most part reserved for the Blessed in the next life.

67. A.1, q.2, fol.6r I.
68. *Ibid.* and a.2, q.1, fol.23v B.
69. A.2, q.1, fol.23v B; ad 1, fol.23v D.
70. A.1, q.2, fol.6v I; a.1, q.3, fol.9r A.

8. SCOTUS'S POSITION

Like Henry, Scotus felt that an assertion of the possibility of human knowledge was a necessary preamble to his consideration of theological topics. But he found Henry's account of how human knowledge is possible to be disastrously wrongheaded. Near the beginning of his commentaries on the *Sentences*,[71] Scotus focuses on what he regards as the most pernicious part of Henry's opinion: viz., the latter's attempt to argue that we cannot have knowledge of the unadulterated truth by purely natural powers on the basis of the created exemplar, but only by means of special divine illumination. Scotus maintains that the premisses that lead Henry to this conclusion "seem to lead to the conclusion that all is uncertain, the opinion of the Academics."[72] Some of Scotus's criticisms of Henry's reasoning have been discussed above. It will not repay us to examine them in further detail, because, in making his case against Henry, Scotus does not always represent Henry's position and intentions correctly. Nevertheless, we have already seen that the general thrust of Scotus's arguments is accurate. He is right to hold that some of Henry's reasons for denying that knowledge based on the created exemplar counts as knowledge of the unadulterated truth would also go to show that the knowledge that Henry thinks is provided by divine illumination in this life, falls short of the certainty demanded by the Academics.

If Scotus thinks that Henry's premisses entail Academic scepticism, he also hopes to forestall a repetition of their "error" by showing how we can have certain and infallible cognition (i) of the first principles of the speculative sciences together with their consequences, (ii) of our own acts, and (iii) of particular and general facts about the physical world. Not that Scotus imagined that he had provided a demonstrative refutation of the Academics' view. Echoing Aristotle, he notes that there is no

---

71. I, d.3, p.1, q.4.
72. *Ibid.*, n.222, (Vaticana III, 135).

use in trying to demonstrate anything to a person who is unwilling to concede that anything is known *per se*, since such people will not grant any premisses from which a proof could proceed; they are "quibblers" who "are not to be convinced."[73] Further, in asserting that we can have certain and infallible knowledge by purely natural powers in this life, Scotus is not really maintaining anything that the Academics could dogmatically deny. Towards the end of his discussion, he claims to have shown how we can have knowledge of "the infallible truth without doubt and deception."[74] Again, speaking about our knowledge of the physical world, he remarks,

> If, then, we neither are in doubt nor are mistaken about the truth of these things, as is clearly the case, we are certain of things cognized through the senses. For where doubt and deception are excluded, there we have certainty.[75]

On Scotus's criterion, it seems that the exclusion of doubt and error suffices for certainty. His discussion does not further clarify whether it is enough that we do not in fact doubt an error-free cognition, or whether doubt must be logically or psychologically impossible. In either case, an Academic sceptic will not deny that we ever have such cognitions, but will question our ability to tell if we do. Moreover, if this is all that Scotus means by 'certainty', it is clear that Henry will not disagree with Scotus's general claim that certain knowledge is possible for human beings in this life by purely natural powers. For although Scotus does not here take any note of it, Henry attributes this sort of certainty both to what he labels "knowledge in the broad sense" and to knowledge based on the created exemplar. Yet, if the certainty Scotus offers is only that measured against Henry's "lower standard," Scotus clearly thinks that it is the only certainty that a reasonable man, who is not a "quibbler," will be interested in.

73. *Ibid.*, n.256, (Vaticana III, 155).
74. *Ibid.*, n.258, (Vaticana III, 156–57).
75. *Ibid.*, n.225, (Vaticana III, 136).

9. KNOWLEDGE OF FIRST PRINCIPLES

First, Scotus tries to show how we can have certain and infallible knowledge of first principles and their consequences by purely natural powers. If we are to have such knowledge this way, we must be able to acquire by purely natural powers the concepts from which such propositions are formulated. Scotus thinks that we can do this through a purely natural process of abstraction that begins with sense experience. The agent intellect illuminates the phantasm produced by sense experiences and abstracts an intelligible species from it. On the basis of this species, a universal concept of the essence or nature of a thing may be formed. Scotus concedes that sometimes the concepts thus formed are unclear. But he maintains, contrary to Henry, that the mind is capable of forming clearer concepts by using the traditional method of division to arrive at the definition of the essence or nature first conceived of. No special divine illumination is needed.[76]

Given an appropriate set of clarified concepts, it will be possible to formulate simple analytic propositions—such as 'The whole is equal to the sum of its parts and greater than any one of them' or 'Horses are animals'—or logical rules—such as the principle of noncontradiction—which are true solely by virtue of the meaning of their terms. Assent to such propositions is necessarily free from error because these propositions are necessarily true. That it is likewise free from doubt, Scotus suggests in two arguments: (a) First, he argues that it is impossible for anyone who grasps the terms of a simple analytic proposition or a logical rule and formulates it, not to recognize its truth.

> ...The terms of principles known *per se* are so identical that it is evident that one necessarily includes the other. Therefore, an intellect compounding these terms [into a proposition], from the very fact that it apprehends them, has present to itself the necessary cause—and indeed the evident cause—of the conformity of that act of compounding to the

76. *Ibid.*, n.259, (Vaticana III, 157).

terms that compose it. This conformity, then, the evident cause of which it apprehends in the terms, is necessarily evident to it...[77]

Scotus is not arguing fallaciously that since the intellect grasps the terms, and the terms are the cause of truth, that the intellect grasps the truth of the proposition. One can be aware of a sufficient cause of x without being aware that it is a sufficient cause of x, and in such a case one would not thereby have any awareness of x. Scotus adds that the terms are the *evident* cause of the truth of the proposition, meaning that it is obvious to anyone who grasps the terms and formulates the proposition that the terms are the cause of the truth of that proposition.

(b) Second, Scotus contends that it is impossible that anyone should grasp the terms of such a proposition and formulate it, and nevertheless deny its truth. For just as it is impossible that contrary properties should exist simultaneously in the same thing, so it is impossible that one contrary should exist simultaneously in the same thing as a sufficient cause of the other contrary exists in. For example, just as it is impossible that the same thing should be simultaneously white all over and black all over, so it is impossible that it should be white all over when there exists in it a sufficient cause of its being black all over. But, following Aristotle,[78] Scotus maintains that having the opinion that p and having the opinion that not-p are just as much contrary properties as being black all over and being white all over. He concludes, therefore, that it is impossible both that one should simultaneously believe a proposition true and believe that same proposition false, and that one should believe a proposition false when there is in one a sufficient cause of one's believing it true. But he has claimed in the first argument that one's grasping the terms of a simple analytic proposition or logical rule and formulating it, is a sufficient cause of one's recognizing its truth. Therefore, it is impossible that one should grasp the terms of such a proposition and formulate it

---

77. *Ibid.*, n.230, (Vaticana III, 138–39).
78. *Metaphysics* IV, 3, 1005b23–24.

and yet deny its truth.[79]

Scotus does not make clear in what sense it is impossible to deny or fail to recognize the truth of such propositions. His appeal to logical principles about the simulutaneous possession of contrary properties might suggest that he thinks this is logically impossible. On the other hand, he says that grasping the terms and formulating the proposition are a sufficient cause of assent. And depending upon what Scotus means by 'cause', there may be ontological necessity in one state of affairs' being the cause of another. Whatever Scotus may have thought, many contemporary philosophers would regard it as conceptually impossible that one should grasp the terms of a simple analytic proposition, formulate it, and yet deny it. For they would take a person's assent, or failure to assent, to such a proposition as criterion of a person's understanding, or not understanding its terms.

Later on in his discussion, Scotus says something apparently inconsistent with his more frequent claim. He admits, as premisses in arguments, that "an indisposed power can err with respect to any proposition whatever, as is clear in the case of dreams"[80] and that "just as it may appear to a dreamer that he sees, so the opposite of any speculative principle known *per se* might appear to him."[81] He thus seems to allow that a dreamer or a madman or anyone else whose cognitive faculties are indisposed might well assent to the opposite of a first principle—something which he has seemed to deny earlier. These remarks can be reconciled, however, if we assume that Scotus's considered opinion is that it is only where the faculty of cognition is not indisposed that grasping the terms of and formulating a simple analytic proposition or logical rule, are sufficient to cause a recognition of its truth, and therefore that only in such cases is it impossible to deny it or fail to assent to it.

One may object even to this more qualified conclusion that many people of sound mind and serious purpose apparently have been able to doubt such propositions. In *Metaphysics,*

79. *Ord.* I, d.3, p.1, q.4, n.231–32, (Vaticana III, 139–140).
80. *Ibid.*, n.256, (Vaticana III, 155–56); cf. n.257, (Vaticana III, 156).
81. *Ibid.*, n.257, (Vaticana III, 156).

Book IV, Aristotle lists a number of philosophers who appear to have denied the law of noncontradiction, maintaining that contradictories are simultaneously true and/or simultaneously false. Again, sceptics have questioned whether following the laws of thought and employing only such inference patterns as the perfect syllogism or *modus ponens* will always lead to consistent results—which is in effect to challenge the soundness of such principles. And it seems that in the face of sufficiently ingenious persuasive arguments, some sane and serious people might be brought to doubt other first principles as well.

It would be open to Scotus to meet this objection simply by adding another qualification to this claim. He might grant that persuasive arguments might undermine one's compulsion to assent or lead one to doubt such propositions, but insist that *in the absence of persuasive arguments* it remains impossible for anyone whose faculties are not indisposed to formulate such a proposition and yet deny it or fail to recognize its truth. Apparently, Scotus does not want to take this line. For later on in his discussion, he declares that while the mind is not compelled to recognize the truth of a necessary conclusion the demonstration of which it does not grasp, and "can even bring up sophistical arguments against that conclusion and on the basis of them dissent from it," nevertheless, "it cannot do this with something that is known first"—i.e., first principles.[82] And he calls Aristotle as his witness, citing the Philosopher's claim that "it is impossible for anyone to believe the same thing to be and not to be, as some think Heraclitus says. For what a man says, he does not necessarily believe."[83] In the same way, Scotus suggests, it may be possible for someone to *say* that he doubts any first principle or to deny it *with his words*, but it is impossible for him actually to *believe* the contrary.

In summary, Scotus thinks that by our purely natural powers we have the concepts from which to formulate simple analytic propositions and logical rules. And no one whose cognitive faculties are not indisposed can formulate them and yet deny

82. *Ibid.*, note added by Scotus at n.246, (Vaticana III, 150).
83. *Metaphysics* IV, 3, 1005b23–25.

them or fail to recognize their truth. Hence, anyone whose cognitive faculties are disposed and who formulates them, will have certain and infallible knowledge of them by Scotus's standards. He adds further that since at least one valid inference pattern—the perfect syllogism—is likewise obvious, "once we are certain about first principles, it is clear how we can be certain about conclusions inferred from them." For "the certainty of the conclusion depends only on the certainty of the principles and the evidence of the inference."[84] Nevertheless, as just noted, it is possible to doubt the consequences of principles whose truth one grasps, so long as it is not clear to one how or whether the conclusion follows from the premiss.

It is important to realize, however, that in showing this, Scotus has not shown that we can be certain about first principles and their consequences according to the standard of the Academics. For they granted when our faculties are disposed, we cannot formulate genuine first principles and yet deny them or fail to recognize their truth. Scotus himself has admitted that when a person's cognitive faculties are indisposed, they can be in error about any proposition, even first principles. And in any case, might we still not overestimate the clarity of our concepts and mistake false propositions for genuine first principles? By what criterion, they will ask, are we to distinguish cases of the latter sort from genuine apprehensions of first principles? Scotus does consider the query as to how we know when our faculties are disposed, although (as we shall see) his account would not satisfy the Academics. But this brings us to the problem of how we can have certain knowledge of our own acts—to which we now turn.

10.   KNOWLEDGE OF OUR OWN ACTS

Scotus begins by saying that where propositions regarding our own acts are concerned, "we are as certain of many of these as we are of first principles and of propositions known *per*

84. *Ord.* I, d.3, p.1, q.4, n.233, (Vaticana III, 140).

se."[85] In support of this, he appeals to Aristotle's remark in *Metaphysics* IV, 6, that those who demand proofs of whether we are asleep or awake "seek a reason of things for which there is no reason; for there is no demonstration of a principle of demonstration."[86] Similarly, Scotus says, other statements about our present mental acts—e.g., 'I understand', 'I hear', and 'I see'—are known *per se*.[87]

Such propositions about our present mental acts and states cannot be on a par with first principles in all respects. For first principles are true solely by virtue of the meanings of their terms. But propositions such as 'I am awake', 'I understand', 'I hear', and 'I see' are contingent propositions and cannot be true solely by virtue of the meanings of their terms. Further, since at least some of these propositons—e.g., 'I hear', 'I see'—can be false of a person when his faculties are indisposed, it will not be impossible for such a person to formulate these propositions and yet deny them. In what ways, then do Aristotle and Scotus think that propositions about our present mental state and acts are like first principles? Principally, I think, in being *non-inferential*. Someone who asks for a demonstration of the fact that he is awake seeks a reason where there is no reason, because there is nothing more obvious from which he could infer it. Apparently, in Scotus's opinion, the same goes for the fact that I understand or hear or see. Scotus remarks that it is very important some contingent propositions are "first and immediate," since "otherwise there would be an infinite regress in contingent propositions or something contingent would follow from a necessary cause—both of which are impossible."[88] It is not clear whether Scotus also thinks that 'I am awake', 'I understand', 'I hear', and 'I see' are *indubitable* when true and formulated by someone whose cognitive faculties are disposed. For once again one might object that even in these circumstances, it is possible to doubt them, since many

85. *Ibid.*, n.236, (Vaticana III, 144).
86. *Ibid.*, n.238, (Vaticana III, 145).
87. *Ibid.*, n.239, (Vaticana III, 145–46).
88. *Ibid.*, n.238, (Vaticana III, 145).

philosophers have done so. And Scotus acknowledges, at least twice in this question[89] the existence of those who demand a proof that one is awake rather than asleep. But in one of these places, he repeats Aristotle's observation that these people seem to distinguish waking from sleeping, well enough for purposes of action,[90] as if this were another case in which philosophers express doubts with their words but do not actually doubt with their minds. If so, his view would be that where such propositions about our own present mental acts or states are concerned, it is impossible that we should formulate them when they are true and yet doubt them or fail to recognize their truth. And this is enough for certain and infallible cognition, according to Scotus's standard.

Scotus's claims regarding our self-knowledge are bolder than some traditionally defended. For example, Augustine concentrates in *Contra Academicos* on showing that there are various propositions—e.g., 'I exist', 'I am alive', 'I think', 'I seem to see the earth or sky',[91] 'This seems white to me',[92] 'This seems bitter', 'This taste is pleasant'[93]—that we can know about ourselves independently of knowing whether we are asleep or awake, sane or insane. And, as Scotus himself notes,[94] Augustine repeats these examples in *On the Trinity*, Book XV, chapter 12, as especially telling against the Academics. But Scotus follows Aristotle in including 'I am awake' among the propositions known *per se*. Further, although he understands 'I hear' and 'I see' in such a way that they may be true even if our perceptions are non-veridical, he follows Aristotle in thinking that we cannot perceive anything unless we are awake. Similarly, he remarks that the intellect is not able to use intelligible species during sleep, so that it is doubtful whether we can understand anything when we are asleep either.[95] It seems on Scotus's view

89. *Ibid.*, n.238, (Vaticana III, 144); n.254–57, (Vaticana III, 154–56).
90. *Ibid.*, n.256, (Vaticana III, 155).
91. III, c.11, sec.24, (CSEL LXIII, 64–65).
92. III, c.11, sec.26, (CSEL LXIII, 66–67).
93. III, c.11, sec.24, (CSEL LXIII, 64–65).
94. *Ord.* I, d.3, p.1, q.4, n.225–28, (Vaticana III, 136–37).
95. *Ibid.*, n.251–52, (Vaticana III, 153).

that 'I see', 'I hear', and 'I understand' all entail 'I am awake'. Hence, the former cannot remain indubitable if the latter is called into question.

This invites the Academics' usual query: "in dreams, I seem to see and seem to hear, whereas in reality I neither see nor hear. Indeed, in dreams it may seem to me that I am awake. How do I distinguish these occasions from those on which I am really awake and really do see or hear?"

Scotus expresses considerable exasperation with such an objection.[96] He says that if the objector is one of those people who hold that nothing is known *per se*, then there is no point in arguing with him. On the other hand, if the objector will grant that something is known *per se* and that an indisposed power can err about anything, then Scotus tries to show him that he should also admit that we can tell when our faculties are disposed and hence when we are awake. He constructs the following argument.

1. Some proposition is known *per se*.

2. Therefore, some proposition can be recognized as being known *per se*. (1)

3. An indisposed power can be in error about anything.

4. Therefore, the intellect understands only when it is disposed (which is only when the person is awake). (3)

5. Therefore, it can be recognized when the intellect is disposed (and when the person is awake). (2 and 4)

2 and 4 do seem to yield 5. But 1 does not entail 2. Perhaps Scotus would say that, nevertheless, one is not in a position to assert 1 unless one has recognized some proposition as being known *per se*. It is not obvious, however, that one might not have some general reason for thinking that something or other is known *per se*. Similarly, 3 does not entail 4. Even if an in-

96. *Ibid.*, n.255–57, (Vaticana III, 154–56).

disposed power can be in error about anything, it does not follow that it is always in error about everything. Perhaps Scotus would argue further that even if by chance an indisposed faculty is sometimes right, we would have criterion for identifying when the indisposed faculty is right. Hence if we are to recognize a case in which the deliverance of a faculty is right, it must be one in which the faculty is disposed. Even if the argument were sound, however, it would not meet the Academics' query. For they have asked how, by what criterion, we can distinguish cases in which we are genuinely awake or genuinely see or hear from those in which we merely appear to be awake, to see, or to hear. Scotus has replied that we recognize that we are awake and that our faculties are disposed in recognizing that something is known *per se*. But if premiss 3 is true, then an indisposed faculty can be mistaken, not only in thinking that it is disposed and that the person is awake, but also about whether something is known *per se*. And the Academic will ask the question with which we ended the previous section: how can we distinguish genuine apprehensions of a first principle from merely apparent ones?

In the final paragraph of article 3, Scotus makes clear how little he cares abut the Academics' objections or standards of knowledge and certainty.

> In reply to the form of this sophistical argument, then, I say that just as it appears to a dreamer that he sees, so the opposite of some speculative principle known *per se* could appear to him. Nevertheless, it does not follow that the latter principle is not known *per se*. And in the same way it does not follow that it is not known *per se* to a hearer that he hears. For an indisposed power can be in error about anything, but a power that is disposed cannot. And it is known *per se* when it is disposed and when it is not. Otherwise, nothing else would be recognized as known *per se*. For one could never tell what would be known *per se* or whether this is something to which the intellect is disposed or to which it would assent in this way.[97]

Here Scotus is saying that the mere logical possibility that one might hold a mistaken belief about *p*, or even the fact that one

97. *Ibid.*, n.257, (Vaticana III, 156).

sometimes does so, does not prevente from knowing *p per se* when one believes it and it is true. And this is so even if there are no infallible signs, according to the Academics' standard, by means of which to distinguish the situations in which one's belief about *p* is true from those in which it is false. Scotus wants to say that 'I see' and 'I hear' are known *per se* in that no one who formulates them when they are true can deny them or fail to recognize their truth. If you ask, "but what is the difference between the cases in which I merely seem to see or hear but do not from those in which I genuinely see or hear?"—he will say that the latter are those cases in which one is awake and one's faculties are disposed. And 'I am awake' and 'My faculties are disposed' are known *per se*, in that no one who formulates these propositions when they are true can deny them or fail to recognize their truth. And that is as much assurance as Scotus thinks it is reasonable to demand.

11. KNOWLEDGE OF THE PHYSICAL WORLD

Finally, Scotus thinks that we can have certain and infallible knowledge about the physical world based on our knowledge of first principles known *per se* together with generalizations about our sense experiences. I shall consider first his account of how we know particular facts about the physical world and then how we know universal generalizations.

In discussing the first, Scotus focuses on the question, "how can a person be certain of those things which fall under the acts of the senses, for instance, that something is white or hot in the way it appears to be?"[98] He distinguishes two sorts of cases. (a) One is that in which "all the senses cognizing the thing make the same judgment about it."[99] When he speaks of "all the senses," it is not clear whether he means "all the senses of a given perceiver" or "all the senses of all of the perceivers cognizing the thing." Perhaps he means both. When all the senses agree

98. *Ibid.*, n.240, (Vaticana III, 146).
99. *Ibid.*

on a given occasion, the problem of deciding which one is more and which one less reliable does not arise. Instead we can focus on whether their agreed deliverances on that occasion are trustworthy.

Scotus thinks that we sometimes can know that they are reliable on the basis of the following principle:

(A) What occurs in most instances by means of something that is not a free cause is the natural effect of this thing.

Working with conceptions of chance and nature derived from Book II of Aristotle's *Physics*, Scotus maintains that (A) is true by virtue of the meaning of its terms. For, on these conceptions, it is a contradiction to say that A's always or very frequently cause B's but they do so merely by chance (where A is a natural cause). A free cause may produce a certain sort of effect very frequently simply because it wills to do so. But the effect of an unfree cause that is not a voluntary agent is either a chance effect or a natural effect. Hence, if an unfree cause always or very frequently produces a certain sort of effect, the effect in question is the one that it is ordained by nature to produce. Given (A), Scotus reasons that

> if the same change in the senses repeatedly occurs in the majority of cases when such an object is present, it follows that the transformation or species produced is the natural effect of such a cause, and thus the external thing will be white or hot or such as it naturally appears to be according to the species so frequently produced.[100]

How do I know that the chair is white? Scotus's answer is that in the majority of cases in the past when I have been in the environs of the chair, it has produced a certain pattern of sensations in me, including a sensation of white color. By (A), I can infer that the chair has inhering in it forms that are naturally apt to produce such sensations in me under those conditions. And what form would be naturally apt to produce sensations of white in a perceiver, but the form of whiteness? Hence the chair

100. *Ibid.*, n.241, (Vaticana III, 147).

must be white. How do I know that fire is hot? Because in the majority of cases in the past when I have approached fire, it has produced sensations of heat in me. Hence, by (A), it must have inhering in it a form that is naturally apt to produce sensations of heat in perceivers—viz., the form of heat. It follows that the fire must be hot. Similarly for other sensible qualities. Scotus's suggestion is that from (A), together with certain generalizations about my past experience, I can have inferential, but certain and infallible knowledge concerning the sensible qualities of particular things.

Scotus's account is, unfortunately, incomplete. He has explained how I can know simple analytic propositions such as (A) (see section 9 above). And if I can have knowledge of my present mental states and acts (see section 10 above), perhaps I can also make knowledgeable generalizations about my past experiences. But (A), together with the fact that I have very frequently had a certain pattern of sensations in the past, do not by themselves entail the conclusion that the chair is white. It is necessary to know in addition that this pattern of sensations was not produced by a free cause—say Descartes' evil demon—simply for its own amusement. And to conclude that this particular chair is white, I must also know that it has been the unfree cause of this pattern of sensations in me on each of many past occasions. Nowhere in this question does Scotus explain how I can acquire such additional knowledge.

(b) As sceptics are fond of pointing out, the deliverances of the senses regarding a given physical object very often disagree. While Scotus would grant that the deliverances of the senses alone would not enable us to discriminate the non-veridical from the veridical perceptions (if any), he is confident that in such cases "we can be certain what is true and which sense is in error" by appealing to a combination of analytic propositions known *per se* and knowledge gained on other occasions from the agreed testimony of the senses.[101] Scotus illustrates this claim with the example of the stick that is partly in the water and partly in the air. In this position it looks broken; but if we

101. *Ibid.*, n.242, (Vaticana III, 147).

run our hand along it, it does not feel broken. And when it is either wholly in water or wholly in air, it does not look broken either. Hence, the senses disagree as to whether or not the stick is broken. Scotus thinks that we can identify the first mentioned visual perception as the mistaken one on the basis of the following principle:

> (B) The harder object is not broken by the touch of something soft that gives way before it.

If 'hard' and 'soft' are regarded as measures of relative impenetrability or penetrability, (B) might be regarded as true by the virtue of the meaning of its terms, as Scotus claims.[102] He then adds that "both the senses of sight and touch attest to the fact that the stick is harder than the water and that the water gives way before it."[103] For instance if we submerge the stick in water and then move it back and forth in the water, it will both look and feel as if the water does not break the stick but rather gives way to it. Thus, by combining our knowledge of the analytic proposition (B) with knowledge acquired from cases in which sight and touch agree, we can judge that sight is wrong in the case first mentioned. Scotus presumably thinks that in all cases in which the senses disagree, there will be some analytic proposition such as (B) and some (actual or possible) set of experiences in which the senses agree that would enable us to identify with certainty which sense or senses are in error on the occasion in question.

(c) Scotus does not think that our knowledge of the physical world is exhausted by our cognition of particulars and their properties. Rather from our experience of numerous particulars, together with (A), we can acquire knowledge of a more general sort. Strictly speaking, (A) licenses the inference from the premiss that A's cause B's very frequently, to the conclusion that B's are what A's are *naturally* ordained to produce. The truth of the premiss is, according to Scotus, "a fact gathered

102. *Ibid.*, n.243, (Vaticana III, 147).
103. *Ibid.*

from experience." How we gather it, he does not explain in detail, but says merely that it involves noticing that *A*'s are a constant factor in each of very many situations in which *B*'s are produced, whereas *C*'s, *D*'s, etc. are not always present.[104] For example, we may observe that the moon is very frequently eclipsed, and discover by examining our experience that the constant factor in each of these eclipse situations is the fact that the earth occupies a certain position between the sun and the moon. We may conclude by (A) that an eclipse of the moon is a natural effect of the earth's taking up that position. Again, we may observe that very many samples of a certain species of herb are hot. (A) entitles us to infer that being hot is a natural effect of the specific form of such herbs.

In introducing this discussion, Scotus suggests that (A) is an even more powerful tool, by means of which

> ...even though a person does not experience every single individual, but only a great many, nor does he experience them at all times, but only frequently, nevertheless a person with this experience knows infallibly that it is so always and in every case.[105]

The suggestion is that given (A) together with the requisite experiences, one can validly infer not merely that *B*'s are the natural effect of *A*'s or that *A*'s naturally cause *B*'s, but also the universal generalization that *A*'s always cause *B*'s. For example, we could infer that the earth's taking up a certain position between the sun and the moon always causes the moon to be eclipsed, and that all herbs of that species are hot. Towards the end of the section, however, Scotus retreats from this position, saying "perhaps we have here no knowledge of the actual union of the terms, but only knowledge of what is apt to be the case."[106] The proposition '*A*'s naturally cause *B*'s', which does follow from (A) together with the requisite experiences, does not entail '*A*'s always cause *B*'s' but only '*A*'s cause *B*'s in most cases and do so unless there is some impediment'. In many

104. *Ibid.*, n.235, (Vaticana III, 142–43).
105. *Ibid.*, n.235, (Vaticana III, 141).
106. *Ibid.*, n.237, (Vaticana III, 144).

cases, it is logically or naturally possible that there should be an impediment. Since heat is a quality really distinct from the specific form of the herb, it is logically possible that the latter exist without the former. And even if the latter produces the former most of the time, it is logically possible that some impediment should prevent it from doing so in this instance.

12.   DOES OCKHAM'S EPISTEMOLOGY HAVE SCEPTICAL CONSEQUENCES?

For Ockham, all certain knowledge either is, or is based on evident cognition. Where our knowledge of contingent states of affairs—whether in the physical world or in our own minds—is concerned, he locates the source of evident cognition in intuitive cognition (see chapter 13 above). There has been more than one attempt in the literature to argue that Ockham's epistemology cannot consistently allow human beings any certainty in the Academics' sense, however. For present purposes, it will be enough to examine two.

(a) In their now notorious discussions, Etienne Gilson and Anton Pegis seize on Ockham's assertion that intuitive cognitions of nonexistents are logically possible as yielding sceptical conclusions regarding our knowledge of the physical world. In Gilson's opinion, Ockham could not assert that an all-powerful God could conserve in us an intuitive cognition of a nonexistent thing

> without endangering what was, according to his own principles, the only type of evident knowledge: the intuition of that which is. If God can conserve in us the intuition of something that is not actually existing, how shall we ever be sure that what we are perceiving as real is an actually existing thing? In other words, if it is possible for God to make us perceive as real an object that does not really exist, have we any proof that this world of ours is not a vast phantasmagoria behind which there is no reality to be found?[107]

107. "The Road to Scepticism," *The Unity of Philosophical Experience*, (New York, 1937), 61–91, at 80–81.

Gilson's idea is that if God could do this, then it would be logically possible for our experience to be just as it is now, even though no mind-independent physical objects exists. And in that case, even if some of our cognitions of physical objects are intuitive and some of our judgments about the physical world are true, our present experience must not contain any infallible signs that they are. Obviously assuming that Ockham reserves the title 'evident' for judgments that are certain in the Academics' sense, Gilson concludes that Ockham could not consistently regard any of our judgments about the physical world as evident. Pegis concurs in Gilson's assessment:

> ...Certainly Ockham thinks that he sees the star when the star no longer exists. Is Gilson wrong in attributing such a view to Ockham? If texts such as this mean anything, there is surely no way of avoiding Gilson's conclusion.[108]

Philotheus Boehner[109] and Sebastian Day[110] have rightly rejected these particular charges as resting on a misunderstanding of Ockham. For according to Ockham, it is true by the definition of 'intuitive cognition' that any judgment caused by an intuitive cognition is evident and therefore true. He explicitly asserts that if God ever did conserve in us an intuitive cognition of a nonexistent object, any judgment caused by that cognition would have to be a judgment that the object did not exist. Thus, Pegis is mistaken in attributing to Ockham the view that if he had an intuitive cognition of a nonexistent star, he would continue to think that the star existed. Again, if God conserved in us all of the intuitive cognitions we now have, while bringing it about that no mind-independent physical objects existed, our experience would—contrary to Gilson's understanding—be

---

108. "Concerning William of Ockham," *Traditio* II (1944): 465–480, at 476.

109. "The Notitia Intuitiva of Non-Existents According to William Ockham," *Traditio* I (1943), 223–275, especially 223, and "In propria causa: A Reply to Professor Pegis," *Franciscan Studies* N.S. V (1945): 37–54.

110. *Intuitive Cognition: A Key to the Significance of the Later Scholastics*, (St. Bonaventure, NY, 1947), 145.

considerably different from what it is now. For we would judge not to exist many objects which we now judge to exist. So long as we are sure that the cognitions we have are intuitive, there can be no reasonable doubt about the truth of the judgments we are caused by them to make.

(b) Nevertheless, it seems that a sound argument for their conclusion could be based on Ockham's remarks in *Quodlibeta* V, q.5.[111] For Ockham explains there in reply to two objections that God cannot cause in us *evident* assent that this thing is present or that whiteness exists when the thing is absent or when the whiteness does not exist, respectively. The reason is that evident judgments are, by definition, true judgments. It is a contradiction to speak of an evident judgment that what is not the case is the case, just as it is a contradiction to suppose that an intuitive cognition causes a false judgment. Ockham goes on to allow, however, that God can cause us to assent to the propositions 'This thing is present' and 'This whiteness exists' when the thing is not present or when the whiteness does not exist. He refers to the act by which we are caused to assent as a "creditive act" and emphasizes that it is an abstractive rather than an intuitive cognition, just as the assent that it causes is not evident.

Clearly, by allowing in these passages that it is logically possible that God should cause us to believe what is false, Ockham is allowing that it is logically possible that God should deceive us. But, the sceptic may wonder, if it is logically possible He should deceive us once, is it not also logically possible that He should deceive us constantly? In that case it would be logically possible that none of the cognitions we take to be intuitive really are intuitive, so that it would be logically possible that our experience be just what it is now and no mind-independent physical objects exist. Ockham's admission that it is logically possible that God should deceive us thus seems to exclude the possibility that we should have knowledge about contingent states of affairs in the physical world that is certain according to the Academics' standard.

111. (OTh IX, 498–500).

Boehner,[112] in effect, objects to the above reasoning that it does not follow from the fact that God can deceive us in the above mentioned way—i.e., by acting together with an abstractive cognition to cause us to assent to a false proposition about some contingent state of affairs in the physical world—that we can never be certain that any of our judgments are evident and therefore true. For where we are dealing with contingent propositions, evident assents are distinguished from such false beliefs in that the former are based on intuitive cognitions and the latter on abstractive cognitions. Ockham himself asserts that experience certifies that we have intuitive cognitions of physical objects.[113] It is tempting to infer from this that he thought there were infallible introspective marks by means of which we could identify intuitive cognitions of physical objects and distinguish them from abstractive cognitions in experience. And if so, given Ockham's definitions, we could thereby identify evident assents to propositions about the physical world and do so with certainty in the Academics' sense and on the basis of introspection alone. And if we can do that, then we can be certain in the Academics' sense that some of our judgments regarding contingent states of affairs in the physical world are true judgments.

Ockham cannot consistently reason this way, however. For one thing, so far from inferring that judgments are evident from the fact that cognitions are intuitive, Ockham actually deduces that we have intuitive cognitions of physical objects[114] and of our own present mental acts[115] from the fact that we have evident cognitions of propositions about them.

Further, Ockham's account of intuitive and abstractive cognition seems to rule out the possibility that introspective marks should provide logically conclusive evidence that a cognition of

---

112. This seems to be Boehner's reasoning in "The Notitia Intuitiva of Non-Existents According to William Ockham," 234–35.

113. *Ord.* I, Prologue, q.1, (OTh I, 23).

114. *Quodl.* I, q.15, (OTh IX, 83); V, q.5, (OTh IX, 496).

115. *Ord.* I, Prologue, q.1, corollary 2, (OTh I, 40, 43); *Quodl.* I, q.14, (OTh IX, 79).

a physical object is intuitive rather than abstractive. His insistence against Scotus that intuitive and abstractive cognitions do not differ in content[116] casts doubt on this possibility. But his definition of 'intuitive cognition' seems to preclude such introspective identification completely. For according to it, that any judgment caused by the cognition is evident and therefore true, is a logically necessary condition for the cognition's being intuitive. In particular, any cognition on which we base a judgment about the physical world will count as intuitive, only if the judgment it causes is a true one. Since Ockham is not a phenomenalist, but thinks that any real physical object exists independently of the mind, it will not be possible to determine by introspection alone whether or not a judgment about the physical word is true. Indeed, before one can be certain whether such a judgment is true, one must first establish whether or not some mind-independent (and therefore non-introspectable) state of affairs obtains. Thus, it will not be possible to use one's certainty that a cognition of a physical object is intuitive as a basis for one's certainty that some judgment about the physical world is evident and hence that some mind-independent state of affairs obtains. For the latter will be epistemologically prior to the former, and not vice versa.

An analogous argument shows that it is impossible that we should gain Academic certainty that any judgment about the physical world is evident on the basis of any other introspectable mark. For it will be a logically necessary condition of a feature's being an infallible introspectable mark (in the Academics' sense of 'infallible') that the judgment it marks is a true one. Consequently, to distinguish genuine from merely apparent occurrences of that feature, I should first have to determine that the judgment so marked was true and hence that some non-introspectable state of affairs obtained. Hence, the epistemological priorities are once again reversed.

Perhaps it will be replied that, on the contrary, Ockham's theory does explain how I can know by introspection alone that my cognition of a physical object is intuitive. For on this ac-

---

116. *Ord.* I, Prologue, q.1, (OTh I, 36–37); d.27, q.3, (OTh IV, 242).

count, if I have an intuitive cognition of a star, that cognition will act together with the intellect to produce in me an intuitive cognition of my intuitive cognition of my intuitive cognition of the star. And the two cognitions together with the intellect will cause me to form the evident judgment 'I have an intuitive cognition of the star'.[117]

This does not show how I can be certain, by the Academics' standard, that my cognition is intuitive, however. For the sceptic does not deny that we have intuitive cognitions, or that we make any true judgments regarding the physical world or our own mental acts. Rather he questions whether we can discriminate a genuine from a merely apparent evident judgment. And he will argue that this is impossible unless there is some infallible sign that distinguishes the former from the latter.

Perhaps it will be said that I can do this by introspection as well, because I can have an intuitive cognition of my intuitive cognition of my intuitive cognition of a star and thereby judge that the second cognition was intuitive just as the first one was. Since Ockham allows that for each cognition, it is possible for me to have an intuitive cognition of it,[118] I can in principle tell with respect to each whether or not it is intuitive and hence whether the judgment it causes is true.

This proposal leads to an infinite regress, however. For I will be certain, by the Academics' standard, that my cognition of a star is intuitive, only if I distinguish genuine from merely apparent intuitive cognitions of intuitive cognitions of intuitive cognitions of a star. If I do that by appealing to yet another intuitive cognition, which I certify by appealing to yet another, etc., it will follow that I will actually be certain, by the Academics' standard, that my cognition of a star is intuitive, only if I am certain that each member of an infinite chain of cognitions is intuitive. But this would involve the simultaneous existence in my mind of infinitely many acts of intellect. And

117. *Ord.* I, Prologue, q.1, (OTh I, 66). This argument was suggested to me by Katherine Delfosse.
118. *Ibid.*, (OTh I, 65–66).

Ockham grants to an objector that this is impossible.[119]

It seems, therefore, that Ockham's account of intuitive and abstractive cognition does not provide for any infallible signs by means of which we can distinguish cases in which we have intuitive cognitions that cause evident judgments from those in which our cognitions are abstractive and our beliefs false. And this is so whether we are concerned with cognitions of physical objects or cognitions of our own mental states. Further, this consequence follows from Ockham's account, even when his admission that God has the power to deceive us is left aside. I conclude that his theory does not allow us any certain knowledge in the Academics' sense.

13.   WAS OCKHAM INTERESTED IN CERTAINTY IN THE ACADEMICS' SENSE?

Gilson and Pegis seem to assume that Ockham was and/or should have been trying to show how we can have certain knowledge of the physical world according to the Academics' standards, and that his failure to do so represents a serious defect in his epistemology. In an earlier paper,[120] I took it for granted that they were right in this assessment. After reexamining the evidence, however, I think it much more probable that Ockham was no more interested in this project than Scotus was, but was content to show how we can have knowledge that is free from doubt and error.

(13.1) First, consider that Ockham clearly regards evident cognition as the paradigm of certain knowledge and locates it as the source of all other certain knowledge. Yet, his primary definition of it—as cognition of a true complex of terms (proposition) a sufficient mediate or immediate cause for which is a non-complex cognition of its terms—includes no stipulation that such a cognition must be distinguishable by infallible signs from mere beliefs. Indeed, as we have seen, the combination of

119. *Ibid.*; cf. chapter 13 above.
120. "Intuitive Cognition, Certainty, and Scepticism in William Ockham," *Traditio* XXVI (1970); 389–398.

this definition with his account of intuitive and abstractive cognition, excludes the possibility that there should be any such infallible introspectable signs. And the above mentioned characteristics of evident cognition correspond closely to those assigned by Scotus to our cognitions of propositions known *per se*: (i) These cognitions are said by Scotus and Ockham, respectively, to be free from error; and (ii) the propositions thus known are said to be such that one cannot formulate them when they are true and fail to recognize their truth. Scotus insists that where propositions known *per se* are concerned, it is altogether impossible that we should formulate them without assenting to them. Ockham's claim is weaker. He does say that a noncomplex apprehension of the terms of such a proposition is a sufficient cause of the evident cognition of it and denotes that the assent cannot be prevented by simple volition not to assent. But he does allow that it might be prevented, if one were confronted with persuasive arguments to the contrary, or if God intervened to prevent the acts of apprehension from causing any judgment (see chapter 13 above). In any case, both agree that when the assents are made, the propositions in question are not actually being doubted and that it is at least difficult, if not impossible, to doubt them. This suggests that in regarding evident cognition as a paradigm of certain knowledge, Ockham did not have his eye on Academic certainty, but the certainty of freedom from doubt and error.

(13.2) Second, there is the fact that, unlike his famous predecessors, Ockham nowhere discusses the Academics' views or arguments in detail. In the course of outlining his own theory of intuitive and abstractive cognition, he mentions their name only once, in quoting the following passage from Augustine's *On the Trinity*, Book XV, chapter 12:

> ...Whereas there are two kinds of things that are known—one of those that the mind perceives by the bodily senses; the other, of those it perceives through itself—these philosophers, viz., the Academics, have chattered a lot against the bodily senses, but they have never been able to cast doubt on those most certain perceptions of true things, which the mind grasps through itself, such as the one I have mentioned 'I

know that I am alive'.[121]

This citation occurs in a context in which Ockham has already settled, to his own satisfaction, the issue of whether we have intuitive cognitions of physical objects and is trying to persuade us that we have them of our own mental acts as well. He does not comment at all on Augustine's mention of Academic scepticism with regard to the senses, but focuses entirely on the latter's positive claim about our non-sensory knowledge. Ockham's neglect of the Academics' arguments could be explained in a number of ways: it could be said either (a) that Ockham was simply ignorant of the considerations raised by the Academics; or (b) that while familiar with them, he failed to recognize their legitimate application to his own theory; or (c) that while familiar with them, he realized their irrelevance to his project of showing that we can have knowledge that is free from doubt and error. (a) seems unlikely. After all, the above quote from Augustine comes from a chapter in which Academic scepticism is the principal topic under discussion. It is, of course, possible that Ockham had not studied Augustine's discussion carefully. But this seems implausible, in view of Ockham's frequent appeal to *On the Trinity*. Further, Ockham shows himself to be very familiar with Scotus's *Ordinatio* and could have become acquainted with the Academics' views by reading Scotus's critique in Book I, d.3, p.1, q.4. It is true that Ockham does not refer to this discussion anywhere in the Prologue or first three distinctions of his own commentary on the *Sentences*. But he cites so many adjacent questions—including every other question in distinction 3, parts 1, 2, and 3—that it would be very strange if he had failed to study this one.[122] Likewise, he frequently refers to Henry's *Summae quaestionum ordinariarum*, and it is therefore conceivable that he would have read Henry's discussion of the possibility of human knowledge, although I have not found a place in which Ockham

121. *Ord.* I, Prologue, q.1, (OTh I, 43).
122. In particular, Ockham cites *Ordinatio* I, d.1, p.1, q.1, 2; p.2, q.1; d.2, p.1, q.1–2, 3; p.2, q.1–4; d.3, p.1, q.1–2, 3; p.2, q.u; p.3, q.1–4.

explicitly cites any part of it. These considerations strongly suggest, although they do not conclusively prove, that Ockham would have been familiar with the views and arguments of the Academics. Given Ockham's usual shrewdness, (b) would have plausibility only if it were thought that Ockham had had to dispatch these issues in a hurry. But it is known that he revised the Prologue and Book I of his *Sentence* commentary at least once before their publication, and his most extensive discussion of sensory illusion was inserted at d.27, q.3 during the course of these revisions.[123] In any case, he returns to these matters in the *Quodlibeta*, which is a later work. Again, if the thrust of the Academics' arguments had been initially obscure to him, a reading of the above mentioned passages from Augustine, Henry of Ghent, or Duns Scotus would surely have clarified the matter for him. The most likely of the three hypotheses is that Ockham did understand the Academics' project and concurred with Scotus's assessment of it.

(13.3) As for Ockham's lengthy discussion of sensory illusion at d.27, q.3, it focuses entirely on refuting Peter Aureol's account. The latter had insisted that what appears must be *something*, even in sensory illusion. But while some philosophers have identified what appears with a sense datum and others with a false proposition that appears true, Aureol insists that it is the thing and its properties that appear. And if either or both do not really exist but are merely apparent, then they will have a non-real mode of existence, which he variously labels "intensional," "seen," or "adjudged" existence.[124] Ockham argues at some length that Aureol's theory is pernicious because positing such unreal entities would destroy direct realism in epistemology and lead to ontological paradox besides.[125] He insists, by contrast, that in sensory illusion it is

123. G. Gál, "Gualteri de Chatton et Guillelmi de Ockham Controversia de Natura Conceptus Universalis," *Franciscan Studies* N.S. XXVII (1967): 191–212, especially 192–99.

124. *Scriptum super primum Sententiarum*, ed. Eligius Buytaert. Cf. I, d.3, sec.14, (II, 696–98).

125. *Ord.* I, d.27, q.3, (OTh IV, 243–44).

often the case that nothing appears; rather it involves the existence in a perceiver of certain acts of apprehension that are apt to produce some of the same effects in that perceiver as veridical sensations do. Ockham does not elaborate on what precisely these effects are in the lower animals that possess sensation only; but in human perceivers, they include mistaken judgment.[126] For example, when a stick that is partly in and partly out of water appears broken, there is no breakage in real or apparent existence,

> ...although the proposition 'The stick is broken' is believed true by the intellect and in the senses there is an apprehension or apprehensions that has (have) enough power (*aequivalens*) to cause in the intellect beliefs of the sort a sensation would cause if the stick were out of the water and appeared broken...[127]

Ockham's primary concern throughout the discussion remains the ontological one of assuring us that particulars never have a non-real mode of existence of the sort Aureol assumes. And although he at one point admits that "deception occurs in many ways" and may sometimes be the result of the clever placement of mirrors by demons,[128] Ockham never worries about how we could infallibly discriminate sensory illusions from veridical acts whose effects they mimic; nor does he here draw back from his conviction that sensory awareness is the beginning of all human knowledge in this life. Similarly, while he insists that imagination may have the same objects under the same aspects as sensation, he never asks how we tell the one from the other.[129] He gives the same account of the source of our knowledge in *Quodlibeta* VI, q.6, where he is defending the logical possibility of intuitive cognitions of nonexistents, again without any concern about the sceptical implications of his remarks.[130]

(13.4) Finally, we must reexamine the context in *Quodlibeta*

---

126. *Ibid.*, (OTh IV, 243–251).
127. *Ibid.*, (OTh IV, 247).
128. *Ibid.*, (OTh IV, 250); cf. *Rep.* II, q.16, (OTh V, 370).
129. *Ibid.*, III, q.3, (OTh VI, 114–124).
130. (OTh IX, 605–606).

V, q.5 of Ockham's famous admission that it is logically possible for God to deceive us. In this question, Ockham defends his distinction between intuitive and abstractive cognition against four objections, the first three of which are raised by Walter Chatton in his commentary on the *Sentences*, Prologue, q.2[131] and the fourth posed by a source unknown to me. Of these, the first and fourth attempt to reduce Ockham's distinction to an absurdity on the ground that if it is accepted, it will be impossible for God to use certain methods to deceive us. Thus, Chatton argues,

> ...Given this distinction, it follows that God would not be able to cause in us an act of cognition through which it would apppear to us that a thing that is absent is present—which is false, since this does not include a contradiction. Proof of the premiss: that cognition is not intuitive, according to you, since through an intuitive cognition a thing appears to be when it is and not to be when it is not. It is not abstractive either, since a thing does not appear to be present through an abstractive cognition.[132]

Ockham replies that his distinction does not force us to deny God the power to bring about any logically possible state of affairs. For Ockham has never said that a thing can not appear to be through an abstractive cognition; rather he has defined abstractive cognition as that by which one cannot have an *evident* cognition that a thing exists or does not exist. And it is in this connection that he maintains that while "...God cannot cause in us such a cognition through which it evidently appears to us that a thing is present when it is absent, since that involves a contradiction,"

> ...Nevertheless, God can cause a creditive act through which I believe that a thing that is absent is present. And I maintain that the creditive cognition will be abstractive, not intuitive...[133]

131. See Jeremiah O'Callaghan, "The Second Question of the Prologue to Walter Catton's Commentary on the *Sentences*: On Intuitive and Abstractive Knowledge," in *Nine Medieval Thinkers*, ed. J. Reginald O'Donnell, 233–269; cf. especially article 3, 246–47.

132. *Quodl.* V, q.5, (OTh IX, 496); cf. O'Callaghan, *op. cit.*, 246.

133. *Quodl.* V, q.5, (OTh IX, 498).

Again, someone objects that

> ...given this [distinction], God would not be able to cause evident
> assent to the contingent proposition 'this Whiteness exists' when
> whiteness does not exist, since the vision of whiteness causes evident
> assent to the proposition 'This whiteness does not exist' and the in-
> tellect would seem to assent to the opposite...[134]

But Ockham replies that while God cannot deceive us by producing "evident assent to the contingent proposition 'This
whiteness exists' when the whiteness does not exist, because a
contradiction follows from this..."

> ...Nevertheless, I grant that God can produce assent of the same as that
> evident assent to the contingent proposition 'This whiteness exists'
> when it does not exist. But the former assent is not evident because
> things are not the way in which the proposition assented to implies
> they are.[135]

Thus, in these interchanges, the logical possibility that God
should deceive us is presented by Ockham's opponents as a
truth it would be absurd to deny, not as a forbidden consequence that it would be scandalous to admit. And Walter Chatton, earlier in the cited question, opines that our experience of
certainty in this life is not so great as to rule out the possibility
that God could cause us to judge things to be otherwise than
they are.[136] It would be wrong to picture Ockham as driven to
admit this possibility only in the face of objections by others.
For there is a little noticed passage in *Reportatio* IV, q.14,
where—without this kind of pressure—Ockham grants that God
could cause in us a habit that would incline us to assent to certain false propositions about the past.[137] The most likely ex-

---

134. *Ibid.*, (OTh IX, 497).
135. *Ibid.*, (OTh IX, 499).
136. O'Callaghan, *op. cit.*, 243: "In reply to the second, I also grant the
conclusion that we do not have so much certainty that God, who can cause a
vision without the thing's being present, could not cause in us an act by
which we would judge things to be otherwise than they are..."
137. Here, too, Ockham is responding to an objection: "Further, God can

planation is that Ockham drew the same conclusion from the Condemnation of 1277 as his contemporaries did, and saw no problem in granting God the power to deceive us.

In conclusion, I have found no positive reason to suppose that Ockham was interested in showing that Academic certainty is possible for human beings, and the above four considerations constitute powerful evidence against that hypothesis. Instead, I am inclined to believe that Ockham was familiar with the views of the Academics, whether by reading Augustine, Henry of Ghent, Duns Scotus, or some other author. But he judged, as Scotus did, that no reasonable person would adopt the Academics' standard of certainty. For if, as Ockham joined others in admitting, it is logically possible that God should deceive us, the Academics' demand for infallible signs by means of which to distinguish genuine from merely apparent instances of knowledge cannot be satisfied. Rejecting their standard, Ockham proceeds to construct a theory according to which we can have knowledge that is free from doubt and error and that ultimately has its causal origin in sensory intuitive cognitions. And he defines 'evident cognition' and 'intuitive cognition' in such a way that it is impossible—even leaving the possibility that God should deceive us aside—that there should be any infallible introspective marks by means of which we could distinguish them from imposters. Nevertheless, Ockham does not explicitly discuss these points, because they do not expose in this theory a failure to do what he intended to do: it is no objection to a theory that attempts to show how we can have certain knowledge according to one standard, that it does not succeed in showing how we can have certain knowledge according to another standard—especially where the latter is a standard that no reasonable person would accept.

---

cause this habit before any act of understanding just as [he can cause it before any] species. Therefore, the habit does not incline one to any past act..." (OTh VII, 311). But the objection is not presented as a *reductio*, which presents the possibility that God should deceive us as one that must be preserved.

14. ADAM WODEHAM'S VIEW

Closer to appreciating the epistemological consequences of God's agreed-upon ability to deceive us as Ockham's secretary, Adam Wodeham. Like Ockham and against Aureol and Chatton, Wodeham insisted that intuitive and abstractive cognitions were to be distinguished, not in terms of some introspective feature of how the object is presented, but in terms of the judgments they are apt to cause. But he followed Chatton in rejecting Ockham's contention that while the intuitive cognition together with the existing and present object suffice naturally to produce a judgment of existence, the intuitive cognition acting alone is naturally apt to produce a judgment of nonexistence. Wodeham argues first that it seems unlikely that a vision of the white Socrates would cause a judgment that Socrates is not white; it is a vision of black Socrates that does that.[138] Again, if the vision of white Socrates naturally has the power to act alone to produce the judgment 'Socrates is not white', it will have and exercise that power even when Socrates is present. Hence, in such cases we would be caused to judge both that Socrates is and that he is not white—which we are not.[139] Again, God could preserve the vision of white Socrates in the presence of white Socrates while suspending the latter's natural power to act together with the former to produce the judgment 'Socrates is white'. If He did, the intuitive cognition of white Socrates would act naturally to cause the false judgment 'Socrates is not white'—which is impossible on Ockham's definition.[140] If Wodeham had confronted Ockham with these arguments, he would not have won his teacher over. To the first, Ockham would agree that visions of white Socrates do not ordinarily produce judgments that Socrates is not white; but this is irrelevant since there are no naturally produced or conserved

138. *Quaestiones in I librum Sententiarum*, Prologue, q.2, Gál's transcription, sec.24, from Cambridge, Gonville and Caius, Cod.281/674, fol.109va.
    139. Q.2, sec.26, fol.109va.
    140. Q.2, sec.27, fol.109va.

intuitive cognitions of nonexistent or non-present objects. To the second, that the presence of the white Socrates is an obstacle that prevents the vision from exercising its natural power to cause the judgment 'Socrates is not white'. To the third, that God can conserve a vision of white Socrates with the power to cause the judgment 'Socrates is not white'; but in such circumstances, the cognition will not count as intuitive. Thinking his arguments sound, however, Wodeham defined an intuitive cognition as "a noncomplex act which is apt to cause evident assent to the truth of a contingent proposition about the present" and insisted with Ockham that it "naturally requires the existence and presence" of its object, while "any other simple and proper or even common apprehension is abstractive."[141] He then explains that evident assent is assent to an evident proposition and notes that 'evident proposition' can be understood three ways: (a) *The first way*, a proposition is evident, if and only if (i) things cannot appear really to be the way it signifies, although (ii) it is possible that one should be convinced by reason and/or experience that they are not that way. For example, someone who sees a stick that is partially submerged in water may form the mental proposition 'The stick in the water is broken', which has the intuitive cognition of the stick and the water among its terms. Under such circumstances, Wodeham says, the proposition cannot help but appear true, even though experience and arguments (perhaps of the sort Scotus proposes; see section 11 above) will convince most people that it is false.[142] By "appearing true," Adam means something in between mere apprehension (we may entertain the proposition 'A man is a donkey', but it does not for that reason appear true) and assent, and he takes it for granted that we will all recognize the difference he has in mind.[143] (b) *The second way*, a proposition is said to be evident, if and only if (i) things cannot not appear really to be the way it signifies, and (iii) things cannot not be as they appear.[144] The new condition (iii) is ambiguous between

141. Q.2, sec.13, fol.109rb.
142. Q.6, sec.66, fol.126ra.
143. Q.6, sec.71, fol.126va.
144. Q.6, sec.66, fol.126ra.

(iii′) when the proposition signifies, things cannot be the way it signifies them to be,

and

(iii″) even if the proposition did not signify, things could not not be as it signifies them to be.

Apparently focussing on (iii″), Wodeham at first suggests that "perhaps every proposition that is evident the second way and categorically signifies that a thing exists, is necessary."[145] But later on, he admits that where the mental propositions 'I am', 'I live' and 'I understand' are formulated from intuitive cognitions, they are evident the second way, presumably in that they satisfy (i) and (iii′).[146] (d) *The third way*, a proposition is evident if and only if (i) things cannot not appear really to be the way it signifies, (iii) things cannot be as they appear, and (iv) given the existing divine ordinances, the existence of the proposition in the mind is apt to necessitate the intellect's assent that things are the way it signifies them to be.[147] Wodeham says that propositions known *per se*, perfect syllogisms, and many rules of inference are evident in this third way.

Having laid down these distinctions, Wodeham considers the objection that

> according to what was said, we could never have evident judgment that things really are the way a true contingent proposition that categorically signifies the existence of an extramental thing, signifies them to be, since no judgment of this kind can be caused by a complex evident the third way...[148]

He makes the following, startling reply:

> ...I grant what is inferred regarding the judgment corresponding to a

145. *Ibid.*
146. Q.6, sec.76, fol.127ra.
147. Q.6, sec.66, fol.126ra–rb.
148. Q.6, sec.68, fol.126va.

contingent truth that signifies an extramental thing. For no such judgment is absolutely evident, by an evidence that excludes every possible doubt. For it is compatible with God's or nature's causing any cognition or possible judgment in the mind that, by God's absolute power, things are not the way the intuitive apprehension signifies them to be. And I grant that every intellect that can be created is of a diminished nature in the sense that it can be deceived about any contingent truth about extramental things, if it categorically asserts that they are or are not thus.[149]

They are not evident the third way apparently because they do not satisfy either condition (iii)—since God could produce or conserve the proposition in the mind, while bringing it about that mind-independent things are not the way it signifies them to be—or condition (iv)—since reason, informing us of the possibility of divine deception, can forestall assent.[150] In another section, he reconsiders his admission that such contingent categorical propositions about mind-independent physical objects are evident even in the first way, when he declares that

> ...Intuitive cognition is not that by virtue of which an evident judgment can be had in the first way unless it is simultaneously evident that God is not conserving the vision miraculously, while annihilating its subject or making it absent. Whether or not it could be [simultaneously evident that God is not doing either of these things], I don't care now. But unless it is, doubt with respect to a contingent truth is not excluded...[151]

Earlier in q.2, Wodeham implies that, in his opinion, there is no way that God Himself could remove this doubt from us:

> Against Ockham's claims and in behalf of my own reply, I argue as follows: for it would not be possible to have any certain judgment that a thing which exists exists or that it does not exist when it does not exist. Therefore, it would be contradictory for God to make us certain about a contingent truth. Proof of the inference: just as God could conserve the vision without the existence of the object, so also He could

149. Q.6, sec.76, fol.127ra.
150. Cf. q.6, sec.77, fol.127ra; sec.101, fol.128rb.
151. Q.6, sec.78, fol.127ra.

conserve any other mental cognition, whether noncomplex or complex without its existing. Therefore, *He could not make us certain by any mental cognition. I grant that there is no cognition by means of which we can be so certain that we could not be deceived by Him, if He wished it.*152

It is clear from the context that Adam thinks of himself as opposing Ockham on this point. Likewise, in q.6, Adam agrees that his position allows no contingent categorical propositions about mind-independent physical objects to be evident,

> ...although Ockham would have to say otherwise. Nor is this surprising, since he supposes that through an intuitive cognition of whiteness it is evidently known that it is when it is and is not when it is not. Therefore, he has to assume that infallible judgment regarding such propositions can be had. But I do not, because I assume that whether or not whiteness exists, the vision of it always inclines one uniformly to a judgment or proposition formed from that vision.153

What goes for propositions about mind-independent physical objects, also applies to mental propositions about one's own mental acts formulated from abstractive rather than from intuitive cognitions.154 Apparently Adam assumes that it is impossible that mental propositions formulated from intuitive cognitions such as 'I exist' or 'I live', to exist and be false, since he allows that they are evident the second way. But since the soul is a distinct created thing from such mental acts, it is not clear why God could not produce or conserve the latter, while destroying the former.

Where mind-independent physical objects are concerned, Wodeham thinks, the most we can be certain about is conditional propositions such as 'This whiteness exists unless God is deceiving me',155 which Wodeham sometimes allows are

152. Q.2, sec.30, fol.109vb, (italics mine).
153. Q.6, sec.77, fol.127ra.
154. Q.6, sec.76, fol.127ra.
155. Cf. q.2, sec.46, fol.110rb; sec.29, fol.109vb; q.6, sec.77–78, fol.127ra.

evident in the third way[156] and sometimes the second way.[157] Perhaps he does not mean to say that every conditional proposition whose consequent is a categorical proposition formed from intuitive cognitions of physical objects is evident in the second and/or third ways. He may wish to retain the ordinary distinction between propositions such as 'The stick in the water is broken' which regularly appear true but usually are judged false on the basis of reason and experience, and those such as 'This whiteness exists' which both appear and are usually judged true, by saying that the conditional 'The stick in the water is broken unless God is deceiving me' is evident the first way, while 'This whiteness exists unless God is deceiving me' is evident the second and/or third way. And Wodeham argues that even these would not be evident, if it were not naturally impossible for an intuitive cognition to be either naturally produced or naturally conserved without its object.[158]

15. NICOLAS OF AUTRECOURT AND THE ACADEMICS

If Ockham was insensitive to and/or uninterested in any sceptical consequences that might be inferred from the logical possibility that we are deceived, his younger contemporary Nicolas of Autrecourt was not. In his two surviving letters to Bernard of Arezzo, as well as his reply to a certain Aegidius who undertook Bernard's defense,[159] Nicolas patiently draws these conclusions, one after another, from Bernard's claims and exhibits the strength of these inferences by pointing out the inadequacy of various objections made to them.

Even so, one must be cautious about seeing Nicolas as the

156. Q.6, sec.77, fol.127ra; sec.101, fol.128rb.
157. Q.6, sec.78, fol.127ra.
158. Q.3, fol.113ra–115rb.
159. Edited together with the letter of Aegidius to Nicolas by Joseph Lappe in *Nicolaus von Autrecourt: Sein Leben, seine Philosophie, seine Schriften*, in *Beiträge zur Geschichte der Philosophie des Mittelalters*, Band VI, Heft 2, (Münster, 1908). I have translated from Lappe's text, to which the page references will be given.

medieval precursor of Descartes or Hume. For his arguments do not go so far as theirs. And it is unclear whether he really accepted them or endorsed their sceptical conclusions. In his first letter to Bernard, Nicolas explicitly regards his demonstration that Bernard's view has sceptical consequences for our knowledge of the physical world and of our own mental acts, as a *reductio ad absurdum* of the latter's position. He summarizes his reaction, commenting

> ...as it seems to me those absurdities follow from your position that follow from the position of the Academics. And therefore, in order to avoid such absurdities, I have defended in disputations held in the court of the Sorbonne the claim that I do have certain and evident cognition of the objects of the five senses and of my own acts.[160]

Nicolas here explicitly regards the position of the Academics and their sceptical conclusions as false and absurd. Further, Nicolas's posture in the greetings and closings of all of the letters is quite unaggressive. He reports that these arguments and objections have occurred to him and that he has been unable to see anything wrong with them. He invites a reply that will show how they are mistaken and thereby bring him and others to a clearer perception of the truth. In one, he even promises, "I will not be obstinate in fleeing from the truth for which I gasp with my whole force of mind."[161] Such remarks might be dismissed as conventional modesty and flattery, but it is conceivable that they are sincere. A diagnosis of Nicolas's true attitude is made the more difficult by the fact that many of the conclusions he deduces against Bernard in these and seven other letters and maintained in his *Sentence*-commentary and several other works, were condemned by the Church. Nicolas submitted to this judgment fully, explaining that he had advanced these conclusions against Bernard only within a certain framework of debate, which they had mutually agreed to. And in Paris, on November 25, 1347, he publicly recanted the condemned theses and burned his writings. As a result of this dark incident

160. 1st Letter, 6*, lines 12–16.
161. 2nd Letter, 14*, lines 1–3.

in intellectual history, it is impossible to compare what he says in the surviving letters with his teaching in more substantial works. It is true that the official lists of condemned theses provide tantalizing clues as to what the lost works may have contained. But since such documents often wrenched statements out of their contexts and distorted their author's intended meaning, they are not reliable guides to Nicolas's real opinions.[162] Whether or not Nicolas held the views he develops in his letters to Bernard, the position merits examination in part for the contrast it provides to those endorsed by Henry of Ghent, Scotus, and Ockham.

16. THE PROPOSED CRITERION OF CERTAIN AND EVIDENT KNOWLEDGE

Nicolas begins his second letter to Bernard by affirming that "all of the certainty that we have" by the natural light[163] "is traced back to the principle"[164] that "contradictories cannot be simultaneously true."[165] The truth of the law of noncontradiction is assured by the fact that "no true law restricts or can contradict it"[166] and that "no power can bring it about that contradictories are simultaneously true."[167] It is the basis of our certainty in that the logical impossibility of error is a necessary condition of certain and evident cognition. Nicolas proposes the following inference:

> It is possible, without any consequent contradiction, that it appear to one that such-and-such is the case and nevertheless that it not be the case.

---

162. For some cautious speculation as to the outlines of his philosophy, see Lappe's discussion, *op. cit.*, 8–31, and Julius Weinberg's book, *Nicolaus of Autrecourt: A Study in Fourteenth-Century Thought*, (Princeton, 1948).

163. Lappe, *op. cit.*, 2nd Letter, 7*, lines 29, 32; 8*, lines 15–17.

164. 2nd Letter, 7*, lines 5–6.

165. 2nd Letter, 6*, lines 32–33.

166. 2nd Letter, 7*, lines 30–31.

167. 2nd Letter, 7*, lines 34–35.

> Therefore, one does not have certain and evident cognition that such-and-such is the case.

And he comments that if I claimed to be certain about something and yet granted the premiss of the above inference, I should have to grant the conclusion and retract my claim to be certain on that occasion.[168] Thus, I shall be said to have certain and non-inferential knowledge of a proposition p on a given occasion, only if it is logically impossible that I should be mistaken in believing p on that occasion. And I can have certain but inferential knowledge of q on the basis of p only if the inference pattern by means of which I derive q from p is traced back, immediately or mediately, to the principle of noncontradiction—i.e., only if it is a contradiction that the premiss(es) should be true and the conclusion false.[169]

Beginning this way, Nicolas is already taking for granted something that Descartes and Hume thought could be questioned: viz., the reliability of reason. If reason is unreliable, then there is no assurance that by strictly adhering to the laws of logic and using only those inference patterns that are based on the principle of noncontradiction, we will not be led to contradictory results. That is, there is no certainty that the principle of noncontradiction will not reduce itself to an absurdity and thereby show itself to be false. When Nicolas assigns this principle axiomatic status, he is thereby refusing to entertain the possibility that reason is unreliable. Further, he explicitly denies what Descartes is thought to have asserted in his "Letter to Mersenne"—that God could bring it about that contradictories are simultaneously true.[170]

---

168. 2nd Letter, 7*. lines 5–19.
169. 2nd Letter, 8*, lines 23–28, corollary 4.
170. In explaining himself to the church authorities, Nicolas says that "quando magister Bernardus predictus et ego debuissemus disputare, concordavimus ad invicem disputando conferre de primo consensu omnium principio, posito a philosopho IIIo *Metaphysice*, quod est: 'Impossibile est aliquid eidem rei inesse et non inesse', loquendo de gradu evidentie qui est in lumine naturali strictissimus. Istis suppositis dixi in predictis epistolis explicite, ut tunc dicebam causa collationis..." (Appendix, 35*, lines 17–25).

According to the above proposed criterion, the logical impossibility of error is a *necessary* condition of certain and evident knowledge. He does not explicitly say that it is also a sufficient condition. On the other hand, he does not here mention any other necessary condition. And when he repeats, in Corollary 3, that "apart from the certainty of faith, there is no other certainty than the certainty of the first principle or what can be traced back to the first principle,"[171] he seems to imply that we are certain regarding the first principle and what can be traced back to it. If he intends it to be a sufficient condition, then it will follow, according to this criterion that we have certain knowledge of any necessarily true proposition that we believe. For since it is contradictory to suppose that such propositions are false, it is likewise contradictory to suppose that they appear to us to be true and yet are false. Thus, if the logical impossibility of error is regarded as a sufficient condition of certainty, it will follow on this criterion as on Scotus's, that we can have certain knowledge of analytic propositions and logical rules, even if there are no infallible signs by means of which we can distinguish cases in which we believe genuine necessary truths from those in which we believe propositions that merely appear to be necessary. The resultant criterion of certain and evident knowledge would thus be less stringent than that of the Academics, where knowledge of necessary truths is concerned. Nevertheless, it would not be simply equivalent to Scotus's or to Henry's criterion of knowledge in the broad sense. For where contingent propositions are concerned, the fact that a true proposition is believed and not doubted, does not imply that it is logically impossible that the belief should be mistaken, but only that the belief is not mistaken. And by the standard Nicolas sets forth, belief in a true contingent proposition would count as knowledge only if it were logically impossible that it should be mistaken.

In any case, Nicolas does not make much use of the positive claim that the logical impossibility of error might be a sufficient condition of certainty. Instead, he concentrates on using the

171. 2nd Letter, 8*, lines 16–17.

fact that it is a necessary condition as a negative test to show that, on Bernard's assumptions, we do not have certain and evident knowledge of many things that we normally suppose ourselves to be certain about. As a preamble to this critique, Nicolas draws some corollaries from his claim that an inference is certain and evident only if it is logically impossible that its premiss(es) be true and its conclusion false. He concludes first that

> (C) In every inference that is immediately derived from the first principle, what the consequent signifies must be really the same as what the whole or a part of the antecedent signifies.

Otherwise, he says, it is clear that the antecedent could be true without the consequent being true.[172] 'Socrates is a man; therefore, Socrates is a man' and 'Socrates is a man; therefore, Socrates is an animal' are certain and evident inferences, and in the former the consequent signifies the whole, in the latter a part, of what the antecedent signifies. In advancing (C), Nicolas must be restricting his attention to inferences by means of which, given certain and evident knowledge of the premisses, one might come to have certain and evident knowledge of the conclusion, and ignoring paradoxical inferences—e.g., 'A triangle has four sides; therefore the moon is made of green cheese' and 'The moon is made of green cheese; therefore either God exists or it is not the case that God exists'—which hold good merely by virtue of having a contradictory premiss or premisses or a necessary conclusion. Given (C), he further infers

> (D) From the fact that one thing is, it cannot be inferred with evidence (an evidence that is traced back to the certainty of the first principle) that another thing is.[173]

---

172. 2nd Letter, 8*, lines 29–34; cf. 9*, lines 21–24, and the Reply to Aegidius, 25*, lines 4–12.
173. 2nd Letter, 9*, lines 15–19; Reply to Aegidius, 25*, lines 4–7.

'Socrates exists; therefore Plato exists' is not a certain and evident inference. For the existence of Plato is neither the whole nor a part of what is signified by 'Socrates exists'. To be sure, an inference such as 'The father of Plato exists; therefore Plato exists (or existed)' is certain and evident. But Nicolas explains that such an inference would not constitute a counterexample to (D). Suppose that Socrates is the father of Plato. 'Father of Plato' is what Ockham would call a connotative term (see Part Two, chapter 10 above) which signifies Socrates directly and Plato obliquely. Hence, in asserting the existence of Socrates under this description one is simultaneously implying the existence, past or present, of his son Plato. And 'Plato exists (or existed)' does, therefore, signify part of what 'The father of Plato exists' signifies. Similarly for other such examples.[174] Where both premiss and conclusion are existential statements, and where the subject term of each is an absolute rather than a connotative term, Nicolas maintains, (D) holds. Ockham and many others would not have accepted (D) in its general form; since they held that a proposition of the form 'x exists', where a proper name, demonstrative, or rigid designatory is substituted for 'x', entails the proposition 'God exists'. Nicolas takes no note of such an exception, however, and wields (D) to generate sceptical conclusions from Bernard's assumptions.

17. NO CERTAIN AND EVIDENT KNOWLEDGE OF OBJECTS INDEPENDENT OF OUR OWN MINDS

Prima facie, it would seem that our best source of certain and evident knowledge of the existence of a given thing would be an act of apprehending the thing itself. Nicolas argues that where things independent of our own minds are concerned, Bernard's assumptions rule out this avenue. Bernard apparently regarded clear and intuitive cognitions as the most perfect and clear of our acts of apprehension. Nevertheless, he allowed that

---

174. Reply to Aegidius, 25*–28*.

(E) Clear and intuitive cognition is that through which we judge that a thing is, whether it is or not;

(F) 'The object does not exist; therefore it does not seem to exist' and 'This object seems to exist; therefore it exists' are not good inferences;

(G) An intuitive cognition of a thing does not necessarily require the existence of the thing.[175]

Obviously from (E), Bernard would admit that it is logically possible that I should have an intuitive cognition of x and thereby judge that x exists, even though x does not exist. Presumably, if this is true of judgments of existence caused by our most perfect acts of apprehension, it is true of those based on less perfect acts of apprehension as well. Hence, however I may apprehend the object, the observation in (F) holds. Nicolas thus concludes that from Bernard's point of view

(H) Every appearance that we have concerning the existence of objects independent of our own minds can be false.

Further, since error is logically possible with respect to all of our judgments of existence,

(J) We cannot be certain, in the natural light, when our appearances concerning the existence of objects independent of our own minds are true or false.[176]

Both Scotus and Ockham would agree with (F). Where x is some object independent of our minds, it does not follow from the fact that I am aware of x and judge that x exists, that x exists. For my act of apprehenson and act of judgment are, by hypothesis, things distinct from x. By (D), it follows that one cannot infer the existence of the latter from the existence of the

175. 1st Letter, 2*, lines 7–18.
176. 1st Letter, 2*, line 19–3*, line 2.

former with evidence and certainty. It is obvious from (E), however, that Bernard defines 'intuitive cognition' differently from both Scotus and Ockham. Scotus defines 'intuitive cognition' as 'an act of apprehension which is of the object as existing and present and which is caused by the existing and present object'. Accordingly, for him, 'intuitive cognition' is a connotative term and (D) does not exclude the inference 'I have an intuitive cognition of x; therefore x exists' as evident. Ockham likewise regards it as true by definition that intuitive cognitions cause only true judgments, and hence would pronounce 'I have an intuitive cognition of x and am thereby caused to judge that x exists; therefore, x exists' an evident inference.

Neither Bernard nor any of his medieval predecessors was a phenomenalist. Hence, they all regarded the objects of the five senses—the so-called sensible qualities such as colors, flavors, odors, textures, temperatures, and sounds—as things independent of our minds. Thus, applying (F), Nicolas concludes that Bernard would find 'Whiteness seems to exist; therefore, whiteness exists' fallacious.[177] And applying (J), he derives

(K) We cannot have certain and evident knowledge of the existence of the objects of the five senses.[178]

Nicolas considers that Bernard might try to avoid these consequences, by maintaining that even though, for example

177. 1st Letter, 3*, lines 5–6.
178. 1st Letter, 3*, lines 2–3; 4*, lines 19–20. In defending against Nicolas's arguments, Aegidius suggests that in view of Nicolas's acceptance of (D) and his claim that we do have certain knowledge of the objects of the five senses, "it is necessary that an intuitive cognition is the same as the thing cognized, since otherwise this would not follow: a thing appears in intuitive cognition; therefore the thing exists..." (Letter of Aegidius to Nicolas, 18*, lines 28–30). If Nicolas had identified colors, odors, flavours, etc. with our intuitive cognitions of them, he would have anticipated the views of George Berkeley. Nicolas does not draw this conclusion anywhere in the letters, however. And while (D) was one of the condemned theses which he recanted (see Lappe's Appendix, 31*, lines 11–15), the view that sensible qualities are to be identified with intuitive cognitions of them was not.

'Whiteness seems to exist; therefore whiteness exists' is fallacious, 'Whiteness seems to exist and the vision of whiteness
is not caused or conserved supernaturally, but is produced by
natural causes alone, together with the general influence of the
first agent; therefore, whiteness exists' does hold good. Nicolas
responds that to regard the latter inference as certain and
evident, one must assume that it is logically impossible that
anything other than God should cause us to have a vision of
whiteness and to judge that whiteness exists when no whiteness
exists. And he asks rhetorically how Bernard has certain and
evident knowledge that the latter is the case.[179]

Again, Nicolas anticipates, Bernard might insist that he has
certain and evident knowledge that only God can cause intuitive cognitions of nonexistents that are clear in a certain
degree, and know in addition that it was not supernaturally
caused, we could evidently infer that it was an intuitive cognition of an existing, not a nonexistent thing. Nicolas's reaction is
that granting Bernard such an inference, he would like to know
how Bernard determines with certainty and evidence on a given
occasion that a particular vision has or has not reached the requisite degree of clarity?[180] Alternatively, one might ask how,
given that a cognition is recognized as having the requisite
degree of clarity, we determine whether it is a naturally caused
intuitive cognition of an existing thing rather than a supernaturally caused cognition of a nonexistent thing? The suggestion is that even if it were allowed that the inference is evident,
we would still not be in a position to have certain and evident
knowledge of its premises.

18.   NO CERTAIN AND EVIDENT OR EVEN PROBABLE
      KNOWLEDGE OF SUBSTANCES OTHER THAN
      OUR OWN MINDS

Conclusion (J) applies generally to all objects existing in-

179. 1st Letter, 3*, line 7–4*, line 12.
180. 1st Letter, 4*, lines 13–17.

dependently of our own minds, and hence to Aristotelian substances as well as to Aristotelian accidents. Nicolas does not
explicitly apply it to substances other than our minds apparently because they "do not appear intuitively." If they did, he suggests, then even "the uneducated would know that such things
exist"—which they do not. It takes philosophical arguments to
bring one to the conclusion that such Aristotelian substances exist.[181]

Scotus and Ockham would agree that human beings (with the
exception of a few saintly persons) do not have intuitive cognitions of God or the angels in this life. They would doubtless also
concur that we do not have intuitive cognitions of the mental
substances of other human beings. And neither allows us intuitive cognitions of material substances in this life (see Part
Three, chapter 13 above).

(J) tells us that even if we could have intuitive cognitions of
material substances, that would not enable us to have certain
and evident knowledge of their existence by Nicolas's standard.
Without such direct awareness of them, the only way we could
hope to learn of their contingent existence is by inferring it
from the existence of sensible qualities of which we do have intuitive cognitions. But we cannot acquire certain and evident
knowledge of the existence of material substances this way for a
double reason: first, as Nicolas has concluded in (K), we cannot
have certain and evident knowledge of the existence of sensible
qualities on the basis of apprehensions of them. And even if we
could, (D) would not allow us certain and evident knowledge of
the existence of something distinct from them on that basis.
Nicolas writes,

> ...granted that there are all those things that appear in a piece of wood
> or in a stone before all discourse, it can be the case—without any con-
> tradiction—that there is no thing there that is called substance. For God
> can bring this about, when nevertheless He cannot bring it about that
> contradictories are simultaneously true. Therefore, it cannot be infer-

181. 2nd Letter, 12*, lines 25–26.

red with evidence from these appearances, that any substance is there.[182]

Hence, it follows that

(L) We cannot have any certain and evident knowledge of the existence of material substances.

And this conclusion would tell as much against Scotus and Ockham as against Bernard.

Nicolas recognizes that the following objection might be made to his reasoning. Suppose that I know with certainty that whiteness exists. Since whiteness is an accident, I know with certainty that an accident exists. But, according to Aristotle's usage, 'accident' means 'something that exists in a subject', and 'substance' means 'the subject of contraries' and hence refers to that in which the accidents inhere. Hence, the inference 'Whiteness exists, therefore, there is a substance in which it exists' is certain and evident by virtue of the meanings of 'accident' and 'substance'.[183]

Nicolas replies that where the meanings of 'accident' and 'substance' are assigned in the above way,

> ...the inference is good. But when it is said that whiteness is an accident, the sense of the proposition is, according to the description assigned to the term 'accident' above, that whiteness is in a subject. I maintain that this is not evident either of itself or from experience...[184]

As we have seen, Ockham regularly uses the term 'accident' in such a way that 'An accident exists; therefore a substance exists' is not a formal inference. For he has insisted that certain qualities are really distinct from substances, and—partly motivated by the doctrine of Transubstantiation (see Part One,

182. Reply to Aegidius, 29*, line 29–30*, line 3; cf. 2nd Letter, 12*, lines 26–29 and 13*, lines 15–29.
183. Reply to Aegidius, 28*, lines 9–20.
184. Reply to Aegidius, 28*, lines 22–26.

chapters 6 and 8)—that it is logically possible for such qualitative things to exist without inhering in any substance at all. Hence, assuming that we could be certain that whiteness exists, we could be certain that whiteness is an accident in Ockham's sense. But we could not use such knowledge to infer the existence of any material substance.

Alternatively, one might try to avoid (L) by arguing that while 'An accident exists; therefore a substance exists' is not evident where 'accident' is taken this second way, 'An accident exists and God is not performing any miracles in this case; therefore a substance exists' is evident.

Nicolas refers us to his first letter for his reply. He would again point out that this second inference is evident, only if it is logically impossible that a creature should cause an accident to exist without inhering in any substance. This is not obviously true, and Nicolas would question how we can know with certainty that there is any logically possible producible state of affairs that can be brought about only by God.[185] He might have questioned further how we can know with certainty that God is not performing any miracles on any given occasion. Although he does not actually do so here, he apparently did, in his fifth letter to Bernard, offer arguments for the stronger conclusion that we cannot have any evident knowledge that anything other than God acts as an efficient cause, and this thesis was condemned.[186]

Of substances other than our own minds, material substances might have seemed prima facie the most accessible. If we cannot have certain and evident knowledge of their existence, a fortiori, Nicolas argues, we cannot have it of the others.[187] Hence,

(M) We cannot have certain and evident knowledge of the existence of any substance other than our own minds.

At this point in his second letter, Nicolas confesses that "although I do not hold the conclusion, yet I have an argument

185. Cf. 1st Letter, 3*, lines 28–34.   187. 2nd Letter, 12*, lines 30–31.
186. Appendix, 32*, lines 21–32.

that I do not know how to dissolve for proving that

> (N) We cannot have any probable knowledge of the ex-
> istence of substances other than our own minds.''[188]

The argument rests on the assumption that

> (O) No one has probable knowledge of some consequent by
> virtue of some antecedent, unless he has certain and evi-
> dent knowledge of whether the consequent existed
> simultaneously with the antecedent at some time.[189]

For instance, assuming that "it was at some time evident to me
that when I put my hand near the fire, I was hot," it can
therefore be "probable for me that if I were now to put my hand
near the fire, I would be hot." Given (O), together with (M), "it
follows that we do not have even probable knowledge of the
existence of substances other than our own minds."[190] Nicolas
seems to have found (N) unpalatable himself. Having offered his
argument, he repeats, "I do not hold the conclusion. May he
[i.e. Bernard] dissolve the argument—certainly there is a way
to do so."[191]

19. NO CERTAIN AND EVIDENT KNOWLEDGE OF OUR OWN PRESENT MENTAL ACTS

Having cast doubt on our ability to have certain and evident
knowledge of objects independent of our own minds, Nicolas
proceeds to extract the further conclusion that

> (P) We cannot have certain and evident cognition of the ex-
> istence of our own present mental acts

188. 2nd Letter, 13*, lines 3–5.
189. 2nd Letter, 13*, lines 6–8.
190. 2nd Letter, 13*, lines 15–16.
191. 2nd Letter, 13*, lines 16–18.

from Bernard's remarks. The argument that Nicolas offers exploits Bernard's claim that

(Q) Our intellect does not have any clear intuitive cognition of our own acts.[192]

Nicolas reasons that

...The intellect which is not certain of the existence of things concerning which it has a clearer cognition, will not be certain of those things concerning which it has a less clear cognition. (But as was said, you are not certain of the existence of objects concerning which you have a clearer cognition than you have concerning your own acts.) Therefore, etc.[193]

While this argument has *ad hominem* force against Bernard, he could not have avoided (P) simply by admitting that we can have clear intuitive cognitions of our own present mental acts. For according to Bernard, the act of apprehension by which we are aware of a given mental act is a distinct mental act.[194] Hence, it is logically possible that one should exist without the other. And assumptions (i)–(iii) could be brought to bear here in the same way as with our awareness of physical objects, to draw the sceptical conclusion stated in (P).

Further, insofar as Scotus and Ockham agree with Bernard in claiming that the act of apprehension by which we are aware of a given mental act is a distinct mental act (see chapter 13 above), they would be liable to the same objection. For it would be logically possible that the act of apprehension of a given mental act should exist while the apprehended act does not exist. Of course, in that case, the act of apprehension would not count as an intuitive cognition for Scotus; and if it caused a judgment of existence, it would not count as an intuitive cognition for Ockham either. But that is only to say that it is logically possible that any act of apprehension of a given mental act should not be

192. 1st Letter, 4*, lines 25–28.
193. 1st Letter, 4*, lines 29–33.
194. 1st Letter, 5*, lines 14–17.

an intuitive cognition and hence logically possible that the judgment caused by any act of apprehension be false. It follows, by the standard Nicolas is using, that no such judgment constitutes certain and evident knowledge of the existence of our own present mental acts.

If this reasoning is sound where our own present mental acts are concerned, it would seem to hold for our awareness of our mental substance as well. Nicolas does not say what sort of awareness Bernard thought we could have of our own minds. Ockham denies that we have intuitive cognitions of our own mental habits and dispositions and hesitates to say whether we can have intuitive cognitions of our own mental substances. But he does insist that the object of a mental act is always something distinct from the mental act (see chapter 13 above). And this admission, together with (D), would seem to preclude any certain and evident knowledge, according to Nicolas's standard.

20.   NO CERTAIN AND EVIDENT KNOWLEDGE OF THE EXISTENCE OF EFFECTS FROM CAUSES OR VICE VERSA

Nicolas has argued from Bernard's assumptions that we cannot have any certain and evident knowledge of the existence of objects independent of our own minds, of our own present mental acts, or of substances other than our own minds. If we cannot have any certain and evident knowledge of the existence of any such things, the question of whether we could come to know the existence of one on the basis of another, or of whether we could recognize causal connections between them, would not arise. Nevertheless, in his Reply to Aegidius, Nicolas makes use of (D) to show that we cannot have certain and evident knowledge of the existence of causes on the basis of their effects, or vice versa. He writes that

> ...where all those things required for an effect are indicated, I will be able to sustain without any contradiction that could be inferred against me that the effect of this sort will not exist. Again, in the course of causes, I will be able to believe reasonably or at least doubt whether

there is any agent whose action is necessarily required for such an effect to be posited. Consequently, I should not believe that when all these things have been posited, necessarily the effect should exist, by such a necessity that there is a contradiction in their being any other way, as is clear enough from what was said before.[195]

Suppose that in the natural course of things, a, b, and c are in fact causally necessary and sufficient for the existence of d. When Nicolas says that "when all of those things required for the effect are indicated, I will be able to sustain without any contradiction that could be inferred against me, that this sort of effect will not be"[196] and "consequently, I should not believe that when all those things are posited, necessarily the effect should exist, by such a necessity that there is a contradiction in their being the other way,"[197] he is merely pointing out that it is logically possible that a, b, and c should exist and not exist. For cause and effect are distinct things, and by (D) the existence of the latter cannot be inferred by a certain and evident inference from the existence of the former. Nicolas evidently repeated this point in his fifth letter to Bernard, and it was condemned in that form by the Church authorities.[198] When Nicolas says that "in the course of causes, I will be able rationally to believe or at least doubt whether there is any agent whose action is necessarily required in order that such an effect should be posited,"[199] he seems to make the converse point: that it is logically possible that d should exist without a, b, and c. Hence, one cannot infer by a certain and evident inference from the existence of d that a, b, and c exist. Nicolas apparently takes both this point and the previous one to hold, whether d comes into existence for the first time or is eternal. If so, this second point seems tantamont to denying that the principle of sufficient reason for production in existence is a necessary truth—which would rob many cosmological arguments for the existence of God of their

195. 29*, lines 10–18.
196. 29*, lines 10–12.
197. 29*, lines 15–18.
198. Appendix, 32*, lines 33–36.
199. Reply to Aegidius, 29*, lines 13–15.

demonstrative force. Perhaps this is why the Church authorities condemned this thesis as "false, heretical, and erroneous."[200] Combining these two points, Nicolas is saying that given any particular thing, we cannot have certain and evident knowledge either that it has or had a cause or that it has or will have any effect. From the list of condemned theses, it seems that in his fifth letter to Bernard, Nicolas explicitly denied that we could have certain and evident knowledge that anything other than God is or could be an efficient cause—in other words, that there is any secondary causality. This contention was likewise condemned as "false and to be revoked."[201]

21.   THE CONDEMNATION OF MEDIEVAL SCEPTICISM

I have already cautioned that Nicolas's own attitude towards the above arguments is uncertain. It is not too much to say, however, that anyone who accepted them and their conclusions would deserve the title "medieval sceptic." Further, the attitude of the Church authorities towards such scepticism in theory of knowledge was—at that time—decidedly negative. They rejected the criterion of certainty and evidence used by Nicolas, listing as "false and to be revoked" his statement that "apart from the certainty of faith, there is no certainty other than the certainty of the first principle and that which can be traced back to the first principle."[202] Further, they condemned its corollary (D)—that the existence of one thing cannot be inferred by a certain and evident inference from the existence of another.[203] Also explicit condemned are conclusions based on (D): viz., (L)—that we cannot have any certain and evident knowledge of the existence of material substances[204]—and his claim that we cannot have certain and evident knowledge of the existence of the cause from the existence of the effect, and vice

200. Appendix, 34*, lines 4–6; cf. lines 1–3.
201. Appendix, 32*, lines 21–32.
202. Appendix, 32*, lines 6–8.
203. Appendix, 31*, lines 13–15.
204. Appendix, 32*, lines 9–11.

versa. I doubt if the fact that (J)— that we cannot be certain, in the natural light, when our appearances concerning the existence of objects independent of our own minds are true or false—and (K)—that we cannot have certain and evident knowledge of the existence of the objects of the five senses—are not explicitly listed indicates any approval of them by the Church authorities. Perhaps, in the case of (K), they were aware of Nicolas's statement in the first letter that he had defended the contrary.[205] Given that Aquinas himself had limited the sort of knowledge that we can have of our own minds, it may be that (P) did not meet with universal disapproval.

* * * * *

POSTSCRIPT:

I think we are now in a position to appreciate how odd it is, at least where general theory of knowledge is concerned, to link Ockham's name with the rise of scepticism. Let us ask, how was Ockham supposed to have manifested these sceptical tendencies?

(a) Not by engaging in extensive discussion of sceptical arguments and conclusions. It is Henry of Ghent who collects and discusses the ancient arguments that human knowledge is impossible. Duns Scotus argues that Henry's own view has the same consequence and explicitly discusses and rejects the Academics' criterion of certainty. And it is left to Nicolas of Autrecourt, making use of similar criterion, to deduce sceptical conclusions once more from assumptions made by Bernard of Arezzo but shared by other thirteenth and fourteenth century philosophers. By contrast, Ockham never gives explicit attention to arguments that human knowledge is impossible or acknowledges the consequences of his own admission that it is logically possible that God should deceive us.

(b) Not by assigning any legitimacy to the Academics' criterion of certainty. It is Henry of Ghent who suggests that

205. 1st Letter, 6*, lines 12–16.

knowledge of the unadulterated truth must meet this standard. And in his letters, Nicolas insists that the only certainty that we have in the natural light apart from the certainty of faith is that which involves the logical impossibility of error. Scotus explains the consequences of accepting the Academics' criterion and rejects it, insisting that we have certain and infallible knowledge when our belief is free from doubt and error. So far from accepting the Academics' standard, Ockham never mentions it. He merely proceeds to argue that we can have certain knowledge beginning with evident cognitions that are caused by a cognition of their terms and free from doubt and error.

(c) It would be reasonable to see Ockham's philosophy as the beginning of a sceptical trend, if his general theory of knowledge were more replete with sceptical consequences than those of his predecessors or contemporaries. Such an evaluation is not justified by the above survey, however. The fact is that none of the philosophers discussed above shows how we can have knowledge, whether of necessary truths or of the physical world, that we can infallibly distinguish from merely apparent knowledge of this kind. Henry tries to soften this conclusion by insisting that the Blessed will have such knowledge in the next life, although he does not really say enough to justify his Augustinian conviction that knowledge obtained in a direct vision of God would be self-certifying. Neither Scotus nor Ockham even tries to show that we can have knowledge that is certain in this sense. And the whole thrust of Nicolas's critique is that, on Bernard's assumptions, one cannot have any knowledge of contingent propositions that is free from the logical possibility of error.

Ockham's epistemology is neither self-consciously sceptical, nor does it have more sceptical consequences than other theories. Further, Ockham shows much less interest in the whole problem than the other philosophers we have discussed. Why, then, have historians of philosophy singled out Ockham's philosophy as marking the beginning of the rise of scepticism? I can think of three reasons.

(d) First, Ockham's admission that it is logically possible that God should deceive us brings Descartes' discussion in the

Meditations to mind. Descartes suggests in *Meditation* I that if it really were logically possible that God should deceive us, we could not have certain knowledge of anything. And he tries to avoid this conclusion by arguing that it is not really logically possible that an omniscient, omnipotent, but perfectly good God should deceive us constantly. His reasoning assumes that in calling God perfectly good, we are assuming that His volitions and actions measure up to a standard that any being would have to meet in order to count as good. And he maintains in *Meditation* IV that God would fall short of these standards if He deceived us constantly. It is worth noting that while Aquinas, Henry of Ghent, and Duns Scotus conceive of God's goodness in such a way that they could make use of this argument, Ockham does not. For—quite apart from whether or not he thinks that we can have logically conclusive evidence that God exists and is omnipotent and perfectly good (see Part Five, chapters 21 and 28)—Ockham's assertion of divine liberty, together with his grounding of ethical distinctions in the concept of obligation rule out any *a priori* demonstration that God is no deceiver. Briefly, on Ockham's view, one can be said to act wrongly (sin), only if one can be under obligation to someone to do something.[206] Rational creatures have an obligation to do whatever God freely commands, which obligation derives from the fact that He is the highest good and is to be loved above all and for His own sake.[207] God cannot be under obligation to anyone to do anything, however.[208] Therefore, He cannot act wrongly (sin), even if He is a deceiver. It might seem, then, that if Ockham had tried to refute scepticism (which he did not), he would have found himself at a disadvantage relative to his predecessors, because of his position in eithics. The importance of this point can be exaggerated, however. For quite apart from the well-known circularity of Descartes' proof, it depends on being able to show that

206. *Rep.* II, q.3–4, (OTh V, 59).
207. *Ord.* I, d.1, q.4, (OTh I, 447); *Rep.* II, q.15, (OTh V, 352–54); *De connexione virtutum,* q.7, a.2, (OTh VIII, 335–36); a.3, (OTh VIII, 358); *Rep.* IV, q.10–11, (OTh VII, 198).
208. *Rep.* II, q.3–4, (OTh V, 59).

God would be doing something evil if He deceived us constantly, even though—as perfectly good—He has not done anything evil in creating us with cognitive faculties that sometimes mislead us. Since the latter is difficult, if not impossible to establish with certainty, the ability to use Descartes' strategy is no great advantage in theory of knowledge.

(e) Second, while Ockham never seriously questioned the possibility of human knowledge in general or of our ability to acquire knowledge of necessary truths and of contingent truths about the physical world and of our own mental acts, he does try to show that our certain knowledge of theological truths is much more limited than his predecessors had imagined (see Part Five below). Some historians of philosophy, such as Gilson and Pegis, have found negative judgment about the scope of natural theology deplorable, and have perhaps regarded such relative pessimism about our ability to know theological truths as scepticism of the worst kind. We shall return to this issue in Part Five, chapter 22 below.

(f) Finally, historians have found it attractive to associate the rise of scepticism with ecclesiastical rebelliousness—and this whether they have regarded the latter developments as good or bad. Of the philosophers discussed in this chapter, Ockham is ecclesiastically the most rebellious. For he was excommunicated for defying Pope John XXII over the issue of Franciscan poverty. By contrast, Henry was on ecclesiastical commissions that sat in judgment of others; and Duns Scotus is on the road to beatification for sponsoring the doctrine of the immaculate conception of the Blessed Virgin Mary. Given these historical facts, historians have found it natural to cast Ockham in the role of medieval sceptic and destroyer of the medieval synthesis. Our survey in this chapter belies such a connection. For it is Nicolas of Autrecourt—at least in his surviving letters to Bernard and Aegidius—not Ockham, who gives a sceptical stance in theory of knowledge explicit development. And the list of condemned theses suggest that in his other letters, he drew sceptical conclusions about the possibility of natural theology that far outrun Ockham's.[209] Yet, by comparison with Ockham, Nicolas was ecclesiastically submissive: he recanted his condemned theses, burned his books, and was made dean of Metz cathedral three years later.

In my opinion, the attempt to identify Ockham as the chief of medieval sceptics is largely misguided and highly misleading and should, accordingly, be abandoned.

209. Lappe, *op. cit.*, Appendix, 31*–45*.